BARRON'S

REAL ESTATE LICENSING EXAMS

SALESPERSON, BROKER, APPRAISER

9TH EDITION

JACK P. FRIEDMAN, Ph.D., MAI, Broker
Licensed Real Estate Broker
Certified General Appraiser
Real Estate Economist, Dallas, Texas
Former Laguarta Professor of Real Estate
Department of Finance/Real Estate Research Center
Texas A&M University

and

J. BRUCE LINDEMAN, Ph.D., Broker
Professor of Real Estate
University of Arkansas
at Little Rock

BARRON'S

© Copyright 2013, 2010, 2005, 2000, 1995, 1990, 1987, 1983, 1979
by Barron's Educational Series, Inc.

All inquiries should be addressed to:
Barron's Educational Series, Inc.
250 Wireless Boulevard
Hauppauge, New York 11788
www.barronseduc.com

ISBN: 978-1-4380-0219-4

ISSN 2152-7334

PRINTED IN THE UNITED STATES OF AMERICA

9 8 7 6

10%
POST-CONSUMER
WASTE
Paper contains a minimum
of 10% post-consumer
waste (PCW). Paper used
in this book was derived
from certified, sustainable
forestlands.

Contents

LIST OF ILLUSTRATIONS

LIST OF TABLES

Preface

In recent years, legal, social, economic, and financial matters affecting real estate have become more complex, creating greater educational needs for those who are engaged in the real estate business. In today's environment, a salesperson, broker, or appraiser cannot survive solely on a pleasant disposition and a neat appearance. Real estate professionals must be aware of and obey federal, state, and local regulations. They need in-depth knowledge of each property being brokered, including its physical surroundings and its economic, legal, social, and political environment.

In recognition of these needs, most states have adopted more stringent standards for the licensure of real estate brokers and salespersons. These standards include more education, more rigorous examinations, or both. Population mobility, the need for licensure reciprocity, increased federal regulation, and greater communication and cooperation between state license law officials have all led to greater uniformity in real estate licensing standards. Also, since 1993 federal law has required that real estate appraisers be state certified. Appraisers (both experienced professionals and new entrants) now must take qualifying examinations that can lead to at least two levels of certification: residential and general. The appraisal sections of this book can now serve the needs of those desiring preparation for appraiser certification as well as those who seek sales or broker licenses.

This book was written as an introduction to real estate, taking into consideration real estate complexities, the need for more knowledge, and the trend toward uniformity among states. It is primarily intended to serve those seeking to meet licensure requirements, but it may also satisfy the needs of persons wanting to know more about real property law, contracts, finance, brokerage, ethics, leasing, appraisal, mathematics, fair housing, truth in lending, and other such topics. For the person just wanting to buy or sell a home, the glossary may serve as a reference for greater understanding of the transaction. It alone can prevent misunderstandings that are costly in terms of time and money.

A careful reading of any document is crucial to understanding it. Many people have unfortunately lost money by failing to read and understand contracts before signing them. Similarly, a careful reading of this book will be helpful toward understanding the complex subject—real estate—that it concerns. Questions have been included at the end of each chapter and comprehensive exams at the end of the book so that you can test your understanding of the material presented, both chapter by chapter and at the end. Though your instructor can be of valuable assistance, the knowledge that you gain will approximate the effort that you expend.

Should you become actively engaged in the real estate business, we wish you success. We hope that all your dealings will be honest and fair. Only in this way can the real estate business become recognized as a profession.

We are grateful to the many people who have aided us in preparing this book. This edition was made possible by Suzanne S. Barnhill and the staff at Barron's, especially Pat Hunter, Senior Editor.

Jack P. Friedman
J. Bruce Lindeman

How to Use This Book

If you are reading this book, you are probably interested in employment in the real estate field. Real estate is a fast-growing, exciting field that offers significant income potential to a person who is willing to work hard and to learn the special features of this interesting business.

If you want to enter the real estate business as a salesperson, broker, or appraiser, then, among other requirements, you will have to take and pass an examination. Potential real estate salespeople and real estate brokers take *licensing* examinations in order to get sales or brokerage licenses. A person whose ambition is real estate appraisal takes a *certification* examination in order to become a certified appraiser. In either case, taking the exam is only one step (you also need educational preparation, for example), but it is a very important one. This book is designed to help you to succeed in taking that important step. To fulfill this purpose, the book has a number of important features that enhance its usefulness to you:

1. This book can be used to study for any licensing or certification examination offered in the real estate field by any state. It covers the material in all nationally distributed examinations as well as those given in states that prepare their own examinations. No matter where you live, this is the book you need.

2. Special emphasis is given to the topics that license applicants find most troublesome on examinations:

   a. Arithmetic and real estate math
   b. Contracts
   c. Closing statements (for broker applicants)

3. Hundreds of sample questions are included at the ends of chapters, covering all the materials discussed.

4. There are *ten* model examinations for you to practice on: three for the salesperson exam, three for the broker's exam, three for appraisal certification exams, and a tenth that may be taken by salesperson and broker candidates.

5. A full and complete glossary is included, along with instructions as to the best study strategy for getting the most out of it.

6. Chapter 23, the final chapter before the model tests, describes the *strategy* and *techniques* of taking examinations so that you can be sure to get every point possible.

Topics

This book is divided into 23 chapters of text, the model examinations (Chapter 24), and a final chapter of answers and explanations. Each chapter covers a specific topic. Some are long, others short. Remember, though, that the material in most of the chapters *complements* the material in the others. This is especially true in Part III, "Real Estate Contracts." The first part of Part III (Chapter 6, "Introduction to Contracts") discusses everything you should know about contracts in general. Each of the other chapters in Part III is devoted to one or more types or parts of real estate contracts. For each of these chapters, all the general material in

Chapter 6 applies to what you are learning. Chapter 7 discusses land description. Chapters 8 through 12 point out the specific characteristics of each type of real estate contract. Chapter 13 is on mortgages and finance, including lending institutions. Chapters 14 and 15 cover appraisal. No matter what exam you're studying for, you should study Chapter 14, but if you aren't preparing for the general appraisal certification exam, you can skip Chapter 15.

Most states have their examinations prepared for them by a testing company, which often administers the examination as well. The three largest testing companies for real estate exams are AMP, PSI, and Pearson-Vue. You can get test information for each of these companies. Some of the largest states prepare their own examinations. It doesn't really matter much to you how the examinations are prepared, because from state to state most of them follow the same format as described in Chapter 23. Your state's examining authority will provide you with a lot of material about the exam you will have to take, including sample questions, information about testing sites and dates, and information about the content of the exam. Inquire whether your state uses only a hard copy paper test or offers it on screen. Some states have introduced computer-driven exams at remote locations, which you may find more convenient. You should also obtain a copy of your state's real estate license laws (available from the same source), because a portion of the examination will cover it. It will come in handy as you study Chapter 5 ("State Real Estate License Law"); space is provided in that chapter for you to write in specific features of your state's laws.

Sample Questions and Examinations

Most chapters are followed by sample questions covering the material contained in the chapter and written in the format most frequently encountered on licensing examinations. You can use these questions to test yourself on what you have read.

When you have finished studying the material in the book, you can take the model examinations in Chapter 24. These will allow you to check your retention of the material you have read and will give you some experience in taking real estate examinations in a format similar to the licensing examination. Each model examination has a 3-hour time limit.

You should not take all the examinations at once. Rather, take one, and then correct it, using the key in Chapter 25. The questions you got wrong will pinpoint the areas in which you need further study. Do this additional studying, and then take the second examination. Once again, use the questions you missed to guide you to still further study. For questions involving mathematics, the answer explanations in Chapter 25 should help you to understand why you missed each question you got wrong and to avoid making the same mistake again. Then take the third examination, once again using the few questions you miss as guides for final study before taking the licensing examination itself.

Taking Examinations

Chapter 23 discusses *techniques* for taking examinations. This chapter will tell you all you must know about how to prepare for an examination, how to approach it, and how to get the highest score possible. *Be sure to read this chapter!* It provides valuable guidelines for taking the licensing examination and will introduce you to the kind of examination you can expect to encounter.

Study Strategy

You should approach your study of the materials you must know in a systematic and sensible way in order to get the most out of it. The following study strategy will be helpful:

1. First, find out everything you can about the licensing examination offered by your state, including where and when it is given, how much it costs, and how to apply. See Chapter 23, "Examination Preparation," for a full checklist of the things you should find out. When you need information, go to your state's real estate regulatory Web site. There you can find out about the exam, when and where it's offered, how much it costs, how to apply, what education requirements you have to meet—in short, everything you need to know. You also can download a copy of your state's license law and regulations. If you can't get on the Internet, or the information you want isn't on the web site, then don't write a letter—TELEPHONE. Even if it's long distance, it only costs a few dollars, and you get the information quickly. Getting a response to a letter can take a week or longer.
2. Next, assemble all the study materials you will need. They include:

   - This book.
   - Your state's Real Estate License Law, Rules and Regulations, disclosure forms, sample contracts, and any other materials provided by the agency.
   - Any study materials *specifically* recommended or required by your state, most particularly, *all* study materials provided by your state's real estate licensing agency; these will tell you what you must know about the special features of your state's laws and practices.

3. Now begin studying. Start with Chapter 2 in this book, "Definitions of Real Estate Terms." Read it carefully, making sure you take note of all the terms. Don't try to understand them all at this point; just become slightly familiar with them.
4. Proceed through the chapters in the order they appear in the book. When you get to Chapter 5 ("State Real Estate License Law"), have your copy of your state's license law handy to refer to.
5. When you have read through Chapter 23 and have answered all the questions at the end of each chapter, take the sample examinations in your field of interest and correct them. Note your weak areas, to be concentrated upon in later study.
6. At this point, read all the study materials provided by your state, and compare your state's practices and laws with those outlined in this book. You will have noted a number of places in this book where you should fill in your state's practice on a particular point—now is the time to do that.
7. Now that you have covered general real estate principles and your state's special materials, take another practice examination.
8. Go over this book again, as well as the materials your state has provided and its license law. Pay particular attention to the problem areas pinpointed by the questions you missed on the first two sample examinations. Take a third examination.

Now you should be ready to take, and PASS, your chosen real estate examination. Be sure to schedule your studying so that you finish up only a day or two before the actual examination; in this way, all the material you have learned will be fresh in your mind.

Definitions of Real Estate Terms

On the following pages is a glossary of real estate terminology. It is quite extensive and probably covers all the terms you might be expected to be familiar with when you take a licensing examination. We suggest that you begin your preparation for the examination by carefully reading over this glossary. This may seem a boring and tedious thing to do, but it will have many advantages. The main benefit is that it will acquaint you with some important terminology used in the real estate business. Once you have studied these terms, the remaining material in this book will be much easier for you to absorb; you will already have some familiarity with most of what you read. In fact, the purpose of the rest of the book is to show you how all the many items defined in the glossary relate to one another in the real estate business.

The best way to study the glossary is to go over it once fairly quickly. Don't skip anything, but don't study it intensely, either. A while later, begin to go over the terms much more carefully, absorbing each definition as it is given. Make sure not to skip over anything: many real estate terms may look familiar because they are composed of familiar words. More likely than not, however, you will find that the *real estate meaning* is *not* the one you are used to. This is one of the more serious problems that many people have with the real estate licensing examinations: you must learn *terminology* and be able to understand and use the special meanings that many words have in a real estate context.

Once you have spent a good amount of time on the terminology, go on through the rest of the book, using the glossary for reference whenever you need to. Later, as the time for the examination approaches, you will find it very helpful to go over the glossary again. It will be a sort of thumbnail review for you to read the terms once again, after you have studied the rest of the book. This will be of considerable help in your final preparation for the examination, especially since you will often encounter strictly definitional questions such as "The term *fee simple* means most nearly——."

Words in italics or small caps are defined in this section or elsewhere in the book.

Glossary

AAA TENANT / *See* TRIPLE-A TENANT.

ABSTRACT OF TITLE / A summary of all of the recorded instruments and proceedings that affect the title to property.

Importance: A person going to buy real estate or lend money on it wants assurance of ownership. Usually an attorney or title insurance company prepares an abstract of title, based on documents in the county courthouse, to be certain of ownership; and only if title is good or marketable does that person buy or make the loan. Typically, *title insurance* is also acquired.

ABUTTING / Adjoining or meeting. *See also* ADJACENT.

ACCELERATED DEPRECIATION / Depreciation methods, chosen for income tax or accounting purposes, that offer greater deductions in the early years. *Straight-line depreciation*, rather than accelerated depreciation, generally applies to buildings bought after 1986.

ACCELERATION CLAUSE / A provision in a loan giving the lender the right to declare the entire amount immediately due and payable upon the violation of a different loan provision, such as failure to make payments on time.

Importance: Without an acceleration clause, a missed payment is just that—one overdue payment. The acceleration clause means the entire loan is due, and the real estate may be foreclosed on.

ACCEPTANCE / The act of agreeing to accept an offer.

Importance: To have a valid contract there must be an offer and an acceptance. The acceptance may be from either party to the other: for example, buyer/seller; landlord/tenant.

ACCESSION / Additions to property as a result of annexing fixtures or alluvial deposits.

ACCESS RIGHT / The right of an owner to get to and from his/her property.

Importance: Property may be or may become encircled by other property. The access right gives an easement by necessity, which allows the owner of landlocked property to cross over adjacent property to reach a street.

ACCRETION / Addition to land through processes of nature, such as deposits of soil carried by streams. *See* alluvium.

ACRE / A measure of land: 43,560 square feet.

ACTION TO QUIET TITLE / *See* QUIET TITLE SUIT.

ACTUAL EVICTION / Expulsion of a tenant from the property.

ADA / Americans with Disabilities Act.

ADJACENT / Lying near but not necessarily in actual contact with.

Importance: When describing the physical proximity of property, the word includes touching property and other nearby parcels, for example, property across the street.

ADJOINING / Contiguous; attaching; in actual contact with.

Importance: In describing the proximity of land, adjoining property is actually touching.

ADJUSTABLE-RATE MORTGAGE (ARM) / A mortgage loan with an interest rate that is allowed to vary during the life of the loan; usually there are *caps* on the amounts by which the interest rate can change annually and over the life of the loan.

Importance: ARMs are often a viable alternative to fixed-rate mortgages, and are especially desirable to the borrower who expects that rates will decline. Often the initial rate is lower than that on a fixed-rate mortgage, and there are caps on the ceiling rate that can be charged if interest rates rise.

ADMINISTRATOR / A person appointed by a court to administer the estate of a deceased individual who left no will.

Importance: If a person dies leaving a will, an executor is usually named to carry out the provisions of the will. When there is no *executor*, an administrator is appointed by the court. The administrator receives a fee.

ADMINISTRATOR'S DEED / A deed conveying the property of a person who died without a will (intestate).

Importance: If a person owned real estate and died without leaving a will, the administrator will give a deed. However, the administrator does not want the potential liability associated with a general warranty deed, so an administrator's deed is used.

ADULT / A person who has attained the age of majority.

Importance: In most states, a person who is 18 years of age is considered an adult. Also, some persons who are married or are in military service may be considered adults though not yet 18. A contract with a minor can be *disaffirmed* by the minor or by that person shortly after he/she becomes an adult.

AD VALOREM / According to valuation.

Importance: Used in describing a property tax rate. *See also* AD VALOREM TAX.

AD VALOREM TAX / A tax based on the value of the thing being taxed. **Example:** If the effective tax rate is 1 percent, the tax will be $1 per $100 of property value.

Importance: In some states, there are several taxing jurisdictions that levy ad valorem taxes. Tax districts include the city, county, and school district.

ADVERSE POSSESSION / A means of acquiring title to real estate when an occupant has been in actual, open, notorious, exclusive, and continuous occupancy of the property for the period required by state law.

Importance: A person can gain title to real estate (or lose title) by acting in a certain way for long enough. In some states, this process may take 3, 5, 10, or 25 years, depending on the circumstances.

AFFIDAVIT / A statement or declaration in writing, sworn to or affirmed before some officer who is authorized to administer an oath or affirmation.

Importance: Some statements must be in the form of an affidavit before they can be recorded. For example, a contractor's lien must be in affidavit form to be perfected.

AFFIRM / To confirm; to ratify; to verify.

AGENCY / The legal relationship between a principal and his/her *agent* arising from a contract in which the principal employs the agent to perform certain acts on the principal's behalf.

Importance: The law of agency governs the rights and obligations of a broker to the principal and of a licensed real estate salesperson to the broker.

AGENCY DISCLOSURE / A written explanation, to be signed by a prospective buyer or seller of real estate, explaining to the client the role that the broker plays in the transaction. The purpose of disclosure is to explain whether the broker represents the buyer or seller or is a dual agent (representing both) or a subagent (an agent of the seller's broker). This allows the customer to understand to which party the broker owes loyalty.

AGENT / A person who undertakes to transact some business or to manage some affair for another, with the authority of the latter. Frequently the term "real estate agent" refers to a licensed salesperson, while a BROKER is called a "broker." Generally, a broker's license requires more experience and education. A salesperson must be sponsored as an active licensee by a licensed broker. **Example:** An owner employs a broker to act as his agent in selling real property; the broker in turn employs salespersons to act as her agents to sell the same property.

Importance: An agent has certain duties to the principal, including loyalty. The agent is to act in the best interest of the principal, even when such action is not in the agent's best interest.

AGREEMENT OF SALE / A written agreement between seller and purchaser in which the purchaser agrees to buy certain real estate, and the seller agrees to sell, upon the terms and conditions of the agreement. Also called *offer and acceptance; contract of sale.*

Importance: When you are buying or selling property, your rights and obligations are described in this document. Offer this document or accept it only when you are satisfied that it contains what you will agree to in a final transaction.

AIR RIGHTS / The right to use, control, or occupy the space above a designated property. **Example:** The MetLife Building in New York City is built on air rights above the Grand Central Railroad Station.

Importance: Most property ownership rights include air rights up to the skies; however, air rights may be limited to a certain height, or, conversely, air rights may be the only property owned, having a floor that begins a stated number of feet above the ground.

ALIENATION / Transferring property to another, as the transfer of property and possession of lands, by gift or by sale, from one person to another.

Importance: In some states, property may be transferred by voluntary alienation, as in a sale for cash, or involuntarily, as in a condemnation.

ALLUVIUM (ALLUVION) / Soil deposited by accretion; usually considered to belong to the owner of the land to which it is added. *See also* ACCESSION.

ALT-A MORTGAGES / Residential property–backed loans made to borrowers who have better CREDIT SCORES than SUBPRIME borrowers but provide less documentation than normally required for a loan application.

Importance: *Alt-A mortgages* typically carry interest rates somewhere between the best rates available and those offered on subprime loans.

AMENITIES / In appraising, the nonmonetary benefits derived from property ownership. **Examples:** pride of home ownership; accessibility to good public schools, parks, and cultural facilities.

Importance: Ownership of real estate may add to one's self-esteem and community involvement.

AMORTIZATION / A gradual paying off of a debt by periodic installments.

Importance: Most mortgages require the payment of interest plus at least some amortization of principal, so that the loan is eventually retired by the amortization payments.

AMORTIZATION TERM / The time required to retire a debt through periodic payments; also known as the *full amortization term.* Many mortgage loans have an amortization term of 15, 20, 25, or 30 years. Some have an amortization schedule as a 30-year loan, but require a *balloon payment* in 5, 10, or 15 years.

Importance: Both the lender and the borrower are assured that the loan will be retired through regular payments without the need to refinance.

ANCHOR TENANT / The main tenant in a shopping center, usually a department store in a regional shopping center or a grocery store in a neighborhood shopping center. Large shopping centers may have more than one anchor tenant. The anchor tenant attracts both customers and other tenants.

ANNUAL PERCENTAGE RATE (APR) / The cost of credit, expressed as an annual interest rate, which must be shown in consumer loan documents, as specified by the Federal Reserve's *Regulation Z* that implements the federal Truth-in-Lending Act.

ANNUITY / A series of equal or nearly equal periodic payments or receipts. **Example:** The receipt of $100 per year for the next five years constitutes a $100 five-year annuity.

ANTICIPATION, PRINCIPLE OF / In real estate appraisal, the principle that the value of a property today is the present value of the sum of anticipated future benefits.

Importance: The anticipation principle serves as the basis for the *income approach* to appraisal.

ANTITRUST LAWS / Federal and state acts to protect trade and commerce from monopolies and restrictions.

APPORTIONMENT / (1) *Prorating* property expenses, such as taxes and insurance, between buyer and seller. (2) The partitioning of property into individual parcels by tenants in common.

APPRAISAL / An opinion or estimate of the value of a property.

Importance: If a buyer is unfamiliar with the value of real estate in an area, it is prudent to require that, as a condition of the agreement of sale, the property be appraised for an amount at least equal to the price being paid. Also, lenders require an appraisal of property as a requirement for making a loan. The borrower will pay the appraisal fee.

APPRAISAL APPROACH / One of three methods used in estimating the value of property: *income approach, sales comparison approach,* and *cost approach.* See each.

Importance: Having three separate methods to estimate the value of property will add confidence to an appraiser's value estimate. However, not all approaches are applicable for all properties.

APPRAISAL BY SUMMATION / *See* COST APPROACH.

APPRAISAL DATE / In an *appraisal report*, the date to which the value applies; distinguished from *report date*.

Importance: Because market conditions change, the appraisal date establishes the conditions for which the value is estimated.

APPRAISAL FOUNDATION / An organization that came into existence in 1987 in an effort to encourage uniform requirements for appraisal qualifications and reporting standards. *See also* UNIFORM STANDARDS OF PROFESSIONAL APPRAISAL PRACTICE.

APPRAISAL INSTITUTE / An organization of professional appraisers that was formed in 1991 by the merger of the American Institute of Real Estate Appraisers and the Society of Real Estate Appraisers. It offers *MAI* and *SRA* designations.

APPRAISAL MANAGEMENT COMPANY (AMC) / A firm that acts as an intermediary between certified or licensed real estate appraisers and clients (often mortgage lenders) seeking appraisal services.

Importance: *Appraisal management companies* became firmly entrenched in the appraisal market when the Home Valuation Code of Conduct was adopted by FREDDIE MAC in 2009. The code required lenders to go through an intermediary to order appraisals so as to prevent lenders from overly influencing the appraisal process. The Code was superseded by the DODD-FRANK WALL STREET REFORM AND CONSUMER PROTECTION ACT in 2010, but AMCs continue as a prominent part of the appraisal market.

APPRAISAL REPORT / A document that describes the findings of an appraisal engagement. Reports may be presented in the following formats: oral, letter, form, or narrative, and may be self-contained, summary, or restricted. *See* UNIFORM STANDARDS OF PROFESSIONAL APPRAISAL PRACTICE.

APPRAISER / One who is qualified to provide a professional opinion on the value of property. All states in the United States offer at least two certifications for real estate appraisers: CERTIFIED GENERAL APPRAISER, awarded to one who is qualified to appraise any property, and CERTIFIED RESIDENTIAL APPRAISER, awarded to one who is qualified to appraise residences with up to four units and vacant lots. State certification requires education, experience, and passing a written examination. Some states offer additional categories for licensees and trainees. Several appraisal organizations offer professional designations. The Appraisal Institute is best known in real estate; it offers the MAI (for income property) and SRA (residential) designations. Others include American Society of Appraisers, International Association of Assessing Officers, International Right of Way Association, National Society of Real Estate Appraisers, and American Society of Farm Managers and Rural Appraisers.

APPRECIATION / An increase in the value of property.

Importance: Appreciation is one of the most significant benefits from real estate ownership. Gains from inflation as well as real income are included.

APPURTENANCE / Something that is outside the property itself but is considered a part of the property and adds to its greater enjoyment, such as the right to cross another's land (i.e., a *right-of-way* or *easement*).

Importance: The right to use another's land for a special purpose can materially affect the value of the subject property.

APR / ANNUAL PERCENTAGE RATE.

ARBITRATION / Process of settling disputes through a neutral third party agreed upon by each side in the dispute. In most cases, arbitration is decided by private firms established to provide this service and is an alternative to filing suit in the public courts.

ARM / *See* ADJUSTABLE-RATE MORTGAGE.

ARM'S-LENGTH TRANSACTION / The "typical, normal transaction," in which all parties have reasonable knowledge of the facts pertinent to the transaction, are under no pressure or duress to transact, and are ready, willing, and able to transact.

ASA / A senior professional designation offered by the American Society of Appraisers. The ASA designation is awarded upon meeting rigorous requirements that include extensive experience, education, and approved sample reports.

AS IS / Without guarantees as to condition, as in a sale.

ASSESSED VALUE or VALUATION / The value against which a property tax is imposed. The assessed value is often lower than the MARKET VALUE due to state law, conservative tax district appraisals, and infrequent reassessment. It may also exceed market value.

Importance: The assessed value of a property is typically a reasonable estimate by the tax assessor, who must periodically review all property in the jurisdiction. By contrast, an appraisal of a single property is more likely to approximate its market value.

ASSESSMENT / A charge against real estate made by a government to cover the cost of an improvement, such as a street or sewer line. *See also* ASSESSED VALUATION.

Importance: Property buyers and owners need to recognize that they may have to pay assessments for municipal improvements that affect their property. Frequently, the owner has little or no influence on the decision.

ASSESSMENT RATIO / The ratio of assessed value to market value. **Example:** A county requires a 40 percent assessment ratio on all property to be taxed. Property with a $100,000 value is therefore assessed at $40,000 (40 percent of $100,000), and the tax rate is applied to $40,000.

ASSESSOR / A government official who is responsible for establishing the value of property for the purpose of *ad valorem taxation*.

Importance: The assessor estimates the value of each piece of real estate in the tax jurisdiction, but does not fix the tax rate or amount.

ASSIGNEE / The person to whom an agreement or contract is sold or transferred.

Importance: This legal term refers to the person who receives the contract.

ASSIGNMENT / The method or manner by which a right or contract is transferred from one person to another.

Importance: Contracts for the sale of real estate are generally assignable, except when financing must be arranged or certain conditions are imposed on a party. In a lease, an assignment gives all the rights of the original tenant to the new tenant.

ASSIGNOR / A party who assigns or transfers an agreement or contract to another.

Importance: Although many contracts can be assigned, the assignor is not necessarily relieved of the obligation. For example, debts cannot be assigned. Another party can assume a debt, but the original borrower remains liable.

ASSUMABLE LOAN / A mortgage loan that allows a new home purchaser to undertake the obligation of the existing loan with no change in loan terms. Loans without due-on-sale clauses, including most FHA and VA mortgages, are generally assumable.

ASSUMPTION OF MORTGAGE / The purchase of mortgaged property whereby the buyer accepts liability for the debt that continues to exist. The seller remains liable to the lender unless the lender agrees to release him/her.

Importance: When entering an agreement for the purchase or sale of real estate, the financing should be checked to determine whether the mortgage is assumable. If the mortgage carries favorable terms and is assumable, this fact will add value to the transaction.

ATTACHMENT / Legal seizure of property to force payment of a debt.

Importance: Property can be taken as security for a debt provided that such action has court approval.

ATTEST / To witness to; to witness by observation and signature.

Importance: Certain documents must be attested to as a condition for recording at the county courthouse.

ATTORNEY-IN-FACT / A person who is authorized to act for another under a power of attorney, which may be general or limited in scope.

Importance: A person may give another the right to act for him/her in some or all matters (*power of attorney*).

The designated person, called an attorney-in-fact, need not be an attorney at law.

AUTOMATED VALUATION MODEL (AVM) / Computerized method for estimating the value of a property. Often used for mass *appraisal* purposes, such as reassessment of a city's property tax base. **Example:** An appraisal firm collected extensive data on home sales and the distinguishing characteristics of each home. By applying an automated valuation model to the data, the firm could quickly estimate a preliminary value of any home in the local market.

AVULSION / The sudden removal of land from one owner to another that occurs when a river abruptly changes its channel.

Importance: If a stream or river is a boundary line, the boundary may change with the addition or removal of land.

BABY BOOMERS / Individuals who were born during the years following World War II, generally defined as 1946–1964. This group represents a sizable portion of the consuming public, and their spending habits and lifestyle have a powerful influence on the economy.

BAILOUT / An effort by the government to provide sufficient financial assistance to prevent the failure of a specific private or quasi-private entity. The program may consist of loans or grants to satisfy outstanding debts or may involve government purchase of an equity position in the firm.

BALANCE, PRINCIPLE OF / In real estate appraisal, the principle that there is an optimal mix of inputs that, when combined with land, will result in the greatest land value. Inputs, or *factors of production,* include labor, capital, and entrepreneurship.

BALLOON PAYMENT / The final payment on a loan, when that payment is greater than the preceding installment payments and satisfies the note in full. **Example:** A debt requires interest-only payments annually for 5 years, at the end of which time the balance of the principal (a balloon payment) is due.

Importance: In arranging financing for real estate, if a balloon is involved, the borrower will need to plan for the large balance that will come due.

BAND OF INVESTMENT / A weighted average of debt and equity rates.

BANKRUPTCY / The financial inability to pay one's debts when due. The debtor seeks relief through court action that may work out or erase debts. There are a number of chapters in bankruptcy law; a certain chapter requires liquidation of all assets to pay off debts, and another chapter allows the debtor to continue operations. Certain property is free from attachment by creditors, depending on state law.

BARGAIN AND SALE DEED / A deed that conveys real estate, generally lacking a warranty. The *grantor* will thus claim to have ownership but will not defend against all claims.

Importance: Sometimes a property owner does not wish to offer a *warranty deed*, but will give more assurance than is offered by a *quitclaim deed*. A bargain and sale deed is a compromise between those two.

BASE AND MERIDIAN / Imaginary lines used by surveyors to find and describe the location of land.

Importance: In states that use a rectangular or government survey method, these lines are similar to latitude and longitude.

BASE LINE / Part of the *government rectangular survey* method of land description. The base line is the major east-west line to which all north-south measurements refer.

BASIC INDUSTRY MULTIPLIER / In economic base analysis, the ratio of total population in a local area to employment in basic industry. *Basic industry* is considered to be any concern that attracts income from outside the local area. The jobs added in basic industry may also contribute to the need for local service jobs (telephone operator, nurse, supermarket clerk, etc.); and, if the workers have families, additional new people may be brought to the area.

BASIS POINT / One 100th of 1%.

BEFORE-AND-AFTER RULE / In an *eminent domain* award, practice followed by many jurisdictions of appraising the property value both before and after the taking, considering enhancement or injury to the property that was the result of *condemnation*.

BENEFICIARY / The person who receives or is to receive the benefits resulting from certain acts.

BEQUEATH / To give or hand down personal property by a will.

BEQUEST / Personal property that is given by the terms of a will.

BILATERAL CONTRACT / A contract under which each party promises performance. *Contrast with* unilateral contract.

BILL OF ASSURANCE / Recorded restrictions affecting a subdivision and a part of all deeds to lots therein.

BILL OF SALE / A written instrument that passes title of personal property from a seller to a buyer.

Importance: A real estate sales agreement is prepared on an *agreement of sale.* A bill of sale is used when furniture and portable appliances are sold.

BINDER / An agreement, accompanied by a deposit, for the purchase of real estate, as evidence of good faith on the part of the purchaser.

Importance: Binders are seldom used in some states because of general agreement and requirements on brokers to use forms specially promulgated for use in their states.

BIWEEKLY LOAN / A mortgage that requires principal and interest payments at two-week intervals. The payment is exactly half of what a monthly payment would be. Over a year's time, the 26 payments are equivalent to 13 monthly payments on a comparable monthly-payment mortgage. As a result, the loan will be amortized much faster than a loan with monthly payments.

BLANKET MORTGAGE / A single *mortgage* that includes more than one parcel of real estate as security.

Importance: When one piece of property is insufficient collateral for a loan, the borrower may be able to satisfy the requirement by putting up more property as security. It is a good idea to negotiate release clauses whereby each parcel can be released from the mortgage when a portion of the loan is paid off, without having to pay off the entire loan.

BOARD OF DIRECTORS / People selected by stockholders to control the business of the corporation.

BONA FIDE / In good faith; without fraud. **Example:** A purchaser pays for property without knowledge of any title defects. In a bona fide sale the seller accepts consideration without notice of any reason against the sale.

Importance: An act in good faith is open, sincere, and honest.

BOND / A certificate that serves as evidence of a debt. *See also* MORTGAGE.

Importance: There are many types of bonds that may be used in real estate. A *mortgage bond* is secured by a mortgage on property. A *completion bond* (also called *performance bond*) is usually issued by a bonding company to assure completion of construction if a contractor fails.

BOOT / In an exchange of like property (i.e., real estate for real estate), boot is unlike property included to balance the value of the exchange.

BOY / Abbreviation for "beginning of year."

Importance: In most leases, rent is due in the beginning of each period. If a commercial lease requires annual payments, rent is due in the beginning of the year (BOY).

BRANCH OFFICE / A place of operation for a real estate firm that is located apart from the main office. The office is owned by the firm owner but is managed by another licensed broker, who may be called an *associate broker* or *broker associate,* and may have other agents working out of the location.

BROKER / A person who is licensed by a state to act for property owners in real estate transactions, within the scope of state law.

Importance: In most states, a person must be licensed as a broker to act in a real estate transaction for another. A licensed real estate salesperson must be sponsored by a broker who accepts responsibility for the salesperson's acts. A broker is regulated by the law of agency, which requires the broker to act in the best interest of the principal.

BROKERAGE / The business of being a *broker*.

Importance: Parties are brought together in a real estate transaction, such as a sale, lease, rental, or exchange.

BROKER'S OPINION OF VALUE (BOV) / An analysis provided by a real estate broker to assist a buyer or seller in making decisions about the listing price of real estate or a suitable bid for purchase; similar to *comparative market analysis.* A fee may or may not be charged. This analysis may not be represented as an APPRAISAL. For mortgage lending purposes, the lender requires an appraisal performed by an APPRAISER who is certified or licensed by the state.

BUBBLE / Situation in which the prices of stock, real estate, or some other asset rise to levels well beyond reasonable VALUATION before "the bubble bursts" and prices eventually return to normal.

BUILDING CAPITALIZATION RATE / In appraisal, the *capitalization rate* is used to convert an *income stream* into one lump-sum value. The rate for the building may differ from that for the land because the building is a wasting asset.

BUILDING CODES / Regulations established by local governments and describing the minimum structural requirements for buildings, including foundation, roofing, plumbing, electrical, and other specifications for safety and sanitation.

Importance: Work on real estate must be in compliance with the building codes, or it will not pass the required inspections.

BUILDING INSPECTION / Inspection of property as it proceeds under construction to ensure that it meets building codes: foundation, plumbing, electrical wiring, roofing, materials. Also, periodic inspection of existing public buildings for health and safety considerations.

BUILDING LINE / A line fixed at a certain distance from the front and/or sides of a lot, beyond which the building may not project.

Importance: When situating improvements on a lot, it is important to observe the building line. Often, one must check with the city to ascertain exactly where this line is.

BUILDING LOAN AGREEMENT / *See* CONSTRUCTION LOAN.

BUILDING PERMIT / Permission granted by a local government to build a specific structure at a particular site.

BULLET LOAN / Typically a loan with a 5- to 10-year term and no amortization. At the end of the term, the full amount is due.

BUNDLE OF RIGHTS THEORY / The theory that ownership of realty implies rights, such as occupancy, use and enjoyment, and the right to sell, bequeath, give, or lease all or part of these rights.

Importance: In a real estate transaction, knowing what one has or is acquiring is vital, because some of the bundle of rights may be missing.

BUYDOWN / Payment of discount points at loan origination in order to secure a lower interest rate; the rate may be bought down for only a few years or for the life of the loan.

Importance: When offered low rate financing on property being bought, one should determine whether the buydown applies to just the first few years or the full term of the loan.

BUYER'S AGENCY AGREEMENT / Contract or verbal understanding that creates the relationship between a potential buyer and a BUYER'S BROKER. Essentially, the broker who is the buyer's agent agrees to represent the interests of the buyer, and the buyer agrees to use the agent in any sales transaction occurring under the terms of the agreement. Although the buyer's broker represents the buyer, the COMMISSION is typically paid by the seller.

BUYER'S BROKER / An agent hired by a prospective purchaser to find an acceptable property for purchase. The broker then represents the buyer and negotiates with the seller in the purchaser's best interest. **Example:** Abel wishes to purchase a small apartment complex. Abel hires Baker, a licensed real estate broker, to find such a property. Baker is acting as a buyer's broker and earns a commission from Abel when an acceptable property is found and the owner is willing to sell.

CANCELLATION CLAUSE / A provision in a contract that gives the right to terminate obligations upon the occurrence of certain specified conditions or events.

Importance: A cancellation clause in a lease may allow the landlord to break the lease upon sale of the building. A lessor may need a cancellation clause if he/she plans to sell the building; the buyer may have another use for it.

CAP / A limit on the amount by which the interest rate on an *adjustable rate mortgage* may be changed; usually there are annual caps and lifetime caps.

Importance: Without caps, interest rates of adjustable rate mortgages can increase without limit. Also, abbreviation for income *capitalization*.

CAPITALIZATION / A process whereby anticipated future income is converted to one lump sum capital value.

Importance: Rental property evaluation is enhanced by the capitalization process. Income is divided by a *capitalization rate* to estimate value, using the following formula:

$$\text{Property Value} = \frac{\text{Rental Income less Operating Expenses}}{\text{Capitalization Rate}}$$

CAPITALIZATION RATE (CAP RATE) / A rate of return used to convert anticipated future income into a capital value. The capitalization rate includes interest and principal recovery.

Importance: *See also* CAPITALIZATION.

CAPITALIZED INCOME / The value estimated by the process of converting an *income stream* into a lump-sum amount; also called *capitalized value*.

CAPTURE RATE / The portion of total sales in the real estate market that are sold by one entity or one project.

CARRYING CHARGES / Expenses necessary for holding property, such as taxes and interest on idle property or property under construction.

Importance: When considering nonrental real estate as an investment, carrying charges should be taken into account.

CASE-SHILLER/S&P HOME PRICE INDEX / A HOME PRICE INDEX developed by economists Carl Case and Robert Shiller for Standard & Poor's Corporation. The index is based on a constant quality, repeat-sale methodology that accounts for variations in the characteristics and location of the single-family homes used. Data on home sales are drawn from local deed records.

Importance: The *Case-Shiller/S&P Home Price Index* is used to calculate the average price appreciation or decline in each of the 20 metropolitan districts covered by the Index.

CASH FLOW / Periodic amounts accruing from an investment after all cash expenses, payments, and taxes have been deducted.

CASH-ON-CASH / *See* EQUITY DIVIDEND.

CAVEAT EMPTOR / "Let the buyer beware." The buyer must examine the goods or property and buy at his/her own risk. In recent years the doctrine has been eroded, especially by the disclosure requirements (regarding property conditions) introduced in many states.

Importance: This was once an accepted condition of sale. Home buyers in some states have much more protection now, as sellers and brokers are required to disclose problems or face possible penalties.

CAVEATS / Warnings, often in writing to a potential buyer, to be careful.

CCIM / *See* CERTIFIED COMMERCIAL INVESTMENT MEMBER.

CC&Rs / Covenants, conditions, and restrictions. These are limitations on land use, usually in a deed, imposed in a subdivision. Protects homeowners by preventing certain uses and assuring uniformity.

CEASE AND DESIST / Order by a court or administrative agency prohibiting a person or business from continuing an activity. Used in real estate brokerage to prevent anti-trust behavior among firms, or in illegal discrimination.

CENSUS TRACT / Geographical area mapped by the U.S. government for which demographic information is available. This information may be used by retailers, real estate developers, and brokers to estimate consumer purchasing power in a market area.

CERCLA / Comprehensive Environmental Response Compensation and Liability Act.

CERTIFICATE OF ELIGIBILITY / Document issued by the DEPARTMENT OF VETERANS AFFAIRS to indicate the recipient's ability to get a home loan GUARANTEED by the agency. The certificate may be obtained by submitting the proper forms to the agency or from a lender participating in the agency's automated certificate program.

CERTIFICATE OF NO DEFENSE / *See* ESTOPPEL CERTIFICATE.

CERTIFICATE OF OCCUPANCY / A document issued by a local government to a developer permitting the structure to be occupied by members of the public. Issuance of the certificate generally indicates that the building is in compliance with public health and *building codes.*

CERTIFICATE OF REASONABLE VALUE (CRV) / Required for a VA-guaranteed home loan, the CRV is based on an appraiser's estimate of value of the property to be purchased. Because the loan amount may not exceed the CRV, the first step in getting a VA loan is to request an appraisal. Although anyone can request a VA appraisal, it is customary for the lender or the real estate agent to do so. The form used is VA Form 26-1805, Request for Determination of Reasonable Value.

CERTIFICATE OF REDEMPTION / Document provided by county tax collectors showing that all past-due property taxes have been paid.

CERTIFIED COMMERCIAL INVESTMENT MEMBER (CCIM) / A designation awarded by the CCIM Institute, which is affiliated with the NATIONAL ASSOCIATION OF REALTORS®.

CERTIFIED GENERAL APPRAISER / A person qualified to appraise any property, under appraiser certification law adopted by all states.

CERTIFIED PROPERTY MANAGER (CPM) / A member of the Institute of Real Estate Management, an organization affiliated with the *National Association of Realtors®.*

CERTIFIED RESIDENTIAL APPRAISER / A person qualified to appraise residences and up to four units of housing, under appraiser certification law. Standards call for less education, less experience, and a less comprehensive examination than are required for a certified general appraiser.

CERTIFIED RESIDENTIAL BROKER (CRB) / A designation awarded by the Realtors National Marketing Institute, which is affiliated with the *National Association of Realtors®.*

CHAIN / A unit of land measurement, 66 feet in length.
 Importance: In surveying, land descriptions sometimes use the chain.

CHAIN OF TITLE / A history of *conveyances* and *encumbrances* affecting a title from the time the original patent was granted, or as far back as records are available. *See also* ABSTRACT OF TITLE.

CHATTEL / Personal property, including autos and household goods and fixtures.
 Importance: Many laws have different applications, depending on whether a property is real estate or chattels. It can be important to know the type of property.

CHATTEL MORTGAGE / A pledge of personal property as security for a debt.

CLAWBACK / Provision in a law or contract that limits or reverses a payment or distribution for specified reasons.

CLEAR TITLE / A title that is free and clear of all *encumbrances.*
 Importance: When buying or selling real estate, it is essential to know whether the title is encumbered or clear. If it is not clear, the effect of the encumbrances on the value or use of the real estate must be checked.

CLIENT / The person who employs a broker, lawyer, accountant, appraiser, and so on.
 Importance: The law describes certain relationships that a professional has with a client. In a real estate transaction it is essential to know exactly what that relationship is. *See also* AGENCY.

CLOSING / (1) The act of transferring ownership of a property from seller to buyer in accordance with a sales contract. (2) The time when a closing takes place.

CLOSING COSTS / Various fees and expenses payable by the seller and buyer at the time of a real estate CLOSING (also called *settlement* or *transaction costs*).

The following are some closing costs:
- BROKERAGE commissions
- lender DISCOUNT POINTS/other fees
- TITLE INSURANCE premium
- deed RECORDING fees
- loan PREPAYMENT PENALTY
- INSPECTION and APPRAISAL fees
- attorney's fees

A rough approximation of a homebuyer's *closing costs* is 2–4% of the purchase price. Similarly, a seller's closing costs may be 3–10% of the sale price. A brokerage commission of 3–7% is included, often paid by the seller.

CLOSING DATE / The date on which the seller delivers the deed and the buyer pays for the property; also called *settlement date*.

Importance: The *agreement of sale* will reflect when closing is to take place. A buyer or seller may be considered to have defaulted on a contract if unable to close by the agreed upon date.

CLOSING STATEMENT / An accounting of funds from a real estate sale, made to both the seller and the buyer separately. Most states require the broker to furnish accurate closing statements to all parties to any transaction in which he/she is an agent.

Importance: This statement shows the accounting, which should be consistent with the agreement of sale. If an error is suspected in the closing statement, the closing should not take place.

CLOUD ON THE TITLE / An outstanding claim or *encumbrance* that, if valid, will affect or impair the owner's title.

Importance: A cloud on title can restrict use and affect ownership. This should be cleared before closing. An attorney or title company should be consulted for assurance of title.

COLLATERAL / Property pledged as security for a debt.

COLOR OF TITLE / That which appears to be good title but is not.

Importance: A person can be fooled by believing he/she is receiving good title. An attorney or title company's input is essential.

COMMERCIAL PROPERTY / Property designed for use by retail, wholesale, office, hotel, and service users.

Importance: Nearly all cities and towns have zoning that restricts the location of commercial property.

COMMINGLE / To mingle or mix, as by the deposit of another's money in a broker's personal account.

Importance: Brokers generally must maintain all *earnest money* in an account that is separate from their personal funds.

COMMISSION / (1) The amount earned by real estate brokers for their services; (2) the official body that enforces real estate license laws.

Importance: (1) Commissions are the way real estate brokers earn money. (2) The Real Estate Commission, in most states, licenses brokers and salespersons and may suspend a license for certain behavior.

COMMITMENT / A pledge or promise; a firm agreement.

Importance: When financing is needed to buy property, a commitment from a lender must be obtained. The loan terms are noted in the commitment, which may include an interest rate lock-in.

COMMON ELEMENTS / Generally, in a *condominium* development, land or a tract of land considered to be the property of the development in which all owners can enjoy use.

Importance: Owners of condominiums share in the use of and payment for common areas, such as walkways, recreational facilities, and ponds. A homeowner's association typically manages the common area.

COMMON LAW / The body of law that has grown out of legal customs and practices that developed in England. Common law prevails unless superseded by other law.

COMMUNITY PROPERTY / Property accumulated through joint efforts of husband and wife and owned by them in equal shares. The doctrine now exists in Arizona, California, Idaho, Louisiana, Nevada, New Mexico, Texas, Wisconsin, and the state of Washington.

Importance: Husband and wife must agree to all real estate transactions involving community property.

COMPARATIVE MARKET ANALYSIS (CMA) / An estimate of the value of property using only a few indicators taken from sales of comparable properties, such as price per square foot.

Importance: Real estate brokers and agents, because they are not state-certified appraisers, may not perform appraisals. So they estimate the value of a subject property using a CMA in order to serve their clients.

COMPARATIVE SALES APPROACH / *See* SALES COMPARISON APPROACH.

COMPARATIVE UNIT METHOD / An appraisal technique to establish relevant units as a guide to appraising the subject property. **Examples:** (1) Parking garages are compared per space. (2) Bowling centers are compared per lane. (3) Land may be sold per square foot or per front foot.

COMPLETION BOND / A legal instrument used to guarantee the completion of a development according to specifications. More encompassing than a performance bond, which assures that one party will perform under a contract under condition that the other party performs. The completion bond assures production of the development without reference to any contract and without the requirement of payment to the contractor.

COMPOUND INTEREST / Interest paid on the original principal and also on the unpaid interest that has accumulated. **Example:** $100 deposited in a 5 percent savings account earns $5 interest the first year. If this interest is not withdrawn, the account's second-year earnings are 5 percent of $105, or $5.25.

Importance: Compound interest is the cornerstone of all financial computations, including monthly mortgage payments and remaining balances.

COMPREHENSIVE ENVIRONMENTAL RESPONSE COMPENSATION AND LIABILITY ACT (CERCLA) / Federal law, known as SUPERFUND, passed in 1980 and reauthorized by SARA in 1986. The law imposes strict joint and several liability for cleaning up environmentally contaminated land. Potentially responsible parties include any current or previous owner, generator, transporter, disposer, or party who treated hazardous waste at the site. Strict liability means that each and every party is liable for the full cost of remediation, even parties who were not contaminators.

COMPS / An appraisal term, short for "comparables," that is, comparable properties.

COMPUTER-AIDED DESIGN (CAD) / The use of a computer for design work in fields such as engineering and architecture; the computer's graphics capabilities replacing work that would traditionally have been done with pencil and paper.

COMPUTERIZED LOAN ORIGINATION (CLO) / Origination of a mortgage loan, usually by someone who is not a loan officer, with the assistance of specialized computer software that ties the originator to one or more mortgage lenders. CLO systems allow real estate brokers to provide a wider array of services.

CONCESSION

1. A business that operates within the property of another business and provides goods or services.

Example: The gift shop in the lobby of a hotel, where a businessman rents space from the hotel to sell newspapers, magazines, and sundries, is a *concession*.

2. Reduction in price, RENT, or other benefit provided to a TENANT or buyer as an inducement to buy or LEASE.

Example: Baker is converting apartments to CONDOMINIUM units. In order to induce tenants to purchase their units, Baker offers a *concession* of a 20% discount on the sales price, available only to current tenants.

CONDEMNATION / (1) The taking of private property for public use, with just compensation to the owner, under *eminent domain*; used by governments to acquire land for streets, parks, schools, and by utilities to acquire necessary property; (2) declaring a structure unfit for use.

Importance: All property is subject to condemnation, though the government must show need. The amount of compensation can be disputed.

CONDITION(S) / Provision(s) in a contract that some or all terms of the contract must be met or the contract need not be consummated. **Examples:**
- Buyer must obtain certain financing.
- House must be appraised at a certain amount.
- City must give occupancy permit.
- Seller must pay for certain repairs.

CONDITIONAL SALES CONTRACT / A contract for the sale of property stating that the seller retains title until the conditions of the contract have been fulfilled.

Importance: Generally, buyers have less of an interest under this type of contract than is conveyed by the receipt of a deed at closing.

CONDO / *See* CONDOMINIUM.

CONDOMINIUM / A system of ownership of individual units in a multiunit structure, combined with joint ownership of commonly used property (sidewalks, hallways, stairs). *See also* COMMON ELEMENTS.

Importance: A condominium can be mortgaged by its individual owner, who must pay assessments for common area maintenance.

CONFORMING LOAN / A mortgage loan that is eligible for purchase by FNMA or FHLMC.

Example: The maximum size of a loan that could be purchased by FNMA or FHLMC, or *conforming loan*, in 2012 was $417,000 when secured by a single-family home (up to $625,500 in certain high-cost areas). The limit is revised each year according to the change in average sales price of conventionally financed single-family homes.

CONFORMITY PRINCIPLE / An appraisal principle that holds that property values tend to be maximized when the neighborhood is reasonably homogeneous in social and economic activity.

CONSENT DECREE / A judgment whereby the defendant agrees to stop the activity that was asserted to be illegal, without admitting wrongdoing or guilt.

CONSIDERATION / Anything of value given to induce entering into a contract; it may be money, personal services, love and affection.

Importance: A contract must have some consideration to be legally binding.

CONSTANT / *See* CONSTANT PAYMENT LOAN.

CONSTANT PAYMENT LOAN / A loan on which equal payments are made periodically so that the debt is paid off when the last payment is made.

Importance: Although each periodic payment is the same, the portion that is interest declines over time, whereas the principal portion increases.

CONSTRUCTION LOAN / A loan used to build on real estate.

Importance: Many construction lenders require, among other things, that the builder obtain a commitment for a permanent loan before they will issue a construction loan. Commercial banks are the most common source of construction loans. The rate is often the prime rate plus 2 percent plus 1 or more discount points. The loan is advanced in stages as the project is completed.

CONSTRUCTIVE EVICTION / An eviction existing when, through the fault of the landlord, physical conditions of the property render it unfit for the purpose for which it was leased.

CONSTRUCTIVE NOTICE / The legal presumption that everyone has knowledge of a fact when that fact is a matter of public record. **Example:** A buys land from B, believing that B is the owner. However, B was a huckster; C owned the property. Because C's deed had been properly recorded, A had constructive notice of C's ownership and cannot claim ownership against C.

CONTIGUOUS / Actually touching; contiguous properties have a common boundary. *See also* ADJOINING.

CONTINGENCY CLAUSE / *See* CONDITION(S).

CONTRACT / An agreement between competent parties to do or not to do certain things for a consideration.

Importance: A valid contract is enforceable in a court of law. All contracts for real estate must be in writing to be enforceable, except leases for less than 1 year.

CONTRACT FOR DEED / *See* LAND CONTRACT.

CONTRACT OF SALE / *See* AGREEMENT OF SALE.

CONVENTIONAL LOAN / A mortgage loan other than one guaranteed by the Veterans Administration or insured by the *Federal Housing Administration.*

Importance: Conventional loans generally require a larger down payment than others, although the required down payment for conventional loans can be decreased with private mortgage insurance.

CONVERTIBLE ARM / An *adjustable rate mortgage* that offers the borrower the option to convert

payments to a fixed-rate schedule at a specified point within the term of the loan. Conversion is made for a nominal fee, and the interest rate on the fixed-rate loan is determined by a rule specified in the ARM loan agreement.

CONVEY / To deed or transfer title to another.

Importance: This term is used to imply a sale or transfer of ownership.

CONVEYANCE / (1) The transfer of the title of real estate from one to another; (2) the means or medium by which title of real estate is transferred.

Importance: This term usually refers to use of a deed, but can also be used for a lease, mortgage, assignment, encumbrance.

COOPERATIVE / A type of corporate ownership of real property whereby stockholders of the corporation are entitled to use a certain dwelling unit or other units of space.

Importance: Special income tax laws allow the tenant stockholders to deduct on their tax returns the housing interest and property taxes paid by the corporation.

CORPOREAL / Visible or tangible. Corporeal rights in real estate include such things as the right of occupancy under a lease.

CO-SIGNER / A person who signs a credit application with another person, agreeing to be equally responsible for the repayment of the loan. *Same as* ACCOMMODATION PARTY.

COST APPROACH / One of the three appraisal methods of estimating value. The estimated current cost of reproducing the existing improvements, less the estimated depreciation, added to the value of the land, gives the appraised value; also called *appraisal by summation.*

Importance: Most properties sell for market value. The cost approach is useful for proposed construction or for estimating the amount of insurance needed.

CO-TENANCY AGREEMENT / Provision in a shopping center lease that requires the operations of one or more other named tenants. If the specified tenant(s) GO DARK, the tenant can significantly reduce rent, reduce payments for common area maintenance, and/or terminate its lease, according to the provision.

COTERMINOUS / Having the same period or termination point (leases).

COUNSELORS OF REAL ESTATE / A professional organization of real estate investment counselors and consultants. Affiliated with the NATIONAL ASSOCIATION OF REALTORS®. Awards the designation of Counselor of Real Estate (CRE). Publishes the journal *Real Estate Issues.*

COUNTEROFFER / Rejection of an offer to buy or sell, with a simultaneous substitute offer.

COVENANTS / Promises written into deeds and other instruments and agreeing to do or not to do certain acts, or requiring or preventing certain uses of the property.

Importance: When buying real estate, it is prudent to determine whether any of the covenants would inhibit or prevent a proposed use of the property.

CPM / *See* CERTIFIED PROPERTY MANAGER.

CRB / *See* CERTIFIED RESIDENTIAL BROKER.

CRE / *See* COUNSELORS OF REAL ESTATE.

CREDIT RATING (REPORT) / An evaluation of a person's capacity for (or history of) debt repayment. Generally available for individuals from a local retail credit association; for businesses from companies such as Dun & Bradstreet; and for publicly held bonds from Moody's, Standard & Poor's, and Fitch's. Individuals have access to their own files.

CREDIT SCORE / A number that purports to predict the probability that a person will default on a loan. Generally, the higher the number, the better risk the individual is considered to be. The score may determine whether the person gets the loan and how favorable the terms will be. The score is estimated from information contained in the individual's CREDIT REPORT. *See also* FICO.

CREDIT TENANT / A shopping center or office building tenant that is large enough, in business long enough, and financially strong enough to be rated at least investment grade by one of the major credit rating services. A property leased to such a tenant may obtain low-interest-rate long-term mortgage financing underwritten on the basis of the tenant's likelihood of honoring its lease.

CREDIT UNION / A nonprofit financial institution federally regulated and owned by the members or people who use its services. Credit unions serve groups with a common interest, and only members may use the available services.

CREDITWORTHINESS / A measure of the ability of a person to qualify for and repay a loan.

CUL-DE-SAC / A street with an intersection at one end and a closed turning area at the other. Often valued in the design of residential subdivisions for the privacy provided to homes on the street.

CURABLE DEPRECIATION / *Depreciation* or deterioration that can be corrected at a cost less than the value that will be added.

Importance: It is economically profitable to correct curable depreciation.

CURTESY / The right of a husband to all or part of his deceased wife's realty regardless of the provisions of her will. Curtesy exists in only a few states.

Importance: Where curtesy exists, it is the husband's counterpart to *dower*.

DAMAGES / The amount recoverable by a person who has been injured in any manner, including physical harm, property damage, or violated rights, through the act or default of another.

Importance: Damages may be awarded for compensation and as a punitive measure, to punish someone for certain acts.

DATE OF APPRAISAL / *See* APPRAISAL DATE.

DEBT/EQUITY RATIO / The relationship of these two components of *purchase capital*. **Example:** Mortgage = \$75,000; equity = 25,000. Therefore, the debt/equity ratio is 3:1. This is equivalent to a 75 percent *loan-to-value ratio* loan.

DECREE / An order issued by a person in authority; a court order or decision.

Importance: A decree may be final or interlocutory (preliminary).

DEDICATION / The gift of land by its owner for a public use and the acceptance of it by a unit of government. **Example:** Streets in a subdivision, land for a park, or a site for a school.

DEDICATION BY DEED / *See* DEDICATION; DEED.

DEDUCTIBLE / The amount of cash that must be paid first by an insured homeowner to cover a portion of a damage or loss. The insurance company will pay the balance of losses exceeding this amount. *See also* TAX DEDUCTIBLE.

Importance: Policies with high deductible amounts are often available at lower premiums than low-deductible policies.

DEED / A written document, properly signed and delivered, that conveys title to real property. *See also* BARGAIN AND SALE DEED, GENERAL WARRANTY DEED, QUITCLAIM DEED, SPECIAL WARRANTY DEED.

DEED IN LIEU OF FORECLOSURE / A deed that conveys a defaulting borrower's realty to a lender, thus avoiding foreclosure proceedings.

DEED OF TRUST / *See* TRUST DEED.

DEED RESTRICTION / A clause in a deed that limits the use of land. **Example:** A deed may stipulate that alcoholic beverages are not to be sold on the land for 20 years.

Importance: A buyer should check that deed restrictions will not inhibit an intended use of property; a seller should consider whether he/she wants to restrict the use of land.

DEFAULT / (1) Failure to fulfill a duty or promise, or to discharge an obligation; (2) omission or failure to perform any acts.

Importance: Upon default, the defaulting party may be liable to the other party(ies).

DEFEASANCE / A clause in a mortgage that gives the borrower the right to redeem his/her property after he/she has defaulted, usually by paying the full indebtedness and fees incurred. **Example:** A late payment on a mortgage or other *default* doesn't necessarily cause the borrower to lose the property. Defeasance may allow redemption, though the loan and fees may have to be paid.

DEFENDANT / The party sued in an action at law.

DEFERRED GAIN / Any gain not subject to tax in the year realized but postponed until a later year.

DEFERRED PAYMENTS / Money payments to be made at some future date.

DEFICIENCY JUDGMENT / A court order stating that the borrower still owes money when the security for a loan does not entirely satisfy a defaulted debt.

Importance: When property is foreclosed on, the amount realized by the sale of the collateral may not satisfy the debt. The lender may be able to get a deficiency judgment to recover the balance owed.

DELAYED EXCHANGE / *See* SECTION 1031; TAX-FREE EXCHANGE, DELAYED.

DELEVERAGE / Become less reliant on debt. Traditionally, the term usually referred to financial leverage in corporations. Since the 2007 debt crisis, usage has broadened to include any entity that suffers from too much debt, including the U.S. government, economic sectors such as real estate, and individuals. Reduces financial risk.

DELIVERY / Transfer of the possession of a thing from one person to another.

Importance: In a real estate transaction there should be delivery of a deed. For example, if an owner dies without giving a deed to a relative while alive, a verbal promise to give the property is inadequate.

DEMOGRAPHY / The study of population characteristics of people in an area, including age, sex, and income.

DEPARTMENT OF VETERANS AFFAIRS / *See* VA.

DEPRECIATION / (1) In appraisal, a loss of value in real property due to age, physical deterioration, or functional or economic obsolescence; (2) in accounting, the allocation of the cost of an asset over its economic useful life.

Importance: It should be recognized that the value of real estate may decline; also, that one can reduce income taxes by claiming depreciation as a tax expense.

DEPRECIATION RECAPTURE / When real property is sold at a gain and ACCELERATED DEPRECIATION had been claimed, the owner may be required to pay a tax at ordinary rates to the extent of the excess accelerated depreciation. Excess depreciation on residential real estate after 1980 is recaptured; all depreciation on commercial property after 1980 is recaptured when an accelerated method had been used, under SECTION 1250 of the INTERNAL REVENUE CODE. **Note:** The importance of *depreciation recapture* for real estate was minimized by the Tax Reform Act of 1986, which mandated straight-line depreciation for buildings bought after 1986.

DEPRESSION / Economic conditions causing a severe decline in business activity, reflecting high unemployment, excess supply, and public fear.

DEVISE / A gift of real estate by will or last testament.

DEVISEE / A person who inherits real estate through a will.

DIRECT CAPITALIZATION / The value estimated by dividing *net operating income* by an overall *capitalization rate* to estimate value. *See also* CAPITALIZATION. **Example:**

Gross income	$100,000
Operating expenses	−40,000
Net operating income	$ 60,000
Capitalization rate	0.12
Value estimate	$500,000

DIRECT SALES COMPARISON APPROACH / *See* SALES COMPARISON APPROACH.

DIRECTIONAL GROWTH / The location or direction toward which a city is growing.

Importance: An investor can often make a profit by purchasing land in the path of a city's growth.

DISCHARGE IN BANKRUPTCY / The release of a bankrupt party from the obligation to repay debts that were, or might have been, proved in bankruptcy proceedings.

DISCOUNT / The difference between the FACE AMOUNT of an obligation and the amount advanced or received. **Example:** Abel sells land for $100,000 and receives a $60,000 mortgage at 7% interest as part of the payment. Abel then sells the mortgage (the right to collect payments on the mortgage) at a $15,000 *discount,* thereby receiving $45,000.

DISCOUNT BROKER / A licensed broker who provides brokerage services for a lower commission than that typical in the market. Generally, the services provided are less extensive than those of a full-service broker or may be unbundled, so that a client may contract for specific services. Many discount brokers charge a flat fee rather than a percentage of the selling price.

DISCOUNTED CASH FLOW / *See* DISCOUNTING.

DISCOUNTED LOAN / One that is offered or traded for less than its face value. *See* DISCOUNT, DISCOUNT POINTS.

DISCOUNTED PRESENT VALUE / *See* DISCOUNTING.

DISCOUNTING / The process of estimating the present value of an *income stream* by reducing expected *cash flow* to reflect the *time value of money*. Discounting is the opposite of compounding; mathematically they are reciprocals.

DISCOUNT POINTS / Amounts paid to the lender (usually by the seller) at the time of origination of a loan, to account for the difference between the market interest rate and the lower face rate of the note (often required when FHA or VA financing is used).

Importance: Discount points must be paid in cash at closing. Buyer and seller should agree, at the time they prepare an agreement of sale, as to who is to pay the points, or what the limits are on the number of points to be paid.

DISPOSSESS PROCEEDINGS / The legal process by a landlord to remove a tenant and regain possession of property.

Importance: If a tenant breaches a lease, the landlord will want to regain possession of the property.

DISTINGUISHED REAL ESTATE INSTRUCTOR (DREI) / A *real estate* teacher, typically of licensing preparation courses, who has been designated by the *Real Estate Educators Association*. **Example:** To qualify as a DREI, Don had to demonstrate classroom teaching techniques to a panel of teachers, who judged his effectiveness. Don also offered experience and expertise in real estate law.

DISTRIBUTEE / A person receiving or entitled to receive land as the representative of the former owner; an heir.

DOCUMENTARY EVIDENCE / Evidence in the form of written or printed papers.

Importance: Documentary evidence generally carries more weight than oral evidence.

DODD-FRANK WALL STREET REFORM AND CONSUMER PROTECTION ACT / Massive overhaul implementing financial regulatory reform, signed into law on July 21, 2010, in response to the financial crisis of 2007–2010. Named for Senator Chris Dodd and Representative Barney Frank and known as the *Dodd-Frank Act.*

DOWER / Under common law, the legal right of a wife or child to part of a deceased husband's or father's property.

Importance: Dower has been generally abolished or severely altered in most states. *Community property* applies in some states.

DREI / *See* DISTINGUISHED REAL ESTATE INSTRUCTOR.

DUAL AGENT / An agent who represents more than one party to a transaction.

DUE DILIGENCE / (1) Making a reasonable effort to perform under a contract. (2) Making a reasonable effort to provide accurate, complete information. A study that often precedes the purchase of property or the underwriting of a loan or investment; considers the physical, financial, legal, and social characteristics of the property and expected investment performance.

DURESS / Unlawful constraint exercised upon a person whereby he/she is forced to do some act against his/her will. **Example:** "Your signature or your brains will be on this contract."

Importance: A person who signs a contract or performs another act under duress need not go through with the agreement.

EARNEST MONEY / A deposit made by a purchaser of real estate as evidence of his/her good faith.

Importance: Earnest money should accompany an offer to buy property. Generally, a broker, attorney, or title company deposits the money in a separate account, beyond the control of the principals, until the contract is completed.

EARNEST MONEY CONTRACT / The term used in some states for an *agreement of sale* contract. In some states preprinted forms, promulgated by the state Real Estate Commission, are available for several types of transactions.

EASEMENT / The right, privilege, or interest that one party has in the land of another. **Example:** The right of public utility companies to lay their lines across others' property.

Importance: Easements allow utility service without requiring the public utility to buy the land. However, a potential real estate purchaser should determine exact locations of all easements to be sure they won't interfere with planned land uses.

ECCR / Easements, covenants, conditions, restrictions. Adds EASEMENTS to CONDITIONS, COVENANTS, and RESTRICTIONS.

ECHO BOOMERS / Generation representing the children of BABY BOOMERS who were born immediately following World War II.

ECONOMIC DEPRECIATION / Loss of value from all causes outside the property itself. **Example:** An expensive private home may drop in value when a sanitary landfill is placed nearby.

ECONOMIC LIFE / The remaining period for which real estate improvements are expected to generate more income than operating expenses cost.

Importance: As land improvements age, they tend to command less rent (in real terms) while maintenance costs rise. The economic life is the expected life of positive contributions to value by buildings or other land improvements.

ECONOMIC OBSOLESCENCE / *See* ECONOMIC DEPRECIATION.

EFFECTIVE GROSS INCOME / For income-producing property, *potential gross income*, less a vacancy and collection allowance, plus miscellaneous income. *See also* GROSS INCOME. **Example:** An office building rents for $12 per square foot and contains 100,000 leasable square feet. A 5% vacancy and collection allowance is expected. A small concession stand provides $1,000 of annual revenue.

Potential gross income:	
$12 × 100,000	= $1,200,000
Less: Vacancy and collection allowance @ 5%	−60,000
Add: Miscellaneous income	+1,000
Effective gross income	$1,141,000

EJECTMENT / An action to regain possession of *real property*, and to obtain damages for unlawful possession.

Importance: Ejectment allows a rightful owner to remove a squatter or trespasser.

EMINENT DOMAIN / The right of the government or a public utility to acquire property for necessary public use by *condemnation*; the owner must be fairly compensated.

Importance: Governments or those with governmental authority can acquire property they need under the Federal Fifth Amendment and state constitutions. As to the amount paid, the parties are entitled to a "day in court."

ENCROACHMENT / A building, a part of a building, or an obstruction that physically intrudes upon, overlaps, or trespasses upon the property of another.

Importance: A *survey* is often required as part of a real estate contract, to determine whether there are any encroachments on the property.

ENCUMBRANCE / Any right to or interest in land that diminishes its value. Included are outstanding mortgage loans, unpaid taxes, easements, deed restrictions, mechanics' liens, and leases.

ENDORSEMENT / The act of signing one's name on the back of a check or note, with or without further qualification; also, the signature itself.

ENTITLEMENT / (1) The right to develop land with government approvals for ZONING density, utility installations, occupancy permits, use permits, streets. (2) In a VA loan, the dollar amount of loan guarantee that the Department of Veterans Affairs (VA) provides to each eligible veteran. VA loan guarantees are available to military veterans who served in the armed services during specified war periods. The guarantee allows the veteran to borrow money to buy a home without the need for a cash DOWN PAYMENT. Generally, LENDERS will lend up to four times the amount of the entitlement with no cash investment by the borrower.

ENVIRONMENTAL ASSESSMENT / A study of the property and area to determine health hazards:

Phase I. To identify the presence of hazards (e.g., asbestos, radon, PCBs, leaking underground storage tanks).

Phase II. To estimate the cost of remediation or cleanup.

Phase III. To remediate the environmental contamination.

ENVIRONMENTAL IMPACT REPORT (or STATEMENT) / Describes probable effects on the environment of a proposed development; may be required by a local government to assure the absence of damage to the environment.

EOY / Abbreviation for "end of year."

Importance: Most mortgage loans call for payments at the end of each period. If the loan requires annual payments, a payment would be due at the end of the year (EOY).

EQUAL AND UNIFORM TAXATION / Principle that all persons of the same class must be treated equally. The same rate and value should apply to property being taxed.

EQUITABLE TITLE / The interest held by one who has agreed to purchase but has not yet closed the transaction.

EQUITY / The interest or value that the owner has in real estate over and above the liens against it. **Example:** If a property has a market value of $10,000, but there is a $7,500 mortgage loan on it, the owner's equity is $2,500.

EQUITY DIVIDEND / The annual *cash flow* that an equity investor receives; same as *cash-on-cash* return.

EQUITY OF REDEMPTION / The right of a real estate owner to reclaim property after default, but before foreclosure proceedings, by payment of the debt, interest, and costs. *See also* DEFEASANCE.

EQUITY YIELD RATE / The rate of return on the *equity* portion of an investment, taking into account periodic *cash flow* and the proceeds from resale. The timing and amounts of *cash flow* after debt service, are considered, but not income taxes.

EROSION / The gradual wearing away of land through process of nature, as by streams and winds.

Importance: Planting vegetation can often prevent soil erosion.

ESCALATOR MORTGAGE / *See* ADJUSTABLE RATE MORTGAGE.

ESCAPE CLAUSE / A provision in a contract that allows one or more of the parties to cancel all or part of the contract if certain events or situations do or do not occur.

ESCHEAT / The reversion of property to the state in the event that the owner dies without leaving a will and has no legal heirs.

Importance: In the absence of a will, the assets of a person who has no legal heirs will escheat to the state.

ESCROW / An agreement between two or more parties providing that certain instruments or property be placed with a third party for safekeeping, pending the fulfillment or performance of some act or condition.

Importance: It is prudent to place money or property in escrow rather than to give it to the other principal of a pending transaction.

ESCROW ACCOUNT / Account where funds are held for safekeeping until needed, usually without interest; in real estate, an account that receives the funds needed for expenses such as property taxes, HOMEOWNER'S INSURANCE, and MORTGAGE INSURANCE when they come due. *See also* TRUST ACCOUNT.

ESCROW AGENT / A neutral third party (such as a lawyer, broker, or title company) who is trusted by buyer and seller to close a transaction. The buyer and seller give instructions with conditions that must be met in order to close.

ESTATE / The degree, quantity, nature, and extent of interest a person has in real or personal property.

ESTATE AT SUFFERANCE / The wrongful occupancy of property by a tenant after his/her lease has expired.

ESTATE AT WILL / The occupation of real estate by a tenant for an indefinite period, terminable by one or both parties at will.

ESTATE FOR LIFE / An interest in property that terminates upon the death of a specified person. *See also* LIFE ESTATE.

ESTATE FOR YEARS / An interest in land that allows possession for a definite and limited time.

ESTATE IN REVERSION / An estate left by a *grantor* for him/herself, to begin after the termination of some particular estate granted by him/her. **Example:**

A landlord's estate in reversion becomes his/hers to possess when the lease expires.

ESTOPPEL CERTIFICATE / A document by which, for example, the mortgagor (borrower) certifies that the mortgage debt is a lien for the amount stated. He/she is thereafter prevented from claiming that the balance due differed from the amount stated. Estoppels apply also to leases.

Importance: The buyer of property on which there is a mortgage or lease should get estoppels to be sure the terms of those agreements are as expected. The right to get estoppel certificates may be written into the lease or mortgage.

ET AL. / Abbreviation of *et alii* ("and others").

ET UX. / Abbreviation of *et uxor* ("and wife").

ETHICS / Principles by which one treats colleagues, clients, and the public in a fair, just, and truthful manner. Adherence to such standards is considered one of the requisites for recognition as a profession.

EVALUATION / A study of the potential uses of a property, but not to determine its present value.

Importance: Evaluations include studies as to the market for and the marketability of a property, feasibility, *highest and best use*, land use, and supply and demand.

EVICTION / A legal proceeding by a lessor (landlord) to recover possession of property.

Importance: Eviction allows a landlord to regain property when a tenant does not uphold the lease. A legal process must be followed.

EVICTION, PARTIAL / A legal proceeding whereby the possessor of the property is deprived of a portion thereof.

EXCESS (ACCELERATED) DEPRECIATION / The accumulated difference between ACCELERATED DEPRECIATION claimed for tax purposes and what STRAIGHT-LINE DEPRECIATION would have been. Generally, *excess accelerated depreciation* is recaptured (taxed) as ORDINARY INCOME upon a sale, instead of receiving more favorable CAPITAL GAINS treatment. *See* DEPRECIATION RECAPTURE.

EXCESS RENT / The amount by which the *rent* under an existing *lease* exceeds the rental rate on comparable existing space.

Importance: Should the lease expire or the tenant break the lease, the new rental rate will probably be at (lower) market rates.

EXCHANGE / Under section 1031 of the Internal Revenue Code, like-kind property used in a trade or business or held as an investment can be exchanged tax free. *See also* BOOT.

EXCLUSIONARY ZONING / Zoning laws of a community that would serve to prohibit low and moderate income housing; considered to be illegal.

EXCLUSIVE AGENCY LISTING / An employment contract giving only one broker the right to sell the property for a specified time and also allowing the owner to sell the property him/herself without paying a commission.

Importance: This is sometimes arranged when an owner wants to continue personal selling efforts while employing a broker. Acceptable to some brokers for some properties.

EXCLUSIVE RIGHT TO SELL LISTING / An employment contract giving the broker the right to collect a commission if the property is sold by anyone, including the owner, during the term of the agreement, and often beyond the term to someone the broker introduced. *Compare* EXCLUSIVE AGENCY LISTING; *contrast with* OPEN LISTING.

EXECUTE / (1) To make out a contract; (2) to perform a contract fully.

Importance: In real estate, unsigned contracts are generally meaningless.

EXECUTED CONTRACT / A contract all terms and conditions of which have been fulfilled.

Importance: When executed, a contract is enforceable.

EXECUTOR / A person designated in a will to carry out its provisions concerning the disposition of the estate.

Importance: The person making a will should name an executor or co-executor who is trustworthy and capable of carrying out the terms of the will. If there is no will and no executor, the court appoints an *administrator*.

EXECUTRIX / A woman who performs the duties of an executor.

EXPENSE RATIO / A comparison of *operating expenses* to *potential gross income*. This ratio can be compared over time and with that of other properties to determine the relative operating efficiency of the property considered. **Example:** An apartment complex generates potential gross income of $1,000,000 annually, and incurs operating expenses of $400,000 over the same time period. The expense ratio of 40 percent can be compared to its historical rate and the same ratios competitive properties. The comparison may disclose reasons for differences that can be used to bolster the property's efficiency.

EXPRESS AGENCY / A clear and explicit relationship between an AGENT and a PRINCIPAL, in the form of either a written contract or an oral understanding. *Contrast with* IMPLIED AGENCY.

EXPRESS CONTRACT / Written agreement that includes elements needed for a valid CONTRACT and specific terms of the contract. *Contrast with* IMPLIED CONTRACT.

FACTORS OF PRODUCTION / In economics, land, labor, capital, and entrepreneurship.

FAIR HOUSING LAW / A federal law that forbids discrimination on the basis of race, color, sex, religion, handicap, familial status, or national origin in the selling or renting of homes and apartments.

FAMILY LIMITED PARTNERSHIP / A limited partnership whose interests are owned by members of the same family. By this arrangement, gift and estate taxes may be reduced. However, owners will not enjoy the freedom of complete ownership or free transferability of interest provided by other ownership vehicles. *See* MINORITY DISCOUNT.

FANNIE MAE / Nickname for Federal National Mortgage Association (FNMA), one of two companies (the other is FHLMC or FREDDIE MAC) that purchase in the secondary market a large share of the residential mortgage loans originated each year. Most of these loans are used to support special bond-type securities sold to investors. *Fannie Mae*, now a semiprivate corporation (a GOVERNMENT-SPONSORED ENTERPRISE) was once an agency of the federal government. On September 8, 2008, in the wake of the financial crisis, Fannie Mae was placed under conservatorship by the FEDERAL HOUSING FINANCE AGENCY. The U.S. government announced 80% ownership of its stock.

FARMER MAC / *See* FEDERAL AGRICULTURAL MORTGAGE CORPORATION.

FARMERS HOME ADMINISTRATION (FmHA) / Former agency of the U.S. Department of Agriculture that administered assistance programs for purchasers of homes and farms in small towns and rural areas. In 1994, the USDA was reorganized, and the functions of the FmHA were transferred to the Farm Service Agency.

FDIC / *See* FEDERAL DEPOSIT INSURANCE CORPORATION.

FEDERAL AGRICULTURAL MORTGAGE CORPORATION / Federal agency established in 1988 to provide a secondary market for farm mortgage loans. Informally called *Farmer Mac*.

FEDERAL DEPOSIT INSURANCE CORPORATION (FDIC) / A U.S. government agency that insures depositors' accounts in commercial banks and savings and loan associations.

Importance: Federal insurance, up to $250,000 per depositor for each insured bank, provides depositor confidence in the banking system and in the individual bank. Banks and savings and loan associations add liquidity to the real estate market.

FEDERAL HOUSING ADMINISTRATION (FHA) / A U.S. government agency that insures to lenders the repayment of real estate loans.

Importance: The FHA is instrumental in assuring that financing is available for housing for low and moderate income levels. Programs include single-family homes, condos, apartments, nursing homes, even new towns.

FEDERAL HOUSING FINANCE AGENCY (FHFA) / U.S. government agency created in 2008 under the Housing and Economic Recovery Act to replace the Federal Housing Finance Board and assume oversight of the FEDERAL HOME LOAN BANK SYSTEM that includes the housing-related GSEs Fannie Mae, Freddie Mac, and the Federal Home Loan Banks.

Importance: Shortly after it was created, the *Federal Housing Finance Agency* was given conservatorship of FANNIE MAE and FREDDIE MAC, providing the agency a strong hand in the ongoing business of the two GSEs. The FHFA was granted enhanced powers to establish standards, restrict asset growth, increase enforcement, and put entities into receivership.

FEDERAL HOUSING FINANCE BOARD / A federal agency created under the FINANCIAL INSTITUTIONS REFORM, RECOVERY, AND ENFORCEMENT ACT (FIRREA) to regulate and supervise the 12 district Federal Home Loan Banks. The Board was abolished in 2008, and its functions were transferred to the newly created FEDERAL HOUSING FINANCE AGENCY (FHFA).

FEDERALLY RELATED MORTGAGE / A MORTGAGE LOAN that is, in some way, subject to federal law because it is guaranteed, insured, or otherwise regulated by a government agency such as the FEDERAL DEPOSIT INSURANCE CORPORATION (FDIC), FEDERAL HOME LOAN MORTGAGE CORPORATION (FHLMC), FEDERAL HOUSING ADMINISTRATION (FHA), FEDERAL NATIONAL MORTGAGE ASSOCIATION (FNMA), the board of governors of the FEDERAL RESERVE SYSTEM, National Credit Union Association (NCUA), Office of the Comptroller of the Currency (OCC), Office of Thrift Supervision (OTS), or Department of Veterans Affairs (VA).

FEDERALLY RELATED TRANSACTION / Real estate transaction that is overseen by a federal agency, including: Federal Reserve Board; FEDERAL DEPOSIT INSURANCE CORPORATION (FDIC); Office of the Controller of the Currency (OCC); Office of Thrift Supervision (OTS); National Credit Union Association (NCUA); FANNIE MAE; FREDDIE MAC; Federal Housing Administration (FHA); and Department of Veterans Affairs (VA).

FEDERAL NATIONAL MORTGAGE ASSOCIATION (FNMA) / *See* FANNIE MAE.

FEE SIMPLE OR FEE ABSOLUTE / Absolute ownership of real property; the owner is entitled to the entire property with unconditional power of disposition during his/her life, and the property descends to his/her heirs and legal representatives upon his/her death intestate.

Importance: When buying real estate, the seller can give only the rights he/she has. A buyer should determine whether complete ownership in fee simple will be received.

FF&E / FURNITURE, FIXTURES, AND EQUIPMENT.

FHA / FEDERAL HOUSING ADMINISTRATION.

FHFA HOUSE PRICE INDEX (HPI) / A home price index compiled by the FEDERAL HOUSING FINANCE AGENCY. The index is based on data taken from loans held by the home mortgage GSEs. Values are available for each state and metropolitan area in the country.

FHA LOAN / A mortgage loan insured by the FHA.

Importance: FHA loans generally reduce the required down payment to 3 percent (sometimes less) but require FHA mortgage insurance, in addition to interest, at 0.5 percent annually.

FIDUCIARY / (1) A person who, on behalf of or for the benefit of another, transacts business or handles money or property not his/her own. (2) Founded on trust; the nature of trust.

Importance: A fiduciary, or a person in such capacity, must act in the best interest of the party who has placed trust.

FILTERING DOWN / The process whereby, over time, a housing unit or neighborhood is occupied by progressively lower-income residents.

FINAL VALUE ESTIMATE / In an *appraisal* of *real estate*, the appraiser's value conclusion. **Example:** An appraiser has determined these three amounts of value based on each appraisal approach:

Cost approach	$600,000
Sales comparison approach	575,000
Income approach	560,000

She then reconciles these amounts, decides which is most relevant, and offers a final value estimate. If the income approach is considered most indicative of purchaser behavior, the amount may be $560,000 to $570,000, depending on the relative weight assigned to each approach.

FINANCIAL FEASIBILITY / The ability of a proposed land use or change of land use to justify itself from an economic point of view.

Importance: Financial feasibility is one test of the *highest and best use* of land, but not the only test. Nor does the financial feasibility of a project necessarily make it the most rewarding use of land.

FINANCING LEASE / A lease wherein lessee becomes lessor to the operating tenant.

FIRREA / Financial Institutions Reform, Recovery, and Enforcement Act.

FIRST MORTGAGE / A mortgage that has priority as a *lien* over all other mortgages.

Importance: Generally, the first mortgage is the one recorded first. When a first mortgage is retired, existing mortgages of lower priority will move up. In case of foreclosure, the first mortgage will be satisfied before other mortgages.

FISCAL POLICY / Decisions by the federal government regarding spending and public finance. Includes decisions on the federal budget, the budget deficit and public debt, and taxation. *Contrast with* MONETARY POLICY.

FISCAL YEAR / A continuous 12-month time interval used for financial reporting; the period starts on any date after January 1 and ends one year later.

FIXED EXPENSES / In the operation of *real estate*, expenses that remain the same regardless of occupancy. *Contrast* VARIABLE EXPENSES. **Examples:** Insurance and interest expenses are expected to be the same, whether or not a building is occupied, so they are fixed expenses. By contrast, the costs of utilities and office cleaning will vary with occupancy.

FIXTURES / Personal property attached to the land or improvements so as to become part of the real estate.

Importance: When buying or selling real estate, it is best to specifically identify which appliances remain and which do not. Otherwise, fixtures remain with the property.

FLOOR LOAN / The minimum that a lender is willing to advance on a *permanent mortgage*. An additional principal amount will be loaned upon attainment of a certain occupancy rate.

FNMA / *See* FEDERAL NATIONAL MORTGAGE ASSOCIATION.

FORBEARANCE / A policy of restraint in taking legal action to remedy a *default* or other breach of contract, generally in the hope that the default will be cured, given additional time.

FORCE MAJEURE / An unavoidable cause of delay or of failure to perform a *contract* obligation on time.

FORECLOSURE / A legal procedure whereby property pledged as security for a debt is sold to pay a defaulted debt.

Importance: Foreclosure gives a lender the right to sell property that was pledged for a debt. All parties to a mortgage contract should recognize its consequences.

FORFEITURE / Loss of money or anything else of value because of failure to perform under contract.

FORM 1099 / Federal income tax form used to report interest, dividends, non-employee compensation, and other income.

FRACTIONAL INTEREST / Ownership of some but not all of the rights in *real estate*. Examples are *easement,* hunting rights, and *leasehold.*

FRACTURED CONDOMINIUM / Housing development containing part rental apartments and part owner-occupied condominiums.

FRAUD / The intentional use of deception to purposely cheat or deceive another person, causing him/her to suffer loss.

Importance: Fraud, intentionally deceiving another, is far worse than misrepresentation, which is an incorrect or untrue statement. Consequently, punishment for fraud is more severe.

FRAUD AND FLIPPING / Illegal practice of purchase and immediate resale, often to defraud an innocent lender.

FREDDIE MAC / Nickname for Federal Home Loan Mortgage Corporation (FHLMC), counterpart to FANNIE MAE as a major purchaser of residential mortgage loans in the secondary market. This company was originally created to buy loans from federally chartered savings and loan associations. Today, there is little difference in the operations of Fannie Mae and Freddie Mac. Together, these companies wield significant influence on the standards required of mortgage borrowers and the types of loans offered. Both companies were placed in conservatorship of the FHFA in 2008 and delisted from the New York Stock Exchange in June 2010.

FREEHOLD / An interest in real estate without a predetermined time span. **Example:** A fee simple or a life estate.

FREE RENT / Space that is occupied but generates no income.

Example: An apartment may be occupied by a resident manager who is partially compensated by *free rent.* Apartment units may be occupied during an initial period of *free rent* offered as a lease CONCESSION. Units may be occupied by firms that supply service to the property owner in exchange for *free rent.*

FRONT FOOT / A standard measurement of land, applied at the frontage of its street line.

Importance: This measure is used for city lots of generally uniform depth. Prices are often quoted as the number of dollars per front foot.

FULL AMORTIZATION TERM / *See* AMORTIZATION TERM.

FULLY AMORTIZED LOAN / A loan having payments of *interest* and *principal* that are sufficient to liquidate the loan over its term; self-liquidating. *See also* AMORTIZATION TERM.

FUNCTIONAL DEPRECIATION / Loss of value from all causes within the property, except those due to physical deterioration. **Example:** A poor floor plan or outdated plumbing fixtures.

FUNCTIONAL OBSOLESCENCE / *See* FUNCTIONAL DEPRECIATION.

FUNDS FROM OPERATIONS (FFO) / A measure of the profitability of a real estate investment trust (REIT). *FFO* begins with net income as derived using generally accepted accounting principles (GAAP). To that it adds depreciation deductions and deductions for amortization of deferred charges, which are noncash deductions. FFO does not consider extraordinary items and gains (losses) on the sale of real estate.

FURNITURE, FIXTURES, AND EQUIPMENT (FF&E) / A term frequently found in the ownership of a hotel or motel. This type of property wears out much more rapidly than other components of a hotel or motel, so an owner or prospective buyer needs to establish the condition, cost, and frequency of replacement of FF&E.

FUTURE VALUE OF ONE / *See* COMPOUND INTEREST.

GAAP / Generally accepted accounting principles. The set of rules considered standard and acceptable by certified public accountants. Accounting deductions are required for real estate depreciation, even for assets that appreciate in value.

GABLE ROOF / A pitched roof with sloping sides.

GAMBREL ROOF / A double pitched roof having a steep lower slope with a flatter slope above.

GAP MORTGAGE / A loan that fills the difference between the *floor loan* and the full amount of the *permanent mortgage.*

GENERAL WARRANTY DEED / A deed in which the *grantor* agrees to protect the *grantee* against any other claim to title of the property and also provides other promises. *See also* WARRANTY DEED.

Importance: This is the best type of deed to receive.

GEOGRAPHIC INFORMATION SYSTEMS (GIS) / A computer mapping program whereby land characteristics and/or demographic information are color coded and often overlaid. The purpose is to determine locations of various business activities and demographics.

GIFT DEED / A deed for which the consideration is love and affection, and no material consideration is involved.

Importance: A gift deed is frequently used to transfer real estate to a relative.

GI LOAN / *See* VA LOAN.

GLA / *See* GROSS LEASABLE AREA.

GLOBAL POSITIONING SYSTEM (GPS) / A network of satellites allowing users with portable GPS devices to determine precise locations on the surface of the Earth. The portable GPS device measures the exact time taken for signals to reach it from at least four different satellites; from this, the instrument can compute its location. Some GPS devices merely report the position in the form of geographic coordinates; others can provide sophisticated maps and driving directions, including turn-by-turn voice narration.

GNMA / Government National Mortgage Association (Ginnie Mae).

GO DARK / Terminate operations; said of an anchor retail tenant in a shopping center. Even though the tenant may continue to pay rent, its absence from the shopping center may cause the shopping center to suffer or close. *See* CO-TENANCY AGREEMENT.

GOOGLE EARTH / Application provided by Google that allows the user to browse satellite images of the world by street address or geographic coordinates (latitude and longitude).

GOVERNMENT RECTANGULAR SURVEY / A rectangular system of land survey that divides a district into 24-mile-square tracts from the *meridian* (north-south line) and the *base line* (east-west line). The tracts are divided into 6-mile-square parts called townships, which are in turn divided into 36 tracts, each 1 mile square, called sections.

Importance: This system is still used in several western states. For urban or suburban purposes the *lot and block number* and/or *metes and bounds* methods predominate.

GOVERNMENT-SPONSORED ENTERPRISE (GSE) / Quasi-governmental organization that is privately owned but was created by the government and retains certain privileges not afforded totally private entities.

Both FANNIE MAE and FREDDIE MAC are *government-sponsored enterprises* that were created by the federal government but transferred to private owners. After 40 years of operation, on September 6, 2008, in response to the financial crisis, 80% of their stock was deemed owned by the U.S. government. Both organizations have the implicit backing of the U.S. Treasury, which allows them to raise funds at lower interest rates than other private concerns and assist housing finance.

GRACE PERIOD / Additional time allowed to perform an act or make a payment before a default occurs.

Importance: Many mortgage contracts have a grace period before a late payment is considered a default. It is usually wise to solve the problem before the grace period expires.

GRADE / (1) Ground level at the foundation of a building; (2) the degree of slope on land (e.g., a 2 percent grade means that the elevation rises 2 feet for every 100 linear feet).

Importance: The grade of land should be checked to determine whether it suits a planned use of the land.

GRADED LEASE / *See* GRADUATED LEASE.

GRADIENT / The slope, or rate of increase or decrease in elevation, of a surface; usually expressed as a percentage. *See also* GRADE.

GRADUATED LEASE / A lease that provides for graduated changes in the amount of rent at stated intervals; seldom used in short-term leases.

Importance: Graduated leases allow rent changes automatically, so that there is no need to revise the entire lease just to change the rent. These are often long-term leases that suit both landlord and tenant.

GRANT / A technical term used in deeds of conveyance of property to indicate a transfer.

GRANTEE / The party to whom the title to real property is conveyed; the buyer.

GRANTOR / The person who conveys real estate by deed; the seller or donor.

GRAYWATER / Household wastewater that is reused for purposes that do not require high sanitation, such as irrigation of household plants and other vegetation. May include waste from bathtubs, wash basins, and laundry appliances but not kitchen sink or dishwasher drainage.

Importance: Programs to encourage the use of *graywater* are used by municipalities as part of an effort to conserve potable water.

GREEN BUILDING / Building that is built or developed specifically to minimize utility costs or to maximize positive environmental considerations (reduce damage to the environment).

Importance: Many environmentally conscious people seek to buy or rent space in *green buildings* to feel they are part of the solution to the world's energy and environmental problems.

GRI / A graduate of the Realtors® Institute, which is affiliated with the *National Association of Realtors*®.

Importance: The GRI designation indicates that a real estate salesperson or broker has gone beyond the minimum educational requirements.

GRM / *See* GROSS RENT MULTIPLIER.

GROSS BUILDING AREA / The total floor area of a building, usually measured from its outside walls.

GROSS INCOME / Total income from property before any expenses are deducted. Gross income may be further described as *potential*, which assumes neither vacancy nor collection losses, or *effective*, which is net of vacancy and collection losses.

GROSS LEASABLE AREA (GLA) / The floor area that can be used by a *tenant*; generally measured from the center of joint partitions to outside wall surfaces. *Contrast with* NET LEASABLE AREA.

GROSS LEASE / A lease of property whereby the landlord (lessor) is responsible for paying all property expenses, such as taxes, insurance, utilities, and repairs. *Contrast with* NET LEASE.

Importance: Landlord and tenant agree in writing as to who pays each operating expense. Otherwise there is strong likelihood for disagreement and litigation.

GROSS POSSIBLE RENT / *See* POTENTIAL GROSS INCOME.

GROSS RENT MULTIPLIER (GRM) / The sales price divided by the rental rate. **Example:** The sales price is $40,000; the gross monthly rent is $400; the GRM = $40,000/$400 = 100. It may also be expressed as an annual figure (8.333), that is, the number of years of rent equaling the purchase price.

Importance: In many investment situations the price is set based on a multiple of the rent level.

GROUND LEASE / An agreement for the rent of land only, often for a long term, at the expiration of which all of the real estate belongs to the landowner.

Importance: Sometimes land can be purchased or leased separately from buildings, thus splitting ownership into components that are more desirable. A property buyer or lessee must be mindful of the lease terms and the effect of such a lease on using or financing the property.

GROUND RENT / The rent earned by leased land.

Importance: Ground leases may be net or gross. In a net lease the *tenant* pays expenses, such as insurance and real estate taxes.

GUARANTOR / A third party to a lease, mortgage, or other legal instrument who guarantees performance under the contract.

GUARDIAN / A person appointed by a court to administer the affairs of an individual who is not capable of administering his/her own affairs.

Importance: An *incompetent* cannot enter a valid contract. It is important to deal with the person's guardian.

HABENDUM CLAUSE / The "to have and to hold" clause that defines or limits the quantity of the estate granted in the deed. **Example:** "To have and to hold for one's lifetime" creates a life estate.

HAMP / *See* HOME AFFORDABLE MODIFICATION PROGRAM.

HANDYMAN SPECIAL / In real estate brokerage jargon, a property that is in need of repair, a *fixer upper*. The implication is that the property is a bargain for someone who can accomplish the repairs economically.

HARP / *See* HOME AFFORDABLE REFINANCE PROGRAM.

HASP / *See* HOMEOWNERS AFFORDABILITY AND STABILITY PLAN.

HEIRS AND ASSIGNS / Terminology used in deeds and wills to provide that the recipient receive a *fee simple* estate in lands rather than a lesser interest.

Importance: These words give the recipient complete ownership, not just an estate for a limited duration of time.

HELOC / *See* HOME EQUITY LINE OF CREDIT.

HEREDITAMENTS / Any property that may be inherited, whether real or personal, tangible or intangible.

HIGHEST AND BEST USE / The legally and physically possible use that, at the time of *appraisal*, is most likely to produce the greatest net return to the land and/or buildings over a given time period.

Importance: To realize the full value of land, the improvements built on it must represent its highest and best use.

HIP ROOF / A pitched roof formed by four walls sloped in different directions. The two longer sides of the roof form a ridge at the top.

HISTORIC DISTRICT / A designated area where the buildings are considered to have some significant historic character. Such designation makes the area eligible for certain federal assistance programs and protects the area from clearance in conjunction with federally sponsored programs.

HOLDER IN DUE COURSE / A person who has taken a note, check, or similar asset (1) before it was overdue, (2) in good faith and for value, and (3) without knowledge that it had been previously dishonored and without notice of any defect at the time it was negotiated to him/her.

Importance: A holder in due course is an innocent buyer of paper (a debt).

HOLDOVER TENANT / A tenant who remains in possession of leased property after the expiration of the lease term.

Importance: A holdover tenant has a *tenancy at sufferance*. The landlord may dictate the terms of occupancy.

HOME AFFORDABLE MODIFICATION PROGRAM (HAMP) / Program of the U.S. Departments of the Treasury and Housing and Urban Development intended to reduce mortgage payments to as little as 31% of verified monthly gross pretax income for homeowners who are not unemployed. *See also* HOMEOWNERS AFFORDABILITY AND STABILITY PLAN (HASP).

More information: Find further information at http://www.makinghomeaffordable.gov/programs/lower-payments/Pages/hamp.aspx. Call 888-995-4673 to discuss this with a government representative.

HOME AFFORDABLE REFINANCE PROGRAM (HARP) / Program set up by the FEDERAL HOUSING FINANCE AGENCY in March 2009 to help UNDERWATER and near-underwater homeowners refinance their mortgages. Unlike the HOME AFFORDABLE MODIFICATION PROGRAM (HAMP), which aims to assist homeowners who are in danger of foreclosure, this program targets homeowners who are current on their monthly mortgage payments but are unable to refinance because of dropping home prices in the wake of the U.S. housing market price correction during 2006–2011.

HOME EQUITY CONVERSION MORTGAGE (HECM) / A reverse mortgage insured by the FEDERAL HOUSING ADMINISTRATION (FHA). The program enables older homeowners to withdraw some of the equity in their homes in the form of monthly payments for life or a fixed term, or in a lump sum, or through a line of credit.

Importance: LENDERS making FHA *home equity conversion mortgages* are insured against loss when the home is sold. FHA insurance often requires that an upfront insurance premium be paid by the borrower, typically out of the proceeds of the loan.

HOME EQUITY LOAN / A loan secured by a second mortgage on one's principal residence, generally to be used for some nonhousing expenditure.

HOMEOWNERS AFFORDABILITY AND STABILITY PLAN (HASP) / U.S. program, announced on February 18, 2009, to help up to nine million homeowners avoid foreclosure. Initial funding of $75 billion was supplemented by $200 billion in additional funding for FANNIE MAE and FREDDIE MAC to purchase and more easily refinance mortgages.

More information: The *Homeowners Affordability and Stability Plan* is funded mostly by the HOUSING AND

ECONOMIC RECOVERY ACT OF 2008. It uses cost sharing and incentives to encourage lenders to reduce homeowners' monthly payments to 31% of their gross monthly income. Under the program, a lender would be responsible for reducing total monthly mortgage payments (PITI) to no more than 38% of the borrower's income, with the government sharing the cost to further reduce the payment to 31%. The plan also involves potentially forgiving or deferring a portion of the borrower's mortgage balance.

HOMEOWNER'S INSURANCE POLICY / An insurance policy designed especially for homeowners. Usually protects the owner from losses caused by most common disasters, hazards, theft, and LIABILITY. Coverage and costs vary widely. Flood insurance is generally not included in standard policies and must be purchased separately.

HOMESTEAD / The status provided to a homeowner's principal residence by some state statutes; protects the home against judgments up to specified amounts.

Importance: In states that honor homesteads, the owner can continue possession and enjoyment of a home against the wishes of creditors.

HOMESTEAD EXEMPTION / In some jurisdictions, a reduction in the assessed value allowed for a person's principal residence.

Importance: In some states, the homestead exemption reduces assessed values for owners; additional exemptions may be claimed by persons past age 65.

HOUSING AND ECONOMIC RECOVERY ACT OF 2008 / Legislation passed to address the subprime housing crisis. The Act created a new regulator for the housing-related GSEs: FANNIE MAE, FREDDIE MAC, and the FEDERAL HOME LOAN BANKS.

More information: Under the *Housing and Economic Recovery Act of 2008*, the FEDERAL HOUSING FINANCE AGENCY (FHFA), which was created by merging the Office of Federal Housing Oversight and the Federal Housing Finance Board, was granted enhanced powers to establish standards, restrict asset growth, increase enforcement, and put entities into receivership.

Importance: Under the Act, the FHFA was given authority to provide capital infusions to Fannie Mae and Freddie Mac to avoid a failure on their obligations, thus increasing confidence in government-sponsored housing finance.

HOUSING STOCK / The total number of DWELLING UNITS in an area.

Example: In 2010, the *housing stock* in the United States comprised approximately 131.7 million units, of which 116.7 million were occupied, with an owner-occupied rate of 65.1%. The housing stock includes mobile homes but excludes GROUP QUARTERS such as prisons, college dormitories, hospitals, hotels, and CONGREGATE HOUSING. The stock also includes approximately 15 million vacant housing units.

HUD / U.S. Department of Housing and Urban Development.

HVAC / An acronym that refers to the climate control system in buildings (heating, ventilation, and air conditioning).

HYPOTHECATE / To pledge a thing as security without having to give up possession of it.

Importance: The word *hypothecate* comes (through Late Latin and French) from a Greek word meaning "to put down as a deposit" and has the same meaning as the French-derived word *mortgage*.

ILLIQUIDITY / Inadequate cash to meet obligations. Real estate is considered an illiquid investment because of the time and effort required to convert it to cash.

IMPACT FEE / An expense charged against private developers by the county or city as a condition for granting permission to develop a specific project. The purpose of the fee is to defray the cost to the city of expanding and extending public services to the development. Though most impact fees are collected from residential property, there can be no discrimination in favor of commercial or industrial property. By law, impact fees cannot be imposed to build new schools.

IMPLIED AGENCY / Occurs when the words and actions of the parties indicate that there is an agency relationship.

IMPROVEMENT RATIO / The value of *improvements* relative to the value of unimproved land. **Example:** Land worth $250,000 was improved with a $750,000 building. The improvement ratio is $750,000/$250,000 or 3:1.

IMPROVEMENTS / Additions to raw land that tend to increase value, such as buildings, streets, sewers.

Importance: An improvement is anything except the raw land. *See also* HIGHEST AND BEST USE.

INCHOATE / (1) Recently or just begun; (2) unfinished, begun but not completed. **Examples:** In real estate, this term can apply to *dower* or *curtesy* rights prior to the death of a spouse, instruments that are supposed to be recorded, and interests that can ripen into a vested estate.

INCOME / The money or other benefit coming from the use of something. Gross sales or income is the full amount received; net income is the remainder after subtracting expenses. Many persons in real estate prefer to use *cash flow* as the measure of income, whereas those in accounting prefer *net income*.

INCOME APPROACH / One of the three appraisal methods used in arriving at an estimate of the market value of property; the value of the property is the present worth of the income it is expected to produce during its remaining life.

Importance: Annual income for rental property can be capitalized into value to estimate the property's worth.

INCOME MULTIPLIER / The relationship of price to income. *See also* GROSS RENT MULTIPLIER.

INCOME PROPERTY / Property whose ownership appeal is that it produces income. **Examples:** Office buildings, shopping centers, rental apartments, hotels.

INCOME STREAM / A regular flow of money generated by a business or investment.

INCOMPETENT / A person who is unable to manage his/her own affairs by reason of insanity, imbecility, or feeblemindedness.

Importance: When conducting business with an incompetent, his/her guardian's consent is required.

INCURABLE DEPRECIATION / (1) A defect that cannot be cured or is not financially practical to cure; (2) a defect in the "bone structure" of a building.

Importance: When appraising real estate using the *cost approach*, incurable depreciation is separated from curable to indicate the actual loss in value sustained by the property.

INDENTURE / A written agreement made between two or more persons having different interests.

Importance: Indentures are used in mortgages, deeds, and bonds. They describe the terms of the agreement.

INDEPENDENT CONTRACTOR / A contractor who is self-employed for tax purposes. When real estate salespeople are self-employed, the broker is not required to withhold taxes.

INDEPENDENT FEE APPRAISER / A person who estimates the value of property but has no interest in the property and is not associated with a lending association or other investor.

INDEX / (1) A statistic that indicates some current economic or financial condition. Indexes are often used to make adjustments in wage rates, rental rates, loan interest rates, and pension benefits set by long-term contracts. (2) To adjust contract terms according to an index.

INDEX LEASE / A lease in which rentals are tied to an agreed upon index of costs. **Example:** Rentals are to increase along with the Consumer Price Index.

Importance: An index lease can provide fairness to both parties in a long-term leasing arrangement.

INDUSTRIAL PROPERTY / Property used for industrial purposes, such as factories and power plants.

Importance: Land to be used for industrial purposes must be zoned for that purpose.

INFLATION / A loss in the purchasing power of money; an increase in the general price level. Inflation is generally measured by the Consumer Price Index, published by the Bureau of Labor Statistics.

Importance: Real estate is considered a hedge against inflation because it tends to be long lasting and holds its value in real terms. As the value of the dollar drops, real estate tends to command more dollars. For example, a home purchased in 1967 for $50,000 was resold in 1976 for $100,000 and in 2013 for $300,000. The home did nothing to cause its price to change; inflation caused the house to command more dollars.

INFRASTRUCTURE / The basic public works of a city or subdivision, including roads, bridges, sewer and water systems, drainage systems, and essential public utilities.

INJUNCTION / A writ or order issued by a court to restrain one or more parties to a suit or a proceeding from performing an act that is deemed inequitable or unjust in regard to the rights of some other party or parties in the suit or proceeding.

Importance: An injunction can prevent a wrongdoing while the legal process continues, that is, before a final judgment is made about the rights of the parties.

INNOCENT PURCHASER / One who buys an asset without knowing of a flaw in the title or property. *See* BONA FIDE purchaser.

IN REM / Latin for "against the thing." A proceeding against *realty* directly, as distinguished from a proceeding against a person (used in taking land for nonpayment of taxes, and so on). By contrast, *in Personam* means "against the person."

INSTALLMENTS / Parts of the same debt, payable at successive periods as agreed; payments made to reduce a mortgage.

Importance: Many debts are paid in installments that include interest for a recent period plus some amount for *amortization*.

INSTALLMENT TO AMORTIZE ONE DOLLAR / A mathematically computed factor, derived from *compound interest* functions, that offers the level periodic payment required to retire a $1.00 loan within a certain time frame. The periodic installment must exceed the periodic interest rate. *See also* AMORTIZATION; AMORTIZATION TERM.

INSTRUMENT / A written legal document, created to effect the rights and liabilities of the parties to it. **Examples:** Deed, will, lease.

INSURABLE TITLE / A title that can be insured by a title insurance company.

Importance: When acquiring real estate, a buyer should determine whether the title is insurable. If not, there are probably valid claims that will affect his/her use or ownership.

INSURANCE / Protection against loss resulting from hazards, such as fire and wind, over a period of time; the property owner's risk is assumed by the insurer in return for the payment of a policy premium.

Examples:
- FLOOD INSURANCE
- HAZARD INSURANCE
- HOMEOWNER'S (INSURANCE) POLICY
- TITLE INSURANCE

INSURANCE COVERAGE / Total amount and type of insurance carried.

Importance: It is conservative to retain insurance coverage based on the replacement value or cost of one's valuables.

INTANGIBLE VALUE / Value that cannot be seen or touched. **Example:** The goodwill of an established business.

INTEREST / (1) Money paid for the use of money; (2) the type and extent of ownership.

INTEREST RATE / (1) The percentage of a sum of money charged for its use; (2) the rate of return on an investment.

Importance: The loan interest rate is an important ingredient in determining the periodic installment payment.

INTERPLEADER / A proceeding initiated by a neutral third party to determine the rights of rival claimants to property or a transaction.

Importance: An escrow agent can call for an interpleader when there is a dispute between the buyer and seller.

INTER VIVOS TRUST / A trust set up during one's lifetime.

INTESTACY / *See* INTESTATE.

INTESTATE / A person who dies leaving no will or a defective will. His/her property goes to his/her legal heirs.

Importance: State law determines inheritance rules for intestates. If there are no heirs, the property *escheats* to the state.

INVESTMENT ANALYSIS / A study of the likely return from a proposed investment with the objective of evaluating the amount an investor may pay for it, the investment's suitability to that investor, or the feasibility of a proposed real estate development.

INVESTMENT PROPERTY / Property that is owned for its income generating capacity or expected resale value. **Example:** Apartments, office buildings, undeveloped land.

INVESTMENT VALUE / The estimated value of a certain real estate investment to a particular individual or institutional investor; may be greater or less than *market value*, depending on the investor's particular situation.

INVOLUNTARY ALIENATION / A loss of property for nonpayment of debts such as taxes or mortgage foreclosure.

INVOLUNTARY LIEN / A lien imposed against property without the consent of the owner (unpaid taxes, special assessments).

Importance: A lien can be created without any action by the landowner.

IRREVOCABLE / Incapable of being recalled or revoked; unchangeable, unalterable.

JEOPARDY / Peril, danger, risk. **Example:** Property pledged as security for a delinquent loan is in jeopardy of *foreclosure*.

JOINT TENANCY / Ownership of realty by two or more persons, each of whom has an undivided interest with *right of survivorship*. **Example:** A and B own land in joint tenancy. Each owns half of the entire (undivided) property. Upon A's death, B will own the entire property, or vice versa.

JOINT VENTURE / An agreement between two or more parties who invest in a single business or property.

JUDGMENT / A court decree stating that one individual is indebted to another and fixing the amount of the indebtedness.

Importance: A judgment is a final determination of the matter, decided by a court.

JUDGMENT CREDITOR / A person who has received a court decree or judgment for money due to him/her.

JUDGMENT DEBTOR / A person against whom a judgment has been issued by a court for money owed.

JUDGMENT LIEN / The claim upon the property of a debtor resulting from a judgment. **Example:** A won't pay his debt to B. After establishing the debt in court, B may be allowed by the court to put a lien on A's real estate.

JUDICIAL FORECLOSURE / Procedure used when a trustee or mortgagee requests court supervision of a foreclosure action.

JUMBO LOAN / A loan whose principal is too large to be purchased by FNMA or FHLMC.

JUNIOR LIEN / *See* JUNIOR MORTGAGE.

JUNIOR MORTGAGE / A *mortgage* whose claim against the property will be satisfied only after prior mortgages have been sold; also called *junior lien*.

Importance: A junior (second, third) mortgage has value as long as the borrower continues payments or the property's value is in excess of the mortgage debts.

LACHES / Delay or negligence in asserting one's legal rights.

Importance: If a person does not act in a reasonable time to assert his/her rights, he/she may be barred from doing so because of the delay.

LAND / The surface of the earth; any part of the surface of the earth. (Note: Legal definitions often distinguish land from water.)

LAND CONTRACT / A real estate installment selling arrangement whereby the buyer may use, occupy, and enjoy land, but no *deed* is given by the seller (so no title passes) until all or a specified part of the sale price has been paid.

Importance: In comparison to a deed, a land contract is easier to foreclose should the buyer fail to make the payments.

LAND LEASE / Only the ground is covered by the lease. *See also* GROUND LEASE.

LANDLORD / A person who rents property to another; a *lessor*.

LANDMARK / A fixed object serving as a boundary mark for a tract of land.

Importance: In surveying, a landmark serves as a reference point.

LAND PATENT / *See* PATENT.

LAND, TENEMENTS, AND HEREDITAMENTS / A phrase used in early English law to express all sorts of *real estate*.

Importance: This is the most comprehensive description of real estate.

LEAD-BASED PAINT / Considered a hazardous material. It is potentially poisonous, and its existence in property is to be disclosed. Its presence is often difficult to determine because applications of lead-based paint may have been covered over by more recent applications of paint that is free of lead.

LEASE / A contract in which, for a consideration called *rent*, one who is entitled to the possession of real property (the *lessor*) transfers those rights to another (the *lessee*) for a specified period of time.

Importance: A lease is an essential agreement, allowing an owner to transfer possession to a user for a limited amount of time.

LEASE ABSTRACT / A synopsis of the major points of a lease.

LEASED FEE / The landlord's ownership interest in a *property* that is under *lease*. *Contrast with* LEASEHOLD.

LEASEHOLD / The interest or estate on which a *lessee* (tenant) of real estate has his/her lease.

Importance: A leasehold can be quite valuable when the tenant's rent is below the market rate and the lease is for a long term.

LEASEHOLD IMPROVEMENTS / Fixtures, attached to *real estate*, that are generally acquired or installed by the tenant. Upon expiration of the *lease*, the tenant can generally remove them, provided that removal does not damage the property and is not in conflict with the lease. **Examples:** Cabinets, light fixtures, window treatments of a retail store in a leased building.

LEASEHOLD VALUE / The value of a tenant's interest in a *lease*, especially when the *rent* is below market level and the lease has a long remaining term.

LEASE WITH OPTION TO PURCHASE / A lease that gives the lessee (tenant) the right to purchase the property at an agreed upon price under certain conditions.

Importance: Because the option allows but does not compel the purchase, it gives the tenant time to consider acquisition.

LEGAL DESCRIPTION / Legally acceptable identification of real estate by the (1) *government rectangular survey*, (2) *metes and bounds*, or (3) *lot and block number* method.

LESSEE / A person to whom property is rented under a *lease*; a tenant.

LESSOR / A person who rents property to another under a *lease*; a landlord.

LETTER OF INTENT (LOI) / The expression of a desire to enter into a CONTRACT without actually doing so.

LEVEL ANNUITY / *See* ANNUITY.

LEVERAGE / The use of borrowed funds to increase purchasing power and, ideally, to increase the profitability of an investment.

Importance: If the property increases in value or yields financial benefits at a rate above the borrowed money interest rate, leverage is favorable, also called positive. But if the rate of property benefits is less than the interest rate, the investor's losses are increased.

LIAR LOAN / Loan in which the proposed borrower provided credit information that was not intended to be verified. *See also* NO-DOCUMENTATION LOAN.

Importance: During the housing boom of 2002–2006, *liar loans* were provided to borrowers who could have asserted an income level that was five times their actual income because their income and employment were not verified before the loan was originated.

LICENSE / (1) Permission; (2) a privilege or right granted by a state to an individual to operate as a real estate broker or salesperson.

Importance: (1) License allows a person to use property for a limited time. (2) In most states, a person must be licensed as a broker (or salesperson) to receive payment for a sale, lease, or other transaction.

LICENSED APPRAISER / Generally, an *appraiser* who meets certain state requirements, but lacks the experience or expertise of a certified appraiser. *See also* CERTIFIED GENERAL APPRAISER; CERTIFIED RESIDENTIAL APPRAISER.

LICENSEE / A person who holds a real estate license.

Importance: In most states, only licensees are entitled to receive compensation for assisting with a real estate transaction. Education and the passing of examinations are requirements of licensing.

LIEN / A charge against property making it security for the payment of a debt, judgment, mortgage, or taxes; a lien is a type of *encumbrance*.

Importance: A lien makes the property collateral for a debt. Some liens may allow the property to be sold to satisfy the debt.

LIFE ESTATE / A freehold interest in land that expires upon the death of the owner or some other specified person.

Importance: A person with a life estate may use the property, but not abuse it, for as long as he/she lives. Then it reverts to the *remainderman*.

LIFE TENANT / A person who is allowed to use property for his/her lifetime or for the lifetime of another designated person. *See also* LIFE ESTATE.

LIKE-KIND PROPERTY / Property having the same nature. *See* SECTION 1031.

LIMITED LIABILITY COMPANY (LLC) / Organization form recognized in many states that may be treated as a partnership for federal tax purposes and has limited liability protection for the owners at the state level. The entity may be subject to the state franchise tax as a corporation. Many states also recognized *limited partnerships*, in which the individual partners are protected from the liabilities of the other partners. These entities are considered *partnerships* for both federal and state tax purposes. **Example:** A limited liability company may be an excellent way to own real estate, because it may provide many of the legal advantages of a corporation and the tax advantages of a partnership. States may impose restrictions, for example, by limiting the number of owners.

LIMITED PARTNERSHIP / PARTNERSHIP in which there is at least one partner who is passive and whose LIABILITY is limited to the amount invested and at least one partner whose liability extends beyond monetary investment. *See* GENERAL PARTNER, FAMILY LIMITED PARTNERSHIP. **Example:** Abel, a syndicator, forms a *limited partnership* with Price, Stone, and Wise. Abel invests his time and talent, is the general partner, and owns 10% of the partnership. Price, Stone, and Wise have each invested $30,000 cash and are limited partners. They buy property with a $90,000 down payment and a $500,000 mortgage. The property drops in value by $250,000. Price, Stone, and Wise lose their equity, and Abel, the general partner, is responsible for additional losses.

LIQUIDATED DAMAGES / An amount agreed upon in a contract that one party will pay the other in the event of a breach of the contract.

LIS PENDENS / Latin for "suit pending"; recorded notice that a suit has been filed, the outcome of which may affect title to a certain land.

Importance: Title to the property under consideration may be in jeopardy.

LISTING / (1) A written employment contract between a *principal* and an *agent* authorizing the agent to perform services for the principal involving the latter's property; (2) a record of property for sale by a broker who has been authorized by the owner to sell; (3) the property so listed. In some states, a listing must be in writing. *See also* EXCLUSIVE AGENCY LISTING, EXCLUSIVE RIGHT TO SELL LISTING, NET LISTING, OPEN LISTING.

LISTING PRICE / The price a seller puts on a home when it is placed on the market. Listing price, or ASKING PRICE, is generally considered a starting place for negotiations between the seller and a prospective buyer.

LITIGATION / The act of carrying on a lawsuit.

LITTORAL / Part of the shore zone of a large body of water.

Importance: Littoral rights differ from *riparian rights*, which pertain to a river or stream.

LOAN CLOSING / *See* CLOSING.

LOAN COMMITMENT / An agreement to lend money, generally of a specified amount, at specified terms at some time in the future. A LOCKED-IN INTEREST RATE may be included.

LOAN CONSTANT / *See* MORTGAGE CONSTANT.

LOAN FRAUD / Purposely giving incorrect information on a loan application to better qualify for a loan; may result in civil liability or criminal penalties.

LOAN-TO-VALUE RATIO (LTV) / The ratio obtained by dividing the mortgage principal by the property value.

Importance: Lenders typically provide loans with a stated maximum loan-to-value ratio. For conventional home loans it is typically 80 percent. In many cases it can be increased to 95 percent if mortgage insurance is purchased. VA and FHA loans may offer higher ratios.

LOCK-IN / An agreement to maintain a certain price or rate for a certain period of time.

Importance: In many *mortgage* commitments the lender agrees to lock-in the interest rate for a certain period, such as 60 days. Sometimes a lock-in is provided only upon payment of a *commitment* fee.

LOT AND BLOCK NUMBER / A land description method that refers to a recorded plat. **Example:** Lot 6, Block F of the Sunnybrook Estates, District 2 of Rover County, Rhode Island.

LOT LINE / A line bounding a lot as described in a survey of the property.

Importance: Lot lines mark boundaries. There may also be building *setback* requirements, or *building lines*, within a lot.

LTV / *See* LOAN-TO-VALUE RATIO.

MAI / A professionally designated member of the Appraisal Institute.

Importance: The MAI designation is one of the most coveted in real estate. Many appraisals of large commercial properties are done by MAIs.

MAJORITY / The age at which a person is no longer a minor and is fully able to conduct his/her own affairs; in some states majority is 18.

Importance: A contract with a minor is voidable by the minor.

MARGIN / A constant amount added to the value of the *index* for the purpose of adjusting the interest rate on an *adjustable rate mortgage*.

MARGINAL PROPERTY / Property that is barely profitable to use. **Example:** The sale of cotton that has been efficiently raised yields $100, but the cotton cost $99.99 to raise. The land is therefore considered marginal land.

MARKET ANALYSIS / A study of the supply and demand conditions in a specific area for a specific type of property or service. A market analysis report is generally prepared by someone with experience in real estate, economics, or marketing. It serves to help decide what type of project to develop and is also helpful in arranging permanent and construction financing for proposed development.

MARKET APPROACH / *See* SALES COMPARISON APPROACH.

MARKET DATA APPROACH / *See* SALES COMPARISON APPROACH.

MARKET PRICE / The actual price paid in a market transaction; a historical fact.

Importance: *Market value* is a theoretical concept, whereas market price has actually occurred.

MARKET STUDY / *See* MARKET ANALYSIS.

MARKET VALUE / The highest price a buyer, willing but not compelled to buy, will pay, and the lowest price a seller, willing but not compelled to sell, will accept. Many conditions are assumed to exist.

Importance: In theory, property would sell for its market value.

MARKETABILITY STUDY / An analysis, for a specific client, of the probable sales of a specific type of real estate product.

MARKETABLE TITLE / A title that a court will consider so free from defect that it will enforce its acceptance by a purchaser; similar to *insurable title*.

MASS APPRAISING / An effort, typically used by tax *assessors*, to determine the salient characteristics of properties in a given submarket, to allow an approximation of value for each. Sophisticated statistical techniques are used frequently in mass appraising.

MATERIAL FACT / A fact that is germane to a particular situation; one that participants in the situation may reasonably be expected to consider.

Importance: In a contract, a material fact is one without which the contract would not have been made.

MECHANIC'S LIEN / A lien given by law upon a building or other improvement upon land, and upon the land itself, as security for the payment for labor done upon, and materials furnished for, the improvement.

Importance: A mechanic's lien protects persons who helped build or supply materials.

MEDIAN PRICE / The price of the house that falls in the middle of the total number of homes sold in that area.

MEETING OF THE MINDS / Agreement by all parties to a contract to its terms and substance.

Importance: When there is a meeting of the minds, the contract is not based on secret intentions of one party that were withheld from another.

MERIDIAN / North-south line used in government rectangular survey.

METES AND BOUNDS / A land description method that relates the boundary lines of land, setting forth all the boundary lines together with their terminal points and angles.

Importance: A person can follow a metes and bounds description on a plat or on the ground.

MILL / One tenth of a cent; used in expressing tax rates on a per dollar basis. **Example:** A tax rate of 60 mills means that taxes are 6 cents per dollar of assessed valuation.

MINERAL LEASE / An agreement that provides the lessee the right to excavate and sell minerals on the property of the lessor or to remove and sell petroleum and natural gas from the pool underlying the property of the lessor. In return, the lessor receives a royalty payment based on the value of the minerals removed.

MINERAL RIGHTS / The privilege of gaining income from the sale of oil, gas, and other valuable resources found on land.

MINOR / A person under an age specified by law (18 in most states).

Importance: Real estate contracts entered into with minors are voidable by the minor.

MINORITY DISCOUNT / A reduction from the MARKET VALUE of an asset because the MINORITY INTEREST owner(s) cannot direct the business operations and the interest lacks marketability.

MISREPRESENTATION / An untrue statement, whether deliberate or unintentional. It may be a form of nondisclosure where there is a duty to disclose or the planned creation of a false appearance. Where there is misrepresentation of *material fact,* the person injured may sue for *damages* or rescind the contract.

MONETARY POLICY / Actions of the Federal Reserve Bank that affect the value of the nation's currency. Monetary policy has a strong influence on market interest rates and the rate of monetary inflation (declining purchasing power of the dollar). *Contrast with* FISCAL POLICY.

MONUMENT / A fixed object and point designated by surveyors to establish land locations. **Examples:** Posts, pillars, stone markers, unique trees, stones, pipes, watercourses.

MORATORIUM / A time period during which a certain activity is not allowed.

MORTGAGE / A written instrument that creates a lien upon real estate as security for the payment of a specified debt.

Importance: The mortgage allows a defaulted debt to be satisfied by forcing a sale of the property.

MORTGAGE BANKER / One who originates, sells, and services *mortgage* loans. Most loans are insured or guaranteed by a government agency or private mortgage insurer.

MORTGAGE BROKER / One who, for a fee, places loans with investors but does not service such loans. On residential loans, the fee is commonly paid by the lender, so that the broker represents the lender rather than the borrower.

MORTGAGE COMMITMENT / An agreement between a lender and a borrower to lend money at a future date, subject to the conditions described in the agreement.

Importance: The terms of the commitment are important, especially the interest rate *lock-in*, if there is one.

MORTGAGE CONSTANT / The percentage ratio between the annual mortgage payment and the original amount of the debt.

MORTGAGEE / A person who holds a *lien* on or *title* to property as security for a debt.

Importance: The mortgagee receives the lien; the *mortgagor* receives the loan.

MORTGAGE LIFE INSURANCE / A policy that guarantees repayment of a mortgage loan in the event of death or, possibly, disability of the MORTGAGOR. Sometimes called MORTGAGE INSURANCE, not to be confused with PRIVATE MORTGAGE INSURANCE.

MORTGAGE MODIFICATION / Legislation and Treasury Department actions aimed at providing lenders with incentives to work with borrowers to avoid foreclosure.

Importance: To avoid foreclosure on homes they held loans on, some banks encouraged *mortgage modifications* to reduce or postpone a homeowner's mortgage payments. Some programs were limited to borrowers who were not in default. *See also* HOME AFFORDABLE MODIFICATION PLAN, HOMEOWNERS AFFORDABILITY AND STABILITY PLAN.

MORTGAGOR / A person who pledges his/her property as security for a loan. *See also* MORTGAGEE.

MOST PROBABLE SELLING PRICE / A property's most likely selling price when not all the conditions required for a *market value* estimate are relevant. **Example:** An appraiser estimated a property's most likely sales price at $100,000, assuming a sale within 20 days, whereas its market value of $120,000 might require up to 6 months to realize.

MULTIPLE LISTING / An arrangement among a group of real estate *brokers*; they agree in advance to provide information about some or all of their listings to the others and also agree that commissions on sales of such listings will be split between listing and selling brokers.

MULTIPLIER / A factor, used as a guide, applied by multiplication to derive or estimate an important value. **Examples:** (1) A *gross rent multiplier* of 6 means that property renting for $12,000 per year can be sold for six times that amount, or $72,000. (2) A population multiplier of 2 means that, for each job added, two people will be added to a city's population.

NAR / *See* NATIONAL ASSOCIATION OF REALTORS®.

NATIONAL ASSOCIATION OF REALTORS® (NAR) / An organization devoted to encouraging professionalism in real estate activities.

Importance: The NAR has strong lobbyists that protect the interest of the real estate community, especially of homeowners. It also has affiliates related to appraising, counseling, and managing real estate.

NEGATIVE AMORTIZATION / An increase in the outstanding balance of a loan resulting from the inadequacy of periodic debt service payments to cover required interest charged on the loan. Generally occurs under indexed loans for which the applicable interest rate may be increased without increasing the monthly payments. Negative amortization will occur if the indexed interest rate is increased.

NET INCOME / In real estate this term is now *net operating income*. In accounting, net income is the actual earnings, after deducting all expenses, including interest and depreciation, from gross sales.

NET LEASABLE AREA (NLA) / For office and retail properties, the portion used exclusively by the tenant; generally excludes hallways, restrooms, and other common areas.

Importance: The rent per square foot may be judged consistently between buildings when it is based on this space measurement.

NET LEASE / A lease whereby, in addition to the rent stipulated, the lessee (tenant) pays such things as taxes, insurance, and maintenance. The landlord's rent receipt is thereby net of those expenses.

Importance: The responsibility for maintenance costs is shifted to the lessee; the lessor is a passive investor.

NET LISTING / A listing in which the broker's *commission* is the excess of the sale price over an agreed upon (net) price to the seller; illegal in some states.
Example: A house is listed for sale at $100,000 net. The broker's commission is $1 if it sells for $100,001. But if it sells for $150,000, the broker receives $50,000.

NET OPERATING INCOME (NOI) / Income from property or business after operating expenses have been deducted, but before deducting income taxes and financing expenses (interest and principal payments).

NLA / *See* NET LEASABLE AREA.

NO-DOCUMENTATION LOAN / Mortgage loan, sometimes called a "no doc," for which the borrower is not required to provide proof of income, employment, or assets. Such loans evolved from *low-documentation loans*, which were originally designed for applicants in the Alt-A loan category, who could satisfy credit standards with high credit scores or low loan-to-value ratios. *See also* LIAR LOAN.

NOI / *See* NET OPERATING INCOME.

NONCONFORMING LOAN / Home mortgage loan that does not meet the standards of, or is too large to be purchased by, FNMA or FHLMC. Typically, the interest rate is at least half a percentage point higher than for a conforming loan.

NONCONFORMING USE / A use that violates *zoning ordinances* or codes but is allowed to continue because it began before the zoning restriction was enacted.

Importance: This allows a prior use to continue, but puts restrictions on future uses of the property.

NONRECOURSE / Carrying no personal liability. Lenders may take the property pledged as collateral to satisfy a debt, but have no *recourse* to other assets of the borrower.

NOTARY PUBLIC / An officer who is authorized to take acknowledgments to certain types of documents, such as *deeds*, *contracts*, and *mortgages*, and before whom affidavits may be sworn.

Importance: Most documents must be notarized as a condition of being recorded.

NOTE / A written instrument that acknowledges a debt and promises to pay.

Importance: A note is enforceable in a court of law. Collateral for the note may be sold to satisfy the debt.

NOTICE TO QUIT / A notice to a tenant to vacate rented property.

Importance: The tenant is permitted to complete the term of the lease, except in cases of *tenancy at will* or *tenancy at sufferance*.

NOVATION / Substitution of a revised agreement for an existing one, with the consent of all parties involved. Technically, any time parties to an existing contract agree to change it, the revised document is a *novation*.

NULL AND VOID / Having no legal validity.

OBLIGEE / The person in whose favor an obligation is entered into.

OBLIGOR / The person who binds him/herself to another; one who has engaged to perform some obligation; one who makes a bond.

OBSOLESCENCE / (1) A loss in value due to reduced desirability and usefulness of a structure because its design and construction have become obsolete; (2) loss due to a structure's becoming old-fashioned, not in keeping with modern needs, with consequent loss of income; and (3) changes outside the property.

Importance: Obsolescence can cause a loss in value just as *physical deterioration* does.

OFFER AND ACCEPTANCE / *See* AGREEMENT OF SALE.

OFFERING PRICE / The amount a prospective buyer offers for a property on the market. When an offer is submitted via a sales contract, it constitutes a bona fide offer for the property.

OFFEROR / One who extends an offer to another.

OFFICE BUILDING / A structure primarily used for the conduct of business, such as administration, clerical services, and consultation with clients and associates. Such buildings can be large or small and may house one or more business concerns.

OFFICE OF FEDERAL HOUSING ENTERPRISE OVERSIGHT (OFHEO) / *See* FEDERAL HOUSING FINANCE AGENCY.

OPEN-END MORTGAGE / A mortgage under which the mortgagor (borrower) may secure additional funds from the mortgagee (lender), usually stipulating a ceiling amount that can be borrowed.

Importance: A development in real estate finance is a line-of-credit home equity loan. This works the same as an open-end mortgage.

OPEN LISTING / A listing given to any number of brokers without liability to compensate any except the one who first secures a buyer ready, willing, and able to meet the terms of the listing or secures the seller's acceptance of another offer. The sale of the property automatically terminates all open listings.

OPEN MORTGAGE / A mortgage that has matured or is overdue and is therefore open to foreclosure at any time.

OPERATING EXPENSE RATIO / A mathematical relationship derived by dividing *operating expenses* by *potential gross income*.

Importance: A comparison of rents for properties would be incomplete without also comparing operating expenses. Apartments generally have operating expense ratios between 30 and 50 percent; this may be exceeded when the lessor pays utilities or the apartments are in low-rent areas. Office buildings often have higher operating expense ratios (40 and 60 percent) because more intensive management and maintenance, such as cleaning services, are provided.

OPERATING EXPENSES / Amounts paid to maintain property, such as repairs, insurance, property taxes, but not including financing costs or depreciation.

OPERATING LEASE / A lease between the lessee and a sublessee who actually occupies and uses the property.

Importance: In an operating lease the lessee runs the property; by contrast, in a *financing lease* the lessee becomes lessor to the operating tenant.

OPERATING STATEMENTS / Financial reports on the cash flow of a business or property. *See* CASH FLOW, RENT ROLL.

OPTION / The right, but not the obligation, to purchase or lease a property upon specified terms within a specified period. **Example:** Moore purchases an *option* on a piece of land. The option cost is $2,500. The option runs 90 days, and the land will cost $1,000 per acre. If Moore wishes to purchase the land, she has 90 days to exercise her right and may buy the land for $1,000 per acre. If she decides not to purchase, she FORFEITS the $2,500 option cost.

OPTIONEE / One who receives or purchases an option.

OPTIONOR / One who gives or sells an option.

OPTION TO PURCHASE / A contract that gives one the right (but *not* the obligation) to buy a property within a certain time, for a specified amount, and subject to specified conditions.

ORAL CONTRACT / An unwritten agreement. With few exceptions, oral agreements for the sale or use of real estate are unenforceable. However, an oral lease for less than 1 year is valid in many states.

Importance: When dealing with real estate, agreements should be in writing.

ORIGINAL EQUITY / The amount of cash initially invested by the underlying *real estate* owner; distinguished from sweat equity or payments made after loan is made.

OUTPARCEL / *See* PAD SITE.

OVERAGE / *See* PERCENTAGE RENT.

OVERALL CAPITALIZATION RATE (OVERALL RATE OF RETURN) / The rate obtained by dividing *net operating income* by the purchase price of the property.

Importance: Rates of return from properties may be compared to each other; or the rate may be divided into income to estimate property value.

OWNERSHIP RIGHTS TO REALTY / Possession, enjoyment, control, and disposition.

PAD SITE / An individual freestanding site for a retailer, often adjacent to a larger shopping center. Also referred to as an *outparcel*.

P&I / Principal and interest (payment).

PACKAGE MORTGAGE / A mortgage arrangement whereby the principal amount loaned is increased to include *personalty* (e.g., appliances) as well as *realty*; both realty and personalty serve as collateral.

PARCEL / A piece of property under one ownership; a lot in a subdivision.

PARTIALLY AMORTIZED LOAN / A loan that requires some payments toward *principal* but does not fully retire the debt, thereby requiring a *balloon payment*. *See also* AMORTIZATION.

PARTIAL OR FRACTIONAL INTEREST / The ownership of some, but not all, the rights in *real estate*. **Examples:** (1) *Leasehold;* (2) *easement;* (3) *hunting rights*.

PARTITION / The division of real property between those who own it in undivided shares. **Example:** A and B own land as tenants in common until they partition it. Thereafter, each owns a particular tract of land.

PARTNERSHIP / An agreement between two or more entities to go into business or invest. Either partner may bind the other, within the scope of the partnership. Each partner is liable for all the partnership's debts. A partnership normally pays no taxes but merely files an information return. The individual partners pay personal income tax on their share of income.

PARTY WALL / A wall built along the line separating two properties, lying partly on each. Either owner has the right to use the wall and has an *easement* over that part of the adjoining owner's land covered by the wall.

PATENT / Conveyance of title to government land; also called a *land patent*.

PAYMENT CAP / A contractual limit on the percentage amount of adjustment allowed in the monthly payment for an *adjustable rate mortgage* at any one adjustment period. Generally, it does not affect the interest rate charged. If the allowable payment does not cover interest due on the principal at the adjusted rate of interest, *negative amortization* will occur.

PERCENTAGE LEASE / A lease of property in which the rental is based on a percentage of the volume of sales made upon the leased premises. It usually provides for minimum rental and is regularly used for retailers who are tenants.

Importance: The retailer pays additional rent only if sales are high; the shopping center owner has an incentive to make an attractive shopping area.

PERCENTAGE RENT / The rent payable under a *percentage lease;* also called *overage*. Typically, the percentage applies to sales in excess of a pre-established base amount of the dollar sales volume.

Importance: Percentage rent provides incentive to a landlord for making a store or shopping area appeal to the market.

PERIODIC ESTATE / A lease, such as from month to month or year to year. Also known as periodic tenancy.

PERMANENT MORTGAGE / A mortgage for a long period of time (more than 10 years).

Importance: A permanent mortgage usually replaces construction or interim financing, and provides steady interest income plus *amortization* payments to the lender. For the borrower it means that there is no need to seek new financing.

PERSONAL LIABILITY / An individual's responsibility for a debt. Most mortgage loans on real estate are *recourse* (i.e., the lender can look to the property and the borrower for repayment). *Contrast with* NONRECOURSE.

PERSONALTY / Personal property, that is, all property that is not *realty*.

Importance: Many laws and terms that apply to real property are not the same as those for personalty. When dealing with both types, appropriate law and terminology must be applied.

PHYSICAL DEPRECIATION (DETERIORATION) / The loss of value from all causes of age and action of the elements. **Examples:** Faded paint, broken window, hole in plaster, collapsed porch railing, sagging frame.

PLANNED UNIT DEVELOPMENT (PUD) / A zoning or land-use category for large tracts that allows several different densities and forms of land use, planned as a single, well-integrated unit.

PLAT / A plan or map of a certain piece or certain pieces of land. **Examples:** A subdivision plat or a plat of one lot.

PLAT BOOK / A public record containing maps of land showing the division of the land into streets, blocks, and lots and indicating the measurements of the individual parcels.

Importance: The tax assessors office, usually in a city or county, maintains a plat book that is open for public inspection.

PLOTTAGE / Increment in the value of a plot of land that has been enlarged by assembling smaller plots into one ownership.

Importance: Combining several small tracts into one ownership can provide a large enough land area for a more profitable use than would be possible otherwise. However, it is often difficult to get several owners to sell, as some hold out for a high price.

PMI / Abbreviation for private mortgage insurance.

POACHER / Someone who trespasses upon another's land for the purpose of illegal hunting, trapping, or fishing. Unlike a squatter, a poacher does not build or occupy a structure on the land but removes property (wildlife) that belongs to the owner.

POCKET CARD / Identification required for *salespersons* and *brokers* in most states.

Importance: Issued by the state licensing agency, it identifies its holder as a licensee and must be carried at all times.

POINTS / Fees paid to induce lenders to make a *mortgage* loan. Each point equals 1% of the loan principal. Points have the effect of reducing the amount of money advanced by the lender, thus increasing the effective interest rate.

POLICE POWER / The right of any political body to enact laws and enforce them for the order, safety, health, morals, and general welfare of the public.

Importance: Government authorities get the power of *eminent domain* through their police power.

POTENTIAL GROSS INCOME / The theoretical amount of money that would be collected in a year if all units in a rental building were fully occupied all year; also called *gross possible rent*.

POWER CENTER / A shopping center with few TENANTS, most of them, junior anchor, or ANCHOR TENANTS. Generally a *power center*'s anchor tenants are "category killers," that is, the dominant retailers in the markets they serve.

POWER OF ATTORNEY / An instrument authorizing a person to act as the agent of the person granting it.

Importance: By using a power of attorney, one can designate a specific person to do everything or just certain limited activities.

PREMISES / Land and tenements; an estate: the subject matter of a *conveyance*.

PREPAYMENT CLAUSE / A clause in a mortgage that gives a mortgagor (borrower) the privilege of paying the mortgage indebtedness before it becomes due.

Importance: Sometimes a penalty must be paid if prepayment is made, but payment of *interest* that is not yet due is waived.

PRESERVATION DISTRICT / A zoning designation to protect and maintain wildlife, park land, scenic areas, or historic districts.

PRICE FIXING / Illegal effort by competing businesses to maintain the same price, such as the commission rate on the sale of real estate.

PRIMA FACIE EVIDENCE / Evidence that on its face will establish a given fact.

PRIMARY LEASE / A lease between the owner and a tenant who, in turn, has sublet all or part of his/her interest.

Importance: The tenant in the primary lease is still responsible to the landlord, even though the sub-tenant(s) occupy the space.

PRINCIPAL / (1) The employer of an *agent* or *broker*; the broker's or agent's client; (2) the amount of money raised by a mortgage or other loan, as distinct from the interest paid on it.

PRIVATE MORTGAGE INSURANCE / Protection for the lender in the event of DEFAULT, usually covering a portion of the amount borrowed. *See also* MORTGAGE LIFE INSURANCE.

PROBATE (PROVE) / To establish the validity of the will of a deceased person.

Importance: Probate relates not only to the validity of a will but also to matters and proceedings of estate administration.

PROBATE COURT / *See* SURROGATE'S COURT.

PROCURING CAUSE / A legal term that means the cause resulting in accomplishing a goal. Used in real estate to determine whether a broker is entitled to a commission.

PRODUCTION BUILDER, PRODUCTION HOME / One who builds homes with plans and specifications that have been replicated in an efficient or assembly-line process. *See also* TRACT HOME; *contrast with* CUSTOM BUILDER.

PROJECTION PERIOD / The time duration for estimating future *cash flows* and the resale proceeds from a proposed real estate investment.

PROMISSORY NOTE / A promise to pay a specified sum to a specified person under specified terms.

PROPERTY / (1) The rights that one individual has in lands or goods to the exclusion of all others; (2) rights gained from the ownership of wealth. *See also* PERSON-ALTY; REAL PROPERTY.

PROPERTY LINE / The recorded boundary of a plot of land.

Importance: A *survey* is performed in order to establish property lines and describe them on a *plat*.

PROPERTY MANAGEMENT / The operation of property as a business, including rental, rent collection, maintenance.

Importance: Property managers remove the daily burden from real estate investors, thus allowing them to be free from daily business operations.

PROPRIETORSHIP / Ownership of a business, including income-producing real estate, by an individual, as contrasted with a partnership or corporation.

PRORATE / To allocate between seller and buyer their proportionate shares of an obligation paid or due; for example, to prorate real property taxes or insurance.

Importance: Many items of expense are prorated between buyer and seller, to the date of closing.

PUD / PLANNED UNIT DEVELOPMENT.

PUR AUTRE VIE / For the life of another. A life estate *pur autre vie* grants a life estate to one person that expires on the death of another person.

Importance: Allows an estate to terminate upon the death of someone other than the life tenant.

PURCHASE AGREEMENT / *See* AGREEMENT OF SALE.

PURCHASE AND SALE AGREEMENT / *See* AGREEMENT OF SALE.

PURCHASE CAPITAL / The amount of money used to purchase real estate, regardless of the source.

PURCHASE CONTRACT / *See* AGREEMENT OF SALE, CONTRACT OF SALE.

PURCHASE MONEY MORTGAGE / A mortgage given by a grantee (buyer) to a grantor (seller) in part payment of the purchase price of real estate.

Importance: Institutional lenders are often unable or unwilling to finance certain types of property, so the seller must accept a purchase money mortgage to facilitate a sale.

QUIET ENJOYMENT / The right of an owner, or any other person legally entitled to possession, to the use of property without interference.

Importance: No interference should be caused by a landlord to a tenant who is in compliance with a lease.

QUIET TITLE SUIT / A suit in court to remove a defect, cloud, or suspicion regarding the legal rights of an owner to a certain parcel of *real property*.

Importance: A potential claimant is told to bring forward his/her claim so its validity can be judged. If it is not valid, the claimant must stop interference with the owner.

QUITCLAIM DEED / A deed that conveys only the *grantor's* rights or interest in real estate, without stating their nature and with no warranties of ownership.

Importance: This deed is often used to remove a possible cloud from the title.

RANGE LINES / In the *government rectangular survey* method of land description, lines parallel to the principal *meridian*, marking off the land into 6-mile strips known as ranges; they are numbered east or west of the principal meridian. *See also* BASE AND MERIDIAN.

RATE OF INTEREST / *See* INTEREST RATE.

REAL ESTATE / Land and all attachments that are of a permanent nature.

Importance: Real estate is distinguished from personal property. At one time real estate was the sole source of wealth and achieved a special place in the law because of its importance.

REAL ESTATE AGENT / *See* AGENT.

REAL ESTATE EDUCATORS ASSOCIATION / A professional organization composed primarily of persons who teach *real estate* in junior colleges and proprietary license preparation schools.

REAL ESTATE INVESTMENT TRUST (REIT) / A *real estate* mutual fund, allowed by income tax laws to avoid the corporate tax if 95 percent of its income is distributed. It sells shares of ownership and must invest in real estate or mortgages.

Importance: A REIT allows small investors to participate in the ownership of large, potentially profitable, real estate projects.

REAL ESTATE SETTLEMENT PROCEDURES ACT (RESPA) / A law that states how *mortgage* lenders must treat those who apply for federally related real estate loans on property with 1–4 dwelling units. Intended to provide borrowers with more knowledge when they comparison shop for mortgage money.

REAL PROPERTY / The right to use real estate, as (1) *fee simple* estate, (2) *life estate*, or (3) *leasehold* estate; sometimes also defined as *real estate*.

REALTOR® / A professional in real estate who subscribes to a strict code of ethics as a member of the local and state boards and of the *National Association of Realtors®*.

Importance: Fewer than half of those licensed to sell real estate are REALTORS®. In many areas a person must be a REALTOR® to participate in the predominant *multiple listing* service.

REALTY / The property rights to real estate.

REAPPRAISAL LEASE / A lease whereby the rental level is periodically reviewed and reset by independent appraisers.

Importance: Landlord and tenant can agree on a long-term lease knowing that the rent will be fair throughout the term because of the reappraisal clauses in the lease.

RECAPTURE CLAUSE / In a contract, a clause permitting the party who grants an *interest* or right to take it back under certain conditions.

RECESSION / Economic slowdown; officially declared after two consecutive quarters of reduced gross domestic product.

RECIPROCAL EASEMENT AGREEMENT (REA) / Agreement between owners of adjacent parcels allowing mutual use of both parcels for certain purposes.

RECISION / *See* RESCISSION.

RECORDING / The act of entering *instruments* affecting the title to real property in a book of public record.

Importance: Recording in this manner gives public notice of the facts recorded.

RECOURSE / The ability of a lender to claim money from a borrower in *default*, in addition to the property pledged as *collateral*.

REDLINING / An illegal practice of a lender refusing to make home loans in certain areas. The term is derived from circling, with red pencil on a map, areas where the institution will not lend.

Importance: If home loans will not be made in a certain area, property values will plummet and neighborhoods deteriorate rapidly. Redlining is an illegal discriminatory practice.

REDUCTION CERTIFICATE / A document in which the mortgagee (lender) acknowledges the sum due on the mortgage loan.

Importance: This is used when mortgaged property is sold and the buyer assumes the debt.

REGULATION Z / Implementation by the Federal Reserve of the federal Truth-in-Lending Act; it specifies how the *annual percentage rate* of a loan is calculated and expressed in consumer loan documents.

REGULATORY TAKING / A series of government limits to property use that constitutes a condemnation of property.

REIT / *See* REAL ESTATE INVESTMENT TRUST.

RELEASE / The act by which some claim or interest is surrendered.

RELEASE CLAUSE / A clause in a mortgage that gives the owner of the property the privilege of paying off a portion of the indebtedness, thus freeing a part of the property from the mortgage.

Importance: Release clauses are frequently used when a mortgage covers more than one property (*blanket mortgage*), so that a particular parcel can be released upon some payment.

RELICTION / Gradual subsidence of waters, leaving dry land.

Importance: Ownership of land beneath a lake, for example, can become more important as reliction occurs.

RELOCATION SERVICE / A company that contracts with other firms to arrange the relocation of employees from one city to another. The service generally handles the sale of the employee's home and purchase of a new home. Furniture moving services may also be included.

REMAINDER / An estate that takes effect after the termination of a prior estate, such as a *life estate*.

Importance: The *remainderman* owns the property outright upon the death of the *life tenant*.

REMAINDERMAN / The person who is to receive possession of a property after the death of a *life tenant*.

Importance: Many people wish to allow a surviving spouse to occupy property for the rest of his/her life, with a child as the remainderman.

REMEDIATION / The cleanup of an environmentally contaminated site. *See* CERCLA.

RENT / The compensation paid for the use of real estate.

Importance: Rent is the most important portion of a lease and may be paid in money, services, or other valuable.

RENT MULTIPLIER / *See* GROSS RENT MULTIPLIER.

RENT ROLL / A list of tenants, generally with the lease rent and expiration date for each tenant.

REPLACEMENT COST / The cost of erecting a building to take the place of or serve the functions of a previous structure.

Importance: Replacement cost often sets the upper limit on value; it is often used for insurance purposes.

REPORT DATE / In an appraisal, usually the date of the last property inspection.

REPRODUCTION COST / The normal cost of exact duplication of a property as of a certain date. Note: Replacement requires the same functional utility for a property, whereas a reproduction is an exact duplicate, using the same materials and craftsmanship.

RESALE PRICE / In a projection of real estate investment performance, the selling price that it is assumed a property could fetch at the end of the projection period. *See also* RESALE PROCEEDS.

RESALE PROCEEDS / Net cash remaining to investor after sale of investment property and paying mortgage payoff and selling costs.

RESCISSION / The act of canceling or terminating a contract. Rescission is allowed when the contract was induced by fraud, duress, misrepresentation, or mistake. *Regulation* Z allows one to rescind certain credit transactions within three business days (not applicable to first mortgages on a home); purchasers of certain land that must be registered by the Department of Housing and Urban Development may rescind within three business days.

RESERVATION PRICE / The highest price a buyer can pay and still achieve his or her primary objectives, such as keeping the monthly payments affordable or paying no more than MARKET VALUE for the property. A buyer will negotiate in hopes of keeping the sales price at or below his or her reservation price.

RESIDENTIAL SALES COUNCIL / An affiliate of the Realtors National Marketing Institute of the *National Association of Realtors*® that provides educational and promotional materials for members, most of whom are involved in residential real estate sales or brokerage.

RESTRAINT ON ALIENATION / A legal situation that would, if allowed to be enforced, prevent property from being sold easily. Restraints on alienation are against public policy, so they cannot be enforced by law.

RESTRICTION / A limitation placed upon the use of property, contained in the deed or other written *instrument* in the chain of title.

Importance: If buying property with restrictions, the buyer should determine its suitability for the uses he/she requires.

RESTRICTIVE COVENANT / *See* RESTRICTION.

REVERSION / The right of a lessor to possess leased property upon the termination of a lease.

Importance: A lease is valid for an established term, after which the lessor receives the reversion.

REVERSIONARY INTEREST / The interest a person has in property upon the termination of the preceding estate.

Importance: A lessor's interest in leased property is a reversionary interest.

REVOCATION / The recalling of a power of authority conferred, as a revocation of a power of attorney, a license, an agency.

Importance: A person with the authority to convey may also have authority to revoke, with reason.

RIDER / An amendment or attachment to a contract.

RIGHT OF SURVIVORSHIP / The right of a surviving joint tenant to acquire the interest of a deceased joint owner; the distinguishing feature of *joint tenancy* and *tenancy by the entireties*.

Importance: The right of survivorship is often used where the joint tenants are closely related.

RIGHT-OF-WAY / (1) The right to use a particular path for access or passage; a type of easement; (2) the areas of subdivisions dedicated to government for use as streets, roads, and other public access to lots.

RIPARIAN OWNER / A person who owns land bounding upon a lake, river, or other body of water.

RIPARIAN RIGHTS / Rights pertaining to the use of water on, under, or adjacent to one's land.

Importance: In most states, riparian rights do not permit property owners to alter the flow of water to their down-stream neighbors.

RISK PREMIUM / The difference between the required interest rate on an investment and the rate on risk-free investments such as U.S. Treasury securities.

ROBO-SIGNER / Epithet applied to persons at banks who signed hundreds of forms each day to proceed with FORECLOSURE without investigating the validity of information on the forms, as was required by law.

Importance: When it was disclosed that thousands of foreclosures were based on documents signed by *robo-signers*, an uproar occurred that embarrassed lenders who were responsible for WRONGFUL FORECLOSURES.

SALE-LEASEBACK / The simultaneous purchase of property and lease back to the seller. The lease portion of the transaction is generally long term. The seller-lessee in the transaction is converted from an owner to a tenant.

SALES ASSOCIATE / In some states, notably Florida, a licensed real estate AGENT who is employed by the designated or employing BROKER. *See* SALESPERSON.

SALES COMPARISON APPROACH / One of three appraisal approaches; also called *market approach* and *market data approach*. Value is estimated by analyzing sales prices of similar properties (comparables) recently sold.

Importance: Virtually all appraisals of homes, and many appraisals of other properties rely most heavily on the sales comparison approach. Two other approaches are *cost* and *income*.

SALES CONTRACT / A contract by which the buyer and seller agree to the terms of sale.

Importance: This document (in some states called an *agreement of sale, a contract of sale*, or an *earnest money contract*) stipulates the rights and responsibilities of buyers and sellers.

SALESPERSON / A person who is licensed to deal in real estate or perform any other act enumerated by state real estate license law, while in the employ of a *broker* licensed by the state.

Importance: A salesperson's license is required for anyone to sell another's property. The salesperson must have a sponsoring broker.

SALES PRICE / The amount of money required to be paid for real estate according to a contract, or previously paid.

SALVAGE VALUE / The estimated value that an asset will have at the end of its useful life.

Importance: Real estate improvements, though long lasting, have a limited useful life at the end of which there may be salvage or scrap value.

SANDWICH LEASE / A lease held by a lessee who sublets all or part of his/her interest, thereby becoming a lessor. Typically, the sandwich leaseholder is neither the owner nor the user of the property.

Importance: The sandwich lessee tries to profit from income tax advantages or the rent differential between the other leases.

S&P/CASE-SHILLER INDEX / *See* CASE-SHILLER/ S&P HOME PRICE INDEX.

SARA / *See* SUPERFUND AMENDMENTS AND REAUTHORIZATION ACT.

SATISFACTION OF MORTGAGE / *See* SATISFACTION PIECE.

SATISFACTION PIECE / An *instrument* for recording and acknowledging final payment of a mortgage loan.

Importance: After a loan has been paid off, the borrower should record a satisfaction of mortgage or satisfaction piece.

SECTION (of Land) / One square mile in the *government rectangular survey*. There are 36 sections in a 6-mile-square township.

SECTION 1031 / The section of the INTERNAL REVENUE CODE that deals with tax-deferred exchanges of certain property. General rules for a tax-deferred exchange of real estate are as follows.

The properties must be
1. exchanged or qualify as a DELAYED EXCHANGE,
2. LIKE-KIND PROPERTY (real estate for real estate), and
3. held for use in a trade or business or held as an investment. *See also* BOOT.

Example: Under *Section 1031*, Lowell trades her APPRECIATED land for Baker's shopping center. EQUITIES are the same. Lowell's adjusted tax basis in the land becomes her adjusted tax basis in the shopping center.

SECURITY INSTRUMENT / An interest in real estate that allows the property to be sold upon a default on the obligation for which the security interest was created. The security interest is more specifically described as a *mortgage* or a *trust deed*.

SEIZIN / The possession of realty by a person who claims to own a *fee simple estate* or a *life estate* or other salable interest.

Importance: Seizin is a covenant needed to transfer ownership to another.

SEPARATE PROPERTY / Property acquired by either spouse prior to marriage or by gift or devise after marriage, as distinct from *community property*.

Importance: In community property states, property that is separate before marriage can remain that way; property acquired during marriage by joint effort is community property.

SETBACK / The distance from the curb or other established line within which no buildings may be erected. *Compare with* building line.

Importance: Setbacks must be observed; if they are violated during construction, the property may have to be razed.

SETTLEMENT DATE / *See* CLOSING DATE.

SETTLEMENT STATEMENT / *See* CLOSING STATEMENT.

SEVERALTY / The ownership of *real property* by an individual as an individual.

Importance: Severalty is distinguished from joint ownership, whereby two or more persons are owners.

SHADOW ANCHOR / An anchor store appearing to be part of a shopping center but situated on land that is owned separately and so not actually a tenant of the shopping center. The shopping center enjoys the traffic generated by the shadow anchor but not the rental income.

SHADOW BANKING SYSTEM / The aggregate system of finance that occurs outside of banks and has therefore not been subject to bank regulation. *See also* DODD-FRANK WALL STREET REFORM AND CONSUMER PROTECTION ACT.

Importance: Components of the *shadow banking system* include HEDGE FUNDS, private equity firms, securitized investment vehicles, and other non-bank financial institutions. An estimated 25–30% of financial transactions occur in the shadow banking system.

SHORT SALE / Arrangement between a MORTGAGOR (borrower) and MORTGAGEE (lender) through which the mortgagor retires the mortgage obligation with a payment of something less than the total outstanding PRINCIPAL BALANCE. Any principal forgiven in the transaction is considered by the IRS to be taxable income to the borrower. At this time Congress is considering a change in tax law to facilitate short sales or WORKOUTS of subprime residential mortgages. (**Note:** This is entirely different from a short sale of stock, which occurs when the seller doesn't own the stock. The broker finds stock to borrow and deliver for the sale, while the seller hopes the value will decline so he can purchase at a lower price than he sold at.)

SINGLE AGENT / A broker who represents, as a FIDUCIARY, either the buyer or the seller, but not both in the same transaction.

SPECIAL ASSESSMENT / An *assessment* made against a property to pay for a public improvement by which the assessed property is supposed to be especially benefited.

Importance: A municipality may install a new sewer line or sidewalk; each owner along the path may be charged a special assessment, in addition to a regular tax.

SPECIAL-PURPOSE PROPERTY / A building with limited uses and marketability, such as a church, theater, school, public utility.

SPECIAL WARRANTY DEED / A deed in which the *grantor* limits the title warranty given to the *grantee* to anyone claiming by, from, through, or under him/her; the grantor. The grantor does not warrant against title defects arising from conditions that existed before he/she owned the property.

Importance: The seller does not guarantee title against all claims—just those while he/she was the owner.

SPECIFIC PERFORMANCE / A legal action in which the court requires a party to a contract to perform the terms of the contract when he/she has refused to fulfill his/her obligations.

Importance: This action is used in real estate because each parcel of land is unique; consequently a contract concerning one parcel cannot be transferred or applied to another.

SPOT ZONING / The act of rezoning a parcel of land for a different use from all surrounding parcels, in particular where the rezoning creates a use that is incompatible with surrounding land uses.

SQUATTER / One who occupies property without permission or legal authority.

SRA / A designation awarded by the *Appraisal Institute.*

Importance: Many of the most qualified residential appraisers have this designation.

STAGFLATION / A term coined in the 1970s to describe an economic situation of stagnant economic condition with inflation.

STAGING / Remodeling and interior decoration to enhance the marketability of a house prior to sale.

STATE-CERTIFIED APPRAISER / *See* CERTIFIED GENERAL APPRAISER; CERTIFIED RESIDENTIAL APPRAISER.

STATUTE / A law established by an act of a legislature.

Importance: Statutes are written laws; laws are also made through judicial interpretation and government administration.

STATUTE OF FRAUDS / A state law that provides that certain contracts must be in writing in order to be enforceable; applies to deeds, mortgages, and other real estate contracts, with the exception of leases for periods shorter than 1 year.

Importance: The statute of frauds requires that contracts involving real estate be in writing.

STATUTE OF LIMITATIONS / A certain statutory period after which a claimant is barred from enforcing his/her claim by suit.

Importance: If a practice continues beyond the statute of limitations the person who is adversely affected may be barred from trying to prevent it.

STATUTORY DEDICATION / The owners of a subdivision or other property file a plat that results in a grant of public property, such as the streets in a development.

STEP-UP LEASE / *See* GRADUATED LEASE.

STIPULATIONS / The terms within a written *contract.*

STRAIGHT-LINE DEPRECIATION / Equal annual reductions in the book value of property; used in accounting for replacement and tax purposes.

Importance: Straight-line provides less depreciation in the early years of an asset than does an accelerated method. Most taxpayers prefer accelerated depreciation because it minimizes current taxes. However, for financial reporting purposes, most companies prefer straight-line because it provides a higher net income.

SUBAGENCY / The relationship under which a sales agent tries to sell a property listed with another agent. This situation is common under a *multiple listing service* (MLS). A listing contract is taken by a listing broker and entered into the MLS, from which any member broker may sell the property. The listing broker and the selling broker split the commission.

SUBDIVIDING / The division of a tract of land into smaller tracts.

Importance: Subdividing allows raw acreage to be developed with streets, utilities, and other amenities added, resulting in lots ready for houses to be built.

SUBDIVISION / A tract of land divided into lots or plots suitable for home building purposes. Some states and localities require that a subdivision *plat* be recorded.

SUBJECT TO MORTGAGE / A method of taking title to mortgaged real property without being personally responsible for the payment of any portion of the amount due. The buyer must make payments in order to keep the property; however, if he/she fails to do so, only his/her equity in that property is lost.

SUBLEASE / A lease from a lessee to another lessee. The new lessee is a sublessee or subtenant. *See also* SANDWICH LEASE.

SUBLET / *See* SUBLEASE.

SUBORDINATED GROUND LEASE / A lease used when the *mortgage* has priority over the *ground lease.*

Importance: In case of a *default*, the unsubordinated interest has a prior claim to the subordinated interest.

SUBORDINATE MORTGAGE / One having a lower priority to another; the subordinate mortgage has a claim in foreclosure only after satisfaction of mortgage(s) with priority.

SUBORDINATION CLAUSE / A clause or document that permits a mortgage recorded at a later date to take priority over an existing mortgage.

Importance: Ordinarily a second mortgage automatically moves up to become a first *lien* when the first mortgage is retired. If the second mortgage has a subordination clause, it will remain a second mortgage when a first mortgage is refinanced.

SUBPRIME / A mortgage loan issued to a party who does not meet the standards set by FNMA and FHLMC for a CONFORMING LOAN.

SUBSURFACE RIGHTS / *Same as* MINERAL RIGHTS.

SUPERFUND / The commonly used name for CERCLA, the federal environmental cleanup law. If a site is on the Superfund list, it is required to be cleaned up by any and all previous owners, operators, transporters, and disposers of waste to the site. The federal government will clean such sites, requiring the responsible parties to pay the cleanup costs. Imposes strict liability.

SUPERFUND AMENDMENTS AND REAUTHORIZATION ACT (SARA) / Law that confirmed the continued existence of SUPERFUND. SARA put more teeth into CERCLA, though SARA provides an innocent landowner defense for a buyer who conducted a Phase I environmental study before the acquisition, with negative results.

SURETY / A person who guarantees the performance of another; a guarantor.

Importance: The surety becomes liable for the contract, just like the original principal. The surety is called when the principal fails to perform some duty.

SURRENDER / The cancellation of a lease before its expiration by mutual consent of the lessor and the lessee.

Importance: Surrender occurs only when both parties agree to it.

SURROGATE'S COURT (PROBATE COURT) / A court having jurisdiction over the proof of wills and the settling of estates and of citations.

SURVEY / (1) The process by which a parcel of land is measured and its area ascertained; (2) the blueprint showing the measurements, boundaries, and area.

Importance: A survey is needed to determine exact boundaries and any *easements* or *encroachments*.

TAG SALE / Sale where individuals mark used household items with tags displaying the price. Tag sales are commonly held on weekends at the vendor's home, often having the merchandise displayed in the front yard or driveway. Tag sales, also called *yard sales* or *garage sales*, are an American tradition.

TALF / *See* TERM ASSET-BACKED SECURITIES LOAN FACILITY.

TARP / *See* TROUBLED ASSETS RELIEF PROGRAM.

TAX / A charge levied upon persons or things by a government.

Importance: Many different types of taxes affect real estate. Most local governments levy an *ad valorem*

tax based on the property value. The federal government and many states have an income tax, but rental property owners may deduct operating expense, interest, and depreciation expense, thereby reducing their taxable income.

TAX DEDUCTIBLE / A type of expense that is allowed under tax law. Tax-deductible expenses can be used to reduce taxable income. *See* TAX DEDUCTION.

Importance: INTEREST and AD VALOREM TAXES are generally *tax deductible* for all types of property. DEPRECIATION, repairs, MAINTENANCE, UTILITIES, and other ordinary and necessary business expenses are *tax deductible* for INCOME PROPERTY.

TAX-FREE EXCHANGE / *See* SECTION 1031.

TAX SALE / The sale of property after a period of nonpayment of taxes.

Importance: Unpaid taxes become a *lien*. Property may be sold for the nonpayment of taxes.

TEASER RATE / An unusually low interest rate offered for the first few months or year of a mortgage loan; used as an enticement to potential borrowers.

Importance: When comparing interest rates on loans offered, a buyer should determine future rate adjustments, as the initial rate may be discovered to be a teaser.

TENANCY AT SUFFERANCE / Tenancy established when a lawful tenant remains in possession of property after expiration of a lease.

Importance: The tenant at sufferance has no estate or title; the landlord may oust the tenant at any time.

TENANCY AT WILL / A license to use or occupy lands and tenements at the will of the owner.

Importance: There is no fixed length of possession. The tenant may leave or may be put out at any time.

TENANCY BY THE ENTIRETIES / An estate that exists only between husband and wife, with equal right of possession and enjoyment during their joint lives and with the *right of survivorship*; that is, when one dies, the property goes to the surviving tenant.

TENANCY IN COMMON / An ownership of realty by two or more persons, each of whom has an undivided interest, without the *right of survivorship*. Upon the death of one of the owners, his/her ownership share is inherited by the party or parties designated in his/her will.

TENANCY IN SEVERALTY / Ownership of real property by an individual as an individual; ownership by one person or by a legal entity.

Importance: Tenancy in severalty is distinguished from *joint tenancy* and/or *tenancy in common*, whereby two or more persons are owners.

TENANT / A person who is given possession of real estate for a fixed period or at will. *See also* LEASE.

TENANT IMPROVEMENTS (TIs) / Those changes, typically to office, retail, or industrial property, to accommodate specific needs of a tenant. TIs include installation or relocation of interior walls or partitions, carpeting or other floor covering, shelves, windows, toilets, and so on. The cost of these is negotiated in the lease.

TENEMENTS / (1) Everything of a permanent nature; (2) anything attached to the soil. In common usage a tenement is a run-down apartment building.

TERM ASSET-BACKED SECURITIES LOAN FACILITY (TALF) / Funding facility under which the Federal Reserve Bank of New York will lend up to $200 billion on a nonrecourse basis to holders of certain AAA-rated asset-based securities (ABS) backed by newly and recently issued consumer and small business loans. On August 17, 2009, the Federal Reserve Board and the Treasury announced that, to promote the flow of credit to businesses and households and to facilitate the financing of commercial properties, the *TALF* program would continue to provide loans against newly issued ABS and legacy commercial mortgage–backed securities (CMBS) through June 30, 2010. TARP guarantees $20 billion of TALF loans.

TERMITES / Insects that bore into wood and destroy it.

Importance: Termite inspections by reputable pest control companies are often required in a real estate transaction. In some places it is customary to require a seller to post a termite bond as assurance that the foundation has been properly treated.

TERMS / Conditions and arrangements specified in a contract.

Importance: Anything lawful may be included in a contract and becomes part of its terms.

TESTAMENT / A will.

TESTAMENTARY TRUST / Created by a will that comes into effect only after the testator's death.

TESTATE / Having made a valid will. *Contrast with* INTESTATE.

TESTATOR / A man who makes a will.

TESTATRIX / A woman who makes a will.

"TIME IS OF THE ESSENCE" / A phrase that, when inserted in a contract, requires that all references to specific dates and times of day concerning performance be interpreted exactly.

TIME VALUE OF MONEY / The concept that money available now is worth more than the same amount in the future because of its potential earning capacity.

TITLE / Evidence that the owner of land is in lawful possession thereof; evidence of ownership. The word is often clarified or qualified by an adjective, such as *absolute, good, clear, marketable, defective, legal*.

TITLE ABSTRACT / *See* ABSTRACT OF TITLE.

TITLE INSURANCE / An insurance policy that protects the holder from any loss sustained by reason of defects in the title.

Importance: The premium is paid once and is good only until ownership changes.

TITLE SEARCH / An examination of the public records to determine the ownership and *encumbrances* affecting real property.

Importance: A title search is typically performed before *title insurance* is issued. If the search shows a title risk, the policy may contain an exception or may not be issued.

TOPOGRAPHY / The state of the surface of the land; may be rolling, rough, flat.

Importance: The topography may affect the way land can be developed, including potential uses.

TORRENS SYSTEM / A title registration system used in some states; the condition of the title can easily be discovered without performing a title search.

TORT / A wrongful act that is not a crime but that renders the perpetrator liable to the victim for damages.

TOWNSHIP / A 6-mile-square tract delineated by *government rectangular survey*.

TOXIC ASSETS / Nontechnical term that supplanted the less dramatic and urgent designation "troubled assets" used during 2007 and 2008 to describe mortgage-related loans and investments that had lost most if not all value in a market that was virtually not functioning. Carried on the books of banks and other financial institutions on a mark to market basis, they were "poisoning" balance sheets and causing a wave of insolvencies.

TRACT / A *parcel* of land, generally held for *subdividing; a subdivision*.

TRADE FIXTURES / Articles placed in rented buildings by the tenant to help carry out a trade or business. The tenant may remove the fixtures before the expiration of the lease, but, if the tenant fails to do so shortly after the lease expires, the fixtures become the landlord's property.

TRADING UP / Buying a larger, more expensive property.

TRAFFIC COUNTS / Generally vehicular traffic tallies performed by the state department of transportation or a local government. These are helpful to determine how to prevent or resolve traffic jams, to plan new roads, or widen existing streets. Retailers use them to determine potential support for a new store.

TRANSACTION BROKER / A broker who provides limited representation to a buyer, seller, or both, but does not represent either in a FIDUCIARY capacity or as a SINGLE AGENT. Does not provide undivided loyalty to either party. Facilitates transaction through assistance but not representation. In some states this term is applied to a broker in an arrangement similar to a no-brokerage agency relationship.

TRANSFER DEVELOPMENT RIGHTS / A type of *zoning ordinance* that allows owners of property zoned for low-density development or conservation use to sell development rights to other property owners. The development rights purchased permit the landowners to develop their parcels at higher density than otherwise. The system is designed to provide for low-density uses, such as historic preservation, without unduly penalizing some landowners.

TRIPLE-A TENANT / A tenant with an excellent credit record; also called *AAA tenant*. **Example:** The U.S. Postal Service and the American Telephone and Telegraph Company are examples of triple-A tenants because they are unlikely to *default* on a lease.

TRIPLE NET LEASE / A lease whereby the tenant pays all expenses of operations, including property taxes, insurance, utilities, maintenance, and repair.

TROUBLED ASSETS RELIEF PROGRAM (TARP) / United States Treasury program set up and funded with $700 billion by the EMERGENCY ECONOMIC STABILIZATION ACT OF 2008. Originally H.R. 1424, this was the ballyhooed "bailout bill," enacted October 2, 2008, when the credit markets were frozen and the American economy seemed to be on the brink of implosion.

TRUST ACCOUNT / A bank account separate and apart and physically segregated from a broker's own funds, in which the broker is required by state law to deposit all money collected for clients; called an *escrow account* in some states.

TRUST DEED / A *conveyance* of real estate to a third person to be held for the benefit of another; commonly used in some states in place of mortgages that conditionally convey title to the lender.

TRUSTEE / A person who holds property in trust for another to secure performance of an obligation; the neutral party in a *trust deed* transaction.

TRUSTEE'S DEED / The deed received by the purchaser at a foreclosure sale; issued by the *trustee* acting under a *trust deed.*

TRUSTOR / The person who conveys property to a trustee, to be held in behalf of a *beneficiary;* in a *trust deed* arrangement, the *trustor* is the owner of real estate and the *beneficiary* is the lender.

UNDERWATER / Slang term used to refer to a property whose debt exceeds its value.

UNDIVIDED INTEREST / An ownership right to use and possession of a property that is shared among co-owners, with no one co-owner having exclusive rights to any portion of the property. *Compare with* PARTITION.

UNEARNED INCREMENT / An increase in the value of real estate due to no effort on the part of the owner; often due to an increase in population.

Importance: *Appreciation* of land in the path of growth is considered an unearned increment because the landowners did nothing to cause it.

UNIFORM COMMERCIAL CODE (UCC) / A group of laws to standardize the state laws that are applicable to commercial transactions. Few of the laws have relevance to real estate.

UNIFORM RESIDENTIAL APPRAISAL REPORT (URAR) / A standard form for reporting the *appraisal* of a dwelling.

Importance: This form is required for use by the major secondary mortgage purchasers. It provides numerous checklists and appropriate definitions and certifications that are preprinted on the form.

UNIFORM RESIDENTIAL LANDLORD AND TENANT ACT (URLTA) / A model law governing residential leasing practice and leases, adopted wholly or in part by about 15 states.

UNIFORM STANDARDS OF PROFESSIONAL APPRAISAL PRACTICE (USPAP) / Standards promulgated by the *Appraisal Foundation* that set forth the requirements for research and reporting with which a professional appraiser is to comply.

UNILATERAL CONTRACT / An obligation given by one party contingent on the performance of another party, but without obligating the second party to perform. *Compare with* BILATERAL CONTRACT.

UNITY / Four unities are required to create a joint tenancy: interest, possession, time, and title. In other words, the joint tenants must have an equal interest arising from the same conveyance, the same undivided possession, and the same use over the same time.

UPGRADERS / People who currently own a home but are seeking to buy what they consider a better home; also called "move-up" buyers. The "upgrade" may involve getting a larger home, a more conveniently located home, or one with special amenities. In almost all cases, the upgrader is looking to spend more for the new home than the proceeds received from selling the old home.

UPLANDS / Land within the mitigation parcel adjacent to surrounding wetlands, often having exotic plant species like the wetlands.

Example: *Uplands* include rangeland, improved pastures, pine flatwoods, and tropical hardwood hammocks all with varying degrees of melaleuca infestation.

UPSIDE-DOWN MORTGAGE / A mortgage loan whose balance is greater than the property providing the security for the loan. A homeowner with such a loan cannot sell the home or refinance the loan without surrendering cash. The homeowner has negative equity in the home. *See also* SHORT SALE, UNDERWATER.

URAR / *See* UNIFORM RESIDENTIAL APPRAISAL REPORT.

URBAN PROPERTY / City property; closely settled property.

Importance: Urban property is more valuable than rural or suburban land because of its greater business activity.

URLTA / *See* UNIFORM RESIDENTIAL LANDLORD AND TENANT ACT.

U.S. GREEN BUILDING COUNCIL / Nonprofit organization that offers LEED certification of GREEN BUILDINGS, educational resources, and a network of chapters and affiliates to support and encourage environmentally sensitive construction of buildings, including homes, and communities.

USPAP / *See* UNIFORM STANDARDS OF PROFESSIONAL APPRAISAL PRACTICE.

USURY / A rate of interest higher than that permitted by law.

Importance: Each state has its own usury laws, with different ceiling interest rates applying to each type of loan. Penalties are severe for usury rates.

VA / Department of Veterans Affairs (formerly Veterans Administration), a government agency that provides certain services to discharged servicemen and women. *See also* VA LOAN OR MORTGAGE.

VA LOAN or MORTGAGE / Home loan guaranteed by the U.S. Department of Veterans Affairs (VA) under the Servicemen's Readjustment Act of 1944 and later. Discharged servicemen and women with more than 120 days of active duty are generally eligible for a VA loan, which typically does not require a down payment.

Importance: The VA guarantees restitution to the lender in the event of default, up to a stated amount.

VALID / (1) Having force, or binding force; (2) legally sufficient and authorized by law.

Importance: A valid contract can be enforced in court.

VALUATION / (1) Estimated worth or price; (2) valuing by appraisal.

Importance: Valuation is the process of estimating the worth of an object.

VALUE / (1) The worth of all the rights arising from ownership; (2) the quantity of one thing that will be given in exchange for another.

Importance: Price is the historic amount that was paid; value is an estimate of what something is worth. Often value is qualified as to a specific type: market, user, assessed, insurable, speculative.

VARIABLE EXPENSES / Property operating costs that increase with occupancy.

VENDEE / A purchaser; a buyer.

VENDEE'S LIEN / A *lien* against property under a *contract of sale*, to secure the deposit paid by a purchaser.

VENDOR / A seller.

VERIFICATION / Sworn statements before a duly qualified officer as to the correctness of the contents of an *instrument*.

VICARIOUS LIABILITY / The responsibility of one person for the acts of another.

VIOLATION / An act, a deed, or conditions contrary to law or the permissible use of real property.

Importance: When there is a violation of a law or contract, the perpetrator may be liable for damages and/or penalties.

VOID / Having no force or effect; unenforceable.

VOIDABLE / Capable of being voided, but not void unless action is taken to void. **Example:** Contracts to real estate entered into by minors are voidable only by the minors.

VOLUNTARY ALIENATION / Legal term describing a sale or gift made by the seller or donor of his/her own free will.

WAIVER / The voluntary renunciation, abandonment, or surrender of some claim, right, or privilege.

Importance: A person may waive a right when that right is not especially important to him/her in the overall transaction.

WARRANTY / A promise or representation contained in a *contract*.

Importance: Usually a seller's warranty pertains to the quality, character, or title of goods that are sold.

WARRANTY DEED / A deed that contains a covenant that the *grantor* will protect the *grantee* against any and all claims; usually contains covenants assuring good title, freedom from *encumbrances*, and *quiet enjoyment*. *See also* GENERAL WARRANTY DEED; SPECIAL WARRANTY DEED.

WASTE / Often found in a mortgage or lease contract, this term refers to property abuse, destruction, or damage (beyond normal wear and tear). The possessor causes unreasonable injury to the holders of other interests in the land, house, garden, or other property. The injured party may attempt to terminate the contract or sue for damages.

WATER TABLE / The distance from the surface of the ground to a depth at which natural groundwater is found.

Importance: The water table may affect the type of buildings that are possible on a parcel of land, and the ability to get well water.

WETLANDS / Land, such as swamps, marshes, and bogs, normally saturated with water. Development may be prohibited, because it could disturb the environment. The U.S. Army Corps of Engineers (COE) and the U.S. Environmental Protection Agency (EPA) have adopted a regulatory definition for administering the Section 404 permit program of the Clean Water Act (CWA) as follows: "those areas that are inundated or saturated by surface or groundwater at a frequency and duration sufficient to support, and that under normal circumstances do support, a prevalence of vegetation typically adapted for life in saturated soil conditions."

WILL / The disposition of one's property to take effect after death.

Importance: If a person dies without a will (*intestate*), the property goes to his/her heirs at law. If a person dies intestate without heirs, the property *escheats* to the state.

WITHOUT RECOURSE / Words used in endorsing a note or bill to denote that the future holder is not to look to the debtor personally in the event of nonpayment: the creditor has recourse only to the property and the borrower is held harmless after foreclosure.

Importance: In *default*, the borrower can lose the property mortgaged, but no other property. There can be no *deficiency judgment*.

WRAPAROUND MORTGAGE / A mortgage that includes in its balance an underlying mortgage. Instead of having distinct and separate first and second mortgages, a wraparound mortgage includes both. For example, suppose that there is an existing first mortgage of $100,000 at 4% interest. A second mortgage can be arranged for $50,000 at 8% interest. Instead of getting that second mortgage, the borrower arranges a wraparound, subject to the first mortgage, for $150,000 at 6%. The first mortgage of $100,000 stays intact (and is included in the $150,000 wraparound). The borrower pays the wraparound lender one payment on the $150,000 wraparound, and the wrap lender remits the payment on the first mortgage to the first mortgage lender.

WRONGFUL FORECLOSURE / A FORECLOSURE that was allegedly performed illegally or incorrectly. *See also* ROBO-SIGNER.

ZILLOW / Popular website that offers data on residential housing prices and sales.

ZIPSKINNY / Data source for demographic information sorted by ZIP code. www.zipskinny.com.

ZONE / An area set off by the proper authorities for specific use, subject to certain restrictions or restraints. Changing the zoning of property usually requires approval by the city council.

ZONING ORDINANCE / An act of city, county, or other authorities specifying the type of use to which property may be put in specific areas. **Examples:** residential, commercial, industrial.

Fundamentals of Real Estate Law

This is the first chapter of subject matter material. Much of what is mentioned in this chapter will be discussed in greater detail in future chapters. Here, however, we are going to summarize real estate law in its entirety, with the exception of license and contract law.

The subject matter of this chapter is a very fertile source of license examination questions, particularly because it concerns things that the average layperson knows little or nothing about. In this manner the examining authorities can make sure that successful licensing applicants have, indeed, studied the laws and customs of the real estate business and know enough about it to be worthy of public trust.

PROPERTY

Property refers to the legal rights to use and enjoy any thing. Strictly speaking, the term *property* does not refer to the things themselves, but to the *legal rights* that a society allows someone with regard to the *use* of and *enjoyment* of these things. In practice, however, we tend to use the word *property* to mean the things themselves, so we don't think it odd for someone to say, "That car is my property." To be absolutely proper, however, he should be saying, "The *rights* to use and enjoy that car are my property."

That may sound like nitpicking, and perhaps it is. When you are speaking of legal matters, though, it is essential to be precise and clear, or you can land in serious trouble. If a contract is drawn up vaguely, or if the description of a piece of land is inexact, the preparer can be held responsible for problems caused by the preparer's negligence.

Property is divided into two kinds: *real property* and *personal property*. Respectively, these are also known as *realty* and *personalty*. Realty is the property rights to real estate; personalty is the property rights to everything else.

Real estate is defined as "land and everything permanently attached to it." A "permanent attachment" is (a) anything that grows on the land, (b) anything that is built upon the land (including roads, fences, etc., as well as buildings), and (c) fixtures. *Fixtures* are items that may appear to be personal property but are considered to be part of the land also. Fixtures may include window air conditioners, major appliances, draperies, and other items of that nature. There is no cut-and-dried definition of a fixture, so many of the court disputes concerning real estate contracts involve misunderstandings concerning what are and aren't fixtures.

Many objects can be either realty or personalty, depending on how they are used. A brick is personalty until it is mortared into place on the wall of a building, at which time it becomes realty. A tree is realty when it is growing, but it becomes personalty when it is cut down. Fixtures are the "gray area," where an argument can be made either way as to the nature of the item. Usually the courts decide such a problem based upon the answers to these questions:

1. How is the item attached to the property? The more "tightly" attached, the more likely it will be considered a fixture.

2. What was the intention of the person who attached it? If he intended it to be a permanent part of the real estate, then it probably will be a fixture.
3. What is the prevailing custom in that particular part of the world? Depending on the location, some things may or may not be considered fixtures. For example, in some places, major appliances, air conditioners, draperies, and the like are considered part of the real estate, whereas elsewhere the seller would be considered perfectly within her rights to take them with her.

Both realty and personalty can be divided into the *tangible* and *intangible*. When we speak of realty, these things are referred to as *corporeal* and *incorporeal*. Corporeal property is the right to use, own, and enjoy real estate directly. The term *incorporeal* concerns the right to use property that actually belongs to another; examples are *easements, rights-of-way*, or mere permission to use someone else's property.

Corporeal property involving real estate is almost always real property as well. Incorporeal real estate property can be either real or personal property. Easements usually are real property; short term leases (in most states leases of one year or less) also are personal property.

ESTATES IN LAND

The collection of rights that someone may have in real estate can be called an *estate* if it is large enough. Estates are divided into two groups: *freehold* and *nonfreehold*. The basic difference is that a freehold estate is of uncertain duration because it extends until the owner chooses to dispose of it or, if he doesn't, until he dies, and we never know just how long that will be. The divisions of freehold estates are *inheritable* and *noninheritable*. Nonfreehold estates involve various kinds of leases. Leases are contracted for specific periods of time, so it is known exactly when these kinds of estates will cease to exist.

Inheritable estates are called *fee simple* estates. Basically these give their owners absolute rights to do whatever they want with the land involved, subject only to the general law, such as zoning and building codes. Most important, as far as the law is concerned, is the right to *dispose* of the estate in any legal manner: by selling it, by giving it away, or by willing it to someone.

Noninheritable estates are called *life estates*. In a life estate arrangement the owner, called the *life tenant*, has the right to use, occupy, and enjoy the property so long as he lives, but upon his death the ownership of the property goes to a predetermined person (or persons) referred to as the *remainderman*. Since the life tenant has rights to the property only so long as he lives, he can transfer to others only those rights. Consequently he may sell his interest to someone, but that person will have to relinquish the property upon the original life tenant's death. The same would happen if the life tenant leased the property to someone and died before the lease expired. Furthermore, the life tenant is considered to be the custodian of the property for the remainderman: he cannot allow the property to deteriorate beyond ordinary wear and tear, because he must protect the remainderman's interest in it.

There is a special form of life estate that is *pur autre vie*. This term is French, meaning "for another life." In such a life estate, the duration is not for the tenant's life, but for that of another person. For example, I purchase a specially built home to accommodate my severely disabled daughter. The purpose is to provide her with a place to reside, with my son, for the rest of her life, after which time I want the home to become the property of a charity. My daughter is legally incompetent and cannot own real estate in her own name. One option that I have would be to grant the home to my son pur autre vie; the "other life" would be that of my disabled daughter. The charity would be the remainderman. My son would be the life tenant so long as my daughter lives; upon her death, the property would revert to the charity.

Nonfreehold estates are leases for specific terms. The lessee, or tenant, has the right (unless she contracts to give it up) to assign or otherwise dispose of her leasehold rights if she has a *leasehold estate*. Furthermore, she has the right to use, occupy, and enjoy the real estate during the period of her lease.

An estate in land requires that its owner have the following rights: the right to *possess* the land, the right to *use* the land, and the right to *dispose* of his estate to someone else. Possession means, basically, just that: the right to occupy the land and make use of it, and to exclude everyone else from the land. A person who has *some* rights to use land, but not *all* possessory rights, is said to have an *interest* in land. An interest occurs when a person has a month-to-month lease that either party can terminate at any time (*tenancy at will*) because no specific duration is mentioned. An interest also occurs when *license to use* is involved; here there is mere permission, and not even a contractual arrangement. This might occur if someone asked permission to come onto your land one afternoon to go fishing.

CREATION OF ESTATES IN LAND

Estates in land are created in the following ways: by *will, descent, voluntary alienation, involuntary alienation*, and *adverse possession*. One receives an estate *by will* if he inherits it by being *so designated in someone's will*. One receives an estate *by descent* if he is *designated by law* as the recipient of some property of a deceased person. This occurs if the person dies *intestate* (with no will); every state has laws governing the disposition of such property.

Some states also have *dower* laws, which have similar effects. Dower laws state that a person's spouse and sometimes his/her minor children are entitled to receive a certain interest in his/her property when he/she dies.Most states have changed their laws (or are in the process of changing them) to give husbands and wives equal rights to one another's estates.

Voluntary alienation is the most common means whereby a person receives estates in land. This term refers to voluntary exchanges, sales, and gifts, wherein the one who gives up the property does so willingly. *Involuntary alienation* occurs where the owner of an estate is forced, in a legal manner, to give up some or all of her rights by the action of law. This most commonly occurs in the case of bankruptcy or of having some other kind of legal judgment entered against one, such as a foreclosure or failure to pay property taxes. Involuntary alienation also occurs by *eminent domain* (see page 55) and by *adverse possession*.

Adverse possession is a special means of acquiring ownership. All states have statutes permitting adverse possession, which is the right of a person who has used another's land actually to receive a legal claim to that land, in fee simple. The ancient idea behind this is that, if the true owner is so uninterested in his land that he does nothing during this period of time to prevent someone else from putting it to use, the community is better off by letting this other person actually have the full rights to the land. Adverse possession cannot be acquired overnight; depending on the state, it takes from 7 to 25 years to establish these rights. The adverse possession must be *open, notorious, continuous*, and *hostile*. This means that the claimant, during the required time period, must have acted completely as if the property were his own, including defending his "rights" against encroachment by others and being perfectly open in his actions. The adverse possession must continue throughout the statutory period; a person can't use someone else's land for the summer of 1984 and later for the summer of 2014 and then claim that he has been using it for 30 years. Further, no tenant can claim against his landlord, because every time a tenant pays rent he legally acknowledges that the person receiving payment is the true owner. Nor may one claim against the government, on the theory that one is already the nominal "owner" of public property. *Easements* (see pages 52–53) also can be acquired by adverse possession; they are called *easements by prescription*.

TENANCIES

Estates in land may be owned in a variety of ways, depending on the number of people involved and their relationship. These various forms of ownership are called *tenancies*. *Tenancy in severalty* is ownership by one person. *Tenancy in common* is a form of ownership by two or more persons. Each one owns an *undivided interest*, which means that he owns a fraction of each part of the realty. In this arrangement, each is entitled to his share of the profits and is responsible to the other owners for his share of the costs and expenses. No part of the land may be disposed of without the consent of all, unless they have a specific arrangement whereby less than unanimity can force a decision. Tenants in common need not own equal shares. They may dispose of their shares in any way they choose, unless they have specifically agreed upon some limitation; this means that A and B may buy real estate as tenants in common and later on B may sell his share to C, making A and C tenants in common. Further, a tenant in common may will his share to someone else or give it away.

Joint tenancy is similar to tenancy in common except for one important difference: joint tenants have the *right of survivorship*. This means that if a joint tenant dies her share is divided proportionally among the surviving joint tenants. Consequently, a joint tenant cannot will her share to someone else. However, she can sell or give her interest away; the new owners will then have the status of tenants in common.

Tenancy by the entireties is a special form of joint ownership allowed only to married couples. In states where it is used, it protects the rights of the family to jointly owned property by providing the same basic rights and responsibilities as joint tenancy while also protecting the property against any foreclosure due to judgment or debt against one of the parties.

Community property is a system that exists in a few states, including the large ones of California and Texas.* Where community property laws exist, half of all property acquired by either husband or wife during a marriage is considered to belong to each partner. These ownership rights transcend death and divorce; consequently, community property states do not have dower or curtesy laws.

All of the forms of tenancy just discussed have to do with freehold estates. There are two major types of tenancies that refer to nonfreehold estates:

Tenancy at will occurs when there is a lease arrangement, but no specific time period is agreed upon. Essentially, then, either party can terminate the arrangement whenever he wants (i.e., at will), so its duration is uncertain.

Tenancy at sufferance occurs when a tenant remains on the property after the expiration of a lease. This differs from tenancy at will in that often some aspects of the original lease contract may be considered to be in force (such as those requiring notice before termination or prohibitions against certain kinds of uses or activities by the tenant). Many states have enacted laws requiring that, even in cases of tenancy at sufferance or tenancy at will, the parties give one another certain minimum notice before termination of the arrangement.

HOMESTEAD LAWS

Many states have what are known as *homestead* laws. These have a number of effects, some of which are similar to those provided by dower and curtesy, and are referred to as *probate homestead*. In many states the homestead laws also protect one's home against certain kinds of judgments and claims. Usually, this protection extends only to a specific dollar amount; the intent of these laws is to ensure that even under the most difficult financial circumstances a homeowner will not lose her entire investment in her home.

LIMITATIONS ON ESTATES AND INTERESTS

Very few estates or interests are completely free of restrictions or encumbrances; one or more of the following will affect most of them: easements, restrictive covenants, or liens.

Easements

An *easement* is the right of one landowner to use land belonging to another for a specific purpose. The most common kinds of easements are access easements, utility easements, and drainage easements. All of these allow someone who is *not* an owner of the affected property to make use of that property for some reason. An *access easement* allows someone to cross a

---

*The others are Arizona, Idaho, Louisiana, Nevada, New Mexico, Washington, and Wisconsin.

property to reach (i.e., obtain access to) another property. These rights exist where one parcel of land is completely blocked by others from access to a public right-of-way. A *utility easement* is a right held by a utility company to put its utility lines on private property, usually for the purpose of providing service to that property. A *drainage easement* requires that a property owner not disturb a natural or man-made drainage pattern that crosses his land.

Easements are created in all the ways that estates are; most commonly, however, they are created by voluntary alienation or adverse possession. In some states, a person who sells a part of his land that does not have direct access to a public right-of-way is legally bound to provide the purchaser with an access easement.

Restrictive Covenants

A *restrictive covenant* is a contract whereby a group of neighboring landowners agree to do (or *not* to do) a certain thing or things so as to mutually benefit all. Covenants most commonly occur in residential subdivisions and are created by the developer as a means of assuring prospective buyers that the neighborhood will be required to meet certain standards. Examples of covenants are prohibitions against using a lot for more than one single-family dwelling, limitations on the minimum size of structures to be built, and specification of architectural style. In some states, the entire collection of restrictions applying to a subdivision is called a *bill of assurance*. Also, in some states, restrictive covenants are called deed *restrictions*.

Liens

Liens are claims against the owner of a property, with that property being usable as security for the claim. Claims for unpaid property taxes are liens, as, in many states, are mortgages. Also, anyone who has done work or provided materials so as to enhance the value of a property may, if not paid on time, secure a *mechanic's lien* against the property. If liens are not paid in the legal manner, the holder of the lien can foreclose against the property. *Foreclosure* is a legal process whereby a person holding a legal claim against a property may have the court order the property to be sold so as to provide funds to pay the claim.

Liens, restrictive covenants, and easements are, legally speaking, *a part of the property* and cannot be separated from it without the consent of all parties involved. A person who is considering buying property must be aware that all encumbrances on the property will remain with it after she acquires title, unless something is done to remove them.

Water Rights

Riparian refers to property that borders on water such as a stream or lake. The owner of such property has *riparian rights*. In most states a riparian property owner cannot accelerate or detain the natural flow of water.

Many western states allow *usufructory rights*, whereby an owner may divert a stream for a beneficial purpose, such as to water a growing crop.

Littoral rights are held by owners of a commercial navigable body of water: lake, ocean, or sea.

Accretion and Erosion

Accretion is an increase in land through the processes of nature. A sudden change in a watercourse can result in a loss of soil, called *avulsion,* or an increase in alluvial deposits, called *alluvium* or *alluvion.*

Erosion is the gradual wearing away of land through the processes of nature. Soil erosion may cause *subsidence.* This could result in a loss of lateral support of a building, diminishing its structural integrity.

CONDOMINIUMS

All states have passed laws that permit the establishment of *condominium* interests in land. *Condominium* is a legal term, describing a certain kind of ownership of land; it does *not* refer to any particular architectural style. In theory, any kind of property, serving any use, can be owned in condominium. In this form of ownership, one has title to a part of a larger piece of property, with the right to use his exclusively and the right to share some of the rest with the other owners. Typically, in a residential condominium one would have the right to use his own dwelling unit, and no right to enter the units owned by others. However, one would share the right, with the others, to use the *common property*, which might include private drives within the project, recreational facilities, common hallways, and elevators. Most important, the law allows an owner of a condominium unit to mortgage and otherwise encumber his unit; if he defaults, a lienholder may force the sale of his unit, but the other owners in the condominium project cannot be held responsible for anything.

A residential condominium development usually has a *homeowners' association* or some similar group that is elected by the owners of the units in the project. The function of the association is to ensure that the common property in the development is taken care of and also to make and enforce whatever rules the owners as a group want to enforce within their private community. Many people who have bought condominium units have found later that the rules and regulations of the association do not permit them to do everything they want to. For example, the association may have a rule limiting overnight guests to no more than two per unit, or requiring that only certain kinds of flowers be planted in the front yards. An owner who may wish to have more guests, or to plant different flowers, can find herself in conflict with the association and can be required to conform to the rules.

Many condominium projects have quite a lot of common property; swimming pools, park areas, parking lots, bicycle paths, tennis courts, clubhouses, and gatehouses are examples. The owners of units in the project own these common elements together, as a group. Their association looks after the common property and assesses each unit owner a fee (called a *condominium fee*), usually monthly, to get the funds necessary to maintain it. An owner who does not pay this fee will usually find that the association has the legal power to file a lien on his unit in order to collect the money.

COOPERATIVES

The *cooperative* form of ownership has existed much longer than condominium, but it is not very common outside major cities, including New York, Miami, and Washington, D.C. In a cooperative, the entire real estate is owned by a *cooperative corporation*. Instead of owning a unit outright, the cooperative owner owns a proportion of the *shares of stock* of the cooperative corporation, along with the right to exclusive use of a particular unit. The owners elect a board of directors that is responsible for the operation of the corporation and, therefore, of the property. Each owner pays monthly assessments to the corporation, which, in turn, pays its property taxes, mortgage payments, maintenance bills, and so forth. A big disadvantage of cooperative ownership is that, if one or more of the owners does not pay, the others will have to make up the difference or face the risk of having the entire property foreclosed.

TITLE AND RECORDATION

A person who owns real estate is said to hold *title* to the land. There is no such thing as "title papers" to real estate, as there are with automobiles and certain other chattels. The term *title* refers to the validity of the available evidence that backs up one's claim to land. Normally, all deeds, liens, restrictions, and easements affecting land are recorded, usually in the courthouse of the county in which the land is located. Some leases, contracts of sale, and other documents may be recorded as well. The object of *recordation* is to provide a means whereby anyone may check the validity of any claim to land. In a legal sense, therefore, the ownership of all land

and all rights to land should be a matter of record. These records are public, which means that anyone may examine them. It also means that anything that is recorded gives everyone *constructive notice* of the information recorded; therefore, in a court of law one is assumed to be aware of all information in the public records.

The total of the evidence in the records will be the validity of the *title* an owner holds. *Good title* is title that cannot be impeached by the records. Title that appears to be good but is not is said to be *color of title*.

EMINENT DOMAIN AND ESCHEAT

There are two special ways in which the government may acquire title to real estate. The most important is *eminent domain*; this is the right of the government to acquire privately owned property to be put to a public use, even if the private owner is unwilling to dispose of it. Government needs this power in order to operate efficiently for the benefit of everyone. Imagine the problems if, when the government decided to build a road, it had to look all over to find willing sellers for land needed for the project—the road might wander all around, and quite possibly it couldn't be built at all.

In an eminent domain situation the government can't just seize the land; it must pay the owner the "fair market value" of the land. However, once the government has established that it needs the land for a legitimate public use, there is no way to stop it. All a landowner can do is to dispute the price being offered; if he thinks it is unfair, he may sue for a higher award and have the court make the final decision. Usually, the government will approach the landowner to work out an amicable arrangement, and quite often the landowner agrees to the offered price and there is no dispute. If, however, the landowner is reluctant or refuses to negotiate, the government will *condemn* the affected land. Condemnation is a legal process whereby the owner is dispossessed of the property and must leave. He retains the right to dispute the price being offered; but once condemnation has begun, a time will come when he must leave the land, which will be transferred to the government whether or not the payment question has been settled. All levels of government have power of eminent domain; also, many states have granted limited eminent domain power to private enterprises such as railroads, and utility companies.

Escheat is a process whereby land for which no legal owner exists reverts to government, which then can dispose of it or use it as it sees fit. Escheat most commonly occurs when someone dies intestate and no legal heirs can be found.

YOUR STATE'S REAL ESTATE LAW

The laws of the states vary considerably. Most state real estate licensing authorities make available literature that explains some of the special provisions of law that affect real estate in that state. To find the answers to the questions on this page, you should study Table 3-1 and the materials from your state. Then check the appropriate boxes and write your other answers in the spaces provided.

1. Does your state have *dower laws*?

   ☐ No   ☐ Yes; they apply to husbands *and* wives

   ☐ Yes, for wives only

   What are the dower rights of wives? _____

   _____

   _____

   What are the dower rights of children? _____

   _____

   _____

2. Is your state a *community property* state?

   ☐ No   ☐ Yes

3. Which tenancies does your state allow?

   Joint tenancy   ☐ Yes   ☐ No

   Tenancy by the entirety   ☐ Yes   ☐ No

   (All states allow tenancy in common, at sufferance, at will.)

4. Does your state have homestead laws?

   ☐ No   ☐ Yes

   If yes, what are the major provisions?

   _____

   _____

5. What is the statutory period for adverse possession in your state?

   For fee simple ownership   _____ years

   For easements   _____ years

   Are there any special situations that would shorten or lengthen the statutory period?

   ☐ No   ☐ Yes

   If yes, what are they?

   _____

   _____

   _____

Table 3-1
**OWNERSHIP AND INTERESTS IN REAL ESTATE:
THE FIFTY STATES AND THE DISTRICT OF COLUMBIA***

State	Joint Tenancy	Tenancy by the Entirety	Community Property	Dower	Homestead	State	Joint Tenancy	Tenancy by the Entirety	Community Property	Dower	Homestead
Alabama	•			•	•	Missouri	•	•			•
Alaska		•			•	Montana	•			•	•
Arizona	•		•		•	Nebraska	•				•
Arkansas	•	•		•	•	Nevada	•		•		•
California	•		•		•	New Hampshire	•				•
Colorado	•				•	New Jersey	•	•		•	
Connecticut	•					New Mexico	•		•		
Delaware	•	•		•		New York	•	•			•
District of Columbia	•	•		•		North Carolina	•	•		•	•
						North Dakota	•				•
Florida	•	•		•	•	Ohio		•		•	•
Georgia				•	•	Oklahoma	•	•			•
Hawaii	•	•		•	•	Oregon	•	•		•	•
Idaho	•		•		•	Pennsylvania	•	•			
Illinois	•				•	Rhode Island	•	•		•	
Indiana	•	•				South Carolina	•				
Iowa	•			•	•	South Dakota	•				•
Kansas	•			•	•	Tennessee	•	•		•	•
Kentucky	•	•		•	•	Texas	•		•		•
Louisiana	See below		•	See below	•	Utah	•	•			•
Maine	•				•	Vermont	•	•		•	•
Maryland	•	•				Virginia	•	•		•	•
Massachusetts	•			•	•	Washington	•		•		
Michigan	•	•		•	•	West Virginia	•	•		•	•
Minnesota	•				•	Wisconsin	•		•	•	•
Mississippi	•	•			•	Wyoming	•	•			•

*The states are arranged alphabetically; each column represents one of five estates or ownership interests. A bullet (•) in a column means that the state *permits* that feature. If there is no bullet, the state *does not permit* it.

Louisiana law comes from French civil law, whereas the law in the other 49 states has evolved from English common law. Therefore, the law in Louisiana is different, and Louisiana license applicants should study that state's law especially diligently. Of the other 49 states:

All permit fee simple estates.

All permit life estates.

All permit individual ownership (tenancy in severalty).

All permit tenancy in common.

All permit condominium.

Questions on Chapter 3

1. Which of the following is most accurately described as personal property?
   - (A) a fixture
   - (B) a chattel
   - (C) an improvement
   - (D) realty

2. Which of the following is *not* corporeal property?
   - (A) a building
   - (B) a leasehold
   - (C) outdoor billboard
   - (D) a fixture

Questions 3–5 concern the following situation:

Mr. Jones died; his will left to Mrs. Jones the right to use, occupy, and enjoy Mr. Jones's real estate until her death. At that time the real estate is to become the property of their son Willis.

3. Mrs. Jones is a
   - (A) remainderman
   - (B) life tenant
   - (C) joint tenant
   - (D) tenant in common

4. Willis is a
   - (A) remainderman
   - (B) life tenant
   - (C) joint tenant
   - (D) tenant in common

5. Mrs. Jones has a
   - (A) fee simple estate in joint tenancy with Willis
   - (B) fee simple estate as tenant in common with Willis
   - (C) life estate
   - (D) life estate in joint tenancy with Willis

6. Which of the following is *not* realty?
   - (A) a fee simple estate
   - (B) a leasehold for indefinite duration
   - (C) lumber
   - (D) a life estate

7. Real estate is defined as
   - (A) land and buildings
   - (B) land and all permanent attachments
   - (C) land and everything growing on it
   - (D) land only

8. A freehold estate is
   - (A) one acquired without paying anything
   - (B) any leasehold
   - (C) any estate wherein one may use the property as he wishes
   - (D) an estate of uncertain duration

9. An item of personalty that is affixed to realty so as to be used as a part of it is
   - (A) a fixture
   - (B) a chattel
   - (C) personal property
   - (D) an encumbrance

10. Which is *not* considered a permanent attachment to land?
    - (A) anything growing on it
    - (B) fixtures
    - (C) chattels
    - (D) anything built upon the land

11. A person who has some rights to use land, but not all possessory rights, is said to have
    - (A) an interest in land
    - (B) an estate in land
    - (C) a life estate in land
    - (D) a tenancy in common

12. A person who has permission to use land, but has no other rights, has
    - (A) tenancy at sufferance
    - (B) tenancy in common
    - (C) license to use
    - (D) a fee simple estate

13. A person receives title to land by virtue of having used and occupied it for a certain period of time, without actually paying the previous owner for it, receives title by
    - (A) will
    - (B) descent
    - (C) alienation
    - (D) adverse possession

14. A person who dies leaving no will is said to have died
    - (A) intestate
    - (B) without heirs
    - (C) unbequeathed
    - (D) unwillingly

15. A person who owns an undivided interest in land with at least one other, and has the right of survivorship, is said to be a
    - (A) tenant in common
    - (B) tenant at will
    - (C) joint tenant
    - (D) tenant at sufferance

16. Tenancy in severalty refers to
    - (A) ownership by one person only
    - (B) ownership by two persons only
    - (C) ownership by at least three persons
    - (D) a special form of joint ownership available only to married couples

17. Dower rights are rights that assure that
    (A) a spouse receives a certain portion of his/her deceased spouse's estate
    (B) dowagers may have property rights
    (C) a homeowner cannot lose his entire investment in his home
    (D) husbands and wives share equally in property acquired during marriage

18. An easement is
    (A) the right to use the property of another for any purpose
    (B) the right to use the property of another for a specific purpose
    (C) a private contract and does not permanently affect the realty
    (D) the right to keep another from using one's land illegally

19. The process whereby a person holding a claim against property can have the property sold to pay the claim is
    (A) a lien
    (B) a covenant
    (C) a mechanic's lien
    (D) foreclosure

20. A person who appears to own property, but does not, is said to have
    (A) good title
    (B) recorded evidence of title
    (C) constructive notice
    (D) color of title

21. Two people who own undivided interests in the same realty, with right of survivorship, have
    (A) tenancy in severalty
    (B) tenancy in common
    (C) tenancy at sufferance
    (D) joint tenancy

22. A fee simple estate is
    (A) a freehold estate
    (B) a life estate
    (C) an estate for years
    (D) an estate in abeyance

23. Which of the following is considered a permanent attachment to land?
    (A) improvements to land
    (B) a fixture
    (C) trees growing on the land
    (D) all of the above

24. A person who has some rights to land, but not all the possessory rights, has
    (A) a life estate
    (B) an interest in land
    (C) an estate at will
    (D) a fixture

25. A person who has color of title to land has
    (A) the appearance of title
    (B) forgeries of state title papers
    (C) a right to one-half the income from the land
    (D) foreign ownership

26. A life estate *pur autre vie* is one in which
    (A) the life tenant must occupy the premises and may not lease them to anyone else
    (B) the duration of the life estate is based upon the duration of the life of someone other than the life tenant
    (C) the life tenant has died
    (D) the life tenant may not occupy the property himself/herself

27. Which of the following would not be real property?
    (A) A lease for one month
    (B) An easement
    (C) Permanent ownership of mineral rights on someone else's land
    (D) A life estate

28. *Adverse possession* may establish
    (A) use of property
    (B) a claim to title
    (C) who owes back taxes
    (D) homestead rights

29. An easement by prescription may establish
    (A) use of property
    (B) a claim to title
    (C) who owes back taxes
    (D) homestead rights

30. Fifty feet of land was added to Apple's farm because a river changed its course. This is an example of
    (A) accretion
    (B) avulsion
    (C) riparian rights
    (D) usufructory

31. Fifty feet of beachfront land was removed by a flood. This is an example of
    (A) riparian rights
    (B) estovers
    (C) avulsion
    (D) emblements

32. As used in real estate practices, the land of a *riparian* owner borders on
    (A) a river
    (B) a stream
    (C) a watercourse
    (D) any of the above

33. A person holding title to real property in severalty would most likely have
    (A) a life estate
    (B) an estate for years
    (C) ownership in common with others
    (D) sole ownership

34. Joint ownership of real property by two or more persons, each of whom has an undivided interest (not necessarily equal) without right of survivorship, is
    (A) a tenancy in partnership
    (B) a tenancy by the entireties
    (C) a tenancy in common
    (D) a leasehold tenancy

35. Generally, the taking of private land by governmental bodies for public use is governed by due process of law and is accomplished through
    (A) exercise of police power
    (B) eminent domain
    (C) reverter
    (D) escheat

36. Governmental land use planning and zoning are important examples of
    (A) exercise of eminent domain
    (B) use of police power
    (C) deed restrictions
    (D) encumbrance

37. After Harry bought his apartment, he started receiving his own property tax bills. This indicates that he has bought into a
    (A) condominium   (C) leasehold
    (B) cooperative   (D) syndicate

38. Helen and David, who are not married, want to buy a house together. To ensure that if one dies, the other automatically becomes the full owner, their deed must state that they are
    (A) tenants in common
    (B) tenants in severalty
    (C) tenants by the entirety
    (D) joint tenants

39. Real property is
    (A) the land
    (B) the land, the improvements, and the bundle of rights
    (C) the land and the right to possess it
    (D) the land, buildings, and easements

40. A house has a built-in bookcase and elaborate chandelier. The buyer is also getting a dinette set and a table lamp. Which is correct?
    (A) The built-in bookcase and chandelier are included in the real estate contract. The lamp and dinette set are chattels and are sold separately.
    (B) All the items must be included in the real estate contract.
    (C) The chandelier is real estate; the other items must be sold on a bill of sale.
    (D) All of the items are real estate because they are sold with the house.

41. Manmade additions to land are known as
    (A) chattels   (C) easements
    (B) trade fixtures   (D) improvements

42. Land can be owned apart from the buildings on it under the arrangement known as a
    (A) net lease   (C) remainder.
    (B) life estate   (D) ground lease.

43. No one seems to own the vacant land next to Mary's house, so she has used it for a pasture for many years. She may have a good chance of obtaining ownership by
    (A) poaching   (C) adverse possession
    (B) foreclosure   (D) eminent domain

44. An abstract of title contains
    (A) the summary of a title search
    (B) an attorney's opinion of title
    (C) a registrar's certificate of title
    (D) a quiet title lawsuit

45. In order to reach the beach, the Smiths have a permanent right-of-way across their neighbor's beachfront property. The Smiths own
    (A) an easement   (C) a deed restriction
    (B) a license   (D) a lien

46. A corporation usually owns property in
    (A) tenancy in severalty
    (B) joint tenancy
    (C) tenancy in common
    (D) tenancy by the entirety

47. Littoral rights for properties abutting the ocean give ownership
    (A) to the mean high water mark
    (B) to a point 100 feet from the shore
    (C) to the state ownership line
    (D) to a point designated by the U.S. Army Corps of Engineers

48. Liability that is limited to the amount invested does not apply to
    (A) partners in a general partnership
    (B) a corporation's shareholders
    (C) limited partners in a limited partnership
    (D) LLPs or LLCs

49. The lumber for a deck that has not yet been built is
    (A) a trade fixture
    (B) real estate
    (C) personal property
    (D) a fixture

50. State law provides for the distribution of an intestate person's property by
    (A) escheat
    (B) intestate alienation
    (C) intestate succession
    (D) involuntary alienation

51. The type of co-ownership that allows an owner's property to be left to his or her heirs is
    (A) tenancy by the entirety
    (B) tenancy in severalty
    (C) tenancy in common
    (D) joint tenancy

52. One who owns a life estate cannot
    (A) sell his interest
    (B) mortgage his interest
    (C) devise his interest
    (D) lease his interest

53. A condominium owner can avoid payment of his or her share of the common expenses by doing which of the following?
    (A) Not using certain common elements.
    (B) Abandoning her apartment.
    (C) Defaulting on mortgage payments.
    (D) None of the above: payment cannot be avoided.

ANSWERS

1. **B**	12. **C**	23. **D**	34. **C**	45. **A**
2. **C**	13. **D**	24. **B**	35. **B**	46. **A**
3. **B**	14. **A**	25. **A**	36. **B**	47. **A**
4. **A**	15. **C**	26. **B**	37. **A**	48. **A**
5. **C**	16. **A**	27. **A**	38. **D**	49. **C**
6. **C**	17. **A**	28. **B**	39. **B**	50. **C**
7. **B**	18. **B**	29. **A**	40. **A**	51. **C**
8. **D**	19. **D**	30. **A**	41. **D**	52. **C**
9. **A**	20. **D**	31. **C**	42. **D**	53. **D**
10. **C**	21. **D**	32. **D**	43. **C**	
11. **A**	22. **A**	33. **D**	44. **A**	

CHAPTER 4

Agency Law

A licensed real estate broker or salesperson is an *agent*; therefore his or her practice comes under the *laws of agency*. He or she is also affected by the real estate license law of his state, a topic that will be discussed in Chapter 5.

An agency relationship involves two parties: the *principal* and the *agent*. The agency relationship is contractual, but it also is covered by the general requirements of agency law. In the real estate business, a broker acts as an agent for his *employer*, or principal, who is the owner of the property for which the broker is seeking a buyer or tenant. A licensed salesperson usually is treated as the agent of the *broker*, because license law does not permit salespersons to act without the supervision of a broker.

A real estate broker is a *special agent*. He is called this because his powers are limited, usually to finding someone with whom his principal can deal. A *general agent* is a person whose powers are broader and may extend far as to commit her employer to action. Note that a real estate broker usually has little or no power actually to commit his principal to anything; the principal may refuse to deal with anyone the broker brings to him, although he still may be liable to pay the broker a commission.

DUTIES OF PARTIES

An agent is employed to deal with third parties on behalf of his principal. The agent is an employee of the principal and must follow his principal's instructions implicitly. Furthermore, he has a duty to act in his employer's best interests, even when doing so means that he cannot act in his own favor. More specifically, agency law requires that the agent abide by the following obligations to his principal:

- He must *obey* his principal's instructions (except, of course, when he is instructed to do something illegal).
- He must be *loyal* to his principal's interests.
- He must act in *good faith*.
- He is expected to use *professional judgment, skill,* and *ability* in his actions. This is particularly true in the case of licensed agents such as real estate brokers, who are assumed to have met certain standards by virtue of having to be licensed.
- He must be able to *account* for all money belonging to others that comes into his possession. Real estate brokers often collect rents, earnest money payments, and other money on behalf of their principals.
- He must perform his duties *in person*. Normally, this would mean that he could not delegate his duties to anyone else unless the principal approved of the arrangement. Because of the nature of the real estate brokerage business and the establishment of the broker-salesperson relationship by all state licensing laws, however, a real estate broker has the implied right to delegate his function to duly licensed salespersons and brokers in his employ.
- He must keep his principal *fully informed* of developments affecting their relationship. A real estate broker should report all offers made on the principal's property, as well as all other information he acquires that may affect the principal's property, price, or other relevant factors.

The principal has obligations to the agent as well. Most of these have to do with money: the principal is obliged to *compensate* the agent for her services, to *reimburse* the agent for expenses paid on behalf of the principal, and to *secure* the agent against any loss due to proper performance of her duties. The principal also has the implied duty to make the agent fully aware of her duties and to inform her fully about anything that will affect her performance.

REAL ESTATE AGENCY CONTRACTS

Agency contracts are *employment* contracts. Consequently, they do not come under the broad heading of real estate contracts and so are not necessarily required by the Statute of Frauds to be in writing (see Chapter 6). The states' real estate licensing laws, however, do require listing contracts to be in writing. In real estate, an agency contract usually is called a *listing*. The details of drawing up these contracts are discussed in Chapter 11. Here, however, we can briefly distinguish among the various kinds of listings. Among listings of property for *sale* are the following:

In an *open* listing the principal agrees to compensate the agent only if the agent actually finds the buyer with whom the principal finally deals. A single owner may have open listings with many brokers, since she is obliging herself to pay only upon performance, and the broker makes his effort at his own risk.

In an *exclusive agency* listing the principal agrees to employ no other broker, and if the property is sold by any licensed agent a commission will be paid to the listing broker. State license law usually requires that any other agent must work *through* a broker having an exclusive listing; the participating brokers must then agree on a means by which they will share in the commission. However, the commission always will be paid to the listing broker, who then may pay a share to the other broker(s) who cooperated in the deal.

An *exclusive-right-to-sell* listing guarantees that the principal will pay the broker a commission regardless of who actually sells the property. This applies even if the principal herself finds the buyer, with no aid at all from the broker. (Note that under an exclusive agency listing the principal does not have to pay a commission if she herself finds the buyer.)

Usage of the term *exclusive listing* varies from one place to another. In some localities the term refers to an exclusive agency; in others it refers to the exclusive right to sell; in still others it refers to both types interchangeably.

A *net* listing is one in which the principal agrees to receive a given net amount. The excess by which the sale price exceeds the net amount goes to the broker as his commission. In many states, net listings are illegal; in many others, they are not illegal but are "frowned upon" or otherwise disapproved of in some quasi-official manner. The big problem with net listings is that the agent is strongly tempted to act in his own interest rather than that of his employer. To illustrate, suppose a net listing contract with a proposed net to the seller of $180,000 is agreed upon. By law, anytime the broker solicits an offer he must report it to the principal. However, let us assume that an offer of exactly $180,000 is made; if the broker transmits it, the seller probably will accept and the broker will receive no compensation. Clearly, there is the temptation to illegally "hide" the offer, and any subsequent offers, until one yielding a satisfactory excess over the listed price is received; obviously such action is contrary to the agent's legal responsibilities to his employer. A further source of trouble with net listings arises when a knowledgeable agent deals with a naïve seller; there may exist an opportunity for the agent to convince the seller to sign a net listing at a low price, thereby guaranteeing the agent a large commission when he finds a buyer who will pay true market value.

THE AGENCY RELATIONSHIP IN REAL ESTATE BROKERAGE

In a *listing contract* (see Chapter 11), the agency relationship is between the owner of the listed real estate and the broker whom the owner hires to sell or lease the real estate. This makes sense; however, in the real estate brokerage business it is very common for other brokers to be involved in the transaction. Brokers very often *cooperate* with one another: they agree to allow one another to seek buyers (or tenants) for each others' listings. If another broker finds a buyer (tenant), then the listing broker agrees to share with that other broker the commission paid by the property owner. This situation leads to the question of whom all these agents actually represent. In *traditional agency*, all agents involved in a cooperated transaction represent *only the seller:* buyers have no agent looking out for their interests. It's called traditional agency because that's the way it was always done until about 20 years ago. At that time the states began to allow *buyer agency*. Buyer agency occurs when the licensee specifically represents the buyer(s), and a contract to that effect is signed. This way, buyers get agency representation: a professional who is looking out for *their* interests. (Buyer agents are compensated with a share of the commission paid by the seller, just as in traditional agency.) More recently, many states have created a "non-agency" brokerage. In this arrangement the licensee isn't really an agent at all; buyer and seller have to look out for themselves and the broker just assists in showing property and moving the transaction along.

Many states now require *agency disclosure* by real estate brokers; upon first contact with a prospective buyer, the broker must provide notification that he actually represents the seller, and does not look out for the specific needs and interests of the buyer. Usually, the law specifies a certain form that must be given to the buyer, and the broker cannot proceed with any dealings with that buyer until the broker has received from the buyer a signed form acknowledging that the buyer understands the agency relationship the broker has with the seller.

Most states now allow *buyer agency*. This is a situation in which a licensed broker or salesperson is the agent of the buyer, rather than of the seller. In such a situation, the loyalty of the licensee is to the buyer rather than to the seller. The states now allow this form of agency in order to provide a means whereby buyers receive the same agency loyalty and service as has always been enjoyed by sellers. Buyer agency also allows licensees to engage in the "selling process" more effectively, because they are not restricted as to the information and advice that they can give to buying prospects.

Single Agent Relationship

In a single agent relationship, the agent may represent either the buyer or the seller. The broker (agent) owes fiduciary duties to the party represented and must disclose these in writing in a residential transaction. The fiduciary duties of a single agent include:

- Dealing honestly and fairly
- Loyalty
- Confidentiality
- Obedience
- Full disclosure
- Accounting for all funds
- Skill, care, and diligence in the transaction
- Presenting all offers and counteroffers in a timely manner, unless a party has previously directed the licensee otherwise in writing
- Disclosing all known facts that materially affect the value of residential real property and are not readily observable

Dual Agency

Suppose a real estate licensee has contracted to be the agent of a prospective buyer, and then begins to show property to that buyer. Suppose, also, that this agent wants to show the buyer property that the agent himself/herself, or the agent's brokerage firm, has listed. In this case, the agent would become the agent of both parties to the transaction. It is clearly impossible to have absolute loyalty to the interests of both parties, so a means has to be devised that allows the licensee to proceed in such a situation. Most states now allow *dual agency* in such cases, though some states prohibit this practice. In order to solve the problem of representing both sides to the transaction, a *dual agency disclosure* has to be presented to, and agreed to, by both the prospective buyer and the owner of the property to be shown. In it, the parties all agree that the licensee's agency relationship with both buyer and seller will be curtailed so as not to compromise the interests of either.

Typically, the dual agency disclosure says, at the very least, that the agent cannot reveal to the seller the highest price the buyer will pay and cannot reveal to the buyer the lowest price the seller will accept. While dual agency is a solution that allows the licensee to show the property in question, it does so by curtailing the agency obligation to both parties. Therefore, some states are trying variations on dual agency, such as requiring, instead, that a different licensee step in, in these situations, to represent one of the parties fully, while the original licensee continues to fully represent the other.

Transaction Brokerage

Many states have adopted a form of brokerage called *transaction brokerage*. A transaction broker signs an agreement with either the buyer or seller or both, stating that the broker does not represent the interests of either party but merely provides brokerage service and general information to both parties. Essentially, the buyer and seller are on their own with respect to looking out for their interests.

In some states, the duties of a transaction broker, which are to be disclosed in a residential transaction, are:

- Dealing honestly and fairly
- Accounting for all funds
- Using skill, care, and diligence in the transaction
- Disclosing all known facts that materially affect the value of residential real property and are not readily observable to the buyer
- Presenting all offers and counteroffers in a timely manner, unless a party has previously directed the licensee otherwise in writing
- Limited confidentiality, unless waived in writing by a party. This limited confidentiality will prevent disclosure that the seller will accept a price less than the asking or listed price, that the buyer will pay a price greater than the price submitted in a written offer, of the motivation of any party for selling or buying property, that a seller or buyer will agree to financing terms other than those offered, or of any other information requested by a party to remain confidential.
- Any additional duties that are entered into by separate written agreement

It should be noted that loyalty, confidentiality, obedience, and full disclosure are not included. In a transaction broker relationship, the seller (or buyer) is considered to be a customer of the broker, not a principal. The customer is not responsible for the acts of the broker-licensee.

In other states, a transaction brokerage relationship is similar to a no brokerage agency relationship, as described below.

No Brokerage Agency Relationship

When buyer and seller have tentatively reached an agreement but seek some help, they may engage a broker with no brokerage relationship. The broker's assistance may be needed to help complete a contract, and payment is by a fixed fee or hourly rate, rather than by commission. There is no agency relationship.

The duties of a licensee who has no brokerage agency relationship with a buyer or seller must be fully described and disclosed in writing to the buyer or seller. The disclosure must be made before the showing of property. When incorporated into other documents, the required notice must be of the same size type, or larger, as other provisions of the document and must be conspicuous in its placement so as to advise customers of the duties of a licensee who has no brokerage relationship with a buyer or seller. Those duties are:

- Dealing honestly and fairly
- Disclosing all known facts that materially affect the value of residential real property which are not readily observable to the buyer
- Accounting for all funds entrusted to the licensee

Other Brokerage Relationships

A 21st-century innovation that is beginning to appear in some states is *designated agency*. This is supposed to solve a problem brought on by buyer agency: suppose a licensee has a buyer agency with someone who is looking for a house. The licensee thinks that the prospect will be interested in a certain home for which this same licensee also has a listing contract. Now the agent is under agency contract to both parties. One solution is to have both buyer and seller agree to a dual agency with the licensee, but, as we have seen, dual agency has its drawbacks. With designated agency, the licensee's principal broker appoints another licensee (the *designated agent*) in the same office to represent one of the parties (usually the buyer), while the original licensee represents *only* the other party in this one situation.

Most states' license laws mandate a *default relationship,* either explicitly (it is spelled out in the law) or implicitly (the law does not specify a default relationship, but it is impossible to apply the law without implying one). This means that upon the "first contact" between a licensee and a buyer (or a seller), a certain form of agency relationship exists by law, unless and until it is replaced by another form. The nature of the default relationship varies from state to state. In some, the default is transaction brokerage. This means that no agency relationship exists until the parties involved agree to one. In some states, the default is seller agency; others have buyer agency as the default.

A key point is that everyone involved in a transaction must be aware of what the agency relationships are before the negotiations for the transaction begin. Exactly when disclosure of buyer agency must be made varies among the states. Some states require that buyer agency be disclosed at first contact with the seller and/or the seller's broker, before an offer actually might be made. Others allow it to be disclosed only when an offer actually is made. This usually is accomplished by including language in the offer (or contract of sale: see Chapter 8) that specifically states that the broker is representing the buyer, even though the buyer's broker will share in the commission paid by the seller.

EARNING THE COMMISSION

Under common law, a broker earns his commission when he produces a buyer (or tenant) with whom the principal is willing to deal. From then on, the risk that the deal actually will go through rests with the principal. However, many listing contracts today put the risk back on the broker by specifying that the commission is not payable until the sale closes.

As mentioned previously, the principal is not obliged to deal with anyone whom the broker brings; that is, the principal, by hiring the broker, incurs no legal responsibility to the *third party*. Consequently, a buyer who is willing to pay the asking price and meet all the conditions set down by the principal in the listing agreement normally will have no legal recourse if the principal refuses to deal with him, unless the buyer's civil rights have been violated.

Nevertheless, the principal's obligations to the broker remain. In the listing agreement an acceptable price and terms of sale are specified. If the broker produces a bona fide offer that meets all these conditions, then the principal is liable to pay the broker a commission even if he chooses not to accept the offer. This is required, because the broker has satisfied the terms of his employment contract, and there *is* a contract between him and the principal. There is *no* contract, however, between the principal and third parties (such as potential buyers), so the principal is not liable to them.

If the broker's principal refuses to pay him a commission that the broker feels he has earned, he may sue in court to receive it. To be successful, he must prove three things:

1. That he was *licensed* throughout the time, beginning with the solicitation of the listing until the closing of the deal and the passing of title (or the notification by the principal that she will not accept an offer that meets the terms of the listing agreement).
2. That he had a contract of employment with the principal. The best evidence here is a written contract, and indeed some state licensing laws require that listings be written to be enforceable.
3. That he was the "efficient and procuring cause" of the sale; that is, that he actually brought about the sale within the terms of the listing contract. In an open listing this would mean that he actually found the eventual buyer. In an exclusive agency listing, he must have found the buyer or the buyer must have been found by a licensed agent. An exclusive-right-to-sell listing effectively defines the broker as having earned a commission when and if the property is sold.

TERMINATION OF AN AGENCY CONTRACT

Agency contracts can be terminated by a variety of events, though some of them are relatively uncommon. In a broad sense, contracts can be terminated in two ways: by the *actions of the parties* to them, or *by law* when certain events occur.

Termination by the actions of the parties includes the following:

The contract is terminated by *performance* when both parties perform their duties as prescribed and the event for which the agency is created ends. In the real estate business, a listing agency contract is terminated by performance when there is a "meeting of the minds" between the principal and the third party found by the agent. Sometimes, however, the contract will specify some other event (usually title closing, in the event of a listing for sale) as the actual termination of the contractual relationship.

The parties may *mutually agree* to terminate the relationship before it has been terminated by performance.

The agent may *resign*. In this case, the agent may be liable to the principal for damages due to his breach of the contract, but he cannot be held to perform under the contract.

The principal may *discharge* the agent. Once again, the principal, too, can be liable for damages due to her breach of the contract, but she cannot be forced to continue the employment of the agent.

The agent may resign, or the principal may discharge the agent, without penalty if it can be proved that the other party was not properly discharging his or her duties under the contract. An agent would be justified in resigning if, for example, his principal did not provide him with enough information to do his job well or required that he perform some illegal act in the execution of his duties. An agent could be discharged justifiably if it could be shown that he was not faithful to his duties or was acting contrary to the interests of the principal.

Termination of the contractual relationship also occurs automatically, *by law*, with the occurrence of certain events, such as the following:

The *death of either party* terminates an agency relationship.

If either party becomes *legally incompetent*, the agency relationship ceases.

Bankruptcy of either party, so as to make continuation of the relationship impossible; terminates the relationship.

Destruction of the subject matter terminates any agency relationship. In real estate this would include such events as the burning down of a house or the discovery of another claim on the title that would make it impossible for the owner of the property to pass good and marketable title.

Questions on Chapter 4

1. A real estate broker is a
   (A) general agent
   (B) special agent
   (C) secret agent
   (D) travel agent

2. Which of the following is *not* required of a single agent with respect to his principal?
   (A) to be loyal
   (B) to provide full disclosure
   (C) to account for his own personal finances
   (D) to deal honestly and fairly

3. A listing contract that says that the broker will receive a commission no matter who sells the property is called
   (A) an open listing
   (B) a net listing
   (C) an exclusive agency listing
   (D) an exclusive-right-to-sell listing

4. Which of the following does *not* terminate an agency relationship?
   (A) making an offer
   (B) the death of either party
   (C) the resignation of the agent
   (D) the destruction of the subject matter

5. To prove her right to a commission a broker must show
   (A) that she was licensed throughout the transaction
   (B) that she had a contract of employment
   (C) that she was the "efficient and procuring cause" of the sale
   (D) all of the above

6. A net listing is one
   (A) that requires the broker to seek a net price for the property
   (B) that is legal in all states
   (C) that most ethical brokers would prefer to use
   (D) in which the broker's commission is the amount by which the sale price exceeds the agreed-upon net price the seller desires

7. Among other things, the principal is obligated to
   (A) compensate the agent for his services
   (B) give the agent full authority to accept or turn down offers
   (C) give the agency the principal's financial statement
   (D) none of the above

8. A real estate agent
   (A) must always represent the seller
   (B) may represent the buyer if the buyer-broker agency is disclosed to all parties
   (C) may not take listings if she represents buyers
   (D) need not disclose a buyer-broker agency relationship

9. A special agent is one
   (A) whose powers are limited to certain specific functions
   (B) who must report to a licensing agency
   (C) who has less then a certain amount of experience as an agent
   (D) who is not a licensed agent

10. Among other things, an agent is obligated to
    (A) act in the principal's best interests unless these conflict with the agent's own interests
    (B) keep an accurate account of all money
    (C) never disclose the agency relationship to anyone
    (D) represent only one principal at a time

11. A no agency brokerage relationship means that
    (A) there is no agency representation
    (B) the broker represents whichever (buyer or seller) he/she meets first
    (C) the broker makes the transaction easy and problem free
    (D) there is no broker involved in the transaction

12. In a dual agency,
    (A) the broker owes complete loyalty to the interests of all parties he/she represents
    (B) the broker is also either the buyer or the seller in the transaction
    (C) there is more than one broker involved in the transaction
    (D) none of the above

13. The rate of commission on a real estate sale is
    (A) typically 6% of the selling price
    (B) mandated at various rates by law
    (C) paid to the salesperson, who gives 50% to the broker
    (D) negotiable between the broker and (typically) seller

14. As a general rule, escrow money received by the broker
    (A) is given to the seller on signing the contract
    (B) may be spent by the broker for repairs to the property
    (C) is deposited in the broker's trust account soon after receipt
    (D) is shared equally by the broker and salesperson

15. An unlicensed employee of a broker who prepares an advertisement to sell a house
    (A) is free to do so
    (B) must have the broker's prior written approval
    (C) must become licensed
    (D) must accurately describe the house

16. An owner who sells property that he developed
    (A) may engage an unlicensed sales staff who receive commissions
    (B) may engage a licensed sales staff who receive salaries only
    (C) must acquire a broker's license
    (D) must acquire a salesperson's license

17. In a transaction broker relationship, the seller or buyer
    (A) is responsible for the broker's acts
    (B) is not responsible for the broker's acts
    (C) is not considered a customer of the broker
    (D) is an agent of the broker

18. In a transaction broker arrangement, parties give up their rights to a broker's
    (A) undivided loyalty
    (B) honest dealings
    (C) use of skill and care
    (D) accounting for funds

19. A way to terminate a brokerage relationship is
    (A) agreement between the parties
    (B) fulfillment of the contract
    (C) expiration of the term
    (D) all of the above

20. A broker with no agency relationship may assist
    (A) the buyer
    (B) the seller
    (C) both buyer and seller
    (D) all of the above

21. A salesperson is _____ of the broker.
    (A) an agent   (C) a paid contractor
    (B) an employee   (D) a Realtor

22. *Prima facie evidence* refers to evidence that is good and sufficient on its face to
    (A) sell real estate
    (B) buy real estate
    (C) establish a given fact
    (D) file a lawsuit

23. Brokerage representation may legally include
    (A) a broker working for the seller
    (B) a broker working as a single agent for buyer or seller (but not both in the same transaction)
    (C) a broker representing neither buyer nor seller but facilitating the transaction
    (D) all of the above

24. Termination of a brokerage relationship may occur as a result of
    (A) bankruptcy of the principal or customer
    (B) death of either party
    (C) destruction of the property
    (D) all of the above

25. When a broker is an agent of the owner, the salesperson is
    (A) a Realtor
    (B) an independent contractor
    (C) a subagent
    (D) an employee

26. A single agent must
    (A) deal honestly and fairly
    (B) be loyal
    (C) provide full disclosure
    (D) all of the above

27. A person who wishes to sell his or her own house
    (A) must employ a broker
    (B) must employ a salesperson
    (C) must employ a Realtor
    (D) may employ any of the above, but is not required to do so

28. Which of the following, when performed for others, are included as real estate services for the purposes of determining licensure requirements?
    (A) buying and selling property
    (B) renting and leasing property
    (C) auction or exchange of property
    (D) all of the above

29. When a broker serves in a single agent capacity, his obligations to the customer include
    (A) loyalty   (C) obedience
    (B) confidentiality   (D) all of the above

30. *Dual agency* is defined as an arrangement in which
    (A) the same broker represents both the buyer and the seller
    (B) the broker is the seller
    (C) the salesperson and the broker split the commission
    (D) the listing broker and selling broker cooperate with each other

31. If a broker uses a title company to hold escrow deposits, the broker must turn over the funds
    (A) on the same day
    (B) in the same time frame as would be required if the broker maintained the account
    (C) when convenient
    (D) at the end of each month

32. If a buyer and seller reach oral agreement over the price and terms of a contract but seek a broker's help to complete written contract forms, the relationship with the broker is likely to be
    (A) single agent
    (B) dual agent
    (C) no brokerage relationship
    (D) any of the above

33. A single agent relationship provides a _____ with a seller.
    (A) fiduciary relationship
    (B) transaction agency
    (C) no business relationship
    (D) subagency

34. When a real estate attorney wants to earn a commission for performing real estate services, he or she must
    (A) become a Realtor
    (B) obtain a real estate license
    (C) join a franchise
    (D) be a member of the bar association

35. It is a good practice for a broker to prequalify
    (A) a prospective buyer   (C) a sales agent
    (B) a seller   (D) all clients

36. The listing expired after 90 days but had a clause that allowed the broker to collect a commission because someone he brought during the listing period bought after expiration. The clause is called
    (A) an extender clause
    (B) an acceleration clause
    (C) a broker protection clause
    (D) a deceleration clause

37. A potential buyer visits a real estate agency asking to view a certain house. The salesperson doesn't know the buyer. He or she
    (A) must show the property
    (B) should take a firearm for self-defense purposes
    (C) may refuse to show the house
    (D) should take whatever safety precautions are necessary

38. In most transactions where there is a broker, the broker represents
    (A) the brokerage   (C) the buyer
    (B) the seller   (D) all of the above

39. A broker is killed in a plane crash. His listings are
    (A) binding on the owners
    (B) transferable to his heirs
    (C) terminated
    (D) transferred to his salespersons

40. *Subagency* is the representation of
    (A) a principal   (C) an agent
    (B) a client   (D) a salesperson

41. A salesperson may accept compensation from
    (A) employing broker only
    (B) co-broker
    (C) principal
    (D) mortgage company

42. In the real estate business, *farming* is
    (A) planting agricultural crops
    (B) specializing in the sale of farms and ranches
    (C) marketing services by concentrating in a geographic area
    (D) cultivating land for sale

43. The buyer gives a $5,000 earnest money check to the seller's broker with instructions not to deposit the check for a week and not to tell the seller that the check has not been deposited. The seller's broker should
    (A) follow the buyer's instructions
    (B) disclose the conditions to the seller
    (C) refuse to accept the check
    (D) notify the Board of Realtors

44. A listing is given to the broker by the
    (A) seller   (C) lawyer
    (B) buyer   (D) lender

45. The seller has accepted an offer. An hour later, the broker receives another offer. The broker should
    (A) tell the seller of the second offer
    (B) reject the second offer on the seller's behalf
    (C) accept the second offer if it is for more money
    (D) seek a better offer from the first buyer

46. Most of the work in a real estate sale is carried out by a licensed salesperson. Who is the legal agent?
    (A) salesperson   (C) lawyer
    (B) broker   (D) principal

47. To be entitled to a commission, a broker with an open listing must prove that he or she
    (A) was the procuring cause of sale
    (B) was licensed
    (C) brought a ready, willing, and able buyer
    (D) all of the above

48. Seller Agent Orange receives three offers on Green's house. He should
    (A) advise Green of the best one
    (B) advise Green of the best two, with a comparison of pros and cons
    (C) advise Green of all three offers
    (D) wait for more offers to come in

49. At a cocktail party, Henry meets a man looking to buy a windmill. Henry has a friend who is looking to sell his windmill, and Henry brokers the deal. To collect a commission, Henry needs a
    (A) business broker's license
    (B) real estate broker's license
    (C) mortgage banker's license
    (D) no license since this is a private arrangement outside Henry's usual business duties

50. A broker's principal role when representing a seller is to
    (A) bring a ready, willing, and able buyer
    (B) advise the buyer as to the suitability of a purchase
    (C) advise the seller as to price and terms
    (D) sponsor salespersons

51. When a broker is a selling agent, his fiduciary obligations to his principal include
    (A) acting in the principal's best interest
    (B) keeping the principal's interest above his own
    (C) keeping the principal informed
    (D) all of the above

52. Commission splits between brokers and salespersons are
    (A) prescribed by law   (C) negotiated
    (B) 50/50   (D) suggested by NAR

53. Appraising, brokerage, consulting, development, economics, finance, and property management are
    (A) activities requiring a state license or certification
    (B) specializations within real estate
    (C) unregulated activities
    (D) economic opportunities

54. An agency relationship can be established by
    (A) an oral agreement
    (B) a written agreement
    (C) an agreement implied by law
    (D) all of the above

55. If the owner informs the broker that he wants single agent representation, what should the broker do?
    (A) decline the assignment
    (B) ask NAR for permission
    (C) ask MLS for permission
    (D) provide the single agency notice at or before taking the listing

56. Mr. and Mrs. Buyer asked broker Bob about the best way to take title to the property they had agreed to buy. What should Bob do?
    (A) advise the Buyers to ask their parents
    (B) advise the Buyers to contact an attorney
    (C) have his accountant advise the Buyers of the best way to take title
    (D) advise the Buyers to contact the county recorder

57. Broker Martin holds $10,000 as earnest money on the purchase made by Will. When can Martin remove the earnest money from the escrow account?
    (A) When the purchase closes escrow.
    (B) When the buyer gives him permission.
    (C) When the seller gives him permission.
    (D) When he needs the money for business expenses, provided it is replaced within five days.

58. A fiduciary relationship could exist between a principal and all of the following *except*
    (A) an appraiser
    (C) a trustee
    (B) a receiver
    (D) an administrator

59. A proper escrow, once established, should be
    (A) not subject to the control of any one interested party
    (B) managed by a licensed broker
    (C) void at the seller's option
    (D) voidable at option of either buyer or seller

60. You are representing seller Sam and bring buyer Bill, your customer, to see the house. Bill makes an offer. Bill has confidentially told you that he went through bankruptcy two years ago, but he thinks he will be financially approved to buy the house. What, if anything, should you do with the information about the bankruptcy?
    (A) Tell Sam.
    (B) Keep the information confidential as Bill expects you to.
    (C) Keep the information confidential unless the deal doesn't go through.
    (D) Contact the bank to verify Bill's financial status.

61. A licensed real estate salesperson can lawfully accept an extra commission in a difficult sale from
    (A) a broker-employer
    (B) the mortgage lender
    (C) an appreciative seller
    (D) a thankful buyer

62. Which of the following is *not* a termination of an agency relationship by operation of law?
    (A) revocation by the principal
    (B) death of the agent
    (C) fulfillment of contract
    (D) expiration of the term

63. A listing agent knows that the house has a roof leak, the water heater is not up to city code, and the seller must sell quickly because of financial difficulties. The agent is showing a potential buyer the property. What can or must the agent legally say?
    (A) "The roof leaks, and the water heater does not meet city code."
    (B) "The seller will take less than the asking price."
    (C) "The seller is in financial difficulty and must sell quickly."
    (D) "The roof leaks, the water heater does not meet city code, and the seller needs a quick sale."

64. Clients may be liable for errors made by brokers or subagents through
    (A) vicarious liability
    (B) casual liability
    (C) absolute liability
    (D) estovers

65. When money is deposited in a broker's trust account, part of which will be used to pay the broker's commission,
    (A) the broker can withdraw his or her share of the money before the real estate transaction is consummated or terminated
    (B) accurate records must be kept on the account
    (C) interest on the account is by law the property of the broker
    (D) the salespeople can withdraw money prior to closing

ANSWERS

1. **B**	14. **C**	27. **D**	40. **C**	53. **B**
2. **C**	15. **B**	28. **D**	41. **A**	54. **D**
3. **D**	16. **B**	29. **D**	42. **C**	55. **D**
4. **A**	17. **B**	30. **A**	43. **B**	56. **B**
5. **D**	18. **A**	31. **B**	44. **A**	57. **A**
6. **D**	19. **D**	32. **C**	45. **A**	58. **A**
7. **A**	20. **D**	33. **A**	46. **B**	59. **A**
8. **B**	21. **A**	34. **B**	47. **D**	60. **A**
9. **A**	22. **C**	35. **A**	48. **C**	61. **A**
10. **B**	23. **D**	36. **C**	49. **B**	62. **A**
11. **A**	24. **D**	37. **D**	50. **A**	63. **A**
12. **D**	25. **C**	38. **B**	51. **D**	64. **A**
13. **D**	26. **D**	39. **C**	52. **C**	65. **B**

State Real Estate License Law

E very state requires that real estate brokers and salespersons be licensed by that state before they can do business. Therefore, each state has a set of laws, referred to as the Real Estate License Law, which describes the process of becoming licensed, the responsibilities of licensees, the administration of the license law, the means of removing licenses from those unfit to keep them, and miscellaneous items. The details of these laws vary from state to state, but many of their general provisions are the same.

UNDERSTANDING YOUR STATE'S LAWS

Every state has at least two kinds of licenses for real estate sales agents: the *broker's license* and the *salesperson's license*. (But note that in a very few states, the titles for these licenses may be somewhat different.) The main difference between the two is that a licensed broker may own and operate and manage a real estate brokerage business; a licensed salesperson *cannot* do any of these things. This means that every state requires licensed salespeople to work for and be under the supervision of a licensed broker. Usually this is referred to as the broker's "holding" the salesperson's license. The license is not actually issued to the salesperson; rather, it is issued to that salesperson's broker. The supervision responsibility of the broker is a serious matter because the broker is liable for anything and everything the salesperson does in the course of the brokerage business. In fact, all agency contracts negotiated by a salesperson actually are contracts between the seller (or buyer) and the *broker,* and not just between the salesperson and the principal.

Some states are beginning to distinguish between two types of broker: the *principal broker* and the *associate broker*. The principal broker is the managing broker, who takes the ultimate responsibility for the actions of all agents in the firm or office. An associate broker may be an assistant manager or merely someone with a broker's license who has chosen to act as a salesperson and have another broker hold his/her license. Some states may have different examination and education requirements for principal and associate brokers.

Before you can study the material in this chapter effectively, you must get a copy of your state's law; every state licensing agency will make available a copy of the state's licensing law to applicants for the licenses. Be sure to study this law carefully! Every state devotes a considerable portion (20–40%) of the licensing examination to a test of the applicant's knowledge of the license law; if you have not studied your state's law, you will have little or no chance to pass the examination.

This chapter will serve as a guide to study of your state's licensing laws. It would be confusing to try to cover the details of every state's variations in this chapter. A better way is to provide this study guide, which you will supplement with a copy of your state's law. The second section of sample questions at the end of the chapter (pages 93–103) is designed to show you the *kinds* of questions you will encounter, as well as to give you an opportunity to demonstrate your knowledge of your own state's law.

Licensing law can be subdivided into several general areas, such as those we use below. Of course, your state may not cover these areas in the same order as we do, but nearly everything in your state's law will be reviewed here. Do not be concerned if you have to skip around in your state's law to follow the study pattern in this book; the authorities don't care whether you know the sequence in which something appears. They want to make sure that you know the *content* of the law; if you follow the study pattern, you *will* know it.

In each section, plenty of blank space is provided for you to note the particular features of your state's law. Sometimes this can be accomplished by actually taping or pasting the relevant part of your state's law in the available space. Other times it will be easier just to make handwritten notes. Be sure to *cross out* items that *do not apply* to your state!

In any event, the study pattern below breaks down the license law into logical segments for the most effective studying.

Before beginning the study pattern, you should *carefully read all the way through your state's law*. This overview will familiarize you with the basic provisions and will make it easier for you to look up items as they are discussed in the study pattern. As you read through the first time:

- Look for notes referring to specific legal cases in which a certain provision was upheld or interpreted.
- Check for explanatory notes providing examples that illustrate important points.
- Be particularly on the watch for portions of the law that have since been repealed or amended! Some states print only the law as it currently stands, but others include all enacted laws relevant to licensing since the original one, even though some may have been repealed or amended later on. In such cases, there usually will be a notation to point out when the repeal or amendment took place. For study purposes, cross out any repealed or otherwise invalid parts of the printed license law you have.
- Look also for provisions that have been enacted but are not yet effective. Often a state law will allow a considerable time after it has passed until it takes effect. This is particularly evident in the case of laws that raise or tighten standards (especially educational) for licensure. Look also for laws containing schedules of provisions that take effect in the future. Many states have adopted schedules by which educational standards for licensure will be raised every so often until a particular goal is reached.
- Be sure to note the way in which the various provisions are numbered or otherwise identified. This will make it easier to understand parts of the law where reference is made to another part of the law.

STUDY PATTERN FOR THE LICENSE LAW

I. Definitions

    A. *Real Estate.* The definition of real estate usually includes most interests in land, buildings, and other improvements. Some states also require licensure for handling investment interests involving real estate (such as syndicates), the sale of businesses, and so on.

_____

_____

_____

_____

B. *Broker.* Note the functions that are defined as those of a real estate broker. Usually there will be many. If your state has associate brokers, how are their functions defined?

_____

_____

_____

_____

_____

C. *Salesperson.* Some states may use a different name, such as associate, for this job. Usually most of the functions will be the same as those for brokers, with the provision that the salesperson is an employee of a broker.

_____

_____

_____

_____

_____

D. *Broker employed by another broker.* Most states provide for this situation; the specific name given to it (associate broker, affiliate broker, employee broker, etc.) varies.

_____

_____

_____

_____

_____

E. *Principal broker and associate broker.* If your state distinguishes between principal brokers and associate brokers, describe the differences between them.

_____

_____

_____

_____

F. *Corporate broker.* Some states provide that a corporation may have a license if it satisfies certain requirements.

_____

_____

_____

_____

_____

G. *Branch offices.* Under what conditions (if any) does your state allow a brokerage firm to have branch offices?

_____

_____

_____

_____

_____

II. Agency Relationships

A. Which of the following agency relationships is allowed in your state?

☐ buyer agency

List restrictions, if any:_____

_____

_____

☐ dual agency

List restrictions, if any:_____

_____

_____

☐ no agency brokerage

List restrictions, if any:_____

_____

_____

☐ transaction brokerage

List restrictions, if any:_____

_____

_____

☐ designated agency

List restrictions, if any:_____

_____

_____

B. Is there a default agency relationship in your state? If so, describe it.

_____

_____

_____

_____

III. Exemptions to the License Law

List here all those who are exempt from your state's license law. Exemption usually include owners of property for sale or lease, those holding an owner's power of attorney, attorneys acting in the exercise of their duties, trustees, certain employees of owners, government, and some others.

_____

_____

_____

_____

IV. Administration of the Law

Most states have a Real Estate Commission that administers the license law. However, some states do not; in these states, the law is administered by a state agency such as the Department of State, or a State Licensing Board or Department.

In any case, you will be asked how this administration is set up and what the organizational pattern is.

If your state has a Real Estate Commission, note the following information: How many commissioners are there? What are their required qualifications (i.e., residence in state, experience, licensed broker, etc.)? What is their compensation? How are they chosen and confirmed and by whom? Is there a required geographical distribution among them? How is the chairperson chosen, and by whom? How are vacancies filled? How long do commissioners serve? Is there a date or time limit for the naming of new commissioners? How frequently does the commission meet? Where does it meet? How many commissioners constitute a quorum?

If your state does not have a Real Estate Commission, look for these answers: Which state agency administers the Real Estate License Law? Where is it located? What, if any, representation is permitted to members of the real estate industry? How is such representation effected: Who appoints whom? Are any qualifications required?

Regardless of whether or not your state has a commission, the following questions will be pertinent: What are the general powers of the agency or commission in the enforcement of the law? How is the *staff* of the agency or commission organized (e.g., does the head have the title of Secretary, Executive Secretary, Commissioner, etc.; are there limits on the size of the staff; who hires them; who determines their pay)? Does the commission or agency have a seal? Where are the offices located?

V. The Licensing Process

You must know *all* the steps to take to get *any* license: broker, associate broker (if applicable), or salesperson. Also, you must know the necessary qualifications to be met by anyone seeking a license. (Section VI is devoted to cataloging the fees that licensees pay.)

A. Must an applicant for either license be sponsored by anyone (either by a person who already has a license or, if a salesperson applicant, by the future employing broker)?

_____

_____

_____

_____

B. What is the minimum age for
   1. salesperson: _____
   2. broker: _____
   3. associate broker: _____

C. How much *general* education must applicants have (e.g., high school or the equivalent)?
   1. salesperson: _____
   2. broker: _____
   3. associate broker: _____

D. What *special* education requirements must licensees meet? Distinguish between education required *before* getting a license and education needed *after* obtaining a license in order to retain the license. Also, are any substitutions (such as experience) permitted for any of these requirements?
   1. salesperson: _____

_____

_____

2. broker: _____

_____

_____

3. associate broker: _____

_____

_____

E. Will changes in the educational requirements that the present law dictates go into effect in the future? What are they, and when do they become effective?

_____

_____

_____

_____

_____

F. Are there any specific *experience* requirements for either license? (Often a broker applicant is required to have been licensed as a salesperson for a certain minimum time.)

_____

_____

_____

_____

_____

G. Are licensees required to be bonded or to contribute to a "real estate recovery fund" or similar fund?

_____

_____

_____

_____

_____

H. Does your state have any other specific requirements?

_____

_____

_____

_____

_____

I. On what grounds can your state refuse to issue a real estate license to an applicant?

_____

_____

_____

_____

_____

VI. Fees

Fill in the blank spaces in the following form to show the fees, and other pertinent information concerning them, that your state requires. The information should be broken down by broker/salesperson; there is a column for each. *Cross out* the fees that your state does not charge.

FEE	BROKER	SALESPERSON	ASSOCIATE BROKER
APPLICATION FEE			
EXAMINATION FEE			
LICENSE FEE:			
(a) Amount of fee			
(b) How often is it payable?			
(c) When is it due?			
RENEWAL FEE:			
(a) Amount of fee if different from license fee			
(b) Penalty for late renewal? How much?			
(c) When is license renewal due?			
TRANSFER FEES:			
(a) To new employing broker			
(b) Change of business address			
(c) Change to different branch of same firm			
(d) Any penalty for frequent transfers?			
DUPLICATE (REPLACEMENT) LICENSE FEE			
REAL ESTATE RECOVERY FUND:			
(a) Payment when becoming licensed			
(b) Later periodic payments			
(c) When are payments due?			
OTHER FEES:			
(a) Reactivating inactive license			
(b) License fee while inactive			
(c) _____			
(d) _____			

VII.   How to Lose a Real Estate License

The license law of your state will spell out a number of practices for which the authorities are allowed to revoke or suspend a license. These practices will be found in the license law itself, in a "code of ethics" or a set of "rules and regulations," or in both places. We have grouped and listed the more common practices and have provided space for you to note any special provisions of your own law. *Cross out* the ones that your state's law does not mention, but *make sure* that your law does not specify the item in somewhat different wording! When in doubt, leave it in. All the practices listed below are poor business practice, at the very least, so even if you aren't sure your state law prohibits one of them, you ought to avoid it anyway. There is space for you to write in comments, if any.

The practices are grouped according to type.

A. MISHANDLING MONEY BELONGING TO OTHERS

1. Commingling trust (or escrow) money with one's own funds.

_____

_____

_____

2. Not remitting funds quickly, once they are received.

_____

_____

_____

3. Salesperson's not remitting funds quickly to broker.

_____

_____

_____

4. Accepting noncash payments on behalf of principal without principal's agreement. (Checks are considered to be cash.)

_____

_____

_____

B. MISREPRESENTATION AND FRAUD

All of these practices are *misrepresentation or fraud*. Some state laws list a number of such practices; others simply say, ". . . for any misrepresentation or fraud . . . ," or some words to that effect.

1. False advertising.

_____

_____

2. Intentionally misleading someone.

_____

_____

_____

3. Acting for more than one party to a transaction without the knowledge of all parties.

_____

_____

_____

4. Using a trademark or other identifying insignia of a firm or organization (such as the National Association of Realtors®) of which one is not a member.

_____

_____

_____

5. Salesperson's pretending to be a broker or to be employed by a broker not his own.

_____

_____

_____

6. Not identifying oneself as a licensee in any transaction in which one is also a party.

_____

_____

_____

7. Taking kickbacks, referral fees, commissions, placement fees, and so on in association with one's duties from persons who are not one's principal, and without the principal's knowledge.

_____

_____

_____

8. Guaranteeing future profits.

_____

_____

_____

9. Offering property on terms other than those authorized by the principal.

_____

_____

_____

10. Pretending to represent a principal by whom one is not actually employed.

_____

_____

_____

11. Failing to identify the broker in all advertising.

_____

_____

_____

12. Others (specify):

_____

_____

_____

C. IMPROPER BUSINESS PRACTICE

1. Failing to submit all offers to the principal.

_____

_____

_____

2. Attempting to thwart another broker's exclusive listing.

_____

_____

_____

3. Inducing someone to break a contract.

_____

_____

_____

4. Accepting a net listing.

_____

_____

_____

5. Failing to put an expiration date in a listing.

_____

_____

_____

6. Putting one's sign on a property without the owner's permission.

_____

_____

_____

7. Failing to post a required bond; failing to keep the bond up to date.

_____

_____

_____

8. Blockbusting.

_____

_____

_____

9. Discriminating.

_____

_____

_____

10. "Steering"

_____
_____
_____

11. Other violation of state, federal, or local fair housing or civil rights laws.

_____
_____
_____

D. FAILURE TO IMPART REQUIRED INFORMATION

1. Failure to leave copies of contracts with all parties involved.

_____
_____
_____

2. Failure to deliver a closing statement to all parties entitled to one.

_____
_____
_____

3. Failure to inform some or all parties of closing costs.

_____
_____
_____

E. IMPROPER HANDLING OR PAYMENT OF COMMISSIONS

1. Paying a commission to an unlicensed person.

_____
_____
_____

2. Paying a commission to a licensee not in one's employ.

_____
_____
_____

3. Salesperson's receiving a commission from anyone other than her employing broker.

_____
_____
_____

4. Unlicensed person receiving or sharing in a commission.

_____
_____
_____

F. AGENCY DISCLOSURE

    1. Failure to disclose to prospective buyers that broker is agent of the seller.

       _____

       _____

       _____

    2. Failure to disclose buyer-broker agency to seller or seller's broker (include when to do so).

       _____

       _____

       _____

    3. Failure to disclose facilitative (transaction) brokerage requirements and limitations.

       _____

       _____

       _____

    4. Required form to use for agency disclosure.

       _____

       _____

       _____

G. OTHER

    1. Being convicted of certain crimes (specify):

       _____

       _____

       _____

    2. Violating any part of the license law.

       _____

       _____

       _____

    3. Making false statements on the license application.

       _____

       _____

       _____

    4. Showing any evidence of "incompetence," "unworthiness," "poor character," and so on. This is a "catch-all" provision usually found at the end of the list of specific offenses to drive home the point that *any* improper action can cost a licensee his license. How does your state phrase this provision?

       _____

       _____

       _____

    5. Other provisions not covered above (specify):

       _____

       _____

       _____

VIII. Revocation Procedure

Every state has a legal process whereby a license can be revoked or suspended. Your state law will spell this out very clearly. Look for the following:

A. Who can make a complaint against a licensee?

_____

_____

_____

B. What form must the complaint take?

_____

_____

_____

C. To whom must it be submitted?

_____

_____

_____

D. What discretion does the authority have with regard to acting on complaints?

_____

_____

_____

E. How are licensees notified of complaints against them?

_____

_____

_____

F. Is there a time limit with regard to the time between the act and the complaint, or the receipt of the complaint and notification of the licensee?

_____

_____

_____

G. What rights does the licensee have?

_____

_____

_____

H. How much time may elapse between a hearing and a decision?

_____

_____

_____

I. May any (or only some) of the parties to a hearing appeal to the courts? If so, which courts? How soon must an appeal be filed?

_____

_____

_____

J. Does a licensee retain her license if an appeal is filed?

_____

_____

K. What are the penalties that the licensing authority may impose directly?

_____

_____

L. What happens to the license of a salesperson or associate broker whose principal broker loses his license?

_____

_____

IX. Handling of Trust Money

Brokers usually keep their principals' money in trust, in the form of rents, earnest money deposits, and so on. The law usually contains provisions regulating such money and its handling. As a rule, it has to be put into a special account called a *trust account* or *escrow account*. Things to look for are: (1) How many different kinds of accounts must be maintained? (2) Can they be interest-bearing; if so, who gets the interest? (3) Must they be deposited in particular banks or with particular agents?

_____

_____

_____

_____

X. Nonresident Licenses

Every state has some regulation regarding out-of-state residents who desire to pursue the real estate business within the state. There are three ways to handle this situation; find the one that your state uses and make the appropriate notes in the space provided below. A state may choose to:

A. Issue nonresident licenses, by requiring nonresidents to take the state's licensing examination. What are the fees such applicants must pay? Do they have to meet all the state's other qualifications? Must they maintain a license in their home state?

B. Prohibit out-of-state residents from operating within the state. The few states that have this provision usually allow the out-of-state licensee to operate within the state provided that all business is funneled through a *resident* licensee.

C. Allow some or all out-of-state licensees to operate on the basis of *reciprocity*; that is, the state will recognize the nonresident's qualification as having been determined by her home state and will issue the applicant an in-state nonresident license on the basis of licensure in a reciprocating state.

_____

_____

XI. Real Estate Recovery Fund

Not all states have real estate recovery funds or similar funds with different names. If yours does not, then cross out this section.

A real estate recovery fund is a fund set up and administered by an agency of the state for the purpose of providing redress for damages caused to members of the public by improper actions by real estate licensees. Usually the money comes from an "assessment" made upon licensees at the time the fund is set up and continuing periodically until the fund reaches a certain level. After that time, if the fund is depleted below a specified point, the assessments begin again and continue until the fund is back to the desired level. Look for the following with regard to the real estate recovery fund:

How does one establish a claim? What process must be gone through before a claim can be paid? What happens to a licensee if a claim is paid because of an improper action on his part? Are there any exceptions to the kinds of claims that may be paid? Are there any time limits within which claims must be made? Are there limits to the dollar amount of any single award?

XII. Regulation of Real Estate Schools

More and more states are requiring some kind of real estate training of applicants and licensees. To assure that the training is proper and effective, some states have amended their licensing laws to give the state real estate licensing agency the power to regulate real estate schools that teach courses used to meet the educational requirements. Look for the following:

Does the law specify any particular curriculum that any or all of the courses must follow? Does the law permit the licensing agency to specify the curriculum? Does the law require that teachers have any particular qualifications? Is the licensing agency given the power to determine the qualifications of teachers?

XIII. Penalties for Violating the License Law

Violation of the license law is a crime. Is it a misdemeanor or a felony or other type of crime? What is the maximum penalty—imprisonment, fine, or both? Is there any provision for repeat offenders? What happens to the license of a licensee who is convicted of violating the law? How does a conviction of violating the law affect a person's future right to get a real estate license?

_____

_____

_____

XIV. Other Provisions

Use this space to note other important provisions of your state's license law that have not been covered so far.

_____

_____

_____

Questions on Chapter 5

You will note that there are two sections of questions for this chapter. The first section is composed of 27 general questions, such as would apply in all states. The answers to these questions appear after them.

The second section is sort of a do-it-yourself question set. A great many questions are provided, but the answers to them depend on the specifics of your state's laws. Therefore, no key to them is given; you must look up the answers in your copy of the law or your notes. More specific instructions appear with the questions in the second set.

GENERAL QUESTIONS

1. A licensee's license must be
   (A) carried in his wallet at all times
   (B) kept on the wall in his home
   (C) posted in a public place in the broker's office
   (D) kept on the wall at the Real Estate Commission

2. A person must be licensed if she is to sell
   (A) her own home
   (B) property belonging to an estate for which she is executor
   (C) property belonging to other clients who pay her a commission
   (D) property she has inherited

3. A broker must place funds belonging to others in
   (A) his office safe, to which only he knows the combination
   (B) a safety deposit box
   (C) an account maintained by the Real Estate Commission
   (D) a trust, or escrow, account

4. License laws forbid
   I. collecting a commission
   II. soliciting for listings before one is licensed
   (A) I only
   (B) II only
   (C) both I and II
   (D) neither I nor II

5. A licensee's license can be revoked for
   (A) closing a deal
   (B) intentionally misleading someone into signing a contract that she ordinarily would not sign
   (C) submitting a ridiculous offer to a seller
   (D) all of the above

6. Real estate licenses, once received,
   (A) remain in effect indefinitely
   (B) are good for a limited period of time
   (C) must be filed in the county records
   (D) may be inherited by the licensee's spouse

7. A broker's unlicensed secretary may
   (A) sell property provided that he does it under the broker's direct supervision
   (B) sell or negotiate deals so long as he does not leave the office
   (C) refer interested clients to the broker or her employed licensees
   (D) all of the above

8. A broker may use escrow moneys held on behalf of others
   (A) for collateral for business loans
   (B) for collateral for personal loans
   (C) to make salary advances to licensees in his employ
   (D) none of the above

9. In order to do business, a licensee must
   (A) make proper application for a license
   (B) pass a licensing examination
   (C) have a license issued by the appropriate state agency
   (D) all of the above

10. A licensee can lose his license for which of the following?
    I. Paying a commission to a nonlicensed person
    II. Using moneys received as commissions to pay office help
    (A) I only
    (B) II only
    (C) I and II
    (D) neither I nor II

11. A licensee can lose her license for
    I. selling properties quickly, at low prices
    II. buying property for her own use from her principal
    (A) I only
    (B) II only
    (C) both of the above
    (D) none of the above

12. Which of the following is not required to have a real estate license?
    (A) A resident manager of an apartment project.
    (B) A resident manager of an apartment project who, for a fee, sells a house across the street.
    (C) A student who sells houses as part of a research project.
    (D) All of the above

13. A licensed salesperson (or whatever such a licensee may be called in your state)
    (A) must be under the supervision of a broker
    (B) can collect commission payments only from his broker
    (C) must have his license held by his employing broker
    (D) all of the above

14. In order to sell property belonging to a trust for which he is trustee, the trustee must have a
    (A) broker's license
    (B) salesperson's license
    (C) trustee's license
    (D) none of the above

15. A person who is employed to sell real estate
    (A) must be licensed
    (B) is an agent
    (C) may be paid a salary or commission
    (D) all of the above

16. A real estate salesperson's compensation is
    (A) 50% of the broker's share
    (B) whatever the seller agreed to
    (C) paid by the broker
    (D) set by state law

17. After one becomes a broker, the most appropriate term for that person is
    (A) REALTOR®
    (B) realtist
    (C) associate
    (D) broker

18. A salesperson may
    (A) open his or her own office
    (B) work out of a broker's branch office
    (C) advertise in his or her personal name
    (D) all of the above

19. Which type of listing is discouraged because it creates a conflict of interest?
    (A) net listing
    (B) open listing
    (C) exclusive listing
    (D) exclusive right to sell

20. Those exempt from licensure include
    (A) people acting for their own ownership interest
    (B) part owners in proportion to their ownership interest
    (C) businesses that sell their own property
    (D) all of the above

21. In a transaction in which the licensed salesperson performed nearly all the work, who is the legal agent?
    (A) salesperson
    (B) broker
    (C) both salesperson and broker
    (D) property owner

22. A cause of action against a real estate licensee for fraud arises when
    (A) the licensee has failed to disclose a material fact
    (B) the licensee has knowingly made an inaccurate statement
    (C) the buyer relied on information provided by the licensee and was damaged
    (D) all of the above conditions are present

23. The best way for a broker acting as a dual agent to minimize his or her risk is to
    (A) hire an attorney
    (B) obtain written permission from both parties to act for both sides
    (C) read the state's real estate law
    (D) provide full disclosure to all parties

24. When representing a buyer in a real estate transaction, a broker must disclose to the seller all of the following *except*
    (A) the buyer's motivation
    (B) the broker's relationship with the buyer
    (C) any agreement to compensate the broker out of the listing broker's commission
    (D) the broker's agreement with the buyer

25. Broker Herman must have an escrow account
    (A) before the state licensing agency will issue his broker's license
    (B) when he holds earnest money
    (C) before his agents can work
    (D) when his personal account is overdrawn

26. Which of the following best describes the role of a broker who seeks a buyer?
    (A) general contractor
    (B) independent contractor
    (C) special agent
    (D) attorney-in-fact

27. How is a buyer's broker typically paid?
    (A) by the buyer at closing
    (B) by a finder's fee paid outside of closing
    (C) by the buyer prior to closing
    (D) by the listing broker through a commission split

ANSWERS

1. **C**	7. **C**	13. **D**	19. **A**	25. **B**
2. **C**	8. **D**	14. **D**	20. **D**	26. **C**
3. **D**	9. **D**	15. **D**	21. **B**	27. **D**
4. **B**	10. **A**	16. **C**	22. **D**	
5. **B**	11. **D**	17. **D**	23. **B**	
6. **B**	12. **A**	18. **B**	24. **A**	

SPECIFIC QUESTIONS CONCERNING YOUR STATE'S LICENSE LAW

No key is provided to the following questions because the answers can differ from one state to another. Try to answer the questions; then check your answers by referring to your state's law and the notes you have made. A good practice is to write your answers lightly in *pencil*. When you check them over after answering the questions, you will be able to erase the incorrect answers and to write in the correct answers in dark pencil or pen. That way, the questions you missed will stand out, and in your future study you will be sure to take note of them as possible weak spots.

Fill-Ins

Fill in the blanks with the words or phrases that reflect the license law of *your* state.

1. The examination fee for a salesperson's license is $ _____.

2. My state will reciprocally issue a real estate license to a licensee from any of the following states: _____

   _____

3. An applicant for a broker's license must be at least _____ years old.

4. A broker must deposit all earnest money payments in an account called a(n) _____

   _____ .

5. To get a salesperson's license, one must have the following general education achievement (high school, college, etc.): _____

6. The maximum imprisonment for violating license law is _____.

7. Three kinds of people who are exempt from license law are _____,
   _____, and _____.

8. The license law is administered by _____.

9. Before taking a licensing examination, a salesperson applicant must have at least _____ classroom hours of instruction in Real Estate Principles.

10. After passing his examination and becoming licensed, a salesperson has _____ months/years to take _____ classroom hours of (specify required subject matter) _____ in order to maintain his licensed status.

11. If a salesperson transfers her employment to a new broker, a transfer fee of $_____ must be paid.

12. The examination fee for the broker's license examination is $_____.

13. Violation of license law is a (misdemeanor, felony, etc.) _____.

14. A salesperson's license fee is $_____ every _____ year(s).

15. License renewal fees must be paid by (date due) _____.

16. A salesperson may collect commission payments from _____.

17. A broker may pay a "referral" fee of up to $_____ to unlicensed persons.

18. If a salesperson's license is renewed late, an additional fee of $_____ must be paid.

19. A broker's license fee is $_____ every _____ year(s).

20. A broker who is employed by another broker pays a license fee of $_____.

21. To take the broker's license examination, a person must have completed the following *real estate* education: _____
_____
_____

22. Nonresident license fees are _____.

23. Only the following have the authority to revoke a real estate license: _____
_____

24. Earnest money deposits paid to brokers must be deposited in the appropriate account within (time limit) _____.

25. A salesperson's license renewal fee is $_____.

26. A broker's license renewal fee is $_____.

27. In the case of a broker who transfers from employment by another broker to independent status, a fee of $_____ must be paid.

28. A salesperson whose license is inactive must reactivate it within _____ years or it will expire.

29. The fee for reactivating an inactive broker's license is $_____.

30. A salesperson may not transfer his employment to a new broker more often than _____ times per year.

31. When a complaint is lodged against a licensee, she must be given at least _____ days' notice of any hearings that will be held.

32. The real estate salesperson's license examination is given _____ times per year.

33. [If your state has associate broker licenses] The education and experience requirements for an associate broker are _____.

34. When a broker's license is renewed late, a late fee of $_____ is charged.

35. If a broker moves his place of business, a fee of $_____ is charged for reissuing new licenses showing the new address.

36. The fee for replacing a lost, stolen, or damaged license is $_____.

37. Real estate licenses must be displayed (where?) _____.

38. Before a person may take the broker's license examination, she must have been a licensed salesperson for at least _____ years.

39. The license fee for a broker's branch office is $_____.

40. After a hearing of a complaint against a licensee, a decision must be rendered within _____ days/months.

True/False

Write *T* for true, *F* for false.

_____ 41. Net listings are illegal in my state.

_____ 42. The Real Estate Commission has the power to specify the curriculum of the courses that licensees and prospective licensees must take to qualify for, or to keep, real estate licenses.

_____ 43. It is illegal to use sellers' powers-of-attorney in order to circumvent the license law.

_____ 44. My state has a real estate recovery fund.

_____ 45. Violation of license law is a misdemeanor.

_____ 46. A person who has lost his real estate license as a result of a violation of license law may never be issued another license.

_____ 47. A convicted felon may not be issued a real estate license.

_____ 48. Brokers may deposit trust and escrow moneys in interest-bearing accounts.

_____ 49. A nonresident of this state may not get any kind of license to do real estate business in this state.

_____ 50. There is no requirement for special real estate education for salespersons.

_____ 51. An out-of-state resident may be issued a license to do real estate business in my state provided that she passes the required examinations, meets educational and age requirements, and pays the specified fees.

_____ 52. When a hearing is held on a complaint against a licensee, the licensee may be represented at the hearing by an attorney.

_____ 53. Complaints against licensees must be submitted to the Real Estate Commission in writing.

_____ 54. Every time a complaint is filed against a licensee, a hearing must be held.

_____ 55. License fees must be paid every 2 years.

_____ 56. The license law requires that, at a specified date in the future, the real estate education required of licensees will be greater than it is now.

_____ 57. In order to take the broker's license examination, a person must satisfy a number of requirements, including at least 3 years' experience as an actively licensed salesperson.

_____ 58. To hold a broker's license a person must be at least 21 years of age.

_____ 59. All licensees must have a high school education or the equivalent.

_____ 60. An applicant for a salesperson's license must be sponsored by a licensed broker.

The following acts concern violations of license law. Write *T* for those that your state's license law specifies as a violation. Write *F* for those that are *not* specified.

_____ 61. Accepting a net listing

_____ 62. Making false statements on license applications

_____ 63. Specifying a closing to occur within 15 days of the signing of a contract of sale

_____ 64. Refusing to convey a ridiculous offer to a principal

_____ 65. A broker's paying a commission directly to another broker's licensed salesperson

_____ 66. Paying a small referral fee to a person who refers a prospect, but takes no other action in the eventual transaction

_____ 67. Inducing a seller to break a listing contract with another broker

_____ 68. Advertising the broker's commission rates

_____ 69. Negotiating a commission rate on a sale

_____ 70. Failing to put an expiration date on a listing

_____ 71. Posting "for sale" signs in violation of local ordinances

_____ 72. Selling a home to a black family in a white neighborhood

_____ 73. Refusing to show a home in a white neighborhood to a black family

_____ 74. Failing to leave copies of contracts with all parties involved

_____ 75. Allowing a person other than a licensed real estate broker to prepare a closing statement

_____ 76. Failing to inform a homebuyer of all closing costs that he must pay

_____ 77. Refusing to negotiate a loan for a buyer

_____ 78. Putting one's sign on property without the owner's permission

_____ 79. Allowing a licensed salesperson to show property without the broker being present

_____ 80. Allowing a salesperson to handle a closing, even if the broker is present and supervising the salesperson

_____ 81. Accepting a placement fee from a loan company without the buyer's or seller's knowledge and consent

_____ 82. Guaranteeing to someone that she will be able to sell a property within 2 years at a profit of 50 percent or more

_____ 83. Intentionally lying in order to induce someone to enter into a contract

_____ 84. Buying property on which one collects a commission without identifying oneself as a licensee

_____ 85. Offering property at a lower price than the seller has authorized in the listing or in a later communication

_____ 86. Failing to identify the broker in all advertising

_____ 87. Placing a blind ad (one in which the fact that the property is being offered by an agent is not stated)

_____ 88. Collecting a commission from more than one party to a transaction

_____ 89. False advertising

_____ 90. Offering for sale property belonging to others, for which one has no listing

_____ 91. A salesperson's not remitting earnest money quickly to his broker

_____ 92. Accepting a postdated check as earnest money after the seller has agreed to this

_____ 93. Commingling trust or escrow money with personal funds

_____ 94. Commingling trust or escrow money with the brokerage firm's general funds

_____ 95. Putting trust or escrow moneys belonging to different people into the same trust or escrow account

_____ 96. Paying license fees for someone else

_____ 97. Doing business while one's license is inactive or is being held by the Real Estate Commission

_____ 98. Secretly collecting a commission from more than one party to a transaction

_____ 99. Attempting to deal directly with a seller who has signed an exclusive listing agreement with another licensee

_____ 100. Selling and renting property from the same office

Multiple-Choice Questions

It is difficult to provide examples of such questions concerning specifics of state law. General examples were given in the preceding section. For reference purposes, we include the following to give you an idea of the *kinds* of multiple-choice questions you may encounter. Note that one answer in some questions is left blank. If none of the other three answers is correct for your state, write the correct answer in the blank. Otherwise, ignore it.

101. License renewal fees are paid
    (A) every year
    (B) every 2 years
    (C) _____
    (D) every 3 years

102. The license fees for brokers/salespersons are
    (A) $50/$20
    (B) the same for both
    (C) $40/$10
    (D) _____

103. In my state it is illegal to
    I. accept a net listing
    II. post "sold" signs on property for which a contract has been accepted
    (A) I only
    (B) II only
    (C) both I and II
    (D) neither I nor II

104. In my state
    (A) buyer-broker agency must be disclosed (when?) _____
    (B) disclosure of the broker-seller agency must be made to buyers
    (C) no agency disclosure is required
    (D) _____

105. Violating license law is punishable by a fine of up to
     (A) $500, imprisonment for up to 6 months, or both
     (B) $500, imprisonment for up to 1 year, or both
     (C) $1000, imprisonment for up to 1 year, or both
     (D) _____

106. Licensees must pay fees for the following:
     (A) transferring employ to another broker
     (B) replacing a lost pocket card
     (C) reactivating an inactive license
     (D) all of the above
     (E) one or two of the above (specify which) _____
     (F) none of the above

107. When a complaint is made against a licensee and a hearing is scheduled, the licensee
     must be given the following advance notice of the hearing:
     (A) 1 week
     (B) 10 days
     (C) 2 weeks
     (D) 1 month
     (E) _____

108. A licensee whose license is inactive or is being held by the Real Estate Commission
     must pay the following fees:
     (A) _____
     (B) the same as active licensees
     (C) half those of active licenses
     (D) $40, broker; $20, salesperson

109. A licensee may appeal a decision made at a hearing for a complaint against him
     directly to
     (A) a circuit court
     (B) the state supreme court
     (C) a federal court
     (D) _____

110. A broker must keep all trust and escrow moneys in
     (A) a separate checking account
     (B) a non-interest-bearing account
     (C) an account that can bear interest
     (D) _____

Questions 111–140 concern your state's Real Estate Commission.

Fill-Ins

Fill in the blanks with the appropriate words or phrases.

111. The Real Estate Commission has _____ members.

112. They serve terms of _____ years.

113. They are appointed by _____.

114. Persons may be nominated for consideration for the post of Real Estate Commissioner by _____.

115. The Chairman of the Real Estate Commission is chosen by _____
_____.

116. The Real Estate Commission must meet (how often?) _____.

117. The Real Estate Commissioners are paid $ _____.

118. The Real Estate Commission meets (where?) _____.

119. The geographical distribution of the homes of the Real Estate Commissioners must be
_____.

120. A Real Estate Commissioner must have been a resident of this state for _____ years prior to assuming her post.

121. A Real Estate Commissioner must hold a _____ license and must have held it for at least _____ years prior to assuming his post.

122. When a vacancy is created on the commission, _____ appoints a new commissioner to fill the unexpired portion of the term.

123. The head of the *staff* of the Real Estate Commission is called _____
_____.

124. The offices of the Real Estate Commission are located at _____
_____.

125. For the commission to transact any business, at least _____ members must be present.

True/False

Write *T* for true, *F* for false.

____ 126. The Real Estate Commission sets the salaries of all people working for it.

____ 127. The Real Estate Commission's budget is composed of all fees and charges it receives from licensees.

____ 128. Real Estate Commission members cannot be reappointed to additional terms.

____ 129. All Real Estate Commission members' terms expire at the same time.

____ 130. Real Estate Commission members must be licensed brokers or salespersons.

____ 131. The Real Estate Commission has no power to revoke or suspend licenses.

____ 132. The Real Estate Commission may deny a license to anyone for any reason.

____ 133. The Real Estate Commission has five members.

____ 134. The Real Estate Commission cannot hold a hearing on a complaint against a licensee unless a quorum is present.

____ 135. The Real Estate Commission has three members.

____ 136. At least one member of the Real Estate Commission must be a member of the general public served by real estate licensees.

Multiple-Choice Questions

Fill in blanks where necessary.

137. The members of the Real Estate Commission, when they assume their posts,
(A) must have been licensed brokers for at least _____ years
(B) must have been residents of the state for at least _____ years
(C) need not be licensed if they represent particular groups (e.g., consumers)
(D) _____

138. The members of the Real Estate Commission
(A) must be REALTORS®
(B) may not participate in the real estate business while holding their posts
(C) must resign if they are sued for improper business practice
(D) _____

139. The Real Estate Commission is responsible for
(A) issuing real estate licenses
(B) conducting hearings on complaints against licensees
(C) setting fees for licenses
(D) more than one of the above (specify which) _____

140. The term of a Real Estate Commissioner is
(A) 2 years
(B) 3 years
(C) 4 years
(D) _____

If your state has a real estate recovery fund (or similar fund), answer questions 141–160. The real estate recovery fund is referred to as the "fund" in these questions, regardless of its specific name in your state.

Fill-Ins

Fill in the blanks with the appropriate words or phrases.

141. When a salesperson first becomes licensed, she must pay $ _____ into the fund.

142. The maximum amount that can be paid on a single claim from the fund is $ _____.

143. The fund must be maintained at a minimum amount of $_____ .

144. When the fund falls below $_____, assessments will be made against all active licensees in the amounts of $_____ for brokers and $_____ for salespersons.

145. Claims must be made against the fund within (time limit) _____ of the time the alleged improper action took place.

146. No more than $ _____ may be paid out of the fund as a result of a single transaction.

147. In my state the name of the fund is _____.

148. If the fund is too low to pay a claim in full, the claim plus _____ percent interest on the unpaid balance will be paid when the fund has risen.

149. A licensee on whose behalf a payment from the fund has been made must pay it back, along with _____ percent interest.

150. When a broker first becomes licensed, he must pay $ _____ into the fund.

True/False

Write *T* for true, *F* for false.

_____ 151. When a claim against the fund has been paid on behalf of a licensee, her license is suspended or revoked and cannot be reissued until she has fully reimbursed the fund.

_____ 152. A claim cannot be made against the fund unless a court judgment has been issued against the affected licensee and it is obvious that he cannot pay the amount in full.

_____ 153. A discharge in bankruptcy does not relieve a licensee of any obligation she may have to the fund.

_____ 154. A licensee may be exempted from fund assessments if he posts a satisfactory bond with the Real Estate Commission.

_____ 155. Money in the fund may be invested in state or federal obligations.

_____ 156. The Real Estate Commission has custody of the fund.

_____ 157. If the fund becomes dangerously depleted, the Real Estate Commission can levy a special assessment on all licensees for the purpose of augmenting the fund.

_____ 158. Claims cannot be paid from the fund unless they are due to fraudulent actions by licensees.

Multiple-Choice Questions

Fill in blanks where necessary.

159. To make a claim against the fund, one must
    (A) secure a court judgment against a licensee
    (B) submit proof that the licensee cannot pay the claim in full
    (C) file the claim within _____ years of the infraction
    (D) _____

160. The assessment to be paid into the fund by new licensees is $ _____ for new salespersons and $ _____ for new brokers.
     (A) $10/$20
     (B) $20/$40
     (C) $50/$100
     (D) _____

If your state permits the Real Estate Licensing Authority to regulate real estate schools, answer questions 161–170.

Fill-Ins

Fill in the blanks with the appropriate words or phrases.

161. The curriculum required of an applicant for a salesperson's license must include _____ hours, distributed as follows: _____
    _____

162. The curriculum required of an applicant for a broker's license must include _____ hours, distributed as follows: _____
    _____

163. Teachers of authorized courses must have the following qualifications: _____
    _____

164. Required courses cannot meet for more than _____ hours per day.

165. A real estate school must be given _____ days' notice of the licensing authority's intention to withdraw the school's approval.

True/False

Write *T* for true, *F* for false.

____ 166. The licensing authority may determine the qualifications of teachers of approved courses.

____ 167. A course cannot meet for more than 3 hours per day.

____ 168. A broker's license applicant must have passed a course providing at least 30 hours of study in the area of valuation and appraisal.

____ 169. The licensing authority must approve all real estate schools, even if their courses do not fulfill the educational requirement for licensure.

____ 170. The licensing authority forbids the offering of courses designed specifically to enable people to pass the licensing examination.

Introduction to Contracts

Most people have a little familiarity with contracts. A popular misconception is that a contract must be filled with obscure, legalistic language and printed in nearly invisible type. Some contracts do appear this way, but these days more and more contracts that consumers encounter are in print that you can see and are written so that they can be understood.

While it is true, as we shall see, that contracts must conform to certain standards, usually the only requirement of the *language* is that it *say clearly what it is supposed to say*. These days there is an admirable trend to simplify and clarify the language of most contracts, eliminating elaborate language that serves no useful purpose.

We can approach the study of contracts with confidence; a little familiarity with them will reveal the basic logic behind the laws and customs that surround them and will eliminate the mystery that usually clouds the layperson's view of these documents.

REAL ESTATE CONTRACTS

The real estate business is dominated by contracts. Buying, selling, mortgaging, leasing, and listing real estate all involve particular kinds of contracts. To become familiar with the real estate business, we must devote a considerable part of our study to contracts *in general*, as well as to the *specific kinds* that concern real estate.

For convenience we divide real estate contracts into two rather loosely defined groups. Our *major* contracts are associated with the kinds of real estate dealings that most frequently occur: these are *listings, contracts of sale, deeds, mortgages*, and *leases*. Other contractual arrangements, which involve particular kinds of circumstances and so are less frequently encountered, constitute our *minor* contracts. Note that this division into major and minor is a grouping we are making for our own convenience. The law and the courts do not make this distinction: to them a contract is a contract, and the parties to all contracts have the same rights of access to the courts and to legal enforcement of their contractual promises.

Real Estate Contracts

Figure 6-1 arranges the major contracts in the order in which they might be encountered in a typical series of transactions. First an owner (a seller) enters into a *listing contract* with a broker; in this contract the seller agrees to pay a commission when the broker has found an acceptable buyer for the listed property. In many states, when a buyer is contacted, the law requires that an *agency disclosure* be made to the buyer by the seller's broker at that time (see Chapter 4 for discussion of agency disclosure). When a buyer becomes interested in the listed property, negotiations begin; if there is a buyer-broker agency relationship (see Chapter 4), disclosure of it must be made to the seller and/or his broker during the negotiations. If the buyer and the seller agree to transact, they will sign a *contract of sale*, in which they agree that at some time in the future the seller will convey the property to the buyer; this conveyance will occur when the *deed* is executed by the seller and delivered to the buyer. The buyer may then seek to borrow part of the cost of the property, so he offers a lender a *mortgage* as collateral for the *note*, which serves as evidence of the debt he owes. Also, he decides to rent part of the premises to someone else, with whom he enters into a *lease* contract.

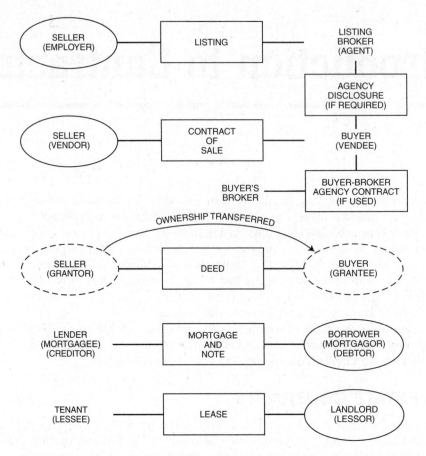

Figure 6-1. Major Contracts. Note: Owners of real estate are circled.

Parties to Contracts

In each of these contracts, the parties have specific names. In a listing contract, the seller is the *employer* and the broker is the *agent*. In the contract of sale, the seller becomes the *vendor* and the buyer is the *vendee*. The parties to the deed are the *grantor* and the *grantee*; the mortgage contract is between the *mortgagor* (owner) and *mortgagee* (lender). The *lessor's* real estate is made available to the *lessee* in a lease contract. Generally, the suffix *-or* refers to the person who conveys rights, privileges, or something else of value to the person whose title has the suffix *-ee*. In subsequent chapters each of the real estate contracts will be discussed in detail, but first we examine the basic principles that apply to all contracts.

What Is a Contract?

A contract is an agreement between two or more *parties*, in which each of the parties pledges to do, or is shown to have done, *something* that will benefit the others. (A contract also can obligate someone *not* to do a certain thing.) This "something" can take a multitude of forms. A common one is a payment of money, though contracts involving no money payment can be perfectly valid. Each of the parties must be shown to benefit, so contracts must involve *exchanges* of benefits. A gives something to B, in return for which B gives something to A. A common example is a purchase: I give money to you, and you give the thing I am buying from you. However, a valid contract need not involve money: I can swap my automobile for your lawn mower, or we can agree that neither of us will build on our land an ugly structure that will be in the line of sight of the other.

Although there are other requirements that must be met, the critical test of the validity of a contract is the issue of whether or not the parties can be shown to benefit from it. The amount of benefit doesn't really matter; but if benefit to one or both parties is totally lacking, then usually there is no contract, for it is an ancient precept of law that no one should give something for nothing. If *any* measurable or identifiable benefit is mentioned in the contract, that will be enough. If you and I sign an agreement that says simply that I will give you my automobile next Tuesday, no court will require me to live up to this promise, because no benefit *to me* is mentioned. However, if our agreement says that I will give you my car next Tuesday in return for one dollar paid by you to me, the courts *will* enforce the agreement against me: it will be a contract because I am receiving some benefit. The fact that my car may be worth much more than one dollar is immaterial here; all that matters is that *both* parties receive *some* benefit: you get my car and I get your dollar.

Enforcement of Contracts

A valid contract has the "force of law" among the parties to it. It is as if they had agreed to "pass" a law among themselves and promised to abide by it. However, when a person violates the provisions of a contract, the police, or a flock of judges and bailiffs, do not descend upon him and demand that he keep his bargain. In fact, the law will do nothing about private contractual disputes unless one of the injured parties petitions the court to intervene. At that point, the law requires the affected parties to appear and to present their arguments. Then the court (i.e., a judge or a jury) makes a decision as to what is to be done, and by whom. (This description, of course, is somewhat oversimplified; resolving a contractual dispute—or any other—in court often consumes considerable time and expense.) It is likely that many violated contracts never reach court because the offended parties do not want the bother of a court case. Even so, there is always that possibility; all parties to a contract have the inherent right to request the court to render judgment if they feel that other parties to the agreement are not living up to it.

Generally, a person who brings a contract to court has two remedies available. First, she can ask that the court require *specific performance* of the offending party, that is, that the court order the other party to live up to the agreement. Often, however, by the time a contract dispute reaches court it is too late for mere performance to do any (or enough) good. In such a case, the injured party may seek *damages*. Here she would claim that she had suffered some loss because of the other party's violation of the contract and would ask that the court order the violator to make the loss good. Note the use of the words *court order* here. Once the court has reached a decision, the parties to the dispute are *required by law* to abide by it.* If they do not, they are in contempt of court and can be jailed or fined if need be. In this manner, behind every contractual arrangement there lies the threat of court action, which can be backed up by potentially severe penalties.

Most contract cases that come to court are not cut and dried. Rarely does a person enter into a contract with the intention to violate it; furthermore, one who *knows* that he is in violation of a contract rarely has the stubbornness (or foolishness) to go ahead with a court showdown he knows he will lose. What usually happens is that *all* parties to a dispute think they are right and the other(s) wrong. The parties *interpret* their agreement differently and are unable to resolve their differences. By taking the matter to court, they ask the court to render a judgment as to who is right and what is to be done.

---

*This assumes that the decision is not appealed. But an appeal only delays an eventual unappealed, or unappealable, decision, which must be respected.

REQUIREMENTS OF VALID CONTRACTS

A contract cannot be considered by a court unless it is valid. While certain kinds of contracts may have additional requirements for validity, *all* contracts must have the following attributes:

1. Mutual agreement
2. Consideration
3. Legally competent parties
4. Lawful purpose
5. Legal form

1. Mutual Agreement

Mutual agreement (often referred to as *offer and acceptance, reality of consent, mutual assent, meeting of the minds*, and similar phrases) means that all parties recognize that an offer has been made and has been accepted by the other parties. All are agreed as to what each party has done, with respect to the contract, as well as to what each party is still required to do in the future. Generally, the parties will agree to do, or not to do, some thing or things, in return for some kind of obligation from the others.

Provided that the other essentials of a contract are present, once an offer has been accepted, a contract exists. The one making the offer is the *offeror*, and the one to whom it is made is the *offeree*. The actions of both of them in creating the contract must be shown to be intentional and deliberate: generally their signatures to a written contract are evidence of this, provided that no fraud, misrepresentation, duress, or mistake is present. However, many binding contracts need not be written; in such cases it is the testimony of the affected parties that provides the evidence that an agreement exists. (Duress, misrepresentation, and fraud are discussed later in this chapter.)

2. Consideration

Legal consideration refers to the "benefit" received by the parties. Each party must be shown to be obligated to do (or not to do) something, in return for some action or nonaction by the other parties to the contract. The benefit can take many forms; all that must be shown is that the party receiving the benefit agreed that it was of use to him and that he was willing to obligate himself in some way in order to get it. Payment of money is always consideration, as is the transfer of ownership of anything that can be shown to have a market value. In addition, the transfer of many *rights* is consideration; for example, a lease transfers rights to use property, but not ownership of the property.

Examples. Here are some examples of consideration in a contract.

1. A pays $50,000 to B. B transfers ownership of the house to A.
2. A pays B $1,200 per month. B gives A the right to use an apartment for each month for which A pays.
3. A pays B $7.50. B lets A watch a movie in B's theater.
4. A agrees not to hang her laundry outside where B and C can see it. B agrees not to hang his laundry where A and C can see it. C agrees not to hang her laundry where A and B can see it.
5. A agrees to use his best efforts to try to find a buyer for B's house. B agrees to pay A a commission of 6% of the sale price if A finds a suitable buyer.
6. A agrees to pay B $392,000 in 60 days, at which time B will transfer to A ownership of a particular house.
7. A pays B $1,000. B gives A the right to purchase B's land for $25,000 at any time of A's choosing during the next 6 months.
8. A transfers ownership of her house to B. B transfers to A the ownership of his parking lot, four albums of rare stamps, two sets of dishes, and a mongrel dog.

9. A pays B $10,000. B transfers to A the ownership of a producing diamond mine in South Africa.
10. A transfers to his son, A, Jr., the ownership of the family estate in return for the "love and affection" that A, Jr. has given to A in the past.
11. A pays B $10,000. B agrees to pay A $126.70 per month for the next 10 years.
12. A pays B $10,000. B gives A the right to have B's house sold if B defaults on her debt to A.

In all of these instances there exists legal consideration; these examples show but a few of the many forms it can take. In many cases it includes the payment of money; in (4), (8), and (10), however, no money changes hands. In most, the consideration involves the parties doing something or performing some act; in (4), however, the parties agree *not* to do something. Examples (2), (3), (4), (7), and (12) include the exchange of rights; (5) includes the exchange of services; and the others involve the exchange of ownership of things.

These are examples of real estate contracts we will examine in more detail later. Example (2) is a *lease*; (4) is a *restrictive covenant*; (5) is a *listing*; (6) is a *contract of sale*; (7) is an *option*; (12) is a *mortgage*; and (1), (8), (9), and (10) are *deeds*. Many of these contracts are purchases of one kind or another; examine (11) closely and you will discover that it is a *loan* or a *note*: A lends B $10,000, which B agrees to repay (at a 9% interest rate) in equal monthly installments of $126.70 for the next 10 years. Example (5) is a *listing*; it is also an *employment contract*, wherein the services of one of the parties are purchased by the other party.

GOOD CONSIDERATION, VALUABLE CONSIDERATION

In all except (10) we have *"valuable" consideration*. Valuable consideration is anything that is of value to practically everyone and thus can be sold for money. Money, of course is "valuable," as is ownership of things, the receipt of someone's services, receipt of various kinds of rights, and the like. However, things such as friendship, love, and affection are not valuable consideration, because their value is entirely subjective. You may set a very high value upon the attention and friendship you receive from your best friend, but to most of the rest of us the attention is valueless, since we don't even know him. Furthermore, a person's affection is not a transferable benefit. Rights, ownership, money, services, and such things can be passed on (or sold) to practically anyone, but you can't sell your best friend's affection to someone else. Consequently, such things as friendship and love are called *"good" consideration*. They are of value to the one who receives them, and if she agrees to transfer benefit in return for them she can be held to her bargain.

The law does *not* require that *equal* consideration accrue to all parties. So long as consideration is there, the law is satisfied, provided of course that no fraud or duress is involved. There is only one exception: the courts will not enforce a contract requiring the simultaneous exchange of different sums of money.

In some cases a contract doesn't have to spell out the exact amount of consideration. Of course, a deed contract ought to describe the real estate very carefully, but often, in deeds, the price paid may be described, for example, as ". . . ten dollars and other good and valuable consideration." Because deeds are recorded, and therefore available to the public to see, many buyers don't want nosy people to find out exactly what they paid for their real estate. This kind of wording, especially for money consideration, is perfectly all right. It says that one has received consideration, and that is all that is necessary.

3. Legally Competent Parties

Competent parties are persons who have the legal right to enter into contractual arrangements. Not all legal persons are human beings: corporations, partnerships, trusts, and some other organizations can also be parties to a contract. You can contract to purchase an automobile from ABZ Auto Sales, Inc., even though this company is not a living, breathing being. Furthermore, not all humans are competent to contract; many are legally unable to do so, and many more may contract only under carefully defined circumstances.

NONHUMAN PARTIES

Usually, each party to a contract must assure himself of the other's legal competence. Although the law places few restrictions upon the possible contracting ability of nonhuman parties, often these organizations will operate under self-imposed restrictions. A corporation's charter, for example, can permit or prevent certain kinds of contractual agreements on the part of the organization; in addition, it can provide that some or all of the permitted functions be carried out in certain ways. For this reason a person who contracts with an organization must assure himself, first, that the outfit is permitted to engage in such a contract, and, second, that the contract is executed and carried out in consistency with the organization's permitted limitations and prescribed methods.

PEOPLE

Among people, there are two major categories of incompetent parties: infants and mentally incompetent persons, along with several minor ones: drunkards, convicts, and others.

a. Infants (or Minors). These are people who have not yet attained the age of majority, which is 18 to 21 in various states. While you may not think that a hulking 17-year-old football star could be incompetent at *anything*, the law says he is. Furthermore, a person who may be immature, ignorant, or naive in business judgment still may be considered by the law to be perfectly competent to take responsibility for her actions if she has attained the age of majority. Minors are not prohibited from contracting, so no law is broken if a minor signs a contract. However, the contract is viewed in a special way by the law: the minor can *void* the contract later on, if he wishes, but adult parties to the contract do *not* have that privilege. The minor may not, however, void (or *disaffirm*) only *part* of the contract; he must abandon it entirely. If he contracts to buy property from an adult, he will have the right to declare the contract void, if he wishes, any time before it is carried out. The adult, however, must honor the contract unless and until the minor actually disaffirms it. If the adult does not keep his bargain, the minor can sue. The adult will receive no help from the courts if the minor disaffirms. However, the minor cannot, say, disaffirm the part of the contract that specifies he must pay for the property, while at the same time requiring the adult to transfer it to him anyway; he must abandon the *entire* contract. Furthermore, if he disaffirms it after the adult has provided him some benefit under it, he may have to pay for (or return) that which he had already received by the time he decided to void the contract.

The whole idea behind the legal specification of some people as incompetent is a matter of protection. An *infant* is considered too young to bind herself to agreements; the law gives her protection by allowing her to void most agreements that she gets herself into. Once an infant attains the age of majority, she becomes an adult and loses this protection, but she *is* given a "reasonable" time beyond the attainment of majority to decide whether she will disaffirm any contracts that she entered into as a minor.

b. Mentally Incompetent Persons. The law also extends this "protection" to other categories of people, the largest being mentally incompetent persons. Unlike infancy, however, mental incompetency (sometimes referred to as insanity) is a state that can come and go. One who is competent (sane) can become incompetent (insane), and one who is incompetent can be cured and so become competent again. Also, it is possible for a person who is under severe stress or suffering from some other transitory disturbance to become so disoriented that the law may extend the protection of incompetence to him during that episode.

Legal protection of a mentally incompetent person takes two forms. First, if he has had a guardian appointed by the court, then all contracts he enters into are *void*, and he had no capacity to contract at all. Notice that the infant's contracts are *voidable*, whereas the contracts of an incompetent person under guardianship are *void*. If the incompetent person has no guardian, his contracts, too, are voidable rather than void. He has the choice to require that his bargains with others be carried out or to disaffirm the contracts.

Neither the infant nor the mentally incompetent person may disaffirm *all* kinds of contracts; generally, courts will enforce against them contracts for *necessaries*. Examples of necessaries are food, clothing, and shelter; sometimes other things are included as well. For example, in some cases contracts for employment or for education may be considered necessaries. Once again, the law is extending another form of protection: an adult usually will not care to contract with an infant or someone else she knows may later plead incompetence and void the contract. Consequently, a truthful incompetent may be at a serious disadvantage if his personal circumstances *require* him to contract. Therefore, the law allows some incompetents what amounts to a limited competency. For things that are "necessary" to them they are allowed to create binding contracts, which they cannot disaffirm and which a court can enforce against them. As a result, competent parties receive the protection *they* seek in a contractual arrangement and any reluctance they may have to deal with an incompetent is eliminated.

c. Other Incompetency. Certain other forms of incapacity "earn" one the legal protection of incompetency. A contract made by a person who is severely intoxicated with alcohol or is under the dominating influence of drugs known to affect judgment may later be considered voidable. Many states consider felon prisoners to be without the right to contract; this situation is described by the rather grim term of *civilly dead*. Usually, when the sentence has been served, and sometimes at the time parole is secured, most rights will be restored.

4. Lawful Purpose

A contract that requires any of its parties to violate the law usually is void. However, if it is possible to do so without impairing the contract's basic purpose, a court will uphold the contract but strike out that part requiring an illegal act. A very good example concerns the Federal Fair Housing Act of 1968. Among other things, this law declared illegal certain restrictive covenants that required buyers of some real estate to agree they would resell only to people of certain racial or cultural backgrounds. At the time the law was enacted, vast numbers of deeds to homes contained such clauses, but that fact did not void those deeds in their entirety. The outlawing of these clauses had no great effect upon the main purpose of the deeds, which was to transfer title to realty in return for consideration. However, if someone had created a special agreement for the sole purpose of restricting the racial or cultural background of purchasers of certain real estate, then that entire contract would have been voided by the enactment of the law. If this kind of agreement came into being after the law was passed, it would be illegal from the beginning and would *never* be a contract.

The essential rule of lawful purpose, then, is that a contract that exists substantially for the purpose of requiring an illegal act is void. So also is a contract in which an illegal act is required, the elimination of which would materially alter the purpose or effect of the contract. When, however, an illegal act is included in a contract but is not essential to the basic intent or purpose of the agreement, a court often will void only the illegal part while letting the rest stand.

5. Legal Form

Some contracts are required to follow a certain form or to be drawn in a certain manner. For example, deeds and contracts of sale require that "legal" descriptions of the property be included; if they are missing or are defective, the entire contract may be invalid. It should be pointed out, though, that much of the wordy, archaic language that frequently appears in contracts is *not* required by any law and appears only as a result of tradition.

STATUTE OF FRAUDS: REAL ESTATE CONTRACTS MUST BE WRITTEN

For most real estate contracts, however, there is one critical requirement with respect to form: generally, all real estate contracts, except (1) listings and (2) leases for 1 year or less, *must be written*. This requirement is an outgrowth of the fact that each state has enacted a law called the Statute of Frauds, which requires that all contracts of certain types be written if legal means are to be used to enforce them. Included in these categories are all contracts in which land or an interest in land is sold and contracts that cannot be performed within 1 year. This latter category, then, includes lease contracts extending for more than 1 year.

As noted in Chapter 4, a listing contract, however, does not require the sale of land or an interest in land among its parties (although it often is tied into such a sale to a third party). It is a contract of *employment*, which is a category not covered by the Statute of Frauds. However, all states, in their real estate licensing laws, require that residential listings, also, be in writing.

The definition of "land or an interest in land" is very specific and also quite broad. It includes future interests, so, in addition to deeds, contracts of sale must be written. It includes partial interests, so mortgages must be written. It includes improvements to land and attachments to it, so contracts involving purchase of buildings or growing plants must be written, even if the actual land beneath them is not part of the transaction. However, once an attachment to land is severed from it (e.g., trees are cut down or crops are reaped), the attachment becomes personal property and is no longer subject to the part of the Statute of Frauds that covers realty. This law usually covers much more than just realty contracts, though, so it is quite possible that many other nonrealty contracts can be required to be written.

DURESS, MISREPRESENTATION, AND FRAUD

All parties to a valid contract must have entered into it willingly and without having been misled as to pertinent facts concerning the arrangement. Consequently, you cannot expect a court to enforce a contract against someone if you pointed a gun at his head to force him to sign, or if you deliberately or unintentionally misled him so that he agreed to its terms, on the basis of this false information. The former kind of situation is described as one of *duress*; the latter is either *misrepresentation* or *fraud*.

Duress

Duress can take any number of forms. When circumstances force a person to do something against her will, one could say that duress exists, but the law does not always see the situation in that way. If the duress is caused by a party who benefits under the contract, then a court usually will recognize it as such; this covers situations such as forcing someone's assent by threatening her illegally. But other circumstance can also create duress: Jones discovers that he has a rare, expensive disease and must sell his home in order to raise money to pay for the cure. A person who buys from him at this time might make an advantageous deal legally, if Jones is in a hurry to sell. If the duress is caused by one's own action, the court is reluctant to recognize it. If you buy a new house and therefore are desperate to sell your old home, that situation is pretty much your own fault. If you create your own duress, you usually have to suffer with it.

Misrepresentation and Fraud

Misrepresentation and fraud go a few steps further: here someone is led into a bad bargain on the basis of false information. Misrepresentation is loosely defined as the *unintentional* giving of false information, whereas fraud is *deliberate*. There is another difference, too: fraud is a *crime* as well as a civil wrong. This means that, whereas a victim of either fraud or misrepresentation is entitled to compensation for what he was misled into losing, a victim of fraud may sue also for punitive damages, which are a form of extra payment required of the culprit as a kind of punishment. Finally, the perpetrator of a fraud may also be prosecuted in criminal court and may end up being convicted and imprisoned.

PROVING MISREPRESENTATION OR FRAUD

A victim must prove three things to show that misrepresentation or fraud exists: (1) that the incorrect information was relevant to the contract she is disputing—that is, it was *material*; (2) that it was reasonable for her to rely on this false information; and (3) that this reliance led her to suffer some loss as a result.

Let's consider an example. Brown considers buying Green's house. Brown asks Green whether the house is free of termites, and Green says that it is. Actually the house is infested. If Brown later buys the house based, in part, upon Green's information and subsequently discovers termite infestation, he may have a case. The point at issue is material: it is reasonable for Brown to base his decision to buy at least partly upon the assurance that no termites inhabit the premises. When he finds them, it is obvious that he has suffered a loss; therefore the first and third conditions are met. Now he must show that it was reasonable to rely upon Green (the owner at the time) to give him accurate information on this matter. If the court agrees with Brown, he has proved his case. If Green knew about the termites and deliberately lied, then he committed fraud. If he truly thought there were no termites, then he misrepresented.

If one or more of the three conditions are missing, fraud or misrepresentation cannot be claimed successfully. If Brown had not bought Green's house, he could not claim relief, because he suffered no loss due to the falsehood. Also, if he had asked a neighbor a few houses away about the termite problem in Green's house and had depended on the neighbor's incorrect information, it is unlikely that he could get help from the court, because he would have great difficulty showing that it was reasonable to rely on a neighbor for this kind of information.

SOME INFORMATION MUST BE DIVULGED

For some kinds of contracts, the law requires that certain information be divulged by at least some of the parties. If it is not, then misrepresentation or fraud may exist. For example, most licensing laws require that brokers inform other parties if the brokers are acting as principals in the contract, as well as agents. Also, most states require a broker to disclose which party she is acting for, especially if more than one party to a transaction is paying her a commission.

DISCHARGE AND BREACH OF CONTRACTS

Contractual arrangements can be terminated in two general ways. *Discharge* of a contract occurs when no one is required to perform under it anymore. *Breach of contract* occurs when one party makes performance impossible, even though other parties are willing, by refusing to do his part or by otherwise preventing discharge of the contract.

Discharge

Discharge can be considered the "amicable" situation in which the parties to a contract agree that the arrangement is terminated. Most often, discharge occurs by *performance*; that is, everyone has done what he has promised to do and nothing more is required of anyone. Other forms of discharge include agreement to terminate a contract, for one reason or another, before it would have been discharged by performance. Such a reason might be the substitution of a new party for one of the original parties; this original party, then, would have had her duties discharged. Sometimes the parties may decide to terminate one agreement by substituting another one for it. Discharge can also occur when the parties simply agree to abandon the contract without substituting a new party or another agreement for it.

STATUTE OF LIMITATIONS

The law limits the time during which contracting parties can take a dispute concerning a contract to court; this is the Statute of Limitations, and in the various states it sets different kinds of limits on different kinds of contracts. Once the limit has passed, a dispute will not be heard in court, so, in that sense, the contract may be said to be discharged, because it can no longer be enforced. It is greatly advisable that any agreement discharging a contract for reasons other than performance or limitation be in writing. Under some situations (particularly when some, but not all, parties have performed or begun to perform under the contract) an agreement discharging an existing contract *must* be in writing.

Breach

Breach occurs when a party violates the provisions of a contract; often this action can be serious enough to terminate the contract by making it impossible to continue the arrangement. The injured parties must seek remedy from the court; usually it takes the form of a judgment for *damages* against the party causing the breach. Sometimes, however, it may be feasible to secure a judgment for *specific performance*, which requires the breaching party to perform as he had agreed. To be successful in court, the injured parties must be able to show that a breach has indeed occurred. Failure by a party to perform entirely as specified in the contract constitutes a breach, as does a declaration that he does not intend to perform. Finally, there is a breach if a party creates a situation wherein it is impossible for every party to the contract to perform as specified. Once any of these events has occurred, there is a breach, and one attribute of a breaching of a contract is that it terminates the obligations of the other parties as well. The person who has breached a contract cannot have that agreement held good against any of the other parties.

Injustice

The court will not enforce a contract if doing so will result in an obvious injustice. While the law is precise, its enforcement is allowed to be compassionate. Consider a case where Smith and Jones come to an *oral* agreement, wherein Smith pays money to Jones, and Jones transfers title to a piece of land to Smith. Smith then builds a house upon the land, whereupon Jones claims title to the land (and to the attachments, including the house) on the grounds that the contract transferring title was oral and therefore invalid. In a case as cut and dried as this, the court would award title to Smith, despite the absence of a written contract, for two reasons. First, there is a principle of law that recognizes an oral contract of this nature provided that the purchaser has "substantially" improved the property; otherwise he clearly would suffer unjustly. Second, if Jones had engineered the entire scheme specifically in order to take advantage of Smith, then Jones's case would be dismissed; a person can't use the law to obtain an unfair advantage over someone else who is acting in good faith.

Outside Circumstances

Finally, a contract can be terminated because of some outside circumstance. For example, new legislation may invalidate some kinds of contracts. The death of one of the parties usually will void a contract; also, if a party becomes ill or injured to the point where she cannot perform, she often can void a contract without penalty. If it turns out that the parties have made a mistake as to what their agreement constitutes, then the contract can be nullified. For example, if Emmett thinks a contract of sale involves his purchase of Joan's property on *First* Street and Joan thinks she has agreed to sell Emmett the property she owns on *Twenty-first* Street, there is no contract, because there hasn't been a meeting of the minds. Finally, if the subject matter of the contract is destroyed, the contract ceases to exist.

Questions on Chapter 6

1. A contract in which an owner of real estate employs a broker for the purpose of finding a buyer for the real estate is a
   (A) deed   (C) listing
   (B) contract of sale   (D) lease

2. A contract in which property is transferred from one person to another is a
   (A) deed   (C) listing
   (B) contract of sale   (D) lease

3. The two parties to a lease contract are the
   (A) landlord and the serf
   (B) rentor and the rentee
   (C) lessor and the lessee
   (D) grantor and the grantee

4. The requirement that all parties to the contract have an understanding of the conditions and stipulations of the agreement is
   (A) reality of consent
   (B) meeting of the minds
   (C) offer and acceptance
   (D) all of the above

5. Consideration that has value only to the person receiving it is
   (A) illegal in any transaction
   (B) good consideration
   (C) valuable consideration
   (D) contingent consideration

6. A person who is too young to be held to a contractual arrangement is called
   (A) youthful
   (B) incompetent
   (C) an emancipated minor
   (D) civilly dead

7. One who is otherwise incompetent to make a contract may be bound to contracts for
   (A) anything but real estate
   (B) real estate only
   (C) necessaries
   (D) food, clothing, and shelter not to exceed $100 per week

8. Which of the following contractual arrangements would be unenforceable?
   (A) A agrees to buy B's house.
   (B) A agrees with B that B shall steal money from C.
   (C) A agrees to find a buyer for B's car.
   (D) A agrees with B that B shall make restitution to C for money stolen by B.

9. The law that requires that most real estate contracts be written to be enforceable is the
   (A) Statute of Limitations
   (B) Statute of Frauds
   (C) Statute of Written Real Estate Agreements
   (D) Statute of Liberty

10. A contract in which A agrees to allow B to use A's real estate in return for periodic payments of money by B is a
    (A) deed   (C) lease
    (B) contract of sale   (D) mortgage

11. When a person deliberately lies in order to mislead a fellow party to a contract, this action is
    (A) fraud
    (B) misrepresentation
    (C) legal if no third parties are hurt
    (D) all right if it is not written into the contract

12. Holding a gun to someone's head to force him to sign a contract is
    (A) attempted murder
    (B) permissible only in exceptional circumstances
    (C) duress
    (D) rude and inconsiderate but not illegal so long as the gun doesn't go off

13. When a party to a contract makes performance under it impossible, the result is
    (A) breach of contract
    (B) discharge of contract
    (C) performance of contract
    (D) abandonment of contract

14. A contract in which A agrees to purchase B's real estate at a later date is
    (A) a deed   (C) a contract of sale
    (B) an option   (D) a lease

15. Contracts made by a minor are
    (A) enforceable at all times
    (B) void
    (C) voidable by either party
    (D) voidable only by the minor

16. Incompetent parties include
    (A) minors
    (B) insane persons
    (C) people with court-appointed guardians
    (D) all of the above

17. The parties to a deed are the
    (A) vendor and vendee
    (B) grantor and grantee
    (C) offeror and offeree
    (D) acceptor and acceptee

18. If A and B have a contractual arrangement and B violates the contract, A may
    (A) do nothing but suffer the consequences
    (B) sue in court for damages and/or specific performance
    (C) call the police and have B arrested unless B agrees to cooperate
    (D) damage B to the extent that she has damaged A

19. A agrees to sell his brand new limousine to B in return for one dollar. Later A wishes to back out of the deal.
    (A) He may not do so.
    (B) He may do so because he is not getting the true value of the limousine.
    (C) He may only require that B pay a fair price for the limousine.
    (D) Both actions are clear evidence of insanity, so the contract is void.

20. A agrees to trade her car to B in exchange for a vacant lot that B owns.
    (A) This is a valid contractual arrangement.
    (B) This is not a contract, because no money changes hands.
    (C) This is not a contract, because unlike items can't be traded.
    (D) This is not a valid contract, because the car is titled in A's name.

21. Two offers are received by the broker at the same time. The broker must
    (A) present both offers
    (B) present only the higher offer
    (C) present only the offer that provides a greater commission
    (D) use his or her best judgment as to which offer to present

22. In a legal sale contract, the seller is often referred to as the
    (A) trustor   (C) donor
    (B) divisor   (D) vendor

23. A contract based on an illegal consideration is
    (A) valid   (C) legal
    (B) void   (D) enforceable

24. A valid purchase and sale agreement must contain
    (A) listing price
    (B) broker's commission
    (C) financing requirements
    (D) purchase price, terms and conditions of sale

25. The terms of a purchase and sale agreement can be changed only
    (A) in writing and signed by all parties to the transaction
    (B) by the broker in a dual agency
    (C) by the title company
    (D) by the attorneys for both parties

26. A person who has the right to act for another is
    (A) a broker
    (B) a witness
    (C) an attorney-at-law
    (D) an attorney-in-fact

27. Which is *not* necessary for a valid contract?
    (A) offer   (C) acceptance
    (B) legal object   (D) due date

28. A contract is accepted with minor modifications. It is
    (A) effective   (C) not binding
    (B) binding   (D) voidable

29. A contract that requires a party *not* to do something is called
    (A) negative
    (B) restraint on alienation
    (C) forbearance
    (D) unjust

30. Which can bind a principal to a contract?
    (A) general agent   (C) subagent
    (B) special agent   (D) attorney-in-fact

31. Broker Bill was given oral instructions to submit an offer for $47,000, but he erroneously prepared an offer for $49,000, which all parties signed. As a result,
    (A) the contract is voidable
    (B) the buyer is exempt
    (C) Broker Bill must forfeit any commission
    (D) the contract is binding

32. A bill of sale is used to convey
    (A) retail store inventory
    (B) leasehold
    (C) leased fee
    (D) all of the above

33. A contract that states the price and terms in writing is
    (A) express   (C) boilerplate
    (B) implied   (D) unenforceable

34. In a contract where there is a dispute because of a contradiction, which holds more weight?
    (A) preprinted form
    (B) words written in
    (C) legalese
    (D) boilerplate

35. A counteroffer is
    (A) good negotiating technique
    (B) rejection of the offer with substitution of a new offer
    (C) an implied contract
    (D) a selling strategy

36. Which of the following is *not* an essential element of a contract?
    (A) offer and acceptance
    (B) consideration
    (C) competent parties
    (D) earnest money

37. Which of the following would *not* have the legal capacity to enter into a valid and enforceable contract for the sale of real estate?
    (A) an illiterate person
    (B) a minor
    (C) a woman in a nursing home
    (D) an authorized officer of a partnership

38. A binder given by a buyer in a real estate transaction
    (A) may be withdrawn by the buyer at any time before the seller signs his or her acceptance
    (B) draws interest in favor of the broker
    (C) must exceed 2% of the sales price
    (D) must be monetary

39. In case of a breach of contract, a party may enforce *specific performance*. What is specific performance?
    (A) A lawsuit for actual and treble damages.
    (B) A lawsuit by the non-defaulting party to specifically collect damages agreed to in the contract.
    (C) A lawsuit to compel action called for in the agreement.
    (D) all of the above

40. A written and signed real estate contract can be voided for which of the following reasons?
    (A) The market value was less than the sales price.
    (B) The market value declines.
    (C) One of the parties failed to read the instrument before signing it.
    (D) One of the parties was an unmarried minor at the time the contract was signed.

41. Meat display cases in a butcher shop are an example of
    (A) fixtures
    (B) personal property
    (C) trade fixtures
    (D) real estate

42. The law requiring that contracts for the sale of real estate be in writing to be enforceable in a court of law is the
    (A) Statute of Conveyance
    (B) Statute of Frauds
    (C) Statute of Enforceability
    (D) Statute of Writing

43. Which of the following statements is true with regard to express and implied contracts?
    (A) An express contract is oral, and an implied contract is created by the parties' actions.
    (B) An express contract is written, and an implied contract is oral.
    (C) An express contract must be in writing, and an implied contract is created by the parties' actions.
    (D) An express contract is stated in words (verbal), whether written or oral, and an implied contract is created by the parties' actions.

ANSWERS

1. **C**	10. **C**	19. **A**	28. **C**	37. **B**
2. **A**	11. **A**	20. **A**	29. **C**	38. **A**
3. **C**	12. **C**	21. **A**	30. **D**	39. **C**
4. **D**	13. **A**	22. **D**	31. **D**	40. **D**
5. **B**	14. **C**	23. **B**	32. **A**	41. **C**
6. **B**	15. **D**	24. **D**	33. **A**	42. **B**
7. **C**	16. **D**	25. **A**	34. **B**	43. **D**
8. **B**	17. **B**	26. **D**	35. **B**	
9. **B**	18. **B**	27. **D**	36. **D**	

Description of Land

Recognized, uniform methods of land description are essential to proper contractual transactions involving land. If the land in a transaction cannot be identified, our legal system will not recognize the transaction as binding. Therefore, proper description of the land involved is an essential part of contracts of sale, deeds, leases, options, mortgages, listings, and virtually all other kinds of real estate contracts.

There are four generally accepted methods of land description in the United States:

1. Rectangular survey
2. Metes and bounds descriptions
3. Lot and block number descriptions
4. Monument or occupancy descriptions

The purpose of all of these is to *identify* real estate. Often, in the terminology of the real estate business, descriptions are called "legal descriptions," giving the impression that there is some particular formula that must be followed. Actually, the only legal point of any importance is that the description be *sufficient to identify the property.* If the property can be identified from the description given, then the description is good. Otherwise, no matter how elaborate it may appear, it is faulty.

Most description methods are designed to demonstrate to a surveyor a means of marking the outline of the land on the ground. Most descriptions do not include buildings; remember that real estate is land *and all attachments to it*, so a description of the land automatically includes all improvements, unless they are *specifically excluded.*

RECTANGULAR SURVEY DESCRIPTIONS

The U.S. government rectangular survey is used in the states indicated in Figure 7-1. If your state is *not* one of them, then you do not have to read this section and can skip to the next section, on metes and bounds.

The government rectangular survey divides the land into squares 6 miles on a side; these are called *townships.* Each township is identified with respect to its distance from the *base line* and the *principal meridian.* There are several sets of principal meridians and base lines throughout the country, so each principal meridian carries a name or number to distinguish it from all the others; each one has a single base line paired with it.

Principal meridians are imaginary lines that run north-south. Base lines are imaginary lines that run east-west. Parallel to the principal meridians and 6 miles apart from each other are other *meridians.* Parallel to the base line are other lines called *parallels*; these are also 6 miles apart. Altogether, this system of north-south meridians and east-west parallels cuts the map up into a grid of 6-mile squares, as in Figure 7-2.

The vertical (north-south) rows of townships are called *ranges*, and the horizontal (east-west) rows of townships are *tiers.* Each township can be identified by labeling the range and tier in which it is found. The ranges and tiers are numbered according to their distances and directions from the principal meridian, or the base line. For example, the principal meridian will have a row of townships on each side of it. The one to the east is called *Range 1 East*, while the one to the west is *Range 1 West.* Similarly, the tier immediately north of the base line is called *Tier 1 North*, while the one below it is *Tier 1 South.*

Figure 7-1.   Government Rectangular Survey

Figure 7-2. Six-Mile Square Grid

To specify a particular township, a description must state both the tier and the range in which the township appears. These specifications usually are given in the form of abbreviations, such as T3N (Tier 3 North) or R4W (Range 4 West). Figure 7-2 identifies a number of townships by this kind of description; note that you simply count the number of ranges (or tiers) from the principal meridian (or the base line) to the particular township, and specify the direction taken. For practice, try to identify all the unmarked townships in Figure 7-2.

Of course, most tracts of land are less than 6 square miles, so it becomes necessary to identify which *part* of the township is the specific piece of land under consideration. This is done by dividing the township into smaller and smaller parcels until the one of interest is all that is left.

All townships are divided into 1-mile squares, as shown in Figure 7-3. Since each township is 6 miles square, it will contain 36 square miles. Each of these is always numbered, as shown in Figure 7-3. Each square-mile tract is called a *section*. Section 1 in any township, then, is the square mile at the very northeast corner of the township; Section 2 is immediately west of Section 1, and so on. Section 21 will be in the fourth row from the top of the township and in the third column from the west. In other words, the north border of Section 21 is 3 miles south of the north boundary of the township; the east border of Section 21 is 3 miles west of the east boundary of the township.

As an example, let us assume that the township illustrated in Figure 7-3 is the one in Figure 7-2 with the sections drawn in; that is, it is T2N, R2E. If, then, we wanted to describe Section 21 of this township, we would write, "Sec. 21, T2N, R2E." We would also have to specify which principal meridian we were using, although in states with only one principal meridian it is not strictly necessary to identify the meridian in a valid description.

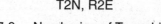

T2N, R2E

Figure 7-3. Numbering of Township Grids

Notice that for each principal meridian there is only *one* T2N, R2E. All other townships using that principal meridian will be in different ranges or tiers, or both. Furthermore, each township has only *one* Section 21. Therefore, a description such as "Sec. 21, T2N, R2E, 5th PM" describes a single square-mile tract of land in eastern Arkansas, on the Fifth Principal Meridian. "Sec. 21, T2N, R2E, Boise Meridian" describes a square-mile tract in southwestern Idaho.

If the tract of land under consideration is smaller than 1 square mile, we must further subdivide the section in which it appears. We do this by dividing the section into quarters or halves; if necessary, we further subdivide the resulting parts until we arrive at the tract we are considering. Figure 7-4 shows examples of how this is done. The entire section can be divided into four quarters: the northeast, northwest, southeast, and southwest quarters. These would be written as NE¼, NW¼, SE¼, and SW¼, respectively. In Figure 7-4 the SE¼ quarter is shown; the others have been further subdivided. The NW$^1/_4$ quarter has been divided into two halves, E½ and W½. The proper descriptions of these subdivisions would be E½, NW¼, Sec. 21, T2N, R2E and W½, NW¼, Sec. 21, T2N, R2E.

The SW¼ quarter of this section has been divided into a number of smaller parcels; the proper description of each is given. The smallest is the shaded tract NW¼, SW¼, NW¼, SW¼, Sec. 21, T2N, R2E. The NE$^1/_4$ quarter of the section has been divided slightly differently: the N½ is divided by the distance from the boundaries of N½, NE¼.

Each square mile contains 640 acres. The quarters, then, contain 160 acres each. Further subdivision yields smaller tracts that can be easily measured in terms of acreage; all the tracts subdivided in Figure 7-4 have the acreage indicated. In any case, it is a simple matter to determine acreage from most rectangular survey descriptions: multiply the series of fractions given in the description; then multiply the result by the 640 acres contained in the section. For example, the NW¼ quarter contains 160 acres: ¼ × 640 = 160. The very small tract cited in the preceding paragraph is NW¼, SW¼, NW¼, SW¼, so its acreage is ¼ × ¼ × ¼ × ¼ × 640 = 2½ acres.

Figure 7-4. Subdivision of a Small Section

Tracts such as those described in the N½, NE¼ subdivision aren't quite as easy to determine, since they aren't described entirely in fractions of the full section. For these, however, it is a relatively simple matter to determine the lengths of the sides in feet; then the total number of square feet can be determined. An acre contains 43,560 square feet; therefore by dividing the square footage of the entire tract by 43,560, we can obtain the acreage of the tract in question.

Sometimes a specific tract cannot be described using a single rectangular survey description; in such cases it is perfectly all right to use several descriptions, each for part of the tract, making sure that all the descriptions together will describe the entire tract. For example, the large L-shaped shaded tract in Figure 7-4 would be described as "E½, NW¼ and S½, NE¼; Sec. 21, T2N, R2E." Note, however, that it is almost always necessary that rectangular survey descriptions be of fairly regular tracts with straight sides. The boundaries almost always must run north-south or east-west. Usually the survey is not a good system for describing irregular tracts, tracts with curved or wandering boundaries, and very small tracts; these are better described using other methods.

One final feature of the rectangular survey description system must be noted: north-south lines on our planet are not parallel because they all meet at the poles. Therefore, the meridians must be adjusted every so often to keep them from getting too close together. This is done by shifting every *fourth* meridian, each 24 miles away from the base line. These meridians, called *guide meridians*, are shown in Figure 7-2. The parallels at which the adjustments take place, that is, every fourth parallel, are called *standard parallels*. Standard parallels and guide meridians are named to indicate their numbers and distance from the respective base line or principal meridian.

METES AND BOUNDS DESCRIPTIONS

Metes and bounds descriptions indicate to the surveyor how to locate the corners of a tract. By locating the corners, one also locates the sides, since they run from corner to corner. Following is a metes and bounds description of Lot 15 in Figure 7-5. This lot is shown enlarged in Figure 7-6.

BEGINNING at a point being the southeast corner of the intersection of Vicious Circle and Alongthe Avenue, thence one hundred and six and forty-hundredths feet (106.40′) north 90°0′0″ east, thence one hundred and twenty feet (120.00′) south 0°0′0″ east, thence seventy-three and fourteen-hundredths feet (73.14′) south 90°0′0″ west, thence one hundred and twenty-four and fifty-three hundredths feet (124.53′) north 15°29′26″ west to the point of beginning; said tract lying and being in Gotham City, Copperwire County, Montana.

Note that a metes and bounds description must have the following components:

1. A properly identified *point of beginning*.
2. *Distance* and *direction* given for each side.

The description above contains all these. The point of beginning is identified as the intersection of two public streets; this is permissible, since a person may always consult the public records to find out exactly where these streets are. From that point, the surveyor is directed to proceed a certain distance, and in a certain direction. By following this description, he can arrive *only* at the specific points described, and these points are the corners of the lot. He will have outlined the particular plot of land in question by following this description; thus it is a good description.

The accuracy of the description is the only point of any consequence in a court of law. The description can progress clockwise or counterclockwise. Directions (north, south, etc.) may be capitalized or not. The description should include, of course, the name of the city (or county) and the state in which the real estate is located.

Figure 7-5.   Block D, Stripmine Estates, Gotham City, Copperwire County, Montana

Often a metes and bounds description may include more language than in the fairly minimal example provided here. Common additional elements are as follows:

1. To define the street rights-of-way, lot lines of adjacent lots, and so on, along which directed lines travel. Example: ". . . thence one hundred feet (100.00') north 63°30'0" west along the southern right-of-way boundary of Thirtieth Street, thence one hundred feet (100.00') north 88°0'0" west along the southern boundary of Lot 44, . . .".

2. To end each direction with the words ". . . to an iron pin . . ." or ". . . to a point . . ." or some other language suggesting that there is a mark on the ground to refer to. More often than not, there is no marker now in existence, though at the time the lot originally was laid out, many years ago, there indeed was. However, over the years these things disappear, erode, and otherwise become invisible.

Figure 7-6.   Lot 15, Block D, Stripmine Estates

3. To refer to actual things on the ground that can be found. If these things are relatively permanent and obvious, they are referred to as *monuments.* Examples: large, identifiable trees, visible streambeds, milestones, stone walls or other constructions, and occasionally genuine monuments placed at a location by the original surveyors for the very purpose of serving as references for descriptions. One serious point to keep in mind is that, if monuments are mentioned in a metes and bounds description, and the directed lines and monuments conflict, then the monuments rule. This means that, if the distance and measurement given say to go 200 feet due north to a certain milestone and the milestone actually is 193 feet, 6 degrees west of north, the latter measurement will rule in the description. For this reason, the inclusion of too many monuments in a description can sometimes cause confusion or error.

4. To add the statement ". . . containing *x* number of acres (square feet, etc.), more or less." This is convenient, but unnecessary; given the measurements and directions supplied by the description, it is always possible to calculate the area of the parcel if need be. The major reason for including the acreage is to protect the grantor against an error in the description that might indicate the transfer of much more (or much less) land. For example, if the description mentions a tract of 100 acres, and the tract actually is only 10 acres, the inclusion of a statement of area would be an immediate indication that the description contained a mistake.

The point of beginning of a metes and bounds description must use a point of reference outside the description of the property itself. In urbanized areas, it is very common to use the nearest intersection of public roads or streets, as in the sample description given. [If that description had been of Lot 14, which is not at the corner, it would have begun as follows:

"BEGINNING at a point on the south boundary line of the right-of-way of Vicious Circle, one-hundred-and-six and forty-hundredths feet (106.40') east of the southeast corner of the intersection of the rights-of-way of Vicious Circle and Alongthe Avenue. . . ."] In government survey states, a point of reference can be a survey location. Many states also have had their own surveys made in all or part of the state, and reference points from these may be used. Indeed, one may refer to any point on earth that can be located using instructions from any publicly recorded document. Once the reference point has been defined, the actual beginning point of the parcel in question is identified by distance and direction from the reference point.

Distance may be expressed in any known unit of measurement, although the most common by far is feet. Directions are given according to the compass. However, in most parts of the United States there are two "sets" of compass directions: magnetic bearings and true bearings. Magnetic bearings refer to the magnetic poles; true bearings, to the geographic poles. If magnetic bearings are used, then, in order to achieve true bearings, they must be corrected for the location at which the survey was made and the date. The reason is that the magnetic pole is not at the same location as the true pole; furthermore, the magnetic pole "drifts" and so is located slightly differently at different times.

By convention, compass bearings are described as numbers of degrees east or west (or south). There are 360 degrees in a full circle, 90 degrees in a right (square) angle. The symbol for *degree* is °, so 90° means 90 degrees. Each degree is divided into 60 *minutes* (symbol:') and each minute is composed of 60 *seconds* (symbol:"). The statement N 44°31'56" E is read as "North 44 degrees, 31 minutes, 56 seconds east."

Due east is exactly 90° away from north, toward the east; it is written as N 90° E. "Due" northeast is half that distance from true north, written as N 45° E. If directions are south of due east or west, they are measured by their deviations from true south. A direction slightly north of due west would be N 89° W; if it were slightly *south* of due west, it would be S 89° W. These and several other examples of various directions are shown in Figure 7-7.

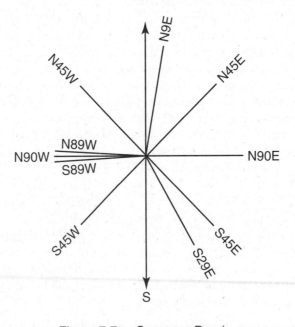

Figure 7-7.   Compass Bearings

LOT AND BLOCK NUMBER

Lot and block number descriptions are common in urban areas where *plats* of subdivisions must be recorded. A plat is a map of the manner in which land is divided into lots; Figure 7-5 is an example of a plat. If the plat is a matter of public record (i.e., has been recorded), it is quite sufficient to refer to it for the legal description of property it illustrates. For example, it would be enough to describe Lot 15 on that plat as "Lot 15, Block D, Stripmine Estates, Gotham City, Copperwire County, Montana." Given this description, a surveyor could look up this subdivision in the records, find the plat of Block D, and from it get all the information he needed to do an accurate survey of the lot.

Lot and block number descriptions are very simple to do and take little space. Therefore, in areas where the records are such that they can be used, they are very popular. It should be pointed out also that reference can be made to *any* recorded document in the preparation of a description. Thus, if lot and block descriptions are impossible, it may be possible simply to refer to a previous deed or other recorded instrument in which a description of the property appears. This should be done however, only if the previous description is exactly the same as the one to be used at present; even so, it is potentially inconvenient in that, whereas copies of plats are easily obtained, and often can be received directly from developers and dealers, old deeds and other documents have to be dug out of the records.

MONUMENT AND OCCUPANCY DESCRIPTIONS

Monument descriptions are similar superficially to metes and bounds descriptions. The difference is that monument descriptions rely entirely upon monuments and specify no distance or direction, except from the monuments themselves to important points of the survey. A monument description might read: "Beginning at the intersection of Highway 9 and County Road 445, thence along the right-of-way of County Road 445 to the end of a stone wall; thence from the end of the stone wall through the center of a large, freestanding oak tree to the center of a streambed; thence along the streambed to the point where the streambed intersects Highway 9; thence along Highway 9 to the point of beginning." Since this description can be followed in order to outline the property, it is a valid description, but there is always the risk that the monuments may move or disappear. These descriptions are used mainly for large rural tracts of relatively inexpensive land, where a full survey may entail much greater expense than is warranted by the usefulness of the land.

Occupancy descriptions are very vague: "All that land known as the Miller Farm"; "All that land bordered by the Grant Farm, Happy Acres Home for the Elderly, the Ellis Farm, and State Highway 42." With this kind of description one must rely on the community's general impression of what constitutes the Miller Farm, the Grant Farm, and so on. Occupancy descriptions are very weak because they indicate no specific boundaries at all. A similar situation arises when street addresses are used as descriptions. Although houses and other buildings usually have address numbers visibly displayed on them, these give no indication at all of the actual extent of the property.

LIMITS OF DESCRIPTIONS

It is important to understand that descriptions, while they may accurately describe land, do not provide any guarantee of *title* to that land. A deed that contains a perfectly usable description of a tract of land may be worthless if the grantor has little or no right to convey title to that particular tract. The mere fact that a deed or contract of sale contains a particular description does not guarantee to the buyer that his claim to the described land will hold up in court. It can only do so if the seller actually had the legal right to transfer the land she described. One cannot sell, give, or otherwise bargain away what one does not own.

Questions on Chapter 7

Answer questions 1–13 only if your state uses the government rectangular survey. If it does not, skip to question 14 and begin there.

1. What is the proper description of the township whose *northeast* corner is 36 miles west of the principal meridian and 6 miles south of the base line?
   - (A) T2S, R7W
   - (B) T1S, R7W
   - (C) T1S, R6W
   - (D) T2S, R6W

2. What is the proper description of the section whose *northwest* corner is 5 miles east of the principal meridian and 2 miles north of the base line?
   - (A) Sec. 23, T1N, R1E
   - (B) Sec. 24, T1N, R1E
   - (C) Sec. 29, T1N, R1E
   - (D) Sec. 25, T1N, R1E

3. How many miles apart are the guide meridians?
   - (A) 12
   - (B) 4
   - (C) 24
   - (D) 18

4. The east-west lines at which guide meridians are adjusted are
   - (A) adjustment lines
   - (B) base line extensions
   - (C) parallels of adjustment
   - (D) standard parallels

5. The number of acres in 1 square mile is
   - (A) 640
   - (B) 5,280
   - (C) 1,000
   - (D) 160

Questions 6–13 concern Figure A, shown below.

Figure A.
Diagram of a Section

6. How many acres does the tract marked A contain?
   - (A) 640
   - (B) 160
   - (C) 80
   - (D) 40

7. How many acres does the tract marked B contain?
   - (A) 640
   - (B) 160
   - (C) 80
   - (D) 40

8. How many acres does the tract marked C contain?
   - (A) 640
   - (B) 160
   - (C) 80
   - (D) 40

9. The description of Tract A is
   - (A) NW¼, NW¼
   - (B) N½, NE¼
   - (C) W½, NW¼
   - (D) W½, N½

10. The description of Tract B is
    - (A) NE¼
    - (B) NE½
    - (C) NE¼, NE¼
    - (D) NE¼, NE¼, N½

11. The description of Tract C is
    - (A) SE¼, SE¼
    - (B) SW¼, SW¼
    - (C) SE¼, SW¼
    - (D) SW¼, SE¼

12. Assume that the illustrated section is Section 8 of a particular township. What section would you be in if you traveled exactly $2\frac{3}{4}$ miles due *south* from the *center* of Section 8?
   (A) Sec. 11
   (B) Sec. 12
   (C) Sec. 20
   (D) Sec. 29

13. Assume that the southeast corner of the section is exactly 28 miles south of the base line and 11 miles west of the principal meridian. In what township is it located?
   (A) T2W, R5S
   (B) T5S, R2W
   (C) T6S, R2W
   (D) T6S, R3W

The remaining questions concern description techniques used in all states.

14. The line behind which all buildings on a lot must be placed is called the
   (A) set line
   (B) setback, or building line
   (C) construction limit
   (D) backup, or setdown line

15. Which of the following is most nearly due west?
   (A) N 88° W
   (B) N 79°66'43" W
   (C) S 89°58'3" W
   (D) W 0°4' N

16. Which of the following would *not* be a proper way to begin a metes and bounds description of Lot 10?
   (A) "Beginning at the southwest corner of Lot 10 . . ."
   (B) "Beginning at the street intersection nearest Lot 10 . . ."
   (C) "Beginning at a point 110 feet northwest of Lot 10 . . ."
   (D) all of the above

17. "All that land known as the Jones Farm" is which kind of description?
   (A) invalid
   (B) occupancy
   (C) metes only
   (D) rural

Questions 18–23 refer to the lot shown in Figure B.

Figure *B.* Block E, Quagmire Village, Metropolis, Elko County, Nevada

18. Which lot has the most footage on Circuit Court?
   (A) Lot 10
   (B) Lot 18
   (C) Lot 20
   (D) Lot 21

19. Which lot has the most street footage?
   (A) Lot 7
   (B) Lot 18
   (C) Lot 20
   (D) Lot 21

20. How many lots border on Circuit Court?
   (A) 9
   (B) 15
   (C) 16
   (D) 21

21. How many lots have sides that are *not* straight?
    (A) 8   (C) 10
    (B) 9   (D) 11

22. How many lots front on more than one street?
    (A) 1   (C) 3
    (B) 2   (D) 4

23. Which lots have the *fewest* straight sides?
    (A) Lots 10, 11, 14, 15, 16, 17, 20
    (B) Lots 10, 11, 14, 16
    (C) Lots 11, 14, 16
    (D) Lots 11, 16

24. A parcel of land is square, ½ mile by ½ mile. How many acres does it contain?
    (A) 40   (C) 320
    (B) 160   (D) 640

25. A township is _____ square mile(s).
    (A) 1   (C) 36
    (B) 4   (D) 64

26. Baselines in the rectangular survey method run
    (A) north and south   (C) northwest
    (B) northeast   (D) east and west

27. The POB in a metes and bounds survey is
    (A) period of basis
    (B) position of boundary
    (C) point of beginning
    (D) pier of boarding

28. The perimeter is 6 miles for each side. The number of townships is
    (A) 1   (C) 3
    (B) 2   (D) 4

29. The perimeter of half a township is _____ miles.
    (A) 36   (C) 4
    (B) 18   (D) 1

30. The principal type of legal land description used in Florida and the United States (except the thirteen original colonies) is
    (A) street numbers
    (B) lot and block
    (C) metes and bounds
    (D) government survey

31. Principal meridians are imaginary lines that run
    (A) north-south   (C) northeast
    (B) east-west   (D) southwest

32. Developers subdivide land and assign lot and block numbers to identify lots in the subdivision. This is a legal description known as
    (A) a block party
    (B) recorded plat description
    (C) developer plat
    (D) lot survey method

33. A township is
    (A) 36 square miles   (C) a small city
    (B) one square mile   (D) 640 acres

34. What is the type of legal description that uses imaginary lines of meridians and baselines?
    (A) metes and bounds
    (B) recorded plat
    (C) lot and block
    (D) rectangular survey

ANSWERS

1. **A**	8. **D**	15. **C**	22. **C**	29. **B**
2. **D**	9. **C**	16. **D**	23. **D**	30. **D**
3. **C**	10. **A**	17. **B**	24. **B**	31. **A**
4. **D**	11. **D**	18. **C**	25. **C**	32. **B**
5. **A**	12. **D**	19. **D**	26. **D**	33. **A**
6. **C**	13. **B**	20. **B**	27. **C**	34. **D**
7. **B**	14. **B**	21. **C**	28. **A**	

CHAPTER 8

Contracts of Sale

A contract for the sale of real estate describes the rights and obligations of the purchaser(s) and seller(s) of real estate. Days, weeks, or months later, at a ceremony called a *closing*, or *settlement*, the seller(s) will deliver a deed that transfers legal title to the property; the purchaser(s) will provide payment for the property as described in the contract of sale.

A contract of sale for real estate is *"the deal."* This means that all the provisions that the parties want, all the "ifs, ands, or buts," must be set forth in this contract; all the negotiation, "wheeling and dealing," "give and take," and such have to occur and be settled *before* the contract of sale exists. Once there is a contract of sale, it is too late for any more negotiation; all the parties to the agreement must abide by it, and none of them can change anything in it unless all other parties agree to the change. Therefore, it's important that the parties to this contract make sure that all the conditions and requirements that they want with regard to the sale and purchase of the real estate are contained in the sale contract.

UNDERSTANDING CONTRACTS OF SALE

It is possible to sell property merely by delivery of a deed in exchange for payment and thus bypass the contract of sale. However, the parties, especially the buyer, face a lot of risk. A title search must be performed to satisfy the buyer that the seller can give ownership, and time is required for such a search. The buyer may also need time to arrange financing. Most lenders will consider real estate loans only after they have studied the contract of sale. In short, it is rare for a transfer of real estate to be completed without such a contract. Furthermore, it is of paramount importance that all parties involved in a transaction understand their contractual obligations and privileges.

Upon completion of the contract of sale, the purchaser (*vendee*) receives an "equitable" title. Equity, in law, attempts to treat things as they should be to be fair and considers the purchaser to have "equitable title," although legal title remains with the seller (*vendor*) until closing. Therefore, if there is a casualty loss—a fire, for example—before closing, the risk may be upon the purchaser. However, considering that equity is intended to be fair, the risk of loss before closing should not pass automatically to the purchaser in all instances. There are situations in which the seller should be responsible and courts will hold him to be so. To avoid potential problems concerning risk of loss, the contract of sale should specify who has the burden of loss prior to closing and which party is obligated to complete the transaction and to receive the proceeds from insurance.

The Statute of Frauds requires that contracts for the sale of real estate be in writing to be enforceable. The *parol evidence* rule prevents oral testimony from being introduced when it conflicts with better (written) evidence. Consequently, care should be exercised in the preparation of a contract of sale.

A contract of sale should contain any *contingency clauses*, or *contingencies*, that the parties want. These "what if?" provisions often allow a buyer or seller to cancel the deal without penalty if something does or doesn't happen (the *if* part). For example, the seller may have her home on the market because her employer is transferring her, but wants to be able to cancel the deal *if* the transfer falls through. A buyer may need to sell his own home in order to be able to buy the seller's property, so he wants to be able to cancel the deal *if* he can't make the sale of his own property within a reasonable time. A great many homebuying contracts of sale are *contingent upon financing*; this means that the buyer can cancel the deal *if* he is unable to get a suitable mortgage loan. Many preprinted contracts of sale have common contingencies already written into them: The buyer can cancel the deal *if* the seller can't provide clear title, *if* the property is severely damaged before closing, *if* termite infestation is found. The seller can cancel the deal *if* the buyer doesn't get financing approval within a certain time.

Many states require that the seller provide the buyer with a *disclosure* of certain conditions, defects, and so on, of the property; if there aren't any, then the seller must provide the buyer with a statement that no such conditions exist. Usually the state mandates a certain form upon which the disclosure is made. If possible, the disclosure must be made available to a prospective buyer before an offer is made, usually when the first contact between prospect and seller and/or listing broker occurs. In a brokered transaction, such disclosure normally will be provided to the broker when the property is listed. The broker then will provide a copy of it to all potential buyers who examine the property. If the transaction is not brokered, it is the seller's responsibility to provide the disclosure to all potential buyers.

A deposit, or *earnest money*, is not necessarily a legal requirement of a contract of sale (the parties' promises to perform in the future usually are sufficient as the required consideration), but is very common that the buyer put down a cash deposit at the time the contract of sale is agreed upon. The function of earnest money is to serve as evidence of his good-faith intentions to perform under the contract. Some states, however, are fussier about the term *earnest money* and specify that it has certain meaning. For example, in some states, if the deposit is called "earnest money," the buyer may abandon the contract at no penalty, except forfeiture of the deposit, and/or the seller can abandon the contract by returning the buyer's deposit and, usually, an additional sum (such as an amount equal to the buyer's earnest money). In these states, therefore, in order to require that buyer and seller go through with the contract, any deposit must be specified to be something (such as a prepayment toward the purchase price) that is *not* what the state defines as earnest money. Check the law in your state.

REQUIREMENTS OF A VALID CONTRACT OF SALE

To assist you in learning about contracts of sale, get a copy of one from a local real estate brokerage office or buy a "generic" one; they are usually available in good stationery stores. You might also be able to download one from a local brokerage's web site or some other source. Note that in some states these contracts may be called something different from contract of sale (in Arkansas, for example, a real estate contract of sale is called *offer and acceptance*). Don't worry about that, though, because whatever they are called where you live, they still are generically contracts of sale.

Like any contract, contracts of sale must conform to the general requirements of contracts as we have already described in Chapter 6. Within contracts of sale themselves, there are six essentials that also must be observed:

1. The interests and identities of the parties
2. Legal description of the real estate
3. The price and how it is to be paid
4. Contingencies and other terms of the sale
5. Settlement date
6. Signatures of the parties

1. Interests and Identities of the Parties

Who is (are) the buyer(s)? Who is (are) the seller(s)? These are the parties to the contract. The name(s) of the seller(s) should be as they are on their recorded deed for the property. The name(s) of the buyer(s) should be as they will be on the new deed.

2. Legal Description of the Real Estate

The real estate has to be described; methods of describing real estate were presented in Chapter 7. Simple descriptions (lot and block number descriptions; uncomplicated rectangular survey descriptions) should be written into the contract, but whoever is writing it should take special care to make sure the description is *accurate*.

If the description is complicated, the chances of error are high, especially with metes and bounds descriptions with all their numbers, directions, and so on. A complicated description often won't be written into the contract but will be *incorporated by reference;* the location of an *existing* accurate version is described instead. Most commonly, the referred document will be one that already is in the public records; the obvious one is the existing recorded deed of the sellers. (If theirs also incorporates a description by reference, then you refer to whatever document that deed refers to.) Because the public records are open to anyone, it is easy to find the referred document and get the description from it. An example of a reference description could be ". . . all that land described in deed from X to Y, dated June 17, 1941, page 133, book 122 of the Coppermine County, Montana, public records." This tells anyone who reads the contract exactly where to find the description. The description by reference can be used only if the real estate currently being transferred is *exactly the same* as described in the referenced description. If any changes have been made to boundaries of the land, then a new description must be written.

Note that land descriptions don't contain any information about improvements to the land (house, drive, etc.). That's okay; remember, real estate is *land and all permanent attachments to it,* so if you acquire the described land you're also getting whatever is on it.

3. The Price and How It Is to Be Paid

The exact price must be described. Usually a buyer doesn't have all the cash to pay for the property and must secure a mortgage loan to be able to complete the purchase. The contract should describe the actual cash amount to be provided by the buyer(s) and the amount of borrowed money that they will provide. If the seller is willing to accept an IOU for all or part of the purchase price (a *purchase money mortgage,* or what we call *seller financing*), that should be included, too. It would be wise for the buyer(s) to insist on including the desired terms of the mortgage loan they need: the maximum interest rate they will pay, the term (15 years, 30 years, etc.), and any other loan terms they consider important—as well as a stipulation that if they can't find the desired loan within a reasonable time, they have the right to cancel the purchase with no penalty.

4. Contingencies and Other Terms of the Sale

These are the "what-ifs" and other specific requirements that the parties agree to. We described one contingency above: "what if" the buyers can't get the mortgage loan they want? Then they can back out of the deal without losing anything. Many of these are written into standard contract forms: the seller must provide "good and marketable" title; the buyer must apply for a loan within ___ days. What if the buyer wants to move in *before* the settlement date (or the seller wants to stay on for a while *after* the settlement date)? Should rent be paid? How much?

5. Settlement Date

A *settlement date* (in some places it's called the *closing date*) must be in a contract of sale. This is the deadline by which the contract requirements should be completed, the deadline by which the buyer must pay for the property and the seller must provide the deed. Without a settlement date there isn't a requirement that the contract be completed; either party could dawdle all they want. If it turns out that the date in the contract is too optimistic (the parties don't have time to complete everything they have to do), the settlement date can always be amended to a later one.

6. Signatures of the Parties

As with any contract, all parties to it must sign it; this is the legal way of showing that they all agree to it. Signatures to a contract of sale don't have to be notarized.

If you look at a contract of sale provided by a brokerage firm, you also will see a section in which the commission to the broker, and when it is to be paid, is described. (Some generic forms from stationery stores include this part, too.) This section actually is a separate contract between seller(s) and broker. It isn't really necessary because their listing contract already obligates the seller to pay the broker, but most brokerage firms include it in their contract-of-sale forms anyway.

Preprinted contracts of sale are almost always used for sales of homes. Suppose there is something already written into the preprinted contract, but the parties *don't* want that part to apply to them? Then we simply cross out that part and have the parties initial or sign near that part of the contract form to acknowledge that they agree to the alteration.

NEGOTIATION (OFFER, COUNTEROFFER, ACCEPTANCE)

Contracts of sale (or any other kind) just don't pop out of the air, ready to go. They are the result of *negotiation*. Negotiation of a contract of sale for real estate usually begins with an *offer* from an interested potential buyer. (The person making the offer is the *offeror*; the person receiving it is the *offeree*.) The buyer probably knows what the seller wants (price, terms, etc.), but very often the buyer won't agree to everything, so the offer will be somewhat different from the seller's desires. The seller will consider the buyer's offer and can either accept it, turn it down, or turn it down and make a "counteroffer" back to the buyer. Now it's the buyer's turn; she may accept the seller's offer, turn it down, or make another offer back to the seller. This can go on for several cycles; eventually either the parties will agree on a final deal, and a contract will be made, or they may decide that it's hopeless and will stop negotiating and go their own ways.

A key element of the negotiation process is that *no one involved is obligated to anyone until a contract exists*. No one is *required* to negotiate; no one is *required* to keep on negotiating once the process has begun. Anyone involved may terminate the process simply by refusing to go on with it. The law lays down some simple rules for the negotiation process.

Once an offer is *accepted*, it isn't an offer anymore: it has become a *contract*. Once a contract exists, the negotiation process ends; because the parties have finally come to an agreement, there's nothing more to discuss. If a party later on decides that he wants some more conditions, it's too late. The contract already exists, and he must abide by it. Of course, he can always approach the other parties and ask to amend the existing contract, but the other parties have no obligation to reopen negotiations.

During negotiation, only one offer can exist at any given moment in time. If A makes an offer to buy B's real estate, an offer exists. It is up to B to decide what to do.

1. She can accept A's offer, and thus create a contract.
2. She can reject A's offer, in which case no offer exists anymore.
3. She can make a counteroffer back to A, in which case A's offer doesn't exist anymore. Now there is *another* offer on the table, from B to A. Making a counteroffer therefore means that two things are being done simultaneously: the offer that was "on the table" is *rejected*, and a new offer is made "the other way."

There's one other thing going on. An offer may be withdrawn *at any time, so long as it has not been accepted*. While B is pondering A's offer, A can, at any time, notify B that the offer is withdrawn. If that happens, that's the end of the offer: it no longer exists. But if, before then, B notifies A that she accepts the offer, the offer doesn't exist anymore *because it has become a contract*. You can't "withdraw" a contract.

If an offer is rejected, it doesn't exist anymore and can't be "resurrected" later on. Consider the following conversation:

Jane: Mike, I'll give you $150,000 for your house.
Mike: No, I need at least $175,000.
Jane: Forget it. That's too much.
Mike: Okay, I'll take the $150,000.

Is there now a contract for Jane to buy Mike's house for $150,000?

NO! Let's take it step by step. First, Jane made an offer to buy Mike's house for $150,000. Mike then counteroffered the house to Jane for $175,000. By doing this, he *rejected* Jane's offer for $150,000 and then replaced her offer to him with *his offer to her* for $175,000. Jane then rejected Mike's offer to her. But she didn't make any other offer back to him. At that point there was no offer on the table at all. When Mike said he'd "take the $150,000," no contract came into being because there wasn't an offer from Jane anymore for him to accept. He had already *rejected* Jane's original offer, so it didn't exist anymore. His statement "Okay, I'll take the $150,000" actually creates a *new* offer *from him to Jane* to sell her the house for $150,000. She doesn't have to accept it. If she does, then Mike and Jane will have a contract. If she says something like "I've changed my mind, I don't want your house," then she has, in turn, rejected Mike's new offer, and there's no offer on the table.

This is a very important aspect of the law of offer and acceptance: *until a contract exists no one has any obligation to anyone else!* If you look at a preprinted contract of sale, you will probably see language on the order of ". . . this offer will remain open until _____." You're supposed to put a date, or a time of day and a date, in the blank space. What does this mean? Must whoever made the offer sit and wait until the deadline to see if the other party accepts the offer? Is that other party guaranteed that length of time to ponder the offer? *NO!* Because this is an offer, no one is obligated to anything. The offeror can withdraw the offer at any time until the offeree accepts it. The only way this language can be interpreted is to mean that if the deadline arrives and the offeree hasn't responded to the offer, then the offer will automatically be *withdrawn* at that time. In effect, this provision is putting a limited lifetime on the offer, and nothing more.

Many real estate agents are apparently unaware of this part of the law. Both your authors have heard of situations when someone wanted to withdraw an offer (maybe they got a better one in the meantime) and the licensee told them, "You can't do that; you've agreed to leave the offer open until that time." This is wrong and could expose the licensee to a lawsuit.

If an offer is accepted by the offeree, it doesn't become a contract until the offeror (or the offeror's agent) has been *notified* of the acceptance. The law says you can't be held to a contract if you don't know that it exists. Because notifying an agent is the same as notifying that agent's principal, if a buyer tells the listing agent that he or she will accept a counteroffer from the seller, the contract exists at that point. Or, if a buyer's agent is notified that the seller accepts an offer from the buyer, there is a contract. (In either case, a professional licensee will immediately call his or her principals to notify them of the acceptance.) Notification doesn't have to be in writing; it can be oral, such as by phone.

Finally, it is common practice, especially in brokered transactions, for offers between potential buyer and seller to be made using contract-of-sale forms. Typically, a buyer wants to make an offer on a home. The buyer (or agent involved) will fill out a contract-of-sale form, with all the terms that the buyer wants written into it. The buyer signs it, and it is submitted to the seller. If the seller accepts the offer, he signs it, and a contract exists once the buyer is notified. The seller presumably is happy because he got an offer he was willing to accept. The buyer is happy because the seller has agreed to all the terms, conditions, price, and so on, that she wanted. Most of the time, though, the offeree does *not* agree with all the terms of the offer. If a counteroffer is made, it is common practice to cross out the parts the offeree doesn't like, write the desired changes in the margins of the form, and add anything else that is desired the same way. The offeree initials or signs by all those changes, signs the document, and submits it to the offeror. (Because the counteroffer rejects the original offer, the original offeror and offeree now have changed places.)

Of course, the new offeree may not like all the changes and might then cross out more stuff, write in more stuff, initial or sign *those* changes, and send it back as a new offer. This process can go back and forth again and again; the cumulative marginal changes and cross-outs can result in a contract form that is becoming an unreadable mess. When it gets to that point, it certainly is good practice to prepare a fresh form with the terms and conditions written into it reflecting the current state of the negotiations.

PARTS OF A REAL ESTATE CONTRACT OF SALE

A contract of sale for real estate will normally contain certain parts. These parts and their purposes are as follows:

PART	PURPOSE
Parties	States the names of the seller (vendor) and buyer (vendee).
Property description	Provides a legal or an adequate description of the subject property and the fixtures included.
Sales price	States the amount to be paid at closing in cash and from the proceeds of financing.
Financing conditions	Purchaser stipulates acceptable conditions of financing, including the type of loan, loan-to-value ratio, interest rate, monthly payments.
Earnest money	Notes the amount of the good-faith deposit presented to the seller or his agent. Also called *hand money* or *escrow money*.
Type of deed	Describes the type of deed to be given at closing (see Chapter 9).
Title evidence	Describes the type of evidence to be considered satisfactory assurance that the seller can give title.
Title approval	Describes the rights of purchaser and seller in the event that the purchaser objects to a flaw in the title.
Property condition	States whatever changes (if any) are required to be made to the property.
Prorations	Calls for the proration of prepaid or unpaid taxes, insurance, rents, etc., between buyer and seller (see Chapter 18).
Loss	Affixes responsibility for casualty losses until closing.
Possession	Establishes a date for possession.
Closing	Establishes a date for closing.
Broker	Acknowledges the existence of a real estate broker, specifies the commission rate, and identifies the principal who will pay the commission.
Default	Describes the obligations of parties in the event one fails to perform.
Contingencies	Describes any "what if" provisions of the contract, and the conditions under which the parties may cancel the contract without penalty.
Miscellaneous provisions	States whatever other provisions buyer and seller agree upon.
Signatures	Principals, brokers, escrow agents.

Questions on Chapter 8

1. Joe offers to buy Susie's house for $225,000. Susie examines Joe's offer and then offers to sell her house to Joe for $250,000. Which of the following is true?
   (A) An offer from Susie to Joe now exists.
   (B) No offer exists.
   (C) Two offers exist: one from Joe to Susie, one from Susie to Joe.
   (D) A contract between Joe and Susie now exists.

2. The law that requires contracts for the sale of real estate to be in writing to be enforceable is the
   (A) Statute of Frauds
   (B) Statute of Limitations
   (C) Statute of Liberty
   (D) parol evidence rule

3. A person who has the power to sign the name of his principal to a contract of sale is a(n)
   (A) special agent   (C) tenant in common
   (B) optionee   (D) attorney-in-fact

4. A valid contract of purchase or sale of real property must be signed by the
   (A) broker   (C) seller only
   (B) agent and seller   (D) buyer and seller

5. Hand money paid upon the signing of an agreement of sale is called
   (A) an option   (C) earnest money
   (B) a recognizance   (D) a freehold estate

6. Joe made an offer to buy Susie's house. The offer says, "This offer will remain open until noon, October 22, 2014." It is now 3 P.M., October 21, 2014. Which of the following is true?
   (A) If Susie does not respond by the deadline, the offer will become a contract.
   (B) Susie must wait until after noon on October 22, 2014, before she can submit a counteroffer.
   (C) Joe must give Susie until noon, October 22, 2014, to consider his offer.
   (D) If Joe has changed his mind, he may now withdraw the offer.

7. A seller of real estate is also known as the
   (A) vendee   (C) vendor
   (B) grantor   (D) grantee

8. In any real estate contract of sale there must be
   (A) an offer and acceptance
   (B) a leasing arrangement
   (C) a mortgage loan
   (D) prepayment of taxes

9. If, upon receipt of an offer to purchase under certain terms, the seller makes a counteroffer, the prospective purchaser is
   (A) bound by his original offer
   (B) bound to accept the counteroffer
   (C) bound by the agent's decision
   (D) relieved of his original offer

10. A contract that has no force or effect is said to be
    (A) voidable
    (B) void
    (C) inconsequential
    (D) a contract of uncertain sale

11. A sales agreement to be enforceable must have
    (A) the signature of the wife of a married seller
    (B) an earnest money deposit
    (C) competent parties
    (D) witnesses

12. A party to a contract of sale normally has the right to
    (A) change the provisions in the contract if it is convenient to her
    (B) change the provisions in the contract if it will save her money
    (C) back out of the contract if she finds a better deal
    (D) none of the above

13. Which of the following would *not* be a contingency clause in a sale contract?
    (A) The settlement will be within 90 days.
    (B) The seller can cancel the deal if the buyer cannot get suitable financing.
    (C) The buyer can cancel the deal if Aunt Minnie won't lend him $10,000.
    (D) The deal is off if the property is infested with termites.

14. Which of the following is *not* true?
    (A) A contract of sale must contain a legal description of the land being sold.
    (B) An unwritten contract of sale is not enforceable in court.
    (C) Once a contract of sale is signed, there is no way to avoid going through with the deal.
    (D) A contract of sale should specify a time limit by which the sale will be closed.

15. A purchase and sale contract included a financing contingency. The purchaser could not obtain the loan required. The purchaser
    (A) forfeits the earnest money
    (B) pays the broker
    (C) is refunded all earnest money
    (D) should not have agreed to buy

16. Simon submits a purchase and sale agreement through the seller's broker. It gives the seller 48 hours to accept. After 24 hours, Simon changes his mind and decides to withdraw the agreement. Simon
    (A) can withdraw anytime before he is notified of its acceptance
    (B) must give the seller the 48 hours, as promised
    (C) will lose his earnest money
    (D) must pay the broker's commission

17. Buyer and seller shake hands on a transaction for a house at $300,000. The contract is
    (A) illegal
    (B) voidable
    (C) unenforceable
    (D) express

18. A buyer's final inspection, usually performed before closing, is called
    (A) due diligence
    (B) due on sale
    (C) a walk-through
    (D) a pre-closing inspection

19. The buyer makes an offer in writing. The seller accepts the offer but makes a small, unimportant change before returning it. There is
    (A) no deal
    (B) a valid contract
    (C) further negotiation
    (D) offer and acceptance

20. A valid contract to purchase real estate must include
    (A) a credit report
    (B) an appraisal report
    (C) a title report
    (D) a legal description

21. Which of the following is a contract that a broker may prepare?
    (A) exclusive listing contract
    (B) purchase and sale agreement
    (C) net listing contract
    (D) all of the above

22. To be effective, a purchase and sale agreement must include
    (A) the purchase price and terms
    (B) the list price
    (C) the closing date
    (D) boilerplate language

23. Brokers may submit
    (A) listing agreements
    (B) purchase and sale contracts
    (C) options
    (D) all of the above

24. In a purchase and sale agreement, the closing date should be
    (A) within 10–15 days
    (B) within 16–20 days
    (C) within 21–30 days
    (D) clearly stated

25. _____ is used to substitute a new borrower, with the lender's approval.
    (A) Assignment
    (B) Assumption
    (C) Novation
    (D) Subject to mortgage

26. An inspection was permitted by a contingency clause to a contract of purchase and sale. The inspection report indicates that multiple repairs are needed, and the buyer doesn't want to purchase the property. Which of the following is true?
    (A) The buyer may get a refund of earnest money if repair costs exceed the limit stated in the contract.
    (B) The buyer must proceed with the purchase if the seller promises to pay for all repairs.
    (C) The buyer may apply the earnest money to the repairs.
    (D) The broker may pay for the repairs out of his or her commission.

27. A purchase and sale agreement signed by buyer and seller is
    (A) a valid contract
    (B) offer and acceptance
    (C) both A and B
    (D) neither A nor B

28. A contract for the purchase of real estate entered into by a 17-year-old is
    (A) enforceable
    (B) voidable by the 17-year-old
    (C) void
    (D) unenforceable

29. A signed purchase and sale agreement is
    (A) voidable by the buyer
    (B) voidable by the buyer with forfeit of any earnest money
    (C) an option
    (D) a binding contract

30. Two weeks after purchase, the buyer discovers oil on the property. The mineral rights are most likely
    (A) property of the state
    (B) owned by the buyer unless reserved by the seller in the deed
    (C) owned by the seller
    (D) subject to litigation

31. If the buyer defaults, the earnest money is usually used as
    (A) a commission to the broker
    (B) a return to the buyer
    (C) advance rent
    (D) liquidated damages

32. Herb is 17 when he signs a contract to lease a small house. After the property manager accepts his offer, the lease contract is
    (A) void
    (B) voidable by Herb
    (C) voidable by either party
    (D) illegal

33. Carol is buying a house and has 30 days in which to obtain a financing commitment as specified in the sales contract. The contract states that Carol must notify the seller within that period if she cannot arrange financing, or risk default if she does not close. The contract states that "time is of the essence" applies to financing approval. Which is true?
    (A) Carol can arrange financing at her convenience.
    (B) The financing approval is automatically extended.
    (C) The lender must check Carol's credit references.
    (D) Carol must adhere to the stated time frame, which will end at 11:59 P.M. on the 30th day.

34. Harry gives Sam a $5,000 payment and a written agreement stating that, on July 1 of the following year, Harry will purchase the property from Sam for $150,000 cash, or Sam may keep the money. This transaction is
    (A) a lease with an option to purchase
    (B) a purchase contract with a delayed settlement
    (C) an option agreement
    (D) a limited partnership

35. Sally has shown Rebecca 11 homes, and Rebecca has selected one and made an offer. An hour later Rebecca changes her mind. Which is true?
    (A) Rebecca has already committed to the first seller and cannot withdraw.
    (B) Rebecca may withdraw the offer but will forfeit the earnest money.
    (C) The broker earned a commission.
    (D) Rebecca may withdraw before the seller accepts the offer.

36. A fixture
    (A) is normally assumed to accompany a property that is sold
    (B) is always assumed to belong to the seller and may be removed
    (C) is usually sold separately from real estate with a bill of sale
    (D) is not considered real estate

37. One who has a right to sign the name of a principal to a contract of sale is
    (A) a special agent
    (B) an attorney-at-law
    (C) an attorney-in-fact
    (D) a broker with a listing

38. Which of the following is true under a contract of sale in which the date of occupancy is later than the settlement date?
    (A) The buyer does not acquire legal title upon settlement.
    (B) The contract should specify whether the seller is to pay rent to the buyer.
    (C) The buyer cannot obtain hazard insurance.
    (D) The seller is the legal owner until occupancy is ended.

39. A prospective purchaser has a legal right to demand which of the following?
    (A) A copy of the broker's employment contract with the seller.
    (B) The return of the earnest money deposit prior to seller's acceptance of the offer to purchase.
    (C) A copy of the plans and specifications of the home.
    (D) A copy of the seller's utility bills for the past year.

40. Which of the following is true regarding the assignment of a sales contract?
    (A) An assignment of the sales contract by the buyer is generally valid.
    (B) Only the original seller can assign rights.
    (C) Assignments relieve the assignor of all obligations.
    (D) Assignment automatically requires the consent of the seller.

ANSWERS

1. **A**	9. **D**	17. **C**	25. **C**	33. **D**
2. **A**	10. **B**	18. **C**	26. **A**	34. **C**
3. **D**	11. **C**	19. **A**	27. **C**	35. **D**
4. **D**	12. **D**	20. **D**	28. **B**	36. **A**
5. **C**	13. **A**	21. **D**	29. **D**	37. **C**
6. **D**	14. **C**	22. **A**	30. **B**	38. **B**
7. **C**	15. **C**	23. **D**	31. **D**	39. **B**
8. **A**	16. **A**	24. **D**	32. **B**	40. **A**

CHAPTER 9

Deeds

To transfer an interest in real estate during his lifetime, the owner (*grantor*) surrenders a *deed of conveyance* to another (the *grantee*). The deed of conveyance, also simply called a *deed*, is covered by the Statute of Frauds; consequently, it must be in writing to be enforceable. Deeds are contracts, and nothing more. They are *not* "title papers" similar to the official documents you get from the state showing that you are the owner of a particular car. Deeds are not "guaranteed" or "backed up" by any government entity. The deed transfers property rights, but those rights are only as "good" as the public records show that they are. Therefore, a deed should be recorded to give the public constructive notice of its existence. Any document recorded in the public records must be *acknowledged*; for most of us that means it must be *notarized*. Notarization is done by a *notary public*, someone who is licensed by the state to be a witness to the authenticity of signatures. In some counties, a few public officials (mayor, county manager, alderman, etc.) may also be authorized to acknowledge documents. The only guarantee provided by the recording entity (usually a county government) is that the recorded document is a true copy of the original; there is no government guarantee of the contents of the document.

TYPES OF DEEDS

There are two basic types of deeds—*warranty* (also known as *general warranty*) and *quitclaim*. Either type is adequate to convey the interest, if any, that the grantor has in property.

The warranty deed contains assurances by the grantor

1. That he has title to the property and the power to convey it (covenant of seizin).
2. That his title is good against claims by others (covenant of quiet enjoyment).
3. That the property is free of encumbrances except as specified (covenant against encumbrances).
4. That he will perform whatever else is necessary to make the title good (covenant of further assurances).
5. That he will forever defend the rights of the grantee (covenant of warranty forever).

The warranty deed is the best type of deed for a grantee to receive.

In contrast, the quitclaim deed carries no warranties whatsoever. The grantor gives up all of his rights to the property without even implying that he has or has ever had any such rights. Should the grantor be possessed of the property in fee simple absolute, then a quitclaim deed serves to transfer complete ownership. However, if a grantor owns nothing, that is exactly what a grantee will receive from the quitclaim deed. The quitclaim deed is usually used to clear up an imperfection in the title, called a *cloud on title*.

A cloud on title (also called a *title defect*) is a circumstance in which the public records are not perfectly clear about who owns or has rights to certain property rights. For example, Elrod wants to buy Sally Smith's real estate. The public records show that Sally, along with her brothers Melvin and Paul, inherited the property from their father some time ago. Sally insists that she is the sole owner, and there is an executor's deed that names only Sally as the grantee from the estate. So, according to the records, the "cloud" is that there is nothing to show that Melvin and Paul ever gave up their rights to inherit. What actually happened is that when their father died, the three siblings agreed that Sally would get the house, and Sally would give up to them her share of their father's stocks and bonds. But the executor failed to get quitclaim deeds for the house from each of the brothers to Sally. Now Sally must get, and record, quitclaim deeds from them to "clear" the title.

A deed that contains some but not all of the covenants of a warranty deed is a *special* or *limited warranty* deed. Special warranty deeds typically contain assurances only against claims that may have originated while that grantor held title. It does not protect against claims that originated previously.

Bargain and sale deeds contain no warranties, only an assurance that the grantor has an interest in the property. A grantor need not state precisely what his interest is or whether the property is unencumbered. It is up to the grantee to ascertain, prior to closing, the grantor's interest in the property.

There are many other types of deeds, including a *trustee's deed* (used to transfer property from a trust); a *referee's deed* in foreclosure; a *sheriff's deed*; and an *administrator's deed*. Most of these are used by persons who must transfer the title of someone else's property. In these situations, the authorized transferor does not wish to personally warranty title from all claims, so the deed given contains a limited warranty. Most of these are grouped into a category called *special warranty* deeds.

DEED REQUIREMENTS

The following elements must be present in a deed for it to be considered valid:

1. A legally competent grantor
2. A designated grantee
3. Consideration—even though only a token amount is shown
4. Words of conveyance
5. The interest being conveyed
6. A description of the property
7. Grantor's proper signature
8. Delivery of the deed and acceptance

PARTS OF A DEED

The traditional deed has the following five parts:

PART OF DEED	PURPOSE
1. Premises	Gives names of parties, exploratory facts, words of conveyance, consideration, legal description of the property
2. Habendum	Is the "to have and to hold" clause, which may describe a limit to the quantity of the estate being granted, such as "to have and to hold forever" or "to have and to hold for life"
3. Testimonium	Contains warranties (if any)
4. Execution	Contains date, signatures, and seal if applicable
5. Acknowledgment	Contains attestation by a public officer, usually a notary public, as to the genuineness of the grantor's signature. (Although acknowledgment is not required to transfer title, it is usually a requirement for the deed to be recorded.)

Figures 9-1 and 9-2 identify the relevant parts of a warranty deed and a quitclaim deed. Note that the quitclaim contains nothing that could technically be called a testimonium. This is so because the quitclaim contains no warranty. The grantee receives whatever interest the grantor may have in the property, but the nature of that interest usually is not stated. Since the grantor will defend against no claim but his own, the document itself is adequate evidence against him. Consequently, no warranty is included.

WARRANTY DEED

STATE OF GEORGIA,

.... County.

THIS INDENTURE, made this ....day of ....

in the year of our Lord Two Thousand and ....

Between...

of the State of............................and County of ....of the first part

and ....

of the State of............................and County of......................................of the second part.

　WITNESSETH: That the said part ....of the first part, for and in consideration of the sum of

....DOLLARS

in hand paid at and before the sealing and delivery of these presents, the receipt whereof is hereby acknowledged, ha....

granted, bargained, sold and conveyed and by these presents do.................grant, bargain, sell and convey unto the said

part ....of the second part, ...heirs and assigns, all that tract and parcel of land

lying and being in...

PREMISES

TO HAVE AND TO HOLD the said bargained premises, together with all and singular the rights, members and appur-

tenances thereof, to the same being, belonging or in any wise appertaining, to the only proper use, benefit and behoof

of ....the said part ....of the second part, ...heirs and assigns forever, IN FEE SIMPLE.

HABENDUM

　And the said part ....of the first part, for..heirs, executors and administrators

will warrant and forever defend the right and title to the above described property unto the said part ....of the

second part,................................heirs and assigns, against the lawful claims of all persons whomsoever.

TESTIMONIUM

　IN WITNESS WHEREOF, That the said part ....of the first part ha ....hereunto set ,......................hand........

and affixed ....seal ...., the day and year above written.

　Signed, sealed and delivered in the presence of:

....(Seal)

....(Seal)

....(Seal)

....(Seal)

....(Seal)

EXECUTION

**ACKNOWL-
EDGEMENT**

Figure 9-1.　Warranty Deed

QUIT-CLAIM DEED

STATE OF GEORGIA, ...County.

THIS INDENTURE, made this ....day of...in the year of our

Lord Two Thousand and ....

between ....of the first part,

and ....of the second part.

WITNESSETH: That the said part ....of the first part for and in consideration of the sum

of ....Dollars,

cash in hand paid, the receipt of which is hereby acknowledged, ...bargained, sold and do ......

by these presents bargain, sell, remise, release, and forever quit-claim to the said part ....of the

second part, ... heirs and assigns, all the right, title, interest, claim or demand which the said

part..................of the first part ha........or may have had in and to ....

PREMISES

with all the rights, members and appurtenances to the said described premises in anywise appertaining
or belonging.

TO HAVE AND TO HOLD the said described premises, unto the said part ....of the second

part heirs and assigns, so that neither the said part ....of the first part nor ....

heirs, nor any other person or persons claiming under ....shall at any time, claim or demand

any right, title or interest to the aforesaid described premises or its appurtenances.

HABENDUM

IN WITNESS WHEREOF, the said part..of the first part ha........hereunto set

hand ......and affixed ....seal, the day and year above written.

(NO TESTI-
MONIUM)

Signed, sealed and delivered in the presence of ....(Seal)

....(Seal)

ACKNOWL-
EDGEMENT

....(Seal)

....(Seal)

EXECUTION

Figure 9-2.   Quitclaim Deed

EXECUTION OF THE DEED

To be considered complete, a deed must be signed by the grantor and delivered to the grantee or delivered in escrow (see below). Occasionally, problems arise when an undelivered deed is found in the grantor's home after his death. The grantee named may claim ownership; but since the grantor never delivered the deed, courts will not agree that transfer was intended.

The requirement for delivery of the deed generally is considered very literally; that is, the grantee actually must have come into physical possession of the document in order for title to be considered transferred to her. The grantee may arrange for her agent to accept delivery for her. A common form of such delivery is *delivery in escrow*. In this situation, the grantor delivers the deed to a trustee or escrow agent, who holds it pending completion of some required action by the grantee (such as payment in full of a note given in payment for all or part of the price). Delivery is considered to have occurred as soon as the escrow agent or trustee received the deed, so title is transferred. However, because the grantee has no deed in her possession, she will have difficulty disposing of the title until she fulfills the necessary requirements to get the deed released to her by the agent.

Questions on Chapter 9

1. X hands Y a deed with the intent to pass title and orally requests Y not to record the deed until X dies. When is the deed valid?
   (A) immediately
   (B) when Y records the deed
   (C) when X dies
   (D) never

2. A quitclaim deed conveys only the interest of the
   (A) guarantee
   (B) property
   (C) claimant
   (D) grantor

3. Which of the following forms of deeds has one or more guarantees of title?
   (A) quitclaim deed
   (B) executor's deed
   (C) warranty deed
   (D) special-form deed

4. The part of conveyance that defines or limits the quantity of the estate granted is
   (A) habendum
   (B) premises
   (C) equity
   (D) consideration

5. The Statute of Frauds
   (A) requires certain contracts to be in writing to be enforceable
   (B) requires a license to operate as a broker or a salesperson
   (C) regulates escrow accounts
   (D) regulates fraud conveyance

6. For a deed to be recorded, it must be in writing and must
   (A) be signed by the grantee
   (B) state the actual purchase price
   (C) be acknowledged
   (D) be free of all liens

7. The most comprehensive ownership of land at law is known as
   (A) an estate for years
   (B) a life estate
   (C) a fee simple
   (D) a defeasible title

8. From the standpoint of the grantor, which of the following types of deeds creates the least liability?
   (A) special warranty
   (B) general warranty
   (C) bargain and sale
   (D) quitclaim

9. The recording of a deed
   (A) passes the title
   (B) insures the title
   (C) guarantees the title
   (D) gives constructive notice of ownership

10. Title to real property may pass by
    (A) deed
    (B) bill of sale
    (C) both A and B
    (D) neither A nor B

11. Real property title may be conveyed by
    (A) adverse possession
    (B) inheritance
    (C) deed
    (D) all of the above

12. A warranty deed protects the grantee against a loss by
    (A) casualty
    (B) defective title
    (C) both A and B
    (D) neither A nor B

13. Recordation of a deed is the responsibility of the
    (A) grantor
    (B) grantee
    (C) both A and B
    (D) neither A nor B

14. Deeds should be recorded
    (A) as soon as possible after delivery
    (B) within 30 days of delivery
    (C) within one year
    (D) none of the above

15. A deed of conveyance must be signed by
    (A) the grantee and the grantor
    (B) only the grantor
    (C) only the grantee
    (D) none of the above

16. A deed to be valid need not necessarily be
    (A) signed
    (B) written
    (C) sealed
    (D) delivered

17. The party to whom a deed conveys real estate is the
    (A) grantee
    (B) grantor
    (C) beneficiary
    (D) recipient

18. Deeds are recorded in the
    (A) county courthouse
    (B) city hall
    (C) Federal Land Book
    (D) state capital

19. A deed must
    (A) contain the street address of the property
    (B) state the nature of the improvement on the land (dwelling)
    (C) contain an adequate description to identify the property sold
    (D) state the total area in the tract

20. What is the maximum number of grantees that can be named in a deed?
    (A) two   (C) ten
    (B) four   (D) there is no limit

21. Property is identified in a deed by the
    (A) habendum   (C) description
    (B) consideration (D) acknowledgment

22. Attestation, by a notary public or other qualified official, of the signature on a deed or mortgage is called an
    (A) authorization   (C) execution
    (B) acknowledgment   (D) authentication

23. For which reason or reasons is a deed recorded?
    (A) to insure certain title
    (B) to give notice of a transaction to the world
    (C) to satisfy a requirement of state law
    (D) to save title insurance cost

24. Ownership of property is transferred when
    (A) the grantor signs the deed
    (B) the grantor's signature has been notarized
    (C) delivery of the deed is made
    (D) the correct documentary stamps are put on the deed and canceled

25. From the point of view of the grantee, the safest kind of deed that can be received is a
    (A) general warranty deed
    (B) special warranty deed
    (C) quitclaim or release deed
    (D) trustee's deed

26. Which of the following statement(s) is (are) true?
    (A) A quitclaim deed transfers whatever interest a grantee has in property.
    (B) A quitclaim deed carries a warranty of good title.
    (C) both A and B
    (D) neither A nor B

27. Joe offers to buy Susie's house for $225,000. Susie examines Joe's offer and then offers to sell her house to Joe for $250,000. Which of the following is true?
    (A) An offer from Susie to Joe now exists.
    (B) No offer exists.
    (C) Two offers exist: one from Joe to Susie, one from Susie to Joe.
    (D) A contract between Joe and Susie now exists.

28. The principal health problem with lead-based paint is
    (A) headaches
    (B) lung cancer
    (C) asbestosis
    (D) ingestion of paint chips by children

29. A *bill of sale* is used to transfer
    (A) assumed mortgage
    (B) subject to mortgage
    (C) trust deed
    (D) personal property

30. If title and possession do not occur simultaneously, there should be an interim
    (A) lease (interim occupancy agreement)
    (B) option
    (C) exchange
    (D) novation

31. _____ means something is left to be done to a contract.
    (A) Executed
    (B) Executory
    (C) Unfulfilled
    (D) Unlisted

32. The date that a construction lien takes is the date
    (A) the project began
    (B) the project was finished
    (C) the bill was presented
    (D) the bill was past due

33. A notary public
    (A) makes the statement
    (B) requires a graduate-level education
    (C) provides acknowledgment
    (D) assures a genuine deed

34. In real estate parlance, *alienation* means
    (A) walking away from a transaction
    (B) offending the seller
    (C) breaking a lease
    (D) transferring title

35. Lead-based paint disclosure is required for residential properties having 1–4 units that were built before
    (A) 1960   (C) 1978
    (B) 1975   (D) 1992

36. Of the following, the best type of deed to receive is a
    (A) special warranty deed.
    (B) trustee deed.
    (C) general warranty deed.
    (D) quitclaim deed.

37. Which of the following provides the most complete form of ownership?
    (A) fee tail
    (B) fee simple absolute
    (C) fee on condition
    (D) leasehold

38. An unpaid mechanic may file a mechanic's
    (A) title   (C) exculpation
    (B) lien   (D) escheat

39. A quitclaim deed will transfer
    (A) with a special warranty
    (B) whatever interest the grantor has
    (C) with a limited warranty
    (D) the leasehold estate

40. To provide security for a loan, the borrower gives a deed to a disinterested third party. This is called a
    (A) junior lien
    (B) general warranty deed
    (C) trust deed
    (D) contract for deed

41. The exercise of eminent domain results in
    (A) seizure
    (B) unjust compensation
    (C) condemnation
    (D) government authority

42. A quitclaim deed is given by the
    (A) grantee   (C) trustor
    (B) trustee   (D) grantor

43. Mortgages and trust deeds are both
    (A) title instruments.
    (B) security instruments.
    (C) binding contracts of sale.
    (D) not recorded.

44. One who receives real estate under a will is a(n)
    (A) escheatee   (C) devisee
    (B) intestate   (D) bequeathee

45. Which instrument is typically used to convey ownership of real estate?
    (A) devise   (C) deed
    (B) lease   (D) mortgage loan

46. Upon marriage in community property states, real property previously owned individually by each party
    (A) becomes jointly owned
    (B) doesn't change
    (C) becomes community property
    (D) is held by a tenancy in common

47. Approximately 43 states do not recognize
    (A) partnerships
    (B) joint tenancy
    (C) community property
    (D) tenancy in common

48. Upon expiration of a life estate, the property passes to the
    (A) life tenant   (C) remainderman
    (B) beneficiary   (D) trustee

49. A widower dies without making a will. His surviving children inherit the property by
    (A) escheat
    (B) law of intestate succession
    (C) estover
    (D) emblements

50. Susan lived rent-free in a remote cabin, with the owner's permission, for 40 years. Susan
    (A) owns the property under adverse possession
    (B) owns the property under prescription
    (C) must pay rent to the owner
    (D) has no ownership interest

51. To be valid, a deed must include
    (A) grantee's signature
    (B) grantor warranty
    (C) property survey
    (D) legal description

52. *Alienate title* means
    (A) inherit property
    (B) sell or convey property
    (C) lease property
    (D) sell to a tenant

53. Herman prepares a deed for his cattle farm to his nephew. Herman dies before delivering the deed. His nephew
    (A) receives nothing
    (B) inherits the farm
    (C) receives the farm when the deed was signed
    (D) receives the farmland but not the cattle

54. An arrangement whereby the seller retains title until final payments have been made is
    (A) an installment sale contract
    (B) a general warranty deed
    (C) an amortizing mortgage
    (D) a bullet loan

55. A bank acquired property through foreclosure. Upon sale of the property, the bank covenants and warrants the property's title only against defects occurring during the bank's ownership. This conveyance is a(n)
    (A) administrator's deed
    (B) general warranty deed
    (C) special warranty deed
    (D) covenant deed

56. A deed is the instrument used to convey ownership of
    (A) personal property
    (B) short-term use of real estate
    (C) real property
    (D) any of the above

57. Which of the following is a voluntary alienation of real property?
    (A) escheat
    (B) condemnation
    (C) foreclosure
    (D) a deed of trust

58. I give my brother permission to live in a house I own until the death of his daughter. This is
    (A) an ordinary life estate
    (B) a life estate *pur autre vie*
    (C) a leasehold interest
    (D) a tenancy for life

59. Which of the following statements regarding deeds is true?
    (A) A general warranty deed gives the least liability to the grantor.
    (B) A quitclaim deed gives the least protection to the grantee.
    (C) A special warranty deed gives the greatest protection to the grantor.
    (D) A bargain and sale deed is voidable in most states.

60. The clause that defines or limits the quantity of the estate being conveyed is the
    (A) habendum clause
    (B) reversion clause
    (C) partition clause
    (D) revocation clause

61. As far as its validity between grantor and grantee is concerned, a signed deed that is not dated, acknowledged, or recorded is
    (A) invalid because of these omissions
    (B) void
    (C) revocable by the grantor
    (D) valid despite these omissions

62. The recording system performs which of the following functions?
    (A) Insures title against loss due to third-party claims.
    (B) Cures major defects in title.
    (C) Gives to the world constructive notice of documents.
    (D) Handles the closing of real estate transactions.

63. A proprietary lease is a unique characteristic of what form of ownership?
    (A) condominium
    (B) cooperative
    (C) timeshare
    (D) PUD

64. Which of the following parties is in the weakest position against a claim of title by a stranger?
    (A) A nonoccupant holder of a warranty deed.
    (B) A nonoccupant holder of an unrecorded quitclaim deed.
    (C) One who holds an unrecorded deed.
    (D) One who holds a recorded quitclaim deed to the property.

65. A deed made and delivered but *not* recorded is
    (A) valid between the parties and valid as to third parties with notice
    (B) valid between the parties and valid as to subsequent recorded interests
    (C) valid between the parties and invalid as to subsequent donees of the property
    (D) invalid between the parties

66. You can be most assured that you are getting fee simple ownership if
    (A) the owner will give a general warranty deed
    (B) the seller can furnish title insurance
    (C) you retain an attorney
    (D) you use an escrow company

ANSWERS

1. **A**	15. **B**	29. **D**	43. **B**	57. **D**
2. **D**	16. **C**	30. **A**	44. **C**	58. **B**
3. **C**	17. **A**	31. **B**	45. **C**	59. **B**
4. **A**	18. **A**	32. **A**	46. **B**	60. **A**
5. **A**	19. **C**	33. **C**	47. **C**	61. **D**
6. **C**	20. **D**	34. **D**	48. **C**	62. **C**
7. **C**	21. **C**	35. **C**	49. **B**	63. **B**
8. **D**	22. **B**	36. **C**	50. **D**	64. **B**
9. **D**	23. **B**	37. **B**	51. **D**	65. **A**
10. **A**	24. **C**	38. **B**	52. **B**	66. **B**
11. **D**	25. **A**	39. **B**	53. **A**	
12. **B**	26. **D**	40. **C**	54. **A**	
13. **B**	27. **A**	41. **C**	55. **C**	
14. **A**	28. **D**	42. **D**	56. **C**	

CHAPTER 10

Leases and Property Management

A lease is a contract that transfers possession of property in exchange for rent. The real estate owner is known as the *landlord* or *lessor*; the user is the *tenant* or *lessee*. The landlord retains a *reversionary right*; that is, he retains the right to use the property upon expiration of the lease. The tenant holds a *leasehold estate*, that is, a personal property interest that gives the tenant the right to use the property for the lease term and under the conditions stipulated in the lease.

With respect to leases, the Statute of Frauds usually requires that only leases for more than one year have to be in writing. This means that in some states it is possible for shorter-term leases (one year or less) to be oral. (But it always is the best practice for any contract to be written; disputing oral contracts in court can get very messy.) You should check your state's laws on leases, though. Some do require that shorter-term leases be written.

TYPES OF LEASEHOLD ESTATES

1. Estate for years
2. Estate from year to year
3. Tenancy at will
4. Tenancy at sufferance

An *estate for years* has a stated expiration date. The period included may be only 1 day or more than 50 years. When the lease term ends, the tenant is to vacate the property.

An *estate from year to year* (also called *periodic estate or estate from period to period*) does not have a fixed expiration date. It is automatically renewed for another period (week, month, year) unless adequate notice for termination is given. One period of notice is generally adequate; less than 1 year is acceptable in the case of a year-to-year lease.

A *tenancy at will* allows the tenant to remain with the consent of the landlord. At any time, either the tenant or the landlord may terminate the agreement. "Emblements" arise by operation of law to give tenants-at-will the right to harvest growing crops.

A tenant who holds property beyond the lease term and without the landlord's consent is a "holdover tenant." The form of estate is called *tenancy at sufferance*. A holdover tenancy has the fewest rights of any leasehold estate.

SOME COMMON LEASE PROVISIONS

Rent

Rent may be payable in any form that the parties agree upon. Typically, rent is payable in money, but it may also be payable in crops, labor, and so on—whatever the landlord and tenant agree upon. *Straight* or *flat* leases call for level amounts of rent. *Step-up* or *step-down*, *graduated*, or *reappraisal* leases provide for fluctuating amounts of rent.

A *percentage lease* requires the tenant to pay, as rent, a percentage of sales. Usually a basic rent is stipulated to guarantee a minimum amount. For example, a lease may require that a retailer-tenant pay $10,000 rent annually, plus 2% of gross sales in excess of $500,000. Should sales be under $500,000, the rent is $10,000; for sales of $600,000, the rent is $12,000, that is, $10,000 basic plus 2% of the $100,000 excess sales.

Operating Expenses

A lease that requires the landlord to pay operating expenses, such as utilities, repairs, insurance, and property taxes, is called a *gross lease*. The lessor considers the rent to be gross income and receives net operating income after he pays operating expenses out of his own pocket. A *net lease* requires the tenant to pay operating expenses. The landlord receives the rent as a net return.

The terms *net* and *gross*, though often used, may be inadequate to describe a lease. *Hybrid*, *seminet*, and *net-net* are used to describe the degree to which a party may be responsible for operating expenses. Careful reading of a lease by interested parties is necessary to avoid misunderstandings.

Escalation

Escalation or *step* provisions are found in long-term gross leases. Should certain operating expenses exceed a designated amount, the increase is passed on to the tenant.

Assignment and Subletting

Unless specifically prohibited in a lease, a tenant has the right to assign or sublet. In either case, the original lessee remains liable to fulfill the lease contract.

An *assignment* occurs when the tenant transfers all the rights and obligations stipulated in the lease to a third party (the assignee).

Should the original tenant wish to keep a portion of the property for his own use or to rent the premises to a third party for a term shorter than his lease, he may sublet. *Subletting* involves a second lease; the original tenant becomes a lessor for part of the property or for the entire property for part of the lease term.

Sale of the Property

When leased property is sold, the lease survives the sale. The tenant is allowed to continue use under the lease terms.

Termination of a Lease

The normal termination of a lease is the result of *performance*. When both landlord and tenant have fulfilled their lease obligations, there is said to be performance.

Another method of terminating a lease is by *agreement*. Landlord and tenant may agree to terminate the lease before its stated expiration date. Compensation may be included in such an agreement.

A *breach* may also cause termination. When either party fails to perform under a lease, there is said to be a breach. Although a breach can terminate a lease, it does not cancel all provisions. The violating party may be held liable for damages. When a tenant has breached a lease, the landlord's remedy is in court. Using a court order, a landlord may eject or *evict* a tenant.

A tenant who vacates property before the fixed expiration date of a lease is responsible for the remaining rent. If the property is eventually leased, the tenant owes only the difference in rent, plus expenses incurred in obtaining a substitute tenant. However, vacating property fails to terminate a lease except by *constructive eviction*. In this form of breach the landlord makes it very difficult or impossible for the tenant to "enjoy" the leased premises as contracted. In effect, the landlord's actions force the tenant to leave. Examples are very noisy repair work that goes on night after night in an apartment building; turning off utilities for long periods of time; closing the parking lot in a retail shopping center.

A *ground lease* is a long-term lease of land or air space. The tenant usually builds whatever improvements are desired. The landlord receives what is called *triple-net* rent; this means that the tenant pays not only operating expenses, but also property taxes and mortgage payments. Ground leases are for very long periods of time, usually 25 to as many as 99 years.

Lease provisions frequently encountered are described below. (Not all of the provisions will be found in every lease.)

PROVISION	PURPOSE
Premises	Describes the property being leased
Term	States the term of the lease
Rent	Describes rental amount, date, and place payable
Construction of building and improvements	Describes improvements for proposed property or property to be renovated to suit tenant
Common area	Describes maintenance of common-use areas, such as those in shopping centers
Taxes	States who will pay ad valorem taxes and escalation amounts
Repairs	States which party is responsible for repairs and maintenance
Alterations	States responsibilities and rights of tenant to alter improvements
Liability insurance	Designates party who is responsible to carry liability insurance and the extent
Other insurance	Designates party who is responsible to carry hazard insurance and the extent
Damage by fire and casualty	Describes operation of lease in the event of a fire or other casualty
Payment for utilities	States which party must pay charges for water, heat, gas, electricity, sewage disposal, and other utilities
Subordination	Describes rights between landlord and tenant in the event of mortgage foreclosure
Certificate of lease status	Obligates tenant to inform mortgage lender of occupancy and rent status
Condemnation and eminent domain	Describes operation of lease in the event of a taking or partial taking of the property
Compliance of law	Requires landlord and tenant to comply with laws and ordinances
Access by landlord	Allows landlord to inspect property
Mechanic's liens	Describes the discharge of mechanic's liens
Assignment and subletting	Limits the tenant's rights to assign or sublet
Nonliability of landlord	Frees landlord from liability due to injury or damage within premises
Right to cure defaults	Allows landlord to cure tenant defaults and require reimbursement
Use	Permits tenant the use of property for specific purposes
Notices	Describes method to serve notice to a party

PROVISION	PURPOSE
Definitions	Defines terms used in the lease
Partial invalidity	Describes operation of lease when parts of lease are held to be invalid
Waiver of redemption	Permits tenant to waive all rights upon lease expiration
Bankruptcy or insolvency	Describes required notice and operation of lease in the event of bankruptcy
Default	Defines lease default
Surrender	Describes how tenant is to leave property upon expiration of the lease
Arbitration	Provides a method to settle disputes
Brokers	Notes whether a broker was involved in lease negotiation
Encumbrances	Describes rights and obligations of parties to deliver and return property (with respect to liens, easements, etc.)
Quiet enjoyment	Agreement by landlord that tenant, while he performs, may have, hold, and enjoy property without interferences
Other restrictions	May limit the leasing of space in a shopping center to a competitor
Entire agreement	States that the written lease is the entire agreement
Percentage clause	Stipulates conditions affecting a percentage lease
Recapture clause	Stipulates that in a percentage lease a lessor may terminate lease if lessee's revenues do not attain a specified level within a certain length of time

LANDLORD-TENANT LAW

Most states and some localities have collected many provisions of lease law and some special enactments into a body of law called *landlord-tenant law*. Most often this body of law applies to residential leasing (apartments, homes, etc.) and specifically defines certain areas of the relationship between the landlord and the tenant. Lease law itself is very old and has been created largely to benefit the owner of the leased property (the landlord). Landlord-tenant law, therefore, tends to concentrate upon *tenants'* rights, although it often also includes specific tenant responsibilities.

Over a dozen states have adopted (some with modifications) a model law called the *Uniform Residential Landlord and Tenant Act*, also known as *URLTA*. This law applies only to residential leasing, with some exceptions such as hotels, motels, and mobile home lots. URLTA concerns such subjects as security deposits, rights of landlord and tenant, and condition of the property. States that have not adopted URLTA as a statute usually have laws covering the same things; however, these laws may, in general, be more favorable to landlords than is URLTA. With or without URLTA, many states and localities have enacted more stringent laws governing tenants' rights. You should check whether your state has laws considering either of the following (note that, if there are only local laws on either subject, they probably won't be covered on state licensing examinations).

Rent Control

Rent control allows government to limit the amount of rents charged. They exist in New York City and in a few other major metropolitan areas where market rents are unusually high.

Withholding Rent

Some states and localities allow tenants to withhold rent if the property doesn't meet certain conditions. These usually involve habitability, safety, and the like or conditions that do not meet building or health codes. In some places the law allows the tenant simply to refuse to pay until the landlord remedies the problem. In others the withheld rent must be used to remedy the illegal condition, if possible, or must be paid into some sort of escrow account pending resolution of the problem. These laws prohibit the landlord from evicting tenants for nonpayment of rent when rent is withheld for reasons allowed by the law. In some states that require an implied *warranty of habitability*, tenants may withhold rent, if premises are "non-habitable," until the landlord remedies the situation. The actual conditions that allow tenants to withhold rent may vary considerably from state to state, although some permit withholding in the case of clear violation of building, safety, sanitation, and health codes.

PROPERTY MANAGEMENT

Property management is the business of seeking and negotiating with tenants for other people's real estate. It is a real estate brokerage function, and property managers in all states are required to hold real estate sales or brokerage licenses. (*Resident managers* of apartment buildings or projects are allowed by most states to function without a license, provided that they do not manage any other properties and are employed either by the property owner or a properly licensed property manager.)

Some brokers who claim to be "property managers" may do little more than find tenants for vacant properties, and collect payment for doing so. Actually, a *professional* property manager does a lot more. In fact, he is able to do everything associated with the proper management of a property, so that the owner need do nothing at all. Property management functions include leasing, negotiating with potential tenants, advertising, developing leasing plans, arranging maintenance and repairs, and paying all bills (out of rent receipts). Of course, property managers are paid for their services. Normally, their payment is a commission on rent payments collected; however, they may instead (or also) receive a flat fee.

Certain special kinds of lease arrangements often are found in managed properties. Retail property (shopping centers, etc.) often features *percentage leases*. In this type of lease, all or part of the tenant's rent is a percentage of her gross business revenues. The theory here is that a well-managed and popular shopping center will generate good business for tenants, and so they will be willing to pay part of their intake as rent. Also, the property manager is encouraged to promote and advertise the shopping center because by doing so he gets more people to come to it, spend more money, and thus generate more rent.

Many percentage leases contain *recapture clauses*. These allow the property manager to void the lease if the tenant does not do at least a certain volume of business within a certain time. In this way the management avoids getting stuck with a poor tenant or one who does not do much business.

Questions on Chapter 10

1. Which of the following statements is correct?
   (A) The tenant is known as the lessor.
   (B) The owner leasing property is the lessee.
   (C) The tenant is the lessee.
   (D) none of the above

2. Under a net lease, who is liable for payment of insurance and repairs?
   (A) lessor   (C) sublessee
   (B) lessee   (D) both A and B

3. A gross lease requires the tenant to pay rent based on
   (A) gross sales   (C) gross profit
   (B) net sales   (D) none of the above

4. A percentage lease requires the tenant to pay a
   (A) percentage of taxes and insurance
   (B) percentage of net income as rent
   (C) percentage of sales as rent
   (D) none of the above

5. A tenant is delinquent in paying rent. The landlord should
   (A) call the sheriff to evict him
   (B) bring a court action
   (C) give him 30 days' notice
   (D) turn off water, lights, etc.

6. A lease that requires the landlord to pay the operating expenses of the property is called
   (A) a gross lease
   (B) an assigned lease
   (C) a percentage lease
   (D) a net lease

7. A lease for less than 1 year
   (A) may be oral
   (B) must be in writing
   (C) may be oral but must be reduced to writing within 1 year
   (D) is always invalid

8. Transfer, by a tenant, of the rights and obligations of an existing lease to another tenant is called
   (A) assignment of lease
   (B) a release
   (C) subletting
   (D) an eviction

9. A contract that transfers possession but not ownership of property is
   (A) a special warranty deed
   (B) an option
   (C) an easement
   (D) a lease

10. When an individual holds property past the expiration of a lease without the landlord's consent, the leasehold estate he has is a
    (A) tenancy at sufferance
    (B) freehold estate
    (C) common of pasturage
    (D) holdover tenant

11. A sublease is a
    (A) lease made by a lessor
    (B) lease made by a lessee and a third party
    (C) lease for basement space
    (D) condition of property

12. A landlord rents a store to a furniture retailer on a percentage lease. On which of the following is the percentage usually based?
    (A) market value   (C) tenant's gross sales
    (B) sales price   (D) tenant's net income

13. Which of the following will *not* terminate a lease?
    (A) performance   (C) surrender
    (B) breach   (D) vacancy

14. When a leased property is sold, what effect does the sale have upon the tenant?
    (A) The tenant must record the lease in the recorder's office.
    (B) The tenant must obtain an assignment from the purchaser.
    (C) The tenant must move out after reasonable notice.
    (D) There is no effect.

15. A lease for more than 1 year *must* be in writing to be enforceable because the
    (A) landlord or tenant might forget the terms
    (B) tenant must sign the agreement to pay rent
    (C) Statute of Frauds requires it
    (D) lease can then be assigned to another person

16. A lease can state that the rent is to be paid in
    (A) labor
    (C) cash
    (B) crops
    (D) any of the above

17. An estate at will is
    (A) a limited partnership
    (B) a tenancy of uncertain duration
    (C) an inheritance by will
    (D) a life tenancy

18. A reversionary interest
    (A) expires when a lease is signed
    (B) allows land to escheat at the termination of a lease
    (C) is a landlord's right to use of property upon expiration of a lease
    (D) constitutes a breach of a lease

19. A leasehold estate is a
    (A) large home built on leased land
    (B) personal property interest in real estate
    (C) landlord's interest in realty
    (D) none of the above

20. Escalation clauses in a lease provide for
    (A) term extensions
    (B) elevator and escalator maintenance
    (C) increased rentals because of higher operating expenses
    (D) purchase options

21. Which of the following statements is true?
    (A) Property managers are required to be licensed in all states.
    (B) Percentage leases are illegal in many states.
    (C) An unlicensed person may solicit tenants for several properties provided that she works for a licensed property manager.
    (D) Property managers do not negotiate leases.

22. Which of the following is true?
    (A) Property management is a real estate brokerage function.
    (B) Resident managers of apartment complexes don't always have to be licensed.
    (C) Property managers usually are paid a percentage of rents collected as their fee.
    (D) all of the above

23. A person who remains on leased property, without the landlord's consent, after the expiration of a lease is
    (A) a tenant at will
    (B) a tenant *par duration*
    (C) a tenant in common
    (D) a tenant at suffrance

24. A lease that requires that all or part of the tenant's rent be based on the tenant's revenues is
    (A) a lease at will
    (C) a percentage lease
    (B) a flat lease
    (D) a gross lease

25. A triple-net lease is one where the tenant pays
    (A) property taxes
    (B) insurance
    (C) maintenance
    (D) all of the above

26. A strip shopping center is a
    (A) regional mall
    (B) neighborhood center
    (C) nonconforming use
    (D) string of neighborhood stores

27. A commercial property investor is typically most interested in
    (A) land value
    (B) current net income
    (C) tax shelter
    (D) appreciation

28. Parallel wooden members used to support floor and ceiling loads are called
    (A) rafters
    (B) joists
    (C) headers
    (D) studs

29. *HVAC* stands for
    (A) high vacancy and collection
    (B) high volume and commissions
    (C) he vacates as convenient
    (D) heating, ventilation, and air conditioning

30. In a typical percentage lease, rent is calculated as a percentage of
    (A) assets of the lessee's business
    (B) net sales of the lessee's business
    (C) gross sales of the lessee's business
    (D) net taxable income of the lessee's business

31. In a tenancy at will, how much notice of intent to terminate must the tenant give the landlord?
    (A) forty-five days if the tenancy is month-to-month
    (B) seven days if the tenancy is week-to-week
    (C) both A and B
    (D) neither A nor B

32. A lease in which the tenant pays maintenance expenses, utilities, and property taxes is a _____ lease.
    (A) gross
    (B) percentage
    (C) leasehold
    (D) net

33. An advantage of being a tenant in a home under a month-to-month lease is
    (A) inflation hedge
    (B) mobility
    (C) income tax deductions
    (D) financial leverage

34. Which of the following has authority to physically evict a tenant from a rental house?
    (A) constable
    (B) sheriff
    (C) policeman
    (D) all of the above

35. A retail tenant in a mall pays monthly rent and in addition pays all property maintenance, taxes, utilities, and cleaning services. This is known as a
    (A) net lease
    (B) percentage lease
    (C) ground lease
    (D) gross lease

36. Michael, a life tenant, decided to remove a back-yard deck and tear down the garage so he could park his car behind the house. Can Ellen, the remainderman, prevent Michael from doing this?
    (A) No. Michael owns a life estate and may use the property during his lifetime as he wishes.
    (B) Yes. A life tenant may not commit waste of any kind.
    (C) No. A life tenant is permitted to remove any improvement on the property.
    (D) Yes, but Michael must pay Ellen an amount equal to the value of the deck and garage.

37. The right of a tenant to take possession of leased premises and not be evicted by anyone who claims superior rights is called the
    (A) covenant of possession
    (B) occupancy guarantee
    (C) covenant of protection
    (D) covenant of quiet enjoyment

38. The sale of a property that is under a long-term lease
    (A) cannot be made unless the present tenant is given an opportunity to terminate the lease
    (B) terminates the lease, and the tenant must negotiate a new lease with the new owner
    (C) terminates the lease upon 45 days' notice by the new owner
    (D) has no effect on the lease as far as the tenant is concerned

39. A tenant's rights under a lease are
    (A) terminated when the property is sold
    (B) usually terminated when the lessor dies
    (C) terminated when the property is mortgaged
    (D) terminated upon a surrender

40. The interest of a tenant in a rented building is called a
    (A) leasehold
    (B) leased fee
    (C) tenant's rights
    (D) tenancy discount

41. Which of the following statements about shopping center leases is true?
    (A) A store's lease in a shopping center is often a percentage lease.
    (B) An index lease requires constant payments over the term of the lease.
    (C) A gross lease is one where the rent is based on an agreed percentage of the gross income.
    (D) A net lease is one where the rent is based on a fixed percentage of the net income.

42. Under a net lease, a tenant would pay a set amount of rent, plus a portion of all the following *except*
    (A) taxes
    (B) insurance
    (C) maintenance
    (D) debt service

43. When leased premises reach a physical condition whereby the tenant is unable to occupy them for the purpose intended, the situation is legally recognized as
    (A) an action in ejection
    (B) constructive eviction
    (C) passive eviction
    (D) dispossess eviction

44. If a tenant defaults on a lease and abandons the property in good condition, for which of the following could the tenant be held liable?
    (A) Balance of the rent plus forfeiture of the security deposit.
    (B) Balance of the rent plus the cost to find a new tenant.
    (C) Decrease in the market value of the property.
    (D) Balance of the rent over the full remaining lease term.

45. The term that describes a tenant's interest in a property is
    (A) a fee simple interest
    (B) a reversionary interest
    (C) a remainder interest
    (D) a leasehold estate

46. A leasehold estate that has a definite beginning and ending date and does not automatically renew is known as
    (A) an estate for years
    (B) a periodic tenancy
    (C) an estate at will
    (D) an estate at sufferance

47. Which of the following parties to a long-term ground lease is the holder of the leased fee?
    (A) grantee
    (B) grantor
    (C) lessor
    (D) lessee

ANSWERS

1. **C**	11. **B**	21. **A**	31. **B**	41. **A**
2. **B**	12. **C**	22. **D**	32. **D**	42. **D**
3. **D**	13. **D**	23. **D**	33. **B**	43. **B**
4. **C**	14. **D**	24. **C**	34. **B**	44. **D**
5. **B**	15. **C**	25. **D**	35. **A**	45. **D**
6. **A**	16. **D**	26. **D**	36. **B**	46. **A**
7. **A**	17. **B**	27. **B**	37. **D**	47. **C**
8. **A**	18. **C**	28. **B**	38. **D**	
9. **D**	19. **B**	29. **D**	39. **D**	
10. **A**	20. **C**	30. **C**	40. **A**	

Listings and Buyer Agency Agreements

A *listing* is a contract of employment between a principal (property owner) and an agent (broker) to sell or lease real estate. Under the terms of the listing contract, the principal agrees to pay the broker a commission when the broker locates a party who is ready, willing, and able to buy or lease the listed property at its list price. Should an offer be tendered for less than the list price, the broker is entitled to a commission only if the transaction is consummated.

A different kind of contract between a real estate broker and his/her client is a *buyer agency agreement*. We usually don't call them listings, though, because the term *listing* has always referred to property for sale.

Normally, the seller pays the commission at closing. It is possible for a buyer to agree to pay a commission in lieu of the seller or in addition to the seller, so long as all parties are aware of the circumstances.

TYPES OF LISTINGS

Listings can be categorized into five broad types as follows:

1. Open listings
2. Exclusive agency listings
3. Exclusive right to sell listings
4. Net listings
5. Multiple listings
6. Limited service listing agreement

Each type is described below.

1. Open Listings

Using an open listing, the principal offers the broker a commission provided that the broker secures a purchaser. The owner reserves the right to list the property with other brokers or to sell the property himself. Thus, the open listing is open to other real estate brokers. All open listings are automatically canceled upon a sale of the property, so that the seller pays no more than one commission to one broker. However, if the owner gave an exclusive listing to a broker and also gave an open listing to a different broker who produced a buyer, the owner is liable for commissions to both brokers.

2. Exclusive Agency Listings

In an exclusive agency listing one broker is employed to the exclusion of all other brokers. The owner retains the right to sell the property herself without paying a commission. However, if the property is sold by a broker other than the listing broker, the listing broker is still entitled to a commission.

3. Exclusive Right to Sell Listings

The exclusive right to sell listing allows the employed broker to collect a commission upon the sale, no matter who sells the property. Whether the employed broker, another broker, or the owner procures a purchaser, a broker with an exclusive right to sell gains his fee upon the sale.

At first glance, such a contract may seem to be to a seller's disadvantage. Even if the seller procures a buyer on her own, or another broker finds one, the listing broker earns a commission. However, this rigid arrangement gives the listing broker the assurance that the property is available for sale by him only. Brokers employed by other types of listings may be dismayed to learn that property has been sold by the owner or another broker. Since this does not occur under an exclusive right to sell, the employed broker has more incentive to devote his efforts and to spend money to promote the sale of the listed property. In recognition of this fact, most real estate boards emphasize the exclusive right to sell listing, particularly for single-family dwellings.

4. Net Listings

In a net listing the property owner fixes the amount that he wishes to receive from a sale. He informs the broker, for example, that he wants a $175,000 check from the sale. The broker may keep any amount as a commission so long as the seller "nets" $175,000. Thus, if the sale price is $175,001, the commission is $1; a sale at $190,000 yields a $15,000 commission.

Generally, net listings are held in poor repute in the real estate brokerage business. In many states they are illegal; in the others they are "frowned upon" or otherwise discouraged by licensing officials. The reason is that they offer too many opportunities for unscrupulous brokers to violate their agency relationships with their principals (the owners who list their properties with them). An owner who isn't knowledgeable about the actual value of her property could be talked into net listing the property at a low price, thereby all but guaranteeing the broker an unusually high payment for selling the property. Even if the listing price is reasonable, brokers may try to "hide" or may illegally turn down offers that the owner probably would accept but that don't provide enough excess for what the broker thinks is an adequate commission. For example, a property is net-listed for $200,000. Obviously, the owner will take any offer of $200,000 or more, since the net listing assures her of receiving the full $200,000 (but no more) from any offer of at least $200,000. A broker who receives an offer of $210,000 may consider his $10,000 share too little, and be tempted to try on his own to negotiate a higher price, turn the offer down, delay transmitting the offer, or otherwise violate his obligation under license law to *immediately* transmit the offer to the owner.

In states that permit net listings, authorities and professional real estate brokerage associations suggest that, when offered a net listing, the broker add her customary charge to the net amount and then inform the seller of the resulting list price. For example, a 6% commission rate added to a $160,000 net figure results in a $170,212.76 offering price. Six percent of $170,212.76 is $10,212.76, leaving $160,000 for the seller. The arithmetic works as follows:

$$\frac{\text{Net Amount to Seller}}{\text{Fraction of Sales Price to Seller}^\circ} = \text{List Price with Commission}$$

$$(^\circ 100\% \text{ less commission})$$

When the $160,000 net figure and the 6% rate of commission are used, the list price becomes:

$$\frac{\$160,000}{0.94} = \$170,212.76$$

5. Multiple Listings

In metropolitan areas, most brokers agree to pool all of their listings. They form a *multiple listing association* to coordinate activities. Through that association, brokers agree to share their exclusive right to sell listings; any cooperating broker may sell property that another has listed. Upon the sale of multiple-listed property, the commission is split between the listing and the selling broker in accordance with the agreement established by the multiple listing association. A small fraction of the commission is paid to the association to cover its expenses of operation, which include the periodic publication, in writing and/or by computer, of the features of all listed property of the brokers belonging to that multiple listing association.

6. Limited Service Listing Agreement

In a limited service listing agreement, the seller agrees to pay the broker a flat fee in advance that is non-refundable, and the broker agrees to perform certain services, such as inclusion of the house in the Multiple Listing Service (MLS), with all inquiries directly to the seller (rather than the broker). The seller may agree to pay a commission (typically 2–4%) to the buyer's licensed representative. The seller may, for an additional fee typically paid at closing, have the listing broker provide seller representation services. Generally, under the agreement, the owner may sell to a buyer he or she procures, without paying a commission.

SELECTING A FORM

No special form is required for a listing. However, it is important to read the form used, to gain an understanding of the type of listing.

AGENCY LAW

A broker is an agent for his principal. The broker's duties, obligations, and responsibilities to his principal are covered by the Law of Agency. Chapter 4 of this book describes this body of law as it pertains to real estate brokerage. Many states require that, upon first contact with a prospective buyer, a broker a salesperson must disclose to the prospect the agency relationship with the seller, if there is one. Ordinarily, this is accomplished by having the buyer sign and return to the agent a form (usually designed and prescribed by law) that describes the agency relationship, so that the prospect realizes that the agent's loyalty is to the seller. Brokers can represent buyers in negotiations and transactions. In such cases they are agents of the buyer, not the seller, and there has to be an agency contract between broker and buyer. Disclosure is required here, too; when negotiations begin with a seller (or seller's broker) of a property the buyer is interested in, the seller and/or listing broker must be notified of the buyer-broker agency relationship.

RATE OF COMMISSION

As a matter of law, commission rates for the sale of real estate are negotiable between the principal and his broker. The rate or amount should be specified in the listing contract to avoid misunderstandings.

LISTING PERIOD

Contracts for the listing of real estate should have a fixed expiration date. Most contracts provide 60 to 120 days for the sale of single-family homes and 6 months to a year for commercial property and apartment complexes. The law does not establish limits, so the actual period agreed upon is a matter of negotiation.

Occasionally, after having been shown a particular piece of property through a broker, a prospect and the property owner may arrange a sale "behind the broker's back." Together they wait for the listing to expire, then contract for the sale without advising the broker, in an attempt to elude the payment of a commission. Despite the fact that the listing has expired, courts are likely to require payment to a licensed broker whose listing expired, if she can show that she was the procuring cause of the sale.

TERMINATION OF LISTINGS

Listing agreements may be terminated either by the parties or by operation of law.

Termination by the parties can occur through:

1. *Performance.* The broker procures a purchaser; the listing contract is terminated when the sale is completed.
2. *Mutual consent.* Both parties agree to terminate the listing.
3. *Expiration of agreed time.* A listing generally has a definite expiration date. If it doesn't, the listing ends after a reasonable period. In many states a listing must have a fixed expiration date.
4. *Revocation by the principal.* At any time, the principal may revoke authority given to the broker. However, the principal may be liable for damages resulting from the breach of contract, but not if he can show the agent to have been negligent in her duties, as by disloyalty, dishonesty, or incompetence.
5. *Revocation by the broker.* An agent may terminate the listing contract or abandon it. However, he may be held liable for damages to the principal because of failure to complete the object of the listing contract.

Termination by law can occur through:

1. *Death of either party.* The death of either the principal or the broker generally causes termination of a listing contract.
2. *Bankruptcy of either party.* Bankruptcy of a principal or an agent normally terminates a contract.
3. *Insanity of either party.* If either party is judged to be insane, he is considered incapable of completing the contract; therefore, the listing contract will terminate.
4. *Destruction of the property.* If the property upon which the agency had been created is destroyed, the agency is terminated.

BUYER AGENCY AGREEMENTS

As agents, real estate brokers don't just represent sellers (in listing contracts); they can also represent buyers. When they do, the broker and buyer execute a *buyer agency agreement.* This contract obligates a broker to represent the buyer and to look out for the buyer's interests. As the buyer's agent, the broker or salesperson can point out other properties that might better suit the buyer's needs, can state that a given property may be overpriced, and can otherwise advise and assist the buyer to get the best possible property to suit the buyer's needs, and at the best possible price. A listing broker or salesperson shouldn't offer this kind of assistance to a potential buyer because it would violate the agency obligation to the seller created by the listing contract.

Most buyer agency agreements are exclusive; that is, the buyer agrees not to employ another broker during the term of the buyer agency contract. Of particular concern is how the buyer's agent will be paid. In "traditional" real estate brokerage, all agents are paid out of the proceeds of the commission paid by the seller to his/her listing broker. Almost everywhere in the United States, buyer agency works the same way. Today's listing contracts typically stipulate that the seller will allow a buyer's agent to be paid from the proceeds of the commission that the seller will pay, and the buyer agency contract usually says that this is how the buyer's broker will be paid. However, the buyer agency contract also describes payment that the buyer must make if the buyer receives out-of-the-ordinary kinds of services from the broker, or if the buyer decides to buy a property that is under a listing contract that does *not* allow commission-sharing with a buyer's broker.

Buyer agency agreements are very popular; the reason is obvious. They give the buyer access to the same level of advice and expertise that sellers have traditionally always had from their brokers.

Buyer agency agreements are subject to the same agency law provisions as listing contracts and may be terminated the same ways as described above for listing contracts. Buyer agency agreements also have limited terms (60–120 days is typical).

You should read your state's license law carefully to find out exactly how buyer agency is treated and what rules and regulations apply to it.

DUAL AGENCY, TRANSACTION BROKERAGE

Dual agency and *transaction brokerage* are special cases of agency. In dual agency, the licensee represents both buyer and seller at the same time. In transaction brokerage (some states call it *facilitative brokerage*), the licensee works with both seller and buyer, and responsibilities to either party are limited. In some states, transaction brokerage is treated as no brokerage agency.

Dual Agency

Dual agency creates potential conflict because it is impossible for a dual agent to provide full agency responsibility to both parties at the same time. Therefore, the dual agency contract severely restricts the actual agency responsibility that the dual agent has. Typically the dual agent cannot tell the seller the maximum price the buyer is willing to pay and cannot tell the buyer the minimum price the seller would accept. Nor can the dual agent tell either party about any particular urgency to transact (or lack of it) that the other party may have. Essentially, the dual agent is pretty much prohibited from giving either party any of the information they would be most eager to get.

Transaction Brokerage

A transaction broker is generally engaged to provide limited representation for a buyer or seller. *Limited representation* means that a buyer or seller is not responsible for the acts of the licensee. Additionally, parties are giving up their rights to the undivided loyalty of the licensee. This aspect of limited representation allows a licensee to assist both the buyer and the seller, but a licensee will not work to represent one party to the detriment of the other party when acting as a transaction broker to both parties.

The duties of a transaction broker, which in some states are to be disclosed in a residential transaction, are as follows:

- Dealing honestly and fairly
- Accounting for all funds
- Using skill, care, and diligence in the transaction
- Disclosing all known facts that materially affect the value of residential real property and are not readily observable to the buyer
- Presenting all offers and counteroffers in a timely manner, unless a party has previously directed the licensee otherwise in writing
- Limited confidentiality, unless waived in writing by a party. This limited confidentiality will prevent disclosure that the seller will accept a price less than the asking or listed price, that the buyer will pay a price greater than the price submitted in a written offer,

of the motivation of any party for selling or buying property, that a seller or buyer will agree to financing terms other than those offered, or of any other information requested by a party to remain confidential.

- Any additional duties that are entered into by separate written agreement

It should be noted that loyalty, confidentiality, obedience, and full disclosure are not included. In a transaction broker relationship, the seller (or buyer) is considered to be a customer of the broker, not a principal. The customer is not responsible for the acts of the broker-licensee.

Transaction brokerage in some states doesn't establish any agency relationship at all. The transaction broker is subject to the same restrictions as the dual agent regarding information for either seller or buyer. The only responsibility the transaction broker has to either party is not to make mistakes in what he does do for them and to exercise due diligence in what he does. Essentially, the transaction broker handles the paperwork, provides the buyer access to listed properties, introduces buyer and seller, supervises negotiations (but doesn't offer advice about price or terms of sale)—that sort of thing. It's up to the buyer and seller themselves to get the other information they need and to conduct the negotiations.

Be sure to check your state's license law very carefully to see if it allows either dual agency (most do) or transaction brokerage (many don't, but it is increasing in popularity). For whichever (or both) is allowed, make sure you understand your state's restrictions and rules regarding them!

Designated Agency

Finally, look to see if your state allows *designated agency*. This is a new, 21st-century "innovation." It is supposed to "solve" the problem that occurs when a licensee has a buyer agency agreement with a buying prospect and want to show that prospect a house for which she also has a listing contract (seller agency). This would create a dual agency situation in which both parties lose a lot of agency representation benefits. Designated agency, in the states that allow it, lets the licensee's managing broker assign one "side" of the transaction to a different agent within the firm. This means that one of the parties suddenly finds himself working with a different agency so long as he is interested in this particular property. However, that agent can give full agency representation, and the other party can get full agency representation from the original agent. Typically, it is the buyer who is assigned to the designated agent; this can't happen, though, without the assigned party's consent. This consent may be written into the original agency contract (listing or buyer agency agreement), or permission may be obtained at the time the designated agency occurs.

Questions on Chapter 11

1. When more than one broker is employed by an owner to sell real estate, there exists
   (A) an exclusive agency listing
   (B) an open listing
   (C) an exclusive right to sell
   (D) a unilateral listing

2. To collect a commission in court, a broker must show that
   (A) he is licensed
   (B) he had a contract of employment
   (C) he is the cause of the sale
   (D) all of the above

3. The broker's responsibility to the owner of realty is regulated by
   (A) the law of agency
   (B) the law of equity
   (C) rendition superior
   (D) investiture

4. What is a real estate listing?
   (A) a list of brokers and salespersons
   (B) a list of property held by an owner
   (C) the employment of a broker by an owner to sell or lease
   (D) a written list of improvements on land

5. Under an open listing
   (A) the seller is not legally required to notify other agents in the case of sale by one of the listing brokers
   (B) the owner may sell the property without paying a commission
   (C) both A and B
   (D) neither A nor B

6. If the listing owner sells her property while the listing agreement is valid, she is liable for a commission under a(n) _____ listing agreement.
   (A) net
   (B) exclusive right to sell
   (C) exclusive agency listing
   (D) open

7. Under an exclusive agency listing,
   (A) the seller may sell by his own effort without obligation to pay a commission
   (B) the broker receives a commission regardless of whether the property is sold
   (C) both A and B
   (D) neither A nor B

8. The listing agreement may not be terminated
   (A) without compensation if the broker has found a prospect ready, able, and willing to buy on the seller's terms
   (B) because of incompetence of the prospect
   (C) if the seller files for bankruptcy
   (D) if the listing agreement is for a definite time

9. A multiple listing
   (A) is illegal in certain states
   (B) is a service organized by a group of brokers
   (C) requires that members turn over eligible listings within 12 days
   (D) causes lost commission

10. Under which type of listing are brokers reluctant to actively pursue a sale, because of the risk of losing a sale to competing brokers?
    (A) an exclusive right to sell listing
    (B) a net listing
    (C) an open listing
    (D) a multiple listing

11. A dual agent
    (A) may perform the same duties for both buyer and seller that she would if she were agent for only one of them
    (B) is severely restricted in the agency duties that she can perform for either party
    (C) may represent either party, but only one of them at a time
    (D) is someone who has more that one property listed

12. Broker Jones is working with buyer Smith and seller Brown in a real estate transaction. Although Jones provides assistance, he is not an agent for either Smith or Brown. Jones is
    (A) a dual agent
    (B) a buyer's agent
    (C) a seller's agent
    (D) a transaction broker

13. A principal may sell her property without paying a commission under
    (A) an open listing
    (B) an exclusive agency listing
    (C) both A and B
    (D) neither A nor B

14. The rate of commission is normally fixed under
    (A) a net listing
    (B) an open listing
    (C) both A and B
    (D) neither A nor B

15. Buyer and seller both may pay a commission so long as
    (A) all parties are aware of the situation
    (B) payments are made to the same broker
    (C) both A and B
    (D) neither A nor B

16. It is possible to terminate a listing by
    (A) revocation by the principal
    (B) revocation by the agent
    (C) both A and B
    (D) neither A nor B

17. An exclusive right to sell listing enables
    (A) the seller to sell the property himself without paying a commission
    (B) cooperating brokers to sell and earn a commission
    (C) both A and B
    (D) neither A nor B

18. Broker Morris has a written agreement with Sarah Lee to find a one-story house with three bedrooms and two baths in Lancaster. What type of agreement does broker Morris have?
    (A) an open buyer's agent agreement
    (B) a dual agency agreement
    (C) an exclusive buyer's agent agreement
    (D) an agency agreement

19. Which of the following would terminate a listing agreement?
    (A) death of the broker
    (B) revocation of the salesperson's license
    (C) an offer to purchase
    (D) expiration of the salesperson's license

20. The Floyds' home was listed with a broker, but they located a buyer and sold the property themselves. However, they were still obligated to pay a brokerage fee. What kind of listing had they agreed to?
    (A) a net listing
    (B) an open listing
    (C) an exclusive right to sell
    (D) a multiple listing

21. If the agent has not located a buyer by the end of the listing period, what happens?
    (A) The listing is automatically extended for an additional 30 days.
    (B) The listing price is reduced by 10%.
    (C) The agency relationship terminates.
    (D) The broker can charge for advertising.

22. A contract in which an owner promises to pay compensation to a broker for providing a buyer but may give listings to other brokers is known as
    (A) an exclusive right to sell
    (B) a net listing
    (C) an open listing
    (D) multiple listing

23. Stephen, a salesperson associated with broker Bob, lists a house for sale for $320,000, with 6% commission due at closing. Three weeks later, the owner accepts an offer of $300,000, brought in by Stephen. Bob's practice is that 45% of commissions goes to the office and the remainder to the salesperson. How much will Stephen make on the sale?
    (A) $18,000
    (B) $10,560
    (C) $9,500
    (D) $9,900

24. Before Mary listed her house, she reserved the right to sell the property to anyone she found without paying a broker. What kind of listing is this?
    (A) exclusive right to sell
    (B) exclusive agency
    (C) multiple
    (D) open

25. Roger has contracted with three brokers to sell his ranch. He has agreed to pay a commission to the broker who brings a ready, willing, and able buyer and who meets his terms. This is a(n)
    (A) exclusive listing
    (B) exclusive right to sell
    (C) open listing
    (D) multiple listing

26. The listing broker will receive a commission fee of 6% on the first $250,000 of the sale price and 4% on any amount above $250,000. If the property sells for $450,000, how much is the total commission?
    (A) $15,000   (C) $27,000
    (B) $18,000   (D) $23,000

27. Which of the following is included in an agent's responsibilities to the party the agent is *not* representing?
    (A) The agent must disclose all material facts to the other party.
    (B) The agent owes no loyalty to the other party.
    (C) The agent must provide all information about the principal.
    (D) The agent must advise the other party.

28. Broker Barb listed Tony's house and subsequently showed it to her sister, who made an offer to purchase. What is Barb's responsibility of disclosure?
    (A) No disclosure is required.
    (B) Barb must disclose her family relationship to the purchaser.
    (C) No disclosure is required if the property is sold at the list price.
    (D) It is a violation of fiduciary duty for Barb to show the property to a relative.

29. Seller Cynthia agrees to let broker Bob keep any amount over the $175,000 that she needs if he sells her house. This is called
    (A) a buyer's listing
    (B) an open listing
    (C) a gross listing
    (D) a net listing

30. A real estate listing usually creates
    (A) a general agency
    (B) a private agency
    (C) a universal agency
    (D) a special agency

31. An exclusive listing agreement should include
    (A) an advertising allowance
    (B) a defined market area
    (C) a definite termination date
    (D) a scaled commission percentage

32. A listing agreement states that the seller will pay the broker any amount over the final sales price plus the seller's closing costs. This is
    (A) illegal in most states
    (B) a net listing
    (C) a triple-net lease
    (D) a highly ethical brokerage practice

33. Broker Michele represented a buyer as a buyer's agent in the purchase of a home listed by broker Susan. How may Michele be paid?
    (A) Only by her client, the buyer.
    (B) Directly by the seller.
    (C) By broker Susan.
    (D) By broker Susan, but a subagency relationship is created.

34. The purposes of a property manager would include all of the following *except*
    (A) maintenance of the property
    (B) preserving the value of the property
    (C) investing the income stream generated by the property
    (D) meeting the goals set by the property owner

35. A properly drafted property management agreement should contain all of the following *except*
    (A) names of owner and manager
    (B) requirement that the manager provide periodic reports to the owner
    (C) fee schedule
    (D) list of approved janitorial companies

ANSWERS

1. **B**	8. **A**	15. **A**	22. **C**	29. **D**
2. **D**	9. **B**	16. **C**	23. **D**	30. **D**
3. **A**	10. **C**	17. **D**	24. **B**	31. **C**
4. **C**	11. **B**	18. **C**	25. **C**	32. **B**
5. **C**	12. **D**	19. **A**	26. **D**	33. **C**
6. **B**	13. **C**	20. **C**	27. **B**	34. **C**
7. **A**	14. **B**	21. **C**	28. **B**	35. **D**

Other Real Estate Contracts

People dealing in real estate may want to accomplish transactions that do not involve the categories of contracts discussed in Chapters 8 through 11. In this chapter you will learn about these other types of contracts including contracts for the exchange of real estate, contracts for deed, options, assignments, and novations.

CONTRACTS FOR EXCHANGE

A *contract for exchange* is used when principals want to exchange property. You may wonder why people would want to swap their real estate, but there are peculiarities in the U.S. Internal Revenue Code that confer tax advantages on some kinds of exchanges. However, these advantages are available only for investment property (property held for rental and income) and property used in one's business. Therefore, people who exchange homes that they live in (their residences) can't use these tax breaks (those who sell their own homes are offered different tax breaks), so a residential broker or salesperson is unlikely to encounter an exchange transaction.

If both properties are agreed by the owners to be of equal value and both are unencumbered, they may be swapped without additional consideration. This transaction may be beneficial to the principals. For example, one person may own land and want income-producing property, whereas the other party may have the opposite holdings and needs. A swap accomplishes the objectives of both parties, even though the properties exchanged are worth much more now than they cost originally.

More often than not, the properties exchanged are of different values. Then the party who gives up the lower-valued property must also give other consideration so that the trade becomes a fair one, acceptable to both parties. Personal property (cash, cars, diamonds, etc.) put into an exchange to equalize the total value of all property exchanged is called *boot*. The party who receives boot may be taxed to the extent of the unlike property received or, if less, to the gain realized. "Unlike" property in a real estate exchange transaction is anything that isn't real estate. "Like-kind" property is real estate. The tax advantage only applies to the like-kind property that is exchanged.

Mortgaged property can be exchanged. Suppose Mr. Jones owns a $10,000 vacant lot free and clear; Mr. Smith owns a $50,000 building with a $40,000 mortgage against it. Since the equity of both is $10,000, the exchange is a fair trade. Smith's boot is relief from a $40,000 debt. Deferred or delayed exchanges are now allowed under Section 1031 (see pages 275 and 294–295), which requires identification of a limited number of possible replacement properties within 45 days, and closing on the one(s) selected within 180 days. There are some other rigid requirements.

Years ago, when a simultaneous exchange was required for income tax purposes, the same broker might have been involved with the buyer and seller, possibly presenting a conflicting situation (which is why such *dual agency* is now illegal in many states). In a deferred exchange, which is the current norm, the broker of the sale and the broker of the replacement property are likely to be entirely different people. It is unlikely that the same broker would be called on as an agent for parties with conflicting interests.

CONTRACTS FOR DEED

In a *contract for deed* (also known as *land contract*, and an *installment land sale contract*), the property seller finances the sale but does not surrender the deed until all payments have been made. This type of contract typically allows the purchaser to gain possession, but not ownership, of the land while paying for it. Because the seller retains the deed until the final payment, he is well protected in the event of default. In many states, because the land is still legally his, he doesn't have to go through foreclosure; he can have the defaulting buyer evicted quickly and regain full possession and ownership of the land. Even in states where foreclosure is required under a contract for deed, the procedure often is less time-consuming and expensive than it would be if the seller were foreclosing a mortgage.

A contract for deed is also known as a *land contract* and an *installment land sale contract*. It is frequently used for the sale of subdivided land, especially in resort communities.

OPTIONS

An *option* gives its holder the right, but *not* the obligation, to buy specific property within a certain time at a specified price. The option need not be exercised. An *optionee* can elect not to purchase the property, in which case amounts paid to acquire the option belong to the property owner, who is the *optionor*.

Consideration must be paid with an option. Upon exercise of the option, the amount paid for the option may or may not apply to the sales price, depending upon the agreement.

An option may be used by a speculator who is uncertain whether a significant increase in the value of the property is forthcoming. Through purchasing an option, she can be assured of a fixed price for the property in a set time span. If the value increase materializes, she exercises the option. Otherwise, she lets it lapse and loses only the cost of the option. The holder of an option may sell the option itself (at a gain or a loss) if she wishes to do so.

ASSIGNMENTS

Assignments refer to the transfer of contracts. Through an assignment, a person may convey to someone else his rights under a contract. A lease may be assigned, as may a contract of sale, a deed, an option, and so on. The person who gives or assigns the contract is the assignor; the receiver, the assignee. It should be noted that the assignor is not automatically relieved of his duties to other parties under the earlier contract. If a lease contract exists and is assigned, for example, the original lessee is still bound to pay rent if the assignee fails to do so.

NOVATIONS

A *novation* is a contract used to substitute a new contract for an existing contract between the same parties. It may also be used to substitute or replace one party to a contract with a different party. Thus, a novation is used to amend an agreement or substitute the parties involved.

A novation must be bilateral: both parties must agree to it. Suppose a home is to be sold, with the buyer assuming the seller's mortgage. Since the seller made a contract to repay the debt, she cannot automatically substitute the new buyer for herself on the debt. Acceptance of the substitution must come from the lender. The process used for this substitution is called a *novation*. In such a case, the original contract has been assigned, while at the same time the assignor has been relieved of her obligations to other parties to the contract.

Questions on Chapter 12

1. Property, unlike real estate, that is used to equalize the value of all property exchanged is called
   (A) listing
   (B) gain
   (C) boot
   (D) equalizers

2. Mr. Hill has a 6-month option on 10 acres at $1,000 per acre. Mr. Hill may
   (A) buy the property for $10,000
   (B) sell the option to another
   (C) not buy the land
   (D) all of the above

3. A contract that gives someone the right but not the obligation to buy at a specified price within a specified time is
   (A) a contract for sale
   (B) an option
   (C) an agreement of sale
   (D) none of the above

4. A contract for deed also is known as
   (A) an installment land sales contract
   (B) a mortgage
   (C) land contract
   (D) both A and C

5. Which of the following best describes an installment or land contract?
   (A) a contract to buy land only
   (B) a mortgage on land
   (C) a means of conveying title immediately, while the purchaser pays for the property
   (D) a method of selling real estate whereby the purchaser pays for the property in regular installments, while the seller retains title to the property

6. Mr. Beans owns land worth $5,000; Mr. Pork owns a house worth $30,000, subject to a $20,000 mortgage that Beans will assume. For a fair trade,
   (A) Pork should pay $5,000 cash in addition
   (B) Beans should pay $5,000 cash or boot in addition
   (C) Beans and Pork may trade properties evenly
   (D) none of the above

7. A speculator can tie up land to await value enhancement, without obligating himself, through the use of
   (A) an installment land contract
   (B) an option
   (C) a contract for deed
   (D) A and C only

8. Ms. Smith wants to buy Jones's house and assume the 6% mortgage. Jones should
   (A) assign the debt
   (B) grant an option on the debt
   (C) ask the lender for a novation to substitute Smith
   (D) none of the above

9. Larry assigned his rights to use leased property to Allen. Allen stopped paying rent. Larry may
   (A) sue Allen for the rent
   (B) not pay the property owner since he hasn't received payment from Allen
   (C) both A and B
   (D) neither A nor B

10. Treasure Homes sold a lot to Mr. Kay under an installment land sales contract. Upon making the down payment, Kay is entitled to
    (A) a warranty deed
    (B) use of the property
    (C) a fee simple estate
    (D) all of the above

11. A like-kind exchange or deferred like-kind exchange is allowed under Section _____ of the Internal Revenue Code.
    (A) 8
    (B) 1031
    (C) 1231
    (D) 1250

12. The sale of land with the deed delivered upon final payment is known as a(n)
    (A) installment land sale contract
    (B) land contract
    (C) contract for deed
    (D) all of the above

13. In a typical land contract, the seller transfers the deed
    - (A) at closing
    - (B) upon receipt of disclosures
    - (C) after the rescission period expires
    - (D) when final payment is made

14. Like-kind exchanges of mortgaged property are based on
    - (A) appraised property value
    - (B) equity value
    - (C) book value
    - (D) adjusted tax basis

15. Before the expiration of an option, the optionee may
    - (A) buy the property
    - (B) choose to do nothing
    - (C) sell the option
    - (D) do any of the above

16. If an option to purchase is exercised, which of the following is true?
    - (A) The option money is automatically applied to the purchase price.
    - (B) The optionor is forced to sell the property.
    - (C) The notice to exercise must be in writing.
    - (D) Closing takes place before the option is exercised.

17. In an option contract, which of the following is true?
    - (A) The seller must sell, but the buyer need not buy.
    - (B) It is specifically enforceable by both parties.
    - (C) The seller may sell or not at his or her option.
    - (D) The buyer must buy.

ANSWERS

1. **C**	5. **D**	9. **A**	13. **D**	17. **A**
2. **D**	6. **B**	10. **B**	14. **B**	
3. **B**	7. **B**	11. **B**	15. **D**	
4. **D**	8. **C**	12. **D**	16. **B**	

Mortgages and Finance

CHAPTER

Most real estate professionals learn very early in their careers that borrowed money is the lifeblood of the real estate business, because nearly all real estate purchases are made with borrowed funds. In addition, most real estate development and construction uses borrowed money. Without access to such funds, these aspects of the real estate business dry up quickly; such cessation of activity has occurred several times during periods of "tight" money, when interest rates are high and loanable funds scarce.

IMPORTANCE OF BORROWED MONEY

There are several reasons for this dependence on borrowed money in the real estate business. Perhaps the most significant reason is that real estate is *expensive*. Even a modest home costs more than $100,000; apartment projects, office buildings, shopping complexes, and the like often cost in the millions. Very few of the more than 66 percent of American families that own their own homes could do so if they had not been able to borrow a significant portion of the price at the time of purchase. Quite simply, very few families have the kind of ready cash necessary to buy a home without borrowing. Similarly, very few real estate developers or builders have enough cash on hand to finance completely the ventures they engage in.

Another fact that contributes to the importance of borrowed money in the real estate business is that real estate is *very good collateral* for loans. It lasts a long time and so can be used to back up loans that have very long repayment terms, such as the 20 to 30 years typical of most home mortgage loans. This enables real estate owners to spread the cost of an asset over a long payment term, so that they can afford more expensive units, as well as to spread the payment over the time they expect to use the asset.

Real estate is *stable in value*. Of course, some real estate values are more stable than others, but generally a lender can expect that real estate collateral will not depreciate quickly and may indeed rise in value.

Real estate investors like to borrow money to buy real estate because it gives them *leverage*. As a simple example, suppose someone buys an apartment complex costing $5 million by putting up $1 million of his own money and getting a mortgage loan for the other $4 million. In effect, he has gained "control" of a $5 million property but has used only $1 million to do it. By borrowing he is able to buy considerably more than if he used only his own money; if he is wise in his choices of the real estate to buy, he may improve his investment profits considerably by borrowing.

MORTGAGES AND NOTES

In the financing of real estate, two important documents are employed: the *loan*, the evidence for which is a *note* or *bond*, and the *mortgage*, which is a pledge of property as security for a debt. A simplified sample of a note and of a mortgage is shown on the next page.

Since the borrower gives the note and mortgage to the lender, the borrower is the *mortgagor*. The lender is the *mortgagee*. (The suffix *-or* always signifies the giver, whereas *-ee* describes the receiver.)

NOTE
Date
I owe you $100,000, payable at the rate of $900 per month for 20 years, beginning next month.
Signed, T. Borrower

MORTGAGE
Date
If I don't pay on the attached note, you can take 34 Spring Street, Hometown, U.S.A.
Signed, T. Borrower

A mortgage and a note are both contracts. Any provisions that are agreed upon may be written into either contract, so long as such provisions are legal. The essential elements of a note are (a) a promise to pay at (b) a fixed or determinable time (c) a certain sum of money (d) to a payee or to bearer, (e) signed by the borrower.

TITLE AND LIEN THEORY

Mortgages (also called *trust deeds* in several states) are viewed either as transfers of property (title theory) or as the creation of a lien (lien theory). Title theory holds that the property is transferred to the lender subject to an automatic return of the property to the borrower upon payment of the loan. Lien theory holds that a mortgage gives the lender a lien on the property, but not title to it.

MORTGAGE LOAN CLASSIFICATION

Mortgages are often classified or described according to particular provisions. Several types of mortgages and their provisions are described below.

VA Mortgages (Also Known as GI Mortgages)

VA loans are made by private lenders to eligible veterans. The VA guaranty on the loan protects the lender against loss if the payments are not made. A VA-guaranteed loan can be used to buy a home, either existing or pre-construction, as a primary residence, or to refinance an existing loan.

BENEFITS OF A VA-GUARANTEED LOAN

- Equal opportunity for all qualified veterans to obtain a VA loan.
- Reusable.
- No down payment (unless required by the lender or the purchase price is more than the reasonable value of the property).
- No mortgage insurance.
- One-time VA funding fee that can be included in the loan.
- Veterans receiving VA disability compensation are exempt from the VA funding fee.
- VA limits certain closing costs a veteran can pay.
- Can be assumed by qualified persons.
- Minimum property requirements to ensure the property is safe, sanitary, and sound.
- VA staff dedicated to assisting veterans who become delinquent on their loan.

WHO IS ELIGIBLE?

Generally, the following people are eligible:

- Veterans who meet length-of-service requirements.
- Service members on active duty who have served a minimum period.
- Certain Reservists and National Guard members.
- Certain surviving spouses of deceased veterans.

KEY UNDERWRITING CRITERIA

- No maximum debt ratio; however, lender must provide compensating factors if total debt ratio is over 41%.
- No maximum loan amount; however, VA does limit its guaranty. Veterans can borrow up to $417,000 without a down payment in most of the country. Find out the limit in any county by visiting www.benefits.va.gov/homeloans/.
- Published residual income guidelines to ensure veterans have the capacity to repay their obligations while accounting for all living expenses.
- No minimum credit score requirement; instead, VA requires a lender to review the entire loan profile to make a lending decision.
- Complete VA credit guidelines are published at www.benefits.va.gov/warms/pam26_7.asp

MAXIMUM POTENTIAL GUARANTY

The maximum amount of guaranty on the loan is calculated as follows:

Loan Amount	Maximum Potential Guaranty
Up to $45,000	50% of the loan amount
$45,001 to $56,250	$22,500
$56,251 to $144,000	40% of the loan amount, with a maximum of $36,000
$144,001 to $417,000	25% of the loan amount
More than $417,000	The lesser of: • 25% of the VA county loan limit, or • 25% of the loan amount

FHA Mortgages

The Federal Housing Administration (FHA), which is part of the Department of Housing and Urban Development (HUD), has many programs that help to provide housing. They insure single-family and multifamily housing loans, nursing home mortgage loans, and loans on mobile homes and other properties.

Section 203(b) is one of the most popular FHA programs. The purpose of 203(b) is to provide mortgage insurance for a person to purchase or refinance a principal residence. The mortgage loan is funded by a lending institution, such as a mortgage company, bank, or savings and loan association, and the mortgage is insured by HUD. To be eligible for a 203(b) mortgage, the borrower must meet standard FHA credit qualifications. Eligible properties are one-to-four-unit structures. The borrower may borrow up to 97% of the purchase price and may include the upfront mortgage insurance premium in the mortgage principal. The borrower will also be responsible for paying an annual premium. More information on this program is available at www.hud.gov/offices/hsg/sfh/ins/sfh203b.cfm.

Conventional Mortgages: Conforming and Jumbo

Conventional mortgages are loans that are neither guaranteed by the VA nor insured by the FHA. Generally, they are the fixed-rate, fixed-principal-and-interest-payment type. In 2012, the maximum amount for a single-family house to conform to FHLMC or FNMA guidelines was $417,000. Loans above that amount are called "jumbo." Jumbo mortgages may be insured privately, with *private mortgage insurance* (called PMI in the mortgage business). Normally, on conventional loans with 80% loan-to-value ratio or less, no PMI is required. However, if the loan is for more than 80% of the lower of (a) the appraised value of the mortgaged property or (b) its sale price, lenders will require PMI, which is paid for by the borrower. Conventional loans may be for as much as 100% of the purchase price, provided that PMI covering the loan amount in excess of 80% loan-to-value can be purchased. As a practical matter, however, the cost of PMI makes loans of much more than 90% loan-to-value so expensive as not to be worthwhile.

Subprime Mortgages

Loans that do not conform to FHLMC or FNMA guidelines may still be available, though typically at higher interest rates. For example, many people without an adequate historical credit record may arrange a loan, called "subprime." One case applies to those who have recently become self-employed and cannot meet FNMA or FHLMC for historical self-employment earnings. Lenders may offer a loan, but because it is not a conforming loan, therefore not marketable to FNMA or FHLMC, and therefore carries higher risk, it will have a higher interest rate.

FICO Score

Fair Isaac Company has developed a credit rating system that most lenders weigh heavily in deciding whether to offer a loan. The system is called FICO. You can get a better understanding of it from *www.fico.com*. It scores one's creditworthiness on a scale of 300 (the worst) to 850 (the best). Major credit bureaus (TransUnion, Experían, and Equifax) apply FICO. Some lenders will exceed typical underwriting criteria for those with high FICO scores.

Purchase Money Mortgages

Sometimes a *seller* provides financing for a purchaser by accepting a mortgage loan in lieu of cash for all or part of the purchase price. A mortgage of this type, where the seller accepts a mortgage loan, is called a *purchase money mortgage*. The seller effectively gives purchase money to the buyer.

Construction Loans and Permanent Mortgages

Construction loans are used by builders or developers to improve land. Construction loan advances are permitted as construction progresses. When commercial property is completed, a *permanent loan* is used to pay off completely the construction loan. Construction loans on single-family homes usually continue until a residence is sold and the occupant arranges permanent financing.

The word *permanent* as it is used in real estate financing is a misnomer. Permanent mortgage loans seldom have terms beyond 30 years, and most will be repaid before their full terms. Although the conventional wisdom is that the typical mortgage loan is outstanding for about 12 years, recent experience has shown a shorter term as declining interest rates have encouraged more frequent refinancing.

Term Loans, Amortizing Loans, and Balloon Payment Loans

A *term loan* requires only interest payments until maturity. At the end of the maturity term, the *entire* principal balance is due.

Amortizing loans require regular, periodic payments. Each payment is greater than the interest charged for that period, so that the principal amount of the loan is reduced at least slightly with each payment. The amount of the monthly payment for an amortizing loan is calculated to be adequate to retire the *entire* debt over the amortization period.

A *balloon payment loan* requires interest and some principal to be repaid during its term, but the debt is not fully liquidated. Upon its maturity, there is still a balance to be repaid.

First and Junior Mortgages

Mortgages may be recorded at county courthouses to give notice of their existence. The mortgage loan that is recorded first in the courthouse against a property remains a *first mortgage* until it is fully paid off. In the event of default and foreclosure, the lender who holds the first mortgage receives payment in full *before* other mortgage lenders receive anything.

Any mortgage recorded after the first mortgage is called a *junior mortgage*. Junior mortgages are further described as *second, third, fourth*, and so on, depending upon the time they were recorded in relation to other mortgage loans on the same property. The earlier a mortgage is recorded, the earlier the mortgagee's claim in a foreclosure action.

Home Equity Lines of Credit

The *home equity line of credit* is like a second mortgage loan, but the borrower does not have to take possession of all of the money at one time. This type of loan is well suited for borrowers who anticipate that they will need more money in the near future, but do not need it immediately.

Setting up a home equity line can be like applying for a credit card. However, because a second mortgage is involved, there is processing, including an appraisal of the property. The application fee may be up to 2% of the line of credit, though some lenders may reduce or even waive this fee. Some plans also charge an annual fee to encourage the borrower to use the line once it has been granted. In addition, many plans require the borrower to take out a minimum amount when the loan is granted.

Home equity lines of credit offer a flexible way to access home equity, thereby financing periodic needs with tax-deductible interest. (Up to $100,000 of home equity loans generate tax-deductible housing interest, whereas personal interest is no longer deductible.) Borrowers may tailor the plan to the way they want to handle the payments and can draw upon the line with checks (good for infrequent, large withdrawals) or credit cards (for frequent, smaller withdrawals).

Budget Mortgages

Budget mortgages require a homeowner to pay, in addition to monthly interest and principal payments, one-twelfth of the estimated taxes and insurance into an escrow account, also called an *impound account*. These mortgages reduce a lender's risk, for the lender is thus assured that adequate cash will be available when an annual tax or insurance bill comes due.

Package Mortgage

Package mortgages include appliances, drapes, and other items of personal property in the amount loaned. The lender tends to exercise more control over a borrower's monthly obligations, and the borrower is able to spread the payment for such items over a lengthy period.

Chattel Mortgage

A *chattel mortgage* is a mortgage on personal property. The property may be a car, boat, furniture, or the like.

Blanket Mortgage

A *blanket mortgage* covers more than one parcel of real estate. *Release provisions* are usually included to allow individual parcels to be released from the mortgage upon payment of part of the mortgage principal.

Open End Mortgage

Using this type of mortgage, the balance is initially increased, that is the funding remains open for an additional amount. A homeowner may buy a place needing extensive repair work. Initially paying, say, $125,000, and initially getting a $100,000 loan, the balance may be increased to, say, $200,000 as repair work progresses.

Flexible Payment Mortgage

In the ARM, the adjusted payment directly follows the change in interest rates, whereas in a flexible payment loan, changes in the interest rate may not be directly felt in the payment; instead there may be payment caps that limit the change in payments. Instead of the payment rising to pay for the higher interest requirement, the principal balance increases. This is called *negative amortization*.

Wraparound Loan

This is really a second mortgage that includes an existing first mortgage in its balance. Suppose property is worth $1 million, and it has a $600,000 first mortgage at a low interest rate, say 4%. A lender might be willing to advance $150,000 at 8% in the form of a second mortgage, but there are negative legal or image characteristics associated with the second mortgage. So the potential second mortgage advances $150,000 in cash and calls the loan a $750,000 wraparound ($600,000 plus $150,000 = $750,000). The interest rate on the wraparound is 6%. The borrower pays the wraparound lender the payment on $750,000, and the wraparound lender pays the first mortgage payment. Where the first mortgage prohibits a second mortgage, then the wraparound may also be prohibited.

Swing Loan

A *swing* loan allows a borrower to "swing a deal." Suppose a homeowner is buying a new house but hasn't sold the old one. A swing loan is provided by a bank for a short term to use as equity in the new house; the loan must be repaid when the old house is sold. Variations include the *bridge loan* and *gap loan*, described below.

Bridge Loan

A *bridge loan* is a short-term loan to cover the period between the construction loan and the permanent loan. There may be a time lag during which a short-term loan is needed.

Gap Loan

A *gap loan* is used to fill in for a shortfall until certain conditions have been met, such as an occupancy percentage rate for an office building. The permanent financing may have a floor amount, payable when construction is complete, and a higher amount, when occupancy reaches a certain level. A gap loan funds the difference until occupancy reaches the specified level.

Construction Loan

A *construction loan* is a loan that funds construction by advancing money in steps as the project is developed. Generally, it is considered to be a high risk and is accompanied by a high interest rate, discount points, and fees. Underwriting is more difficult for a proposed project than for one that exists on the market. The construction lender does not want to advance more than is put in the project, so the loan is made in increments: when the land is purchased, streets and utilities installed, foundations, framing, roofing, and so on. Before providing a construction loan, a lender generally requires a commitment for permanent financing when an income property is built.

For a *subdivision loan,* release provisions allow parcels to be removed as collateral so the lots may be sold. To release a lot requires a payment against the loan.

Home Equity Loan

For a household that is house rich and cash poor, a *home equity loan* may be a tempting way to finance a child's college education, medical bills, or another purpose. A home equity loan is likely to be simply a second mortgage, but it carries a lower rate than other types of consumer finance.

Land Contract

In a *land contract,* also called a contract for deed, an installment sales contract, or an agreement for sale, title does not pass until the final payment is made. This is often used to finance recreational or resort property or for buyers with poor credit ratings.

Sale-Leaseback

A lease and a loan share many of the same characteristics, so a lease can be structured to be like a loan. Instead of borrowing to raise money and repaying the loan, one can sell property and lease it back for a long term (25 or 30 years). The sale generates cash (like borrowing a mortgage), and the rental payments are like mortgage payments. At the end of the lease term there may be a purchase option at a small amount for the property user. This is sometimes a method to arrange 100% financing and to control property without a legal purchase.

MORTGAGE REPAYMENT

For decades only one mortgage repayment method was available for home loans: *fixed-interest, fixed-payment amortization.* On these loans, the interest rate was always the same, the monthly payment was always the same, and when all the scheduled payments had been made, the loan balance was paid in full. Beginning in the 1970s, however, a variety of other methods entered the mortgage market. Today, the most popular loans are fixed-rate mortgages (FRMs) and adjustable rate mortgages (ARMs), each of which has several variations.

Fixed-Rate Mortgages

The *fixed-rate mortgage (FRM)* is the most popular modern mortgage instrument. It features an interest rate that does not change; it is "fixed" over the life of the loan. Fixed-rate loans can have any term up to 30 years (even longer in certain restricted government-subsidized programs). The most popular term, however, is 30 years, followed by 15 years and 20 years. In a typical FRM the monthly payment remains the same throughout the loan term; by the end of the term the loan has been completely repaid to the lender. However, there are some plans in which the monthly payment is not always the same; the most common of these are graduated payment mortgages and balloon mortgages.

GRADUATED PAYMENT MORTGAGE (GPM)

The GPM is designed to allow a relatively low monthly payment in the first years of the loan; the payment is increased by some amount (or percentage) every year until it becomes high enough to fully amortize (pay off) the loan over the remaining term. Typically, this final payment level will be reached after 5 to as many as 10 years. One unpleasant feature of most GPMs is *negative amortization* in the early years. The loan amount actually goes up instead of down at first, because the payments during the first 3 to 5 years aren't even enough to pay the accumulating interest on the loan; the unpaid interest is added to the loan amount, which keeps growing until the payments become high enough to cover the interest.

BALLOON MORTGAGE

The balloon mortgage features reasonable monthly payments, but a term too short to allow for the loan to be fully paid. Therefore, at the end of the term a large final payment the ("balloon" payment) is due. A typical arrangement is for the borrower to make payments as though the loan had a 30-year term; however, after 10 or 15 years the loan comes due and the entire unpaid balance must be paid.

Adjustable-Rate Mortgages

Adjustable rate mortgages (ARMs) feature interest rates that change every so often. A change in the interest rate, of course, usually means a change in the amount of the monthly payment as well. ARMs were first introduced in the 1970s, but did not become really popular with borrowers until the 1980s, by which time several modifications had been introduced that helped overcome consumer reluctance. When ARMs were first offered, a wide variety of terms and conditions were available. Nowadays the ARM has been fairly well standardized into a few popular versions that have many features in common. All have *periodic adjustment*, an interest rate based upon some *index* of interest rates, and both periodic and lifetime *caps* on interest rates.

The *period* of the loan is the frequency at which adjustments occur; common periods are 6 months and 1 year, but longer periods (3 to 5 years) are gaining in popularity. Today most ARMs have the interest rate adjusted every year. Interest rates aren't adjusted arbitrarily; they are based upon an *index* of interest rates. The ARM contract specifies the index used and the *margin*. Each time the rate is adjusted, this margin will be added to the index rate to get the new rate for the ARM loan for the following period.

The *caps* are limits on changes in the interest rate. The *periodic cap* limits the amount of change for any one period; the *lifetime cap* provides upper and lower interest rate limits that apply for the entire life of the loan. The most popular cap arrangements are "1 and 5" (limited largely to FHA and VA loans) and "2 and 6." The first number is the periodic cap; the second, the lifetime cap. An "annual ARM with 2 and 6 caps" will be adjusted every year (annually), by no more than 2 percentage points (the periodic cap) above or below the previous year's rate, and over the life of the loan the interest rate can't rise by more than 6 percentage points (the lifetime cap) above the original rate. ARMs are popular with lenders, who don't want to get stuck with low-interest loans in a period of rising rates, but have been difficult to "sell" to borrowers, most of whom are unwilling risk a rise in interest rates, which would increase their loan payments. The mortgage industry is addressing this concern with a variety of features and concessions tied to ARM loans. The most popular and effective of these are *convertibility* and *teaser rates*.

The convertibility feature, which is not an automatic part of all ARM loans, allows the borrower to convert the ARM loan to an FRM loan at some time in the future, usually 3, 4, or 5 years after the loan is originated. Typically a fee, usually 0.5 to 1% of the loan amount, is charged for conversion. The appeal of convertibility is that the loan doesn't have to be an ARM forever, and the borrower feels "safer" with the ARM because of the conversion privilege.

Teaser rates are unusually low *initial* interest rates. They are very common in ARMs with annual (or shorter) adjustment periods. An interest rate that is attractively low for the first year or two of the ARM translates into low initial payments and thus into genuine money savings for the borrower. Teaser rates can have another useful effect: if the lifetime cap applies to the initial loan rate, then the maximum interest rate on the loan will be relatively low as well. Teaser rates are typically 3 or more percentage points below current FRM interest rates. For example, if FRM loans are available at 4% interest for 30-year mortgages, the teaser rate for a 30-year annual ARM with 2 and 6 caps probably will be around 1%. This would result in a lifetime cap of 1% + 4%, or 5%. Even if, a year after origination, the interest rate were to rise by the full 2% annual cap, the second year's rate would be 3%, still a full point less than the original FRM rate.

To illustrate, for a 30-year FRM for $500,000 at 4% interest, the monthly payment would be $2,387.08. An ARM of $500,000, with a 1% teaser rate, would require a monthly payment of $1,608.20 for the first year, and a maximum possible payment (at 3% interest) of $2,091.12 the second year. The ARM borrower would be more than $9,346 ahead the first year and another $3,552 ahead the second year, for a total cash savings of $12,898 over the first two years. This "money in the pocket" provides many borrowers with a strong incentive to choose the ARM, particularly if it also has the convertibility feature

ARMs with longer adjustment periods (3, 5, and even 7 years) are becoming more popular. If they have teaser rates, these rates are much closer to the FRM rate (1% to 1.5% less, at the most); periodic caps on these loans are higher, although a lifetime cap of about 6% is common.

Others

REVERSE MORTGAGE (RM)

Here the lender makes the payments to the borrower, gradually advancing money to a (typically elderly) homeowner. The amounts advanced, plus interest, become the principal of the loan. Payments to the lender are deferred until a sale of the property, the death of the homeowner, or a time when the balance owed approaches the market value of the home. RMs also can be arranged whereby money, borrowed against the home, is used to purchase an annuity contract that will pay the homeowner for life. The homeowner then pays the mortgage interest with income from the annuity. The primary borrower must be at least age 62 to qualify for the FHA program.

BIWEEKLY MORTGAGES

Here the lender figures the monthly payment on a 30-year amortizing loan, then requires half to be paid every 2 weeks. Because there are twenty-six 2-week periods in a year, this is the equivalent of paying for 13 months per year. As a result the loan is retired in 18 to 22 years. For borrowers who are paid every 2 weeks, such a mortgage may fit the budget well. However it may not appeal to those who are paid monthly.

PRIMARY MORTGAGE MARKET

The primary mortgage market consists of institutions that originate mortgages. These mortgages can then be sold on what is called the secondary mortgage market.

Savings and Loan Associations

Savings and loan associations actively originate residential mortgages in the United States. Most sell the loans in the secondary market.

Commercial Banks

Commercial banks originate many residential mortgages; they are more active, however, in the construction loan field and in other types of lending. They have a great deal of latitude in the types of activity in which they engage, but strict limitations are imposed for each type.

Mutual Savings Banks

Mutual savings banks have no stockholders; they operate for the benefit of depositors. Some invest in residential mortgages.

Life Insurance Companies

Life insurance companies invest a relatively small amount of their total assets in residential mortgage loans. They are quite active in permanent mortgage loans on income-producing property, including apartments, shopping centers, and office buildings.

Mortgage Companies

Mortgage companies, also known as *mortgage bankers* and *mortgage brokers*, are the most common sources of home mortgages. They originate almost two-thirds of all residential mortgages. However, these businesses do not lend their own money; they are not financial institutions. Rather, they originate and service home mortgage loans on behalf of large investors (insurance companies, banks, pension funds, and the like) in mortgage loans. Mortgage bankers receive a fee for originating loans and fees for servicing them: collecting payments, holding escrows, dunning late payers, and so on. Mortgage brokers originate loans but do not service them.

SECONDARY MORTGAGE MARKET

Federal National Mortgage Association

The *Federal National Mortgage Association* (also known as *FNMA* or *Fanny Mae*) is a federally chartered, privately owned and managed corporation. It does not make direct loans to homeowners; rather, it purchases first mortgage loans, many originated by mortgage bankers, in the secondary mortgage market. FNMA thereby aids in the liquidity of mortgage investments, making mortgages more attractive investments. FNMA presently owns a significant percentage of all residential mortgages.

Federal Home Loan Mortgage Corporation

The *FHLMC*, or *Freddie Mac*, is a privately owned corporation that, like FNMA, buys mortgages on the secondary market. It buys much of its inventory from savings and loan associations and commercial banks. It also sells participations in pools of mortgages.

Government National Mortgage Association

The *Government National Mortgage Association* (*GNMA* or *Ginnie Mae*) is a U.S. government entity that encourages low-income housing. It will guarantee packages consisting of FHA or VA loans.

Farmers Home Administration

This agency, *FmHA*, which has regional branches, provides financing for the purchase and operations of farms and rural homes and guarantees loans on such properties made by others.

LENDER CRITERIA

Institutional lenders perform a process called *underwriting*. The purpose of this is to assess the risks of making the loan. They look at the property and the borrower. As to the property, the lender typically arranges for an appraisal (cost is paid by the borrower), which will provide information about the property's value, its location, and market conditions, including comparable sales.

The lender will get a credit report on the borrower, financial statements, and letters from employers concerning salary, term of employment, and prospects for the continuation of employment. Lenders will verify bank accounts and other assets of the borrower, as well as liabilities.

For a conventional loan on a single-family home, the lender will normally require a 20% down payment. This would be a *loan-to-value ratio* of 80%. If the borrower seeks a greater loan-to-value ratio, he will be required to get private mortgage insurance (PMI). Up to 90 and 95% loan-to-value ratios may be obtained. For a duplex or four-unit property, a larger down payment (25%) is normally required.

Lenders have certain guidelines to follow if they want to have a truly marketable loan— that is, a loan that can be sold to FNMA or FHLMC. This is called a *conforming* loan. The lender will provide a *qualifying* ratio of housing payments to gross income of 28% and a ratio of total fixed payments to gross income of 36%. For example, suppose the Andersons earn $10,000 per month. The maximum housing payment they would be allowed is $2,800 per month, including principal, interest, taxes, and insurance. When payments on other long-term debt, such as car loans, are considered, the maximum allowed would be $3,600 (36%). These guidelines may be exceeded by applicants with high FICO scores.

Many lenders will offer *nonconforming* loans to those who don't qualify. These loans won't conform to FNMA/FHLMC guidelines, and a higher rate of interest is charged. But they may allow a marginal borrower to purchase the home desired. Nonconforming loans include jumbo, subprime, and Alt-A.

With income-producing property, a lender will also look to the debt coverage ratio and insist that the net operating income from the property exceed debt service by a comfortable margin that is by 25% or more. So a debt service coverage ratio of 1.25 times net operating income may be required.

When considering a loan on the stock in a cooperative apartment, lenders will consider the risk. If it is an existing, sold-out development, it is less risky than one that is to be built or converted from rental apartments. For those, the developer or sponsor's filings of stock with the attorney general may offer clues as to the likelihood of success.

MORTGAGE LOAN DISCOUNTING

Points

One *point* is 1% of the amount of the loan. Some mortgage loan charges are expressed in terms of points. These charges are either *fees* or *discounts*. Typical fees expressed in points are origination fees, conversion fees (ARM to FRM; see page 182), prepayment penalties, and so on. The actual dollar amount of such a fee depends upon the dollar amount of the loan involved. For example, most new mortgage loans have origination fees. Usually, the fee is about one point, or 1% of the loan amount. For a loan of $100,000, then, the fee will be $1,000 (1% of $100,000); for a loan of $75,000 the fee will be $750, and so on.

Discount points are something else, although they, too are expressed as percentages of the loan amount. Discounts are paid at origination in order to reduce the interest rate on the loan. (You can think of discounts as somewhat like interest paid in advance.) Depending upon the amount of the discount required, a lender will offer a variety of interest rates on new mortgage loans. For example, a "menu" of interest rates might be: 6.5 + 0, 6.25 + 1.25, 6.0 + 2.5. These mean that the lender will offer an interest rate of 6.5% with no discount (usually called "par"); 6.25% in return for a payment of 1.25% of the loan amount (a 1.25-point discount); and 6% in return for a 2.5-point discount. For a $100,000 loan from this menu, the borrower's interest rate will be 6.5% if no discount is paid, 6.25% if $1,250 is paid in advance, and 6% for an advance payment of $2,500. Why would anyone pay discounts? Actually, many borrowers don't. However, *sellers* often do for a variety of reasons, usually concerned with making a sale more attractive to a buyer.

Discounts also are used as *buydowns*, often in association with teaser interest rates. Buydowns substitute an initial charge for interest later in the loan. Most often they are used to provide an unusually low interest rate during the early period of a loan. For example, if the "normal" rate of interest is 7%, a lender may offer a buydown (for a fee of about 5.5% of the loan amount) that will give the loan an interest rate of 5% the first year, 6% the second, and 7% the third. After the third year, the interest rate will be 7% for the rest of the loan period.

Prepayment Penalties and Privileges

Nearly all home mortgage loans allow the borrower to pay off the principal balance without penalty at any time. Many commercial property mortgages require a penalty, such as 3% of the outstanding balance, for early debt retirement. The penalty diminishes over time.

Acceleration Clauses

An *acceleration clause* states that the full principal balance becomes due upon certain default. If one or more payments are past due (depending on the agreement), the entire loan becomes due. It is common for residential mortgage loans to have a "due on sale" clause. A due on sale clause will cause the loan to become payable when the property is sold, even when the loan is not in default.

Loan Assumption

Property offered for sale may be encumbered by a loan bearing a low interest rate, which makes it attractive to the real estate purchaser. The buyer may pay the seller for his equity (the difference between the property value if free and clear and the amount of debt) and then *assume* the loan. The purchaser then becomes liable for the loan and its required payments. The original borrower, however, is not automatically freed from his obligation. He may ask the lender for a *novation* (see page 172) which serves to release him from responsibility, and then substitute the new property owner as the sole debtor. In the absence of a novation, the lender may look to the property and to both the original borrower and the subsequent purchaser for repayment.

Rather than assume a loan, a purchaser may agree to take the property *subject* to a mortgage loan. In doing so, the buyer acknowledges the debt, but it does not become her personal liability. In the event of default, she stands to lose no more than her investment.

Usury

Every state has laws prescribing maximum permitted interest rates. Charging a higher interest rate than that permitted by law is considered *usury*. Penalties for usury differ widely from state to state.

Estoppel Certificate

An *estoppel certificate* is a statement that prevents its issuer from asserting different facts at a later date. For example, a mortgage originator may wish to sell the mortgage loan (the right to collect payments) to another. The loan purchaser may ask for an estoppel certificate, whereby the borrower states the amount he owes. Later, the borrower is stopped from asserting that he owed less at the time he signed the estoppel certificate.

Releasing from Property Mortgages

Four methods by which property may be released from mortgages are:

1. *Satisfaction piece.* This document from the lender states that the loan is paid off and that the lender releases property from the lien.
2. *Parcel or land release.* This releases part of mortgaged property from the mortgage, usually upon payment of part of the debt.

3. *Postponement of lien.* The lien is not satisfied but is subordinated, meaning that it assumes a lower priority.

4. *Foreclosure.* This is described in detail below.

Foreclosure, Deficiency Judgments, and Equity of Redemption

Upon certain default, a lender may be allowed to go through an authorized procedure, known as *foreclosure,* to have the property applied to the payment of the debt. Should the property sell at foreclosure for more than the unpaid first mortgage loan plus the expenses of the foreclosure action, the excess belongs to the junior lenders, if any. After all lenders have received full payment, any excess funds go to the borrower.

It is more likely that the proceeds from a foreclosure will be inadequate to pay mortgage indebtedness. In this case, the lender may attempt to get a *deficiency judgment* for the amount of the loan that remains unpaid. This requires the borrower to pay the deficiency personally. Deficiency judgments are difficult to establish in many jurisdictions. Commercial property mortgagors are frequently able to negotiate *exculpatory* clauses in their loans. Exculpatory clauses cause loans to be *nonrecourse*; when such a clause exists, a defaulting borrower may lose the real estate that he has pledged, but he is not personally liable for the debt. The lender may look only to the property as collateral.

Should property be foreclosed, the borrower has the right to redeem the property by repaying in full the principal owed. This is known as *equity of redemption* and must be exercised within the time period prescribed by state law. In some states, the right must be exercised before the actual foreclosure sale; in others, the right remains for up to 2 years after such a sale.

2008 FINANCIAL CRISIS

In late summer 2008, a financial crisis erupted. While there is plenty of blame to go around, events that led to the crisis may be summarized as follows.

The bubble in housing prices began to reverse in the fall of 2006 in many places, notably parts of California and Florida, which had enjoyed a boom in prices since 2000.

Boom Times

During the boom, lending standards were greatly relaxed, with lenders expecting that house price inflation would prevent losses. Borrowers were able to get nearly 100% financing even if their credit was substandard. No-documentation (no-doc) and low-documentation (low-doc) loans were available in which the lender performed little due diligence (documentation) to ascertain the borrower's creditworthiness. These were also called "liar loans" because borrowers could lie about their income and employment without being investigated.

Loans were sold on Wall Street in packages called *collateralized mortgage obligations* (*CMOs*). To maximize the price, these were sold in pieces, called *tranches*, that ranged from high credit to what became known as *toxic*, depending on the priority of claim in default.

Beginning of the Crisis

Beginning in 2007, many lenders began to struggle at the start of a wave of home foreclosures. Both home investors and users began to default on mortgages because home prices dropped, which put the owners "upside-down," meaning negative equity (they owed more than the property was currently worth), many without the resources to make monthly payments.

Snowballing Crisis

The mortgage crisis snowballed, with a growing number of homeowner defaults. Many lenders became unable to meet their obligations or to sell their inventory of mortgage loans and foreclosed houses.

In August 2008, Fannie Mae, Freddie Mac, and other real estate lenders collapsed, many of those being supported only by federal government bailouts in September 2008; others failed. Commercial banks, investment banks, and savings associations collapsed, including icons that were rescued or restructured with government intervention or no longer exist, including:

AIG Insurance	U.S. government credit facility, $85 billion, September 16, 2008
Bear Stearns	Bought by JPMorgan Chase May 30, 2008
Countrywide	Bought by Bank of America January 11, 2008
Fannie Mae	Placed in U.S. government conservatorship September 7, 2008
Freddie Mac	Placed in U.S. government conservatorship September 7, 2008
IndyMac	Failed July 11, 2008
Lehman Brothers	Declared bankruptcy September 15, 2008
Merrill Lynch	Bank of America announced intent to buy September 14, 2008, closed purchase January 1, 2009
Wachovia	Merged with Wells Fargo December 31, 2008
Washington Mutual	Placed in FDIC receivership September 25, 2008

Government Intervention

In an effort to prevent a collapse of lending activity, the U.S. government passed legislation. Some of the most significant pieces of legislation are abbreviated: HAMP, HARP, HASP, TALF, and TARP. They are described below.

The **Home Affordable Modification Program (HAMP)** of the U.S. Departments of the Treasury and Housing and Urban Development was intended to reduce mortgage payments to as little as 31% of verified monthly gross pretax income for homeowners who are not unemployed.

The **Home Affordable Refinance Program (HARP)** was set up by the Federal Housing Finance Agency in March 2009 to help underwater and near-underwater homeowners refinance their mortgages. Unlike the Home Affordable Modification Program (HAMP), which aims to assist homeowners who are in danger of foreclosure, this program targets homeowners who are current on their monthly mortgage payments but are unable to refinance because of dropping home prices in the wake of the U.S. housing market price correction during 2006–2011.

The **Homeowners Affordability and Stability Plan (HASP)**, announced on February 18, 2009, was designed to help up to nine million homeowners avoid foreclosure. Initial funding of $75 billion was supplemented by $200 billion in additional funding for Fannie Mae and Freddie Mac to purchase and more easily refinance mortgages.

The **Term Asset-backed Securities Loan Facility (TALF)** is a funding facility under which the Federal Reserve Bank of New York will lend up to $200 billion on a nonrecourse basis to holders of certain AAA-rated asset-based securities (ABS) backed by newly and recently issued consumer and small business loans. On August 17, 2009, the Federal Reserve Board and the Treasury announced that, to promote the flow of credit to businesses and households and to facilitate the financing of commercial properties, the TALF program would continue to provide loans against newly issued ABS and legacy commercial mortgage–backed securities (CMBS) through June 30, 2010. TARP guarantees $20 billion of TALF loans.

The **Troubled Assets Relief Program (TARP)** is a United States Treasury program set up and funded with $700 billion by the Emergency Economic Stabilization Act of 2008.

Originally H.R. 1424, this was the ballyhooed "bailout bill," enacted October 2, 2008, when the credit markets were frozen and the American economy seemed to be on the brink of implosion.

Effect of Government Programs

The long-term effect of these government programs has yet to be determined. In the short term, in 2008–2009, they prevented the mortgage market from becoming frozen and helped to stabilize the banking industry. They provided hope for many homeowners to avoid default or foreclosure.

Aftermath

The aftermath of the crisis is that it has taken many years and significant agony to play out. People have realized that real estate does not always appreciate in value. Lenders have relearned to apply high standards to qualify buyers for mortgage loans and have come to understand their own vulnerability to failure.

Questions on Chapter 13

1. A type of mortgage in which the lender makes periodic payments to the borrower, who is required to be age 62 or older in the FHA program, is called:
   (A) Opposite
   (B) Accelerate
   (C) Reverse
   (D) Deficit

2. A conventional mortgage is
   (A) amortizing
   (B) guaranteed by the FHA
   (C) not guaranteed by any government agency
   (D) approved by the VA

3. A chattel mortgage is usually given in connection with
   (A) realty   (C) personal property
   (B) farms   (D) commercial property

4. The lending of money at a rate of interest above the legal rate is
   (A) speculation   (C) both A and B
   (B) usury   (D) neither A nor B

5. One discount point is equal to
   (A) 1% of the sales price
   (B) 1% of the interest rate
   (C) 1% of the loan amount
   (D) none of the above

6. Discount points in FHA and VA loans are generally paid by the
   (A) lender   (C) seller
   (B) purchaser   (D) broker

7. The main appeal of VA mortgages to borrowers lies in
   (A) low interest rates
   (B) minimum down payments
   (C) an unlimited mortgage ceiling
   (D) easy availability

8. When a loan is assumed on property that is sold,
   (A) the original borrower is relieved of further responsibility
   (B) the purchaser becomes liable for the debt
   (C) the purchaser must obtain a certificate of eligibility
   (D) all of the above

9. An estoppel certificate is required when the
   (A) mortgage is sold to an investor
   (B) property is sold
   (C) property is being foreclosed
   (D) mortgage is assumed

10. An owner who seeks a mortgage loan and offers three properties as security will give
    (A) a blanket mortgage
    (B) an FHA mortgage
    (C) a conventional mortgage
    (D) a chattel mortgage

11. A clause in a mortgage or accompanying note that permits the creditor to declare the entire principal balance due upon certain default of the debtor is
    (A) an acceleration clause
    (B) an escalation clause
    (C) a forfeiture clause
    (D) an excelerator clause

12. Which of the following statements is (are) false?
    (A) VA loans are insured loans.
    (B) FHA loans are guaranteed loans.
    (C) both A and B
    (D) neither A nor B

13. A second mortgage is
    (A) a lien on real estate that has a prior mortgage on it
    (B) the first mortgage recorded
    (C) always made by the seller
    (D) smaller in amount than a first mortgage

14. A large final payment on a mortgage loan is
    (A) an escalator   (C) an amortization
    (B) a balloon   (D) a package

15. A requirement for a borrower under an FHA-insured loan is that he
    (A) not be eligible for a VA or conventional loan
    (B) have cash for the down payment and closing costs
    (C) have his wife sign as coborrower
    (D) certify that he is receiving welfare payments

16. A mortgaged property can
    (A) be sold without the consent of the mortgagee
    (B) be conveyed by the grantor's making a deed to the grantee
    (C) both A and B
    (D) neither A nor B

17. In the absence of an agreement to the contrary, the mortgage normally having priority will be the one
    (A) for the greatest amount
    (B) that is a permanent mortgage
    (C) that was recorded first
    (D) that is a construction loan mortgage

18. The mortgagor's right to reestablish ownership after delinquency is known as
    (A) reestablishment
    (B) satisfaction
    (C) equity of redemption
    (D) acceleration

19. The Federal National Mortgage Association is active in the
    (A) principal mortgage market
    (B) secondary mortgage market
    (C) term mortgage market
    (D) second mortgage market

20. The money for making FHA loans is provided by
    (A) qualified lending institutions
    (B) the Department of Housing and Urban Development
    (C) the Federal Housing Administration
    (D) the Federal Savings and Loan Insurance Corporation

21. Amortization is best defined as
    (A) liquidation of a debt
    (B) depreciation of a tangible asset
    (C) winding up a business
    (D) payment of interest

22. A mortgage is usually released of record by a
    (A) general warranty deed
    (B) quitclaim deed
    (C) satisfaction piece
    (D) court decree

23. Loans from savings and loan associations may be secured by mortgages on
    (A) real estate
    (B) mobile homes
    (C) both A and B
    (D) neither A nor B

24. The borrower is the
    (A) mortgagee
    (B) creditor
    (C) mortgagor
    (D) both A and B

25. In an amortizing mortgage, the
    (A) principal is reduced periodically along with the payment of interest for that period
    (B) principal is paid at the end of the term
    (C) lenders have greater security than in an unamortizing mortgage
    (D) loan-to-value ratio does not exceed 30%

26. A term mortgage is characterized by
    (A) level payments toward principal
    (B) interest-only payments until maturity
    (C) variable payments
    (D) fixed payments including both principal and interest

27. Mortgage bankers
    (A) are subject to regulations of the Federal Reserve System
    (B) are regulated by federal, not state, corporation laws
    (C) act as primary lenders
    (D) earn fees paid by new borrowers and lenders

28. The seller of realty takes, as partial payment, a mortgage called
    (A) sales financing
    (B) note toting
    (C) primary mortgage
    (D) purchase money mortgage

29. A state in which a borrower retains title to the real property pledged as security for a debt is a
    (A) lien theory state
    (B) title theory state
    (C) creditor state
    (D) community property state

30. A state in which a mortgage conveys title to the lender is known as a
    (A) lien theory state
    (B) title theory state
    (C) conveyance state
    (D) community property state

31. A biweekly mortgage requires
    (A) monthly payments to increase by
        predetermined steps each year
    (B) payments every two weeks
    (C) that the lender share profits from resale
    (D) none of the above

32. The use of reverse annuity mortgages
    (A) is widespread because of inflation
    (B) helps elderly people who are house rich
        but cash poor
    (C) is losing importance with inflation
    (D) none of the above

33. The Federal Housing Administration's role in
    financing the purchase of real property is to
    (A) act as the lender of funds
    (B) insure loans made by approved lenders
    (C) purchase specific trust deeds
    (D) do all of the above

34. The instrument used to remove the lien of a
    trust deed from record is called a
    (A) satisfaction lien
    (B) release deed
    (C) deed of conveyance
    (D) certificate of redemption

35. The type of mortgage loan that permits borrow-
    ing additional funds at a later date is called
    (A) an equitable mortgage
    (B) a junior mortgage
    (C) an open-end mortgage
    (D) an extensible mortgage

36. A loan to be completely repaid, principal and
    interest, by a series of regular, equal installment
    payments is a
    (A) straight loan
    (B) balloon-payment loan
    (C) fully amortized loan
    (D) variable-rate mortgage loan

37. The instrument used to secure a loan on
    personal property is called a
    (A) bill of sale
    (B) trust deed
    (C) security agreement
    (D) bill of exchange

38. A secured real property loan usually consists of
    (A) financing statement and trust deed
    (B) the debt (note) and the lien (deed of trust)
    (C) FHA or PMI insurance
    (D) security agreement and financing statement

39. When a loan is fully amortized by equal monthly
    payments of principal and interest, the amount
    applied to principal
    (A) and interest remains constant
    (B) decreases while the interest payment
        increases
    (C) increases while the interest payment
        decreases
    (D) increases by a constant amount

40. A *subordination clause* in a trust deed may
    (A) permit the obligation to be paid off ahead
        of schedule
    (B) prohibit the trustor from making an addi-
        tional loan against the property before the
        trust deed is paid off
    (C) allow for periodic renegotiation and adjust-
        ment in the terms of the obligation
    (D) give priority to liens subsequently recorded
        against the property

41. *PMI* stands for
    (A) public money interest
    (B) payments made on investments
    (C) principal and mortgage interest
    (D) private mortgage insurance

42. High loan-to-value ratio loans generally are
    accompanied by
    (A) FHA insurance   (C) PMI
    (B) VA guarantees   (D) any of the above

43. Low interest rates cause
    (A) higher inflation rates
    (B) housing to be more affordable
    (C) higher loan-to-value ratios
    (D) owner financing to be more readily available

44. Rental income received appears on
    (A) balance sheet
    (B) cash flow statement
    (C) both of the above
    (D) neither of the above

45. A trust deed will always have a(n)
    (A) acceleration clause
    (B) assumability clause
    (C) prepayment penalty
    (D) lis pendens

46. Virtually all deeds of trust will have a clause that states that the full principal is due upon certain default. This is called a(n)
    (A) release clause
    (B) acceleration clause
    (C) novation clause
    (D) assignability clause

47. A VA loan amount is based on
    (A) Certificate of Reasonable Value
    (B) term of military service
    (C) secondary mortgage market
    (D) FNMA loan limits

48. In a fully amortizing loan,
    (A) the payment toward principal increases as the loan is amortized
    (B) the payment toward interest decreases as the loan is amortized
    (C) the principal and interest payment remains constant
    (D) all of the above

49. Most investors' principal motivation is
    (A) income tax shelter
    (B) housing the needy
    (C) increasing prestige
    (D) making a profit

50. Because of its illiquidity, large size, and lack of portability, investors expect commercial real estate to provide _____ return, compared to marketable securities.
    (A) a higher   (C) the same
    (B) a lower   (D) an unknown

51. When the buyer pays the cost with a lump-sum check and the seller delivers the deed, the arrangement is a
    (A) purchase money mortgage
    (B) contract for deed
    (C) contract for purchase and sale
    (D) closing

52. After a mortgage is paid off, most lenders are expected to
    (A) keep all records for five years
    (B) send a recorded satisfaction piece
    (C) file a lien
    (D) refinance the loan upon request

53. The bank agreed to lend Ira $300,000, with his house as collateral. Of this amount, Ira received $200,000 immediately and could borrow the $100,000 balance in installments. This is called
    (A) an open-end mortgage
    (B) a blanket mortgage
    (C) an amortizing loan
    (D) a P&I mortgage

54. A loan that is approved quickly and has a low down payment usually has
    (A) higher costs and interest rate
    (B) lower costs and interest rate
    (C) a longer amortization period
    (D) an adjustable rate

55. Two months in a row a homeowner failed to make payments on his trust deed, so the lender recorded a notice of default. The borrower
    (A) cannot stop foreclosure
    (B) must repair his credit report
    (C) may walk away
    (D) may request reinstatement

56. A loan from the seller to the buyer is called a
    (A) bullet loan
    (B) home equity loan
    (C) junior mortgage
    (D) purchase money mortgage

57. The Truth-in-Lending Law is also known as
    (A) RESPA   (C) Regulation Z
    (B) USPAP   (D) FREC

58. The purpose of prequalifying a buyer is to
    (A) determine the buyer's ability to pay
    (B) exclude other agents
    (C) earn a fee for this effort
    (D) determine buyer preferences and taste

59. Leverage is
    (A) a broker's employment of a salesperson
    (B) using cash for all purchases
    (C) using credit cards
    (D) using borrowed money to complete an investment purchase

60. A mortgage loan that includes two or more properties is
    (A) an acquisition and development mortgage
    (B) a total lien mortgage
    (C) a blanket mortgage
    (D) a participation mortgage

61. A *callable* loan is
    (A) one that the lender may call "due" at any time
    (B) one on which the lender may increase the interest rate
    (C) one on which the borrower can prepay the principal without penalty
    (D) one that allows the borrower to draw against a line of credit

62. When property is sold "subject to" a mortgage, the person primarily responsible for repayment is
    (A) the buyer
    (B) the lender
    (C) the one who assumes the loan
    (D) the seller

63. Fannie Mae is
    (A) an originator of mortgage loans
    (B) a purchaser of mortgage loans
    (C) an agency of the Federal Housing Administration
    (D) a branch of the Federal Reserve

64. The seller would have the least financing exposure in
    (A) new financing by buyer
    (B) purchase money mortgage
    (C) assumption of loan by buyer
    (D) purchase "subject to" mortgage

65. A first-time buyer's down payment source may be
    (A) savings
    (B) a gift from a relative
    (C) a personal loan
    (D) any of the above

66. A lender should consider which of these factors before issuing a loan?
    (A) property value
    (B) borrower's credit rating
    (C) down payment
    (D) all of the above

67. A real estate investment trust requires at least _____ shareholders.
    (A) 10   (C) 100
    (B) 35   (D) 1,000

68. The most important function of the FHA is to
    (A) make loans   (C) purchase loans
    (B) insure loans   (D) sell loans

69. Which of the following participate(s) in the secondary loan market?
    (A) Fannie Mae   (C) Ginnie Mae
    (B) Freddie Mac   (D) all of the above

70. Private mortgage insurance protects the
    (A) buyer's heirs   (C) buyer's income
    (B) lender   (D) investment value

71. *P&I* in real estate finance stands for
    (A) property and investments
    (B) property and inventory
    (C) principal and interest
    (D) principal and inventory

72. A clause in a mortgage that limits the owner's liability to the property is
    (A) recourse   (C) assumption
    (B) subordination   (D) exculpatory

73. The seller has agreed to pay two points to the lending institution to help the buyers obtain a mortgage loan. The house was listed for $320,000 and is being sold for $300,000. The buyers will pay 20% in cash and borrow the rest. How much will the seller owe to the lender for points?
    (A) $6,400   (C) $5,120
    (B) $4,800   (D) $6,000

74. The lender's underwriting criteria specify a maximum housing expense to income ratio of 28%. If the applicant proves annual earnings of $75,000 in the previous year, and that salary is continuing, the maximum monthly PITI would be
    (A) $2,100   (C) $2,800
    (B) $1,750   (D) $2,700

75. Which of the following is an advantage of a biweekly mortgage payment plan?
    (A) The borrower pays less per month in return for a longer term.
    (B) It is equivalent to 12 monthly payments each year.
    (C) There are lower interest rates.
    (D) The loan is paid off sooner than it would be with 12 monthly payments.

76. Common covenants found in a mortgage include all of the following *except*
    (A) keep the property in good repair
    (B) pay all current real estate taxes
    (C) provide unlimited access to the mortgagee
    (D) not damage any improvements securing the loan

77. The function of the Federal Housing Administration (FHA) is to
    (A) lend money
    (B) insure loans
    (C) guarantee loans
    (D) buy loans

78. The buyer who agrees to pay an existing loan but does not take personal responsibility
    (A) assumes the loan
    (B) takes the property subject to the loan
    (C) subordinates the loan
    (D) forecloses on the loan

79. In general, the lien with first claim on the real estate is the
    (A) largest one
    (B) one that is signed
    (C) one that was recorded first
    (D) one that is foreclosed

80. When a borrower is required to maintain an escrow account with the lending institution, money in that account may be used to pay the homeowner's
    (A) Realtor
    (B) utility bills
    (C) property taxes or insurance
    (D) life insurance

81. Which of the following describes a mortgage package?
    (A) A loan that is packaged with other loans to sell to the secondary market.
    (B) A standardized loan package to be used in financing the purchase of a single-family home.
    (C) A loan with more than one parcel of real estate as collateral.
    (D) A loan with both real and personal property as collateral.

82. Which one of the following does not affect the interest rate adjustment in an adjustable-rate mortgage loan?
    (A) index
    (B) equity value
    (C) margin
    (D) cap

83. To secure a loan in some states, the borrower conveys title to the property to a disinterested third party for safekeeping. In this situation, the document required is a
    (A) general warranty deed
    (B) deed of trust
    (C) involuntary conveyance
    (D) mortgage

84. What is the definition of a mortgage?
    (A) A promise to repay a loan under specific terms and conditions.
    (B) A pledge of personal liability in case of delinquency.
    (C) A description of the loan and the collateral on that loan.
    (D) A pledge of property as collateral for a debt.

85. In a fixed-rate amortized loan, which one of the following does not vary from month to month?
    (A) monthly principal and interest payment
    (B) interest paid
    (C) principal paid
    (D) remaining principal balance

86. A property is foreclosed and sold for nonpayment of the mortgage loan. The sale does not cover the remaining balance of the mortgage loan. The bank goes to court to collect the shortfall, which is called a
    (A) judicial foreclosure
    (B) statutory redemption
    (C) equitable redemption
    (D) deficiency judgment

87. A young married woman's income is discounted by 40% by a bank when she applies for a mortgage loan because she is of childbearing age. This is
    (A) illegal discrimination
    (B) legal discrimination because of the business aspects of banking
    (C) legal because she might quit her job and be unable to make payments
    (D) legal because protection of depositors' money supersedes other laws

88. Which of the following is not an obligation of the mortgagor?
    (A) maintain the property
    (B) keep hazard insurance in force
    (C) get permission for alterations
    (D) advise the mortgagee of a change in the escrow account balance

89. A mortgage is best described as what type of lien?
    (A) involuntary and general
    (B) trust or estate
    (C) voluntary and specific
    (D) involuntary and specific

90. A person buys a furnished house and wishes to finance the purchase of both the house and the furniture through a mortgage loan. He tries to get
    (A) a blanket mortgage
    (B) a purchase-money mortgage
    (C) a temporary loan
    (D) a package mortgage

91. Buying real property "subject to the mortgage" is
    (A) a type of condition loan
    (B) a mortgage bought by FHA and sold to Ginnie Mae
    (C) taking title to property with no personal responsibility for paying the mortgage loan
    (D) the right to foreclose without going to court

92. Which one of the following is true when the seller takes back a mortgage from the buyer as part payment for the sale?
    (A) The seller retains possession of the property until the debt is paid.
    (B) The seller retains legal title.
    (C) A second mortgage may not be placed on the property by the buyer.
    (D) This is a purchase-money mortgage.

ANSWERS

1. C	20. A	39. C	58. A	77. B
2. C	21. A	40. D	59. D	78. B
3. C	22. C	41. D	60. C	79. C
4. B	23. C	42. D	61. A	80. C
5. C	24. C	43. B	62. D	81. D
6. C	25. A	44. B	63. B	82. B
7. B	26. B	45. A	64. A	83. B
8. B	27. D	46. B	65. D	84. D
9. A	28. D	47. A	66. D	85. A
10. A	29. A	48. D	67. C	86. D
11. A	30. B	49. D	68. B	87. A
12. C	31. B	50. A	69. D	88. D
13. A	32. B	51. D	70. B	89. C
14. B	33. B	52. B	71. C	90. D
15. B	34. B	53. A	72. D	91. C
16. C	35. C	54. A	73. B	92. D
17. C	36. C	55. D	74. B	
18. C	37. C	56. D	75. D	
19. B	38. B	57. C	76. C	

Appraisals

REQUIREMENTS FOR APPRAISAL LICENSING

Most states have at least two appraiser classifications; some have as many as four.

- **Certified residential appraiser.** This designation allows its holder to appraise residential properties of one to four units, having no limit on the value.
  Education. Requires 200 classroom hours of precertification education, including coverage of the Uniform Standards of Professional Appraisal Practice, and an associate degree or higher or 21 semester hours in certain courses.
  Experience. 2,500 hours.
- **Certified general appraiser.** This designation allows its holder to appraise any property of any value.
  Education. Requires 300 classroom hours of precertification education, including coverage of the Uniform Standards of Professional Appraisal Practice, and a bachelor's degree or higher or 30 semester hours in certain courses.
  Experience. 3,000 hours.
- **Licensed appraiser.** This designation allows its holder to appraise residential properties of one to four units valued up to $1 million.
  Education. Requires 150 classroom hours of precertification education, including coverage of the Uniform Standards of Professional Appraisal Practice.
  Experience. 2,000 hours in no less than 12 months.
- **Registered appraiser.** This is an "apprentice" or "trainee" designation that does not require an examination.
  Education. Requires 75 classroom hours of precertification education, including coverage of the Uniform Standards of Professional Appraisal Practice.
  Experience. None

Appraisal Examinations

No examination is required to be a registered appraiser in the states that offer that designation. All three of the examinations for the other designations consist of 100 questions, and candidates are given four hours for completion. A score of 75% is passing for all exams.

To apply for an appraisal license in most states, an applicant must:

1. Be 18 years old or older.
2. Have a high school diploma or equivalent.
3. Provide evidence of successful completion of the educational requirements.
4. Make it possible for the Appraisal Board to begin an inquiry as to competence and qualifications by disclosing records of crimes or proceedings, mental disabilities, and disclosures of suspensions or revocations of other professional licenses.

Government Regulation of Appraisers

At one time, anyone could claim to be an appraiser, since there was no mandatory test of the skills required to estimate property value. The higher qualifications of some individuals were (and still are) recognized by professional designations conferred by appraisal associations, but such designation was not a requirement for practice as an appraiser. Since the early 1990s, however, a real estate appraiser must be licensed or certified in his or her state in order to appraise property in a federally related transaction. Since federally related transactions include any in which an FDIC-insured bank, FNMA, FHLMC, or GNMA, is involved, probably 90% or more of real estate appraisals are now prepared by a state-licensed or -certified appraiser. A licensed real estate broker or salesperson may appraise real estate in situations where there is not a federally related transaction.

Government regulation was imposed as a result of the savings and loan debacle of the 1980s, when numerous savings institutions collapsed, largely as a result of defective or nonexistent real estate appraisals. An appraisal serves as evidence that a loan is properly supported by collateral and thus serves to protect our nation's financial institutions.

WHAT IS AN APPRAISAL?

An *appraisal* is an expert's opinion of value. Appraisals are used in real estate when a professional's opinion of value is needed. Because each property is unique and is not traded in a centralized, organized market, value estimates require the collection and analysis of market data.

To understand what appraisals are, please examine the preceding definition more closely. By *an expert,* we mean a person with the competence and experience to do the type of analysis required. You can get opinions of value from the sales agent, the owner, the tenant, or anyone else familiar with the property. However, these opinions may not be very useful and probably won't be convincing as evidence of value. Usually, an appraisal expert has attained some type of designation through formal study and examination by a recognized body such as the state or a professional organization.

An *opinion* is a judgment supported by facts and logical analysis. The appraiser considers all available information that reflects on the value of the property and then follows a logical process to arrive at an opinion. The result is not merely a guess but a careful reading of the facts in the case.

As shown in Figure 14-1, The Appraisal Process, the preparation of an appraisal report is an eight-step problem-solving exercise that begins with *defining the problem*—for example, "to estimate market value." The second step is to *plan the appraisal*. The third is *data collection and verification*. Fourth, the *highest and best use* of the site is considered, and fifth, the *land value* is estimated. Three *approaches to appraisal*—*cost, sales comparison,* and *income* (or capitalization) are applied as a sixth step. Each approach provides an independent value estimate. The seventh step is *reconciliation,* in which the value estimates from the three approaches are considered and a *final value conclusion* is reached. The last step is a written *report.* Each of these steps will be covered in more detail later in the chapter.

WHY APPRAISALS ARE NEEDED

An appraisal may be sought for any of a number of purposes, including the following:

1. To help buyers and/or sellers determine how much to offer or accept.
2. To assist lenders in determining the maximum prudent amount to lend on real estate.
3. To arrive at fair compensation when private property is taken for public use.
4. To determine the amount to insure, or the value loss caused by a natural disaster.
5. To determine the viability of a proposed building, renovation, or rehabilitation program.
6. To assist in corporate mergers, reorganizations, and liquidations.
7. To determine taxes due, including income, gift, estate, and ad valorem taxes.

The following sections present some other specialized uses of appraisal.

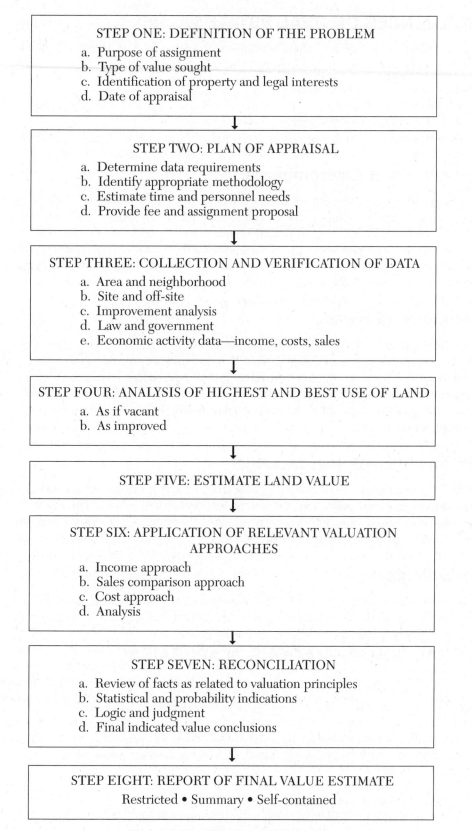

STEP ONE: DEFINITION OF THE PROBLEM

a. Purpose of assignment
b. Type of value sought
c. Identification of property and legal interests
d. Date of appraisal

STEP TWO: PLAN OF APPRAISAL

a. Determine data requirements
b. Identify appropriate methodology
c. Estimate time and personnel needs
d. Provide fee and assignment proposal

STEP THREE: COLLECTION AND VERIFICATION OF DATA

a. Area and neighborhood
b. Site and off-site
c. Improvement analysis
d. Law and government
e. Economic activity data—income, costs, sales

STEP FOUR: ANALYSIS OF HIGHEST AND BEST USE OF LAND

a. As if vacant
b. As improved

STEP FIVE: ESTIMATE LAND VALUE

STEP SIX: APPLICATION OF RELEVANT VALUATION APPROACHES

a. Income approach
b. Sales comparison approach
c. Cost approach
d. Analysis

STEP SEVEN: RECONCILIATION

a. Review of facts as related to valuation principles
b. Statistical and probability indications
c. Logic and judgment
d. Final indicated value conclusions

STEP EIGHT: REPORT OF FINAL VALUE ESTIMATE
Restricted • Summary • Self-contained

Figure 14-1. The Appraisal Process

Source: INCOME APPRAISAL ANALYSIS, Jack P. Friedman and Nicholas Ordway, © 1988. Adapted by permission of Prentice Hall, Inc., Upper Saddle River, New Jersey.

INFLUENCES ON REAL ESTATE VALUE

Forces affecting real estate values operate on the international and national, regional, and local community levels. These forces can be categorized as follows:

1. Physical and environmental
2. Economic-financial
3. Political-governmental-legal
4. Sociological

Physical and Environmental

Physical and environmental forces include such factors as dimensions, shape, area, topography, drainage, and soil conditions, as well as utilities, streets, curbs, gutters, sidewalks, landscaping, and the effect of legal restraints (zoning, deed restrictions) on physical development.

Nuisances and hazards are also to be considered, including contaminated air and water and environmentally hazardous building materials such as asbestos, PCBs, certain types of mold, and urea formaldehyde.

Economic-Financial

The fixed location of land and its immobility distinguish land from other assets. Land is dependent on where it is and what surrounds it. Urban land derives its value from its location. The most significant determinants of value are the type of industry in the area, employment and unemployment rates and types, interest rates, per capita and household income, and stability. These matters also affect the individual property, including real estate prices and mortgage payments.

Political-Governmental-Legal

Political-governmental-legal factors focus on the services provided, such as utilities, spending and taxation policies, police and fire protection, recreation, schools, garbage collection, and on planning, zoning, and subdivision regulations. Building codes and the level of taxes and assessments are also important considerations.

Sociological

Sociological factors are concerned with the characteristics of people living in the area, the population density and homogeneity, and compatibility of the land uses with the needs of residents.

LEGAL CONSIDERATIONS IN APPRAISAL

Appraisers are expected to know and consider legal matters affecting real estate in making their appraisals. These matters are covered elsewhere in this book. Specific topics and coverage follow:

A. Real estate vs. real property (Chapters 2 and 3)
B. Real property vs. personal property (Chapters 2 and 3)
   1. Fixtures
   2. Trade fixtures
   3. Machinery and equipment
C. Limitations on real estate ownership (Chapters 2 and 3)
   1. Private
      a. Deed restrictions
      b. Leases

   c. Mortgages
   d. Easements
   e. Liens
   f. Encroachments
  2. Public
   a. Police power
    (1) Zoning
    (2) Building and fire codes
    (3) Environmental regulations
   b. Taxation
    (1) Property tax
    (2) Special assessments
   c. Eminent domain
   d. Escheat
 D. Legal rights and interests (Chapters 3 and 10)
  1. Fee simple estate
  2. Life estate
  3. Leasehold interest
  4. Leased fee interest
  5. Other legal interests
   a. Easement
   b. Encroachment
 E. Forms of property ownership (Chapter 3)
  1. Individual
  2. Tenancies and undivided interest
  3. Special ownership forms
   a. Condominiums
   b. Cooperative
   c. Timesharing
 F. Legal descriptions (Chapter 7)
  1. Metes and bounds
  2. Government survey
  3. Lot and block
 G. Transfer of title (Chapter 9)
  1. Basic types of deeds
  2. Recordation

TYPES OF VALUE APPRAISED

There are numerous types of value that the appraiser may be asked to estimate.

Market Value

Market value is the major focus of most real property appraisal assignments. Both economic and legal definitions of market value have been developed and defined. A current economic definition agreed upon by agencies that regulate federal financial institutions in the United States of America is:[1]

  The most probable price which a property should bring in a competitive and open market under all conditions requisite to a fair sale, the buyer and seller each acting prudently and knowledgeably, and assuming the price is not affected by undue stimulus. Implicit in this definition is the consummation of a sale as of a specified date and the passing of title from seller to buyer under conditions whereby:

---

[1] *Dictionary of Real Estate Appraisal,* 5th ed. (Chicago: Appraisal Institute, 2010), p.123; definition 3.

- Buyer and seller are typically motivated;
- Both parties are well informed or well advised, and acting in what they consider their best interests;
- A reasonable time is allowed for exposure in the open market;
- Payment is made in terms of cash in U.S. dollars or in terms of financial arrangements comparable thereto; and
- The price represents the normal consideration for the property sold unaffected by special or creative financing or sales concessions granted by anyone associated with the sale.

Value Contrasted with Cost and Price

Value, cost, and price are not the same. *Value* is a measure of how much a purchaser would likely be willing to pay for the property being appraised. *Cost* is a measure of the expenditures necessary to produce a similar property. Depending on several factors, this cost could be higher or lower than the current value. *Price* is the historic fact of how much was spent on similar properties in past transactions. Neither past prices nor cost will necessarily represent a fair measure of current value.

Other Types of Value

Although market value is the most common value sought, an appraiser may be asked to estimate some other value needed for a specific purpose. Included are such values as *loan value*, *insurable value*, *book value*, *rental value*, *fair value*, *salvage value*, *investment value*, and many others.

LOAN VALUE OR MORTGAGE VALUE

Loan or *mortgage value* is the same as market value. Property serving as collateral for a loan or mortgage is normally valued at market value.

INVESTMENT VALUE

Investment value is the estimated value of a certain real estate investment to a particular individual or institutional investor. It may be greater or less than market value depending on the investor's particular situation. For example, the investment value of vacant land in the path of growth would be greater for a young, aggressive investor who has time to wait for fruition than for an elderly widow who needs available cash for living expenses. Similarly, the investment value of a tax shelter is greater for a high-tax-bracket investor than for a tax-exempt pension plan.

VALUE IN USE AND VALUE IN EXCHANGE

Value in use, which tends to be subjective because it is not set in the market, is the worth of a property to a specific user or set of users. It considers the value of the property when put to a specific use as part of a going concern. For example, the use of a factory where automobiles are assembled may have a high value to the manufacturer, even though the market value of the property is difficult to measure and may be low because there are few interested buyers. Value in use is distinguished from *value in exchange*, which is the value of a commodity, in terms of money, to people in general rather than to a specific person. Value in exchange is a more objective measure and is commonly identified with market value.

ASSESSED VALUE

The *assessed value* (or *assessed valuation*) is the value of property established for property tax purposes. Although tax assessors try to value most property at market value (or some specified fraction of market value), the fact that they must assess a great number of properties periodically on a limited budget often means that assessed values are quite different from market values.

INSURABLE VALUE

The *insurable value* of a property is the cost of total replacement of its destructible improvements. For example, suppose a home that sold for $100,000 ten years ago would cost $200,000 to rebuild today, not including land cost. Its insurable value would be $200,000 even if its current market value, including the land, was only $175,000.

GOING-CONCERN VALUE

Going-concern value is the worth of a business, such as a hotel, based on its operations. The replacement cost of the property may be much more or much less than the business is worth.

Comparative Market Analysis

Very often, property owners want to get an idea of what their real estate is worth, without paying for a full appraisal. For example, a homeowner may contact a broker or salesperson to list her house, and will accept the broker's or salesperson's judgment of its value or amount for a house to be listed and put on the market. A broker may not wish to spend the time to prepare a full-blown appraisal just to solicit a listing, even if she is perfectly qualified to do so. Further, unless the broker is licensed or certified by the state, the appraisal could not be used to support a loan by a federally chartered bank or savings association.

A Comparative Market Analysis (CMA) will be prepared by the broker or salesperson for this purpose. Unlike the standard preprinted forms required for Fannie Mae/Freddie Mac residential appraisals, there is no standard form for a CMA. Brokers are free to include whatever information they wish to use, and present it in any manner.

A CMA is likely to show recent sales of other houses in the neighborhood, and salient characteristics. It may also show properties currently for sale on the market. Consider the data in Table 14-1.

Table 14-1
COMPARATIVE MARKET ANALYSIS

Property	Price	Date	Sq. Ft.	# Bedrooms	# Baths	Stories	Per SF
Subject	?	Now	2,000	4	2	1	?
Comp 1	$420,000	Last year	2,100	4	2	2	$200.00
Comp 2	$380,000	Last year	1,950	3	1.5	1	$194.88
Comp 3	$470,000	Six months	2,250	4	2.5	1	$202.88
Asking 1	$430,000	Now	2,050	3	2	2	$209.74
Asking 2	$450,000	Now	2,100	3	2	1	$214.28

This particular CMA might be used to judge a market range (highest and lowest prices per square foot). However, it offers no information on special features, the age or condition of the houses, nor how long it took to sell them or how long the existing listings have been on the market. So, a CMA is not as detailed or thorough as an appraisal, though it may provide a reasonable indication of property value.

Comparative (Residential) Market Analysis

A *comparative (residential) market analysis* (CMA or RMA) provides information on the current situation of the housing market. It tries to answer the question, "How is the market?" A response might be, "There are currently 102 homes for sale in northeast Tallahassee. Twenty homes were newly listed last month, and 27 sold last month. The average time on the market for those that sold was 62 days. Of those that sold, 67% were in the $400,000–$500,000 price range, with 10% in the $500,000–$600,000 range and 5% above $600,000. Eight percent were below $300,000, and 10% were between $300,000 and $400,000. Houses with fewer than two full bathrooms are not doing well. About half of the buyers are local 'move-ups,' with the other half transferees. Prices seem to be rising slightly."

As is apparent, the purpose of an RMA is to describe the current condition of the real estate market. This may help answer the question of whether this is a good time to buy or sell and whether prices are rising or falling.

Automated Valuation Models

Automated Valuation Models (AVMs) apply complex statistical techniques to data on comparable sales to offer an estimate of value. AVMs are often used by those offering home equity loans who don't want to incur a $350–$400 appraisal fee. For a typical fee of $50, a value estimate is provided, which may consider the size, age, location, and number of rooms in the house. If a lender wants greater assurance of value than an AVM offers, he may ask for a site visit or a full appraisal.

Evaluations

An *evaluation* of real estate is a study that does not lead to an estimate of market value. An evaluation may be performed to consider the feasibility of a proposed use (feasibility study), the highest and best use of the property, or a market study that considers the supply and demand in the current market for a certain type of land use.

ECONOMIC PRINCIPLES

Economics involves combining the *factors of production* to result in a product that is worth more than the cost of the individual factors. The factors of production are land, labor, capital, and entrepreneurship. For example, to produce a bushel of wheat may require $1 for land rent, $1 for labor, $1 for equipment, and $1 for the business management and risk-taking entrepreneur. This is a total of $4, so the farming operation would not occur unless the expected selling price was $4.01 or more per bushel. Many economists recognize only three factors of production, regarding profit as the owners' compensation for their risk taking and inputs of management and entrepreneurship. Certain economic principles are associated with real estate valuation. The major principles are explained below.

Anticipation

Anticipation is determination of the present worth of income or other benefits one expects to receive in the future from the ownership of property. For income-producing properties, value is based on the anticipated net receipts from the operation of the assets plus any amounts to be received upon resale.

Balance (Proportionality)

For any type of land use, there are optimal amounts of different factors of production that can be combined to create maximum land values. Land, labor, capital, and entrepreneurship can be combined in different proportions, as is demonstrated by the number of houses that may be erected on a parcel of land. Values are maximized when factors are in proportion, or *balance* is achieved.

Change

Real estate values tend not to remain constant, but to vary over time. New technology and social patterns create new demands for real estate. Demographic *changes* create needs for different kinds of housing. People's desires and tastes undergo transitions. Neighborhoods go through a life cycle of growth, maturity, decline, and renewal. Any of these factors and many others can change the utility of real estate at a given location.

Objects wear out. New businesses are started, and others end. The land use pattern is modified by private and public actions. Money supply and interest rates fluctuate. Economic conditions create opportunities or stifle growth.

Competition

When profits exceed the income necessary to pay for the factor of production, *competition* will tend to enter the market, causing average net incomes to fall. This principle is important to an analyst attempting to estimate the value of property that is selling above the cost of its replacement. Its high cost attracts builders and developers, who can earn a large profit from new construction.

Conformity

Conformity is a measure of how well the architectural style and levels of amenities and services offered by a real estate development meet market needs and expectations. A project that fails to conform to market standards is likely to suffer a financial penalty. This does not mean, for example, that all buildings in a particular location must be of the same architectural style. However, the architectural styles and the land use must be compatible. Consider the consequences of building a brightly painted Victorian house replete with architectural gingerbread in a neighborhood of split-level houses. Consider also what would happen if a municipal incinerator were constructed next to a nursing home. The nursing home might have to close because of the health hazard posed by the smoke and other pollution.

Contribution

Contribution is the amount by which the value or net income of an economic good is increased or decreased by the presence or absence of some additional factor of production. Contribution is the value increment or detriment to an economic good by the addition of some new factor, rather than the actual cost of the new factor itself. In real estate, some things add more than their cost of production, whereas others may actually detract from value. For example, a new exterior paint job may improve the appearance of a house and make it more salable. On the other hand, a potential buyer may regard a swimming pool as a liability rather than an asset.

An example of the principle of contribution would be a builder's deliberation over whether to add a tennis court to an apartment complex. The cost of this feature is $25,000. With the added tennis court, the complex is worth $1,100,000. Without it, it is worth only $1,000,000. Thus, the tennis court would add $75,000 to the overall value. Since the cost of adding this amenity is less than its contribution, a prudent builder would construct the tennis court.

Increasing and Decreasing Returns

As resources are added to fixed agents in production, net returns will tend to increase at an increasing rate up to a certain point. Thereafter, total returns will increase at a decreasing rate until the increment to value is less than the cost of resource unit input. A common problem faced by the owners of land is the determination of how intensively their land should be developed. Development should become more intensive as long as profit increases. For example, the profit on a downtown office building, to be sold above cost, may increase with the height of the building, up to a point. Above that height, the profit may decline.

Opportunity Cost

Opportunity cost is the return forfeited by not choosing an alternative. A person with $25,000 to invest may choose to buy equity in a rental residence rather than to purchase a certificate of deposit. The opportunity cost is the interest not received on the CD.

Substitution

The maximum value of a property is set by the lowest price or cost at which another property of equivalent utility may be acquired. This *substitution* principle underlies each of the three traditional approaches to value used in the appraisal process: (1) direct sales comparison, (2) income, and (3) cost. A rational purchaser will pay no more for a property than the lowest price being charged for another property of equivalent utility. Likewise, it is not prudent to pay more for an existing project if another one of equivalent utility can be produced, without unreasonable delay, for a lower cost. If an investor is analyzing an income stream, the maximum price is set by examining the prices at which other income streams of similar risk and quality can be purchased.

Supply and Demand

Supply is the quantity of goods, such as real estate, available at a given price schedule; *demand* is the quantity of goods desired at this price schedule. Demand is based on the desire of potential purchasers to acquire real estate, provided that they also have sufficient sources of financing to act on their desires. Together, supply and demand interact to establish prices.

In the long run, supply and demand are relatively effective forces in determining the direction of price changes. An excessive supply or lack of demand will tend to depress price levels. A contrary pressure, which serves to raise prices, occurs when there is either an inadequate supply or a high demand.

Surplus Productivity

Surplus productivity is the net income attributed to land after the costs of labor, capital, and entrepreneurship have been paid. Because land is physically immobile, the factors of labor, capital, and entrepreneurship must be attracted to it; therefore, these factors are compensated first. If any money is left over, this residual amount is paid as rent to the owner. In economic theory, land is said to have "residual value" and has worth only if a surplus remains after paying for the other factors of production.

REAL ESTATE MARKETS AND ANALYSIS

This topic is concerned with the characteristics of the real estate market, the analysis of use of additional space (absorption), the role of money and capital markets, and the financing terms available for a property. Market analysis and absorption are discussed below. Mortgages and finance were considered in Chapter 13.

Real Estate Markets

Real estate is not a single market but consists rather of a series of submarkets with different desires and needs that can change independently of one another. Consequently, real estate markets are said to be *segmented*. The market for retail space in north Atlanta may be quite different from that in east, west, or south Atlanta. Even within the directional quadrants there are significant differences, depending on the distance from downtown and from the nearest major artery or intersection. Within a narrow geographic area there may be a saturation of one type of retail space but not enough of another. For example, neighborhood shopping centers, which typically have a supermarket and a drugstore as anchor tenants, may be abundant, whereas there is no convenient regional mall.

Availability of Information

One key to successful appraisal is the ability to locate reliable, consistent data. Sources of market data for rental income and expense are described below.

NATIONALLY DISSEMINATED RENTAL AND OPERATING EXPENSE DATA

Certain national organizations collect information from owners and managers in major cities regarding local rents and operating expenses. Such information can be used judiciously to determine whether the data for a particular property appear consistent with experience reported nationally. Because the real estate market is fragmented, a data source appropriate for the specific property must be used.

Office Buildings. The Building Owners and Managers Association (BOMA) International provides information on office building rental rates and operating expenses experienced by its members in major U.S. cities. BOMA's address is

Building Owners and Managers International
1101 15th Street NW, Suite 800
Washington, DC 20005
www.boma.org

Shopping Centers. The Urban Land Institute (ULI) releases a new edition of *Dollars and Cents of Shopping Centers* every two years. ULI's address is

Urban Land Institute
1025 Thomas Jefferson Street, Suite 500W
Washington, DC 20007
www.uli.org

Apartments, Condominiums, and Cooperatives. The Institute of Real Estate Management (IREM) of the National Association of REALTORS® periodically provides the *Income/Expense Analysis* for various types of buildings (elevator, walk-up, others) in different cities. IREM's address is

Institute of Real Estate Management
430 N. Michigan Avenue
Chicago, IL 60611
www.irem.org

Hotels and Motels. One source of information on national and local trends is STR Global. Its address is

STR Global
735 E. Main Street
Hendersonville, TN 37075
Phone: (615) 824-8664
Fax: (615) 824-3848
www.strglobal.com

LOCAL SOURCES OF REAL ESTATE DATA

Local organizations often collect real estate data, usually for membership use or sale to interested parties. These include the following:

Local Boards of REALTORS. Most metropolitan areas have a Board of REALTORS, or other broker group, that sponsors a multiple listing service (MLS). Upon the sale of property listed through the MLS, the broker must supply information about the completed transaction. Each property sold and its terms of sale are therefore available on computer or in a published book. Some REALTOR boards provide information to members only; some share with other real estate organizations.

Local Tax Assessing Offices. Assessing offices usually keep a file card on every property in the jurisdiction, noting property characteristics, value estimate, and data from which the estimate was derived. Many jurisdictions are notified of every sale or building permit, for immediate update of affected properties.

Local Credit Bureaus and Tax Map Companies. These may have data on certain parcels; since their main business is not evaluation, however, they are not regular sources.

University Research Centers. University research centers, many of which are supported by state broker and salesperson license fees, may have aggregated data on real estate transactions collected from other sources throughout the state. These data are often helpful in identifying trends established over time and by city for various types of property. Additional research and educational information may also be available from such centers.

Private Data Sources. Many real estate investors retain files on their property. They will often share information, usually for reciprocity rather than payment.

Property Owners. Property owners' records include permanent records such as deeds, leases, and copies of mortgages (lenders have the original mortgage documents), as well as periodic accounting and tax return information about a property's recent past. An owner's report may be of limited immediate use, however, because it may be disorganized, contain extraneous information, or be arranged poorly for appraisal purposes. Also, data from a single property cannot offer a broad perspective on the market.

Demand for Property

An appraiser must always be concerned about the demand for a property. People must want to use the property enough to pay the rent asked. If the demand to use the property is high, the demand to buy the property will also be high. High demand means top rents, low vacancies, and good resale prospects. Poor demand means rent reductions, high vacancies, and a property that is hard to sell.

The following are the key items that produce demand for real estate:

Economic growth in the local area increases demand for all properties. New jobs and more residents increase the need for developed real estate. Rising incomes mean higher rents and prices, as well as more retail sales.

Good-quality property raises demand. A property should have all the standard features expected in the market, plus something extra that the competition doesn't have. Appearance, features, size, and services are valued in the market.

A *good location* improves demand. Location can make a poor-quality property profitable, while a good property in the wrong place can suffer.

A *competitive price* can increase demand. If a property is less than ideal, it may be able to compete on the basis of price. It is important to know what segment of the market the property is intended to serve and to price accordingly.

The *cost of alternatives* also determines demand. Apartments are more popular when house prices are high. Houses sell better when interest rates are low.

The demand for a type of property can be estimated by a market analysis. This will indicate whether there is room for more of that type of property in the market. The demand for a specific property can be determined by comparing its features, location, and price to those of similar properties.

MARKET ANALYSIS

Market analysis is the identification and study of current supply and demand conditions in a particular area for a specific type of property. Such a study is used to indicate how well a particular piece of real estate will be supported by the market. It identifies the most likely users of the project and determines how well they are being served by the existing supply of properties. In essence, the study shows whether there is a need for a new project, or whether an existing project has a good future.

For example, suppose a developer is considering construction of new luxury apartments in a certain town. A market study will first examine the sources of demand for the units. It will identify a *target market*: the type of tenants most likely to be attracted to the property. Description of the target market may include family income, typical family structure, and the features that potential buyers will desire in a residence. The analysis will then survey the market area and use all relevant available data sources to see how many people of this type exist and where they live. A good study will project growth trends in the target market, since a likely source of tenants will be new arrivals.

Next, the study will examine supply conditions. The number and the location of similar properties are identified. A survey of vacancies indicates how well supply matches demand. Features and characteristics of competing properties should be described, and some indication of market rents found. In addition, any new projects that will come along should be identified.

An appraiser should determine whether the market is unbalanced. When the supply of a certain type of real estate is short, rents and prices may be high, but only temporarily. New competition will add to the supply and drive prices down. By contrast, when a market is over-supplied, the price must be low enough to offer an attractive investment.

Market analysis is used to estimate the pace of rent-up or sales for a new project. This *absorption rate* may be expressed as an overall rate ("The market needs 1,000 new apartment units per year") or as a specific rate for the project ("Given current competition, the project should capture 200 new rentals per year"). An absorption rate estimate is important in projecting the revenue production of a property.

A market analysis may indicate that there is little demand for the type of project envisioned. Then a change in plans is needed; the project can be redirected to a different target market. The study may also be used to help in the design of the project. It may identify some feature lacking in the existing supply that, if included in the proposed project, will offer a competitive advantage. At the same time, it may be necessary to offer the standard features of the competition. The market study will also help in pricing the product for the indicated market target.

FEASIBILITY ANALYSIS

A *feasibility study* tests not only market conditions but also the financial viability of a proposed project. It is not enough to describe the market for rental units; one must also explore whether the cost of production can be maintained at a price that allows a profit or meets some investment objective.

THE VALUATION PROCESS

As noted earlier in this chapter, the steps in the appraisal or valuation process are as follows:

1. Define the problem to be solved.
2. Plan the appraisal.
3. Collect and verify data.
4. Analyze the highest and best use of the land.
5. Estimate the land value.
6. Apply relevant valuation approaches.
7. Reconcile the value indications and make a final value estimate.
8. Report the final value estimate.

Define the Problem

In defining the problem to be solved, the appraiser must ascertain a number of items. A definition of value should be formulated at the outset of the valuation process. The property to be valued and the property rights to be appraised must be identified. Also, the date of the estimate of value must be determined. The use of the appraisal should be addressed, in order to determine the needs and requirements of the client. Finally, the appraiser must consider and set forth any special limiting conditions that will be part of the appraisal.

Plan the Appraisal

The second step is planning the appraisal. This includes determining the data needed and identifying potential data sources, identifying the methodology to be applied, estimating the time and personnel needed, estimating the fee, and scheduling the work to be performed.

Collect and Verify Data

Part three of the valuation process involves gathering data related to the subject property and its environs (region and immediate neighborhood), and comparable market data. A narrative report often starts with national trends, then proceeds to the region and local area. General data gathering relates to the region in which the property is located and the interaction of social, economic, governmental, and environmental forces. A neighborhood description is included. A *neighborhood* is an area of complementary land uses that may be delineated by natural barriers, political boundaries, income levels of inhabitants, or streets.

The appraiser, in gathering specific data and completing research into general data, should seek to identify any factors that directly or indirectly influence the subject property, so that these factors can be considered in the appraisal. Specific data are those related directly to the subject property. These include site data, improvement data, zoning data, ad valorem tax data, and market data. *Market data* is a broad term referring to all real estate sales, listings, leases, and offers that are used in developing the three approaches to value (see pages 215–223). Thus, data requirements are set by the appraisal problem to be addressed. Not only must data be collected, but also the accuracy of the collected information must be verified.

Analyze the Highest and Best Use

After describing and analyzing the subject environs, site, and improvements, the appraiser analyzes the *highest and best use* of the property. The highest and best use analysis for improved properties has a twofold purpose: (1) to determine the highest and best use of the site as if vacant, and (2) to analyze the highest and best use of the property as improved. The highest and best use of the site as if vacant is required so that land with similar highest and best uses can be used for comparison purposes in the land value estimate section of the appraisal. Also, the existing improvements are evaluated in regard to the highest and best use of the site as if vacant. If the existing improvements do not conform to this use of the site, changes or modifications should be considered. The highest and best use of a property is a very crucial conclusion, as the three approaches to value are developed on the basis of this determination.

Estimate the Land Value

The next step in the valuation process involves estimating the value of the site as if vacant. In determining this value, consideration must be given to the highest and best use of the site. One or more of the following methods can be used to arrive at an indication of the value of the site as if vacant:

1. Sales comparison
2. Allocation
3. Extraction
4. Subdivision development
5. Land residual technique
6. Ground rent capitalization

Apply Valuation Approaches

After the site value estimate, the three approaches to value: the cost approach, the sales comparison (market) approach, and the income approach are developed. Sometimes, one or more of the three approaches is not applicable to a given property and is not developed in the appraisal. In this case, the appraiser should state why the approach is not applicable. This can be determined, however, only by careful analysis of the property being appraised in relation to the analytical tools available to the appraiser. A short explanation of each approach follows; the three approaches are considered in detail later in this chapter.

COST APPROACH

The cost approach is based on the principle of substitution. It recognizes that buyers often judge the value of an existing structure by comparing it with the cost to construct a new structure of the same type. In developing the cost approach, the appraiser estimates the cost to replace or reproduce the improvements, deducts depreciation (if any), and then adds to this figure the estimated value of the site or land as if vacant. The major limitation of this approach is the difficulty in estimating accrued depreciation, particularly when depreciation is present in more than one form.

SALES COMPARISON APPROACH

The sales comparison approach (formerly called *market approach*) recognizes that no informed and prudent person will pay more for a property than it would cost to purchase an equally desirable substitute property (the principle of substitution). In developing this approach, the appraiser locates sales of properties similar to the property being appraised (called *comparable sales*) and provides details describing them in the appraisal report. These sale properties are then compared to the property being appraised, and adjustments are made for differences between each such property and the property under appraisal. The reliability of this approach is directly related to the quality and quantity of the sales data.

INCOME CAPITALIZATION APPROACH

The income capitalization approach is based on the principle of anticipation, which states that value is created by the anticipation of future benefits to be derived from ownership of a given property. The appraiser is primarily concerned with the future benefits to be derived from operation of the subject property—the net operating income (NOI), or cash flow. The steps in this approach include estimating potential gross income by comparison with competing properties, deducting a market derived vacancy and collection loss allowance, and estimating expenses (derived from historical and/or market experience) to determine a projected stream of net operating income. The income stream is then capitalized into an indication of value by using capitalization rates extracted from competitive properties in the market, or by using other techniques when applicable.

Reconciliation

It should be noted that all three approaches are closely interrelated, and that all three use market data: the cost approach utilizes data from the market on labor and materials costs, the direct sales comparison approach analyzes sales of similar properties, and the income capitalization approach determines the market investment return rates. Also, data and conclusions from one approach are often used in one or more of the other approaches. If good data are available for application of all three approaches, the resulting indications should fall within a narrow range.

Among the factors considered in the final estimate of value are the accuracy, reliability, and pertinence of the information available for each approach. Major considerations in the *reconciliation* of value indications are which approach has the best data, which is the most likely to be free of error, and which is the most reliable for the type of property being appraised. A final value estimate should be rounded so as not to give a false impression of the precision associated with an opinion.

Report

Three types of written reports for real estate appraisals prepared under USPAP are

1. Self-contained
2. Summary
3. Restricted use

A *self-contained report* provides all details about the property and the data used to appraise it. A *summary report* can summarize many of the details, which are included in work papers. A *restricted use report* is abbreviated so much that its use is usually restricted to one party such as the property owner, who knows all about the property and doesn't need extensive explanations in a report.

A *form report* is a summary report placed on a preprinted form, generally used for one- to four-family dwellings. An *oral report* may be provided to client; however, all the research must have been performed before providing the oral report and must be retained in the appraiser's files.

PROPERTY DESCRIPTION

The site, improvements, and construction design must be described in an appraisal to allow the reader to understand the physical qualities of the property.

Site Description

The size and shape of the site are described, and any impediment to development or any superior qualities are noted. If a parcel is narrow or awkwardly shaped, this fact is mentioned. Road frontage (or lack of access) and topography are noted. Zoning is described, detailing allowable uses and the current use. The appraiser should note, with reference to maps, whether the property is in a flood-prone area. The availability of utilities at the site, including water supply and sewers, gas and electricity, and, if appropriate, cable television, is noted.

Improvements Description

The size, condition, and utility of the improvements must be described in the appraisal report, accompanied by photographs of the property, both inside and out. Photographs give the reader a visual impression in addition to the written description of the information to be conveyed. Anything relevant about the usefulness (or lack thereof) and condition of the property is described.

Basic Construction and Design

When plans and specifications are available, the appraiser can refer to them in describing the design and construction. Otherwise, he must rely on visual impressions and answers to questions provided by owners, lessees, or neighbors. At the least, the report should describe the foundation (concrete slab, pier and beam), framing, finish (inside and out), and electrical and mechanical systems.

The usefulness of the building is important. Functionality is affected by such factors as ceiling height for warehouse space, pedestrian traffic flow for retail locations, and layout of office space for office buildings.

HIGHEST AND BEST USE ANALYSIS

Highest and best use is defined as follows:

> *The reasonably probable and legal use of vacant land or an improved property, which is physically possible, appropriately supported, financially feasible, and that results in the highest value. The four criteria the highest and best use must meet are legal permissibility, physical possibility, financial feasibility, and maximum profitability.*[2]

The four criteria are applied in sequential order. Potential uses are narrowed through the consideration of each criterion so that, by the time the last criterion is applied, only a single use is indicated. A property often will have numerous uses that are physically possible; a lesser number that are both physically possible and legally permissible; fewer still that are physically possible, legally permissible, and financially feasible; and only a single use that meets all four criteria.

As the definition implies, there are two types of highest and best use: the highest and best use of land or a site as if vacant, and the highest and best use of property as improved. The highest and best use of land or a site as if vacant can be specifically defined as follows:

> *Among all reasonable, alternative uses, the use that yields the highest present land value, after payments are made for labor, capital, and coordination. The use of a property based on the assumption that the parcel of land is vacant or can be made vacant by demolishing any improvements.*[3]

In valuing an improved parcel, consideration should be given to the additional value, if any, of the improvements. The highest and best use of property as improved is defined as follows:

> *The use that should be made of a property as it exists. An existing property should be renovated or retained as is so long as it continues to contribute to the total market value of the property, or until the return from a new improvement would more than offset the cost of demolishing the existing building and constructing a new one.*[4]

[2]*The Dictionary of Real Estate Appraisal,* 5th ed. (Chicago: Appraisal Institute 2010), pp. 93–94.
[3]Ibid.
[4]Ibid.

Highest and Best Use of the Land as if Vacant

This type of use forms the basis of land value in the cost approach. Four tests are employed in the effort to determine the highest and best use of land. The first three are physical, legal, and financial. Uses that meet the first three tests are then considered to determine which is the maximally productive. Highest and best use analysis assumes that any existing building can be demolished.

PHYSICALLY POSSIBLE

The appraiser describes the uses surrounding the site and in the neighborhood, along with the traffic flow on the subject's street and nearby thoroughfares. Visibility and access are described as they affect potential uses. The size and shape are considered, and the question of whether these attributes lend themselves to certain uses or are impediments is discussed. Nearby transportation systems (bus, subway, rail) are also considered. Availability of utilities is a physical factor that can limit or impede development.

LEGALLY PERMISSIBLE

Legal restrictions include private restrictions and existing public land use regulations—in most cities, zoning. Often, only a title search by a competent attorney will uncover deed restrictions. It is therefore recommended that a title search be made if any question regarding deed restrictions arises. If common restrictions (e.g., utility and drainage easements) exist, the appraiser can state whether they appear to adversely affect the site's development potential. The appraiser should specify what is allowed within the zoning classification.

FINANCIALLY FEASIBLE

The financial feasibility of the physically possible and legally permissible uses of the site is considered. In this analysis, consideration is given to the supply and demand levels for residential, retail, and industrial properties within the area.

MAXIMALLY PRODUCTIVE

On the basis of surrounding existing uses, most probable type of use and, within this range, possible alternatives (e.g., office/warehouse or office/laboratory for industrial property) are stated. Although a great deal of judgment is involved, the appraiser provides a conclusion as to the highest and best use. This use need not be one that can be implemented immediately, but may be something to consider for the future.

Highest and Best Use of the Property as Improved

When the property is already improved with a substantial building, there are only two practical alternatives for the subject: razing the improvements or continued operation as improved. When the improvements have lost much of their utility because of their effective age, obsolescence, and condition, demolition could be considered. However, it is often not economically feasible to demolish when there is sufficient income and utility to justify continued operation of the building for an interim period.

APPRAISAL MATHEMATICS AND STATISTICS

Math concepts in appraisal fall into two categories:

1. The math of real estate finance, which is covered in Chapter 15.

2. Statistical concepts of mean, median, mode, range, and standard deviation, which follow.

- *Mean*—the average of a set of numbers. It is found by adding the amounts and dividing by the number of items.
- *Median*—the middle item in a ranking.
- *Mode*—the most popular amount, that is, the one that occurs most frequently in a list.
- *Range*—the difference between the largest and the smallest numbers in a list.

For example, consider seven homes that sold for the following amounts:

Number	Price
1	$ 300,000
2	340,000
3	400,000
4	420,000
5	480,000
6	480,000
7	540,000
Total	$2,960,000

The *mean*, or average, is found by totaling all the prices and then dividing by the number of sales (seven). In this example, the mean is $422,857. The *median* is $420,000, as three houses sold for more and three for less. The *mode* is the most popular price—in this case, $480,000, as two houses sold for that price and only one for every other price. The *range* is from $300,000 to $540,000, or $240,000.

- *Standard deviation*—a term used to describe the variance of the observations from the mean. It is important to remember that 66% of observations fall within one standard deviation from the mean, and 95% fall within two standard deviations.

SALES COMPARISON APPROACH

The sales comparison approach is based primarily on the principle of substitution, which holds that a prudent individual will pay no more for a property than it would cost to purchase a comparable substitute property. The approach recognizes that a typical buyer will compare asking prices and seek to purchase the property that meets his or her wants and needs for the lowest cost. In developing the sales comparison approach, the appraiser attempts to interpret and measure the actions of parties involved in the marketplace, including buyers, sellers, and investors.

Collection of Data

Data are collected on recent sales of properties similar to the subject, called *comparables* (*comps*). Sources of comparable data include Realtor publications, public records, buyers and sellers, brokers and salespersons, and other appraisers. Salient details for each comp are described in the appraisal report. Because comps will not be identical to the subject, some price adjustment is necessary. The idea is to simulate the price that would have been paid if the comp were actually identical to the subject. Differences that do not affect value are not adjusted for. If the comp is *superior* to the subject, an amount is *subtracted* from the known sales price of the comp. *Inferior* features of the comp require that an amount be *added* to the comp's known sales price. From the group of adjusted sales prices, the appraiser selects an indicator of value that is representative of the subject.

Selection of Comparables

No set number of comparables is required, but the greater the number, the more reliable the result. How are comps selected? To minimize the amount of adjustment required, comps should be closely similar to the subject. How current and how similar the comps are depends on the availability of data. Comps should be verified by calling a party to the transaction. The appraiser must ascertain that comps were sold in an *arm's length* market transaction; that is, that the sales price or terms were not distorted by, for example, the fact that buyer and seller were relatives.

The following are common shortcomings in the selection process:

- The sale occurred too long ago. (The market may have changed since the sale took place.)
- The location is too different. (Location and surroundings have important effects on value.)
- Special financing was used in a comparable sale. (The price may have been based in part on favorable financing terms.)
- Too few comparables can be found. (One or two sales may not represent the market.)
- The comparable was not an open market transaction. (A sale to a relative or an intra-company sale, foreclosure, or the like is not considered an open market or arm's length transaction.)

When the subject is unusual or when market activity is slow, one or more of these problems may be unavoidable. However, if this is the case, the problem(s) should be acknowledged and taken into consideration when the final value opinion is rendered.

Steps in Approach

The steps involved in developing the sales comparison approach are as follows:

1. Research the market to obtain information pertaining to sales, listings, and sometimes offerings of properties similar to the property being appraised.
2. Investigate the market data to determine whether they are factually accurate and whether each sale represents an arm's length transaction.
3. Determine relevant units of comparison (e.g., sales price per square foot), and develop a comparative analysis for each.
4. Compare the subject and comparable sales according to the elements of comparison, and then adjust each sale as appropriate.
5. Reconcile the multiple value indications that result from the adjustment of the comparables into a single value indication.

Units of Comparison

Units of comparison (see step 3 above) are defined as "the components into which a property may be divided for purposes of comparison."[5] For example, apartment complexes are typically analyzed on the basis of one or more of the following three units of comparison: sales price per square foot of rentable area, sales price per apartment unit, and gross income multiplier. Land is sold by the acre, front foot (along a road or street), square foot, and developable unit. All appropriate units of comparison should be analyzed for the property type being appraised, and the resulting value indications reconciled to a single indicated value or value range. The best unit of comparison for any property is the unit that is considered important in the market for that property type.

Adjustments are usually required to compare the comparable properties selected to the subject property. The adjustments may be applied either to the total sales price or to the unit or units of comparison. Income multipliers are not normally adjusted, however. The comparable sales are adjusted for differences in *elements of comparison*, which are defined as "the characteristics or attributes of properties and transactions that cause the prices paid for real estate to vary."[6] The adjustment process is an effort to isolate the amount paid for different features or sizes; thus it rests on the principle of contribution.

---

[5]Ibid., p. 202.
[6]Ibid., p. 66.

Use of Units of Comparison in Appraisals

Real estate is more easily appraised using units of comparison. Just as meat is sold by the pound, fabric by the yard, precious metals by the troy ounce, and liquids by the fluid ounce, quart, or gallon, real properties are compared by a unit of comparison after adjustments are made to comparables to obtain a uniform quality level. The unit of comparison used may vary depending on the property type or use. Units of comparison may be used in all approaches to value.

Land

Farm land and large vacant tracts are normally sold by the *acre* (1 acre equals 43,560 square feet). Valuable tracts are sold by the *square foot*, although land along a highway suitable for commercial development or waterfront property may be sold by the number of *front feet* (length along the highway or shoreline). A certain minimum or typical depth is associated with the frontage. Another way that land may be sold is per unit of allowable development. For example, when zoning permits 12 apartment units per acre, the price may be $120,000 per acre (or stated as $10,000 per developable unit).

Improved Property

Improved properties may be sold by varying units of measurement, depending on their use. For example, office or retail space may be sold on a per-square-foot, motels on a per-room, and theaters on a per-seat basis. However, quality, condition, and other elements are also considered, and an adjusted price is estimated before the units are compared so that the units of comparison are truly comparable.

Elements of Comparison

The following *elements of comparison* should be considered in the sales comparison approach:

1. Real property rights conveyed
2. Financing terms
3. Conditions of sale
4. Market conditions on date of sale
5. Location
6. Physical characteristics

Adjustments for these are made to the actual selling price of the comparable property.

Real Property Rights Conveyed

In most situations, fee simple title will be conveyed. However, when the comparables differ from the subject in the extent of rights conveyed, adjustment is required. The appraiser must also be aware of the effects of easements and leaseholds on the price and must apply adjustments accordingly.

Financing Terms

Generally, the seller will receive cash from the sale, even when the buyer arranges a loan from a third party. When the property is sold with special financing, however, the price will be affected. Therefore, when the seller provides financing or pays points or excessive fees for the buyer's loan, the price received should be adjusted to a cash equivalent to result in the market value. Terms of financing, whether good or poor, affect the price but not the value.

Conditions of Sale

In some transactions, sellers or buyers may be unusually motivated, so that the price agreed upon does not necessarily reflect market value. This is true in cases of foreclosure and bankruptcy, as well as transactions in which a buyer requires a certain adjacent parcel for business expansion. A parent may sell property to a child at a bargain price, or a stockholder may sell to his wholly owned corporation at a high price, both in relation to the market. An appraiser must adjust these non-arm's-length transactions to the market, or not use them as comparables.

Market Conditions on Date of Sale

Especially during periods of inflation or local economy changes, it is possible to determine shifts in price levels over time. In a rising market, a comparable property sold just a few months ago would fetch a higher price if sold now. For this reason it is important to identify the date of sale of each comparable. Unless a comparable sale is very recent, an adjustment may be needed for market conditions.

Location

Since real estate prices are greatly affected by location, an adjustment is warranted for this characteristic when a comparable's location differs significantly from the subject's. Because each location is unique, the adjustment is often subjective. For retail properties, traffic count is often a key variable.

Physical Characteristics

Physical characteristics of the property warrant adjustment. These characteristics include age, condition, construction, quality, maintenance, access, visibility, and utility.

The Adjustment Process

Adjustments may be made in terms of percentages or in dollar amounts. Either the total sales price may be adjusted, or the adjustments can be applied to one or more units of comparison. The adjustments should be made in sequential order, with the adjustment for real property rights always made first, the adjustment for financing terms then made to the sales price adjusted for real property rights conveyed, and so on. Adjustments for location and physical characteristics can be grouped together as a single cumulative amount or percentage. If characteristics are interrelated or interdependent, then cumulative percentage adjustments may be used. If they are independent, however, each should be applied to the actual price of the comparable property.

The *paired sale* technique is useful in adjusting for just one feature. If other sales are found for properties that are similar except for just one feature, the value of that feature can be captured. It is then applied to the comparable properties.

After adjustment, the sales will indicate a range in total value or unit value for the property being appraised. If the sales data are highly comparable, and the sales occurred in a reasonably efficient market, the range in indicated values should be tight. When market conditions are imperfect and comparable sales data are limited, however, the range in indicated values may be wider.

In reconciling the value indications provided by the comparable sales, the appraiser should consider the amount of adjustment required for each sale. Sales requiring lesser degrees of adjustment are typically more comparable and are given greater weight than sales requiring greater adjustment. Other factors must be considered, however, including the reliability of the sales data and the degree of support of the required adjustments. After consideration of these factors, a final point value or value range is set forth.

COST APPROACH

The cost approach to appraising is predicated on the assumption that the value of a structure does not exceed the current cost of producing a replica of it. This tends to hold true when a site is improved with a new structure that represents the highest and best use of the site.

Typically, an appraiser estimates the reproduction cost of the subject property, then subtracts for depreciation. The market value of the site (land prepared for use) is then added to the depreciated reproduction cost to arréve at a final estimate of value.

Steps in the cost approach, also called the *summation approach*, follow:

1. Estimate the value of the site as if vacant and available to be put to its highest and best use as of the date of the appraisal.
2. Estimate the reproduction or replacement cost new of the improvements.
3. Estimate all elements of accrued depreciation, including physical, functional, and economic obsolescence.
4. Subtract the total accrued depreciation from the replacement cost new of the improvements to determine the present worth of the improvements.
5. Add the estimated depreciated worth of all site improvements.
6. Add the total present worth of all improvements to the estimated site value to arrive at the value of the property as indicated by the cost approach.

The procedure for estimating land value was described in the sales comparison approach.

Site Value

A *site* is land that has been cleared, graded, and improved with utility connections so that it is ready to be built upon. In a real estate appraisal, the site value is typically estimated even though the purpose of the appraisal is to estimate the value of the entire property, the improved real estate. The site value is estimated as part of the cost approach.

Site value may also give information about the entire property. For example, suppose that the site value is almost equal to the improved property value; this fact may provide a clue about the highest and best use of the property. It may help also in analyzing the possibility of replacing the existing building, or give information on the useful life of the present improvements.

There are several ways to estimate site value; sales comparison, land residual, allocation, extraction, and plottage and assemblage are discussed below.

SALES COMPARISON

The sales comparison technique for land is similar to that described above for improved properties, but it is easier to apply to land because there are fewer factors to consider. It is the most commonly used technique for land valuation.

LAND RESIDUAL

Improved properties may generate annual income. If the building value is known, the income attributable to the building may be subtracted from the total income; the difference is the income to the land. That amount may be converted to a land value by dividing by a capitalization rate (rate of return).

ALLOCATION

Allocation is a method of estimating land value as a fraction of total value. Suppose that, for the type of property in question, data from numerous comparables indicate that land is typically 25% of total value. The land value for the subject property is then estimated at 25% of total value unless there is some reason not to apply this technique (such as the presence of excess land on the subject).

EXTRACTION

The *extraction* method of estimating land value involves subtracting the depreciated cost of improvements from the total value of the property. It is used to best advantage when the improvements have little value.

PLOTTAGE AND ASSEMBLAGE

These terms relate to combining two or more parcels of land. The combination is called *assemblage*. When the combined parcel is worth more, because of increased utility, than the parcels would be if sold separately, the increment of value added is called *plottage*.

Reproduction Cost Versus Replacement Cost

Reproduction cost is the cost of building a replica; *replacement cost* is the cost of replacing the subject with one that has equivalent utility but is built with modern materials and to current standards of design and function. Replacement cost new tends to set the upper limit on current value.

Measuring Reproduction Cost or Replacement Cost

Four methods of measuring reproduction or replacement cost are as follows:

1. *Quantity survey*, whereby each type of material in a structure is itemized and costed out (the price of each nail, brick, etc., is reflected). Overhead, insurance, and profit are added as a lump sum.
2. *Unit-in-place*, whereby the installed unit cost of each component is measured (e.g., exterior walls, including gypsum board, plaster, paint, wallpaper, and labor). Equipment and fixtures are added as a lump sum.
3. *Segregated cost* or *trade breakdown*, which is similar to the unit-in-place method except that the units considered are major functional parts of the structure, such as foundation, floor, ceiling, roof, and heating system. Fixtures and equipment are added as a lump sum.
4. *Comparative unit*, whereby all components of a structure are lumped together on a unit basis to obtain the total cost per square foot or cubic foot. Costs include materials, installation, and builder's overhead and profit.

Cost Services

Companies that provide cost data, either through on-line computer services or as hard copy, include Marshall & Swift/Boeckh, R.S. Means, and Dodge (McGraw-Hill).

Cost Indexes

Cost indexes are prepared, using a construction inflation index, to update costs from the latest price schedules to the present time. Another index, a local multiplier, is printed for selected cities to show the variation from the benchmark region or city.

Depreciation

Depreciation is a reduction in value, due to all sources, from cost new. *Accrued depreciation* is the total loss of value from all causes, measured from reproduction cost new. Depreciation is broken down into three elements—physical, functional, and external or economic—and each is further classified as curable or incurable.

Physical Deterioration

Physical deterioration is a reduction in the utility of improvements resulting from an impairment of physical condition and is commonly divided into curable and incurable components. *Curable physical deterioration* considers items (referred to as "deferred maintenance") that a prudent purchaser would anticipate correcting immediately upon acquisition of the property. It is assumed that the cost of effecting the correction will not be greater than the anticipated gain in value accrued by virtue of correcting the problem. This estimate is usually computed as a cost to cure. *Incurable physical deterioration* refers to items that cannot be physically or economically corrected.

Functional Obsolescence

Functional obsolescence is a loss of value due to characteristics inherent in the structures themselves. It results in a decreased capacity of the improvements to perform the functions for which they were intended, in accordance with current market tastes and standards of acceptability. Something becomes outmoded. As mentioned above, functional obsolescence consists of curable and incurable items.

CURABLE FUNCTIONAL OBSOLESCENCE

Curable functional obsolescence may be the result of either a deficiency or an excess. The measure of a deficiency is the excess cost to cure, whereas the measure of an excess is the reproduction cost of the superadequacy, less physical deterioration already charged, plus the cost to cure. As noted, in order for an item to be considered curable, the necessary cost to cure must not exceed the anticipated increase in value due to the cure.

INCURABLE FUNCTIONAL OBSOLESCENCE

Incurable functional obsolescence is caused by either a deficiency or an excess that, if cured, would not warrant the expenditure. In other words, the owner/purchaser would not be justified in replacing items whose cost would exceed the anticipated increase in value. If caused by a deficiency, obsolescence is estimated as the capitalized value of the rent loss due to the condition. An excess is measured by the reproduction cost of the item, less physical deterioration already charged, plus the present worth of the added cost of ownership due to the subject property and other factors relating to this property.

External or Economic Obsolescence

External or economic obsolescence is a diminished utility of the structure due to negative influences from outside the site. It is almost always *incurable* on the part of the owner, landlord, or tenant. External obsolescence can be caused by a variety of factors, such as neighborhood decline; the property's location in a community, state, or region; market conditions; or government regulations.

Depreciation Calculations

There are a number of ways to calculate the value loss from depreciation. These include the economic age-life method, the breakdown method, and market extraction. Definitions of two important terms are offered below as an aid to understanding depreciation calculations.

Economic life is the period over which improvements to real estate contribute to the value of the property. Economic life establishes the capital recovery period for improvements in the traditional residual techniques of income capitalization. It is also used in the estimation of accrued depreciation (diminished utility) in the cost approach to value estimation.

Effective age, as applied to a structure, is the age of a similar structure of equivalent utility, condition, and remaining life expectancy, as distinct from *chronological age*; that is, effective age is the age indicated by the condition and utility of the structure. If a building has had better than average maintenance, its effective age may be less than the actual age; if there has been inadequate maintenance, it may be greater. A 40-year-old building, for example, may have an effective age of 20 years because of rehabilitation and modernization.

ECONOMIC AGE-LIFE METHOD

The ratio between the effective age of a building and its total economic life is its *economic age-life.* To estimate the building's incurable physical depreciation, this ratio is applied to the cost of the building or components after deferred maintenance has been subtracted.

BREAKDOWN METHOD

With this method, the loss in value is separated into physical, functional, and external causes.

Cost Approach Example
Replacement Cost New

Office/warehouse building:		
(24,208 SF @ $41.56/SF)		$1,006,084
Site improvements and equipment:		
Parking lot	$150,000	
Signage, landscaping, misc.	10,000	
Subtotal, site improvements		160,000
Subtotal, hard costs		$1,166,084
Developer/contractor profit:		
Building cost new @ 15%		174,912
Ad valorem taxes @ 2.6% × $140,000		3,600
Marketing, misc.		2,000
Replacement cost new		1,346,596
Less: Accrued depreciation:		
Physical depreciation (based on direct cost)		
Curable	$120,000	
Incurable	802,686	
Subtotal	$922,686	
Obsolescence		
Functional	100,000	
External	220,000	
Subtotal	$320,000	
Total accrued depreciation		−1,242,686
Estimated present value of improvements		103,910
Add: Estimated land value		140,000
Indicated land value via cost approach		$243,910
Rounded to:		$240,000

Cost Approach Estimate of Value $240,000

INCOME APPROACH

Most of the income approach methodology will be found in the general certification section of Chapter 15. All appraisal candidates, however, are expected to understand gross rent multipliers (or gross income multipliers) and to be able to estimate income and expense.

Gross Income Multiplier

The *gross income multiplier* is simply the sales price divided by the rental income, generally on an annual basis. For example, if a building sold for $1,200,000 and earns $200,000 a year in rent, the multiplier is 6 ($1,200,000/$200,000 = 6). This multiplier is often used on a monthly rent basis, especially for houses. If a home sold for $120,000 and rents for $1,000 per month, the monthly multiplier is 120. The multiplier is applied to the subject's rent to estimate its value.

Generally, the gross rent multiplier is used as a sales comparison measure for income property. It may be used as the income approach for single-family housing.

Estimate of Income and Expenses

The income most commonly used is called *net operating income (NOI)*, which is found for rental properties as follows:

1. Estimate *potential gross income* (the rental collected if all units are rented for an entire year).
2. Subtract a vacancy and collection allowance.
3. Subtract *operating expenses.* These include insurance, maintenance and repairs, real estate taxes, utilities, and other expenses essential to the operation of the property.

   Operating expenses are categorized as fixed or variable. *Fixed expenses* remain constant regardless of occupancy, whereas *variable expenses* go up and down depending on occupancy.

   Another category of operating expenses consists of reserves for the replacement of appliances, carpets, and other short-lived assets. Since these may last only 5–10 years, an amount is set aside annually as a provision to prevent distorting the income in the year these assets are replaced.

   Interest and principal payments and depreciation are *not* operating expenses.

The result—(1) minus (2) and (3)—is net operating income. NOI is then divided by a capitalization rate, which is the rate used to convert an income stream into a lump sum capital value. The capitalization rate must be adequate to provide for a return on the entire investment, as well as a recovery of the portion of the property that is subject to depreciation.

The rate of return on the entire investment can be estimated as in the following example:

> ***Basic Rate:***
> *Safe, liquid rate of return on investment*
>   *(U.S. government bonds, insured savings)* — 1%
> *Provision for illiquidity* — 1%
> *Provision for investment management* — 1%
> *Provision for risk* — 2%
> *Rate of return on investment* — 5%
> *Plus capital recovery: 80% of cost represented by improvements,*
>   *which are subject to a 40-year life = 80% × 2½% (straight-line*
>   *annual depreciation)* — 2%
> *Capitalization rate* — 7%

If net operating income is estimated at $100,000, the resulting value is $100,000 ÷ 0.07 = $1,428,571, rounded to $1,429,000. The formula employed is as follows:

$$\text{Value} = \frac{\text{Income}}{\text{Capitalization Rate}}$$

PARTIAL INTERESTS

The residential appraiser is expected to know the effects of certain partial interests, namely:

- Leaseholds and leased fees
- Life estates
- Easements
- Timeshares
- Cooperatives
- Undivided interests in common areas

Leaseholds and Leased Fees

When property is leased, the tenant has a *leasehold*. This may be a valuable interest, particularly when the lease rent (called the *contract rent*) is below market rent and the lease is for a long term. The landlord's position is called *leased fee*. An appraiser should determine the effect of a lease on the market value of the fee simple and ascertain the definition of value being sought. Is it a leased fee value, or fee simple unencumbered?

Life Estates

A *life estate* allows a person to use property for his or her own lifetime or for the life of another person (*pur autre vie*). Upon death, the remainderman becomes the sole owner. Thus, the market value of the property is divided between two persons: one with the right of use for life and another whose use commences upon the life tenant's death.

Easements

An *easement* is the right to use property owned by another for a specific purpose. For example, billboards may be erected on easements, and power company transmission line paths and other land needed for utilities are often provided by the use of easements. Easements may enhance the value of real estate when they generate adequate revenue (billboard rent), attract desired services (utilities to the property), or provide access to other properties. They may detract from value when they represent nuisances (unsightly utility wires), indicate flood plains, or prevent alternative profitable property uses. Unless easements are specifically excluded by the appraisal report, an appraiser should ascertain the effect of easements on property being considered as well as easements on others' properties that the subject property owner can enjoy.

Timeshares

A *timeshare* is the right to use property for a given period of time each year. Often used for resort property, a timeshare may be ownership of a specific apartment unit for a specific period, such as the first week in April of each year, or it may represent the right to use any of a number of identical units in a condominium development for any week during a certain period (with prices varying for peak and off-season periods). The price of a weekly timeshare, when multiplied by 52 weeks, may exceed two to three times the value of the unit if sold in its entirety, but timeshare ownership often includes amenities (such as utilities, laundry service, and periodic redecoration) that would not be included in ownership of the unit itself.

Cooperatives

Some apartment buildings, especially in New York, are owned as cooperatives (co-ops). A corporation owns the building and can mortgage it. Stockholders own certain shares, which give each stockholder the right to occupy a certain unit. Stockholders are generally tenants and must pay their pro rata shares of maintenance expenses. Special tax laws allow the tenants to deduct interest on the mortgage and real estate taxes. An appraiser must recognize the valuation process for this type of property and understand how the stock is valued.

Undivided Interests In Common Areas

Condominiums provide for separate ownership of individual units with the right to mortgage each unit. Common areas such as walkways, recreational facilities, and exterior walls are owned jointly. Each condo owner owns a share of the common area and may use it, as may all other condo owners.

APPRAISAL STANDARDS AND ETHICS

The Uniform Standards of Professional Appraisal Practice (USPAP) have been developed by the Appraisal Foundation. Appraisers belonging to an organization that is a member of the Appraisal Foundation adhere to these standards. The following are highlights of certain parts of the USPAP.

Preamble

- The appraisal must be meaningful and not misleading in the marketplace.
- The appraiser is to observe all the ethical standards set forth below.
- Certain competency provisions are to be observed.
- If departure provisions are utilized, the rules concerning their use must be observed. A departure provision is a provision for the appraiser to depart from the standards. For example, a departure provision allows an approach to be waived provided that the appraiser explains why that approach was not used.
- Users of an appraiser's services are encouraged to demand work in conformance with the standards.

Ethics

To promote and preserve the public trust inherent in professional appraisal practice, an appraiser must observe the highest standards of professional ethics. The ETHICS RULE of USPAP is divided into four sections: Conduct, Management, Confidentiality, and Record Keeping.[7]

CONDUCT

- An appraiser must perform assignments ethically and competently in accordance with USPAP and any supplemental standards agreed to by the appraiser in accepting the assignment. An appraiser may not engage in criminal conduct. An appraiser must perform assignments with impartiality, objectivity, and independence, and without accommodation of personal interests.
- In appraisal practice, an appraiser must not perform as an advocate for any party or issue.
- An appraiser must not accept an assignment that includes the reporting of predetermined opinions and conclusions.
- An appraiser must not communicate assignment results in a misleading or fraudulent manner. An appraiser must not use or communicate a misleading or fraudulent report or knowingly permit an employee or other person to communicate a misleading or fraudulent report.

---

[7]The sections that follow are taken from Appraisal Standards Board, *Uniform Standards of Professional Appraisal Practice,* 2012–2013 edition (Washington, DC: Appraisal Foundation). Comments and footnotes have been omitted.

- An appraiser must not use or rely on unsupported conclusions relating to characteristics such as race, color, religion, national origin, gender, marital status, familial status, age, receipt of public assistance income, handicap, or an unsupported conclusion that homogeneity of such characteristics is necessary to maximize value.

MANAGEMENT

- The payment of undisclosed fees, commissions, or things or value in connection with the procurement of an assignment is unethical.
- It is unethical for an appraiser to accept an assignment, or to have a compensation arrangement for an assignment, that is contingent on any of the following:

  1. the reporting of a predetermined result (e.g., opinion of value);
  2. a direction in assignment results that favors the cause of the client;
  3. the amount of a value opinion;
  4. the attainment of a stipulated result; or
  5. the occurrence of a subsequent event directly related to the appraiser's opinions and specific to the assignment's purpose.

- Advertising for or soliciting assignments in a manner that is false, misleading, or exaggerated is unethical.

CONFIDENTIALITY

- An appraiser must protect the confidential nature of the appraiser-client relationship.
- An appraiser must act in good faith with regard to the legitimate interests of the client in the use of confidential information and in the communication of assignment results.
- An appraiser must be aware of, and comply with, all confidentiality and privacy laws and regulations applicable in an assignment.
- An appraiser must not disclose confidential information or assignment results prepared for a client to anyone other than the client and persons specifically authorized by the client; state enforcement agencies and such third parties as may be authorized by due process of law; and a duly authorized professional peer review committee except when such disclosure to a committee would violate applicable law or regulation. It is unethical for a member of a duly authorized professional peer review committee to disclose confidential information presented to the committee.

RECORD KEEPING

- An appraiser must prepare a workfile for each appraisal, appraisal review, or appraisal consulting assignment. The workfile must include:

  1. the name of the client and the identity, by name or type, of any other intended users;
  2. true copies of any written reports, documented on any type of media;
  3. summaries of any oral reports or testimony, or a transcript of testimony, including the appraiser's signed and dated certification; and
  4. all other data, information, and documentation necessary to support the appraiser's opinions and conclusions and to show compliance with this Rule and all other applicable Standards, or references to the location(s) of such other documentation.

- An appraiser must retain the workfile for a period of at least five (5) years after preparation or at least two (2) years after final disposition of any legal proceeding in which the appraiser provided testimony related to the assignment, whichever period expires last.
- An appraiser must have custody of his or her workfile, or make appropriate workfile retention, access, and retrieval arrangements with the party having custody of the workfile.

Competency

The appraiser must properly identify the problem to be addressed and have the knowledge and experience to complete the assignment competently. If the appraiser does not have the required knowledge or experience, she must

1. Disclose this fact to the client before accepting the engagement.
2. If engaged, take all steps necessary to complete the assignment competently.
3. Describe the deficiency and the steps taken to complete the assignment competently.

Standards

The following are some standards to be followed in appraising real estate.

- *Standard 1.* In developing a real property appraisal, an appraiser must identify the problem to be solved and the scope of work necessary to solve the problem, and correctly complete research and analysis necessary to produce a credible appraisal. An appraiser must be aware of, understand, and correctly employ the recognized methods and techniques necessary to produce a credible appraisal.
- *Standard 2.* In reporting the results of a real property appraisal, an appraiser must communicate each analysis, opinion, and conclusion in a manner that is not misleading.
- *Standard 3.* In performing a review assignment, an appraiser acting as a reviewer must develop and report a credible opinion as to the quality of another appraiser's work and must clearly disclose the scope of work performed.
- *Standard 4.* In developing a real property appraisal consulting assignment, an appraiser must identify the problem to be solved, determine the scope of work necessary to solve the problem, and correctly complete the research and analyses necessary to produce credible results.
- *Standard 5.* In reporting the results of a real property appraisal consulting assignment, an appraiser must communicate each analysis, opinion, and conclusion in a manner that is not misleading.

Questions on Chapter 14

1. All of the following types of broad forces affect value *except*
   (A) physical
   (B) intellectual
   (C) political
   (D) social
   (E) economic

2. Social, economic, governmental, and environmental influences that affect property value are called
   (A) laws
   (B) forces
   (C) factors
   (D) consequences
   (E) impacts

3. Compared with other assets, real estate is
   (A) immobile
   (B) expensive
   (C) long-lived
   (D) mortgageable
   (E) all of the above

4. The truly distinguishing characteristic of real estate as compared with other assets is
   (A) large size
   (B) long life
   (C) high price
   (D) uniqueness
   (E) fixed location

5. The primary economic distinguishing characteristic of land is
   (A) homogeneity
   (B) high cost
   (C) immobility
   (D) slow depreciation
   (E) no depreciation

6. Urban land derives its value primarily from its
   (A) size
   (B) natural beauty
   (C) concentration of population
   (D) location
   (E) buildings

7. Which of the following is a basic component of value?
   (A) utility
   (B) scarcity
   (C) demand coupled with purchasing power
   (D) transferability
   (E) all of the above

8. The value of real estate is determined in the market mainly by its
   (A) price
   (B) productivity
   (C) mortgage
   (D) size
   (E) height

9. Which of the following is an important governmental influence on neighborhood values?
   (A) zoning code
   (B) income level
   (C) owner occupancy
   (D) flood plain mapping
   (E) ethnic concentration

10. *Realty* is best defined as rights in
    (A) land
    (B) improvements on and to land
    (C) buildings
    (D) fixtures
    (E) real estate

11. Built-in appliances are legally classified as
    (A) real estate
    (B) trade fixtures
    (C) chattels
    (D) personal property
    (E) amenities

12. The term improvements to real estate refers to
    (A) buildings only
    (B) buildings, fences, walkways, etc.
    (C) trees and buildings
    (D) all of the above
    (E) none of the above

13. Rights of condemnation are held by a
    (A) state government agency
    (B) local agency or authority representing a federal government agency
    (C) utility company
    (D) small municipality
    (E) all of the above

14. Eminent domain requires
    (A) appraisal processes for the estimation of real property value
    (B) just compensation for specific types of financial loss
    (C) due process for the taking of property through condemnation
    (D) both A and B
    (E) both B and C

15. Zoning and environmental protection regulations represent the exercise of
    (A) land use politics
    (B) public use
    (C) escheat
    (D) eminent domain
    (E) police power

16. All of the following are considered legal encumbrances *except*
    (A) leases
    (B) utilities
    (C) zoning
    (D) mortgages
    (E) liens

17. *Real property* is defined as
    (A) leased and unleased space
    (B) rights in realty
    (C) land and all improvements
    (D) the right to use or occupy real estate
    (E) realty

18. Which of the following expires upon the owner's death?
    (A) fee tail
    (B) remainder interest
    (C) simple interest
    (D) life estate
    (E) estate for years

19. The most complete interest in real property is
    (A) fee tail
    (B) joint tenancy
    (C) tenancy in common
    (D) fee simple
    (E) life estate *pur autre vie*

20. A deed should be recorded in order to
    (A) give constructive notice of the transaction
    (B) comply with federal and state law
    (C) pass title
    (D) make the deed a legal document
    (E) establish the priority of claim of the purchaser

21. Property description is necessary to
    (A) identify and locate the subject property
    (B) identify the property rights being appraised
    (C) find the appropriate section in the report
    (D) find the official map coding of the subject property
    (E) tell where the property deed is recorded

22. One way in which land may be legally described is by
    (A) highest and best use
    (B) acreage
    (C) mailing address
    (D) metes and bounds
    (E) front footage

23. "Block 17, lot 5 of the Woodcreek Subdivision" is an example of a land description using which of the following systems?
    (A) lot and block
    (B) rectangular method
    (C) metes and bounds
    (D) government survey
    (E) monuments survey

24. A value estimate is a
    (A) estimate of a selling price
    (B) prediction that property will sell for exactly the amount named
    (C) projection or extrapolation of historic price to future price
    (D) sophisticated guess by expert
    (E) promise or option to buy

25. *Loan value* is the same as
    (A) investment value
    (B) market price
    (C) replacement value
    (D) book value
    (E) market value

26. *Mortgage value* is synonymous with
    (A) market price
    (B) liquidation value
    (C) market value
    (D) assessed value
    (E) insurable value

27. An objective kind of value that can be estimated for property bought and sold in the market is called
    (A) value in use
    (B) value in exchange
    (C) economic value
    (D) potential value
    (E) insurable value

28. In appraisal, "market value" is most commonly identified with
    (A) value in use
    (B) value in exchange
    (C) assessed value
    (D) listing value
    (E) none of the above

29. Price and value are
    (A) not necessarily the same
    (B) synonymous
    (C) different, depending on financing terms
    (D) close together in an inactive market
    (E) used interchangeably in a report

30. Market price is the amount for which a property
    (A) should sell
    (B) was sold
    (C) will sell
    (D) could sell
    (E) would be appraised

31. All of the following statements are true *except:*
    (A) *Real property* refers to items that are not permanently fixed to a part of the real estate.
    (B) Appraising is the art and science of estimating the value of an asset.
    (C) Assets typically requiring appraisal include real and personal property.
    (D) Asset values change with time.
    (E) Markets change with supply and demand.

32. *Investment value* is best described as
    (A) market price
    (B) market value
    (C) the cost of acquiring a competitive substitute property with the same utility
    (D) the present worth of anticipated future benefits to a certain individual or institutional investor
    (E) value in exchange

33. Assessed value is usually based on
    (A) cost value
    (B) book value
    (C) market value
    (D) insurable value
    (E) replacement cost

34. The principle of anticipation
    (A) is future oriented
    (B) is past oriented
    (C) involves the "as of" date for an appraisal
    (D) predicts the loan-to-value ratio for the subject property
    (E) is substitution oriented

35. Which principle of value best affirms that value is the present worth of expected future benefits?
    (A) supply and demand
    (B) balance
    (C) substitution
    (D) anticipation
    (E) conformity

36. What principle states that value levels are sustained when the various elements in an economic or environmental mix are in equilibrium?
    (A) anticipation
    (B) equivalence
    (C) substitution
    (D) balance
    (E) highest and best use

37. The fundamental valuation principle underlying the sales comparison process is
    (A) contribution
    (B) substitution
    (C) conformity
    (D) change
    (E) anticipation

38. Which principle of value best affirms that the maximum value of a property generally cannot exceed the cost of its replacement?
    (A) increasing and decreasing returns
    (B) supply and demand
    (C) substitution
    (D) balance
    (E) anticipation

39. The fact that the value of a property tends to equal the cost of an equally desirable substitute is an example of the principle of
    (A) balance
    (B) substitution
    (C) contribution
    (D) diminishing returns
    (E) supply and demand

40. The principle of substitution holds that a purchaser will pay no more for a property than
    (A) the maximum he can afford
    (B) the cost of acquiring an equally desirable substitute
    (C) the price of a previously owned property
    (D) the price of a property with greater utility
    (E) none of the above

41. The function(s) of a real estate market is (are) to
    (A) facilitate exchanges
    (B) set prices
    (C) allocate resources
    (D) adjust supply to demand
    (E) all of the above

42. In estimating current market value, an appraiser assumes all of the following *except that:*
    (A) The buyer is typically motivated.
    (B) The parties are knowledgeable.
    (C) A reasonable time will be allowed for market exposure.
    (D) The property will be marketed by a professional expert.
    (E) The property will be sold for cash or equivalent terms.

43. In which market are there many potential buyers but few properties available?
    (A) demand
    (B) buyer's
    (C) seller's
    (D) low-priced
    (E) normal

44. A perfect market occurs when
    (A) there are numerous buyers and sellers who are knowledgeable and free to trade
    (B) all products are interchangeable and can be transported to better markets
    (C) the government allocates supply and demand perfectly
    (D) all of the above are true
    (E) A and B only are true

45. The identification and study of a pertinent market is called
    (A) market analysis
    (B) neighborhood review
    (C) property research
    (D) market segmentation
    (E) market interaction

46. If the typical occupancy rate in an area is 95 percent, what conclusion would you most likely draw about a subject property that has 100 percent occupancy?
    (A) Advertising is average.
    (B) The rents are high.
    (C) The rents are low.
    (D) Management is incompetent.
    (E) New construction will occur soon.

47. Which type of studies test the ability of various proposed improvements to meet investment objectives?
    (A) market
    (B) feasibility
    (C) marketability
    (D) cost-benefit
    (E) prospectus

48. A decrease in land value is the result of
    (A) functional obsolescence
    (B) physical deterioration
    (C) market forces
    (D) wear and tear
    (E) obsolescence

49. To estimate market value, an appraiser follows the
    (A) appraisal report
    (B) valuation process
    (C) evaluation methodology
    (D) appraisal guidelines
    (E) report evolution technique

50. In appraising, the most important judgment is probably called for in
    (A) projecting selling rates
    (B) reconciling value indications
    (C) selecting good comparable data
    (D) performing neighborhood analysis
    (E) making rental market estimates

51. An "as of" date is specified in appraisals to
    (A) show when the appraiser inspected the property
    (B) indicate the prevailing price level
    (C) indicate the market conditions on which the value is estimated
    (D) indicate when the buyer agreed to purchase the property
    (E) indicate the value as of the closing date

52. An appraisal of real estate
    (A) guarantees its value
    (B) assures its value
    (C) determines its value
    (D) estimates its value
    (E) segments its value

53. Residential appraisers generally provide an estimate of
    (A) market price
    (B) mortgage loan value
    (C) cash value
    (D) assessed value·
    (E) market value

54. Commercial real estate appraisers are most frequently asked to estimate
    (A) assessed value
    (B) liquidation value
    (C) insurable value
    (D) market value
    (E) intrinsic value

55. Legal transactions that frequently require appraisals are
    (A) income-tax-deductible charitable contribution of property, estate tax, and property settlement upon divorce
    (B) damage lawsuits, loan foreclosures, and security for bail bonds
    (C) company merger, tax basis, and loan assumptions
    (D) all of the above
    (E) none of the above

56. Knowledge of land value is required for all of the following *except*
    (A) condemnation actions
    (B) fire insurance
    (C) property taxation
    (D) a ground lease
    (E) a grazing lease

57. A market value estimate provided in an appraisal
    (A) changes with the use to which it is put
    (B) changes with the function of the appraisal
    (C) remains the same regardless of whom the appraisal is prepared for
    (D) depends upon the use or function of the appraisal
    (E) always reflects market value

58. In preparing an appraisal, definition of the problem identifies all of the following *except*
    (A) the real estate being appraised
    (B) the highest and best use for the property
    (C) the real property rights
    (D) the date of the value estimate
    (E) the use to which the appraisal will be put

59. In appraising, the data requirements are set by the
    (A) client
    (B) lender
    (C) seller
    (D) appraisal problem
    (E) appraiser

60. The requirement to verify data in an appraisal report vary according to
    (A) the appraiser's "gut feelings" about the reliability of the data
    (B) the purpose and intended use of the appraisal report
    (C) legal restrictions on the property
    (D) the type of value being sought
    (E) the use to which the property has been put

61. A property's immediate environment is
    (A) its pivotal point
    (B) a "comp" grid
    (C) a neighborhood
    (D) the adjacent uses
    (E) a natural boundary

62. The life cycle of a neighborhood illustrates the principle of
    (A) substitution
    (B) highest and best use
    (C) change
    (D) conformity
    (E) anticipation

63. The data required for an appraisal assignment are established by the
    (A) lending association
    (B) appraiser
    (C) buyer
    (D) Office of Thrift Supervision
    (E) nature of the appraisal problem

64. Which of the following exhibits is *least* frequently used in an appraisal?
    (A) a photograph of the subject property
    (B) an aerial photograph of the surrounding area
    (C) a plot plan
    (D) a floor plan
    (E) a photograph of a comparable property

65. In which market is the direct sales comparison approach most applicable?
    (A) seller's
    (B) buyer's
    (C) reasonable
    (D) active
    (E) calm

66. The criteria for determining highest and best use include all of the following *except*
    (A) physical possibility
    (B) financial feasibility
    (C) legal permissibility
    (D) maximal productivity
    (E) effect on community welfare

67. The three approaches to estimating value are
    (A) cost, income, and replacement
    (B) replacement, income, and reproduction
    (C) cost, direct sales comparison, and income capitalization
    (D) reproduction, cost, and income
    (E) market, building residual, and multiplier

68. In appraising a dwelling built 50 years ago, the appraiser usually relies on the
    (A) current reproduction cost
    (B) original construction cost
    (C) current replacement cost
    (D) direct sales comparison approach
    (E) superior construction technique

69. Which approach would be best when appraising a 15- to 20-year-old house?
    (A) cost
    (B) feasibility study
    (C) sales comparison
    (D) income capitalization
    (E) replacement cost new less accrued depreciation

70. The appraiser's final value estimate should be based on
    (A) an average of the three value indications given by the three approaches to value
    (B) a weighing of the reliability of the information analyzed in each of the three approaches to value
    (C) an average of the values in the three closest comparable sales
    (D) the correlation technique
    (E) adjustments for the most recent indicators in the local market

71. Before reconciliation the appraiser should
    (A) reinspect the subject property
    (B) evaluate the reliability of each approach to value
    (C) review the overall appraisal process and check for technical accuracy
    (D) seek the property owner's opinion
    (E) average the results from the approaches used

72. Since each value approach has its own strengths and weaknesses, an appraiser should
    (A) choose the approach that is the most popular with lenders
    (B) choose the approach that is the most popular with buyers
    (C) weigh the strengths and weaknesses of each approach and decide which is the most reliable for the subject property
    (D) weight each approach equally
    (E) use the approach that the client feels is most appropriate

73. The cost approach is often given more weight in the appraisal of
    (A) old or obsolete buildings
    (B) single-family houses more than 10 years old
    (C) new buildings or special-use buildings
    (D) commercial and industrial properties
    (E) vacant land

74. In reconciliation and conclusion of value, the appraiser should
    (A) describe the relevance of each value approach explored
    (B) discuss the reliability of the data used
    (C) provide arguments to justify his or her final conclusion of value
    (D) explain his or her judgments and reasoning
    (E) do all of the above

75. Value indications are reconciled into a final value estimate
    (A) throughout the appraisal
    (B) after the report of defined value
    (C) after each approach is completed
    (D) at the preliminary stage to let the client know what result to expect
    (E) after all three approaches have been completed

76. During the reconciliation process, an appraiser should ask:
    (A) How appropriate is each approach?
    (B) How adequate are the data?
    (C) What range of values do the approaches suggest?
    (D) all of the above
    (E) A and C only

77. Which of the following is the longest and most detailed type of appraisal report?
    (A) restricted use
    (B) summary
    (C) self-contained
    (D) oral
    (E) detailed

78. All of the following are main sections in the typical narrative appraisal report *except*
    (A) introduction
    (B) engagement letter
    (C) description, analyses, and conclusion
    (D) addenda
    (E) valuation

79. An oral appraisal report
    (A) is not worth the paper it is written on
    (B) must be supported by a work paper file
    (C) is unethical
    (D) is impossible
    (E) is a legitimate substitute for a written report

80. Standardized residential form reports
    (A) are adequate for all appraisals
    (B) may not be as detailed or complete as written reports
    (C) are seldom adequate for appraisals
    (D) allow little space for neighborhood analysis
    (E) are difficult to computerize

81. The highest and best use of a site is its
    (A) existing use
    (B) most probable use that is legally and physically possible and provides the highest financial returns
    (C) immediate next use
    (D) ordinary and necessary use
    (E) least expensive use

82. The important reason(s) for inspecting and analyzing the subject site is (are) to
    (A) ascertain its highest and best use
    (B) note any unusual characteristics
    (C) find comparable sales
    (D) be certain the property exists
    (E) all of the above

83. The length of a tract of land along a street is called the land's
    (A) depth
    (B) width
    (C) frontage
    (D) abutment
    (E) lineage

84. The number of square feet in 1 acre is
    (A) 64,000
    (B) 460
    (C) 440
    (D) 43,560
    (E) 34,560

85. The livable square footage of a single-family residence is usually measured from the
    (A) total interior (including interior walls)
    (B) inside room dimensions
    (C) interior plus basement
    (D) exterior
    (E) exterior, with adjustment for wall width

86. The most important item an appraiser needs for recording data during a building inspection is a
 (A) plat map
 (B) tape measure
 (C) checklist
 (D) clipboard
 (E) blank paper

87. A large home built in an area of small cottages is an example of
 (A) overimprovement
 (B) underimprovement
 (C) land regression
 (D) functional obsolescence
 (E) environmental aesthetics

88. The period over which a building may be profitably used is its
 (A) actual life
 (B) physical life
 (C) useful life
 (D) normal life
 (E) effective age

89. An improvement's remaining economic life is
 (A) its chronological age
 (B) its effective age
 (C) the future time span over which the improvement is expected to generate benefits
 (D) its effective age minus its chronological age
 (E) its effective age plus its chronological age

90. To be considered as a possible alternative for highest and best use, a use must be
 (A) physically and legally possible and financially feasible
 (B) physically and legally possible
 (C) already in existence and legal
 (D) physically possible and appropriate
 (E) legal and profitable

91. When applying the concept of highest and best use of land as if vacant, the assumption is made that
 (A) any existing building can be demolished
 (B) zoning cannot be changed
 (C) the basic characteristics of a site can be changed
 (D) vacant land produces maximum income
 (E) land is not subject to erosion

92. The highest and best use of land as if vacant forms part of the basis for
 (A) mortgage equity analysis
 (B) a property rights adjustment
 (C) an operating expense estimate
 (D) the cost approach
 (E) the square footage approach

93. The best assurance of appraisal accuracy results from the use of
 (A) the greatest number of adjustments
 (B) a gross dollar amount of adjustments
 (C) a large number of truly comparable properties
 (D) a net dollar amount of adjustments
 (E) market segmentation

94. The direct sales comparison approach to appraising derives an estimate of value from
 (A) sales of comparable properties
 (B) comparison of the architecture of properties
 (C) comparison of loans made on properties
 (D) original costs of comparable properties
 (E) checking prices in the *Wall Street Journal* stock market report

95. A gross rent multiplier is often used in the
 (A) direct sales comparison approach for single-family housing
 (B) income approach for income property
 (C) income approach for single-family property
 (D) cost approach
 (E) back-door approach to valuation

96. Gross rent multiplier analysis is
 (A) required in almost every residential appraisal
 (B) applicable to every residential appraisal
 (C) applicable to residential property valuation only
 (D) part of the direct sales comparison approach to valuation of commercial properties
 (E) seldom used for houses

97. In estimating site value, the direct sales comparison approach
 (A) does not apply to older residences
 (B) is the most reliable method available
 (C) is considered inferior to other methods
 (D) is used only when the subject property is unimproved
 (E) is used for real estate but not for personal property appraisals

98. In an open market transaction, the subject property sold would not be
    (A) listed for at least 30 days
    (B) listed on a multiple listing service
    (C) advertised in local newspapers
    (D) sold to a relative
    (E) closed by a title company

99. The minimum number of comparable sales needed to apply direct sales comparison is
    (A) 3
    (B) 4
    (C) 10
    (D) 30
    (E) no set number

100. Physical units of comparison include
    (A) seats in a theater
    (B) rooms in a hotel
    (C) square feet of a house
    (D) cubic feet of a warehouse
    (E) all of the above

101. A nine-story office building without an elevator would suffer from which type of depreciation?
    (A) locational obsolescence
    (B) functional obsolescence
    (C) external obsolescence
    (D) physical deterioration
    (E) accounting depreciation

102. A comparable sale has four bedrooms compared to the subject's three bedrooms. The fourth bedroom is worth $30,000. What do you do with that number?
    (A) Add it to the comparable's sale price.
    (B) Subtract it from the comparable's sale price.
    (C) Add it to the subject's value.
    (D) Subtract it from the subject's value.
    (E) Nothing—do not use this sale as a comparable.

103. The sales comparison approach requires an appraiser to make adjustments to value. How are the adjustments posted on a grid?
    (A) If the comparable is better, subtract value; if worse, add value.
    (B) If the comparable is better, add value; if worse, subtract value.
    (C) If the subject is better, subtract value; if worse, add value.
    (D) If the subject is better, add value; if worse, subtract value.
    (E) A grid is not the place to post adjustments.

104. The method of estimating replacement or reproduction cost that requires you to know the original cost of construction of the building is
    (A) square foot
    (B) quantity survey
    (C) unit in place
    (D) index
    (E) exact measurement

105. An appraiser uses all of the following approaches in developing an opinion of value for real estate *except*
    (A) cost approach
    (B) replacement approach
    (C) income approach
    (D) sales comparison approach
    (E) capitalization of income approach

106. "The total number of years a building is considered to contribute to the value of the property" is a good definition of
    (A) chronological age
    (B) effective age
    (C) economic life
    (D) depreciable term
    (E) usable age

107. A rate or ratio that relates net operating income to the value of income property is
    (A) the gross rent multiplier
    (B) the capitalization rate
    (C) the depreciated cost factor
    (D) the effective gross income factor
    (E) equity yield rate

108. To estimate the appraised value of an income-producing property, the appraiser will
    (A) divide the NOI by the cap rate
    (B) divide the cap rate by the NOI
    (C) multiply the NOI by the cap rate
    (D) divide the equity dividend rate by NOI
    (E) none of the above

109. The subject property of an appraisal has a one-car garage and no fireplace. Two similar nearby properties sold in the last month, and each one has a two-car garage and a fireplace. In making adjustments to use the sold properties as comparables, the appraiser will
    (A) subtract value from the comparables
    (B) use two properties with one-car garages and no fireplace that sold last year
    (C) add value to the comparables
    (D) use the recorded sales prices of each property
    (E) consult with active brokers in the local market

110. The economic life of a building has come to an end when
    (A) the rent produced is valued at less than a similar amount of money invested
    (B) the reserve for depreciation equals the cost to replace the building
    (C) the building ceases to represent the highest and best use of the land
    (D) the value of the land and the building equals the value of the land alone
    (E) the building is vacant and cannot be rented

111. A capitalization rate incorporates return on
    (A) land and building and recapture of building
    (B) land and building and recapture of land
    (C) land and recapture of land and building
    (D) building and recapture of land and building
    (E) recapture of building only

112. All of the following are examples of external obsolescence *except*
    (A) population density
    (B) wear and tear
    (C) zoning
    (D) special assessments
    (E) rent control

113. The gross income multiplier is derived by dividing the sales price by
    (A) the monthly net income
    (B) the monthly effective income
    (C) the annual net income
    (D) the annual gross income
    (E) vacancy and collection allowance

114. In using the market comparison approach to appraisal, the appraiser considers
    (A) the sales price of comparable properties
    (B) the acquisition cost to the present owner
    (C) income tax rates
    (D) property tax assessments
    (E) the listing price of the subject

ANSWERS

1. **B**	24. **A**	47. **B**	70. **B**	93. **C**
2. **B**	25. **E**	48. **C**	71. **C**	94. **A**
3. **E**	26. **C**	49. **B**	72. **C**	95. **C**
4. **E**	27. **B**	50. **B**	73. **C**	96. **D**
5. **C**	28. **B**	51. **C**	74. **E**	97. **B**
6. **D**	29. **A**	52. **D**	75. **E**	98. **D**
7. **E**	30. **B**	53. **E**	76. **D**	99. **E**
8. **B**	31. **A**	54. **D**	77. **C**	100. **E**
9. **A**	32. **D**	55. **A**	78. **B**	101. **B**
10. **E**	33. **C**	56. **B**	79. **B**	102. **B**
11. **A**	34. **A**	57. **C**	80. **B**	103. **A**
12. **B**	35. **D**	58. **B**	81. **B**	104. **D**
13. **E**	36. **D**	59. **D**	82. **E**	105. **B**
14. **E**	37. **B**	60. **B**	83. **C**	106. **C**
15. **E**	38. **C**	61. **C**	84. **D**	107. **B**
16. **B**	39. **B**	62. **C**	85. **D**	108. **A**
17. **B**	40. **B**	63. **E**	86. **C**	109. **A**
18. **D**	41. **E**	64. **B**	87. **A**	110. **D**
19. **D**	42. **D**	65. **D**	88. **C**	111. **A**
20. **A**	43. **C**	66. **E**	89. **C**	112. **B**
21. **A**	44. **E**	67. **C**	90. **A**	113. **D**
22. **D**	45. **A**	68. **D**	91. **A**	114. **A**
23. **A**	46. **C**	69. **C**	92. **D**	

Certified General Appraiser

This chapter is of interest primarily to those who wish to become licensed as certified general appraisers. Much of the material will be of interest also to brokers, salespersons, and other appraisers but is not presently required by licensing examinations for those groups.

LEGAL CONSIDERATIONS IN APPRAISAL

Property is generally classified as either real or personal. Whatever is more or less permanently affixed to land or buildings is *real property*; all other property is *personal property*. Questions frequently arise as to whether or not fixtures are part of the real estate in question; if they *are* part, they are included in the appraised value.

Trade Fixtures

A *trade fixture* is attached to a rented facility by a tenant who uses that fixture in conducting a business. No matter how trade fixtures are attached to real estate, they are personal property. Some examples are booths, counters, and bar stools in a restaurant, tanks and pumps in a service station, and shelves in a retail store. The tenant may remove these at the expiration of the lease.

In determining whether an item is a trade fixture, courts will consider:

1. *The manner of attachment.* Personal property can generally be removed without damage.
2. *The adaptation of the article to the real estate.* Items that are built specifically to be installed in a particular building and are unlikely to be used in another are probably real estate.
3. *The intent of the parties when the property was attached.*

Machinery and Equipment

An appraiser needs to know whether or not to include these items in the real estate value estimate. For example, in a hotel there may be equipment in laundry facilities, guest exercise rooms, or restaurants that could be considered either real or personal property. In the office section of a warehouse, there could be heating, ventilation, and air conditioning equipment, lighting, and plumbing facilities for office workers. Depending on the same criteria described for fixtures, the appraiser has to classify the machinery and equipment as real or personal property.

TYPES OF VALUE

All types of value were covered in Chapter 14 except *going-concern value*. This is the difference between the market value of a business and the market value of its assets. For example, a restaurant may be worth $1 million as a business even though its building, land, furniture, fixtures, and equipment have an aggregate market value of only $600,000. The $400,000 excess is the going-concern value.

When appraising business real estate, such as a hotel or motel, retail store, or storage service facility, an appraiser needs to recognize the difference between the business value and the real estate value. The value conclusion will, of course, depend on what is being appraised.

ECONOMIC PRINCIPLES

All of these principles were discussed in Chapter 14 except *opportunity cost*, that is, the cost of an opportunity forgone by not choosing it. For example, suppose an investor buys mortgages on real estate that yield 8% rather than corporate bonds yielding 7%. The opportunity cost is the 7% yield on the bonds that were not bought.

Similarly, if an appraiser accepts an assignment for $8,000 that requires his full-time effort for a month, requiring him to turn down another assignment at $6,000 because of a time conflict, the $6,000 is the opportunity cost.

REAL ESTATE MARKET ANALYSIS

The three items of the Examination Content Outline that were not covered in Chapter 14 are *existing space inventory*, *current and projected space surplus*, and *new space*.

Existing Space Inventory

Existing space may be inventoried and categorized for a market or market segment. For example, for each office building in a city, a database may be used that includes, at a minimum, the following information:

Building name	*Year built*
Building location	*Class (A, B, C)*
Square feet retail	*Occupancy rate*
Square feet office	*Effective rent rate*
Rent rate asked	*Typical lease terms*

The database can then be sorted in various ways: by amount of space in each section of the city or by class, rent range, vacancy rate, and so on.

Current and Projected Space Surplus

Using the database model described above, one can estimate an occupancy ratio for each part of the city and class of building, for example, and can then compare historical absorption rates with existing surplus space to estimate future occupancy. This comparison must be tempered by knowledge of specific important changes to come, such as the impending relocation of a corporate headquarters to another city. The analysis will provide insights as to the likelihood of a tightening of supply or a surplus of space.

New Space

The planning or engineering department of the city can provide information on the issuance of permits authorizing new construction. Since these permits will be for specific buildings, they will provide locations and sizes that may be added to the database. Construction and leasing activity will be recognized for new space; together these can offer a picture of the supply of space for the next 2 to 3 years in an office market, for example.

APPRAISAL MATH AND STATISTICS

All compound interest functions are reserved for the appraiser general certification examination. There are six of these functions; each is described below. All six functions are variations on the compound interest formula, which holds that interest in each period is based on the initial principal plus accrued but unpaid interest earned in prior periods. The six functions (and their column locations in standard six-function tables) are as follows:

- Future value of $1 (Column 1)
- Future value of an annuity of $1 per period (Column 2)
- Sinking fund factor (Column 3)
- Present value of $1 (Column 4)
- Present value of an annuity of $1 per period (Column 5)
- Installment to amortize $1 (Column 6)

Future Value of $1

This function is compound interest. Interest that has been earned and left on deposit becomes principal. In the next period, that principal will earn interest along with the initial principal. The formula for compound interest is as follows:

$$S^n = (1 + i)^n$$

where S^n = sum after n periods; i = periodic rate of interest; n = number of periods.

Table 15-1 indicates the growth of a $1.00 deposit that earns 10 percent compound interest for 5 years. Figure 15-1 illustrates the growth of $1.00 at compound interest.

Although Table 15-1 illustrates a compounding interval of 1 year, compounding may occur daily, monthly, quarterly, or semiannually. Interest rates are usually stated at a nominal annual figure, such as 10 percent, but more frequent compounding increases the effective rate. The general formula is the same: $S^n = (1 + i)^n$.

Table 15-1
FUTURE VALUE OF $1
$1.00 Deposit at 10% Interest Rate for 5 Years

Year		Compound Interest and Balance
0	Deposit	$1.00
1	Interest earned	0.10
1	Balance, end of year	1.10
2	Interest earned	0.11
2	Balance, end of year	1.21
3	Interest earned	0.121
3	Balance, end of year	1.331
4	Interest earned	0.1331
4	Balance, end of year	1.4641
5	Interest earned	0.1464
5	Balance, end of year	$1.6105

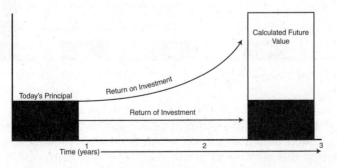

Figure 15-1. Growth of Principal at Compound Interest

Future Value of an Annuity of $1 Per Period

This function offers the future value of a series of equal amounts deposited at the ends of periodic intervals. It is the sum of all these individual amounts, each deposited at the end of an interval (period), plus appropriate interest. Note that this differs from the future value of $1 factor in two ways. First, the future annuity factor is based on a series of deposits, whereas the future value of $1 involves a single deposit. Second, the accumulation is based on a deposit at the end of each interval, whereas compound interest is based on a deposit made at the beginning of the total period.

The formula for the future value of $1 per period is as follows:

$$S_n = \frac{s^n - 1}{i} \quad \text{or} \quad \frac{(1 + i)^n - 1}{i}$$

where S_n = future value of annuity of $1 per period; i = periodic interest rate; n = number of periods considered.

Table 15-2 shows the annual interest earned and end-of-period balances of the future value of an annuity of $1 per period at 10% interest. Figure 15-2 is an illustration of the function for four periods.

Table 15-2
FUTURE VALUE OF AN ANNUITY OF $1 PER PERIOD
Illustrated at 10% Interest Rate for Four Periods

End of period 1, initial deposit	$1.00
Interest, period 1	0.00
Balance, end of period 1	1.00
Interest, end of period 2	0.10
Deposit, end of period 2	1.00
Balance, end of period 2	2.10
Interest, end of period 3	0.21
Deposit, end of period 3	1.00
Balance, end of period 3	3.31
Interest, end of period 4	0.331
Deposit, end of period 4	1.00
Balance, end of period 4	$4.641

Figure 15-2. Accumulation of $1 per Period (Future Value of an Annuity). *A*, *B*, *C*, and *D* each represent $1 deposited at the end of a year. Each deposit earns compound interest from the date deposited until the date on which a terminal amount is sought. Thus, all deposits and interest are allowed to accumulate. The terminal value is the sum of all deposits plus compound interest.

Sinking Fund Factor

This factor shows the deposit that is required at the end of each period to reach $1.00 after a certain number of periods, considering interest to be earned on the deposits. It is the reciprocal of the future value of an annuity of $1 per period.

For example, at a 0% rate of interest, $0.25 must be deposited at the end of each year for 4 years to accumulate $1.00 at the end of 4 years. If, however, the deposits earn compound interest at 10%, only $0.215471 need be deposited at the end of each of the 4 years.

Table 15-3 indicates how four periodic deposits grow to $1.00 with interest. Figure 15-3 offers a graphic presentation of the same data.

Table 15-3
SINKING FUND FACTOR
Illustrated to Reach $1.00 in Four Periods at 10% Interest Rate

Deposit, end of period 1	$0.215471
Interest for period 1	0.000000
Balance, end of period 1	0.215471
Interest for period 2	0.021547
Deposit, end of period 2	0.215471
Balance, end of period 2	0.452489
Interest for period 3	0.045249
Deposit, end of period 3	0.215471
Balance, end of period 3	0.713209
Interest for period 4	0.071321
Deposit, end of period 4	0.215471
Balance, end of period 4	$1.000000

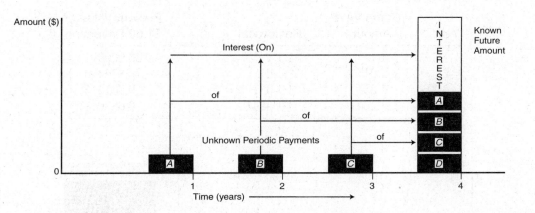

Figure 15-3.   Sinking Fund Factor. *A, B, C,* and *D* are equal amounts deposited at the end of each year. Each deposit earns compound interest for the period of time it remains on deposit. At the end of the time period considered, the depositor can withdraw the terminal value. The sinking fund factor is computed in such a way that the terminal value will always equal $1.

Present Value of $1

This factor offers the value now of $1 to be received in the future. Money has a time value; a dollar to be received in the future is worth less than a dollar now. The amount of discount depends on the time between the cash outflow and inflow and the necessary rate of interest or discount rate.

Since the purpose of investing is to receive returns in the future, applying the present value of $1 factor to anticipated future income is a crucial step in valuing an investment. When applying a present value factor, the terms *discounting* and *discount rate* are used, as contrasted with *compounding* and *interest rate*, which are used in computing future values. Mathematically, the present value of a reversion is the reciprocal of the future value of $1.

For example, at a 10% discount rate, $100.00 that is expected 1 year from now has a present value of $90.91. As an arithmetic check, consider that, if an investor has $90.91 now and earns 10% during the year, the interest will amount to $9.09, making the principal in 1 year $100.00 ($90.91 original principal + $9.09 interest).

An investor who will get $100.00 in 2 years and pays $82.64 now receives a 10% annual rate of interest. As a check, consider that, after 1 year, $82.64 will grow to $90.91 with 10% interest, then to $100.00 in 2 years.

The formula for the present value of $1 is as follows:

$$V^n = \frac{1}{(1+i)^n} \quad \text{or} \quad \frac{1}{S^n}$$

where V = present value of $1; i = periodic discount rate; n = number of periods.

Table 15-4 shows the present value of a reversion at 10% interest for 4 years. Figure 15-4 illustrates the present value of $1.

Table 15-4
PRESENT VALUE OF $1
Illustrated at 10% Interest Rate for 4 Years

Year	Compound Amount	Reciprocal		Present Value of $1.00 Reversion
1	1.1	1/1.1	=	$0.909091
2	1.21	1/1.21	=	0.826446
3	1.331	1/1.331	=	0.751315
4	1.4641	1/1.4641	=	0.683013

Figure 15-4.   Present Value of a Reversion

Present Value of an Annuity of $1 Per Period

An ordinary annuity is a series of equal payments beginning one period from the present. It is also defined as a series of receipts. For example, the right to receive $1.00 at the end of each year for the next 4 years creates an ordinary annuity.

Table 15-5 shows the present value of an annuity of $1 each year for 4 years at a 10% interest rate. Figure 15-5 provides an illustration.

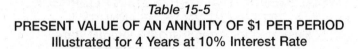

Table 15-5
PRESENT VALUE OF AN ANNUITY OF $1 PER PERIOD
Illustrated for 4 Years at 10% Interest Rate

Year	Present Value of Reversion	Present Value of Annuity
1	$0.9091	$0.9091
2	0.8264	1.7355
3	0.7513	2.4868
4	0.6830	3.1698

Figure 15-5.   Present Value of an Ordinary Annuity

Installment to Amortize $1 (Loan Constant or Mortgage Constant)

This function shows the periodic payment required to retire a loan, with interest. It is the sum of the interest (or discount) rate and the sinking fund factor. It is the reciprocal of the present value of an annuity of $1 per period. This factor, which shows the constant payment necessary to amortize a loan in equal periodic installments, considers the term, interest rate, and principal of the loan.

As the interest rate increases or the amortization term shortens, the required periodic payment is increased. Conversely, lower interest rates and longer repayment periods reduce the required periodic payment. Each level payment in the installment to amortize $1 factor is a blend of interest and a reduction of the original principal.

The formula for the installment to amortize $1 is as follows:

$$\frac{1}{a_n} = \frac{i}{1 - V^n} \quad \text{or} \quad \frac{1}{a_n} = \frac{i}{1 - \dfrac{1}{(1 + i)^n}}$$

where a_n = present value of annuity of $1 per period; i = interest rate; n = number of periods; V^n = present value of $1.

Table 15-6 shows that the installment to amortize $1 is the reciprocal of the present value of an annuity of $1 factor. Figure 15-6 illustrates the distribution of periodic payments to interest and principal retirement.

Table 15-6
**INSTALLMENTS TO AMORTIZE $1 AS RECIPROCAL
OF PRESENT VALUE OF ANNUITY**
Illustrated for 4 Years at 10% Interest Rate

Year	Present Value of Annuity	Installment to Amortize $1
1	$0.9091	$1.10
2	1.7355	0.5762
3	2.4868	0.4021
4	3.1698	0.3155

Figure 15-6.   Mortgage Payment Application (Installment to Amortize $1)

As an example of use, suppose that a $100 loan requires four equal annual payments at 10% interest. The required payment will be $31.55. As a check, one can construct an amortization schedule as shown in Table 15-7.

Table 15-7
AMORTIZATION SCHEDULE FOR A $100 LOAN
Level Payments at 10% for 4 Years

Year	Loan Balance at Beginning of Year	Add Interest at 10%	Less Interest and Principal Payment	Balance at End of Year
1	$100.00	$10.00	$31.55	$78.45
2	78.45	7.85	31.55	54.75
3	54.75	5.48	31.55	28.68
4	28.68	2.87	31.55	-0-

SALES COMPARISON APPROACH

Chapter 14 covers most of the details associated with sales comparisons. Here, gross income multipliers and overall rates are discussed, along with certain units of comparison, mineral rights and other vertical interests, and tenant improvements.

Gross Income Multipliers

Gross income multipliers can be used to compare comparable properties to the subject property. The *gross income multiplier (GIM)* indicates the relationship between the annual revenues from a property and its selling price or value. In nearly all situations, the sales price is several times greater than the revenues and therefore is the numerator, with the revenues the denominator. The resulting factor is expected to be greater than 1, most frequently between 4 and 20.

Potential Gross Income Multiplier

Potential gross income (PGI) is the amount that would be received from rental properties if all units were fully occupied all year. For example, if a building contained 100 apartments, each renting for $1,000 per month, the PGI would be 100 × $1,000 × 12 months, or $1,200,000. If this building were to sell for $10 million, the *potential gross income multiplier (PGIM)* would be 8.333 ($10,000,000 ÷ $1,200,000).

Effective Gross Income Multiplier

Effective gross income (EGI) is determined by subtracting an allowance for vacancy and collection losses from potential gross income. In the example above, if the appropriate allowance percentage rate is 5% of the $1,200,000 potential gross income, the allowance is $60,000. The EGI is therefore $1,200,000 minus $60,000, or $1,140,000. The *effective gross income multiplier (EGIM)* is the selling price divided by the EGIM, that is, $10,000,000 ÷ $1,140,000, or 8.772.

Overall Rate of Return

The *overall rate of return* is the percentage relationship between the *net operating income (NOI)* and the sales price. Since NOI is a revenue amount, this ratio is almost always less than 1, typically 0.05 to 0.30.

NOI is EGI minus operating expenses (OE). Operating expenses are payments that must be made to run the property, but not financing expenses, such as interest, nor depreciation. Operating expenses include maintenance and repairs, payroll and payroll taxes, real estate property taxes, advertising, utilities, management fees, grounds maintenance, and replacement reserve.

Suppose, in the preceding example, that annual operating expenses are $440,000. Then NOI is $1,140,000 (EGI) minus $440,000 (OE), or $700,000. The overall rate of return is

$$\frac{\text{NOI}}{\text{Sales Price}} = \frac{\$700,000}{\$10,000,000} = 7\%$$

Units of Comparison

The certified general appraiser is expected to be knowledgeable about some less obvious units of comparison, including those for specialized properties, such as motels and theaters. Units of comparison for these include the price per room for a motel and the price per seat for a theater. The computation is straightforward: after appraisal adjustments are made for the elements of comparison described below, the adjusted price is divided by the number of units.

An appraisal should emulate market conditions; for example, in the case of multiscreen theaters, the number of screens may become a unit of comparison.

Mineral Rights and Other Vertical Interests

A real estate appraiser is not expected to be a geologist or to be able to value subsurface rights (*mineral rights*), but she must recognize that in certain regions the minerals may have value. When some comparables sell with mineral rights and some without, the appraiser must take care to make the appropriate adjustments from the comparables to the subject property. The paired-sale technique (see Chapter 14) may be useful for this purpose.

An appraiser may need also to value other *vertical interests*, such as *air rights* (the right to build above property, starting from a certain height) and tunneling.

Tenant Improvements

Tenant improvements, known in the trade as TIs, are allowances given to a tenant to adapt the property for his use. For example, a retail tenant agrees to a 5-year lease at a rent of $25 per square foot per year. The landlord offers bare walls and will advance $15 per square foot, before occupancy, for the tenant to adapt the property to his use. If costs exceed the allowance, the tenant will be responsible.

When comparing rents, an appraiser must also consider TIs. One building may offer a low rent but contribute no TIs, whereas another has higher rents and a generous TI allowance. The appraiser must understand the market so as to properly estimate the market rent for the subject property.

SITE VALUE

Two methods of estimating site value, in addition to those given in Chapter 14, are *ground rent capitalization* and *subdivision analysis*. These methods apply only in certain situations.

Ground Rent Capitalization

In a few places, notably Hawaii, Baltimore, and Manhattan, there is a high concentration of ground lease ownership; that is, the building owner does not own the land but, as a tenant, leases it from the landowner. An appraiser can estimate land value by *capitalization*, that is, by dividing the annual rent by an appropriate capitalization rate. As a simple example, suppose that the rent on a lot in Baltimore is $120 per year, renewable forever. The appropriate rate of return on investment is 6%. Then the land value is $120 ÷ 0.06 = $2,000.

Subdivision Analysis

Subdivision analysis is a method of estimating the maximum that a subdivider can pay for a tract of land. This method involves a sales estimate (usually monthly or quarterly) and a cost estimate over time. Cash flows are then discounted to a present value.

The example shown in Table 15-8 was prepared on an annual basis. As can be seen from the table, $137,285 is the maximum that can be paid for land, and still allow the subdivision to be developed, under the assumptions shown.

INCOME APPROACH

A certified general appraiser is expected to know how to appraise income-producing property on the basis of the revenue it is expected to generate. A number of techniques used for this purpose are described below.

Table 15-8
SUBDIVISION DEVELOPMENT ANALYSIS

	Year			
	1	2	3	4
Lost sales units	0	10	15	20
Price per lot		$ 20,000	$ 22,000	$ 25,000
Total sales	-0-	200,000	330,000	500,000
Costs:				
Engineering	$ 40,000			
Utility installation	70,000	100,000		
Clearing and grading	50,000			
Advertising	25,000	25,000	25,000	25,000
Streets and sidewalks	50,000	50,000	60,000	-0-
Permits	10,000			
Contractor's overhead and profit	10,000	10,000	10,000	10,000
Legal and accounting	15,000			
Interest	20,000	15,000	15,000	15,000
Entrepreneurial profit			50,000	50,000
Total costs	$290,000	$200,000	$160,000	$100,000
Cash flow (total sales less Total costs)	(290,000)	-0-	170,000	$400,000
Discount rate @ 10%	× .90909	× .8264	× .7513	× .683
Present value	(263,636)	-0-	$127,721	$273,200
Sum of present value	$137,285			

Estimation of Income and Expenses

Income property valuation begins with an estimate of income and expenses, which was described, to a limited extent, under the sales comparison approach. The levels of income generated by a given property range from a top level, potential gross income, to a bottom level, owner's cash flow. Table 15-9 on the next page is a chart of income levels.

In addition to income, operating expenses must be considered, and an operating statement derived.

Potential Gross Income

Potential gross income is the rent collectible if all units are fully occupied.

TYPES OF RENT

In estimating potential gross income, the appraiser distinguishes between *market rent* (economic rent) and *contract rent*. Market rent is the rate prevailing in the market for comparable properties and is used in calculating market value by the income approach. Contract rent is the actual amount agreed to by landlord and tenant. If the leases are long-term, contract rent is important in calculating investment value.

Market rents represent what a given property should be renting for, based on analysis of recently negotiated contract rents for comparable space—but only those that are considered bona fide "market" rents. The market rent should be the amount that would result from a lease negotiated between a willing lessor and a willing lessee, both free from influence from outside sources.

Table 15-9
LEVELS OF REAL ESTATE INCOME

	Potential gross income
Less:	Vacancy and collection allowance
Plus:	Miscellaneous income
Equals:	**Effective gross income**
Less:	Allowable expenses
	Maintenance and operating
	Administrative
	Utilities
	Real estate taxes
	Replacement reserves
	Etc.
Equals:	**Net operating income**
Less:	Debt service
	Mortgage principal
	Mortgage interest
Equals:	**Before-tax cash flow**
	(Cash throw-off or equity dividend)

RENTAL UNITS OF COMPARISON

Rents must be compared in terms of a common denominator. Typical units of comparison are square foot, room, apartment, space, and percentage of gross business income of the tenant, as shown in Table 15-10.

Table 15-10
RENTAL UNITS OF COMPARISON
FOR TYPES OF INCOME-PRODUCING PROPERTY

Rental Unit of Comparison	Type of Income-Producing Property
Square foot	Shopping centers, retail stores, office buildings, warehouses, apartments, leased land
Room	Motels, hotels, apartment buildings
Apartment	Apartment buildings
Space	Mobile home parks, travel trailer parks, parking garages
Percentages of gross business income	Retail stores, shopping centers, restaurants, gas stations

When the square foot unit is used for an office building or shopping center, the appraiser should note that some leases are based on *net leasable area* (*NLA*) and others on *gross leasable area* (*GLA*). NLA is the floor area occupied by the tenant. GLA includes NLA plus common areas such as halls, restrooms, and vestibules. An office building with 100,000 square feet of GLA may have only 80,000 square feet of NLA, a difference of 20%. When leases are compared, it must be known whether rent is based on GLA or NLA.

Effective Gross Income

Effective gross income is the amount remaining after the vacancy rate and collection (bad debt) allowances are subtracted from potential gross income and miscellaneous income is added. Calculating effective gross income is an intermediate step in deriving the cash flow.

VACANCY AND COLLECTION ALLOWANCE

The losses expected from vacancies and bad debts must be subtracted from potential gross income. These losses are calculated at the rate expected of local ownership and management.

MISCELLANEOUS INCOME

Miscellaneous income is received from concessions, laundry rooms, parking space or storage bin rentals, and other associated services integral to operating the project.

Operating Expenses

The potential list of operating expenses for gross leased real estate includes

- Property taxes: city, county, school district, special assessments
- Insurance: hazard, liability
- Utilities: telephone, water, sewer or sewage disposal, electricity, gas
- Administrative costs: management fees, clerical staff, maintenance staff, payroll taxes, legal and accounting expenses
- Repairs and maintenance: paint, decoration, carpet replacement, appliance repairs and replacement, supplies, gardening/landscaping, paving, roofing
- Advertising and promotion: media, business organizations

FIXED VERSUS VARIABLE EXPENSES

Operating expenses may be divided into two categories. *Fixed expenses* do not change as the rate of occupancy changes. *Variable expenses,* on the other hand, are directly related to the occupancy rate: as more people occupy and use a building, variable expenses increase.

Fixed expenses include property taxes, license and permit fees, and property insurance. Variable expenses generally include utilities (such as heat, water, sewer), management fees, payroll and payroll taxes, security, landscaping, advertising, and supplies and fees for various services provided by local government or private contractors. There may be a fixed component in expenses normally classified as variable—for example, a basic fixed payroll cost regardless of the occupancy rate.

REPLACEMENT RESERVE

Provision must be made for the replacement of short-lived items (e.g., carpeting, appliances, and some mechanical equipment) that wear out. Such expenditures usually occur in large lump sums; a portion of the expected cost can be set aside every year to stabilize the expenses. A replacement reserve is necessary because the wearing out of short-lived assets causes a hidden loss of income. If this economic fact is not reflected in financial statements, the net operating income will be overstated. An appraiser should provide for a replacement reserve even though most owners do not set aside money for this purpose.

Net Operating Income

Net operating income (NOI) is estimated by subtracting operating expenses and the replacement reserve from effective gross income. Any interest or principal payments are not considered in computing NOI.

NOI for each comparable sale should be estimated in the same way that the subject property's NOI is considered. All relevant income and operating expenses are included in consistent amounts or rates to uniformly apply a capitalization rate. Each dollar of error in stating NOI will be multiplied, perhaps by 10 or more, in the resulting value estimate.

Operating Statement Ratios

Operating statement ratios are informative comparisons of expenses to income. The *operating expense ratio* is the percentage relationship of operating expenses to potential or effective gross income. There are typical ratios for each type of property in a market area, and much higher or lower ratios may be a clue to the effectiveness of management policies, efficient or inefficient.

The *net income ratio* is the reciprocal of the operating expense ratio. It tells what the fraction of property net operating income is compared to potential gross income. The *break-even ratio* is the occupancy rate needed to have zero cash flow. It is the sum of operating expenses plus debt service, divided by potential gross income.

Income Capitalization

Income capitalization is a process whereby a stream of future income receipts is translated into a single present-value sum. It considers

1. Amount of future income (cash flow)
2. Time when the income (cash flow) is to be received
3. Duration of the income (cash flow) stream

A *capitalization rate* is used to convert an income stream into a lump-sum value. The formula used is as follows:

$$V = \frac{I}{R}$$

where V = present value; I = periodic income; R = capitalization rate.

Direct Capitalization

Direct capitalization involves simple arithmetic division of two components to result in a capitalized value, as shown below:

$$\text{Property Value} = \frac{\text{Net Operating Income}}{\text{Overall Rate of Return}}$$

The appraiser considers other properties that have been sold and the net operating income generated by each to derive an *overall rate of return* (OAR). A market-derived OAR is then divided into the subject's NOI to estimate the latter's value.

OVERALL CAPITALIZATION RATE

To derive an overall capitalization rate from market data, the appraiser must select similar properties that have sold recently and are characterized by income streams of risk and duration similar to those of the subject property. If sufficient comparables are available, an OAR can be derived directly from the market and the appraiser can use direct capitalization to convert forecast NOI into a market value estimate.

To illustrate, suppose an appraiser has found the following data:

Comparable	NOI	Sales Price	Indicated OAR
#1	$240,000	$2,000,000	0.120
#2	176,000	1,600,000	0.110
#3	210,000	2,000,000	0.105

If adequate data of this nature were consistently available, appropriate overall rates could be developed for all types of properties, and other methods of capitalization would be of little importance. Unfortunately, reliable, verified sales data are not plentiful, and caution should be exercised in using this capitalization method. The comparability of the sale properties to the subject property must be analyzed carefully. Appropriate application requires that the comparables considered be consistent in these respects:

- Income and expense ratios
- NOI calculations
- Improvement ratio
- Remaining economic life
- Date and terms of sale

The simplicity of direct capitalization makes it attractive, even though complex relationships of income, expenses, and rates of return may underlie the computation. Various ways to derive rates are described in this chapter.

The *overall capitalization rate* must include a return on and a return of investment. Return *on* investment is the compensation necessary to pay an investor for the time value of the money, risk, and other factors associated with a particular investment. It is the interest paid for the use of money, also referred to as *yield*. Return *of* investment deals with repayment of the original principal, referred to as *capital recovery*. The capitalization rate taken from the market presumably incorporates other factors, such as expected inflation, income tax effect on the property, and interest rates and loan terms. However, this is a presumption, without actual numbers being tested to validate the expectation.

The yield rate is a rate of return on investment. Since real estate tends to wear out over time, though its economic useful life may be 50 years or longer, an investor must receive a recovery *of* the investment in addition to a return on it. There are three ways to provide a return of investment:

1. Straight line
2. Annuity
3. Sinking fund at safe rate

Straight Line. The straight-line technique is useful when building income is forecast to decline. Under a straight-line method, an annual depreciation rate is computed as an equal percentage for each year of the asset's life. When the life is 50 years, the rate is 2% per year, totaling 100% over 50 years. Thus, 2% would be added to the 10% return on investment to provide a 12% capitalization rate. That rate is divided into the estimated building income to derive an estimate of building value.

Annuity. An annuity method is useful when the income is projected to be level annually for a finite life. The appraiser determines the capital recovery rate at the sinking fund factor at the investment's rate of return. At 10% return on investment for 50 years, this factor is 0.000859, offering a total capitalization rate of 0.100859 (0.10 + 0.000859).

Sinking Fund at Safe Rate. The sinking fund factor at a safe rate is used when reinvestment assumptions are conservative. The 5% sinking fund factor for 50 years is 0.004777. This provides a capitalization rate of 0.104777 (0.10 + 0.004777) when given a 10% rate of return on investment.

Band of Investment

Net operating income from real estate is typically divided between mortgage lenders and equity investors. Rates of return can be weighted by the portions of purchase capital contributed, to result in a rate of return applicable to the entire property. This method is called the *band of investment*. The yield or interest or discount rate is then used to capitalize all of the NOI into one lump-sum property value. This value would assume that a capital recovery provision is unnecessary since neither amortization nor recovery of equity invested is considered.

For example, suppose that lenders typically contribute 75% of the required purchase capital and seek an 6% rate of return on investment. Equity investors want a 9% rate of return on investment. The yield or discount rate for the entire property would be 6.75%, as shown in Table 15-11. This rate consists purely of interest and assumes no principal retirement of the loan and no capital appreciation or depreciation of the equity investment. Further, all of the NOI is paid each year to each investor, mortgage and equity. Repayment of all purchase capital will be made upon a resale of the property at an indefinite time in the future.

Table 15-11
RATES OF RETURN FOR A MORTGAGED PROPERTY

Source of Funds	Portion of Purchase Capital		Rate of Return on Investment		Weighted Rate
Mortgage	0.75	×	0.06	=	0.0450
Equity	0.25	×	0.09	=	0.0225
Yield or discount rate for entire property					0.0675

Gross Income Multipliers

In the case of multipliers, gross rent (income) estimates are frequently used by investors. The estimated annual gross income is multiplied by a factor that has been derived as an accurate representation of market behavior for that type of property. A monthly gross income multiplier is typically used for residential housing, whereas annual multipliers are used for other types of property.

Ease of computation makes a rent multiplier a deceptively attractive technique. For appropriate application, however, everything about the subject being appraised and the comparables used must be alike, including the lease terms, tenant strength, operating expenses, and physical setting. The rent multiplier is, at best, a crude measuring device.

Residual Techniques

Residual techniques can be applied to income-producing property. The term *residual* implies that, after income requirements are satisfied for the known parts of the property, the residual, or remaining, income is processed into an indication of value for the unknown part. The three most commonly used types are (1) land, (2) building, and (3) equity residual techniques.

LAND RESIDUAL TECHNIQUE

The land residual technique is useful when improvements are relatively new or have not yet been built. Their values (or proposed costs) can be closely approximated, as can their estimated useful lives. For example, suppose recently constructed real estate improvements cost $1 million and have a 50-year economic useful life. The appropriate rate of return on investment is 10% because that rate is competitive with other investment opportunities perceived to have equal risk. Straight-line capital recovery is considered appropriate for the improvements. The annual recovery rate is 2% (100% ÷ 50 years = 2% per year), so the total required rate of return for the improvements is 12%. Annual net operating income for the first year is estimated to be $150,000. The improvements require a 12% return on $1 million of cost, which equals $120,000 of income. Subtracting this amount from the $150,000 net operating income leaves a $30,000 residual for the land. This amount, capitalized in perpetuity at 10%, offers a land value of $300,000. Capitalization of land income in perpetuity is appropriate because land is thought to last forever. This technique is summarized in Table 15-12.

Table 15-12
**LAND RESIDUAL TECHNIQUE—STRAIGHT-LINE
CAPITAL RECOVERY FOR BUILDINGS**

Net operating income (first year)	$ 150,000
Less: Income attributable to improvements:	
10% (on) + 2% (of) = 12%; 0.12 × $1,000,000	− 120,000
Residual income to land	$ 30,000
Capitalized at 10% return on investment in perpetuity	$ 300,000
The total property value is then estimated at $1.3 million ($1 million for improvements plus $300,000 for land).	

The land residual technique is used also in estimating the highest and best use of land. Costs of different proposed improvements can be estimated, as can the net operating income for each type of improvement. A capitalization rate is multiplied by the estimated improvement cost, and the result subtracted from forecast net operating income. The result is forecast land income. Whichever type or level of improvement offers the highest residual income to land is the highest and best use of the land, subject to legal and physical constraints.

BUILDING RESIDUAL TECHNIQUE

The building residual technique works in reverse of the land residual technique. When the land value can be estimated with a high degree of confidence (as when there are many recent sales of comparables), income attributable to the land is subtracted from net operating income. The residual income is attributable to the improvements and can be capitalized to estimate their value. Then the capitalized value of the improvements is added to the land value to obtain a total property value estimate.

As an example of the building residual technique, suppose that the land value is estimated at $200,000 through a careful analysis of several recent sales of comparable vacant tracts of land. A 10% discount rate is considered appropriate. Of the estimated $150,000 of annual NOI, $20,000 is attributable to the land. Capital recovery for land income is unnecessary since the land will last forever. The $130,000 balance of NOI is attributable to the improvements, which would be worth $1,083,333 using a straight-line capital recovery rate and 50-year life. The building residual technique is summarized in Table 15-13.

Table 15-13
BUILDING RESIDUAL TECHNIQUE

Net operating income	$ 150,000
Less: Income to land: 10% of $200,000	$ − 20,000
Income to improvements	$ 130,000
Improvement value at straight-line capital recovery: (over 50 years) $130,000 ÷ 0.12	$ 1,083,333

EQUITY RESIDUAL TECHNIQUE

The equity residual technique is an effort to estimate the value of the property when the mortgage amount and terms are known. Net operating income is calculated as in other techniques, and debt service is subtracted to result in cash flow. The cash flow is capitalized at an appropriate equity dividend rate to obtain equity value, which is added to the mortgage principal to provide a value estimate.

Owner's Cash Flow from Operations

In this technique, net operating income is forecast for a number of years to some period in the future when a property sale is expected to occur. The cash flows from operations and resale are discounted by an appropriate discount rate, then totaled to offer a property value estimate.

Adjustments to Capitalization Rates

Depending on lease and market information, net operating income may be forecast to be level, to grow, or to decline. An appraiser must use known information and provide market evidence for the projections.

Financial results from real estate depend on lease terms and economic conditions. If the tenant's credit is triple A and the lease is long term at a fixed net rental rate, income should be assured. If the tenant's credit rating is not high, or the lease is not net or its term is short, value will depend on such factors as inflation, competition, interest rates, and economic conditions.

Current values may be strongly affected by expectations of future resale prices. An appraiser must therefore consider resale expectations when selecting a capitalization rate. This "cap rate" is raised when value decline is expected in the future, lowered when appreciation is anticipated.

Estimating Resale Price

REVERSION

It is sometimes helpful to estimate a resale price based on expectations for the future. The resale price, less selling costs and outstanding debts, has a present value that, added to the present value of net operating income for each year, may be used to estimate today's value. The estimated resale price is diminished by selling expenses, including commissions and legal expenses, to result in proceeds from sale. Table 15-14 shows how a $1,000,000 resale price is diminished by transaction costs.

Table 15-14
RESALE PRICE DIMINISHED BY TRANSACTION COSTS

Resale price		**$1,000,000**
Less seller's estimated expenses of sale:		
Title insurance policy	$ 3,000	
Attorney's fees	4,500	
Release of lien	200	
Survey of property	600	
Escrow fees	500	
Recording fees	200	
Broker's professional service fee (commission)	40,000	
Subtotal		− 49,000
Estimated receipts to seller		**$ 951,000**

OTHER METHODS OF RESALE PRICE ESTIMATION

The resale price can be estimated in several other ways. First, today's market value with a percentage annual growth or depreciation rate is applied. This method assumes that future values are related to today's value, often adjusted by expected inflation. Second, income forecast for the year after the sale is capitalized to obtain a resale price. Third, the sales price of encumbered property may be the cash flow after debt service, capitalized at an equity dividend rate, and added to the mortgage balance.

Measuring Rate of Cash Flow

Cash flow is usually defined as the amount left after debt service. The rate of cash flow can be derived in two ways: dividend and yield.

Equity Dividend Rate

The *equity dividend rate* (also called *cash-on-cash return*) is cash flow divided by the equity paid for the property. The result is a measure of cash return on investment. When cash flow can be measured accurately, it may be divided by a market-derived equity dividend rate to obtain the equity value. Equity value, plus mortgage balance, offers a property value estimate.

Debt Coverage Ratio

The *debt coverage ratio* indicates a lender's margin of safety. It is computed by dividing net operating income by debt service. Lenders typically want a ratio ranging from at least 1.1 for the safest property, secured by a net lease from a tenant with triple A credit, up to 1.2 to 1.5 for apartments or office buildings and a minimum of 2.0 for recreational property.

Discounted Cash Flow (Yield) Capitalization

By contrast to first-year capitalization techniques, yield capitalization rates employ compound interest/present value factors. These rates are typically found in six-function compound interest tables, described on pages 241–246, which offer a precise value for periodic cash flow and reversion based on a specific rate of return on investment.

Discounted Cash Flow Application

Discounted cash flow capitalization is best applied when income from the property and a resale price can be forecast with reasonable certainty. This requires income forecasts of rents, operating expenses, and tenant improvements, as previously discussed.

The key to discounted cash flow is the *discounting process*, which is based on the fact that money to be received at some time in the future is worth *less* than money received today. The value that we assign to such *future incomes* is called *present value*, or *present discounted value*. Exactly what the present value of a future income is will depend on the answers to two questions: (1) when will the income accrue and (2) what is the *discount rate*? The discount rate is a rate of return, similar to an interest rate, that measures the risk and time value of the income to be received. How a discount rate is arrived at is discussed below, but there are a couple of basic rules that are useful: (1) the longer we have to wait for a future income, the less it is worth to us *today* (i.e., the lower is its present value), and (2) the higher the discount rate applied to a future income, the lower its present value (and vice-versa).

Appraisers value an income property by examining the net income that the property can be expected to provide in the future, and then finding a present value for that income. This can be done fairly easily using six-function tables or a financial calculator. However, most states don't allow applicants for licenses to use financial calculators (not yet, anyway), so we will take a brief look at the math involved.

Essentially, we derive a present value for each part of the future income stream, and then add all the values. For example, suppose we are appraising a property that will produce a net income of $10,000 per year for 5 years; at the end of 5 years it can be sold for $50,000. (This one-time income at the end of the holding period, either sale price or salvage value, is called a *reversion* by real estate appraisers.) Let's assume that we're using a discount rate of 12%. This means that we need a return of 12% a year (compounded) for this investment. To simplify, let's assume also that the incomes accrue at the *end* of each year. Then our income stream will be $10,000 a year for 4 years, with a fifth-year income of $10,000 *plus* the sale proceeds of $50,000, for a total fifth-year income of $60,000. Our income stream looks like the column below headed "Income."

Time	Income	Factor		Present Value
Year 1	$10,000	1/1.12 =	0.892857	$ 8,928.57
Year 2	$10,000	1/(1.12)2 =	0.797194	7,971.94
Year 3	$10,000	1/(1.12)3 =	0.711780	7,117.80
Year 4	$10,000	1/(1.12)4 =	0.635518	6,355.18
Year 5	$60,000	1/(1.12)5 =	0.567427	34,045.61
	Present value total			**$64,419.10**

We arrived at a present value of about $64,400. What we're saying, with this number, is that a future income of $10,000 a year for 5 years, plus a reversion of $50,000 at the end of 5 years, when discounted at 12% a year, is worth about $64,400 *today*. In other words, $64,400 invested today, at 12% annual return, will yield the income we project for the property.

How exactly did we do this? Let's look at the first year's income of $10,000. We don't get it for a year, but we have to pay for it *now*. Basically, we ask, "How much money, invested today, will grow to $10,000 in 1 year, given a 12% annual return?" This first year's income, then, will have a present value of $10,000/1.12 because we are looking for an amount that, once it has earned a 12% return, will *become* $10,000. What we did in the table was to figure out the *factor* for 12% for 1 year, which is the decimal equivalent of 1/1.12, and then multiply it by $10,000. The advantage of this method is that, once we figure out what 1/1.12 is, we can use that number to get the present value of *any* amount to be received 1 year from now at a rate of 12%.

For the 12% *factors* for periods beyond 1 year, we just divide by 1.12 *again* for *each* year longer that we have to wait for the income. For the present value of the second year's income, we multiply $10,000 by 1/1.12 *twice* (once for each year): $10,000 × 1/1.12 × 1/1.12, which is the same as $10,000 × 1/(1.12)2. For the third year we use 1/(1.12)3, and so on. Once we've figured out the present value of each of the five annual incomes, we just add them. You can check these numbers out yourself. For each year's income, start with the present value. Multiply it by 1.12; do this for each year that you have to wait, and you should end up with $10,000 for each of the first 4 years, and $60,000 for the fifth year.

YIELD RATE SELECTION

An appraiser can attempt to construct a yield rate using the *buildup method,* by identifying the components of a required rate of return. Although there is general agreement in identifying the components (see below), the proportion of each component in the overall rate is arbitrary. Furthermore, the buildup is unnecessary because an investor acquires the entire property, which provides one rate. Although the buildup method is theoretical, it helps us to understand capitalization rates and to compare them with non-real estate investments.

To construct a built-up rate, begin with a liquid, risk-free rate, such as the rate on passbook accounts offered by financial institutions whose depositors' accounts are insured by a U.S. government agency. The rate is the minimum that must be paid as compensation for the time value of money.

Add to this risk-free rate a provision for the risk associated with the specific type of real estate being appraised. For example, risk is low where there is a strong tenant with captive customers, but high for property leased to weak tenants who have fickle customers.

Provisions must be made for illiquidity. *Liquidity* is a measure of how quickly an asset can be converted into cash. Compared to stocks and bonds, real estate is illiquid, particularly in a weak market or tight-money economy.

The burden of investment management must also be included. This is the decision making required of the investor and is distinguished from the everyday process of property management.

The components of the buildup method and their proportions in the overall built-up rate are summarized as follows:

Risk-free rate	*5%*
Risk of subject property	*3%*
Illiquidity of subject property	*2%*
Investment management	*1%*
Rate of return on investment	*11%*

Selecting the appropriate yield rate depends on numerous factors, especially the availability of accurate market data. An appraiser must consider the duration, quality, and amount of income from the property forecast for each future year. Other relevant factors include the earnings or yield rate required by the market and the portion of investment that is subject to capital recovery.

Ratio capitalization requires a realistic estimate of net operating income, which is divided by a supportable capitalization rate. The mathematical composition of the cap rate is derived from the market, tempered by property performance expectations.

VALUATION OF PARTIAL INTERESTS

The certified general appraiser is expected to have an extensive knowledge of partial interests in real estate. These include interests in a lease, lease provisions, and the identification of the various ownership positions within a property having different risk features.

Lease Interests

A *subleasehold* may be carved out of a lease interest. A subleasehold is the interest of the tenant's tenant; that is, a tenant may sublease his property, becoming a landlord to another tenant. The subtenant's interest may be valuable.

Renewal options in a lease give the tenant the right, but not the obligation, to extend the lease at whatever rent and terms are described in the option. This encumbrance can affect the value of the property either positively or negatively.

Tenant improvements must be analyzed to determine how they affect the property value. Are they to remain after the lease expires? Would a substitute tenant find them useful and pay a premium for them, or would they be expensive to demolish on demand?

Concessions granted in the market or by the property to attract tenants must be assessed. For example, suppose an office building rents for $25 per square foot on a 5-year lease, with the first year free. The property is appraised in the second year of the lease. Is the correct rent $25/per square foot or much less? How much rent can be capitalized? The appraiser needs to understand the market.

Lease Provisions

NET VERSUS GROSS LEASES

A lease is typically referred to as *net* or *gross*, although most leases are neither absolutely net nor absolutely gross. In an absolute net lease the tenant (lessee) pays taxes, insurance, and operating expenses: maintenance, including repairs, alterations, replacements, and improvements, ordinary or extraordinary repairs whether interior or exterior, and so on. A net lease is the most straightforward approach for a single-tenant structure. The terms *triple-net* and *net-net-net* lease are often used to indicate a greater degree of net-ness than that for other leases.

As to specific taxes, tenants pay taxes, special assessments, and the like; however, tenants do not pay obligations of the landlord (lessor), such as gift, income, inheritance, franchise, or corporate taxes, or a tax on the rental receipts of the landlord.

The real estate owner is a passive investor when a net lease is used, relying on net rent to provide a return on investment. The property is the owner's investment, not a business.

With a gross lease the landlord pays all operating expenses. The owner must become a businessperson, keeping firm control over operating expenses and assuring that money spent to comply with the lease is spent prudently.

With a *stop* (or *escalation*) clause in a gross lease, the landlord pays a base-year amount for the expense and the tenant pays the increase in expense each year. A net lease or stop clauses reduce the need for frequent rent adjustments, cost of living indexes, or short-term leases.

OPERATING EXPENSES

A properly written lease should specify whether landlord or tenant pays for each operating expense. It should also specify that the responsible party must present proof of payment, such as a paid property tax bill or insurance policy in conformity with requirements of the lease, to provide assurance of protection from risks covered by the lease. If the lessee in a net lease does not supply the information, the lessor should request it.

Percentage Leases

A *percentage lease*, commonly used for a retail tenant, provides incentive to the landlord to make the property attractive and thus encourage retail sales. The landlord must be prepared to audit the tenant's retail sales records and to enforce provisions of the lease that protect the lessor's rights to a percentage of sales.

Most percentage leases require a fixed *minimum base rent* plus a percentage rent based on gross sales in excess of a certain amount. The base rent is often set as an anticipated average amount of sales per square foot for the particular type of business. For example, suppose industry norms for a ladies' fashion shop indicate that sales of $200 per square foot (SF) are typical. Rent for a 10,000-SF shop could be $100,000 per year plus 5% of sales above $2 million (10,000 SF × $200 typical sales = $2,000,000). Percentage rents would be imposed only when sales exceed the norm of $200/SF of floor area.

Different types of businesses have different typical percentage rents. For example, a jewelry store or other retailer selling luxury items tends to be relatively small, and has a high markup and low inventory turnover in comparison to a grocery or discount store. The percentage rental rate thus tends to be higher for the luxury or specialty store.

Certain lease provisions are necessary to assure fairness to both parties in administering a percentage lease. Monthly or annual sales reports may be required; and the landlord may have the right to hire an auditor, whose fee will be paid by the tenant if sales are understated or by the landlord if no discrepancies are found.

Cost of Living Index

Leases for multiple years without rent adjustments result in hardships to landlord or tenant during highly inflationary or deflationary periods. A long-term lease may have a *cost of living adjustment* that calls for changes in rent based on the change in some published index.

The index used and the frequency and amount of adjustment are negotiable. The Consumer Price Index (CPI), published by the Bureau of Labor Statistics of the U.S. Department of Labor, is usually chosen because of its frequency of computation and publication. A lesser known local index tied to rental rates, operating expenses, or real estate values may be satisfactory but can introduce elements of instability or potential manipulation, possibly resulting in litigation.

The adjustment period may be a single year or a multiple of years. This period should be short for a gross lease but may be longer for a net lease. With a net lease the landlord has less financial exposure to the risk of inflation because the tenant pays operating expenses.

The degree of adjustment may be only part of the full change in the index selected. For example, if 50% of the index was selected as the multiplier and the index rose by 20%, rent would increase by 10%. This provides some protection to the landlord (who perhaps bought the property with preinflation dollars) but does not inflict the full effect of inflation on the tenant.

Excess Rent

Excess rent is the difference between contract and market rents; the term implies that the tenant is paying more than would be paid for comparable property. If a property has several leases, the appraiser should prepare a schedule with the expiration date of each lease to assist in estimating the quality and duration of the income stream.

Valuation Considerations

A property may have been fractionated, that is, split into different interests. For example, there may be two mortgages and/or a land lease. The appraiser needs to determine the volatility of income, the priorities of cash distributions, and the risks and rewards for each interest. In doing so, the value to each party having a fractional interest can be estimated by the appraiser.

SUMMARY

The certified general appraiser is expected to have knowledge of income property valuation techniques and an understanding of their applications to specialized properties and interests that are beyond the expectations for a residential appraiser, broker, or salesperson.

Questions on Chapter 15

1. The fact that rents tend to be set by the market for equally desirable space reflects the principle of
   (A) balance
   (B) substitution
   (C) externalities
   (D) supply and demand
   (E) conformity

2. The net income that remains after the proper costs of labor, capital, and entrepreneurship have been paid is
   (A) surplus rent
   (B) opportunity cost
   (C) effective income
   (D) land rent
   (E) contract rent

3. All of the following are essential to the viability of an industrial district *except*
   (A) labor
   (B) materials
   (C) transportation
   (D) high technology
   (E) entrepreneurship

4. The present and future demand for a property and its absorption rate are considered in a
   (A) valuation report
   (B) market feasibility study
   (C) market segmentation study
   (D) highest and best use analysis
   (E) narrative appraisal

5. Real estate markets
   (A) are national in scope
   (B) do not meet the criteria for a perfect market
   (C) are centralized in nature
   (D) consist of used property only
   (E) are prevalent in former Communist countries

6. The federal discount rate, which is the interest rate that banks pay on the funds they borrow from the Federal Reserve, is most closely linked to
   (A) the inflation rate
   (B) the prime rate
   (C) long-term yield rates
   (D) interest rates on 30-year bonds
   (E) municipal bond rates

7. Credit-regulating devices used by the Federal Reserve include
   (A) moral suasion
   (B) reserve requirements
   (C) the federal discount rate
   (D) the Federal Open Market Committee
   (E) all of the above

8. Monetary policy helps control inflation by
   (A) regulating the money supply
   (B) encouraging rent control
   (C) reducing taxes
   (D) refusing to balance the budget
   (E) using a noncalendar year

9. The secondary mortgage market is where
   (A) mortgage bankers originate mortgage loans
   (B) second mortgages are originated
   (C) existing mortgages are bought and sold
   (D) the FNMA and GNMA make mortgage loans
   (E) the RTC searches for buyers of savings and loan associations

10. When inflation is expected to be high, investors tend to avoid
    (A) equity investments
    (B) long-term fixed-income investments
    (C) short-term investments
    (D) money market instruments
    (E) tangibles

11. Mortgage financing affects
    (A) equity dividends from real estate
    (B) equity yields from real estate
    (C) monetary policy
    (D) fiscal policy
    (E) both A and B

Questions 12–14 are based on the following information:

A $1,500,000 loan is issued with 5 discount points. The loan bears an 8% interest rate and has a 9% mortgage constant, with annual payments.

12. The original annual payment was
    (A) less than $120,000
    (B) $120,000
    (C) $135,000
    (D) more than $150,000
    (E) none of the above

13. The annual mortgage constant is
    (A) 8%   (D) 9.75%
    (B) 8.25%   (E) above 9.75%
    (C) 9%

14. What is the amount of the loan discount?
    (A) less than $75,000   (D) $150,000
    (B) $75,000   (E) more than $150,000
    (C) $100,000

15. Which of the following is a valuation study?
    (A) market value appraisal
    (B) market and marketability study
    (C) absorption analysis
    (D) feasibility study
    (E) technical impact study

16. Generally, the *least* reliable sources of sales data are
    (A) bankers
    (B) appraisers
    (C) newspaper articles
    (D) brokers
    (E) sellers

17. Operating income data do *not* include
    (A) vacancy rate
    (B) reproduction cost
    (C) operating expenses
    (D) utilities provided by the owner
    (E) lease terms

18. Industrial buildings are typically measured in terms of
    (A) gross living area
    (B) gross building area
    (C) net leasable area
    (D) gross rentable area
    (E) interior area

19. The appropriate time adjustment for a property is concluded to be an increase of 7% per year compounded. The time adjustment for a comparable sales property that sold for $40,000 two years ago is
    (A) −$5,796
    (B) −$5,600
    (C) −$2,800
    (D) +$5,600
    (E) +$5,796

20. How much must be deposited today, in a bank that pays 10% rate of interest with annual compounding, in order to realize $10,000 in 4 years?
    (A) $40,000
    (B) $9,077
    (C) $6,830
    (D) $4,000
    (E) $2,500

21. Ms. Brown has just paid $5 for a purchase option on some land. The option gives her the right to buy the property for $10,000 at the end of 2 years. The $5 paid for the option will not be applied to the purchase price. How much must Ms. Brown put aside today, in a bank that pays a 10% rate of interest with monthly compounding, to achieve a balance of $10,000 in 2 years?
    (A) $12,100
    (B) $10,000
    (C) $8,194
    (D) $6,720
    (E) $5,000

22. A sample of 100 residences had an average square footage of 1,500 with a standard deviation of 120 and normal distribution. This means that
    (A) about two out of three have between 1,380 and 1,620 sq. ft.
    (B) about nine out of ten have between 1,380 and 1,620 sq. ft.
    (C) almost every home has between 1,140 and 1,560 sq. ft.
    (D) almost every home has between 1,380 and 1,620 sq. ft.
    (E) none of the 100 homes has any standard construction defect

23. In problem 22, two standard deviations would be
    (A) 50 homes
    (B) 1,500 sq. ft.
    (C) 240 sq. ft.
    (D) 67% of all homes
    (E) none of the above

Questions 24–28 are based on the following information:

Eleven recent sales of rental income property provided the following data:

Sale Number	Sales Price	Gross Monthly Rent
1	$162,000	$1,500
2	184,000	1,600
3	152,000	1,440
4	160,000	1,470
5	183,000	1,580
6	134,000	1,400
7	144,000	1,350
8	176,000	1,560
9	132,000	1,350
10	183,000	1,650
11	153,000	1,380

24. The range of gross rent multipliers is
    (A) 675 to 825
    (B) 66,000 to 92,000
    (C) 95.7 to 115.8
    (D) 150
    (E) none of the above

25. The mean monthly rental is
    (A) $1,350
    (B) $1,400
    (C) $1,470
    (D) $1,480
    (E) none of the above

26. The median monthly rental is
    (A) $1,350
    (B) $1,400
    (C) $1,470
    (D) $1,480
    (E) none of the above

27. The mode of the monthly rentals is
    (A) $1,350
    (B) $1,400
    (C) $1,470
    (D) $1,480
    (E) none of the above

28. The best estimate of the gross rent multiplier is
    (A) 92
    (B) 100
    (C) 108
    (D) 116
    (E) none of the above

29. In the sequence of adjustments in the sales adjustment process, the item adjusted for first should usually be
    (A) location
    (B) terms of financing
    (C) size
    (D) time
    (E) it makes no difference which is first

30. The land development method in appraisal is used to estimate the value of vacant acreage that is ready to be subdivided. This method requires
    (A) study of current sales of subdivided lots
    (B) projection of land development costs
    (C) RTC approval
    (D) both A and B
    (E) none of the above

Questions 31–36 are based on the following information:

You are appraising a 20-acre tract of unimproved land. The site is zoned for single-family residential use. All utilities are available along the street on which the land fronts. From the engineers who will plat the proposed subdivision, you learn that 20% of the land area will be used for streets and sidewalks. You find that zoning will permit four lots per acre of net developable land after deducting streets. Research indicates that lots similar to those that will be available on the subject land sell for $18,000 and that the entire tract can be developed and sold in 1 year. You find that 40% of the sale price of each lot must be allocated to selling costs, overhead, contingencies, carrying cost, and developer's profit. Finally, your research discloses that 2,000 feet of streets (including water, storm sewer, and sanitary sewer lines) must be installed at a cost of $80 per foot.

31. How many lots can be developed?
    (A) 20
    (B) 64
    (C) 80
    (D) 88
    (E) 16

32. What is the gross sales price from the sale of all lots?
    (A) $288,000
    (B) $360,000
    (C) $1,152,000
    (D) $1,440,000
    (E) $1,584,000

33. What is the cost of installing streets and water and sewer lines?
    (A) $16,000
    (B) $32,000
    (C) $64,000
    (D) $160,000
    (E) none of the above

34. What is the total of selling cost, overhead, contingencies, carrying costs, and developer's profit?
    (A) $144,000
    (B) $460,800
    (C) $576,000
    (D) $633,600
    (E) none of the above

35. What is the total cost of development and overhead, including developer's profit?
    (A) $304,000
    (B) $320,000
    (C) $620,800
    (D) $733,600
    (E) none of the above

36. What is the developer's potential profit on the 20-acre tract?
    (A) less than $160,000
    (B) $160,000
    (C) $531,200
    (D) $1,152,000
    (E) $1,440,000

37. When there is a dearth of recent land sales data, which technique may the appraiser use to estimate land value?
    (A) land residual
    (B) property residual
    (C) building residual
    (D) mortgage residual
    (E) property reversion

38. The annual net operating income from an apartment house is $22,000. With a capitalization rate of 11%, the indicated market value is
    (A) $2,420
    (B) $126,000
    (C) $176,000
    (D) $200,000
    (E) $242,000

39. A small office building sold for $120,000. The monthly net operating income is $1,300 per month. What was the overall capitalization rate?
    (A) 1.08%
    (B) 9.2%
    (C) 10.8%
    (D) 12%
    (E) 13%

40. For which of the following would the lowest ratio of operating expenses to gross income be incurred by the landlord?
    (A) resort hotel
    (B) net-leased retail store
    (C) office building
    (D) apartment building
    (E) nursing home for the elderly

41. The band-of-investment technique is most useful when equity investors are primarily concerned with
    (A) land appreciation rates
    (B) building tax shelters
    (C) gross rent multipliers
    (D) equity capitalization rates
    (E) noise abatement

42. Which of the following is the preferred method of deriving a capitalization rate?
    (A) summation
    (B) band of investment
    (C) direct comparison
    (D) bank of investment
    (E) monetary policy

43. Capitalization is employed in the
    (A) cost approach
    (B) direct sales comparison approach
    (C) income approach for income properties
    (D) income approach for residential properties
    (E) none of the above

44. Capitalization is the process whereby
    (A) income is converted to an indication of value
    (B) syndicates are formed
    (C) an asset is removed from accounting records
    (D) both A and B
    (E) none of the above

45. The operating expense ratio for income property is typically
    (A) between 4 and 10
    (B) under 100%
    (C) under 10%
    (D) under 2%
    (E) more than 10

46. In determining income and expenses, the first step is
    (A) a lease and rent analysis
    (B) an effective gross income estimate
    (C) an operating expense estimate
    (D) a reconstructed operating statement
    (E) a market analysis

47. A forecast using discounted cash flow analysis would include
    (A) income, vacancy, and operating expenses
    (B) an economic analysis
    (C) reversion at the end of the holding period
    (D) discounting expected future cash flows to a present value
    (E) all of the above

48. If the overall capitalization rate for income property were to increase while estimated net operating income remained the same, the resulting value estimate would
    (A) increase
    (B) decrease
    (C) remain the same
    (D) any of the above could occur
    (E) none of the above would occur

49. Estimated income property values will decline as a result of
    (A) increased net cash flows
    (B) lower capitalization rates
    (C) lower vacancy rates
    (D) increased discount rates
    (E) higher standard of living

50. *Income capitalization* is the term used to describe the process of estimating the value of income property by studying expected future income. This process
    (A) converts the net operating income of a property into its equivalent capital value
    (B) reflects the time value of money by reducing or discounting future income to its present worth
    (C) focuses on the present worth of future benefits
    (D) uses market interest rates
    (E) all of the above

51. When estimating the value of an income-producing property, the appraiser will *not* consider
    (A) income taxes attributable to the property
    (B) the remaining economic life of the property
    (C) potential future income
    (D) net operating income
    (E) expected future income patterns

52. In income capitalization, value is measured as the present worth of the
    (A) forecast reversion with a growth factor
    (B) forecast cash flow capitalized in perpetuity
    (C) forecast effective gross income (EGI) plus the reversion
    (D) forecast net operating income plus the reversion
    (E) cost of production

53. Income capitalization techniques are typically *not* used in valuing
    (A) retail properties
    (B) apartment buildings
    (C) office buildings
    (D) motels
    (E) single-family residences

54. The lump sum that an investor receives upon resale of an investment is called
    (A) net income
    (B) gross income
    (C) equity dividend
    (D) reversion
    (E) residual

55. The most commonly used capitalization rate is the
    - (A) income rate
    - (B) composite capitalization rate
    - (C) interest rate
    - (D) overall rate
    - (E) underall rate

56. An ordinary annuity is
    - (A) level in amount and timing
    - (B) different from a variable annuity
    - (C) received at the end of each period
    - (D) a stream of income
    - (E) all of the above

57. The procedure used to convert expected future benefits into present value is
    - (A) residual analysis
    - (B) capitalization
    - (C) market capitalization
    - (D) equity capitalization
    - (E) compounding

58. A reconstructed operating statement for an owner-operated property should include
    - (A) income tax
    - (B) book depreciation
    - (C) management charges
    - (D) wages earned outside the property
    - (E) imputed interest

59. *Yield* is defined as
    - (A) overall capitalization
    - (B) stopping to review work
    - (C) letting another speak first
    - (D) rate of return on investment
    - (E) rate of return of investment

60. Which of the following is a specific expense item rather than a category?
    - (A) replacement reserve
    - (B) property taxes
    - (C) operating expenses
    - (D) fixed charges or expenses
    - (E) variable expenses

61. In yield capitalization, investor assumptions are
    - (A) accrued
    - (B) critiqued
    - (C) regulated
    - (D) questioned
    - (E) simulated

62. The basic formula for property valuation via income capitalization is
    - (A) $V = IR$
    - (B) $V = I/R$
    - (C) $V = R/I$
    - (D) $V = SP/GR$
    - (E) $V = I/F$

63. All of the following consider the time value of money *except*
    - (A) net present value
    - (B) discounted cash flow
    - (C) internal rate of return
    - (D) payback period
    - (E) compound interest

64. A rent survey of apartment buildings reveals that one-bedroom units have a considerably higher occupancy factor than two-bedroom units. If the subject property contains only two-bedroom units, the appraisal should probably project
    - (A) an average of the vacancy factors for all units surveyed
    - (B) a higher vacancy factor than was found for one-bedroom units
    - (C) a lower vacancy factor than was found for one-bedroom units
    - (D) the same vacancy factor as was found for one-bedroom units
    - (E) Projection from the information provided is impossible.

65. The quality of a forecast future income stream is indicated by its
    - (A) amount
    - (B) length
    - (C) timing
    - (D) mortgage
    - (E) risk

66. The total anticipated revenue from income property operations after vacancy and collection losses are deducted is
    - (A) net operating income
    - (B) before-tax cash flow
    - (C) effective gross income
    - (D) potential gross income
    - (E) property residual income

67. Which of the following is used in direct capitalization?
    (A) internal rate of return
    (B) overall capitalization rate
    (C) building capitalization rate
    (D) mortgage capitalization rate
    (E) equity yield rate

68. Which of the following statements is true?
    (A) If the overall yield on the property is less than the mortgage rate, favorable leverage occurs.
    (B) When negative leverage occurs, the owner receives a cash yield on the property that is greater than if the property were not financed.
    (C) If the overall property yield equals the mortgage rate, the owner receives an additional yield on his investment by trading on the equity.
    (D) Financing the property at higher rates of interest than the overall rate may not be beneficial to the owner in terms of yield on the equity investment.
    (E) When a property generates cash flow, its owner pays tax on the money received.

69. Which of the following statements is true?
    (A) An investor usually considers the return from a property in the light of the risk being assumed.
    (B) An investor who assumes higher risk usually expects lower investment yield.
    (C) Higher-risk investments are generally associated with lower investment returns.
    (D) To maximize the overall risk position, the investor may wish to diversify real and/or personal property investments.
    (E) The lowest-risk investment is real estate.

70. Capitalization rate is
    (A) the annual rent divided by the purchase price
    (B) annual income and all gains or losses prorated to an effective annual amount— an internal rate of return
    (C) the percentage or decimal rate that, when divided into a periodic income amount, offers a lump-sum capital value for the income
    (D) unchanging with time
    (E) none of the above

Questions 71–75 are based on the following information:

A $12 million office building is purchased with an 80% loan-to-value ratio mortgage, payable over 30 years at 11% interest with monthly payments of $91,423. At 100% occupancy, rents would be $2 million. The vacancy trend in the area is 2.5%. Operating expenses amount to $650,000, including $50,000 placed in a replacement reserve. The land is considered to be worth $2 million.

71. What ratio, expressed as a percentage, is between 80 and 85?
    (A) improvement
    (B) overall rate
    (C) mortgage constant
    (D) vacancy
    (E) operating expense

72. What ratio, expressed as a percentage, is between 10 and 11?
    (A) improvement
    (B) overall rate
    (C) mortgage constant
    (D) vacancy
    (E) operating expense

73. What ratio, expressed as a percentage, is between 11 and 12?
    (A) improvement
    (B) overall rate
    (C) mortgage constant
    (D) vacancy
    (E) operating expense

74. What ratio, expressed as a percentage, is between 30 and 40?
    (A) improvement
    (B) overall rate
    (C) mortgage constant
    (D) vacancy
    (E) operating expense

75. What ratio, expressed as a percentage, is between 0 and 5?
    (A) improvement
    (B) overall rate
    (C) mortgage constant
    (D) vacancy
    (E) operating expense

76. Investors for apartments are seeking a 10% cash-on-cash return in the current market. The current interest rate on a 30-year mortgage for this type of property is 12% with monthly payments. Lenders will fund up to a 75% loan-to-value ratio. What is the overall rate of return using the band of investment technique?
   (A) 10%–10.5%
   (B) 10.51%–11%
   (C) 11.01%–11.25%
   (D) 11.26%–12%
   (E) none of the above

Questions 77–81 are based on the following information:

A certain older office building in the heart of a downtown metropolitan area currently generates $40,000 net operating income. Income is expected to decline systematically over the estimated 10 remaining years of the building's useful life. Therefore, straight-line capital recovery (declining income to the building) is considered appropriate. The land is currently valued at $250,000, based on numerous recent sales of comparable properties. For this type of property, investors want a 10% interest (yield to maturity) rate.

77. How much of the first year's $40,000 net operating income is attributable to the land?
   (A) $15,000   (D) $30,000
   (B) $20,000   (E) $40,000
   (C) $25,000

78. How much of the net operating income is attributable to the building?
   (A) $15,000   (D) $30,000
   (B) $20,000   (E) $40,000
   (C) $25,000

79. What is the building capitalization rate, assuming straight-line capital recovery?
   (A) 5%   (D) 20%
   (B) 10%   (E) 25%
   (C) 15%

80. What is the value of the building, using the building residual technique?
   (A) $75,000   (D) $130,000
   (B) $100,000   (E) $140,000
   (C) $125,000

81. What is the combined value of the building and land?
   (A) $275,000   (D) $330,000
   (B) $300,000   (E) $340,000
   (C) $325,000

Questions 82–86 are based on the following information:

A freestanding retail store is under a triple net lease for the next 25 years, with $20,000 rent payable at the end of each year. The tenant has a purchase option to buy the property at the end of the lease term for $150,000. The property is free and clear of debt. For this situation, investors seek a 12% rate of return on investment.

82. What is the present value of the rental income?
   (A) less than $100,000
   (B) $100,000 to $150,000
   (C) $150,000 to $175,000
   (D) $175,000 to $200,000
   (E) $200,000 to $250,000

83. On the assumption that the tenant will exercise her purchase option, what is the present value of the reversion?
   (A) less than $10,000
   (B) $10,000 to $20,000
   (C) $20,000 to $100,000
   (D) $100,000 to $150,000
   (E) more than $150,000

84. What is the present value of the property?
   (A) less than $100,000
   (B) $100,000 to $150,000
   (C) $150,000 to $175,000
   (D) $175,000 to $200,000
   (E) $200,000 to $250,000

85. What is the overall rate of return?
   (A) 10%–10.5%
   (B) 10.5%–11%
   (C) 11%–11.25%
   (D) 11.25%–11.5%
   (E) more than 11.5%

86. What is the equity dividend rate?
   (A) 10%–10.5%
   (B) 10.5%–11%
   (C) 11%–11.25%
   (D) 11.25%–12%
   (E) none of the above

87. The most common type of partial-interest appraisal involves
   (A) a leased property
   (B) a timeshare residence
   (C) a condominium
   (D) rezoning
   (E) condemnation

88. When contract rent exceeds market rent, the leasehold interest
   (A) is subleased
   (B) must be appraised
   (C) has no positive value
   (D) should be mortgaged
   (E) is the same as the leased fee

89. Lease provisions may describe all of the following *except*
   (A) rental payments and the term of use and occupancy
   (B) whether landlord or tenant pays operating expenses
   (C) rent escalations and renewal or purchase options
   (D) the credit rating of the tenant
   (E) assignment or subletting rights

90. *Overage rent* is the
   (A) actual rent over the entire lease term
   (B) percentage rent above guaranteed minimum rent
   (C) amount by which contract rent exceeds market rent
   (D) rent that is past due
   (E) rent the property could command in the open market if not subject to its lease

91. A lease normally states all of the following *except*
   (A) agreed terms of occupancy
   (B) rental payments
   (C) tenant's responsibilities and obligations
   (D) financing of the property
   (E) actions causing default

92. All of the following lease provisions are advantageous to the lessee *except*
   (A) an escape clause
   (B) a renewal option
   (C) a purchase option
   (D) an escalation clause
   (E) All of the above are advantageous.

93. Homeowners' associations are usually found in
   (A) planned unit developments (PUD)
   (B) condominiums
   (C) timeshares
   (D) both A and B
   (E) none of the above

94. If a $54,000 investment in real estate generates gross earnings of 15%, the gross monthly return most nearly is
   (A) $819
   (B) $705
   (C) $675
   (D) $637
   (E) $8,100

95. In arriving at an effective gross income figure, an appraiser of rental property makes a deduction for
   (A) real property taxes
   (B) repairs
   (C) vacancy
   (D) depreciation
   (E) replacement reserves

ANSWERS

1. **B**	20. **C**	39. **E**	58. **C**	77. **C**
2. **D**	21. **C**	40. **B**	59. **D**	78. **A**
3. **D**	22. **A**	41. **D**	60. **B**	79. **D**
4. **B**	23. **C**	42. **C**	61. **E**	80. **A**
5. **B**	24. **C**	43. **C**	62. **B**	81. **C**
6. **B**	25. **D**	44. **A**	63. **D**	82. **C**
7. **E**	26. **C**	45. **B**	64. **B**	83. **A**
8. **A**	27. **A**	46. **A**	65. **E**	84. **C**
9. **C**	28. **C**	47. **E**	66. **C**	85. **A**
10. **B**	29. **B**	48. **B**	67. **B**	86. **E**
11. **E**	30. **D**	49. **D**	68. **D**	87. **A**
12. **C**	31. **B**	50. **E**	69. **A**	88. **C**
13. **C**	32. **C**	51. **A**	70. **C**	89. **D**
14. **B**	33. **D**	52. **D**	71. **A**	90. **B**
15. **A**	34. **B**	53. **E**	72. **B**	91. **D**
16. **C**	35. **C**	54. **D**	73. **C**	92. **D**
17. **B**	36. **C**	55. **D**	74. **E**	93. **D**
18. **B**	37. **A**	56. **E**	75. **D**	94. **C**
19. **E**	38. **D**	57. **B**	76. **D**	95. **C**

CHAPTER 16

Taxation and Assessment

Real estate, because it is valuable and also hard to hide, has been subject to tax for nearly all of human history. Consequently, it is easy for officials to assess taxes on real estate. The property tax is an ad valorem tax; that is, it is based on the *value* of the thing being taxed. In effect, then, the tax bill on a large, valuable property should be more than the bill on a small, relatively low-valued one.

The property tax usually is the major source of income for city and county governments. In a sense, this may be just, because the real estate that provides the bulk of the taxes collected also benefits greatly from many of the services local government pays for with the property taxes it collects. Most important of these is fire protection, which accrues almost exclusively to real estate. Police protection and the provision and maintenance of local streets and roads also provide obvious benefits. Nearby, locally provided public amenities such as schools and parks make many kinds of real estate more valuable. The control of real estate development through zoning and building codes also tends to preserve the values of existing real estate improvements, as does the provision of planning services. In addition, local courthouses store the records that are necessary for the documentation of title to real estate.

TAX ASSESSMENT

Real estate taxation is relatively straightforward, but some elements can be fairly confusing unless the process is studied carefully.

Because the tax is based upon the value of the real estate, some method must exist for determining the values of all parcels of real estate in the taxing jurisdiction. For this purpose, local governments usually have a *tax assessor's* office, although it often goes by a different name. The function of the office is to set a valuation upon each parcel of taxable property in the jurisdiction. Sometimes this is done by actually appraising each property, but this method is very expensive except for the most valuable properties. More often, the assessment is arrived at by simpler means. Frequently the indication of value made when a property is sold will be used to determine the sale price, which, it is assumed, is very close to the true value. (In states that use documentary stamps or deed transfer taxes the approximate sale price often can be deduced from the value of the stamps affixed to the deed or from the amount of transfer tax paid.) Often all assessments will be adjusted by some specific formula each year to take account of inflation or other reasons for overall value changes. Building permits serve to pinpoint new construction and additions to existing buildings; aerial photography accomplishes the same objective.

More often than not, a single property will be in *more* than one taxing jurisdiction. Most commonly, a property may be in a particular county, as well as in a specific city or town, and each may levy taxes. Many areas have independent school districts as well. Furthermore, there can be a multiplicity of other kinds of taxing districts, depending upon what state and local laws will allow and provide for. Usually, however, a single assessing agency will provide a valuation for all taxing jurisdictions that affect a given property; this is done because assessment is an expensive process and duplication of effort is thereby avoided.

Every jurisdiction provides some means whereby property owners can appeal assessments they consider unjust. The exact method of appeal varies considerably across the country. You should find out how it is done in your state.

EXEMPTION FROM PROPERTY TAXES

Not all real estate is subject to the real property tax; some of it is *exempt*. Exactly what is exempt and what is not is a matter decided by both state and local laws. Some kinds of property, however, are exempt almost everywhere. Primary among these is any property owned by government. This exemption seems to make sense: it would be peculiar for the government to pay taxes to itself. Of course, there are several governments; although it is conceivable that they could pay taxes to one another, they don't. Therefore, *all* government-owned property, no matter which government owns it, is exempt from property taxes. In some areas, where a very large proportion of the property is government-owned, this situation can work a hardship on local taxpayer-owners of property, especially when the government-owned property receives many of the services paid for by local taxes. Examples of such "problem" areas are state capitals, Washington, D.C., and many small cities and towns that provide school and other services for large government (usually military) establishments. In such cases the benefiting branch of government often will provide some direct grant of money to the affected local government to make up for the unpaid property tax.

Some privately owned property may also be exempt from tax. Most areas will exempt certain kinds of land uses that seem to provide other benefits to the community, making them desirable even when exempt from property tax. These uses usually include churches, nonprofit private schools, and some other charitable organizations. In some localities, *all* property owned by such organizations is exempt from tax; however, the current trend is toward granting the exemption only to property that actually is used by the organization for its basic purposes. In such an area, then, a church building used for religious purposes would be exempt, but an apartment project owned by the church would not be—even if all its profits went to the church.

PAYMENT OF TAXES

Past-due property taxes automatically become a lien on the property so affected. If the taxes remain unpaid, the taxing government eventually can foreclose and have the property sold in order to pay the taxes. A tax lien takes priority over all other liens, including mortgages, even ones that have been entered on the records before the tax lien.

Normally, a property owner has a considerable period of time between the time the taxes actually are levied and the date payment is due. The specific schedule followed varies from state to state and sometimes even among localities within a state. As a matter of fact, a property owner whose land falls into more than one taxing district may find that the various districts have differing collection schedules.

A homeowner often is spared the chore of remembering when taxes are due, because his mortgage lender requires him to make a supplemental payment into an escrow account with each monthly payment. This money mounts up to create a fund from which the lender pays taxes (and usually insurance) when they are due. Generally the lender is contractually responsible to the borrower for paying the taxes out of these funds; if a mistake is made, or a penalty is required for late payment, the lender can be held liable to the borrower.

CALCULATION OF PROPERTY TAXES

To calculate property taxes, three figures are necessary: the *appraised valuation* of the property, the *assessment ratio*, and the *tax rate*. The assessment ratio is applied to the appraised valuation to obtain the *assessed value*. Then, the tax rate is applied to the assessed value in order to find the tax due. In effect, the tax rate will be a certain proportion, such as 7.66% of the assessed valuation, or $76.60 per $1,000 of valuation, or 76.6 mills per dollar of valuation. All three of these represent the same tax rate, expressed in three different ways.

To determine the tax rate, it usually is easiest to turn the rate into a percentage figure, because that can be easily applied to the assessed valuation through simple arithmetic procedures. Rarely, however, is the tax rate expressed as a percentage; instead, it usually is given as a *millage rate*. A millage rate specifies how many *mills* must be paid for each *dollar* of assessed valuation. A *mill* is $\frac{1}{10}$ of a cent; therefore, there are 1,000 mills in 1 dollar. The millage rate, then, shows how many *thousandths* of the assessed valuation must be paid in tax.

Millage rates are easy to convert to percents: percents measure hundredths, so to change a millage rate to a percentage rate, *the decimal point is moved one place to the left*. This is the same as dividing by 10, since there are 10 thousandths in each hundredth. Consequently, a millage rate of 77.6 is the same as 7.76%. Sometimes the millage rate is expressed as so many dollars per thousand dollars of assessed valuation. In either case, the figure is in thousandths, so the numerical value is the same: 77.6 mills *per dollar* is the same as $77.60 per thousand dollars.

Once the tax rate is expressed as a percent, the next step is to determine the assessed valuation to which it must be applied. In some states and localities, the assessed valuation is the same as the market value of the property as estimated by the tax assessor. In others, however, only part of the market value is subject to tax. Sometimes the taxable amount is fixed by state law; in other localities, the local government determines the taxable portion of the estimated value. Often the figure so arrived at will be altered even further. Many states have a *homestead exemption*, which exempts a certain proportion of the assessed valuation from taxation. Often older homeowners get special exemptions, as do low-income homeowners in a few areas. Once these exemptions are determined, they are subtracted from the assessed valuation to arrive at the net figure upon which the tax is based. However, a further element of confusion can enter the picture: many properties are subject to tax by more than one jurisdiction, and the method of calculating assessed valuation, and the exemptions that may be allowed, can vary among them.

When the assessed valuation subject to tax has been determined, the tax rate is applied to it to determine the tax to be paid. For example, assume that a property has a taxable assessed valuation of $100,000, and the millage rate is 77.6, or 7.76%; then 7.76% of $100,000 will be the tax to be paid. This is found by changing the percentage into a decimal and multiplying: $0.0776 \times \$100,000 = \$7,760$. The tax, then, is $7,760.

OTHER TAXATION ISSUES

Economic Impact of Taxation

Economists classify taxes in relationship to the impact on ability to pay. A tax is "regressive" when those with low income pay a higher proportion of their means than others. For example, poor people pay the same tax on a loaf of bread as the wealthy. A tax is "proportional" when it taxes proportionally to taxpayer means. Ad valorem property taxes are proportional because people buy housing according to affordability. A tax is "progressive" when the wealthy pay more. Income tax rates increase with higher income, so the income tax is progressive.

Independent Contractor vs. Employee

An independent contractor works for him/herself, pays self-employment taxes, and pays estimated income taxes.

By contrast, an employee pays Social Security tax. From his or her paycheck, the employer deducts income taxes, Social Security tax, and other withholdings. The employer must also contribute to Social Security and other programs.

Most real estate brokers prefer to treat salespersons as independent contractors. They may do so provided they don't exercise certain controls, such as what hours the person works, ownership of tools and supplies the person uses (vehicles, computer), or payment of dues.

INCOME TAXATION

Income tax laws are numerous and complex. Some highlights affecting real estate are indicated below, distinguished between those that affect personal residences and those that apply to income property.

Personal Residence Income Taxation

It is important to maintain permanent records concerning the acquisition of a personal residence. The initial cost serves as the basis for determining gain or loss, and that can stay with the owner through sales and purchases of subsequent homes.

HOME ACQUISITION DEDUCTIONS

The acquisition of a home gives rise to a tax deduction for discount points on a mortgage loan. Provided the discount points are for interest (not for services) and are customary in the area, they may be taken as an interest deduction. Since 1994, the Internal Revenue Service has allowed the deduction for discount points to a buyer even when the points have been paid by the seller. Points incurred to refinance a personal residence are treated differently from original debt. Points in a refinancing must be amortized (spread out equally each period over the life of the loan).

HOMEOWNERSHIP TAX DEDUCTIONS

The two principal tax deductions allowed a homeowner (including a condominium or cooperative apartment owner) are for property taxes and interest expense. You may deduct on up to two residences for your cost, plus up to an additional $100,000 of debt. The maximum federal income tax rate at this writing is approximately 35%, so the tax savings reduces the largest homeownership expense by up to that percentage.

HOME SALE

A married couple may exclude up to $500,000 of gain on the sale of a principal residence. A single individual may exclude up to $250,000 of gain. There are limits as to the frequency of exclusion and requirements for a principal residence.

Income Taxation of Income Property

The purchase of income-producing real estate ordinarily does not generate immediate income tax deductions. A buyer should, however, indicate how much was paid for land, how much for real estate improvements, and how much for personal property. Except for land that is not depreciable, depreciation for real estate improvements and personal property generate tax deductions.

OPERATIONS OF INCOME PROPERTY

Rental income is included as business income on Schedule C of the tax return. Expenses of business operations are tax deductible. These include not only interest and ad valorem taxes but also maintenance and repairs, management, insurance, and all other reasonable and necessary expenses to operate the property. Depreciation is a noncash expense that serves to reduce taxable income. Because depreciation provides a deduction without a cash payment, it is considered very favorable for owners. Under present tax law, apartment owners may depreciate their property (not land) over a 27½-year term. Owners of other property types, such as office buildings, warehouses, shopping centers, and so on, must use a 39-year depreciable life. Depreciation reduces the tax basis for property, which could cause a taxable gain upon resale.

RESALE

The adjusted tax basis is subtracted from the resale price of real estate to derive the taxable gain. The adjusted tax basis is original cost less depreciation plus capital improvements. This gain is generally taxable as a capital gain. However, certain types of depreciation tax deductions may be taxable as ordinary income upon a sale.

EXCHANGE

Under Section 1031 of the Internal Revenue Code, there are opportunities to postpone the tax on a gain. One must identify potential replacement property within 45 days of the sale date of the previously owned property and close within 180 days of the sale. The old and new properties must be held for use in a trade or business, or held as an investment. The realized gain will be taxable to the extent that the seller receives unlike property, including cash, which is called *boot*.

CHECKLIST FOR YOUR STATE'S AND LOCALITY'S PROPERTY TAXATION PRACTICES

Obtain the answers to the following questions from the literature supplied by your state's licensing agency or from the local tax assessor's office in your area.

What proportion of the estimated market value is subject to tax? _____ %

Are any of the following exemptions applicable to the tax base?
- ☐ Homestead exemption
- ☐ Old-age exemption
- ☐ Exemption for the poor
- ☐ Other(s): _____

Is it possible for a property to be subject to taxes by more than one governmental body?
- ☐ No; taxes are levied only by _____
- ☐ Yes; these include:
  - ☐ State government
  - ☐ County (parish) government
  - ☐ City (township) government
  - ☐ School district
  - ☐ Special assessment district
  - ☐ Improvement district
  - ☐ Other(s): _____

Questions on Chapter 16

1. An ad valorem tax is based on
   (A) income earned
   (B) the value of the thing being taxed
   (C) the size of the thing being taxed
   (D) something other than A, B, or C

2. The property tax is a form of
   (A) sales tax   (C) income tax
   (B) ad valorem tax   (D) excise tax

3. The major source of income for local government usually is
   (A) income taxes   (C) property taxes
   (B) licenses and fees   (D) parking meters

4. Which of the following is (are) always exempt from real property taxes?
   (A) income-producing property owned by a church
   (B) government-owned property
   (C) most restaurants
   (D) a private, for-profit school

5. A millage rate of 84.5 mills is the same as
   (A) $84.50 per $1,000
   (B) 8.45%
   (C) both A and B
   (D) none of the above

6. If a property is assessed at $60,000 and the millage rate is 32.5, the tax is
   (A) $19.50   (C) $1,950
   (B) $195.00   (D) $19,500

7. The appraised valuation of a property is $85,000. The property tax is based on 20% of appraised valuation. The city tax is 50 mills; the county tax is 40 mills. Which of the following is true?
   (A) The city tax is $1,850.00.
   (B) The county tax is $850.00.
   (C) The city and county taxes combined add up to $1530.00.
   (D) The city and county taxes combined add up to $7650.00.

8. A lien for unpaid property taxes
   (A) can be sold at auction
   (B) takes priority over all other liens
   (C) cannot exist unless taxes are at least 36 months overdue
   (D) is a form of adverse possession

9. Which of the following is *not* a good reason why real property taxes are so popular?
   (A) Real estate ownership is easy to hide.
   (B) Real estate is valuable.
   (C) Real estate is easy to find.
   (D) Real estate can be foreclosed to provide payment of unpaid tax levies.

10. Real property taxes are justifiable because
    (A) real property benefits from many services provided by property taxes
    (B) real property owners are wealthy and can afford to pay taxes
    (C) real property taxes are legal everywhere, whereas many other kinds of taxes are not
    (D) none of the above

11. A tax-deductible front-end interest cost on a mortgage loan or deed of trust for a newly purchased home is called
    (A) interest abatement
    (B) discount points
    (C) interest in advance
    (D) prepaid mortgage insurance

12. A tax deduction for business property that requires no cash outlay is
    (A) interest expense
    (B) vacancy loss expense
    (C) depreciation expense
    (D) management expense

13. The two most important income tax deductions for homeowners are for _____ and
    _____.
    (A) repairs, maintenance
    (B) mortgage interest, repairs
    (C) mortgage interest, property taxes
    (D) mortgage payments, sales taxes

14. The initial cost of an asset, increased by capital expenditures and reduced by depreciation expense, from which gain or loss is measured, is
    (A) basic adjustment
    (B) basal metabolism
    (C) adjustment of base
    (D) adjusted basis

15. The federal income tax exemption on the gain from the sale of a personal residence held long enough by a married couple is up to
    (A) $25,000   (C) $250,000
    (B) $125,000   (D) $500,000

16. The federal income tax exemption on the gain from the sale of a personal residence held long enough by a single individual is up to
    (A) $25,000   (C) $250,000
    (B) $125,000   (D) $500,000

17. Cash or other unlike property included to equalize values in a tax-free Section 1031 exchange is called
    (A) slipper   (C) parity
    (B) equity   (D) boot

18. A Real Estate Investment Trust (REIT) must
    (A) be closely held (five or fewer owners)
    (B) distribute nearly all of its taxable income
    (C) own stocks or bonds
    (D) be the same as a limited partnership

19. Federal income tax rates are generally
    (A) regressive   (C) progressive.
    (B) neutral   (D) none of the above

20. Federal income tax deductions for a principal residence include
    (A) mortgage interest
    (B) real estate taxes
    (C) uninsured casualty losses, over a certain amount
    (D) all of the above

21. A homeowner, on his or her federal income tax return, may not deduct
    (A) fixing-up expenses
    (B) cost of a new porch
    (C) repainting
    (D) any of the above

22. The report of a sale to the IRS is normally made on Form 1099 by
    (A) buyer
    (B) seller
    (C) broker
    (D) closing agent

23. In a tax-free exchange under Section 1031 of the Internal Revenue Code, *boot* is
    (A) "unlike" property that may be taxable
    (B) like-kind property
    (C) given by a TIC
    (D) an equity kicker

24. Harold bought 20 acres for $125,000 and sold the land three years later for $230,000. On his income tax return he reports
    (A) short-term capital gain of $105,000 in the year of sale
    (B) long-term capital gain of $105,000 in the year of sale
    (C) ordinary income of $105,000 in the year of sale
    (D) annual income of $35,000

25. A principal difference between an independent contractor and an employee is
    (A) dress code
    (B) income taxation
    (C) fiduciary relationship
    (D) public service

26. Indications of independent contractor status include
    (A) freedom of hours to work
    (B) use of own vehicle
    (C) payment of own professional dues
    (D) all of the above

27. The business relationship between broker and salesperson for income tax purposes is usually
    (A) employer-employee
    (B) independent contractor
    (C) single agent
    (D) self-employment

28. The term most closely associated with real estate taxes is
    - (A) ad valorem
    - (B) appraised value
    - (C) market value
    - (D) net income tax

29. The assessment ratio can be used to
    - (A) determine the tax rate
    - (B) convert market value to value in use
    - (C) convert market value to assessed value
    - (D) determine property tax exemptions

ANSWERS

1. **B**	7. **C**	13. **C**	19. **C**	25. **B**
2. **B**	8. **B**	14. **D**	20. **D**	26. **D**
3. **C**	9. **A**	15. **D**	21. **D**	27. **B**
4. **B**	10. **A**	16. **C**	22. **D**	28. **A**
5. **C**	11. **B**	17. **D**	23. **A**	29. **C**
6. **C**	12. **C**	18. **B**	24. **B**	

Real Estate Investment

Real estate has been the path to riches for many investors. In addition, it has provided security and income to those who had the foresight to build an estate. Success in real estate investing requires knowledge, capital, and the willingness to take risks. An investor must know how to select properties, when to buy and sell, how to finance and operate a rental property.

FUNDAMENTALS OF REAL ESTATE INVESTMENT

Real estate has proven itself to be a lucrative investment through the years. There are many ways to invest in real estate and each offers distinct benefits. About two thirds of Americans own their own homes, and this basic level of real estate investment frees them from dependence on a landlord, and hopefully provides financial rewards in the form of value appreciation. In addition to their homes, many people have acquired small holdings of income property. Often self-managed, these properties provide periodic income, some of which is tax sheltered, and opportunity for appreciation gains.

Investors may put their money into a limited partnership or a Real Estate Investment Trust (REIT). This is like a mutual fund for real estate. Through such entities, investors can own a part of large properties or diversified holdings. This form also provides the advantages of professional property and investment management.

Investment Advantages

Regardless of the form of investment, investors look for several advantages from real estate. Real estate often offers higher cash returns than alternative investments. In part, this can be attributed to greater risk and difficulty of resale (illiquidity) associated with the property. Returns may be increased by using borrowed money, called leverage. Real property tends to be a good hedge against inflation since rents may be increased as costs rise. Well-located properties may even beat inflation and offer resale profits from appreciation in value. Finally, tax shelter has traditionally been an attraction of real estate investment. Opportunities for tax shelter have been diminished by recent tax law changes. However, in some cases, tax benefits still exist. Each of these attractions are described in greater detail in this chapter. Real estate investments cover a wide range from the relatively secure to the highly speculative. In general, the most secure investments emphasize current income production from highly creditworthy tenants. Speculative investments emphasize appreciation potential from future developments.

Investment Drawbacks

There are serious drawbacks to real estate investing. One factor that limits the field of real estate investors is the size of the required investment. A down payment on even a modest rental home requires several thousand dollars. Purchasing a sizable commercial property or assembling a diversified portfolio of properties means a much larger investment, certainly beyond the means of the typical investor. Syndicators overcome this problem by gathering a group of investors each of whom purchases shares of a large property or inventory of properties. Partnership interests may be acquired for as little as $1000. Furthermore, the investor may buy into several partnerships to gain further diversification.

Real estate is an *illiquid* investment. This means that, once the investment is made, it is difficult to get money out quickly. It takes at least several weeks, and sometimes months, to sell a property. Market conditions may prevent a sale at a reasonable price. If liquidity is desired, you may purchase shares in a publicly traded syndication, or a REIT. Many of these are traded on the major stock exchanges and offer immediate conversion to cash.

Since real estate is a physical asset, it requires ongoing management. Purchase of a property is like buying a small business. The owner is responsible for maintaining the property and keeping it productive. Professional property managers or resident managers can be hired to take on many of these responsibilities. The owner still must decide on tenant selection, rental rates, marketing, alterations, and when to sell.

Real estate markets are local in nature. There is a shortage of available information about current prices, rental, and vacancy rates. The typical purchaser is in the market infrequently and cannot stay attuned to current conditions. Therefore, it is difficult to decide on the best offering price for a property or rental rate to charge.

Aside from the size of the investment, the costs of purchasing a property are increased by transaction expenses. These include sales commissions, attorney fees, title insurance, appraisal and surveying costs, loan fees, and transfer taxes. A seller may pay as much as ten percent of the price of the property in transaction costs. In addition, the buyer may pay five or more percent. These costs tend to make real estate a long-term investment. Short-term profits would have to be substantial to offset transaction costs.

Real estate is *immobile*. For the investor, this means the performance of the property is determined by local market conditions. The demand for the property may be depressed by an economic downturn or an abundant supply of similar properties. The property cannot be moved to another location where conditions are better. In addition to local market conditions, a property is affected by the quality of the neighborhood and what happens to surrounding properties. Therefore, location is a major factor in a property's performance. Furthermore, these conditions may change over time. A big part of investment analysis involves evaluating trends in the local market and surrounding area.

What you can do with your property is subject to government policies. On a broad scale, government influence on interest rates and economic trends will affect demand for the property. On a local scale, government can limit your use of the property through zoning ordinances, building codes, health codes, and environmental laws. In some places a residential project may come under rent controls. Decisions to extend streets and utilities can change the attractiveness of your property. For these reasons, real estate investors often take an active interest in the affairs of their local government.

INVESTMENT ANALYSIS

Investment analysis is deciding if a particular investment opportunity is a good choice. A projection of expected investment returns is helpful in making the decision. Since the return from real estate investments depends on future rent, operating expenses, financing, and tax considerations, an estimation of what these will be will help you estimate how the property will perform. Projections may be the main determinant of the decision or may supplement other sources of information. The important thing to remember is that projections are only as good as the assumptions used to make them.

Pro Forma Statements

Pro forma statements show expected returns from operating a property. One of the most important results is cash flow, the money produced by an investment that you get to keep. Basically, this amounts to the cash, if any, left over after all expenses have been paid. Expenses include those to operate the property and to meet all loan requirements.

Cash flow represents the money produced by operating the investment. It does not reflect any appreciation gains that may eventually be received at resale nor equity buildup due to mortgage amortization. Since these types of return are realized only in the future, cash flow is a measure of the current performance of the investment. For that reason, some investors base their decision to acquire a property on a simple *cash-on-cash* return. This measure is cash flow divided by the required equity investment. For example, a property which is expected to produce a cash flow of $10,000 per year and requires a cash investment of $100,000, has a cash-on-cash return of ten percent.

The following is an example of how to calculate the cash flow from a real estate investment.

STATEMENT OF OPERATIONS
PRO FORMA

Total rental income if building full (Potential Gross Income)		$200,000
Less allowance for vacancies and bad debts		10,000
Effective Gross income		$190,000
Operating expenses:		
Management	$ 10,000	
Maintenance	25,000	
Utilities	7,000	
Property taxes	15,000	
Insurance	3,000	
Repairs	10,000	
Total operating expenses		70,000
Net operating income		$120,000
Debt service (mortgage payments):		
Principal	$ 5,000	
Interest	80,000	
Total debt service		85,000
Before-tax cash flow		$ 35,000

A property seller or broker may offer a *pro forma statement of operations,* such as the one above, as part of a sales presentation. The rental income may be attractive estimates rather than actual amounts earned by the property. Or, operating expenses may be based on last year's rates while property taxes, insurance, or utilities have jumped in the current year. You may have to recast the amounts to determine what you are likely to incur in costs or receive in cash flow. Get the owner's rent roll, which is a list of the tenants, space occupied (i.e., apartment number), and rent, and compare the figures to the pro forma statement. Or look at actual operating statements, not forecasts.

Expected cash flow can be an indication of how speculative an investment is. When appreciation rates are high, it is not uncommon for properties to be purchased with negative cash flow. The investor expects to have to "feed" the property (pay the cash flow deficit out of other income or capital reserves) until the property is sold. An expected large profit at resale offsets the period of negative cash flow. In other cases, investors may purchase properties with turn-around potential—those that are currently losing money but which may become productive given renovation or marketing effort. These properties are expected to have negative cash flow for a time, but eventually produce positive income and resale profits. In any case, where the cash-on-cash return is low or negative, the investment is speculative in nature. Eventual returns are based on anticipated improvements in market conditions or the appeal of the property, and this introduces risk that the improvement will not materialize.

Short-term analysis can be used to screen properties. The following indicators may be calculated quickly with a few bits of information that are based on current performance:

GROSS RENT MULTIPLIER

This is the total gross rent divided by the price of the property. The lower the number, the less you are paying for the gross income.

OVERALL RATE OF RETURN OR CAPITALIZATION RATE

This is the net operating income (rent less operating expenses) divided by the value of the property. This measure is preferred to the gross rent multiplier because it accounts for operating expenses. Also, it offers a percentage rate, which is a customary way to express rate of return.

CASH-ON-CASH RETURN OR EQUITY DIVIDEND RATE

This is the cash flow divided by the required equity investment, and is especially useful when you know how the property will be financed. You may use before-tax or after-tax cash flow. If after-tax cash flow is used, you should adjust the returns on alternative types of investment for taxes to make a meaningful comparison.

Long-term analysis requires more information and assumptions since you are projecting several years into the future. If you are considering a property whose value is likely to increase or decrease in the near future, or if inflation is significant, long-term analysis is probably worthwhile. The analysis requires that you project growth rates for rents, operating expenses, and property value. Changes in debt service and taxes are also considered. The result of the analysis can be a measure of yield to maturity called the *internal rate of return*. This is the projected annual rate of return over the entire holding period. It can be used to compare other investments with the same holding period. Alternatively, you may calculate the *net present value* of the investment based on your required rate of return. This is often useful when comparing investments that require different levels of cash investment or when putting together a portfolio of several investments. Fortunately, there are computer programs available to do long-term investment analysis.

INVESTMENT STRATEGY

Investment Life Cycle

Like most things, a real estate investment has a beginning and an end. You purchase a property (or share in a partnership) and later sell it, hopefully for a profit. In between, the property may provide income if well managed. This middle period of operation may be long or short, depending on market conditions and the reasons for buying the property. Because of high transaction costs, most investors end up holding real estate for several years.

There are important considerations at each stage of the life cycle of the investment.

Purchase

The investor will be concerned with getting the right property at a good price and with favorable financing terms. The property should fit the investment objectives. If cash flow is desired, pick a property with proven ability to produce cash flow. If you want appreciation, pick a property with potential for increased value. The price you pay will have a lot to do with appreciation. If you pay above market value, the property will have to improve for you to break even. Financing may determine whether the property makes money or even whether you can keep the property. You must decide how much leverage to use, knowing that high leverage increases possible returns but may reduce income.

Operation

During this phase, the property should produce some cash flow. This is the income to you as an investor. Some properties have negative cash flow, which means you must pay some expenses out of your pocket. A part of cash flow may be due to tax benefits. Depending on your tax situation, these benefits allow you to shelter some property income from taxes. Remember that cash flow may vary from year to year and it depends on your ability to keep a sufficient amount of paying tenants and minimize operating expenses.

Sale

The main benefit from sale is capital gain, the profit on the sale. To make a profitable sale, you will want to maximize the sales price and minimize taxes on the sale. The highest price depends on the timing of the sale. You want to sell when the market is strong. Sometimes, a better price can be had if you are willing to help finance the purchase. To limit your exposure to taxes, you may wish to structure the sale as an *installment sale*. This allows you to spread the income from the sale over several years and may reduce the tax rate on the gain. Also, you may want to arrange an exchange. If properly done, an exchange can avoid payment of taxes altogether.

The key to a successful investment is to consider all of the income expected through the cycle, and its timing, to determine whether it is worth the cost.

WHEN TO SELL

How long should investment real estate be held? Its optimal holding period varies with the property type, market conditions, and each individual investor. Perhaps the most important factor is what you'll do with the money.

Do you plan to spend the money on a new boat, or reinvest it wisely? If you really just want to buy the boat, then investment strategy doesn't matter. However, as an investor considering the sale, think about the net amount you'll realize and how you'll reinvest it. If you can't equal or exceed the return that you'll get from continuing to hold the property, keep what you have. You might consider refinancing, which allows you to get some money out of the property without selling it.

Here's an example: Suppose you bought a rental house a few years ago for $50,000 and now it's worth $100,000. It generates annual income of $10,000, net of operating expenses. If you sell, you'll pay a brokerage commission ($6000), expenses of sale ($3000), and income taxes ($11,000). You'll be left with $80,000 to reinvest. Suppose the best investment opportunity is one that yields 8%; that will provide only $6400 annually, much less than the $10,000 you're now getting. If you can't exceed $10,000 of income on a new investment opportunity, keep the house. But if the $80,000 is needed to go into a business that promises to pay a 50% annual return, sell the house. The rate of return is like a speedometer—if your vehicle is too slow, get a faster one, if you can.

Considering a sale requires more thought than just estimating a rate of return, because it must include risk factors. The problem becomes more complex when debt is involved. As to risk, a bond may provide more safety, whereas the business venture may be much riskier than the rental house. So your personal judgment must temper a higher rate with increased risk of loss or volatility. As to financing, one must subtract the debt on property owned to determine exactly how much money will be realized from a sale. This adds more mathematics to the problem. The effect of depreciation and capital gains can add complications to the income tax estimate.

Highly leveraged real estate that appreciates in value will provide a very high yield on the equity investment. To sustain such a high yield, there is a temptation to sell and buy another larger, highly leveraged property in a year or two. However, this sort of pyramiding is financially dangerous—like playing "double-or-nothing"—one loss and you're completely wiped out. A longer holding period tends to be safer, and you eliminate the risk associated with a new purchase.

Sometimes cash can be extracted from real estate by refinancing, thus extending the optimal holding period. Refinancing costs money but eliminates most of the expenses of a sale, including income taxes. Refinancing may provide the cash for a new boat or additional investment. But be sure you can handle the increased payments of a new loan with increased principal.

AVAILABLE FINANCING

Arranging the best financing can be as important as negotiating the best price for a property. Before you talk to a lender, however, you should understand how the various terms of a loan can affect your investment.

Interest Rate

Interest is a charge for the use of money. The lower the rate, the more attractive the loan. The degree of leverage is also important. Many investors will pay a significantly higher interest rate in order to enjoy a lower cash down payment and therefore be able to exercise more leverage. Some equity investors will pay higher prices for property to achieve more leverage. Sellers sometimes accommodate by providing financing to buyers or by paying *discount points* on a buyer's loan, but they will try to raise their price to compensate. Consequently, prices are generally increased by favorable financing.

Degree of Leverage

When interest rates are low, the loan amount is usually limited by the *loan-to-value* (L/V) ratio. When rates are high, the *debt coverage ratio* (DCR) usually sets the maximum loan amount. For conservative lenders, the L/V ratio is usually in the range of 65 to 70%. Other lenders may use L/V ratio criteria of 75 to 80%. A conservative DCR is around 1.25.

Amortization Term

The longer the amortization term of a mortgage loan, the lower the annual debt service, and therefore the greater the annual cash flow. However, once loan terms are stretched beyond 30 years, the annual mortgage payment requirement declines, but the change is quite small. Annual debt service can never become less than the interest due on the principal balance. Many loans on income property become due years before being fully amortized. These are called *balloon payment* loans.

Prepayment Privileges

In this circumstance, the borrower has the right to pay off the remaining debt before it is due. Some loans include penalties for prepayment, although usually the penalty declines with time. For example, the penalty may be 3% if the loan is prepaid during the first five years, 2% for the next five years, then declining by 0.5% for each of the following years until there is no penalty. Some mortgage loans are locked in for the first five to ten years; prepayment without the lender's consent is prohibited.

Exculpation

Exculpation is freedom from liability. When a mortgage loan includes an exculpatory clause, the property is the sole collateral for the loan. Should the property be foreclosed, the lender can look only to the property for full satisfaction of the debt, not to other property you own. In the absence of exculpation, you are usually personally liable for the debt. *Nonrecourse* is another term used to describe mortgages with exculpatory clauses; the lender's only recourse in the event of borrower default is to the property itself, not to your personal assets.

Assumability

This right allows the borrower to transfer the mortgage loan with the property to another party. Since the new owner may not be as good a credit risk as the original owner, lenders often reserve the right to approve a loan assumption. In recent years, some lenders have been willing to approve changes routinely, provided that they can *escalate* (increase) the interest rate on the debt. Such provisions in mortgage loans make assumption privileges less attractive. Despite lender approval of changes in assumption, original borrowers remain liable for the mortgage debt. So if there is a default on an assumed loan, sellers are liable, but they can try to collect from their buyer. By contrast, if the buyer took the property "subject to" the loan, but did not assume it, the sellers remain solely liable for default.

Call or Acceleration Provisions

These provisions effectively permit balloon payments. Although the loan has a 25 or 30 year term, lenders, at their option, can accelerate payment of the principal after ten or fifteen years, regardless of whether the loan is in default. This obviously puts the lender in a strong position. Upon reaching the "call" date, the lender can force repayment or escalate the interest rate.

Subordination

Moving a mortgage loan to a lower priority. The priority of a lender's claim is where the lender stands in line for collection after a foreclosure. Land financed by a seller with a first mortgage and now ready for development is not acceptable collateral for a construction lender. Construction lenders want a first lien. If the holder of an existing mortgage is willing to subordinate, the existing mortgage will be reduced to a second lien position to allow a first lien for the new mortgage. If a subordination clause will be needed, you should attempt to insert it initially; lenders are reluctant to reduce collateral later. Subordinated loans are more favorable to borrowers because they increase the flexibility of first-mortgage financing.

PROPERTY TYPES AND INVESTMENT CHARACTERISTICS

Real estate comes in many different forms and can be leased or financed in so many different ways that the lease or mortgage will alter its investment characteristics. These characteristics vary from very passive investments to management-intensive ones, and from the lowest to the highest levels of risk.

Apartments

OWNERSHIP

Traditionally dominated by independent individuals or partnerships. Relatively little in institutional, corporate or large developer portfolios.

CHARACTERISTICS

Individual investors have been attracted to rental housing for several reasons.

1. Familiarity with housing
2. Liberal borrowing opportunities
3. Management need and ability
4. Tax incentives offered by government to encourage housing

ATTRACTIVE FEATURES

1. Leverage opportunities
2. Ability to respond quickly to market conditions (short leases)
3. Greater liquidity than other real estate investments
4. Tax shelter for high bracket investors
5. Inflation hedge
6. Greater immunity to recession than other property types

RISKS

1. Rent control
2. Competition
3. Local economy dependence

Office Buildings

OWNERSHIP

Dominated by institutional, corporate, or large developer portfolios.

CHARACTERISTICS

The institutional investor and large developer is attracted to office buildings because of:

1. Perceived quality and quantity of income stream
2. Large capital requirement prevents others from bidding
3. Ability to acquire competent property and investment management services

ATTRACTIVE FEATURES

1. Cash flow
2. Ability to respond to market conditions
3. Long-term nature of investment and physical asset: attractive for long-term investors such as pension funds and insurance companies
4. Inflation hedge
5. Perceived long-term stability
6. Expected diversification benefits vs. securities

RISKS

1. Effect of recession on space needs
2. Competition
3. Local economy dependence
4. Functional obsolescence

Shopping Centers

OWNERSHIP

Shopping center investors may be categorized into the following groups:

1. Major national and regional shopping center developers
2. Local shopping center developers
3. Commercial property investors
4. Institutional investors and Pension Funds
5. Investment Banking and Security firms
6. Syndications and Real Estate Investment Trusts
7. Foreign investors

PHYSICAL CHARACTERISTICS

1. Unified architectural treatment for the building or buildings, providing space for tenants that are selected, and managed as a unit for the benefit of all tenants
2. Unified site, suited to the type of center called for by the marketplace
3. An easily accessible location within the trade area with adequate entrances and exits
4. Sufficient on-site parking to meet the demands generated by the retail commercial users
5. Service facilities
6. Site improvements, such as landscaping, lighting, and signage, to create a desirable, attractive, and safe shopping environment

7. Tenant grouping that provides merchandising interplay among stores and the widest possible range and depth of merchandise
8. Surroundings that are agreeable and comfortable for shopping and that create a sense of identity and place

ATTRACTIVE FEATURES

1. Long-term viability from long-term leases with selected creditworthy tenants.
2. Financial stability and security when there are financially strong national chain stores as tenants.
3. Value enhancement and appreciation through the sales performance of tenants.
4. Limitations on expense exposure with "net" leases and periodic recycling opportunities.

RISKS

1. Locational obsolescence
2. Leasing, when terms of tenants become undesirable
3. Financing, when interest rates or payment requirements are burdensome
4. Tenant use requirement in lease
5. Expense pass-through
6. Governmental activities: ordinances, rules, statutes or governmental laws, or regulations

CATEGORIES OF SHOPPING CENTERS

Shopping centers are divided into five distinct categories: the strip/convenience center, the neighborhood shopping center, the community shopping center, the regional shopping center, and the super-regional shopping center.

TABLE 17-1
CHARACTERISTICS OF SHOPPING CENTERS

Center Type	Leading Tenant (Basis for Classification)	Typical GLA* (Square Feet)	General Range in GLA (Square Feet)	Usual Minimum Site Area (Acres)
Strip/convenience	Varies	13,000	Under 30,000	Under 3
Neighborhood	Supermarket	70,000	30,000–125,000	3–10
Community	Junior department store, large variety, discount, or department store	200,000	125,000–400,000	10–40
Regional	One or more full-line department store(s)	600,000	400,000–800,000	40–100
Super-regional	Three or more full-line department stores	1,200,000	800,000 and up	60–120

*GLA=Gross Leasable Area

Source: International Council of Shopping Centers

Industrial Properties

OWNERSHIP

1. Corporate users
2. Developer/investors
3. Joint ventures with developers and users
4. Pension funds
5. Life insurance companies
6. Long-term individual investors

INVESTMENT CHARACTERISTICS

1. Cash flow
2. Stable values
3. Long life

RISKS

1. Tenant default
2. Environmental obsolescence
3. Local economic conditions
4. Illiquidity
5. Functional obsolescence
6. Environmental problems

TYPES OF USES

1. Service center
2. Office warehouse
3. Distribution
4. Manufacturing
5. Research and development

Location

An expression in real estate is that the three key aspects of success are "location, location, location." Very similar buildings can have very different values depending on where they are located. In fact, the value of undeveloped land is almost totally determined by where it is located.

The reason location is so important is that real estate is more than just space in an economic sense. Its surroundings have a lot to do with how useful the property is. One big reason to buy or rent a piece of property is to be near other activities.

The type of location desired varies with the type of property:

For *residential properties,* people will want to be relatively close to their job and shopping, but not so close that there is a lot of traffic in their neighborhood. Being in a good school district is important to many home buyers. The neighborhood should be pleasant and well-cared for. A prestigious address can add a great deal of value. If the property has apartments, being on a bus route might be important.

Stores and shopping centers need visibility and traffic flow. The property should be near areas where shoppers live or work, depending on the type of stores. Big stores should not be too close to their competitors, but small stores often like to be near big stores, hoping to attract shoppers coming and going to the larger store.

Office buildings should be close to business activities. Lawyers want to be near courthouses or government offices; consultants want to be near corporate headquarters or banks; doctors need to be near hospitals or nursing homes, and other businesses need to be near customers. Because of the necessity to be close together, downtown areas used to be the best place for offices. Today, suburban locations may be just as valuable because of improvements in communications.

Industrial properties should be close to the source of their materials and labor. They have great need for good transportation, with heavy industry often locating on rail lines or near seaports. A good highway is almost a necessity.

In real estate, the best locations get the top dollar. As an investor, you have to look at more than the property alone. Remember, however, that the quality of a location can change over time. Sometimes, a lesser location can become the best place to be.

SOURCES OF MARKET DATA FOR INCOME AND EXPENSES

In addition to the sources listed in Chapter 14, the following may be helpful:

LOCAL SOURCES OF REAL ESTATE DATA

Local organizations often collect real estate data, usually for membership use or sale to interested parties. These include the following:

- Local Board of Realtors/Multiple Listing Service
- Local tax assessor's office
- Local credit bureaus, and tax map reproduction firms
- University research centers
- Private brokerage or appraisal firms

LOCAL BOARDS OF REALTORS

Most metropolitan areas have a Board of Realtors, or other broker group, that sponsors a multiple listing service (MLS). Upon the sale of property listed through MLS, the broker must supply information about the completed transaction. Each property sold and its terms of sale are therefore available on computer or in a published book. Some realtor boards provide information to members only; some share with other real estate organizations.

LOCAL TAX ASSESSOR'S OFFICES

Assessor's offices usually keep a file on every property in the jurisdiction, with property characteristics, value estimate, and how the estimate was derived. Many jurisdictions are notified of every sale or building permit, for immediate update of affected properties.

LOCAL CREDIT BUREAUS AND TAX MAP COMPANIES

These may have data on certain parcels; since their main business is not evaluation, they are not a regular source.

UNIVERSITY RESEARCH CENTERS

University research centers, many of which are sponsored by broker and salesperson state license fees, may have aggregated data on real estate transactions collected from other sources throughout the state. This data is often helpful in identifying trends established over time, and by city, for various types of property. Additional research and educational information may be available from such centers.

PRIVATE DATA SOURCES

Many real estate appraisers and brokers retain file data for property owned by their clients and others. They will often share information, usually for reciprocity rather than payment.

PROPERTY OWNER

Property owner's records include permanent records such as deeds, leases, and copies of mortgages (lenders have the original mortgage document), as well as periodic accounting and tax return information about the property's recent past. An owner's report may be of limited immediate use, however, because it may be disorganized, have extraneous information, or be arranged poorly for appraisals. Also, data from a single property cannot offer a broad perspective on the market.

RETURN ON INVESTMENT

Return on investment is the actual earnings from the investment; this is apart from any returns which represent repayment (called amortization) of the principal invested. The difference is like distinguishing the fruit from the tree on which it grows. Both can be sold for money, but selling the tree provides a different type of income than would picking the fruit each year.

In real estate, it is sometimes difficult to determine how much of income is return *on* investment and how much is a return *of* investment. For example, if you rent a property that depreciates in value, some of the rental income must go toward significant repairs, or the eventual possibility of replacing the building when it becomes useless from age or obsolescence.

Why is this important? It makes a difference in evaluating the performance of the investment. The return on investment determines how well your money is invested. Return of investment affects risk of capital. The sooner your investment is recovered, the less risk there is of losing it.

Measures of return on investment include the *equity dividend rate,* based on a one-year analysis, and the *internal rate of return,* based on a multiyear projection (see DISCOUNTED CASH FLOW ANALYSIS). Consider that the rate of return you get includes these:

A SAFE RATE

This is the rate you could get if you put your money into a perfectly safe, liquid investment, such as a federally insured passbook savings account.

A LIQUIDITY PREMIUM

This compensates you for the difficulty of, and time required, to sell your property. Stocks and bonds may be sold at market value within a moment's notice, whereas selling real estate may take months or years.

A MANAGEMENT PREMIUM

This is for the burden of monitoring and making decisions about the investment.

A RISK PREMIUM

This accounts for the chance that you may not get all your money back or that the return will be lower than expected.

You may use a buildup approach to evaluating the return on a particular investment. Consider a real estate investment that promises an annual return of 14% before taxes. You would hold the property for at least ten years. The safe liquid rate, as measured by the current yield on passbook savings accounts, is 5%. The real estate looks like a superior investment. But you must remember to account for the premiums included in the rate. The following increased rates are estimates that will vary with the type of property, economic situation, and tenant or user.

The real estate is difficult to sell, so add another 3% for illiquidity. The real estate requires more investment decisions, add 2%. Finally, there is much more risk that the real estate will deviate from the promised return. Add 4% more. The built-up rate is now 14%. Using these estimates, the real estate should offer at least a 14% rate of return on investment. If it doesn't, you might be better off with the savings account.

Return of Investment

Hopefully, any investment will provide a stream of future income. A portion of this income represents the *return of* the investor's original invested cash. Any excess is a *return on investment*. The return of investment may appear in a lump sum at the end of the investment term. For example, if you deposit money in a savings account or buy a certificate of deposit, your money is refunded when you close the account. In other cases, the return may a part of the periodic income stream. If you were to borrow a self-amortizing mortgage loan, the principal is paid down with each payment. At maturity there is no lump sum payment.

The return from a real estate investment is less clear-cut. Whether periodic income includes return of investment depends on how much is realized at resale. Consider an investment of $100,000 that provides an annual cash flow of $15,000. If the property is sold later for $100,000, the resale proceeds provide all of the return *of* investment and all of the annual cash flow is return *on* investment. If the sale is made for less than $100,000, a portion of the annual cash flow is actually return *of* investment.

Guard against investments that offer illusory returns. Suppose someone offers you an investment that provides a 20% return each year for five years. If there is no resale amount, you will have just received your money back with absolutely no return on investment.

Likewise, if a property produces negative cash flow, all return of and on investment is pushed to resale. During times of rapid inflation, investors may purchase properties strictly for appreciation. The price paid is often so high that net operating income fails to cover debt service. In effect, the investor must invest new capital in the property each year. The hope is that resale proceeds will be sufficient to return the original investment, all annual cash flow deficits, and provide a return on investment. Be sure that the expected value enhancement is sufficient to cover the long wait to receive returns, with compound interest.

By contrast, if you receive periodic income, and then sell for a profit, the resale proceeds not only provide the return of capital but some return on investment as well.

The use of depreciation tax deductions affects the pattern of return. Depreciation allows you to receive some return on investment before resale through tax savings. If your property depreciates in value at the same rate as it is depreciated for tax purposes (resale price equals adjusted tax basis), all tax savings due to depreciation deductions is return of investment, not a return on investment.

In summary, consider the entire cycle of an investment, from purchase to resale, all of the investment returns and contributions, and their timing.

Risk

Risk is the chance that things will not turn out as planned. Since no one knows what will occur in the future, risk is an unavoidable fact of life. However, it is possible to anticipate or forecast the future and project a reasonable range of possible outcomes. This is what is meant by the term calculated risk. It does not imply that risk can be precisely measured, but that sources of risk can be identified. In this way, it is possible to rank investment opportunities according to their riskiness.

Why would an investor choose to take more risk? Greater risk ought to mean the chance of higher returns. Risk not only introduces the chance that the return will be lower than expected, but also that it will be higher. (For example, the potential reward from playing the lottery is much higher than the maximum yield from a savings account, but you typically lose your entire "investment" in the lottery, which you won't do in the savings account.) Since most people are averse to risk, high risk ventures must offer a high potential return to attract investors. Put another way, society often rewards those who are willing and able to take risks. Therefore, to get a high return, you must accept higher risk.

Most people are said to be risk-averse. This normally means that people prefer less risk to more risk. However, some investors are more sensitive to risk than others. Some are prone to worry about things going wrong and are probably better off with relatively risk-free investments. It should be recognized that no investment is truly risk-free. Real estate rises and falls in value. It is illiquid. Even investing in government-insured passbook accounts exposes the investor to the *purchasing power risk* that inflation will wipe out any real return.

Some investors have a greater *capacity* to undertake risk. This capacity depends on the consequences of the investment not working out as planned. If you need cash flow from the investment for the basic necessities of life, you have a low capacity for risk. Any reduction in income would be serious. Likewise, if the invested income is your entire wealth, risk capacity is low. You could weather a reduction in cash flow but would be harmed by loss of capital. An investor with *venture capital*, which is money that he or she is willing to place at risk, can take on more risk. Some investors have what they call "play money" that is not crucial to their financial support and which they can use for speculative ventures. It is important to determine how much risk you are prepared to take and choose investments accordingly.

There are different types of risk. Possibly the most familiar type is *business risk*. This is the chance that the investment will not perform as expected. It may turn out that more capital investment is needed to keep the property going. For example, a major component of the building may fail unexpectedly and need replacing. Or a storm may damage the building. Revenues may drop due to a rise in vacancies or the need to lower rental rates. Operating expenses may increase. Expected appreciation may not be realized when the property is sold. It is even possible that changes in tax laws may affect the return over time. Some of these risks can be reduced by using *hazard insurance*. Others may be minimized by diversifying investment among different locations and types of property.

A second type of risk is *financial risk*. This is the chance that you will be unable to make the debt service payments on the property and thus become insolvent. Financial risk is increased by the use of *leverage*. The more money borrowed to purchase the property, the higher the chance that a declining net operating income will fail to cover debt service. This is especially a problem if you are poorly capitalized or have most of your capital tied up in illiquid assets. This is why any investment is made more risky by using financial leverage. (Likewise, leverage increases the potential return). The use of short-term financing also exposes you to *interest rate risk*. This is the chance that interest rates will increase and adversely affect return. Such financing as balloon loans or adjustable rate mortgages present the possibility that debt service costs will increase if interest rates rise.

TAX CONSIDERATIONS

One of the traditional attractions of real estate investment is its ability to generate tax losses. These losses arise from certain deductions and credits that reduce taxable income but do not require cash outlays. In other words, a property may show a loss for tax purposes, yet produce positive *cash flow*. When this occurs, the loss is said to shelter income from taxation. Reduced taxes are a form of investment income.

Most of the expenses associated with rental property are deductible from taxable income. These include operating expenses and interest payments on the mortgage loan. Mortgage principal repayment is never deductible. (If the property is your personal residence, you may deduct property taxes and interest payments.)

While business expenses are deductible for rental property, they represent real cash outlays. Therefore, they do not provide tax shelter. Deductions for tax depreciation reduce taxable income but do not require cash outlays. Rather, they are a way of accounting for the gradual decline in value of man-made structures. You are allowed to deduct a portion of the property's original value each year to compensate for this decline in value. These deductions can shelter part or all of the income produced by the property. Except for high income investors, you may also shelter income up to $25,000 that is earned from sources outside the property by showing tax losses of the property.

While tax shelter has long been an advantage of real estate investment, it is very limited in today's tax environment. For properties placed in service after 1986, depreciation deductions are based on a life of 27.5 years for residential properties and 39 years for nonresidential properties. The amount of annual deduction is approximately 1/27.5, or 1/39, of the purchase price of buildings. Land is not depreciable. In most cases, depreciation deductions under this schedule are too small to provide shelter. Any tax losses produced may be applied only against *passive income*. Basically, passive income is produced by rental properties. This prevents many real estate losses from offsetting income from wages, salaries, or other types of investments, such as dividends or interest earnings. If you *actively participate* in the management of the property, up to $25,000 of nonpassive income may be offset by passive losses. This begins to be phased out as adjusted gross income (AGI) rises above $100,000, and it is eliminated at $150,000 of AGI. "Active participation" refers to investors who own property directly and make most of the investment decisions.

Even under these restrictions, depreciation does reduce taxes on the income from the property. In addition, it may be possible to put together a tax strategy whereby investments with tax losses are matched with properties with passive income. The result could be a source of tax-free income.

An example serves to show how tax shelter is calculated:

ASSETS

Purchase cost of entire property	$1,150,000
Land purchase cost	150,000
(land cannot be depreciated)	
Building cost	$1,000,000
Divide building cost by depreciable life, in this case 27.5 years, to derive annual depreciation.	$36,363
(or multiply by the IRS factor which is .0364 per year)	

OPERATING STATEMENT

Rental collections	$ 150,000
Less operating expenses	$ 50,000
Less interest paid	85,000
Less depreciation	36,363
Taxable income from property	$ –21,363

Because the income is negative, the property provides over $21,000 of tax shelter to be applied against income from other passive investments. Any unused losses may be carried forward to future tax years.

As a special incentive, the tax code sometimes provides tax credits for certain types of investment expenses. In the past, credits have been given for purchasing capital equipment (such as elevators), rehabilitating historically significant structures, and for taking energy conservation measures. Credits are applied directly against taxes owed rather than as deductions against income. Credits may be available for investors who build, renovate or purchase housing for low-income tenants.

DEPRECIATION/INCOME TAX DEDUCTIONS

A key to real estate investments is depreciation claimed for federal income tax purposes. The Internal Revenue Service allows an owner of business or investment property to claim depreciation as a business expense, even when the property increases in value. Land is not considered to wear out so depreciation cannot be claimed on it. Appliances, carpets, and furniture can be depreciated over a relatively short life, and buildings over a longer period. The exact life to be used has changed frequently. Almost every time the tax law has changed in recent years, the depreciable life has been changed. Usually tax changes affect new owners, whereas present owners continue the depreciable life they started with.

Depreciation allows a tax deduction without the owner paying for it in cash. This gives the owner the best possible benefit—a tax deduction that doesn't reduce cash flow. For example, suppose an investor buys a small building for $100,000 and is allowed a 27.5-year depreciable life using the straight-line method of depreciation. The owner may claim a tax deduction of $3640 annually (the first year can be less depending on the month the property was acquired). This deduction reduces the owner's taxable income which will in turn save income taxes. The deduction was created merely by a bookkeeping entry and can be claimed even though the property rises in value. Thus the owner gains by reducing taxes on property that provides cash flow from rents and would otherwise generate taxable income.

However, the taxpayer must be prepared to return the benefits received from depreciation when the property is sold. There is a concept called *basis*—the point from which gain or loss is measured. In general, basis begins as the price paid for the property. As you claim depreciation as a tax deduction, you reduce the basis. This increases the gain when property is sold. If the investment remains the same in value, or rises, all of the depreciation becomes taxable as a gain when sold. In this way, depreciation that was claimed while owning the property generates taxable gain on a sale, unless the property actually loses value more quickly than the investor depreciates it on his/her tax return.

Tax depreciation should not be confused with an actual reduction or loss in value. Tax depreciation does not measure the actual loss in value of property sustained in a year. It is an arbitrary deduction allowed by tax law.

To summarize, depreciation claimed for tax purposes allows the investor to save on taxes, perhaps having to pay them back later. It is not a measure of a property's loss in value.

TAX-FREE EXCHANGES

In most real estate investment programs, there comes a time when you need to change properties. Your property may have grown in value and now it is time to move up to a larger property. You may want to get into a different type of property, such as moving from rental housing to an office building. If you move, you may want to keep your investments close at hand. You may have several small properties and want to consolidate into one large property.

Many have found that the best way to change properties is thorough exchanging. They merely trade properties with another investor. This may be simpler than selling the property and reinvesting in a new one. It means you need only one transaction instead of two (or more). Financing is often exchanged along with the property, so you don't necessarily need to get a new loan. There is no need to get out of the market and then get back in, taking the chance that the market changes during that time.

Another big advantage of exchanging is that you may save taxes. If your property has appreciated, you will owe taxes on capital gains when you sell. An exchange can let you defer paying those taxes until some time in the future when you sell the new property. To do this, you must trade for other investment real estate (the property traded or received can't be your home). If you end up with some cash from the exchange, you may have to pay some taxes. In most cases, you will need to trade up in the exchange. If you end up with a smaller debt, you may have to pay some taxes. However, in cases where you pay some taxes, they may be less than if you sold your property for cash.

The rules of a tax-free exchange are described in Section 1031 of the Internal Revenue Code. They now allow a sale to qualify as a tax-free exchange, provided that, within 45 days, replacement property is identified, and is purchased within 180 days. Be sure to enlist professional tax advice when considering a trade.

Questions on Chapter 17

1. Investment real estate may offer
   (A) cash flow
   (B) appreciation in value
   (C) income tax shelter
   (D) all of the above

2. REIT is a
   (A) Really Energized Income Tax
   (B) Real Estate Investment Trust
   (C) Real Estate Income Target
   (D) none of the above

3. A REIT is like
   (A) tenancy in common
   (B) a joint tenancy
   (C) community property
   (D) a mutual fund

4. Refinancing is
   (A) arranging a new loan to replace an existing loan
   (B) a wraparound mortgage
   (C) done to postpone income taxes
   (D) reduces operating expenses

5. Depreciation claimed for income tax purposes
   (A) reduces cash flow
   (B) reduces taxable income
   (C) increases potential gross income
   (D) increases operating expenses

6. A list of tenants, their space identified, and rent amounts, is called
   (A) an operating statement
   (B) a tenant list
   (C) a rent roll
   (D) an operating role

7. One of the important drawbacks to direct real estate investing is
   (A) illiquidity
   (B) location
   (C) small size
   (D) disclosure requirements

8. Instead of selling property and paying a tax on the gain, one may prefer
   (A) a capital gain
   (B) Section 1231
   (C) a tax-free exchange
   (D) ordinary income

9. A projection of what is expected to occur from operating a property is a _____ statement.
   (A) conforming
   (B) nonconforming
   (C) consistent
   (D) pro forma

10. Neighborhood, community, regional, are descriptive of
    (A) apartments
    (B) office buildings
    (C) warehouses
    (D) shopping centers

11. Casualty insurance is
    (A) financing expense
    (B) capital expenditure
    (C) fixed expense
    (D) variable expense

12. Taxable gain on the sale of commercial real estate is calculated by
    (A) sales price minus the basis
    (B) adjusted sales price minus the basis
    (C) realized selling price minus the adjusted tax basis
    (D) contract sales price minus the adjusted tax basis

ANSWERS

1. **D**	4. **A**	7. **A**	10. **D**
2. **B**	5. **B**	8. **C**	11. **C**
3. **D**	6. **C**	9. **D**	12. **C**

Real Estate Mathematics and Problem Solving

The mathematics problems you will encounter on the licensing examination are most likely to be in the form of *word problems*, that is, problems that describe a situation for which you have to find a mathematical answer. Here is an example of a simple word problem:

> *I have three apples. John has four apples. How many apples do John and I have together?*

Here is an example of a very complicated word problem:

> *Ms. Jones owns a building that is rectangular in shape: 40 ft. × 66 ft. 3 in. She wishes to construct a sidewalk around the perimeter of the building. The sidewalk will be made of concrete and crushed stone. It will be 4 ft. wide and will be poured to a depth of 3½ in. The composition will be 85% concrete and 15% crushed stone. Concrete costs $313.00 per cubic yard. Crushed stone is $27.83 per ton; 1 cu. yd. of crushed stone weighs 3,282 lb. 15 oz. Labor required to construct the sidewalk is $19 per hour; in 1 hour a laborer can finish 188 sq. ft. of sidewalk. The laborer must be paid for at least 4 hours every time he works, even if it takes him less time to finish the job. How much will the sidewalk cost?*

In spite of the complicated appearance of the second problem, the process for solving it is basically the same as the process for solving the first:

1. *Read* the question.
2. Determine *what* is being asked for.
3. Determine *how* to arrive at the answer.
4. *Calculate* the answer.
5. *Check* the answer.

The last step is particularly important, especially when the problem is a complicated one; you have to make sure that you did all the calculations correctly, or your answer will be wrong. On most examinations, knowing *how* to do a problem will get you no credit; you must provide the *correct answer* as evidence that you know how to do that particular problem. You should be aware of one more fact: on mathematics questions offered in a multiple-choice format you have both an advantage and a possible disadvantage.

The advantage, which is always present, is that *you are given the correct answer to the problem!* Obviously, it *must* be among the ones you are to choose from; all you have to do is to figure out *which* one it is.

A possible disadvantage is that some of the *incorrect* answers may be answers you would arrive at by making common mistakes. You may be lulled into choosing the incorrect answer by assuming that, since your calculations gave you an answer that appears among the ones you must choose from, it *must* be correct. You should especially be on your guard if one of the choices given is something like "none of the above" or "none of the other answers is correct." This kind of choice *may* mean that none of the answers is correct, but it may also be included as a red herring.

Mistakes on mathematics problems may result from:

1. Incorrect reading of the problem. *Solution*: Read carefully!
2. Misunderstanding what is being asked for. *Solution*: Read carefully and slowly; you have plenty of time, so don't rush!
3. Not knowing how to do the problem correctly. *Solution*: Study this chapter carefully, so that you know how to approach all kinds of problems.
4. Incorrect calculation of the answer. *Solution*: Study the methods of calculation for all kinds of real estate problems, as outlined in this chapter.
5. Mistakes in arithmetic. *Solution*: Check your work, to make sure that you did your arithmetic correctly.

Note that these five common sources of errors can be controlled by applying the five steps in problem solving offered at the beginning of this chapter.

In discussing the various kinds of real estate mathematics problems, we are going to assume in this chapter that you have an adequate knowledge of basic arithmetic. Have your calculator ready before you tackle the sample problems; use this opportunity to become familiar with the calculator, if you aren't already. You must get used to doing these kinds of problems with a calculator because you'll be using one for the exam.

MEASUREMENTS AND TERMS

Measurements of Lengths and Areas

Many real estate problems involve *measurements* of lengths and areas. You will be assumed to know at least the measurements listed below.

Linear measures:

12 inches	=	1 foot
3 feet	=	1 yard
5,280 feet	=	1 mile

Area measures:

144 square inches	=	1 square foot
9 square feet	=	1 square yard
640 acres	=	1 square mile

Most of these measures you already know, but here is one that *you absolutely must remember:*

1 acre = 43,560 square feet

Burn this into your memory! You can bet the farm (and all of its acreage) that you'll be asked questions that *require* you to know the number of square feet in an acre.

Special Terms You Should Know

Also, you must know the following special *terms* used in real estate measurement; these are illustrated in Figure 18-1.

Depth refers to the straight-line distance from the front-lot line to the rear-lot line. If these lot lines aren't parallel, the term *depth* will refer to the *longest* straight-line distance between them. The lot shown in Figure 18-1 has a depth of 272 feet.

Figure 18-1.   Real Estate Measurement

Frontage is the *lineal distance* (see *lineal foot* below) of the lot line that is also a part of a public street or other right-of-way. Frontage of corner lots usually is expressed as separate figures for the distance fronting on each of the streets the lot bounds. This would also apply to very deep lots that border streets at both ends, and so on. The frontage of the lot in Figure 18-1 is 133 feet.

Front foot refers to the distance that a lot borders on a street. For the lot illustrated in Figure 18-1, we can say that it has *133 feet of frontage* or that it has *133 front feet*. (To say that the lot has 133 front feet of frontage is redundant.)

Lineal foot refers to the distance between two particular spots. Note that lineal feet need not be a *straight* measure; rather, the term refers to the number of feet traveled while following a *particular path connecting the particular points involved.* In real estate, this term is used normally to describe irregular lot sides (such as the east side of the lot in Figure 18-1, which is 363 lineal feet on a lot that has only 272 feet of depth), irregular paths along roads, and so on.

Right-of-way (*R.O.W.*) refers to the area owned by the government within which a road is located. On maps, plats, and so on, the term R.O.W. usually refers to the width of the right-of-way area (which usually exceeds *pavement* width).

Approaches to Solving Problems

You are assumed to be familiar with the basic methods of calculating distance, area, and volume; here we will confine ourselves to particular kinds of real estate problems that you will encounter. Most of them can be characterized as specific *forms* of problems that are easy to recognize.

Before showing how to deal with them, however, we should pass on one very crucial hint for solving these kinds of problems:

Draw a picture of the problem, if you possibly can. Then, with the picture as your guide, go through the problem step by step.

We cannot stress this process too much. By drawing a picture of the problem, you can *look* at it. A picture really is valuable, especially if it helps you to visualize a problem. (Sometimes, of course, the problem on the exam will include a picture or diagram. But if it doesn't, supply your own!) Then when you do the problem, work it very carefully, step by step. Even if you feel you can take some shortcuts, or do part of it in your head, DON'T! Solving problems this way may be boring or tedious, but it helps to eliminate mistakes.

Math Problem Set A

The following problems deal with lengths, areas, and measures. The answers, along with the methods of solution, are given at the end of the chapter. Use the space below each question to work it out.

1. Brown's home measures 55 ft. long and 30 ft. wide. The outside walls are $8\frac{1}{2}$ ft. high. Brown is going to paint these walls and wants to know how much the paint will cost him. There are two doors, each 3 ft. × $7\frac{1}{2}$ ft., one picture window 12 ft. × 5 ft., and 6 windows $2\frac{1}{2}$ ft. × 4 ft. The doors and windows will not be painted. Each gallon can of paint will cover 320 sq. ft. and will cost $9.98.

2. Ms. Orsini wishes to subdivide her 76-acre tract into building lots. She will have to use 665,000 sq. ft. of land for streets, roads, parks, and so on. If the zoning code requires that each lot have at least 7,500 sq. ft., what is the *maximum* number of lots that she can develop out of this land?

3. Steinfeld has a building that measures 65 ft. long × 35 ft. deep. One of the 65-ft. sides fronts directly on the sidewalk; he wants to build a sidewalk 8 ft. wide to surround the building on the other three sides. If the sidewalk costs $1.15 per square foot to build, what will be the total cost?

4. Johnson's lot is rectangular and contains 313 sq. yd. If the frontage is 41 ft., how deep is the lot?

5. A triangular plot of land is 500 ft. wide at the base and 650 ft. deep to the point of the triangle. What is the value of this lot, at $600 per acre?

6. *If your state uses the rectangular government survey, do this problem:*

   Huang purchased the NW¼ of the SE¼ of a section of land. A road 66 ft. wide goes due north-south through the parcel, splitting it into two pieces. Huang did *not* acquire title to the road. How much land did he get?

PERCENT PROBLEMS

A great many real estate problems involve percents; these include commissions, interest, mortgage payments, loan discounts (points), depreciation, profit and loss, and return on investment. We will discuss each of these, but it should be remembered that the mathematics involved is the same for all of them: you will be looking for one of three things—a base, a rate, or a result.

Every percent problem can be stated as one of three variations of the following statement:

$$A \text{ is } B \text{ percent of } C.$$

Numerical examples of such a statement are "14 is 50% of 28" and "63 is 90% of 70." Of course, if you know all three numbers, you don't have a problem.

All percent problems are like the statement above, except that one of the numbers is missing: the problem is to find that missing number.

Type 1:	*A is B percent of ?*	*(C is missing.)*
Type 2:	*A is ? percent of C*	*(B is missing.)*
Type 3:	*? is B percent of C*	*(A is missing.)*

The solutions to these problems are as follows:

$$A = B \times C$$
$$B = A \div C$$
$$C = A \div B$$

An easy way to remember these is that A is B multiplied by C. To find either B or C, you divide A by the other. Here are some examples illustrating the three variations of the percent problem:

1. What is 88.5% of 326?   (? is B percent of C.)
2. 16 is what percent of 440?   (A is ? percent of C.)
3. 43 is 86% of what?   (A is B percent of ?.)

The solutions are as follows:

1. The missing item is A. $A = B \times C$. $A = 0.885 \times 326$. $A = 288.51$.
2. The missing item is B. $B = A \div C$. $B = 16 \div 440$. $B = 0.0363636 = 3.63\%$
3. The missing item is C. $C = A \div B$. $C = 43 \div 0.86$. $C = 50$.

Commission Problems

Commission problems naturally are very popular on real estate examinations because most licensees are paid in commissions. A real estate commission is simply what the employer pays the agent for performing his function. Most often, the commission is a portion of the sale price received by a seller because of the efforts of the agent to secure a buyer. Typical commission rates vary from as low as 1% or less to over 10%, depending on the kind of property, the prevailing custom in the area, and the success of the agent, or the employer, in negotiating the listing contract.

The simplest commission problems are like this one:

> *Jones sells Smith's house for $311,800. Jones's commission is 7% of the sale price. What is her commission, in dollars?*

Here the solution is to find 7% of $311,800: $0.07 \times \$311,800 = \$21,826$.

This *same* problem, which is the type 1 described above, can also be stated as a type 2 or type 3 problem:

> *Type 2:*   *Jones sells Smith's house for $311,800 and receives a commission of $21,826. What is her commission rate?*
>
> *Type 3:*   *Jones sells Smith's house and receives a commission of $21,826, which is 7% of the sale price. What was the sale price?*

These problems are simple. To make them more "interesting," they are often expanded in one of two ways. The first way is to make them more complicated, and there are two methods of doing that. The second way is to develop the question *backwards*; this often traps many unwary examinees, but if you pay attention it won't fool you.

First, let's look at the more elaborate kinds of commission problems. The two methods used are (a) to have you calculate the salesperson's share of a total commission and (b) to make the means of determining the commission more complicated.

Here (a) is illustrated:

> *O'Reilly sells Marino's house for $180,000. The commission is 6½% of the sale price. O'Reilly's broker receives 45% of this amount from the listing broker as the selling broker's share. O'Reilly herself is entitled to 60% of all commissions that she is responsible for bringing in. How much does O'Reilly get?*

This may look complicated, but it is just three consecutive simple percent problems.

(1) How much was the total commission? A is 6½% of $180,000; A = $11,700.
(2) O'Reilly's broker received 45% of this amount. A is 45% of $11,700 = $5,265.
(3) O'Reilly gets 60% of that amount. A is 60% of $5,265 = $3,159.

This is the second kind (b):

> *Albertson sold Harding's house for $115,000. The commission rate is 7% of the first $50,000 of the sale price, 4% of the next $50,000, and 1.5% of everything over that. What was Albertson's total commission?*

Once again, we have several simple percentages to calculate: 7% of the first $50,000 is $3,500; 4% of the next $50,000 is $2,000; adding $2,000 to $3,500 yields a commission of $5,500 on the first $100,000 (or $50,000 + $50,000). This leaves a balance of $15,000, to which we apply the commission rate of 1½% to get another $225, for a total commission of $5,725.

This question could have been complicated further by going an additional step and asking, What was the effective commission rate on the sale? Here the question is, "What percent of the sale price is the actual commission?" First we say, $5,725 is ? percent of $115,000. Then we take the additional step: B = 5,725 ÷ 115,000 = 0.0498, so the percentage = 4.98%.

Now let's turn to the other general category of complicated commission problems—those in which the question is developed *backwards*. Here the question is phrased like this:

> *Baker sold her house; after paying a 7% commission she had $260,400 left. What was the sale price of the house?*

Many people will find 7% of $260,400, add it on, and GET THE WRONG ANSWER!! Their mistake is that the commission should be figured on the *sale price*, and they are figuring it on what the seller had left *after* the commission was paid. The way to solve these problems is simple: If Baker paid a 7% commission, then *what she had left* was 93% (or 100% − 7%) of the sale price. Now the problem becomes a familiar variation: $260,400 is 93% of ? C = $260,400 ÷ 0.93 = $280,000.

As you can see, this question is "backwards" in that you don't actually have to figure the dollar amount of the commission. On your examination be sure to look out for these kinds of problems; the best way to spot them is to follow the rule of *reading* the question and *then* trying to determine what you are asked to do.

You should be aware of the terminology used in commission figuring. The *commission* is the dollar amount arrived at by applying the *commission rate* to the *sale price*. If you are asked for the "commission," you are being asked to tell *how many dollars and cents* the commission payment was. If you are asked for the "commission rate" or the "rate," you are being asked to provide the *percent rate* of the commission.

Interest Problems

Interest is money paid to "rent" money from others. It is typically expressed as an annual percentage rate; that is, for each year that the money is borrowed, a certain percentage of the loan amount is charged as interest. Interest will most often be stated in annual percentage terms even for loans that have a duration of much less than 1 year. As an example, the "interest rate" on charge accounts, credit card accounts, and the like may be charged monthly, and the bill may be due within a month, but the interest rate still is expressed as an annual rate. This practice is becoming even more prevalent as a result of federal truth-in-lending laws, which *require* that the annual percentage rate (APR) be stated.

Usually, for short-term arrangements a monthly or quarterly rate will also be specified. If you are given only an annual rate and are required to calculate based on a monthly or quarterly rate, simply divide the annual rate by 12 to get the monthly rate, and by 4 to get the quarterly rate. If a problem gives a monthly or quarterly rate, multiply a monthly rate by 12 or a quarterly rate by 4 to get the annual rate. For example:

> *A rate of 12% annually is 1% monthly and 3% quarterly.*
> *A rate of 9½% annually is 2.375% quarterly or 0.791666 . . . % monthly.*
> *A rate of 0.6% monthly is 1.8% quarterly or 7.2% annually.*

Interest is calculated in two ways, *simple* and *compound*.

Simple interest is calculated quite straightforwardly. To determine the interest charge for any period of time, we calculate the proportional interest, based on the annual rate. If the annual rate is 6%, interest for 2 years is 12%, interest for 6 months is 3%, and so on.

When *compound interest* is used, interest is charged on unpaid interest, as well as on the unpaid debt. This adds a complicating element to the calculation, since some sort of adjustment may be necessary to allow for the fact that interest is not being paid periodically, but is being allowed to accumulate over all or part of the term of the debt. Since in real life most debts are paid in monthly installments, one does not frequently encounter interest compounding in the payment of debts. One *does* encounter it in savings accounts, where a well-advertised feature is that, if a depositor does not withdraw the interest his principal earns, it is added to his balance and begins to earn interest too.

Before compound interest can be calculated, the compounding frequency must be given. This is expressed in units of time. Compounding can be daily, quarterly, semiannually, annually—indeed it can be over any period of time, even "continuously." Given a compounding term, interest is figured by first deriving an interest rate for the term involved. Then interest is calculated for *each* term, taking into account the fact that some or all of the interest earned so far may not have been paid out. Here is an example:

> *Berger borrows $1,000 at 8% annual interest. The interest is compounded quarterly. How much interest will Berger owe after 9 months?*

First we must change the annual rate to a quarterly rate: 8 ÷ 4 = 2, so the quarterly interest rate is 2%.

For the first quarter, interest is 2% of $1,000, or $20.

To calculate interest for the second quarter, we add the first quarter's interest to the balance to get $1,020, upon which interest for the second quarter is due. Therefore, the second quarter's interest is 2% of $1,020.00, or $20.40. In effect, for the second quarter there is $20 interest, again, on the initial balance of $1,000, plus another 40¢ interest on the unpaid $20 of interest earned in the first quarter.

Interest for the third quarter of the 9-month period will be based on a balance of $1,040.40, which is the original balance plus the interest accumulated in the first two quarters. Therefore, interest for the third quarter is 2% of $1,040.40, or $20.81. The total interest for the 9 months (three quarters) will be $20.00 + $20.40 + $20.81, or $61.21.

Notice that compound interest will amount to *more* than simple interest, if the interest period extends over more than one compounding term. We can show this with the same problem, this time assuming that simple interest is paid. In this case, the interest is $20 each quarter, for a total of only $60, compared to the $61.21 charged under compound interest. The reason is that, with simple interest, interest is calculated only on the original loan balance. Compound interest includes interest on earned but unpaid interest as well as on the original principal, so a larger amount becomes subject to interest once the first compounding term has passed.

In real estate problems, interest questions usually involve *mortgage loans* and *loan discounts*, or *points*.

MORTGAGE LOANS

Mortgage loans are like any other loans in that interest is charged for the use of someone else's money. Usually these loans require monthly payments, with part of the payment used to pay the interest due since the last payment and the remainder used to reduce the amount of the loan (the *principal*). Eventually, in this manner the loan will be fully paid off.

A very common question on this type of loan concerns the interest payable in any given month. This requires you to calculate the loan balance for that month before you can find the interest payment due. Here is an example:

> *Smith borrows $30,000 on a 30-year mortgage loan, payable at 9% interest per year. Payments are $241.55 per month. How much interest is to be charged in each of the first 3 months?*

The first step in the solution is to determine the *monthly* interest rate, since mortgage interest payments are made monthly. Therefore, we divide the annual rate of 9% by 12 and get an interest rate of ¾% or 0.75% per month.

Now we can find the interest payable in the first month, which is $0.0075 \times \$30,000.00 = \$225.00$. The total monthly payment is $241.55, so after the $225.00 interest is paid, there remains $241.55 - $225.00 = $16.55 to be used to reduce the loan. This means that the loan balance for the second month is $30,000.00 - $16.55 = $29,983.45.

Now we calculate interest for the second month: $0.0075 \times \$29,983.45 = \$224.88$. This means that in the second month $241.55 - $224.88 = $16.67 is used to reduce the loan, leaving a balance of $29,983.45 - $16.67 = $29,966.78 for the third month.

The third month's interest, then, will be $0.0075 \times \$29,966.78 = \$224.75$. We can tabulate these results as follows:

Month	Loan Balance	Loan Payment	Interest	Loan Payoff
1	$30,000.00	$241.55	$225.00	$16.55
2	29,983.45	241.55	224.88	16.67
3	29,966.78	241.55	224.75	16.80
4	29,949.98	. . . . . .	. . . . . .	. . . . . .

This kind of loan is called *self-amortizing, equal payment*. The monthly payments are equal. However, as the loan balance is reduced a little each month, the portion of the payment representing interest decreases monthly, while the portion going to reduce the loan increases.

In some loans, called *level principal payment loans*, the loan amount is reduced the *same* amount with each payment. This means that the payments themselves get smaller each time, as the interest due decreases because the loan balance is decreasing. Here is an example:

> *Smith borrows $24,000 for 10 years at an annual rate of interest of 12%. He pays it back in the level principal payment manner each month. What will be his payments for the first, fourth, and tenth months?*

The first thing we must do here is to calculate the amount of the monthly level principal payment. Since 10 years is 120 months, the monthly principal payment is $24,000 ÷ 120 = $200. The monthly interest rate is 12% ÷ 12 = 1%.

In the first month, the entire $24,000 is on loan, so the payment is the level $200 payment plus 1% of $24,000, which is another $240. Therefore, the first month's total payment is $200 + $240 = $440.

For the fourth month, Smith will owe the original balance of $24,000 *less* the $200 payments that were made for each of the first 3 months. That amount totals $600, so for the fourth month he owes $24,000 − $600 = $23,400. Then, 1% of $23,400 is $234; this added to the level payment of $200 gives a payment of $434 for the fourth month.

The payment for the tenth month is calculated in the same way. At that time, nine payments will have been made, so the loan will have been reduced by 9 × $200 = $1800, leaving a loan amount of $22,200. Since 1% of that amount is $222, the full payment for the tenth month will be $422.

LOAN DISCOUNTS

The purpose of loan discounts is briefly explained in Chapter 13 ("Mortgages and Finance"). A loan discount is very simple to calculate, since it is merely a given percentage of the loan amount. You should be aware of the terminology, though, since these discounts often are referred to as *points*. One discount point is the same as a charge of 1% of the loan amount. Therefore, a discount of three points (often just referred to as "three points") is 3% of the loan amount. Frequently, a problem involving discounts will require you first to determine the loan amount; this can trap the unwary examinee, who makes the mistake of calculating the discount based on the purchase price instead of the *loan amount*. Here is an example:

> *Murgatroyd bought a home costing $154,900. She got a 95% loan, on which there was a charge of 3¾ points. What was the discount in dollars and cents?*

First we calculate the loan amount, which is 95% of $154,900: 0.95 × $154,900 = $147,155.

Now we can calculate the discount, which is 3¾ points, or 3¾% of the loan amount: 0.0375 × $147,155 = $5,518.31.

Depreciation

Although the tax laws allow all sorts of complicated ways to calculate depreciation, the only one you have to worry about on licensing examinations is the simplest one, which is called *straight-line depreciation*. Straight-line depreciation assumes that the property depreciates an *equal* amount each year.

We will not argue here whether real estate does or does not, in fact, depreciate. Some does and some does not seem to. However, there are many reasons why one should be aware of the possibility of depreciation, not the least of which is that in the long run a real estate asset *will* wear out. The 50-year-old house that is being offered for ten times the original cost of construction also has a new roof, modernized heating and air-conditioning, new wiring, carpeting, kitchen installations, and plumbing. Nearly every visible surface has been repainted and remodeled.

When calculating depreciation, you must know the *useful life* of the property (sometimes referred to as *economic life*, or just plain *life*). Once you know this, you can easily calculate an annual *depreciation rate*: divide the useful life, in years, *into* 100% to get the percent rate of depreciation per year. For example:

> *10-year life: 100% ÷ 10 = 10% depreciation per year*
> *50-year life: 100% ÷ 50 = 2% depreciation per year*
> *35-year life: 100% ÷ 35 = 2.857% depreciation per year*

Once this has been done, most depreciation problems become only slightly elaborated versions of the standard three types of percentage *problems*. For example:

(a) *Madison owns a building for which he paid $550,000. If it has a total useful life of 30 years, what is its value after 5 years?*

(b) *Madison owns a building for which he paid $550,000. If it has a 40-year life, in how many years will it be worth $426,250?*

(c) *Madison owns a building worth $550,000. If it depreciates to $440,000 in 9 years, what is the total useful life?*

(d) *If a building depreciates at a 2½% per year, in how many years will it be worth 85% of its original value?*

Here is how the answer to each of these is found:

(a) Here you are asked to determine the value after 5 years, so you must determine how much the building depreciates each year. A 30-year life yields 3⅓% depreciation per year. Five years' depreciation, then, is 16⅔%. Therefore, in 5 years the building will be worth 83⅓% (100% − 16⅔%) of its original value: 0.8333 × $550,000 = $458,333.33, its value after 5 years.

(b) Here you want to know how long it takes for a certain depreciation to take place. A 40-year life is depreciation at 2½% per year. $426,250 is 77½% of $550,000 (426,250 ÷ 550,000). 100% − 77½% = 22½% total depreciation. At 2½% per year, that would take 9 years to accumulate (22.5 ÷ 2.5 = 9).

(c) Here you have to determine the useful life. $440,000 is 80% of $550,000 (440,000 ÷ 550,000 = 0.80). Therefore, the building depreciates 20% in 9 years, or 2.2222 . . . % per year. Divide this figure into 100% to get the total number of years required for the building to depreciate fully: 100 ÷ 2.2222 = 45. Thus, the useful life is 45 years.

(d) In this problem you don't have to calculate the depreciation rate, since it is given to you (2½% per year). If the building depreciates to 85% of its original value, it will have depreciated 15%. 15% ÷ 2½% = 6 years' worth of depreciation.

Profit and Loss

Calculation of profit and loss is another slightly different version of the three types of percentage problems. The important thing to remember is that profit and loss are always expressed as percentages of *cost*. Cost is the original price that the seller paid for the property when he acquired it. If *his* selling price is higher than cost, he has a profit. If it is lower, he has a loss.

The *dollar value* of profit or loss is the difference between purchase price and sale price.

The *rate* of profit or loss is the percentage relationship between the purchase price and the dollar value of profit or loss.

Here are some examples:

(a) *Martin bought her house for $449,500 and sold it later for $559,000. What was her rate of profit?*

(b) *Samson Wrecking Company mistakenly tore down part of Habib's home. Before the home was damaged, it was worth $300,000. Afterward, it had sustained 28% loss. What was its value after the wrecking?*

(c) *Harrison sold his home for $420,500 and made a 45% profit. What had he paid for the home?*

Here are the solutions:

(a) First, determine the dollar value of the profit: $559,000 − $449,500 = $109,500. Then determine what percentage proportion the dollar value is of the *purchase price* ($109,500 is ? percent of $449,500). 109,500 ÷ 449,500 = 24.36%.

(b) The loss was 28% of the original value of $300,000: 0.28 × $300,000 = $84,000. $300,000 − $84,000 = $216,000 value afterward.

(c) The original price of the house, plus 45%, is now equal to $420,500. Therefore, $420,500 is 145% of the original price of the home (? is 145% of $420,500). 420,500 ÷ 1.45 = $290,000. As a check, Harrison's profit is $130,500 ($420,500 less $290,000), which is 45% of $290,000 ($130,500 ÷ $290,000 = 0.45).

Return on Investment

The concept of return on investment is very similar to the concept of interest payments on loans. In the investment case, an investor spends money to buy an income-producing asset. She wants to make money from it; otherwise there is no point to the investment. She calculates her return and expresses it as a *percentage* of her investment being paid back to her each year. In a sense, she can be thought of as "lending" her money to the investment and having it "pay" her "interest" on her money.

It is possible to make deceptively simple-sounding investment questions so complicated that they can best be answered with the aid of a computer or a very sophisticated calculator. This fact needn't concern you, though. On licensing examinations the questions are kept simple enough that they can be calculated quickly by hand or, in states that allow their use, with simple, hand-held calculators that do no more than add, subtract, multiply, and divide.

If you think of return on investment problems as similar to interest problems, you should have no trouble with them. Here are some examples:

(a) *Bennett owns a building that cost him $650,000. How much income should the building produce annually to give Bennett a 15% return on his money?*

(b) *Maximilian paid $435,000 for a triplex apartment building. All units are identical. He lives in one unit and rents the other two. The total net income per month from rental is $3,550. What annual rate of return is he getting on his investment in the rental units?*

(c) *What monthly income should a building costing $385,000 produce if the annual return is to be 15%?*

Here are the solutions:

(a) The building should produce an income each year of 15% of $650,000: 0.15 × $650,000 = $97,500.

(b) This problem involves a lot of steps, but they are simple ones. First we must determine how much of the purchase price should be allocated to the two rental units. Since all three are the same, one-third of the purchase price ought to be allocated to each. This means that two-thirds of the price should be allocated to the two rental units: ⅔ × $435,000 = $290,000. Next we must determine the annual dollar amount of income received. The monthly income is $3,550, so the annual income is $3,550 × 12 = $42,600. Now we must find out what percent $42,600 is of $290,000: $42,600 ÷ $290,000 = 14.69%, the annual rate of return.

(c) Here we must calculate a monthly dollar income. The annual income must be 15% of $385,000, or $57,750. The monthly income is one-twelfth of that amount, or $4,812.50.

Math Problem Set B

Here are some practice problems involving percents. The questions cover all of the kinds we have just discussed, including common variations. Answers are given at the end of the chapter.

1. Peters sold her home for $248,500 and made a 42% profit. How much did she pay for the home?

2. Rodriguez's home cost $499,000. He financed the purchase with a 90% loan. The discount was three points. How much was the dollar amount of discount?

3. Going back to problem 2, assume that the interest rate on Rodriguez's loan was 7% per year and that the loan was for a 25-year period. How much interest would be payable with the first payment?

4. Talbot sold her building for $484,437.50. She had owned it for 7 years and had originally paid $575,000 for it. What was the annual rate of depreciation?

5. Sam Zealous, the real estate agent, sold I. M. Sellar's home for him. After paying Zealous a commission of 7½% of the sale price, Sellar ended up with $184,907.50. What was the sale price?

6. Winken, Blinken, and Nod are partners in the ownership of a certain property worth $440,000. The property produces a 21% return per year, in income collected monthly. Winken owns a 37% share of the building. How much is Winken's monthly income from the property?

7. In problem 6, Blinken owns a 22% share and Nod owns the rest. If $198,000 originally was paid for the property, what would be the dollar value of Nod's share of the profit if the partners were to sell the property today for its current value? What rate of profit does this represent?

8. Bernie, a real estate salesman for Gettum Realty, Inc., gets 52½% of all real estate commissions he brings into the firm. Bernie just sold Fred's home for $447,500. Fred had listed the home with a different broker in the same Multilist group as Bernie's broker. According to the Multilist rules, the listing broker received 40% of the commission, and the selling broker received the rest after a fee of 3% of the commission was paid to the Multilist group to cover its expenses. How much (dollar amount) of the 6½% commission on this sale was paid to Bernie?

9. Mr. Selkirk borrowed $5,000 to install new kitchen appliances in his home. The loan was for 1 year, with no payments to principal to be made until the loan term was past. The interest rate was 10½% per year, with the interest payable quarterly. How much was the quarterly interest payment? If the interest had been allowed to compound quarterly, how much *extra* interest would Mr. Selkirk have had to pay in excess of simple quarterly interest?

10. Ms. Jessup just sold for $625,000 a building she bought 8 years earlier for $930,000. What was the percentage rate of her loss? What was the annual rate of depreciation she sustained?

PRORATION

Proration, which is a necessary input into the calculation of closing statements, normally will come up only on examinations for broker's licenses. If you are seeking a brokerage license, you should cover the material in this section. Appraisal or salesperson candidates can skip it.

Two kinds of prorating methods are in common use. The most widely used one employs the *statutory year*; the other, the *actual year*.

The function of proration is to distribute equitably the costs of a particular charge that two or more people must share. In real estate, these costs usually are created by transactions associated with a title closing, in which allocations are made for charges that apply over the period in which both buyer and seller own the property. The most commonly prorated items are these:

- Real property taxes
- Property insurance
- Interest on assumed mortgage loans
- Prepaid or later-paid rentals

Property taxes are usually paid by the year; when a transaction occurs in the middle of a year, part of that year's property tax usually will be deemed, by the parties to the sale, to be payable by each one. Note that the government that collects the taxes does *not* prorate them; it collects the *full* amount of the taxes from whoever owns the property at the time the taxes are due. If, when the sale occurs, the year's property taxes have *already* been paid, the seller will have paid them and the buyer must recompense the seller for the portion of the taxes that apply to the part of the year when the buyer will own the property. On the other hand, if the taxes are due *after* the close of the sale, the buyer will have to pay them in full, for the entire year, when they come due. At the closing the seller pays the buyer for the share that applies during the period of the tax year when the seller owned the property.

Insurance usually is paid in advance. Often insurance policies are multiyear policies, although the premiums generally are payable annually. On licensing examinations, however, problems that involve closing often assume that the entire multiyear premium was paid at once when the policy was purchased; this is a device to see whether examinees read the questions completely. Since insurance usually is paid in advance, the buyer, if he assumes the existing insurance policy, recompenses the seller for the prepaid unused portion of the policy that the buyer gets from her.

When the buyer assumes the seller's mortgage loan, and the closing date is not the day after the loan payment is due and paid, the month's interest must be prorated between buyer and seller. Loan payments are due at the end of the monthly payment periods. When the next payment is due, the buyer will have to pay it in full, including the interest for an entire month during which he actually owned the property only part of the time. Therefore, the seller will have to pay the buyer for her share of the mortgage interest.

Rents work the other way, since they are payments *to* the owner rather than *by* the owner. Rent usually is paid in advance, but it is possible to have a situation where rent is paid at the *end* of the month or lease period. If rent is paid in advance, the seller will have been paid a full month's rent for the month in which the closing occurs; she must pay the buyer his prorated share of that month's rent already received. If the rent is paid at the end of the month, the buyer will get a full month's rent covering the month of sale, and he must recompense the seller for the period during which she owned the property. Because of these two types of situations examinees must read rent questions carefully.

Computing Prorations

To compute prorations an examinee must know three things:

1. How much—in money—is the item to be prorated?
2. To whom is payment to be made?
3. How much time is involved?

The discussion above covers the question of who pays whom what charges, but in summary we can state two easily remembered rules:

1. If the item was paid *before* closing, the buyer recompenses the seller.
2. If the item will be paid *after* closing, the seller recompenses the buyer.

These rules are fair because the seller had to pay all items due before closing, and the buyer will have to pay everything that comes due after closing.

Calculation of the amount of money due in the payment will vary, depending on the complexity of the problem. Sometimes the amount is specified exactly; other times it will have to be calculated. It is quite popular in licensing examinations to require the examinee to calculate the property tax bill before he can begin to prorate it (see Chapter 16). Usually the insurance premium and rentals will be given, since it is difficult to incorporate a sensible calculation method for them into a problem. Proration of the interest on assumed mortgages is another favorite candidate for calculation.

Calculation of the proration itself includes apportioning the time involved among the parties. Rent and interest usually are apportioned over 1 month, taxes over 1 year, and insurance over 1 or more years.

To prorate correctly, you must have two important pieces of information:

1. Who (buyer or seller) is supposed to "have" the day of closing?
2. Which calculation year (statutory or calendar) is being used?

You must be given this information somewhere in the examination. If you can't find it, ask one of the examination supervisors.

THE CLOSING DAY

The day of closing can be counted either as the buyer's first day or as the seller's last day. Which it is to be usually reflects local custom, so we can't state a general rule (although in the East and the South, the closing day most often is considered the seller's, while it tends to be the buyer's in the West).

THE STATUTORY YEAR

Prorating items over a full year can involve very messy calculations, since everything has to be divided by 365 (or 366), the number of days in a year. Many banks and other financial institutions therefore have substituted the 360-day "statutory year" as a means of simplifying calculation. This system assumes the year to be made up of twelve 30-day months. Numbers such as 360 and 30, while large, can be divided easily by many other numbers, so that calculations involving them are less cumbersome.

For items paid monthly, such as interest and rent, the statutory year rarely is used, since its application can create visible distortion in 31-day months and, especially, in February. However, spread over a year or more, the error introduced with the statutory year becomes very small, so it is sometimes used for calculation of prorated taxes and insurance.

To prorate an item using the statutory year, first find the payment for the full period. Next, divide this payment by the number of months in the period to get the monthly cost, and divide the monthly cost by 30 to find the daily cost. After determining who pays whom, and for what length of time, you can calculate the prorated payment.

Using the statutory year was helpful when calculations were made by hand or with adding machines; now that calculators and computers are in common use, dividing by 365 (or 366) instead of 360 isn't such a big deal. As a result, the recent trend has been to use the actual year instead of the statutory year.

THE ACTUAL YEAR

If using the statutory year is forbidden, the actual year must be used. In this case, you need to calculate how many days of the period must be paid for. You then multiply this sum by the *daily* cost of the item to get the prorated payment. The difficulty comes in the fact that to get the daily rate you must divide the annual rate by 365, or 366 in leap years. Further, it often is confusing to try to count days elapsed in a significant part of a year, especially when dealing with odd beginning and ending dates. To try to figure how many days elapse between January 1 and July 26 of a given year is bad enough; to calculate the number of days that elapsed from, say, October 23 of one year to March 14 of the following year is even worse. If you must use the actual year, you have no alternative; you need to remember the number of days in each month and whether or not you're dealing with a leap year. Be sure to keep your calculator in good working order, and to be familiar with its use, to help you make actual-year computations.

ROUNDING IN PRORATION

One very important warning is necessary here. When you are calculating prorations, always carry your intermediate results (i.e., daily and monthly charges) to *at least two decimal places beyond the pennies*. Do *not* round to even cents until you have arrived at your *final* answer, because when you round you introduce a tiny error. This is acceptable with respect to your final answer, but intermediate answers will later be operated on, including multiplication by fairly large numbers. Each time a rounded number is multiplied, the rounding error is multiplied also! To prevent such errors from affecting your final result, always carry intermediate steps to at least two extra decimal places beyond what your final answer will have.

Proration Examples

Here is an example of proration for each of the four commonly prorated items: rent, interest, taxes, insurance.

RENT

Rent usually is paid in advance.

> *The closing date is May 19, 2014, and rent is payable for the calendar month on the first of each month. Who pays whom what in the proration of rent of $795 per month?*

Since the seller received the May rent payment on May 1, he should pay the buyer the portion of rent covering the part of the month *after* the closing date. May has 31 days; the closing date is May 19. Therefore, the buyer will own the property for $31 - 19 = 12$ days during May. The daily rent for May is $\frac{1}{31}$ of the monthly rent, since there are 31 days: $795.00 \div 31 = 25.6452 (remember to carry to two extra decimal places). The buyer's share of the rent, then, is $12 \times $25.6452 = 307.7424, which rounds to $304.74. (Note that if we had rounded the daily rental to $25.65 and then multiplied by the 12 days, the result would have been $307.80, or 5¢ too much.)

INTEREST

Interest is paid after it has accrued. Normally, the interest period ends the day *before* a payment is due—that is, a payment due on the first of the month covers the preceding month; one due on the 18th of the month covers the period from the 18th of the preceding month through the 17th of the current one.

The closing date is September 22, 2014. Interest is payable, with the payment on the 16th of the month. The loan amount as of September 16, 2014, is $448,100. The interest rate is 6¼% per year. If the loan is assumed, who pays whom what for prorated interest?

We have to calculate the monthly interest due and determine how much of that amount is paid by whom. First, the dollar amount of interest—this is $\frac{1}{12}$ of 6¼% of the loan balance of $448,100: $\frac{1}{12} \times 0.0625 \times \$448,100 = \$2,333.85$. Note that we rounded off the monthly interest, because the lender does that, too, each month.

The period involved here is 30 days, since September has that length. The seller will have to pay the buyer for all of the interest between September 16 and September 22, since on October 16 the buyer is going to have to pay the full month's interest. The seller will own the property for 7 days of that time. (At a glance, this appears incorrect since $22 - 16 = 6$. However, the seller owns the property on both the 16th and the 22nd, so we must add a day. Another way is to count the days on our fingers, starting with the 16th and ending with the 22nd.)

Now we must determine the daily interest charge, which is $\$2,333.85 \div 30 = \$77.7950$. We multiply this by 7 to get the seller's share for 7 days: $\$77.7950 \times 7 = \$544.565$, which rounds to $544.57.

TAXES

Taxes are usually assessed for a full year, so we would use the statutory year for calculation, if permitted.

The closing date is April 27, 2014. Taxes are $1,188.54 per year. The tax year is March 1 to February 28 (or 29) of the following year. Who pays whom how much in prorated taxes? Use both the statutory and the actual year, assuming (a) that taxes are paid on June 1 and (b) that taxes are paid on March 15 of the tax year.

This sample problem is probably more complex than any you will encounter on a licensing examination, but it demonstrates all the possibilities.

In situation (a) the seller pays his share to the buyer, since the taxes are due after the closing date and so must be paid by the buyer. In situation (b) the buyer pays the seller her share, because the taxes for the full tax year were paid by the seller before the closing date.

Statutory Year Calculations. The closing date is April 27, 2014, and the tax year begins March 1, 2014. Therefore the seller owns the property for 1 month and 27 days:

Note that we did not use April 27, the closing date, in this calculation, because we consider the closing date as belonging to the seller. April 28, then, is the first day that the seller does *not* own the property, and so we must count from that day.

The seller's share is for 1 month and 27 days. The total tax payment is $1,188.54 per year. Dividing by 12 yields a monthly tax charge of $99.0450. Dividing this amount by 30 yields a daily tax charge of $3.3015.

1 month @ $99.0450	=	$99.0450
+ 27 days @ $3.3015	=	+ 89.1405
Total seller's charge		$188.1855 = $188.19

The seller's share is $188.19, so the buyer's share is the rest, or $1,188.54 − $188.19 = $1,000.35.

In situation (a), then, the seller pays the buyer $188.19.

In situation (b) the buyer pays the seller $1,000.35.

Actual Year Calculations. When calculating using the actual year, we reduce everything to days. The year has 365 days,* so, using the same problem, the daily tax charge is $1,188.54 ÷ 365 = $3.25627. The seller owns the property for a total of 58 days: 31 days of March and 27 days of April of the tax year. Therefore the seller's share is 58 × $3.25627 = $188.8654 = $188.87. The buyer's share would be $1,188.54 − $188.87 = $999.67.

In situation (a), taxes are paid on June 1 and the seller pays the buyer $188.87.

In situation (b), taxes are paid on March 15 and the buyer pays the seller $999.67.

Note two things about this calculation. First, the results are 68¢ different from those obtained with the statutory year method; this discrepancy occurs because of the different calculation technique. Second, when the daily charge was calculated, it was carried to *three* extra decimal places. In the actual year calculation, we might have to multiply by a number as large as 365, and the rounding error would be multiplied by that much. Carrying to three extra decimal places reduces this error.

INSURANCE

> *A 3-year insurance policy, dated October 22, 2012, is assumed on the closing date of August 11, 2014. The full 3-year premium of $559.75 was paid at the time the policy was bought. Who pays whom what if this policy is prorated?*

First we calculate the monthly insurance charge, which is $\frac{1}{36}$ (3 years, remember) of the premium of $559.75: $559.75 ÷ 36 = $15.5486. The daily charge is $\frac{1}{30}$ of that amount: $15.5486 ÷ 30 = $0.5183.

Now we must calculate how long the buyer will use the policy. If the policy is dated October 22, 2012, then it expires on October 21 (at midnight) of 2015.

The buyer will own the policy for 1 year, 2 months, and 10 days. He will pay the seller the prorated share, since the seller paid for the full 3 years when she bought the policy. (Now we just go ahead and figure 1 year and 2 months to be 14 months, to save the problem of calculating the annual premium.)

14 months @ $15.5486	=	$217.6804
10 days @ $0.5183	=	+ 5.1830
Total payable to seller		$222.8634 = $222.86

Calculating insurance according to the actual year can be cumbersome. To do this we ought to calculate first the annual premium, which is $\frac{1}{3}$ of $559.75 = $186.58333. The daily premium charge is this amount divided by 365: $186.58333 ÷ 365 = $0.51119. Note that once again we are carrying actual year calculations to an extra *three* decimal places.

---

*Except leap years, which have 366 days.

Math Problem Set C

Here are some proration problems for you to practice with. Answers are given at the end of the chapter.

1. The closing date is June 26, 2014. Taxes are collected on a calendar-year basis and are payable on June 1 of each year. Taxes for the year are $3,899.50. A one-year insurance policy, dated May 2, 2014, is to be assumed by the buyer. A full one-year premium of $1,444.85 was paid when the policy was issued. A mortgage loan with a balance of $288,230.11, as of June 1, 2014, will be assumed. It has an interest rate of 5¼% per year; payments are made on the first of the month. Part of the property is rented, with rent of $550 per month payable in advance on the first of the month. Use the statutory year. Who pays whom what at closing?

2. The closing date is December 15, 2013. Taxes are $982, and cover the period from May 1, 2009, to April 30, 2014; they are not due and payable until the last day of the tax year. An insurance policy of 1 year, dated March 19, 2014, and costing $360, is to be assumed. The property is not rented, and the loan is not to be assumed. Use the *actual* year. Who pays whom what?

3. Use the statutory year for insurance and taxes. The closing date is April 20, 2014. Taxes are $1,188 per year and are payable in four quarterly installments due March 31, June 30, September 30, and December 31 of each year. Quarterly tax payments are equal. An insurance policy costing $1,046.55 for 5 years, dated July 16, 2011, is to be assumed. The property is not rented. Who pays whom what?

4. The closing date is September 25; use the statutory year. In this area, two property taxes are paid. A $555.10 *city* tax must be paid by August 15, while a $303.25 *county* tax must be paid by October 15. Taxes cover the calendar year in which they are paid. What is the *net* amount payable? Who pays it to whom?

HINTS ON HANDLING MATHEMATICAL PROBLEMS ON EXAMINATIONS

Now that the different kinds of mathematics problems that appear on licensing examinations have been discussed, a few remarks dealing with the proper ways to approach them are in order.

You should remember that your objective on the examination is to get a passing grade. It is *not* necessary that you get 100%—only enough to pass. Mathematical problems can be terrible time-consumers; therefore you should devote your time at the outset to the problems that do not take a lot of time. Save the complicated ones for later, when you have had the chance to answer all the "easy" questions. Many examinees determinedly tackle the mathematics first or spend tremendous amounts of time on a very few problems, only to find later that they have to rush just to have a chance of getting to every question on the examination.

Try to determine just how long a problem will take *before* you tackle it. If it's going to take a lot of time, postpone it. Then when you get back to the time-consuming questions, do first those that are worth the most points. This may mean that you will turn in your examination without finishing one or two of the really long arithmetic problems. That doesn't mean you're stupid—it means you're smart. Instead of slaving away over the few points these unfinished problems represented, you used your time to build up a good score on the other parts of the examination that could be answered quickly. However, before turning in your test paper, try to mark an answer for *every* question, even math problems not attempted. You might just guess the right answer!

Another point to remember concerning arithmetic questions is that you may not need all the information given. After you read the question and determine just what you are being asked to do, begin to search for the information you need to provide the answer. Do not assume that just because some information is included you must find some way of using it in your solution. Fairly often extra information has been included just to sidetrack or confuse examinees whose arithmetic skills make them unsure of themselves.

Answers

Math Problem Set A

1. **$39.92** total cost

   The house is 55 ft. × 30 ft., or 170 ft. around. Since it is $8\frac{1}{2}$ ft. high, the total wall area is
   $$170 \text{ ft.} \times 8.5 \text{ ft.} = 1{,}445 \text{ sq. ft.}$$
   Now we must subtract for doors, the picture window, and other windows:
   - Doors: 3 ft. × 7.5 ft. = 22.5 sq. ft. each
   - Picture window: 12 ft. × 5 ft. = 60 sq. ft.
   - Windows: 2.5 ft. × 4 ft. = 10 sq. ft. each

   Unpainted area includes:

2 doors @ 2.5 sq. ft.	45 sq. ft.
Picture window	60 sq. ft.
6 windows @ 10 sq. ft.	60 sq. ft.
Total unpainted area	165 sq. ft.

   If 165 sq. ft. are unpainted, then 1280 sq. ft. (1,445 − 165) must be painted. A gallon of paint covers 320 sq. ft. Therefore, we will need:
   $$1{,}280 \text{ sq. ft.} \div 320 \text{ sq. ft.} = 4 \text{ gal. of paint @ } \$9.98 = \mathbf{\$39.92} \text{ total cost}$$

2. **352** lots

   76 acres is 3,310,560 sq. ft. (76 × 43,560). Subtracting 665,000 sq. ft. for roads, parks, etc., leaves 2,645,560 sq. ft. to be devoted to lots. Each lot must be 7500 sq. ft.
   $$2{,}645{,}560 \text{ sq. ft.} \div 7500 \text{ sq. ft.} = 352.74$$
   Therefore, Orsini can get no more than **352** lots out of the land.

3. **$1,389.20** total cost

The following diagram shows that the walk can be divided into two parts, each 43 ft. × 8 ft., and one part 65 ft. × 8 ft. These contain 344 + 344 + 520 = 1208 sq. ft. If 1 sq. ft. costs $1.15, then 1208 sq. ft. cost 1208 × $1.15 = **$1,389.20**.

4. **68.707** ft.

There are 9 sq. ft. in 1 sq. yd., so the lot contains 313 × 9 = 2,817 sq. ft. If the plot is rectangular, with frontage of 41 ft., the depth must be

$$2{,}817 \text{ sq. ft.} \div 41 \text{ ft.} = \textbf{68.707 ft.}$$

5. **$2,238.29** total value

The formula for the area of a triangle is $A = \frac{1}{2} \times B \times H$. The base ($B$) is 500 ft.; the height, or depth (H), is 650 ft.

$$500 \text{ ft.} \times 650 \text{ ft.} = 325{,}000 \text{ sq. ft.}$$
$$325{,}000 \text{ sq. ft.} \times \tfrac{1}{2} = 162{,}500 \text{ sq. ft.}$$
$$162{,}500 \text{ sq. ft.} \div 43{,}560 \text{ sq. ft.} = 3.73049 \text{ acres}$$

The land is valued at $600 per acre, so the total value is

$$\$600 \times 3.73049 \text{ acres} = \textbf{\$2,238.29}$$

6. **38** acres

One section (1 square mile) contains 640 acres. (You have to know that fact.) The NW¼ of the SE¼ of a section, then, contains

$$\tfrac{1}{4} \times \tfrac{1}{4} \times 640 = 40 \text{ acres}$$

Now we must determine how much of that 40-acre tract is taken up by the road. The road is 66 ft. wide. The 40-acre tract is ¼ mi. on a side (draw a diagram, if necessary, as shown); ¼ mi. is 1,320 ft. (or 5,280 ft. ÷ 4). Therefore, the road is 66 ft. × 1,320 ft., since it crosses the entire tract.

$$1{,}320 \text{ ft.} \times 66 \text{ ft.} = 87{,}120 \text{ sq. ft.}$$
$$87{,}120 \text{ sq. ft.} \div 43{,}560 \text{ sq. ft.} = 2 \text{ acres}$$

If the road contains 2 acres, then Huang ended up with the rest of the 40 acres, or **38** acres.

Math Problem Set B

1. **$175,000** purchase price
   If Peters sold her home for $248,500 and made a 42% profit, then $248,500 is 142% of her purchase price: $248,500 ÷ 1.42 = **$175,000** purchase price.

2. **$13,473** discount on loan
   First the amount of the loan, 90% of $499,000, is $449,100. The three-point discount is 3% of the loan amount: 0.03 × $449,100 = **$13,473** discount.

3. **$2,619.75** interest the first month
   The interest for the first month will be ¹⁄₁₂ of the annual interest on the full loan amount, since none of it will have been paid back during the first month of the loan. 0.07 × $449,100 = $31,437 annual interest. $31,437 ÷ 12 = **$2,619.75** interest the first month.

4. **2¼%** depreciation per year
   The building had depreciated a total of $575,000 − $484,437.50 = $90,562.50. Next we determine what percentage $90,562.50 is of $575,000: 90,562.50 ÷ 575,000 = 15¾%. This had occurred over 7 years, to give an annual rate of 15¾% ÷ 7 = **2¼%** depreciation per year.

5. **$199,900** sale price
   If Sellar paid a 7½% commission, his $184,907.50 represents 92½% of the sale price (100% − 7½% = 92½%). $184,907.50 is 92.5% of ?. $184,907.50 ÷ 0.925 = **$199,900** sale price.

6. **$2,849** is Winken's share of the monthly income.
   The building produces an annual income of 21% of $440,000: 0.21 × $440,000 = $92,400 annual income. $92,400 ÷ 12 = $7,700 monthly income to the building. Winken gets 37% of this: 0.37 × $7,700 = **$2,849** monthly income going to Winken.

7. **$99,220** Nod's share; **122.22**% rate of profit
   Since Winken owns 37% and Blinken owns 22%, Nod must own 41%. The total profit is $440,000 − $198,000 = $242,000. Nod's share is 41% of this: 0.41 × $242,000 = $99,220. Note that the *rate* of profit for the entire building is the same as the rate of profit for each of the three investors. This just means that each of them experienced the same growth in wealth as did the entire investment. If you are skeptical about this, work it out for each of the investors. For the entire building, the profit of $242,000 is 122.222. . . % of the original purchase price of $198,000. For Nod's share, we can calculate his original share as 41% of the $198,000 purchase price: 0.41 × $198,000 = $81,180. **$99,220** is **122.22**. . . % of $81,180 (99,220 ÷ 81,180).

8. **$8,704.40** paid to Bernie
   This problem is elaborate and time consuming, but not difficult. First we determine what percentage of the total commission goes to Bernie's broker. If the other broker gets 40% and the Multilist group gets 3%, that leaves 57% for Bernie's broker. Second, we figure the dollar amount of Bernie's broker's share of the commission. The total commission is 6½% of $447,500: 0.065 × $447,500 = $29,087.50. Bernie's broker gets 57% of that amount: 0.57 × $29,087.50 = $16,579.90. Bernie gets 52½% of that: 0.525 × $16,579.90= **$8,704.40**.

9. **$131.25** quarterly payment; **$21.04** more per year for compounding
   The simple interest due quarterly is ¼ of the annual interest, which is 10½% of $5,000, or 0.105 × $5,000 = $525. The quarterly simple interest is $525 ÷ 4 = $131.25.

   To find accumulated compound interest requires additional computation. We already know, from the calculations we just did, that the interest for the first quarter is $131.25. For the second quarter, then, we will have $5,000.00 + $131.25 = $5131.25 on which to calculate interest. Thus, ¼ × 0.105 × $5,131.25 = $134.70, the interest due for the *second* quarter. At this point, a total of $265.95 of unpaid interest has accrued ($131.25 + $134.70), so for the third quarter interest must be calculated on $5,265.95: ¼ × 0.105 × $5,265.95 = $138.23. At the end of the third quarter a total of $404.18 in unpaid interest has accrued ($265.95 + $138.23); therefore, for the fourth quarter interest will be calculated on $5,404.18. The interest for the fourth quarter is ¼ × 0.105 × $5,404.18 = $141.86, giving a total interest for the year of $546.04 ($404.18 + $141.86).

   Simple interest would have been 4 × **$131.25** = $525.00, so with compound interest a total of **$21.04** more is paid ($546.04 − $525).

10. **32.8%** loss; **4.1%** annual depreciation rate
    The total amount of the loss is $930,000 − $625,000 = $305,000. This is 32.8% of $930,000 ($305,000 ÷ $930,000 = 0.328). Profit and loss are calculated based on the *purchase* price originally paid. Since this depreciation occurred over an 8-year period, the annual depreciation rate is **32.8%** ÷ 8 = **4.1%**.

Math Problem Set C

1. Taxes: **$1,993.08** payable to seller
   Insurance: **$1,224.11** payable to seller
   Interest: **$1,092.87** payable to buyer
   Rent: **$73.33** payable to buyer
   Taxes: June 26 represents 5 months and 26 days that the seller will own the property during the year. He has already paid the taxes, since they were due June 1. Therefore, the buyer must pay the seller for the 6 months and 4 days that she will own the property. One month's taxes is $3,899.50 ÷ 12 = $324.9583. One day's taxes is $324.9583 ÷ 30 = $10.8319.

6 months @ $324.9583	=	$1,949.7498
4 days @ $10.8319	=	+ 43.3276
Total taxes payable to seller		$1,993.0774 = **$1,993.08** rounded

   Insurance: The policy expires May 1, 2015, so the buyer will own it for 10 months and 5 days. The monthly charge is $1,444.85 ÷ 12 = $120.4042. The daily charge is $120.4042 ÷ 30 = $4.0135.

10 months @ $120.4042	=	$1,204.0420
5 days @ $4.0135	=	+ 20.0675
Total insurance payable to seller:		$1,224.1095 = **$1,224.11** rounded

   Interest: The next payment is due July 1; it includes all the interest for June and will be paid by the buyer. The seller must therefore pay the buyer his share (26 days) of the June interest. One year's interest is $288,230.11 × 0.0525 = $15,132.0808. One month's interest is $15,132.0808 ÷ 12 = $1,261.0067. One day's interest is $1,261.0067 ÷ 30 = $42.0336. The seller owes the buyer 26 days of interest: 26 × $42.0336 = $1,092.8736, or **$1,092.87** rounded.

   Rent: The seller has been paid the $550 rent for the entire month of June; the buyer will own the property for 4 days in June, so the seller owes the buyer 4 days' worth of June rent. One day's rent proration is $550.00 ÷ 30 = $18.3333. Four days' worth of rent is 4 × $18.3333 = $73.3332, or **$73.33** rounded.

2. Taxes: **$616.10** payable to buyer
   Insurance: **$91.73** payable to seller
   Taxes: The taxes due cover from May 1 to December 15 for the seller, who has to pay his share to the buyer at closing, since the buyer will be liable for the entire year's tax bill at the end of the tax year. One day's tax charge is $982.00 ÷ 365 = $2.69041. The seller owns the property for 229 days (31 days each in May, July, August, and October; 30 days each in June, September, and November; and 15 days in December): 229 × $2.69041 = $616.10389 = **$616.10** payable to the buyer.
   Insurance: One day's insurance is $360 ÷ 365 = $0.98630. The buyer must pay the seller, since the seller paid the full premium when the policy was bought. The buyer will own the property from December 16 (the day after closing, for prorating purposes!) through the expiration of the policy on March 18. She will own it for 93 days (16 in December, 31 in January, 28 in February, 18 in March): 93 × $0.98630 = $91.7259 = **$91.73** payable to the seller.

3. Taxes: **$66** due to buyer
   Insurance: **$468.04** due to seller
   Taxes: Taxes here are paid quarterly and not annually. The closing date is April 20, so the March 31 payment already has been made. The only payment that must be prorated is the June 30 payment, since it covers a period in which both buyer and seller will own the property. Quarterly taxes are $1,188.00 ÷ 4 = $297.00. Monthly taxes are $297.00 ÷ 3 = $99.00. Daily taxes are $99.00 ÷ 30 = $3.30. These numbers all come out even, and no rounding will be necessary, so no extra decimal places are required.
   The seller will own the property for the 20 days of April during the second quarter. Therefore, he must pay the buyer 20 × $3.30 = **$66** for his share of the second quarter's taxes.
   Insurance: The 5-year policy cost $1,046.55; 1 year's insurance charge is $1,046.55 ÷ 5 = $209.31. One month's charge is $209.31 ÷ 12 = $17.4425. One day's charge is $17.4425 ÷ 30 = $0.5814. The policy expires July 15, 2012.
   The buyer will own the policy for 2 years, 2 months, and 25 days.

2 years @ $209.31	=	$418.62
2 months @ $17.4425	=	34.885
25 days @ $0.5814	= +	14.535
Total due seller for insurance		**$468.04**

4. Seller owes **$76.75** to buyer.
   In this problem, part of the tax is payable before the closing (by the seller) and part is payable after the closing (by the buyer). The seller owns the property for 8 months and 25 days of the year; the buyer owns it for 3 months and 5 days.
   City tax: This is payable by the buyer to the seller, since it was paid August 15. One month's tax is $555.10 ÷ 12 = $46.2583; one day's tax is $46.2583 ÷ 30 = $1.5419. The seller receives payment for 3 months and 5 days, or $146.48 from the buyer.
   County tax: This is payable by the seller to the buyer, since it is due *after* closing. The tax is $303.25 ÷ 12 = $25.2708 monthly; daily it is $25.2708 ÷ 30 = $0.8424. The seller owes a total of $223.23 to the buyer. Therefore, the seller owes a net of $223.23 − $146.48 = **$76.75** to the buyer.

CHAPTER 19

Closing Statements

Quite some time ago, it was common practice for real estate brokers (but not salespeople) to prepare the *closing statements* (also called *settlement statements, escrow statements*) for the transactions they and their salespeople effected. Therefore, it is traditional for several questions about closing statements to appear on *broker's* license examinations. Salesperson's examinations rarely have anything more than an occasional very simple question about closing statements. Nowadays, although licensing laws usually require brokers to make sure that a closing statement is provided to both buyer and seller, common practice is for someone other than the broker actually to prepare the statement. Often the lender providing a new mortgage loan for the buyer will do so; otherwise closings can be handled by *title companies, abstract companies,* or *escrow agents.*

PURPOSE OF CLOSING STATEMENTS

Closing statements provide an accounting of all funds involved in a real estate transaction. These statements show the amount that the buyer must pay and that the seller will receive from the transaction. Buyer and seller each are given an accounting of all items they must pay for or are credited with in the transaction. Brokers should prepare a reconciliation for each sale as well, to "button up" the statements.

DEBITS AND CREDITS

You need not be a bookkeeper to understand closing statements. Two columns are shown for the buyer and two for the seller. The two columns for each party are a debit column and a credit column. Totals of debit and credit columns for the same party must agree with each other.

Listed in the debit column are amounts that the party being considered, buyer or seller, is charged for. Listed in the credit column are those that the party will receive credit for. Cash is needed to balance.

As a simple example, assume the sale of a $520,000 house on July 30, 2014. Assume that the seller has already paid taxes of $6,859.24 for the entire 2014–2015 fiscal year ended June 30, 2015. The seller should be credited with the payment of $520,000 for the house and $6,306.68 of prepaid taxes for the remainder of the 2014 year (July 31, 2014, to June 30, 2015, during which time the buyer will own the house). Cash will be the offsetting debit.

The buyer will be debited for the house and paid-up taxes; cash is the offsetting credit. The closing statements will appear as follows:

| | Seller | | Buyer | |
	Debit	Credit	Debit	Credit
Real property		$520,000.00	$520,000.00	
Prepaid taxes		6,306.68	6,306.68	
Cash due from buyer				$526,306.68
Cash due to seller	$526,306.68			
Totals	$526,306.68	$526,306.68	$526,306.68	$526,306.68

(NOTE: If you cannot easily tell how the $6,306.68 of prorated property tax was calculated, you should review the "Proration" section in Chapter 18.)

Now let's consider the same transaction except that we will add two more items: A broker was involved, who earned a commission of $31,200 for making the sale; also, the buyer must pay $300 for a survey. The seller is to pay the broker's commission, so the seller's statement will show a debit of $31,200 for that. The buyer's statement will show a debit of $300 for the survey. The new closing statement will appear as follows:

	Seller		Buyer	
	Debit	Credit	Debit	Credit
Real property		$520,000.00	$520,000.00	
Prepaid taxes		6,306.68	6,306.68	
Sales commission	$31,200.00			
Cash due from buyer			300.00	$526,606.68
Cash due to seller	$495,106.68			
Totals	$526,306.68	$526,306.68	$526,606.68	$526,606.68

An item that affects only one party is shown as a debit or a credit *only on the statement of the party affected.* For example, if the sales commission is paid by the seller, the amount appears only on the seller's closing statement. If the buyer pays for a survey, it appears only as a debit to him.

Items of value that are sold, exchanged, or transferred between buyer and seller are shown in *opposite* columns of *both* parties. For example, the transferred property is shown as a credit to the seller *and* as a debit to the buyer. *Never should an item transferred, exchanged, or taken over be shown as a credit to both parties or as a debit to both.* If an item is transferred, sold, or exchanged, it is a debit to one party and a credit to the other.

Items usually *debited* (charged) to the buyer that are likely to be encountered include the following:

1. Purchase price of the real property
2. Purchase price of personal property
3. Deed-recording fees
4. Title examination
5. Title insurance
6. Hazard insurance
7. Survey
8. Appraisal fee (sometimes charged to seller)
9. Prepaid taxes
10. Loan assumption fees

Items that are likely to be *credited* to the buyer are:

1. Earnest money deposits
2. Proceeds of a loan he borrows
3. Assumption of a loan
4. Mortgage to the seller (purchase money)
5. Current taxes unpaid to closing
6. Tenant rents paid in advance (the seller collected these)
7. Balance due to close (paid by buyer to close)

Items likely to be *debited* to a seller are:

1. Sales commission
2. Current but unpaid taxes
3. Existing debt, whether assumed or to be paid off
4. Loan prepayment penalties
5. Discount points for buyer's VA or FHA loan. Discount points on *conventional* loans may be charged to buyer or to seller depending on contractual arrangements, custom in the area, local law, and so on.
6. Rent received in advance
7. Deed preparation

Items usually *credited* to a seller are:

1. Sales price of real property
2. Sales price of personal property
3. Prepaid taxes
4. Prepaid insurance (only if policy is assumed by buyer)
5. Escrow balance held by lender

Comprehensive Sample Problem

Abe Seller and Will Buyer are to close on Seller's house on January 30, 2015. The purchase price is $520,000. In addition, Buyer will pay $2,600 for appliances. Seller is to pay a commission of 6% of the sale price to XYZ Realty, Inc. County property taxes for calendar 2013 were $6,859.24 and were due on January 15, 2015. They were paid in full on that date by Mr. Seller. Since the house is in an unincorporated area, there is no city property tax.

The property was occupied by Ms. Happy Tenant, whose lease survives the sale. Her monthly rental is $3,100, paid on the first of each month. Rent is to be prorated to the date of closing.

Abe Seller owes $353,108.48 on a mortgage loan carrying an interest rate of 11¾%, which must be paid off at closing, plus interest for the entire month of January. He will also incur a 1% mortgage prepayment penalty. In addition, he has agreed to pay two discount points on Mr. Buyer's $490,000 VA mortgage loan.

Mr. Buyer will take over Mr. Seller's hazard insurance policy. The policy anniversary date is January 26, 2015. Mr. Seller has not yet paid the $2,920 premium, so Mr. Buyer will have to pay it at a later date.

At closing, Mr. Seller will be charged $500 for a termite inspection. Mr. Buyer will pay $300 for a survey, $500 for an appraisal and credit report, $264 for trust deed recording fees, and $48 to record the warranty deed. He will also be charged $2,680 for title insurance. Mr. Buyer will execute a trust deed in favor of Mr. Seller to secure a purchase money mortgage loan of $30,000 from Mr. Seller to Mr. Buyer. An $8,000 earnest money deposit from Mr. Buyer is being held in escrow by XYZ Realty, Inc., to be applied to the purchase price at closing.

Using Figure 19-1, Settlement Statement Worksheet, and the information given above, complete the closing statement. Figure 19-2, Completed Statement Worksheet, is a completed worksheet for this problem.

SETTLEMENT STATEMENT WORKSHEET

SETTLEMENT DATE:	BUYER'S STATEMENT		SELLER'S STATEMENT	
	DEBIT	CREDIT	DEBIT	CREDIT

Figure 19-1.   Settlement Statement Worksheet

SETTLEMENT STATEMENT WORKSHEET

SETTLEMENT DATE: 1/30/15	BUYER'S STATEMENT		SELLER'S STATEMENT	
	DEBIT	CREDIT	DEBIT	CREDIT
Purchase price	$520,000.00			$520,000.00
Earnest money		$8,000.00		
Trust deed		490,000.00		
Second trust deed		30,000.00	$30,000.00	
Prorated taxes	6,306.68			6,306.68
Prorated insurance		32.00	32.00	
Prorated rent		100.00	100.00	
Personal property purchase	2,600.00			2,600.00
Trust deed payoff			353,108.48	
Accrued mortgage interest			3,310.40	
Prepayment penalty			3,531.08	
Brokerage commission			31,200.00	
Discount points			9,800.00	
Termite inspection			500.00	
Deed recording	48.00			
Trust deed recording	264.00			
Survey	300.00			
Appraisal and credit report	500.00			
Title insurance	2,680.00			
Due from buyer/to seller		$4,566.68	$97,324.72	
	$532,698.68	$532,698.68	$528,906.68	$528,906.68

Figure 19-2.   Completed Settlement Statement Worksheet

BROKER'S RECONCILIATION

A broker's reconciliation worksheet is used to assure that all cash receipts and disbursements are accounted for properly. Like a closing statement, it has two columns, which can be described as "cash receipts" and "cash disbursements," respectively. The totals of the two columns must agree.

The reconciliation can be prepared using the following steps:

1. Go down the debit column of the purchaser's closing statement.

    A. List the items that the broker will pay from the purchaser's account in the "disbursements" column of the reconciliation.
    B. On a separate worksheet called "Loan Proceeds," list the items that the new mortgage lender will receive directly from the buyer or will withhold from the loan amount.

2. Go down the credit column of the buyer's closing statement.

    A. List on the broker's reconciliation, as a receipt, all cash paid by the buyer. Be sure to include the earnest money and cash paid at closing.
    B. On the top of the loan proceeds worksheet, list the amounts of mortgage money supplied at closing. Do not include assumed mortgages or those taken by the seller in partial payment.

3. Go down the debit column of the seller's closing statement.

    A. List any amounts to be paid by the broker on behalf of the seller as a "disbursement" on the broker's reconciliation.
    B. List the sales commission as a disbursement on the broker's reconciliation.
    C. On the loan proceeds worksheet, list the balance of loans to be paid off, accrued interest, prepayment penalties, and discount points charged to the seller.

4. Go down the credit column of the seller's closing statement. If the seller has paid cash and not received something from the buyer in return, it must be reconciled.

Items not selected in steps 1–4 include the property being sold and prorated charges. These items will not appear on the broker's reconciliation.

5. On the loan proceeds worksheet, sum all items, excluding the principal of the new loan, which was written on top of the previous page. Subtract the sum from the new loan principal to get the loan proceeds, and insert that amount as a receipt on the broker's reconciliation.
6. Total the receipts and the disbursements columns of the reconciliation. They should agree to complete the reconciliation.

Amounts shown in each column should be received/disbursed by the broker who has earned a commission.

LOAN PROCEEDS WORKSHEET

Amount borrowed on new loan		$490,000.00
Less: Discount points	$ 9,800.00	
Existing mortgage loan payoff	353,108.48	
Prepayment penalty	3,531.08	
Accrued interest payable	3,310.40	
	$369,749.96	–369,749.96
Loan proceeds		$120,250.04

Figure 19-3 shows a broker's cash reconciliation statement for the sample problem described in the preceding section.

Address: 1999 Somewhere Parkway   Closing Date: January 30, 2015
Mr. Abe Seller   Mr. Will Buyer
(Seller)   (Buyer)

	Receipts	Disbursements
From Buyer		
Earnest Money Deposited	8,000.00	
Check for Balance	4,566.68	
To Seller		
Check for Balance		92,324.72
Expenses		
Real Estate Commission		31,200.00
Preparation of Warranty Deed		
Preparation of Security Deed and Promissory Notes		
Title Fees		
Recording ~~Security Deed~~ Trust Deed		264.00
Recording Warranty Deed		48.00
Survey		300.00
Special Assessments		
First Trust Deed Proceeds	120,250.04*	
Appraisal and Credit Report		500.00
Termite Inspection		500.00
Title Insurance		2,680.00
	132,816.72	132,816.72

*See worksheet attached.

Figure 19-3.   Cash Reconciliation Statement

REAL ESTATE SETTLEMENT PROCEDURES ACT

The *Real Estate Settlement Procedures Act* (RESPA) covers most residential mortgage loans used to finance the purchase of one- to four-family properties. Included are a house, a condominium or cooperative apartment unit, a lot with a mobile home, and a lot on which a house will be built or a mobile home placed using the proceeds of a loan.

Purpose of RESPA

The purpose of RESPA is to provide potential borrowers with information concerning the settlement (closing) process so that they can shop intelligently for settlement services and make informed decisions. RESPA does not set the prices for services; its purpose is merely to provide information about settlement (closing) and costs.

Materials to Be Received Under RESPA

Under RESPA, a person who files a loan application for property covered must receive from the lending agency a pamphlet titled *Settlement Costs and You* and a good-faith estimate of the costs of settlement services. The lender has 3 business days after receiving a loan application to mail these materials. From that time until settlement, the loan applicant has an opportunity to shop for loan settlement services. One business day before settlement, if the loan applicant requests, he has the right to inspect a Uniform Settlement Statement (pages 332–333), which shows whatever figures are available at that time for settlement charges. At settlement the completed Uniform Settlement Statement is given to the borrower or his agent. When there is no actual settlement meeting, the Uniform Settlement Statement is mailed.

Uniform Settlement Statement (HUD-1 Form)

As discussed, the Uniform Settlement Statement (usually called the *HUD-1 Form*) is used in all RESPA-affected transactions (which include practically all residential transactions). The form is shown in Figure 19-4; it has been filled in using the same information as in the comprehensive sample problem described on pages 325–326. Note that one item not mentioned in the sample problem is flood insurance, and no dollar figure is given on the form. Instead the notation "P.O.C" ("paid outside closing") is used to show an item that may be important to the deal at hand, but was paid for or otherwise settled by the parties before closing.

SETTLEMENT COSTS AND YOU

The pamphlet *Settlement Costs and You* contains information concerning shopping for services, homebuyer's rights, and homebuyer's obligations. It also includes a sample Uniform Settlement Statement (HUD-1 Form) and describes specific settlement services. In addition, it provides information concerning a comparison of lender costs and describes reserve accounts and adjustments between buyer and seller.

REQUIREMENT TO REPORT TO THE INTERNAL REVENUE SERVICE

The Federal Tax Reform Act of 1986 created a new requirement that brokers and/or settlement agents report the details of some real estate transactions to the U.S. Internal Revenue Service. The primary responsibility lies with the settlement agent, the person who actually handles the closing.

If there is no settlement agent, the responsibility rests with the buyer's broker and the seller's broker, in that order. Not all transactions need be reported.

CHECKLIST FOR YOUR STATE'S PRACTICES

(1) Does your state have a deed transfer (documentary) tax?

☐ No

☐ Yes. How is it calculated? _____

Who pays it?   ☐ Buyer   ☐ Seller

(2) How are property taxes assessed in your state? (See checklist for Chapter 16, "Taxation and Assessment.") _____

_____

A. **Settlement Statement**

U.S. Department of Housing and Urban Development

OMB Approval No. 2502-0265 (expires 9/30/2006)

B. Type of Loan

1. ☐ FHA	2. ☐ FmHA	3. ☐ Conv. Unins.	6. File Number:	7. Loan Number:
4. ☒ VA	5. ☐ Conv. Ins.			8. Mortgage Insurance Case Number:

C. Note: This form is furnished to give you a statement of actual settlement costs. Amounts paid to and by the settlement agent are shown. Items marked "(p.o.c.)" were paid outside the closing; they are shown here for informational purposes and are not included in the totals.

D. Name & Address of Borrower:	E. Name & Address of Seller:	F. Name & Address of Lender:
WILL BUYER 404 W. MAIN SOMEWHERE	ABE SELLER 915 OAK ST. SOMEWHERE ELSE	W.E. GOTCHA 4821 BIGG BLDG. ANYPLACE

G. Property Location:	H. Settlement Agent: DUE ITRIGHT & CO.	
915 OAK ST.	Place of Settlement: 4372 BIGG BLDG. ANYPLACE	I. Settlement Date: 1-30-15

J. Summary of Borrower's Transaction		K. Summary of Seller's Transaction	
100. Gross Amount Due From Borrower		**400. Gross Amount Due To Seller**	
101. Contract sales price	520,000.00	401. Contract sales price	520,000.00
102. Personal property (APPLIANCES)	2,600.00	402. Personal property (APPLIANCES)	2,600.00
103. Settlement charges to borrower (line 1400)	3,792.00	403.	
104.		404.	
105.		405.	
Adjustments for items paid by seller in advance		Adjustments for items paid by seller in advance	
106. City/town taxes to		406. City/town taxes to	
107. County taxes to	6,306.68	407. County taxes to	6,306.68
108. Assessments to		408. Assessments to	
109.		409.	
110.		410.	
111.		411.	
112.		412.	
120. Gross Amount Due From Borrower	532,698.68	**420. Gross Amount Due To Seller**	528,906.68
200. Amounts Paid By Or In Behalf Of Borrower		**500. Reductions In Amount Due To Seller**	
201. Deposit or earnest money	8,000.00	501. Excess deposit (see instructions)	
202. Principal amount of new loan(s)	490,000.00	502. Settlement charges to seller (line 1400)	41,500.00
203. Existing loan(s) taken subject to		503. Existing loan(s) taken subject to	
204. PURCHASE MONEY MORTGAGE	30,000.00	504. Payoff of first mortgage loan	353,108.48
205.		505. Payoff of second mortgage loan	
206.		506. 1ST MORTGAGE INTEREST	3,310.42
207.		507. 1ST MORTGAGE PREPAY PENALTY	3,531.08
208.		508. PURCHASE MONEY MORTGAGE	30,000.00
209.		509.	
Adjustments for items unpaid by seller		Adjustments for items unpaid by seller	
210. City/town taxes to		510. City/town taxes to	
211. County taxes to		511. County taxes to	
212. Assessments to		512. Assessments to	
213. PRORATED INSURANCE	32.00	513. PRORATED INSURANCE	32.00
214. PRORATED RENT	100.00	514. PRORATED RENT	100.00
215.		515.	
216.		516.	
217.		517.	
218.		518.	
219.		519.	
220. Total Paid By/For Borrower	528,132.00	**520. Total Reduction Amount Due Seller**	431,581.96
300. Cash At Settlement From/To Borrower		**600. Cash At Settlement To/From Seller**	
301. Gross Amount due from borrower (line 120)	532,698.68	601. Gross amount due to seller (line 420)	528,906.68
302. Less amounts paid by/for borrower (line 220)	(528,132.00)	602. Less reductions in amt. due seller (line 520)	(431,581.96)
303. Cash ☒ From ☐ To Borrower	4,566.68	603. Cash ☒ To ☐ From Seller	97,324.72

Section 5 of the Real Estate Settlement Procedures Act (RESPA) requires the following: • HUD must develop a Special Information Booklet to help persons borrowing money to finance the purchase of residential real estate to better understand the nature and costs of real estate settlement services; • Each lender must provide the booklet to all applicants from whom it receives or for whom it prepares a written application to borrow money to finance the purchase of residential real estate; • Lenders must prepare and distribute with the Booklet a Good Faith Estimate of the settlement costs that the borrower is likely to incur in connection with the settlement. These disclosures are manadatory.

Section 4(a) of RESPA mandates that HUD develop and prescribe this standard form to be used at the time of loan settlement to provide full disclosure of all charges imposed upon the borrower and seller. These are third party disclosures that are designed to provide the borrower with pertinent information during the settlement process in order to be a better shopper.

The Public Reporting Burden for this collection of information is estimated to average one hour per response, including the time for reviewing instructions, searching existing data sources, gathering and maintaining the data needed, and completing and reviewing the collection of information.

This agency may not collect this information, and you are not required to complete this form, unless it displays a currently valid OMB control number.

The information requested does not lend itself to confidentiality.

Figure 19-4. HUD-1 Form

L. Settlement Charges

		Paid From Borrowers Funds at Settlement	Paid From Seller's Funds at Settlement
700. Total Sales/Broker's Commission based on price $ 520,000 @ 6 % = 31,200			
Division of Commission (line 700) as follows:			
701. $ 31,200 to XYZ REALTY			
702. $ to			
703. Commission paid at Settlement			31,200.00
704.			
800. Items Payable In Connection With Loan			
801. Loan Origination Fee %			
802. Loan Discount 2 %			9,800.00
803. Appraisal Fee to			
804. Credit Report 500 to MESSUP, INC.		500.00	
805. Lender's Inspection Fee			
806. Mortgage Insurance Application Fee to			
807. Assumption Fee			
808. HAZARD INSURANCE TO MILFORD INS. AGENCY			P.O.C.
809. FLOOD INSURANCE TO MILFORD INS. AGENCY			P.O.C.
810.			
811.			
900. Items Required By Lender To Be Paid In Advance			
901. Interest from to @$ /day			
902. Mortgage Insurance Premium for months to			
903. Hazard Insurance Premium for years to			
904. years to			
905.			
1000. Reserves Deposited With Lender			
1001. Hazard insurance months@$ per month			
1002. Mortgage insurance months@$ per month			
1003. City property taxes months@$ per month			
1004. County property taxes months@$ per month			
1005. Annual assessments months@$ per month			
1006. months@$ per month			
1007. months@$ per month			
1008. months@$ per month			
1100. Title Charges			
1101. Settlement or closing fee to			
1102. Abstract or title search to			
1103. Title examination to			
1104. Title insurance binder to			
1105. Document preparation to			
1106. Notary fees to			
1107. Attorney's fees to			
(includes above items numbers:)			
1108. Title insurance 2,680.00 to RJL TITLE CO.		2,680.00	
(includes above items numbers:)			
1109. Lender's coverage $			
1110. Owner's coverage $			
1111.			
1112.			
1113.			
1200. Government Recording and Transfer Charges			
1201. Recording fees: Deed $ 48.00 ; Mortgage $ 264.00 ; Releases $		312.00	
1202. City/county tax/stamps: Deed $; Mortgage $			
1203. State tax/stamps: Deed $; Mortgage $			
1204.			
1205.			
1300. Additional Settlement Charges			
1301. Survey $300 to JONES LAND SURVEY		300.00	
1302. Pest inspection to ABC TERMITE CO.			500.00
1303.			
1304.			
1305.			
1400. Total Settlement Charges (enter on lines 103, Section J and 502, Section K)		3,792.00	41,500.00

Figure 19-4. HUD-1 Form (*continued*)

Questions on Chapter 19

1. The purchase price is shown on the purchaser's closing statement as
   (A) a debit
   (B) a credit
   (C) both A and B
   (D) neither A nor B

2. The purchaser's earnest money held by a broker until closing is shown as
   (A) a debit to the purchaser
   (B) a credit to the seller
   (C) both A and B
   (D) neither A nor B

3. If property taxes for the current year have not yet been paid, they should be shown as
   (A) a credit to the buyer
   (B) a debit to the seller
   (C) both A and B
   (D) neither A nor B

4. A tenant paid rent at the beginning of the month. The sale of the property takes place during the middle of the month. The rent is prorated by
   (A) crediting the seller
   (B) debiting the buyer
   (C) both A and B
   (D) neither A nor B

5. The buyer has arranged new financing for property. Closing statements, with respect to the mortgage principal, should show
   (A) a credit to the buyer
   (B) a debit to the seller
   (C) both A and B
   (D) neither A nor B

6. The seller will pay a broker's commission. The commission is shown as
   (A) a credit to the seller
   (B) a debit to the seller
   (C) a debit to the buyer
   (D) A and C only

7. The buyer will take over the seller's insurance policy. The premium has been paid by the seller. The unexpired premium should be shown as
   (A) a credit to the seller
   (B) a debit to the buyer
   (C) both A and B
   (D) neither A nor B

8. The seller will accept a second mortgage from the buyer. The amount owed is shown as
   (A) a credit to the buyer
   (B) a debit to the seller
   (C) both A and B
   (D) neither A nor B

9. The sale price of personal property to be paid for at closing is shown as
   (A) a credit to the buyer
   (B) a debit to the seller
   (C) both A and B
   (D) neither A nor B

10. An existing mortgage on the property is to be assumed by the buyer. The closing statements show the mortgage principal as
    (A) a credit to the buyer
    (B) a debit to the seller
    (C) both A and B
    (D) neither A nor B

11. The buyer must pay $100 for a survey and credit report at closing. The settlement statements show
    (A) a debit to the buyer
    (B) a credit to the seller
    (C) both A and B
    (D) neither A nor B

12. The buyer has arranged a 4½% VA mortgage loan with two discount points. The discount points are shown as
    (A) a debit to the seller
    (B) a debit to the buyer
    (C) both A and B
    (D) neither A nor B

13. The buyer is to assume the seller's mortgage loan and must also maintain the tax and insurance escrow account held by the mortgage lender. The escrow account balance is shown as a
    (A) debit to the buyer
    (B) credit to the seller
    (C) both A and B
    (D) neither A nor B

14. The tenant has a $250 security deposit in an account to be taken over by the buyer. At closing, the security deposit should be shown as a
    (A) credit to the buyer (C) debit to the buyer
    (B) credit to the seller (D) B and C only

15. The seller incurs a prepayment penalty to pay off his mortgage loan. The penalty is shown as
    (A) a credit to the seller
    (B) a debit to the seller
    (C) a credit to the buyer
    (D) B and C only

16. The buyer, in connection with her new financing, must establish, at closing, a $500 escrow account for taxes and insurance. The escrow deposit is shown as
    (A) a debit to the buyer
    (B) a credit to the buyer
    (C) a credit to the seller
    (D) A and C only

17. The buyer will pay for deed recording and title insurance at closing. These items are shown as
    (A) a credit to the buyer
    (B) a debit to the buyer
    (C) a credit to the seller
    (D) A and C only

18. RESPA is intended to
    (A) regulate charges for settlement services
    (B) provide information about settlement services to home loan applicants
    (C) both A and B
    (D) neither A nor B

19. After a home loan application is filed, how many business days does a lender have to provide a good faith estimate of settlement charges?
    (A) 1
    (B) 2
    (C) 3
    (D) 15

20. Upon the loan applicant's request, he has the right to inspect
    (A) the seller's credit report
    (B) a final Uniform Settlement Statement
    (C) the broker's financial statement
    (D) a Uniform Settlement Statement with whatever figures are available

21. The title company checks records of the
    (A) county clerk
    (B) county recorder
    (C) federal court
    (D) all of the above

22. On a closing statement, which is a debit to the buyer?
    (A) purchase price
    (B) new mortgage loan
    (C) down payment cash
    (D) all of the above

23. Who performs a title search prior to a purchase?
    (A) buyer
    (B) seller
    (C) broker
    (D) title company and closing attorney

24. RESPA requires the lender to provide a good-faith estimate of closing costs within _____ business day(s) after loan application.
    (A) 1
    (B) 2
    (C) 3
    (D) 5

25. Under RESPA, a closing statement must be delivered
    (A) at closing
    (B) three days after closing
    (C) ten days after closing
    (D) when the buyer requests it

26. Which party is most likely to demand title insurance as a prerequisite to participating in the purchase?
    (A) buyer
    (B) seller
    (C) mortgage lender
    (D) attorney

27. The closing date in a purchase and sale
    agreement should be
    (A) filled in by the broker
    (B) within 30 days following the contract
    (C) set for a date after loan approval
    (D) clearly stated

28. At closing, which is expected to be prorated?
    (A) taxes
    (B) rental income
    (C) both A and B
    (D) neither A nor B

29. An escrow or settlement agent is often used for
    all of the following purposes *except*
    (A) to determine that outstanding and unpaid
        liens will be satisfied
    (B) to see that the purchase price is paid and
        all checks have cleared the bank
    (C) to handle the signing of documents and
        the closing
    (D) to prepare the tax documents

ANSWERS

1. A	7. C	13. C	19. C	25. A
2. D	8. C	14. A	20. D	26. C
3. C	9. D	15. B	21. D	27. D
4. D	10. C	16. A	22. A	28. C
5. A	11. A	17. B	23. D	29. D
6. B	12. A	18. B	24. C	

Fair Housing Law

The federal Fair Housing Act, Public Law 90–284, was enacted into law on April 11, 1968, as Title VIII of the Civil Rights Act of 1968.

PURPOSE

The purpose of the Fair Housing Act is expressed by Section 801 of the law, which states:

> It is the policy of the United States to provide, within constitutional limitations, for fair housing throughout the United States.

The following explanation of the need for fair housing is quoted directly from *Understanding Fair Housing*, U.S. Commission on Civil Rights.°

> *Housing is a key to improvement in a family's economic condition. Homeownership is one of the important ways in which Americans have traditionally acquired financial capital. Tax advantages, the accumulation of equity, and the increased value of real estate property enable homeowners to build economic assets. These assets can be used to educate one's children, to take advantage of business opportunities, to meet financial emergencies, and to provide for retirement. Nearly two of every three majority group families are homeowners, but less than two of every five nonwhite families own their homes. Consequently, the majority of nonwhite families are deprived of this advantage.*
>
> *Housing is essential to securing civil rights in other areas. Segregated residential patterns in metropolitan areas undermine efforts to assure equal opportunity in employment and education. While centers of employment have moved from the central cities to suburbs and outlying parts of metropolitan areas, minority group families remain confined to the central cities, and because they are confined, they are separated from employment opportunities. Despite a variety of laws against job discrimination, lack of access to housing in close proximity to available jobs is an effective barrier to equal employment.*
>
> *In addition, lack of equal housing opportunity decreases prospects for equal educational opportunity. The controversy over school busing is closely tied to the residential patterns of our cities and metropolitan areas. If schools in large urban centers are to be desegregated, transportation must be provided to convey children from segregated neighborhoods to integrated schools.*
>
> *Finally, if racial divisions are to be bridged, equal housing is an essential element. Our cities and metropolitan areas consist of separate societies increasingly hostile and distrustful of one another. Because minority and majority group families live apart, they are strangers to each other. By living as neighbors they would have an opportunity to learn to understand each other and to redeem the promise of America: that of "one Nation indivisible."*

°From *Understanding Fair Housing*, U.S. Commission on Civil Rights, Clearinghouse Publication 42, February 1973, p. 1.

PROPERTY COVERED

The federal Fair Housing Act of 1988 extended the property covered to all single or multi-family dwelling units, with the few exceptions noted below. A *dwelling* is defined as any building or structure designed as a residence to be occupied by one or more families; included are mobile-home parks, trailer courts, condominiums, cooperatives, and time-sharing units. Community associations and "adult-only" communities are clearly included unless they qualify under an exception.

Housing-for-the-elderly-only communities are built and operated for older persons: specifically, 100% of the units must be occupied by residents 62 years of age or older, or 80% of the units must be occupied by at least one person age 55 or older, *and* significant facilities and services designed for use by elderly persons must be in place. Special facilities include an accessible physical environment, communal dining facilities, social and recreational programs, the availability of emergency and other health care facilities, and other amenities intended for the elderly. The apartments must publish and adhere to policies that demonstrate an intent to serve persons aged 55 and over.

Apartment complexes with four or fewer units are exempt from the federal Fair Housing Act when the owner occupies at least one unit, and single-family homes sold or rented by an owner are exempt. However, the exemption applies only to persons owning no more than three properties at one time and is subject to other restrictions. In selling, the owner may not use a real estate salesperson or broker and may not print, publish, or otherwise make any reference to preference, limitation, or discrimination on the basis of race, color, religion, sex, national origin, familial status, or handicap.

DISCRIMINATION IN SALE OR RENTAL

Section 804 of the Fair Housing Act makes it unlawful to do any of the following:

(a) *To refuse to sell or rent after the making of a bona fide offer, or to refuse to negotiate for the sale or rental of, or otherwise make unavailable or deny, a dwelling to any person because of race, color, religion, sex, national origin, familial status, or handicap.*

(b) *To discriminate against any person in the terms, conditions, or privileges of sale or rental of a dwelling, or in the provision of services or facilities in connection therewith, because of race, color, religion, sex, national origin, familial status, or handicap.*

(c) *To make, print, or publish, or cause to be made, printed, or published any notice, statement, or advertisement, with respect to the sale or rental of a dwelling that indicates any preference, limitation, or discrimination based on race, color, religion, sex, national origin, familial status, or handicap, or an intention to make any such preference, limitation, or discrimination.*

(d) *To represent to any person because of race, color, religion, sex, national origin, familial status, or handicap that any dwelling is not available for inspection, sale, or rental when such dwelling is in fact so available.*

(e) *For profit, to induce or attempt to induce any person to sell or rent any dwelling by representations regarding the entry or prospective entry into the neighborhood of a person or persons of a particular race, color, religion, sex, national origin, familial status, or handicap.*

1988 AMENDMENTS

Amendments to the federal Fair Housing Act that became law in 1988 extended protection to familial status and handicap. Familial status refers to members of a family. The amendment prohibits discrimination against people with children, adults living with, or in the process of acquiring legal custody of, anyone under age 18, and pregnant women.

The physically and mentally handicapped are also covered. *Handicap* is defined as a mental or physical impairment that substantially limits a person's major life activities; included are persons with records of impairment. Current drug addicts, persons convicted of drug-related felonies, and transvestites are not protected as handicapped under the law, but alcoholics are covered.

The law also appears to prohibit restrictions that would prevent the handicapped from using necessary aids. For example, a person who requires a seeing-eye dog should be allowed to have one even if pets are otherwise prohibited in an apartment building. Similarly, that person would be allowed to take the dog through the hallway, even if dogs are generally prohibited in public parts of the building.

Today, nearly all dwelling units are subject to the Fair Housing Law.

DISCRIMINATION IN NEW CONSTRUCTION

Under the 1988 amendments, newly constructed multifamily facilities (four or more units) must be accessible to the handicapped. In buildings with elevators, the handicapped must have access to 100% of the units, but only ground-floor units of garden-type apartments are required to be accessible.

Common areas in buildings must be accessible to all handicapped persons, and doors and hallways must be wide enough to allow passage of wheelchairs.

New living units must be constructed in a way that allows access for the handicapped, including the appropriate location of light switches, plugs, and environmental controls. Bathroom walls must be reinforced to allow future installation of grab rails, and the occupant must be allowed to install them. Requirements for removal, when the handicapped person vacates, are uncertain.

DISCRIMINATION IN FINANCING

Section 805 of the Fair Housing Act applies to transactions after December 31, 1968. It states that it is unlawful for

> *any bank, building and loan association, insurance company or other corporation, association, firm or enterprise whose business consists in whole or in part in the making of commercial real estate loans, to deny a loan or other financial assistance to a person applying therefore for the purpose of purchasing, constructing, improving, repairing, or maintaining a dwelling, or to discriminate against him in the fixing of the amount, interest rate, duration, or other terms or conditions of such loan or other financial assistance, because of the race, color, religion, sex, or national origin of such person or of any person associated with him in connection with such loan or other financial assistance or the purposes of such loan or other financial assistance, or of the present or prospective owners, lessees, tenants, or occupants of the dwelling or dwellings in relation to which such loan or other financial assistance is to be made or given: Provided, that nothing contained in this section shall impair the scope or effectiveness of the exception contained in Section 803(b).*

Section 803(b) exempts a single-family house sale or lease by owner, if certain provisions are met. This exemption was described on page 338.

Federal law also prohibits lending institutions from *redlining*. Redlining is a practice whereby lenders designate certain areas as "too risky" and refuse to make loans on property in those areas. (The term *redlining* refers to outlining those areas in red on a map.) Before it was outlawed, redlining by lenders usually affected low-income areas and, particularly, areas whose populations were composed largely of minorities.

DISCRIMINATION IN BROKERAGE SERVICES

Section 806 of the Fair Housing Act states:

> *After December 31, 1968, it shall be unlawful to deny any person access to or membership or participation in any multiple-listing service, real estate brokers' organization or other service, organization, or facility relating to the business of selling or renting dwellings, or to discriminate against him in the terms or conditions of such access, membership, or participation, on account of race, color, religion, sex, national origin, familial status, or handicap.*

BLOCKBUSTING

Blockbusting, that is, the soliciting of homeowners by unscrupulous real estate agents, brokers, or speculators who feed upon fears of homeowners, is prohibited by the Fair Housing Act. Blockbusters attempt to buy properties at very low prices from whites in racially transitional neighborhoods and then broker or sell them to blacks at high prices. Some blockbusters deliberately incite panic and white flight to achieve their greedy, unlawful goal.

TWO SPECIFIC EXEMPTIONS

There are two specific, limited exemptions to the Fair Housing Laws. One exemption allows a religious organization to discriminate with respect to its noncommercial property. It does not, however, allow this exemption if the religion discriminates on the basis of race, color, sex, national origin, familial status, or handicap with respect to its membership. The other exemption allows private clubs that provide lodging as an incident to their main purpose to give preferential treatment to club members.

ENFORCEMENT BY THE FEDERAL GOVERNMENT

Any person who claims to have been injured by a discriminatory housing practice or who believes that he will be irrevocably injured by a discriminatory housing practice that is about to occur (hereafter "person aggrieved") may file a complaint with the Secretary of the Department of Housing and Urban Development (HUD). Complaints must be in writing, must state the facts, and must be filed within 1 year after the alleged discriminatory housing practice occurred. The Attorney General conducts all litigation in which the Secretary of HUD participates as a party pursuant to the Fair Housing Act.

ENFORCEMENT BY PRIVATE PERSONS

The rights granted to private persons by the Fair Housing Act may be enforced by civil action in appropriate U.S. district courts without regard to the amount in controversy, and in appropriate state or local courts of general jurisdiction. A civil action must be commenced within 1 year after the alleged discriminatory housing practice occurred.

Upon application by the plaintiff and in such circumstances as the court may deem just, a court of the United States in which a civil action under this section has been brought may appoint an attorney for the plaintiff and may, upon proper showing, authorize the commencement of a civil action without the payment of fees, costs, or security. A court of a state or subdivision thereof may do likewise to an extent not inconsistent with the law or procedures of the state or subdivision.

The court may grant as relief, as it deems appropriate, any permanent or temporary injunction, temporary restraining order, or other order, and may award to the plaintiff actual damages, injunctive or other equitable relief, and civil penalties up to $50,000 ($100,000 for repeating violators), together with court costs and reasonable attorney fees in the case of a prevailing plaintiff, provided that said plaintiff, in the opinion of the court, is not financially able to assume said attorney's fees.

PENALTY FOR INJURY, INTIMIDATION, DISCOURAGEMENT

Under Section 901 of the Civil Rights Act of 1968 (Title IX) whoever

A. injures or threatens to injure or interfere with any person because of his race, religion, color, sex, national origin, familial status, or handicap, and who is selling, leasing, occupying, financing, etc., dwelling, or

B. intimidates persons who deal with others in housing on account of race, religion, color, sex, national origin, familial status, or handicap, or

C. discourages others from dealing with others in housing on account of race, religion, color, sex, national origin, familial status, or handicap

shall be fined up to $1,000 or imprisoned for up to 1 year, or both. If bodily injury results, the penalty is a fine of $10,000 maximum or up to 10 years in prison, or both. If death results, the wrongdoer shall be imprisoned for any term of years or for life.

OTHER FAIR HOUSING LAWS

The Fair Housing Act was not the first law intended to prevent discriminatory practice in housing. The Supreme Court of the United States, in the 1917 *Buchanan* case, prohibited, on constitutional grounds, local governments from requiring residential segregation. This ruling is noteworthy because in 1896 the Supreme Court had established the doctrine that legally compelled segregation in such areas as public transportation and public education was constitutionally permissible. The Buchanan decision destroyed the doctrine as it applied to housing. In 1948, in *Shelley* v. *Kraemer*, the Supreme Court struck down as unconstitutional the legal enforcement of racially restrictive covenants.

The executive branch of the government took fair housing action for the first time in 1962, when President Kennedy issued an executive order on equal opportunity in housing. Although it represented a significant legal step forward, this executive order was limited. Its guarantee of nondiscrimination was restricted largely to housing provided through the insurance and guaranty programs administered by FHA and its sister agency, the Veterans Administration (VA), after the date of the order's issuance (November 20, 1962). Housing financed through conventional loans was not covered by the President's order, which also left hundreds of thousands of existing housing units receiving FHA and VA assistance immune from the nondiscrimination mandate. In fact, barely 1% of the nation's housing was covered by President Kennedy's executive order.

In 1964, Congress enacted Title VI of the Civil Rights Act of 1964, prohibiting discrimination in any program or activity receiving federal financial assistance. Among the principal programs affected by this law were low-rent public housing, a program directed to providing housing for the poor, and urban renewal. Like President Kennedy's executive order, Title VI excluded conventionally financed housing. It also excluded most FHA and VA housing that the executive order covered. Less than half of 1% of the nation's housing inventory was subject to the nondiscrimination requirement through Title VI.

In 1968, Congress enacted Title VIII of the Civil Rights Act of 1968, the federal Fair Housing Law. This law, which is the one described at the beginning of the chapter, prohibits discriminatory practices by all real estate brokers, builders, and mortgage lenders.

In June 1968, two months after enactment of Title VIII, the Supreme Court of the United States, in the landmark case of *Jones* v. *Mayer*, ruled that an 1866 civil rights law passed under the authority of the Thirteenth Amendment (which outlawed slavery) bars all racial discrimination in housing, private as well as public.

Today, over 90% of all U.S. housing is subject to the Fair Housing Law.

THE AMERICANS WITH DISABILITIES ACT

The Americans with Disabilities Act (ADA), passed in 1992, considerably broadens the scope to which society in general must accommodate persons with disabilities. Many provisions of the act address discrimination in employment and access to public services. However, some of the most pervasive problems facing disabled persons have necessarily been involved with real estate: buildings are the most "barrier-prone" part of the physical environment. Narrow doors and hallways, variations in floor levels that require the negotiation of stairs, built-in facilities too high for the wheelchair-bound—the list of problems goes on and on.

Most new construction that may serve the public in general (almost anything except single-family housing) must meet barrier-free standards. Also, existing businesses with 15 or more employees must eliminate physical barriers that prevent disabled workers or customers from "functioning in the marketplace"; this requirement obviously requires considerable "retrofitting" of existing real estate.

Questions on Chapter 20

1. The 1968 Fair Housing Act prohibits housing discrimination on the basis of
   (A) race and color
   (B) race, color, and religion
   (C) race, color, religion, and national origin
   (D) race, color, religion, national origin, sex, familial status, or handicap

2. The prohibitions of the 1968 Fair Housing Act apply to privately owned housing when
   (A) a broker or other person engaged in selling or renting dwellings is used
   (B) discriminatory advertising is used
   (C) both A and B
   (D) neither A nor B

3. The prohibitions of the 1968 Fair Housing Act apply to
   (A) multifamily dwellings of five or more units
   (B) multifamily dwellings of four or fewer units if the owner occupies one of the units
   (C) both A and B
   (D) neither A nor B

4. A single-family house privately owned by an individual owning fewer than three such houses may be sold or rented without being subject to the provisions of the Fair Housing Act unless
   (A) a broker is used
   (B) discriminatory advertising is used
   (C) both A and B
   (D) neither A nor B

5. The limiting of sale, rental, or occupancy of dwellings owned or operated by a religious organization for noncommercial purposes, provided that membership in said religion is not based on race, color, or national origin,
   (A) is prohibited by the Fair Housing Act
   (B) is prohibited by the Civil Rights Act
   (C) both A and B
   (D) neither A nor B

6. A single-family house privately owned by an individual owning fewer than three such houses may be sold or rented without being subject to the provisions of the Fair Housing Act if
   (A) no more than one such house is sold in any 2-year period
   (B) a broker is employed to sell the house
   (C) both A and B
   (D) neither A nor B

7. What are the broker's responsibilities under the 1968 Fair Housing Act?
   (A) to show all houses to all prospects
   (B) to treat all prospects equally
   (C) both A and B
   (D) neither A nor B

8. Complaints about discrimination may be brought
   (A) to the Secretary of Housing and Urban Development
   (B) directly to court
   (C) both A and B
   (D) neither A nor B

9. If a minority prospect asks to be shown homes in white neighborhoods, the broker
   (A) obliges and shows homes in white neighborhoods
   (B) responds and shows homes as requested
   (C) both A and B
   (D) neither A nor B

10. The 1968 federal Fair Housing Law states that it is illegal to discriminate against any person because of race, color, religion, national origin, sex, familial status, or handicap
    (A) in the sale, rental, or financing of housing or residential lots
    (B) in advertising the sale or rental of housing
    (C) both A and B
    (D) neither A nor B

11. The broker's obligation in complying with the requirements for equal opportunity in housing is
    (A) to replace white residents with minority homeowners
    (B) to avoid any acts that would make housing unavailable to someone on account of color
    (C) both A and B
    (D) neither A nor B

12. The Civil Rights Act of 1968
    (A) makes it illegal to intimidate, threaten, or interfere with a person buying, renting, or selling housing
    (B) provides criminal penalties and criminal prosecution if violence is threatened or used
    (C) both A and B
    (D) neither A nor B

13. Court action may be taken by an individual under the Fair Housing Act
    (A) only if a complaint is filed with HUD
    (B) if action is taken within 1 year of the alleged discriminatory act
    (C) if the alleged discriminatory act occurred on public property
    (D) if the alleged discriminatory act caused damage of at least $500

14. Which is exempt from the federal Fair Housing Act of 1968?
    (A) salesperson selling lots in a subdivision
    (B) salesperson renting apartments in a building with 10 units
    (C) owner renting vacant single-family unit
    (D) none of the above

15. If a landlord refuses to rent to a minority prospective tenant with a poor credit record,
    (A) federal fair housing laws are violated
    (B) the minority applicant should report this violation
    (C) there is no violation
    (D) the landlord may face a significant fine

16. Sullivan wants to rent an apartment but is confined to a wheelchair. At Sullivan's request, the landlord must
    (A) build a ramp at the landlord's expense
    (B) build a ramp at Sullivan's expense
    (C) do nothing
    (D) reduce the rent to Sullivan's affordability level

17. A seller asks his broker about the race of a potential buyer. The broker
    (A) must answer the question if a single agent
    (B) violates fair housing laws if he answers the question
    (C) may answer the question because of the Constitutional right to free speech
    (D) may tell the seller but no one else

18. Which Constitutional amendment provides support by banning racial discrimination?
    (A) Second
    (B) Third
    (C) Twelfth
    (D) Thirteenth

19. Broker Bob is showing houses to Joe Chen, who is of Chinese ancestry. Bob shows Joe houses in a neighborhood of predominantly Chinese-American residences because Bob thinks Joe would feel more at home there. This is
    (A) illegal steering under fair housing laws
    (B) superior and tactful service
    (C) done for Joe's benefit
    (D) effective sales technique

20. Where the dominant population base of an area consists of minorities,
    (A) brokers need not be concerned with fair housing laws
    (B) brokers must still observe fair housing laws
    (C) there are no reporting requirements
    (D) violation of fair housing laws is not possible

21. The Civil Rights Act of 1968 prohibits
    (A) integration
    (B) greenlining
    (C) discrimination in housing
    (D) school busing

22. Familial status refers to
    (A) families with two or more children
    (B) families with children under age 18
    (C) the earning capacity of the family
    (D) RESPA

23. Broker Barb is acting as a buyer's agent for Joe. Joe asks whether any people of a certain race live in a specific neighborhood. How should Barb respond?
    (A) She should advise Joe that, under fair housing laws, she cannot provide that information.
    (B) She should advise Joe of the race of all the neighbors she is aware of.
    (C) She should advise Joe that he should contact the demographic agency to obtain the information.
    (D) She should advise Joe to contact the school district to obtain the information.

24. A broker has contacted owners in a certain subdivision and advised them that several members of a particular race have bought homes in the area. The broker has offered to list properties at a reduced rate and encouraged the owners to sell quickly. This is
    (A) steering
    (B) profiling
    (C) blockbusting
    (D) scaring

25. Ellen owns a two-family house and lives in one side. She wants to advertise the other side as nonsmoking. Can she legally do so?
    (A) yes, because the right to smoke is not protected by law
    (B) yes, because she owns the house
    (C) no, because a property owner cannot advertise discriminatory practices
    (D) no, because smoking is perfectly legal

26. A tenant applicant confined to a wheelchair is interested in renting a patio home. A request is made to the landlord to allow the tenant to build an access ramp. Which of the following is true?
    (A) The tenant's application may be rejected.
    (B) The landlord must allow the tenant to make the modification at the tenant's expense.
    (C) The landlord is required to pay for modifications to the property to accommodate the access.
    (D) The landlord may collect an additional deposit to assure compliance.

27. No federal fair housing laws are violated if a landlord refuses to rent to
    (A) families with children
    (B) tenants of Indian descent
    (C) deaf persons
    (D) college students

28. The federal ban on discrimination based on familial status is intended to provide equal access to rentals for
    (A) unmarried couples under 25
    (B) people with children
    (C) single tenants
    (D) the elderly

29. The Civil Rights Act of 1866 prohibits
    (A) zoning
    (B) redlining
    (C) open housing
    (D) racial discrimination

30. A minority group is moving into an area immediately adjacent to an old subdivision. ABC Realty offers to list homes in the subdivision at a lower-than-usual commission rate if the owners list within 45 days. There is no mention of race, and the broker acts in good faith. Which of the following is true?
    (A) Such practice is not illegal.
    (B) Brokers cannot lower their standard rate of commission.
    (C) The broker's license can be revoked for this action.
    (D) This is blockbusting.

31. A couple of Greek ancestry looking for a house asks a real estate agent to show them houses in Greek neighborhoods. Which of the following is correct?
    (A) The agent must accommodate this request because the buyers requested it.
    (B) The agent should tell the buyers that he will show them houses in a number of different neighborhoods.
    (C) The agent should refuse to show any houses to the buyers.
    (D) The agent should agree, then show the buyers houses in other neighborhoods.

32. Advising people on which neighborhoods they would be happy in may be construed as an illegal activity called
    (A) steering
    (B) canvassing
    (C) redlining
    (D) blockbusting

33. "Whites only" is the advertisement for a house that's for sale. This is
    (A) legal if the house is owner-occupied
    (B) illegal unless a real estate agent is used
    (C) legal because it's a one-family house
    (D) illegal

34. The Aggie Oaks Apartments advertising states that families with children are welcome. The management has allocated a certain section of the complex for residents with children, and those tenants must pay an additional security deposit for each child under twelve. Is this discriminatory?
    (A) No, because families with children are welcome to the complex.
    (B) Yes, based on marital status.
    (C) Yes, based on familial status.
    (D) No, because children are not a named protected class.

35. Armando and Maria Rios agreed to sign a buyer's agreement with a real estate agent who showed them homes in predominantly Hispanic areas only. This is an example of
    (A) boycotting certain neighborhoods
    (B) thoughtful customer service
    (C) cultural sensitivity
    (D) steering

36. Agent Curt has been asked by his seller not to advertise in a Spanish-language newspaper. Curt and his office would not violate the law if
    (A) the paper does not serve the market area of his office
    (B) he doesn't like the paper's editorial positions on many issues
    (C) his seller directed him in writing
    (D) his office has never used the paper because of the high rates charged by the paper

ANSWERS

1. D	9. C	17. B	25. A	33. D
2. C	10. C	18. D	26. B	34. C
3. A	11. B	19. A	27. D	35. D
4. C	12. C	20. B	28. B	36. D
5. D	13. B	21. C	29. D	
6. A	14. C	22. B	30. A	
7. B	15. C	23. A	31. B	
8. C	16. B	24. C	32. A	

CHAPTER 21

Truth-in-Lending Law

Regulation Z of the Federal Reserve System, known as the Truth-in-Lending Act, became effective on July 1, 1969. Amendments established on April 1, 1981, became mandatory on April 1, 1982. The provisions affecting credit transactions in real estate are emphasized here, although the act covers other types of credit.

The purpose of Regulation Z is to let borrowers and consumers know the prevailing cost of credit so that they can compare costs among various credit sources and thus avoid the uninformed use of credit. Regulation Z also regulates the issuance of credit cards and sets maximum liability for their unauthorized use. In addition, it provides a procedure for resolving billing errors that occur in open end credit accounts. Regulation Z does not set maximum or minimum interest rates or require any charge for credit.

COVERAGE

Generally, Regulation Z applies to each individual or business that offers or extends credit when four conditions are met:

1. The credit is offered or extended to consumers.
2. The offering or extension of credit is done regularly (see definition of *creditor* below).
3. The credit is subject to a finance charge or is payable, pursuant to a written agreement, in more than four installments.
4. The credit is primarily for personal, family, or household purposes.

DEFINITION OF CREDITORS

Creditors are those who must comply with Regulation Z. A *creditor* is defined for this purpose as a person who arranges or extends credit more than 25 times a year (or more than 5 times in a year in the case of transactions secured by a dwelling).

The term *creditor* does not include a person who arranges seller financing of a dwelling or real property. However, a real estate broker may be a creditor in the following situations:

1. The broker acts as a loan broker to arrange for someone other than the seller to extend credit, provided that the extender of credit (the person to whom the obligation is initially payable) does not meet the *creditor* definition.
2. The broker extends credit, provided that the broker otherwise meets the *creditor* definition.

PENALTIES FOR VIOLATION OF REGULATION Z

A lender who fails to make disclosures as required under the Truth-in-Lending Act may be sued for actual damages plus twice the amount of the finance charge, as well as court costs and attorneys' fees. The finance charge portion of damages is subject to a minimum of $100 and a maximum of $1,000. If lenders are convicted in a criminal action for willfully or knowingly disobeying the act or the regulation, they may be fined up to $5,000, imprisoned for up to 1 year, or both.

EXEMPT TRANSACTIONS

The following transactions are exempt from the Truth-in-Lending Law:

1. Business, commercial, agricultural, or organizational credit.
2. Extension of credit to other than a natural person, including credit to government agencies.
3. Credit over $25,000 not secured by real property or a dwelling.
4. Extension of credit that involves public utility service.
5. Securities or commodities accounts.
6. Home-fuel budget plans.

ANNUAL PERCENTAGE RATE

Regulation Z takes ten printed pages to define *annual percentage rate (APR)*. Briefly summarized, APR means the true interest rate charged for the use of money.

FINANCE CHARGE

Definition

The *finance charge* is the cost of consumer credit as a dollar amount. It includes any charge payable directly or indirectly by the consumer, and imposed (directly or indirectly) by the creditor, as part of or a condition of the extension of credit. It does not include any charge of a type payable in a comparable cash transaction.

EXAMPLES

1. Interest, time-price differential, and any amount payable under an add-on or a discount system of additional charges.
2. Service, transaction, activity, and carrying charges, including any charge imposed on a checking or other transaction account to the extent that the charge exceeds the charge for a similar account without a credit feature.
3. Points, loan fees, assumption fees, finder's fees, and similar charges.
4. Appraisal, investigation, and credit report fees.
5. Premiums or other charges for any guarantee or insurance that protects the creditor against the consumer's default or other credit loss.
6. Charges imposed on a creditor by another person for purchasing or accepting a consumer's obligation, if the consumer is required to pay the charges in cash, as an addition to the obligation, or as a deduction from the proceeds of the obligation.
7. Premiums or other charges for credit life, accident, health, or loss-of-income insurance, written in connection with a credit transaction.
8. Premiums or other charges for insurance against loss of or damage to property, or against liability arising out of the ownership or use of property, written in connection with a credit transaction.
9. Discounts for the purpose of inducing payment by a means other than the use of credit.

The following charges are not finance charges:

1. Application fees charged to all applicants for credit, whether or not credit is actually extended.
2. Charges for actual unanticipated late payment, for exceeding a credit limit, or for delinquency, default, or a similar occurrence.
3. Charges imposed by a financial institution for paying items that overdraw an account, unless the payment of such items and the imposition of the charge were previously agreed upon in writing.

4. Fees charged for participation in a credit plan, whether assessed on an annual or other periodic basis.
5. Seller's points.
6. Interest forfeited as a result of an interest reduction required by law on a time deposit used as security for an extension of credit.
7. The following fees in a transaction secured by real property or in a residential mortgage transaction, if the fees are bona fide and reasonable in amount:

   a. Fees for title examination, abstract of title, title insurance, property survey, and similar purposes.
   b. Fees for preparing deeds, mortgages, and reconveyance, settlement, and similar documents.
   c. Notary, appraisal, and credit report fees.
   d. Amounts required to be paid into escrow or trustee accounts if the amounts would not otherwise be included in the finance charge.

8. Discounts offered to induce payment for a purchase by cash, check, or certain other means.

Premiums for certain types of insurance are also excludable if certain conditions are met, and certain taxes and fees prescribed by law are excludable.

CONTENT OF DISCLOSURES

The following are disclosure requirements for closed-end loans. Most real estate mortgages are considered closed-end because there are no subsequent credit advances. For each transaction, the creditor shall disclose the following information as applicable:

1. **Creditor.** The identity of the creditor making the disclosures.
2. **Amount financed.** The "amount financed," using that term, and a brief description such as "the amount of credit provided to you or on your behalf." The amount financed is calculated by

   a. determining the principal loan amount or the cash price (subtracting any down payment);
   b. adding any other amounts that are financed by the creditor and are not part of the finance charge; and
   c. subtracting any prepaid finance charge.

3. Itemization of amount financed.

   a. A separate written itemization of the amount financed. (Good faith estimates of settlement costs for transactions subject to the Real Estate Settlement Procedures Act [RESPA] are acceptable substitutes.) These items include

      i. The amount of any proceeds distributed directly to the consumer.
      ii. The amount credited to the consumer's account with the creditor.
      iii. Any amounts paid to other persons by the creditor on the consumer's behalf. The creditor shall identify those persons. (Generic names or general terms are acceptable for certain persons such as public officials, credit reporting agencies, appraisers, and insurance companies.)
      iv. The prepaid finance charge.

   b. The creditor need not comply with paragraph 3-a above if the creditor provides a statement that the consumer has the right to receive a written itemization of the amount financed, together with a space for the consumer to indicate whether it is desired, and the consumer does not request it.

4. Finance charge. The "finance charge," using that term, and a brief description such as "the dollar amount the credit will cost you."
5. Annual percentage rate. The "annual percentage rate," using that term, and a brief description such as "the cost of your credit as a yearly rate."
6. Variable rate. If the annual percentage rate may increase after consummation, the following disclosures must be included:

   a. The circumstances under which the rate may increase.
   b. Any limitations on the increase.
   c. The effect of an increase.
   d. An example of the payment terms that would result from an increase.

7. Payment schedule. The number, amounts, and timing of payments scheduled to repay the obligation.

   a. In a demand obligation with no alternative maturity date, the creditor may comply with this paragraph by disclosing the due dates or payment periods of any scheduled interest payments for the first year.
   b. In a transaction in which a series of payments varies because a finance charge is applied to the unpaid principal balance, the creditor may comply with this paragraph by disclosing the following information:

      i. The dollar amounts of the largest and smallest payments in the series.
      ii. A reference to the variations in the other payments in the series.

8. Total of payments. The "total of payments," using that term, and a descriptive explanation such as "the amount you will have paid when you have made all scheduled payments."
9. Demand feature. If the obligation has a demand feature, that fact shall be disclosed. When the disclosures are based on an assumed maturity of one year, that fact shall also be disclosed.
10. Total sale price. In a credit sale, the "total sale price," using that term, and a descriptive explanation (including the amount of any down payment) such as "the total price of your purchase on credit, including your down payment of $_____." The total sale price is the sum of the cash price, the items described in paragraph 2-b, and the finance charge disclosed under paragraph 4 above.
11. Prepayment.

    a. When an obligation includes a finance charge computed from time to time by application of a rate to the unpaid principal balance, a statement indicating whether or not a penalty may be imposed if the obligation is prepaid in full.
    b. When an obligation includes a finance charge other than the finance charge described in paragraph 11-a above, a statement indicating whether or not the consumer is entitled to a rebate of any finance charge if the obligation is prepaid in full.

12. Late payment. Any dollar or percentage charge that may be imposed before maturity due to a late payment, other than a deferral or extension charge.
13. Security interest. The fact that the creditor has or will acquire a security interest in the property purchased as part of the transaction, or in other property identified by item or type.
14. Insurance. The items required by law in order to exclude certain insurance premiums from the finance charge.
15. Certain security interest charges. The disclosures required by law in order to exclude from the finance charge certain fees prescribed by law or certain premiums for insurance in lieu of perfecting a security interest.
16. Contract reference. A statement that the consumer should refer to the appropriate contract document for information about nonpayment, default, the right to accelerate the maturity of the obligation, and prepayment rebates and penalties. At the creditor's

option, the statement may also include a reference to the contract for further information about security interests and, in a residential mortgage transaction, about the creditor's policy regarding assumption of the obligation.

17. Assumption policy. In a residential mortgage transaction, a statement as to whether or not a subsequent purchaser of the dwelling from the consumer may be permitted to assume the remaining obligation on its original terms.

18. Required deposit. If the creditor requires the consumer to maintain a deposit as a condition of the specific transaction, a statement that the annual percentage rate does not reflect the effect of the required deposit.

Disclosure for Certain Residential Mortgage Transactions

1. Time of disclosure. In a residential mortgage transaction subject to the Real Estate Settlement Procedures Act the creditor shall make good faith estimates of the disclosures described above before consummation, or shall deliver or place them in the mail not later than three business days after the creditor receives the consumer's written application, whichever is earlier. (See Figures 21-1, 21-2, and 21-3.)

2. Redisclosure required. If the annual percentage rate in the consummated transaction varies from the annual percentage rate disclosed by more than 1/8 of 1 percentage point in a regular transaction or more than 1/4 of 1 percentage point in an irregular transaction, the creditor shall disclose the changed terms no later than consummation or settlement.

Mortgage Savings and Loan Assoc.

Date:

ANNUAL PERCENTAGE RATE The cost of your credit as a yearly rate.	FINANCE CHARGE The dollar amount the credit will cost you.	Amount Financed The amount of credit provided to you or on your behalf.	Total of Payments The amount you will have paid after you have made all payments as scheduled.
10.85 %	$106,500.74	$44,605.66	$151,106.40

Your payment schedule will be:

Number of Payments	Amount of Payments	When Payments Are Due
360	$419.74	Monthly beginning 6/1/2014

This obligation has a demand feature.

You may obtain property insurance from anyone you want that is acceptable to Mortgage Savings and Loan Assoc. If you get the insurance from Mortgage Savings and Loan Assoc. you will pay $ ___150-/year___

Security: You are giving a security interest in:
☒ the goods or property being purchased.
☐ _____

Late Charge: If a payment is late, you will be charged $ _____5_____ % of the payment.

Prepayment: If you pay off early, you may have to pay a penalty.

Assumption: Someone buying your house may, subject to conditions, be allowed to assume the remainder of the mortgage on the original terms.

See your contract documents for any additional information about nonpayment, default, any required repayment in full before the scheduled date, and prepayment refunds and penalties.

_____
e means an estimate.

Figure 21-1.   Sample of Mortgage with Demand Feature

| ANNUAL PERCENTAGE RATE
The cost of your credit as a yearly rate. | FINANCE CHARGE
The dollar amount the credit will cost you. | Amount Financed
The amount of credit provided to you or on your behalf. | Total of Payments
The amount you will have paid after you have made all payments as scheduled. |
|---|---|---|---|
| 9.00 % | $83,452.22 | $44,000.00 | $127,452.22 |

State Savings and Loan Assoc.   **Account number**

Your payment schedule will be:

Number of Payments	Amount of Payments	When Payments Are Due
360	$354.03	Monthly beginning 6/1/2014

Variable Rate

The annual percentage rate may increase during the term of this transaction if the prime rate of State Savings and Loan Assoc. increases. The rate may not increase more often than once a year, and may not increase by more than 1% annually.

The interest rate will not increase above 15.00 %. Any increase will take the form of higher payment amounts. If the interest rate increases by 1 % in one year, your regular payment would increase to $ 385.64.

Security: You are giving a security interest in the property being purchased.

Late Charge: If a payment is late, you will be charged 5% of the payment.

Prepayment: If a you pay of early, you ☐ may ☐ will not have to pay a penalty.

Assumption: Someone buying your house may, subject to conditions, be allowed to assume the remainder of the mortgage on the original terms.

See your contract documents for any additional information about nonpayment, default, any required repayment in full before the scheduled date, and prepayment refunds and penalties.

e means an estimate.

Figure 21-2.   Sample of Variable-Rate Mortgage

Subsequent Disclosure Requirements

1. Refinancings. A refinancing occurs when an existing obligation that was subject to this part of Regulation Z is satisfied and replaced by a new obligation undertaken by the same consumer. A refinancing is a new transaction requiring new disclosures to the consumer. The new finance charge shall include any unearned portion of the old finance charge that is not credited to the existing obligation. The following shall not be treated as a refinancing:

a. A renewal of a single payment obligation with no change in the original terms.
b. A reduction in the annual percentage rate with a corresponding change in the payment schedule.
c. An agreement involving a court proceeding.
d. A change in the payment schedule or a change in collateral requirements as a result of the consumer's default or delinquency, unless the rate is increased, or the new amount financed exceeds the unpaid balance plus earned finance charge and premiums for continuation of insurance of certain types.
e. The renewal of optional insurance purchased by the consumer and added to an existing transaction, if disclosures relating to the initial purchase were provided as required by this subpart.

Convenient Savings and Loan   **Account number:**

ANNUAL PERCENTAGE RATE The cost of your credit as a yearly rate.	FINANCE CHARGE The dollar amount the credit will cost you.	Amount Financed The amount of credit provided to you or on your behalf.	Total of Payments The amount you will have paid after you have made all payments as scheduled.
15.37 %	$177,970.44	$43,777	$221,548.44

Your payment schedule will be:

Number of Payments	Amount of Payments	When Payments Are Due
12	$446.62	Monthly beginning 6/1/2014
12	$479.67	" " 6/1/2015
12	$515.11	" " 6/1/2016
12	$553.13	" " 6/1/2017
12	$593.91	" " 6/1/2018
300	varying from $637.68 to $627.37	" " 6/1/2019

Security: You are giving a security interest in the property being purchased.

Late Charge: If a payment is late, you will be charged 5% of the payment.

Prepayment: If you pay off early, you
☒ may   ☐ will not   have to pay a penalty.
☒ may   ☐ will not   be entitled to a refund of part of the finance charge.

Assumption: Someone buying your house cannot assume the remainder of the mortgage on the original terms.

See your contract documents for any additional information about nonpayment, default, any required repayment in full before the scheduled date, and prepayment refunds and penalties.

e means an estimate.

Figure 21-3.   Sample of Graduated-Payment Mortgage

2. Assumptions. An assumption occurs when a creditor expressly agrees in writing with a subsequent consumer to accept that consumer as a primary obligor on an existing residential mortgage transaction. Before the assumption occurs, the creditor shall make new disclosures to the subsequent consumer, based on the remaining obligation. If the finance charge originally imposed on the existing obligation was an add-on or a discount finance charge, the creditor need only disclose:

a. The unpaid balance of the obligation assumed.
b. The total charges imposed by the creditor in connection with the assumption.
c. The information required to be disclosed under section 226.18(k), (l), (m), and (n) of Regulation Z.
d. The annual percentage rate originally imposed on the obligation.
e. The payment schedule under section 226.18(g) and the total of payments under section 226.18(h), based on the remaining obligation.

RESCISSION

The right to rescind (cancel) a transaction is called *recission*. Most lending contracts have a 3-day right of recission period; in other words, anytime during the first 3 *business days* after the transaction is agreed to, the borrower can decide to cancel the transaction without penalty. The practice of many lenders is not to advance funds until this 3-day period has expired. One significant exception to the right of recission concerns real estate loans that are part of a contract of sale (i.e., they represent seller financing that is agreed to in the sale contract).

To rescind a credit transaction, the borrower may notify the creditor of the rescission by mail, telegram, or other written means of communication. Generally, the right to rescind expires on midnight of the third business day following the loan transaction, delivery by the creditor of the notice of the right to rescind, or delivery of all material disclosures, whichever occurs last.

Effect of Rescission

A consumer who exercises his right to rescind is not liable for any finance or other charge, and any security interest becomes void upon rescission. Within 20 days after receipt of a notice of rescission, the creditor shall return to the consumer any money or property given as earnest money, down payment, or otherwise, and shall take any action necessary or appropriate to reflect the termination of any security interest created under the transaction. If the creditor has delivered any money or property to the consumer, the consumer may retain possession of it until the performance of the creditor's obligations under this section. Then the consumer shall tender the property to the creditor, except that, if return of the property in kind would be impracticable or inequitable, the consumer shall tender its reasonable value. Tender of property shall be made at the location of the property or at the residence of the consumer, at the option of the consumer. Tender of money shall be at the creditor's place of business. If the creditor does not take possession of the property within 20 days after tender by the consumer, ownership of the property vests in the consumer without obligation on his part to pay for it.

RESIDENTIAL MORTGAGE TRANSACTIONS: SUMMARY OF DISTINCTIONS

There are five parts of Regulation Z that provide different treatment for residential mortgage loans as compared to other types of credit. These are as follows:

1. Certain fees in connection with a residential mortgage can be excluded from finance charges. These are fees for title examination, title insurance, title abstract, survey, preparing deeds and mortgage documents, notary, appraisal and credit report, and amounts paid into an escrow account if such amounts are not otherwise included in a finance charge.
2. In a residential mortgage transaction, the creditor must include a statement as to whether a subsequent purchaser of the dwelling may assume the remaining obligation on its original terms.
3. The timing of disclosure under Regulation Z for residential mortgage transactions, which are also covered by the Real Estate Settlement Procedures Act (RESPA), coincides with RESPA's requirements.
4. When a mortgage loan is assumed, the creditor must look at the intentions of the party assuming it to determine the required disclosures. If this party will use the property as a principal dwelling, disclosures applicable for such use are necessary, even if the original borrower did not use the property for that purpose.
5. A transaction to construct or acquire a principal dwelling is not eligible for the right of rescission. The lien status (first or junior mortgage) does not matter. However, a transaction that is separate from the purchase, such as one to improve a residence, is covered by this right of rescission.

Questions on Chapter 21

1. The purpose of Regulation Z is to
   (A) set the maximum interest rates that may be charged
   (B) let borrowers know the cost of credit
   (C) both A and B
   (D) neither A nor B

2. Regulation Z applies to
   (A) all real estate salespersons and brokers
   (B) all retail stores
   (C) wholesale establishments only
   (D) none of the above

3. Regulation Z covers
   (A) borrowing from relatives
   (B) borrowing by a business
   (C) real estate credit transactions
   (D) inheritances

4. Under Regulation Z, borrowers must be told in writing of
   (A) the annual percentage rate for credit
   (B) the total dollar amount of the finance charge
   (C) both A and B
   (D) neither A nor B

5. Which of the following must be included as a "finance charge" for real property credit transactions?
   (A) fee for title insurance
   (B) fee for deed preparation
   (C) monthly payment, in dollars
   (D) none of the above

6. The annual percentage rate (APR) means the
   (A) true interest rate charged
   (B) total dollar amount of finance charges
   (C) monthly payment, in dollars
   (D) percentage of loan paid off each year

7. Under Regulation Z, a borrower may have the right to cancel, within 3 days, a
   (A) second mortgage used to improve his dwelling
   (B) first mortgage loan used to purchase his dwelling
   (C) home-improvement loan more than 1 year old
   (D) none of the above

8. To cancel a credit transaction, the borrower must inform the lender, within 3 days,
   (A) by phone   (C) both A and B
   (B) in writing   (D) neither A nor B

9. If a borrower cancels the contract within the 3-day period, she is responsible for
   (A) a 10% finance charge
   (B) a 1% finance charge
   (C) 3 days' interest
   (D) none of the above

10. The maximum penalty for conviction, in a criminal action, for willfully disobeying Regulation Z is up to
    (A) a $5000 fine
    (B) 1 year's imprisonment
    (C) both A and B
    (D) neither A nor B

11. Under the federal Truth-in-Lending Law, two of the most critical facts that must be disclosed to buyers or borrowers are
    (A) duration of the contract and discount rate
    (B) finance charge and annual percentage rate
    (C) carrying charges and advertising expense
    (D) installment payments and cancellation rights

12. An advertisement states, "$500 down." Under Regulation Z, it must also state
    (A) broker's address
    (B) salesperson's name
    (C) total price
    (D) annual percentage rate

13. Under the Truth-in-Lending Act, the lender must disclose
    (A) annual percentage rate
    (B) simple rate of interest
    (C) second mortgage source
    (D) Cost of Funds Index

14. The Truth-in-Lending Act is also known as
    (A) USPAP
    (B) NAR
    (C) Regulation Z
    (D) FNMA

15. Regulation Z requires disclosure of
    (A) recording costs
    (B) attorney fees
    (C) title costs
    (D) annual percentage rate

16. RESPA requires the proposed lender to give
    the borrower
    (A) a brochure
    (B) an estimate of closing costs
    (C) both A and B
    (D) neither A nor B

17. The Real Estate Settlement Procedures Act
    (RESPA) applies to
    (A) all real estate financing
    (B) contracts for deed
    (C) second mortgages only
    (D) financing of one- to four-family residences

18. Mortgage lenders may not discriminate on the
    basis of age, but they need not lend to
    (A) parents of more than two children
    (B) childless couples
    (C) part-time workers
    (D) minors

ANSWERS

1. **B**	5. **D**	9. **D**	13. **A**	17. **D**
2. **D**	6. **A**	10. **C**	14. **C**	18. **D**
3. **C**	7. **A**	11. **B**	15. **D**	
4. **C**	8. **B**	12. **D**	16. **C**	

Subdividing, Building and Development, Environmental Concerns

Subdividing is the process of acquiring raw land and improving it to the point where it is prepared to be built on. At that point it is called a site and it can be sold to a builder or a prospective homeowner who will build on it. *Building* is putting a structure on the site. *Development* is both activities combined, usually including financing.

Subdividing is more than just preparing a map showing the boundaries of each lot. First, a subdivider gains control of the land through an option or contract. He may buy the land, though most subdividers don't want to use their own money at that point. A subdivider wants to be assured of financing before paying for the land.

LAND

The value of land depends on what is around it. Land is a prisoner of its environment, so its location is crucial. Attributes of land may be described in four categories: physical, financial-economic, legal-political, and social. Physical characteristics include size, shape, topography, eye appeal, access to utilities, climate, and soil quality. Financial-economic issues include employment and unemployment in the area, wage rates, industry type and growth, interest rates, and inflation rates. Legal-political matters include zoning, building codes, and taxation. Social forces include school quality, hospitals, houses of worship, and availability of services. A key determinant of land value is the rate of inflation and expectations. This is because tangibles such as land are considered a hedge against inflation.

The value of land is most often appraised using a direct sales comparison (market) approach. Another method is by land development, whereby the final aggregate selling price of the lots are estimated and, working backwards, one subtracts the cost of development and adjusts for time and risk.

The cost of the finished lots for a homesite is typically four to five times the cost of the raw land. For example, if the raw land is purchased for $40,000 per acre, a finished lot of one-quarter acre can be expected to sell for $40,000 to $50,000.

The subdivider must have appropriate zoning for end use. For example, the land may be zoned R-1, which in that jurisdiction allows four houses per acre; or R-2, which may allow six houses. The subdivider must engage an architect and engineer to examine the subdivision and file a plat to be approved (map of the subdivision) by the planning and zoning and the engineering departments of the city.

A building permit must be obtained from the city before ground can be broken. The municipality's engineer checks the suitability of the land for the planned building. Later, assuming construction progresses, the city's inspector will inspect the foundation, heat and ventilation system, wiring, and plumbing and roofing, for compliance with the building code. Upon completion of construction, a certificate of occupancy will be issued.

ACQUISITION AND DEVELOPMENT LOANS

Often a commercial bank is the likely source of an acquisition and development loan. Such loans generally carry interest at the prime rate plus three to five discount points. The loan is funded in stages, as the development proceeds. A subdivision or any other construction loan is considered high risk. Until sales occur in sufficient quantity, money is poured in without any coming out. It is the financial equivalent of swimming underwater. Economics in the area could change, as could the national economy. Home building is sensitive to interest rates and local growth, especially employment. Buyers are fickle—building a home is easily put off.

The first funds loaned are to purchase the land. Then, as the land is graded and potential drainage problems are cured, another installment is due. Connecting utilities to each lot— electricity, natural gas, water, sewer, and perhaps cable television, are costly. Another construction draw is due. Paving streets and putting in sidewalks deserve another draw. Advertising and selling expenses must be funded. So the construction loan balance is increased in steps, with the lender assuring that work has been done before advancing the money.

When lots are to be sold, they must be released from the subdivision loan to allow for construction financing of the house. Generally, these release provisions require more money for a given lot than the proportionate amount of subdivision loan. For example, if there is a $3 million loan on a 100 unit development, or $30,000 per lot, the loan may require that $40,000 be paid to release a lot from the subdivision loan. That way the lender forces the subdivider to stay with the project and earn a profit only after the development has proven its success through a near sell-out.

To keep loans and costs under control, the subdivider will build in phases, having enough inventory of lots to satisfy demand, but not too much, because of cost considerations.

City inspectors will examine the work at various stages to give approvals. Approvals are generally to determine compliance with city codes for safety reasons, but they are also to protect the public. Installation of pipes must be done properly to insure they won't leak natural gas, will carry sewage without leaking, and that water pipes won't get contaminated. Inspectors also assure that electrical connections are safe.

Generally, lots are considered a sale of real estate and may be sold by licensed real estate brokers and salespeople. If lots are offered for sale out of state, the subdividers must file a statement with the Office of Interstate Land Sales Registration. This is to make buyers aware of risks, especially buyers who might not visit the property. This is often the case for resort property.

DEVELOPMENT

Development is not only getting the land prepared for use, it is also building on it and often financing a permanent loan. Matters to be considered when developing real estate are the site, market, financial feasibility, lease, financing, and construction.

Site—Zoning and Adjacent Land Uses

A site must have proper zoning before development can begin. Frequently, sites suitable for residential development are not zoned that way, or those intended for retail use are not zoned for commercial. Then, there must be an exploration of the attitudes of the local residents, municipal zoning staff, and the various governmental bodies that approve a proposed project, such as the Zoning Board of Appeals and City Council.

Proximity of Competition and Traffic-Generating Businesses

Conditions outside the site affect the success of the proposed development. Adjacent uses may generate desirable or undesirable traffic depending upon the type of business. For example, fast food restaurants typically find that shopping centers, high schools, and theaters are desired traffic generators. A residential development wants quiet neighbors. Both would tend to feel that salvage yards, factories, and auto dealerships generate undesired traffic.

Size and Shape

Most developments need some street frontage. Rectangular sites are preferred for some uses because they make the most efficient layout for building, parking, and access.

Traffic Access, Count, and Curb Cuts

A user must be able to enter and exit a site safely without causing traffic congestion. Although many developers prefer at least two curb cuts, some cities will not allow more than one curb cut for small development of under, say, 150 feet of frontage.

Visibility

Some uses, such as retail properties, require good visibility. Poor visibility of a site is related to accessibility: a site that is difficult to see is also difficult to enter. A person traveling at 35 miles per hour should be able to see the property (or its sign) in time to enter the parking area safely. Corner lots generally provide better visibility and access than interior lots. Sign requirements vary by city; one should check with the planning or zoning department.

Topography, Drainage, and Utilities

A flat site is preferred for commercial development, whereas many homebuyers prefer land with scenic qualities—a lake, stream, or hillside. The contour of the land affects the site development and building design. A level or gently sloping (less than three percent) grade is easier to build on; slopes of more than five percent require special consideration. Low-lying areas with poor drainage may require storm sewers, water retention ponds, or structural building considerations. The unavailability of gas, water, sewer, or electric service at or near the site is a major problem.

Parking and Landscaping Requirements

For a commercial development, the parking area must support the property's image of attractiveness and convenience. Therefore, the layout, dimensions and arrangements, grading, paving, landscaping, and lighting must all be considered in the site planning process.

FINANCIAL FEASIBILITY

There are two methods of trying to assure the financial feasibility of a proposed development. One is to determine the cost (or operating expenses and debt service) that a completed building will incur. The price (or rental rate) is established to exceed that sum by a reasonable amount, depending on the equity capital required. This method is appropriate when attempting to build a unique structure with special market acceptance. However, when building into a competitive market, determine the going price (or rental rate) in the market. Then construction and related building costs must be kept within a strict budget so that market rents will be ample to pay for debt service and operating expenses, and to provide an adequate return on equity. Costs to be included are:

- Land
- Land acquisition fees
- Interest during construction
- Construction loan fees
- Permanent loan fees
- Permits
- Building and paving
- Site work
- Utility hookups
- Legal and accounting
- Builder's and developer's profit

LEASING

The lease is the key to developing real estate for a nonspeculative rental project. It allows property development and reduces risk for all parties who may be concerned—the landlord, tenant, lender, developer, builder, and investor.

The strength of a lease provides the basis for issuing credit. An institutional lender will provide a commitment for permanent financing based on the terms of a lease and credit standing of a tenant. The lease should specify, in sufficient detail, all aspects of the development. The permanent lender is obligated to fund the project upon completion of all terms described in the lease. The commitment need not be funded if the lease terms are not met, for example, if the completed building differs from the lease specifications or doesn't meet building codes, or there are other unfulfilled lease provisions. A permanent financing commitment paves the way to construction financing. When financing is arranged, the money is available to begin the project.

FINANCING

The two types of real estate financing are equity and debt. Equity funds are the owner's money in the property. Debt funds are obtained from third parties, predominantly from financial institutions.

Equity Financing

When the prospective owner's cash resources are insufficient to provide needed equity, other sources may be available. A partnership is one option. Joint ventures are similar to partnership agreements, but are for owning and operating one specific business; they terminate upon disposition of that business.

Debt Financing

Under normal circumstances, financing for a newly built real estate development is obtained from two different lenders: a long-term (permanent) lender, and an interim (construction) lender. The permanent lender issues a takeout commitment that promises to repay the construction loan upon project completion. Only with a takeout commitment (or acceptable substitute), can a construction loan be arranged. The borrower prefers a permanent loan commitment from a long-term lender rather than a short-term lender.

Financing alternatives include a permanent loan (with or without participation) or a miniperm or balloon loan. Each may be structured to pay interest only for a specified period followed by amortization at a specified rate, with level payments, or an adjustable-rate mortgage (ARM). The ARM rates on commercial properties are usually indexed to short-term rates such as the prime or U.S. treasury bill rate. Rate adjustments may have annual caps and a ceiling on the rate over the life of the ARM.

Participation mortgages provide an inflation hedge to the lender as compensation for increasing market interest rates. The borrower gives up a portion of annual earnings and pays annual debt service plus a percentage of gross income or net operating income above a specified level. Lenders prefer to use gross income because values are easier to validate.

Lenders

Savings and loan associations, commercial banks, and mortgage bankers are the primary sources of loans for housing.

Mortgage REITs finance every step of a real estate development. REITs may originate loans or purchase them from other originators. *Pension fund* investment managers typically place a portion of their assets in bank trust departments, trust companies, and life insurance companies. These assets are placed in commingled funds for investment in real estate equities and mortgages.

Insurance companies are interested in investing in commercial real estate mortgages, often through mortgage bankers who have correspondents. *Finance companies* are construction and gap financing lenders for commercial real estate. Underwriting criteria are competitive with commercial banks. Loan structures are also similar. Finance companies will accept more risk in higher L/V ratios than commercial banks with corresponding higher commitment fees, points, and interest rates.

THE LOAN PROCESS

The loan process includes four steps. In *loan submission,* a comprehensive package of the borrower's financial condition and the project's characteristics and feasibility is presented to the lender. *Loan processing* includes analysis of the loan submission to verify borrower and project information submitted. *Loan underwriting* includes analysis of the borrower's creditworthiness and project feasibility to reach a lending decision. Negotiations between borrower and lender are needed to reach an agreement regarding loan terms. *Loan closing* activates the borrower and lender decisions and establishes contractual arrangements.

CONSTRUCTION FINANCING

The construction loan is secured by the land and subsequent improvements. The lender expects the loan to be repaid in a lump sum when construction is completed. For commercial property, with key tenants committed, and a permanent loan package arranged, the developer-borrower can shop for an interim (construction) loan. Institutional loans, other third party loans, and joint ventures, are three options usually available for construction financing.

The lender usually contracts with an independent architect or engineer and legal counsel to conduct the inspections. On each disbursement, county records are examined to be sure that no new liens have been filed. Typically, funds are disbursed to cover costs up to five to ten percent less than work in place plus stored materials.

Ten percent of the total construction loan amount is typically retained after construction completion, disbursed when the lender has verified that all subcontractors, materialmen, and the general contractor have been paid and no mechanics' liens have been filed on the property. With the final disbursement, the construction lender expects the property to be occupied and the permanent loan to be funded, paying off the interim loan.

These steps do not eliminate construction and economic risks. Construction risks include stoppages due to labor problems, unfavorable weather, unanticipated increase in construction costs, errors in plans and specifications, poor construction management, misappropriation of construction funds, and developer insolvency. Economic risks include market change that reduces demand, neighborhood decline, poor space design and construction defects, and poor marketing analysis leading to incorrect pricing and marketing strategy.

PHYSICAL DEVELOPMENT

To physically develop the property, the landowner must act as a builder or hire a construction firm. If the landowner is the general contractor and developer, construction knowledge is essential. Since many landowners do not have the required time or expertise, most projects are built by firms in the construction business.

CONSTRUCTION ARRANGEMENTS

A contractor will agree to do the specified work by a certain date for a fixed price or a certain markup above cost. Generally, contracts are complex and consist of several documents including:

1. Invitation to bid
2. Instructions to bidders
3. General legal conditions of the contract
4. Supplementary operating conditions of the contract
5. Technical specifications
6. Drawings and blueprints
7. Bid bond
8. Contract agreement(s)

  a. Owner-architect
  b. Owner-contractor
  c. Contractor-subcontractor

9. Performance bond

The construction requirements and specifications of the project are exposed for bids; generally, the contract is awarded to the low bidder unless there are extenuating circumstances.

There are several cost estimation services available to help estimate the cost of alternative construction features; three are the *Boeckh Building-Cost Manual*, the *F. W. Dodge Construction Cost Manuals*, and the *Marshall Valuation Service*.

To reduce the chances for conflict between owners, architects, engineers, and contractors, standardized contract documents are commonly used. The American Institute of Architects offers a variety of forms that are frequently used. The National Society of Professional Engineers, the American Public Works Association, and the Associated General Contractors of America also provide standardized contract forms.

TYPES OF CONTRACTS

Although there are many variations, most contracts fall into one of the following categories and are awarded through competitive bidding, negotiation, or a joint venture.

A *fixed-price contract* requires the contractor to complete the project for a specific dollar amount. With a *guaranteed-maximum-price contract*, the owner pays for only the actual cost incurred (including a contractor's fee) within the maximum price guarantee. A *cost-plus contract* reimburses the contractor for actual costs incurred plus an additional percentage or fixed amount.

SELECTING A CONTRACTOR

There are several questions to be raised in selecting a contractor. Does the contractor have prior experience building similar projects? Can a list of these projects be provided, along with original cost estimates and the actual cost of each? Does the contractor have experience building in the local area?

Building regulations, labor supplies, and the source of materials vary with each city; a contractor not familiar with local conditions may have conflicts, time delays, or greater expenses.

Also, it is easier to check the references of a local contractor with lenders, government agencies, trade unions, and building supply houses.

Will the contractor provide a financial statement to indicate that (a) the firm has sufficient funds to be responsible for specific performance, (b) the firm is able to handle the cash flow requirements, and (c) there are no excessive short-term debts that might create problems after the project is started? Who are the subcontractors to be used for each major activity area? What is their reputation for quality and reliability, and their relationship with the general contractor? The general contractor is only as good as the subcontractors used.

CONDOMINIUMS AND COOPERATIVES

Developers or converters of a proposed condominium or cooperative, or any other shared housing arrangement, in most states must file a statement indicating their plan. The developer must provide disclosure of the plans. This includes an architect's or engineer's report, past or expected expenses, management arrangements, and other legal and financial arrangements. It should include the conditions, covenants, and restrictions of use.

Condominium and co-op converters must follow specific rules in their community, depending on the converter's plans to allow for eviction of existing nonbuyers or a noneviction plan.

Housing offerings are printed in red on at least part of the first page (red herrings) upon preliminary review, then final plans are printed in black ink.

ENVIRONMENTAL CONSIDERATIONS

Increased environmental sensitivity has raised the liability of those involved in real estate. Every gas station could have a leaking tank, pump, or pipe that contaminates ground water. Dry cleaners and car washes may use chemicals that, if released, are harmful. Even seemingly innocent property uses such as golf courses and agricultural land are suspect because of fertilizer and pesticide applications.

Recently, the Federal Home Mortgage Corporation proposed guidelines of due diligence for environmental standards of single-family homes which, until now, were defined as noncontaminating. A house may host radon (suspected of causing lung cancer), have had pesticides liberally applied to the lawn, have urea formaldehyde or asbestos insulation. It may be near a landfill, or have been built on contaminated land. Due diligence for the investigation of homes is being proposed. It would require an inspection of records of prior ownership and land use, and an inspection of the property.

Liability

Superfund is the common name for the 1980 law that affects many issues of real estate contamination. Superfund, reauthorized in 1986 as SARA, includes stronger clean-up standards, disclosure requirements, and funding. *Superfund* requires the clean-up, but pays only in extreme situations, and it can render property worthless. It imposes liability on those involved with hazardous materials, liability that is *strict, joint and several, and retroactive.* Liability is created by Superfund in any connection with the property: as an owner, operator, generator, or transporter. Strict means that it doesn't matter whether such a person acted knowingly or reasonably—that person bears liability. The absence of negligence or other wrongdoing is not a defense. There are some legal defenses, but they are limited.

Joint and several liability means that every responsible party is liable for the full cost. The government or Superfund claimant may find anyone with a "deep pocket" to pay costs, and it doesn't have to sort out who was responsible for how much damage. Huge clean-up costs could conceivably be assessed against someone who took title for an instant during a closing to facilitate a transaction, but otherwise had no involvement with the property. The unlucky party would be responsible for the full amount, but could seek reimbursement from other responsible parties.

Retroactive liability means that it reaches back to prior owners and operators. This overrides "as is" clauses in sales contracts. It also precedes any mortgage lien.

Activities

Activities that may cause contamination include manufacturing, assembly, repair, laboratory, storage, machine shop services, and cleaning. A partial list of types of businesses that may be perpetrators includes any that use, manufacture, or supply products to these uses: electronics, leathers, paints, pesticides, petroleum, pharmaceutical, plastics, refining, smelting, or textiles. In addition to those activities, events that may cause serious problems include fires, explosions, spills, and tank, pump, and pipe leaks.

Contaminated Items

Contamination can be found in buildings, soil, and groundwater. Within a building, asbestos may have been used for insulation and pipe-wrapping. There is no problem unless the asbestos is friable, which means it crumbles. Interior components of a building may have thick residues of chemicals that were used—these may have migrated through concrete floors into the soil.

Contamination that spreads through groundwater can cause problems to adjacent property. An extensive site assessment might be needed to determine the extent of damage.

Detection

A proper site assessment by a qualified professional is the best approach when considering a purchase. More and more lenders are requiring one as a requisite for a mortgage loan on commercial or industrial property, as contaminants can render a property worthless, and a foreclosure makes the lender an owner who is liable. Site assessment costs range from a few thousand to hundreds of thousands, and include drilling tests, electrical conducting, ground penetration, and laboratory analysis. An aerial photograph may help identify suspect points including ditches, landfills, lagoons, pits, ponds, tanks, and waste piles.

Other methods of due diligence to determine detection include reviewing public records and newspapers and checking with the local fire department and state or federal environmental or pollution agencies.

A Phase I assessment should be performed by a buyer as part of the due diligence acquisition process; it will help avoid clean-up liability under Superfund. Phase II is to estimate the cost of clean-up, and Phase III is to perform the work.

ACQUISITION DUE DILIGENCE

Due diligence relates to the process of inquiring about the property before buying. Because buyers and brokers are not engineers or geologists, it is in their best interest to hire qualified personnel to inspect the property.

Every house should be inspected for wood-destroying insects by a qualified, licensed pest control operator. Termites, carpenter ants, old house borers, and other pests should be discovered and the damage assessed. A qualified inspector will check the plumbing, electrical, and mechanical systems. Finally, a structural engineer may be helpful to determine soundness.

Commercial properties may need those types of inspectors, and a high level engineer. Environmental inspections may include searching for contaminants such as lead-based paints, the presence of underground storage tanks, groundwater contaminants from adjacent properties, asbestos, and pollution from the subject property into the air and water.

Due diligence for income property also includes a review of market conditions including proposed competition, tenant leases, and often financing availability.

Questions on Chapter 22

1. Subdividing is a process of
   (A) passive investment in land
   (B) clearing land of unwanted debris
   (C) preparing land to be built on
   (D) building on land

2. A developer is
   (A) the same as a subdivider
   (B) one who subdivides, builds, and generally finances
   (C) a builder and tenant
   (D) a broker who builds

3. Land appraisal is most frequently done by which approach?
   (A) income
   (B) replacement cost
   (C) sales comparison
   (D) all of the above

4. Construction loan funds are
   (A) provided in steps as construction progresses
   (B) loaned at the start of a project
   (C) loaned at the completion of a project
   (D) always the same dollar amount as permanent loan funds

5. Land for commercial uses ideally is on a (an)
   (A) slope or grade
   (B) heavily travelled street or road
   (C) in a residential neighborhood
   (D) interstate freeway

6. Banned health hazard products include all except
   (A) radon
   (B) asbestos
   (C) radioactive materials
   (D) Drano

7. Construction cost sources include all except
   (A) Wiley
   (B) Dodge
   (C) Boechk
   (D) Marshall

8. In most states, a condominium converter must
   (A) not renew leases of tenants
   (B) file a plan and provide disclosure
   (C) make a special deal with each tenant over age 65
   (D) not evict anyone under any circumstances

9. Before breaking ground, a _____ must be obtained from the city.
   (A) construction loan
   (B) red herring
   (C) occupancy plan
   (D) building permit

10. The final stage of building inspection is the granting of a
    (A) prospectus
    (B) certificate of occupancy
    (C) inspection certificate
    (D) conforming use certificate

11. A nonconforming use
    (A) is allowed to continue unless the building is damaged
    (B) is grandfathered
    (C) was conforming before a zoning change
    (D) all of the above

12. Private restrictions on the use of land may be created by
    (A) private-land use controls
    (B) written agreement
    (C) general plan restrictions in subdivisions
    (D) all of the above

13. Covenants, conditions, and restrictions (CCRs) are usually recorded by a document called
    (A) a plat
    (B) subdivision rules
    (C) Declaration of Restrictions
    (D) common area designations

14. If CCRs and zoning conflict with each other,
    (A) the more stringent rules apply
    (B) either can be followed
    (C) courts or mediation will be needed to settle
        the matter
    (D) the developer will decide what to do

15. A *turnkey* project is one that is
    (A) under development
    (B) under contract
    (C) complete and ready for use or occupancy
    (D) under lease

16. A development has restrictive covenants.
    These may not regulate
    (A) exterior paint color
    (B) fences
    (C) satellite dishes
    (D) race of owner

17. Zoning ordinances typically regulate the
    (A) number of occupants allowed per dwelling
        unit
    (B) uses of each parcel of land
    (C) maximum rent that may be charged
    (D) building code

18. Tony's Pizzeria has signed a purchase contract
    with X Oil Company to purchase a parcel of
    property. X Oil Company has failed to disclose to
    Tony's that toxic substances were dumped on the
    property over a ten-year period. When this omis-
    sion is discovered by Tony's, the contract is
    (A) valid
    (B) voidable
    (C) void
    (D) unenforceable

19. If an area is rezoned industrial and a commercial
    establishment may continue its operation in that
    area, this is an example of
    (A) variance
    (B) nonconforming use
    (C) conditional use permit
    (D) spot zoning

20. You want to build your house 10 feet closer to
    the road than the zoning ordinance permits.
    You will likely try to get
    (A) a zoning ordinance change
    (B) a variance
    (C) a deed restriction amendment
    (D) a nonconforming use

ANSWERS

1. **C**	5. **B**	9. **D**	13. **C**	17. **B**
2. **B**	6. **D**	10. **B**	14. **A**	18. **B**
3. **C**	7. **A**	11. **D**	15. **C**	19. **B**
4. **A**	8. **B**	12. **D**	16. **D**	20. **B**

Examination Preparation

STUDYING FOR THE EXAM

You can't expect to walk into the examination room cold and pass with flying colors. You have to be ready for the exam. This means more than just doing a lot of reading and trying to cram your head full of facts. You have to be psychologically ready and properly prepared to take the examination so that you can *do your best* on it. To do this you have to acquire the following things:

1. Knowledge
2. A positive attitude
3. Information about exam taking
4. Confidence
5. Rest

Let's take these things one by one.

1. Knowledge. Of course you have to have the knowledge to get through the examination; this means knowing the subject matter well. Begin by studying this book and your state's license laws. Also, if your state provides special examination preparation materials, study those, too. You can't expect to acquire all the requisite knowledge if you start just a short while before the examination. You should follow a *reasonable* study schedule so that you will be at maximum readiness the day of the examination (see Chapter 1).

2. A positive attitude. Your attitude should be one of confidence; after all, if you have worked hard to learn all the real estate concepts, then you DO know the required material. The exam simply is the place where you get your chance to demonstrate that you are qualified for a real estate license.

3. Information about exam taking. Some people panic at the prospect of taking an exam and end up doing badly as a result. This sort of thing does happen; but if you look at the examination in the proper perspective, it won't happen to you. If you are concerned about taking an examination after having been out of school for such a long time, the thing to do is to practice: take the model examinations in Chapter 24. Set up actual "examination conditions." Give yourself a time limit, and go right through each practice exam just as if it were the real thing. Use all the examination-taking techniques you'll read about in this chapter. Each model exam has a key at the end of the book so that you can grade your own performance. To guide your future study, note the areas where you did well and those where you did badly. Do this for *each* practice examination: first take the exam and grade it, then do more studying in your weaker areas before you take the next one.

In this way you'll accomplish three important objectives. First, you'll get used to the examination situation. Second, you'll gain practice in answering the kinds of questions featured on most real estate license examinations. Third, you'll be able to keep track of the subject areas where you need more study and practice.

4. Confidence. Here are the areas of subject matter that examinees worry most about: (a) arithmetic, (b) contracts, and (c) for broker examinees, closing statements. We have included detailed sections on all of these, as well as on all other real estate subjects. The arithmetic you need to know is exactly the same sort you had to do for homework in the sixth and seventh grades. Contracts inspire awe because they're supposed to be the province of lawyers. By now you know that a contract is just a piece of paper on which people put down facts concerning an agreement they've made. In regard to a contract, all you have to be sure of is to write what you are supposed to and to be clear in what you say. Even property description doesn't have to look like mumbo-jumbo. Metes and bounds descriptions just need to tell where the boundaries of a property lie; rectangular government survey descriptions use a peculiar but very high-powered shorthand that's easy to learn; lot and block number descriptions are great because they're simple and explicit.

Closing statements worry broker examinees because they look so mysterious. Actually, they're nothing but a record of where people's money goes in a real estate transaction. Once again, the important thing is accuracy. Also, if you think a bit about most of the items involved, it is easy to see if they should be paid by (or to) the seller or the buyer. All that's left is to line up all the numbers neatly so that they can be added easily. The tricky part about closing statements usually is the prorating of various items. As Chapter 18 explains, there is nothing mysterious about prorating; however, the calculations are long and clumsy, so there's room for error to sneak in if you're not careful.

Throughout this book an important aim has been to explain everything thoroughly. If you understand the subjects discussed, you should have no confidence problem: you *know* the basic principles of real estate.

5. Rest. Don't stay up studying the night before the exam! No one is at his best when he's tired or short of sleep. The day before the exam should be one of rest and relaxation.

You can, however, design a little last-minute study session that actually will help you, without disturbing your relaxation. Prepare a brief outline of the *important* points on which you know you need special effort. If contracts bug you, make a list of all the contracts and a brief description of each. Study this material for one-half hour in the morning, one-half hour in the afternoon, and one-half hour in the evening, but finish your studying *at least* two hours before bedtime. In that way you'll be strengthening your weaknesses, but you won't be spending so much time on studying that it interferes with the really important task at hand: getting yourself relaxed. The morning of the examination, if you have time, you can spend another half hour going over those notes one last time.

TWO IMPORTANT RULES

Your objective when you take any examination is to get as high a score as possible. The way to do that is to provide as many right answers as you can. This leads us directly to the most important rule of all in taking examinations.

ALWAYS ANSWER EVERY QUESTION. Even if you have to guess, write down an answer. If you leave the question blank, you can be certain that it will be counted as wrong because a blank answer is a wrong answer. If you guess, there is always the chance that the guess will be correct. Boiled down, the situation is as simple as this: you know you will get the question wrong if you leave it blank, but if you guess at an answer you may guess the right one.

The second rule is SKIP THE HARD QUESTIONS AT FIRST AND SAVE THEM FOR LAST. Many people start at the beginning of an examination and work their way through, one question at a time, until they run out of time. If they encounter a hard question, they battle with it for a long time and won't go on until they've licked it (or it has licked them). These people are lucky to get to the end of the exam before they run out of time; if they don't get to the end, they never even see some of the questions—and they might have been able to answer enough of those questions to earn a passing grade on the exam. On all of the national examinations, all questions are worth the same. Most independent states score their examinations that way too. So what sense is there in spending 15 minutes, half an hour, or more on a single question, when you can use that same time to read and answer a couple of *dozen* questions correctly? (The materials you get from your state's licensing authority will tell you what kinds of questions to expect and how they are counted.)

When you take the exam, start at the beginning. Read the instructions, then read the first question. Answer it if you can, and then go on to number 2. Answer that one if you can, and then go on to the next and the next and the next. When you come across a hard question that you have to think about, or that will take a lot of time to answer even if you know exactly how to get the answer (some arithmetic problems can be like that), skip it for the time being. Come back to it later, after you have gone all the way through the exam and answered all the questions that you can do fairly quickly. Be sure to make some kind of note for yourself of the questions you skip, so you'll remember to go back to them!

STRATEGIES FOR HANDLING COMMON TYPES OF QUESTIONS

In order to know how to attack your state's particular examination, you have to be familiar with the special strategies for handling specific kinds of questions.

Multiple-Choice Questions

This is a multiple-choice question:

The title of this chapter is
(A) How to Hammer a Nail
(B) Examination Preparation
(C) I Was an Elephant for the FBI
(D) none of the above

The national examinations are composed entirely of multiple-choice questions. The essence of this kind of question is that you must choose one of the answers as the correct one.

Always remember that with a multiple-choice question *you are looking at the right answer*! You just have to pick it out. Your strategy for answering such questions is as follows:

1. Read the question *completely* and *carefully*. Many people miss little key words such as *if*, *not*, *but*, and *except* that can completely change or limit the meaning of a sentence.
2. If the answer is obvious to you, mark it properly and go on to the next question. Then forget about the question you have just answered. Almost always the answer you pick first is the right one, and you will very rarely improve an answer by coming back and stewing over it later.
3. If the answer is not obvious, begin the guesswork strategy. First look for all the choices that you know are wrong. You may not be sure of the right answer, but that doesn't mean you can't find some answers you know are wrong. Then guess an answer from the ones that are left.

   Remember to make your guesses educated. Usually you will be able to guide your guesswork by using some of your knowledge. You may be able to decide that a certain answer is much more likely to be right than the others. Always be sure to eliminate answers you *know* are wrong in order to limit your choices and thus improve your chances of guessing the right one. However, if it looks as though a long time will be needed to reach even a guesswork answer, skip the question and come back to it later if you have the time.

USING COMPUTER ANSWER FORMS

Figure 23-1 is an example of a computer examination form. Forms like these used to be the standard for all kinds of examinations, but their use is declining in favor of touch-screen computers. Even so, you can make a few copies of the form to mark your answers to the model exams in this book—or you can simply circle your answers directly on the book pages.

If you have to use one of these answer forms, you will be given the form and a *test booklet*. The examination questions and instructions will be written in the test booklet; you will "code" your answers onto the answer sheet. Usually you will be asked to make no marks at all on the test booklet; you should put your name and any other identification asked for in the appropriate spaces on the answer sheet. Remember one critical rule: *Do not make any marks at all on either the test or the answer sheet unless and until you are instructed to.* Normally the test booklet will contain very detailed and specific instructions on how to enter the necessary information on the answer sheet; in addition, the people administering the examination will give an oral and visual presentation on the same subject.

Figure 23-1.   Computer Examination Form

Using these answer sheets is really quite simple. Below is an example of a set of answer spaces for three different questions:

```
1  ⸬A⸬   ⸬B⸬   ⸬C⸬   ⸬D⸬
2  ⸬A⸬   ⸬B⸬   ⸬C⸬   ⸬D⸬
3  ⸬A⸬   ⸬B⸬   ⸬C⸬   ⸬D⸬
```

For each question you have four answers to choose from: A, B, C, and D. (For the appraiser exams, there are five answer choices.) When you have picked your answer, enter it on the examination form by *shading* the appropriate space with your pencil. Suppose, for example, you choose C:

⸬**C**⸬   ▬◖▬

Here are three easy sample questions. Answer them by shading the appropriate space in the answer set that follows.

1. If John has two apples and I have three, together we have
   (A) 4   (C) 6
   (B) 5   (D) 7

2. The capital of France is
   (A) London   (C) Paris
   (B) Washington   (D) Des Moines, Iowa

3. Those things in the middle of your face that you see with are
   (A) eyes   (C) nose
   (B) ears   (D) fingernails

```
1  ⸬A⸬   ⸬B⸬   ⸬C⸬   ⸬D⸬
2  ⸬A⸬   ⸬B⸬   ⸬C⸬   ⸬D⸬
3  ⸬A⸬   ⸬B⸬   ⸬C⸬   ⸬D⸬
```

The answers are obvious: 1 is B, 2 is C, 3 is A. The properly marked answer form is as follows:

```
1  ⸬A⸬   ▬■▬   ⸬C⸬   ⸬D⸬
2  ⸬A⸬   ⸬B⸬   ▬■▬   ⸬D⸬
3  ▬■▬   ⸬B⸬   ⸬C⸬   ⸬D⸬
```

There are two things you must be careful of with respect to using computer answer forms. First, make sure you have enough pencils. Be certain that you are or are not required to bring your own pencils; if you are, get ordinary #2 pencils—the kind you can buy at any stationery store. And bring a little hand pencil sharpener along, too. After you sharpen a pencil, be sure to blunt the point by scribbling on some scratch paper before marking the answer form. You don't want to poke holes in it.

Second, our strategy of skipping the hard questions and saving them to the last means that you have to *make absolutely certain that you are putting the answer in the right space for that question!* Be especially careful here. The computer is very stupid! If you put answer marks in the wrong spaces, it will count them wrong.

By the way, the computer form used on the exam you take may be slightly different from the sample form shown here. However, it will be used in just the same way we use ours.

ON-SITE SCORING SYSTEMS
(KEYPADS AND TOUCH SCREENS)

Pencil-and-paper examinations are being replaced by various kinds of computerized exams. One form uses a "keypad" attached to a small terminal (screen) that displays the questions and the answer choices. You enter your choice of answer on the keypad, which also has keys allowing you to "erase" an answer, "scroll" back and forth in the exam, skip a question, and so on. Other forms use what appears to be a typical desktop personal computer, complete with a normal keyboard. The most common kind of computerized testing system uses a touch screen. It looks like a normal computer monitor, but to register your responses you tap the screen at appropriate places. If you've ever used the do-it-yourself checkout line at a supermarket, or a do-it-yourself photo machine at a drugstore, you've used a touch screen.

Whatever the system used, you usually can get some literature ahead of time that explains how to use the system. Naturally, it is important to know as much about it as you can in advance. Also, before you take the exam, the administrators will provide a detailed explanation and demonstration of how to use the equipment. Whatever the system, usually the instructions for using it (entering answers, erasing, scrolling, etc.) either appear on the screen (usually at the bottom or top) or can be accessed easily.

There are two major advantages to these devices. First, the machines make it easier to skip around within the exam without losing track of where you are and without any risk that you will put your answers in the wrong spaces. Second, most of the machines allow for instant scoring of your exam. When you are done, you "lock" the machine by pressing a special key. After that time, you no longer can enter or change answers. At that point, the administrators of the exam can instantly provide your score, since your answers are entered into the computer already. Usually you will be given a sheet that will tell you which questions you answered correctly and which you missed. In some examining centers, if the exam isn't over yet, you may be allowed to check your answers against the exam you just took and so tell exactly where you went wrong on the questions you missed.

Model Examinations

Following are ten model practice final examinations for you to take under conditions similar to those you will experience when you take the actual exam. The first three are sample salesperson licensing exams and should be taken by all applicants for the salesperson's license. Examinations 4, 5, and 6 are sample broker's licensing exams. Prospective brokers should take these in addition to the salesperson exams. One salesperson and one broker exam have 100 questions; the rest have 80.

Examinations 7, 8, and 9 are sample appraiser certification exams; each has 100 questions. Residential certification applicants need answer only the first 75 questions in each exam; general certification applicants should answer all 100.

We suggest that applicants for broker's licenses or appraiser certification take the salesperson's exams as well as the ones they are practicing for. Because all the material covered in the typical salesperson's licensing examination is also covered in the broker's license exam and in both types of appraiser certification exams, valuable additional practice will be gained by taking the salesperson's exam.

Examination 10 is a compilation of additional questions that may be found on any of the exams and should be taken by both salesperson and broker applicants.

Note that the practice exams contain no questions on license law; the reason for this is that each state's law varies. For this subject matter, go over your notes, materials you obtained from the examination authorities, and the text and questions in Chapter 5.

Model Examination 1
SALESPERSON

See page 485 for the answer key. Math problems are worked out on page 489.

1. If, upon receipt of an offer to purchase under certain terms, the seller makes a counteroffer, the prospective purchaser is
   (A) bound by his original offer
   (B) bound to accept the counteroffer
   (C) bound by the agent's decision
   (D) relieved of his original offer

2. A broker who makes profitable investments with earnest money deposits
   (A) must share 50% of the profits with the owners of the money he used
   (B) has done something illegal
   (C) may keep all the profits
   (D) must turn over the profits to the state's licensing authorities

3. A real estate broker must comply with
   (A) agency law
   (B) her state's real estate licensing law
   (C) both A and B
   (D) neither A nor B

4. Smith makes an offer on Jones's property and states that the offer will remain open for 3 days. The day after Smith has made the offer, he decides to withdraw it since Jones has neither rejected nor accepted it.
   (A) Smith cannot do this.
   (B) Smith can do this only if Jones was planning to reject the offer anyway.
   (C) Smith must give Jones at least half the remaining time to make a decision.
   (D) Smith may withdraw the offer.

5. In order to sell property belonging to a trust for which she is trustee, the trustee must have
   (A) a broker's license
   (B) a salesperson's license
   (C) a trustor's license
   (D) none of the above

6. Appraised valuation is $250,000. Tax is based on 20% of appraised valuation. City tax is 50 mills; county tax is 40 mills. Which of the following is true?
   (A) City tax is $2,500.
   (B) County tax is $20,000.
   (C) City and county tax add up to $6,000.
   (D) None of the above

7. Under Truth-in-Lending, the lender must advise the borrower of the loan's
   (A) owner   (C) seller
   (B) annual percentage rate   (D) closing date

8. In the absence of an agreement to the contrary, the mortgage normally having priority will be the one that
   (A) is for the greatest amount
   (B) is a permanent mortgage
   (C) was recorded first
   (D) is a construction loan mortgage

9. A development in which a person owns her dwelling unit and, in common with other owners in the same project, also owns common property is
   (A) a leased fee
   (B) a condominium
   (C) a homestead
   (D) none of the above

10. Which of the following is true?
    (A) A condominium owner need not pay condominium fees that he feels are too high.
    (B) Condominium units are attached housing units.
    (C) Condominium is an ownership form, not an architectural style.
    (D) Condominiums cannot be rented.

11. The money for making FHA loans is provided by
    (A) qualified lending institutions
    (B) the Department of Housing and Urban Development
    (C) the Federal Housing Administration
    (D) the Federal Savings and Loan Insurance Corporation

12. License law forbids
    (A) soliciting for listings before one is licensed
    (B) collecting a commission from more than one party to a transaction
    (C) showing property to other licensees
    (D) the purchase by a broker of property that she has listed

13. The term REALTOR®
    (A) is a registered trademark
    (B) refers to anyone who has a real estate license
    (C) refers to anyone who sells real estate
    (D) none of the above

14. Complaints about housing discrimination may be brought
    (A) to the Secretary of Housing and Urban Development
    (B) directly to court
    (C) either A or B
    (D) neither A nor B

15. Which of the following is (are) ALWAYS exempt from real property taxes?
    (A) income-producing property owned by a church
    (B) government-owned property
    (C) most restaurants
    (D) a private, for-profit school

16. Tenancy in severalty refers to
    (A) ownership by a married couple
    (B) ownership by one person
    (C) ownership by people who are related, but not married
    (D) ownership by unrelated people

17. For every contract of sale there must be
    (A) an offer and acceptance   (C) a broker
    (B) a mortgage loan   (D) good consideration

18. Real estate brokers can lose their licenses for which of the following?
    (A) using moneys received as commissions to pay office help
    (B) representing the buyer in a transaction
    (C) refusing a listing
    (D) paying a commission to a nonlicensed person

19. A broker must keep all earnest money deposits in
    (A) her office safe
    (B) her business checking account
    (C) an escrow or trust account
    (D) a savings account

20. Eminent domain is
    (A) the right of the government to take private property for public use
    (B) the extent to which state boundaries reach out to sea
    (C) an ancient form of ownership not common today
    (D) the right of the federal government to pass laws that supersede state law

21. An 8-year-old building was worth $190,000 after depreciating at a rate of 3% per year. What was its original value?
    (A) $195,700   (C) $250,000
    (B) $235,600   (D) $277,778

22. Flaherty's mortgage loan is for $200,000 and carries an annual interest rate of 6%. Monthly payments are $1,200. How much will the principal be reduced by the *second* monthly payment?
    (A) $200.00   (C) $1,499.00
    (B) $201.00   (D) $1,500.00

23. Bernard signs a listing that guarantees the listing broker a commission payment if the sale is effected by any licensed agent. This is
    (A) an open listing
    (B) an exclusive agency listing
    (C) an exclusive right to sell listing
    (D) a net listing

24. Macrae negotiates with Ortez to list Ortez's property once Macrae is issued his real estate license. When the license is issued, Ortez signs a listing with Macrae.
    (A) The listing is valid.
    (B) The listing is invalid.
    (C) The listing is valid only at the listing price.
    (D) Macrae can collect only half the normal commission.

25. A licensee can lose his license for
    (A) selling properties quickly, at low prices
    (B) buying property for his own use from his principal
    (C) splitting a commission with another participating broker
    (D) none of the above

26. A type of mortgage in which the lender makes periodic payments to the borrower, who is required to be age 62 or older in the FHA program, is called:
    (A) Opposite
    (B) Accelerate
    (C) Reverse
    (D) Deficit

27. A conventional mortgage is
    (A) amortizing
    (B) guaranteed by FHA
    (C) not guaranteed by a government agency
    (D) approved by the VA

28. Among other things, the principal is obligated to
    (A) compensate the agent for her services
    (B) reimburse the agent for expenses incurred on behalf of the principal
    (C) both A and B
    (D) neither A and B

29. Which of the following is NOT required to have a real estate license?
    (A) the resident manager of an apartment project
    (B) the resident manager of an apartment project who, for a fee, sells a house across the street
    (C) a student who sells houses as part of a research project
    (D) all of the above

30. Recordation of a deed is the responsibility of the
    (A) grantor
    (B) grantee
    (C) both A and B
    (D) neither A nor B

Model Examination 1

Questions 31–34 refer to the Far Hills Estates diagram below.

Far Hills Estates

31. Which of following statements is (are) true?
    (A) Four lots in Block E have frontage on two streets.
    (B) Iron Road has more lots fronting on it than any of the other streets on the plat.
    (C) both A and B
    (D) neither A nor B

32. Which lot has the greatest footage on Wood Lane?
    (A) Lot 11, Block E
    (B) Lot 12, Block E
    (C) Lot 1, Block L
    (D) Lot 19, Block E

33. Which lot has the greatest depth?
    (A) Lot 4, Block L
    (B) Lot 7, Block E
    (C) Lot 5, Block E
    (D) Lot 16, Block E

34. Which of following statements is (are) true?
    (A) The lots on the westerly side of Dale Road should appear in Block F.
    (B) There is no indication of where to find a plat of the easterly side of Lambert Drive.
    (C) both A and B
    (D) neither A nor B

35. The part of conveyance that defines or limits the quantity of the estate granted is
    (A) habendum
    (B) premises
    (C) equity
    (D) consideration

36. The Statute of Frauds
    (A) requires certain contracts to be in writing to be enforceable
    (B) requires a license to operate as broker or salesperson
    (C) regulates escrow accounts
    (D) regulates the estate owning real estate

37. A warranty deed protects the grantee against a loss by
    (A) casualty
    (B) defective title
    (C) both A and B
    (D) neither A nor B

38. Brown's building rents for $8,500 per month. The building's market value is $470,000. Taxes are 75 mills, based on 40% of market value. What percentage of the building's income must be paid out in tax?
    (A) 6.9%
    (B) 10.7%
    (C) 13.8%
    (D) 34.5%

39. Henderson bought a home for $420,000. Four years later he sold it for $599,000. What is the average annual rate of appreciation?
    (A) 9.92%
    (B) 10.65%
    (C) 13.12%
    (D) 42.62%

40. The income approach to appraisal would be most suitable for
    (A) a newly opened subdivision
    (B) commercial and investment property
    (C) property heavily mortgaged
    (D) property heavily insured

41. Real estate is defined as
    (A) land and buildings
    (B) land and all permanent attachments to it
    (C) land and everything growing on it
    (D) land only

42. A second mortgage is
    (A) a lien on real estate that has a prior mortgage on it
    (B) the first mortgage recorded
    (C) always made by the seller
    (D) smaller in amount than a first mortgage

43. Depreciation can be caused by
    (A) physical deterioration   (C) economic obsolescence
    (B) functional obsolescence   (D) all of the above

44. Regulation Z applies to
    (A) all real estate salespersons and brokers
    (B) all retail stores
    (C) all wholesale establishments
    (D) none of the above

45. Perkins bought 11 lots for $21,000 each. He keeps four and sells the remaining lots for a total of $28,000 more than he originally paid for all of them. What was the average sale price of each lot that he sold?
    (A) $21,000   (C) $37,000
    (B) $33,000   (D) $49,000

46. One discount point is equal to
    (A) 1% of the sales price   (C) 1% of the loan amount
    (B) 1% of the interest rate   (D) none of the above

47. Which of the following is NOT realty?
    (A) fee simple estate   (C) lumber
    (B) leasehold for indefinite duration (D) life estate

48. A lease can state that the rent is to be paid in
    (A) labor   (C) cash
    (B) crops   (D) any of the above

49. A mortgaged property can be
    (A) sold without the consent of the mortgagee
    (B) conveyed by the grantor making a deed to the grantee
    (C) both A and B
    (D) neither A nor B

Questions 50 and 51 refer to the diagram below of a house and a lot.

50. How many square feet are there in the house?
    (A) 384
    (B) 1,200
    (C) 1,584
    (D) 2,000

51. What percentage of the area of the lot is taken up by the house?
    (A) 13½%
    (B) 17.6%
    (C) 22.2%
    (D) 24.0%

52. Regulation Z covers
    (A) borrowing from relatives
    (B) borrowing by a business
    (C) real estate credit transactions
    (D) inheritances

53. A contract that gives someone the right but not the obligation to buy at a specified price within a specified time is
    (A) a contract of sale
    (B) an option
    (C) an agreement of sale
    (D) none of the above

54. The prohibitions of the 1968 Fair Housing Act apply to
    (A) multifamily dwellings of five or more units
    (B) multifamily dwellings of four or fewer units if the owner occupies one of the units
    (C) single-family dwellings
    (D) none of the above

55. Consideration that is of value only to the person who receives it is called
    (A) good consideration
    (B) near consideration
    (C) valuable consideration
    (D) no consideration

56. An easement in gross
    (A) covers an entire property and all parts of it
    (B) extends to one person only
    (C) extends to the general public
    (D) occurs when the public has used private land without hindrance for a certain period of time

57. A condominium homeowner's association may
    (A) require that certain owners sell their units and leave
    (B) assess fees for the upkeep of common property
    (C) practice discrimination, if it is done subtly
    (D) none of the above

58. If government takes private property it must
    (A) make just compensation for the property taken
    (B) require the property for a public use
    (C) both A and B
    (D) neither A nor B

59. The lot shown above sold for $78,300. What was the price per square foot?
    (A) $4.17   (C) $2.90
    (B) $3.56   (D) $2.45

60. A salesperson receives 60% of the total commission on a sale for $315,000. The salesperson received $15,120. What was the rate of commission?
    (A) 4.8%   (C) 6¾%
    (B) 6%   (D) 8%

61. A millage rate of 84.5 mills is the same as
    (A) $84.50 per $1,000   (C) both A and B
    (B) 8.45%   (D) neither A nor B

62. A single-family house privately owned by an individual owning fewer than three such houses may be sold or rented without being subject to the provisions of the Fair Housing Act unless
    (A) a broker is used
    (B) discriminatory advertising is used
    (C) both A and B
    (D) neither A nor B

63. The transfer, by a tenant, of certain rights and obligations of an existing lease to another tenant is called
    (A) assignment of lease
    (B) a release
    (C) subletting
    (D) an eviction

64. A "contract for deed" is also known as
    (A) an installment land sales contract
    (B) a land contract
    (C) both A and B
    (D) neither A nor B

65. Nadel buys a new house costing $188,000. Land value is 15% of total price. The house contains 1733 sq. ft. What is the cost per square foot of the house alone (not including the land)?
    (A) $16.44
    (B) $92.21
    (C) $109.64
    (D) $127.20

66. Salesman Jones works for a broker. Jones receives 42% of all commissions he brings in. Jones sells a home for $140,700, at a 6½% commission. What is the *broker's* share of the proceeds?
    (A) $3,841
    (B) $5,304
    (C) $9,146
    (D) $1,407

67. Rent for a 90 ft. by 60 ft. office is $6,300 per month. What is the annual rent per square foot?
    (A) $14
    (B) $11
    (C) $7.56
    (D) $140

68. An estoppel certificate is required when the
    (A) mortgage is sold to an investor
    (B) property is sold
    (C) property is being foreclosed
    (D) mortgage is assumed

69. An owner who seeks a mortgage loan and offers three properties as security will give
    (A) a blanket mortgage
    (B) an FHA mortgage
    (C) a conventional mortgage
    (D) a chattel mortgage

70. Ferraro bought a lot for $20,000 in 1993 and spent $130,000 to build a house on it in 1995. Today the house has increased 40% in value while the lot has increased 800%. What is the combined value of house and lot today?
    (A) $180,000
    (B) $182,000
    (C) $210,000
    (D) $362,000

71. A contract that has no force or effect is said to be
    (A) voidable
    (B) void
    (C) avoided
    (D) voidiated

72. Which of the following statements is (are) false?
    (A) FHA loans are insured loans.
    (B) VA loans are guaranteed loans.
    (C) both A and B
    (D) neither A nor B

73. To be enforceable, a sales agreement must have
    (A) the signature of the wife of a married seller
    (B) an earnest money deposit
    (C) competent parties
    (D) witnesses

74. A broker listed a house for $350,000, at a 6% commission. The eventual sales price was $315,000. How much less was the broker's commission that it would have been if the house had sold at the listed price?
    (A) $210
    (B) $2,100
    (C) $18,900
    (D) $35,000

75. How many square feet are there in 1¼ acres?
    (A) 10,890
    (B) 44,649
    (C) 54,450
    (D) 152,460

76. Under Regulation Z, borrowers must be informed in writing of
    (A) the annual percentage rate
    (B) the total dollar amount of the finance charge
    (C) both A and B
    (D) neither A nor B

77. An item of personalty that is affixed to realty so as to be used as a part of it is
    (A) a fixture
    (B) a chattel
    (C) personal property
    (D) encumbered

78. The requirement that all parties to a contract have an understanding of the conditions and stipulations of the agreement is
    (A) consenting realty
    (B) a proper offer
    (C) good and valuable consideration
    (D) mutual agreement

79. A deed of conveyance must be signed by
    (A) the grantee and the grantor
    (B) only by the grantor
    (C) both A and B
    (D) neither A nor B

80. In the application of the income approach to appraising, which of the following statements is true?
    (A) The higher the capitalization rate, the lower the appraised value.
    (B) The higher the capitalization rate, the higher the appraised value.
    (C) The present value is equal to future income.
    (D) none of the above

Model Examination 2
SALESPERSON

See page 485 for the answer key. Math problems are worked out on page 491.

NOTE: In this model examination all the arithmetic questions (questions 91–100) are grouped at the end, but you may expect that in some states the math questions will be scattered throughout the examination.

1. Jackson's will left to Mrs. Jackson the right to use, occupy, and enjoy Jackson's real estate until her death. At that time the real estate will become the property of their children. Mrs. Jackson is a
   (A) remainderman
   (B) life tenant
   (C) joint tenant
   (D) tenant in common

2. To prove his right to a commission, the broker must show
   (A) that he was licensed throughout the transaction
   (B) that he had a contract of employment
   (C) that he was the "efficient and procuring cause" of the sale
   (D) all of the above

3. Contracts made by a minor are
   (A) enforceable at all times
   (B) void
   (C) voidable by either party
   (D) voidable only by the minor

4. Mr. Beans owns land worth $25,000; Mr. Pork owns a house worth $150,000, subject to a $100,000 mortgage, which Beans will assume. For a fair trade,
   (A) Pork should pay $25,000 cash in addition
   (B) Beans should pay $25,000 cash in addition
   (C) they may trade properties evenly
   (D) none of the above

5. From the standpoint of the grantor, which of the following types of deed creates the least liability?
   (A) special warranty
   (B) general warranty
   (C) bargain and sale
   (D) quitclaim

6. The lending of money at a rate of interest above the legal rate is
   (A) speculating
   (B) usury
   (C) both A and B
   (D) neither A nor B

7. A licensee's license must be
   (A) carried in her wallet at all times
   (B) posted in a public place in the broker's office
   (C) kept on the wall at the licensee's home
   (D) kept on the wall at the Real Estate Commission

8. The parties to a deed are the
   (A) vendor and vendee
   (B) grantor and grantee
   (C) offeror and offeree
   (D) acceptor and acceptee

9. A person must be licensed if he is to sell
   (A) his home
   (B) property belonging to an estate for which he is executor
   (C) property belonging to other clients who pay him a commission
   (D) property that he has inherited

10. Which of the following is NOT an appraisal approach?
    (A) cost   (C) income
    (B) sales comparison   (D) trade

11. The most comprehensive ownership of land at law is known as
    (A) estate for years   (C) fee simple
    (B) life estate   (D) defeasible title

12. Each of the following pairs of words or phrases describes the same extent of land EXCEPT
    (A) 1 acre—43,560 square feet
    (B) 1 mile—5,280 feet
    (C) 1 square mile—460 acres
    (D) 1 section—640 acres

13. In order to sell property, one must
    (A) have a realtor's license
    (B) belong to a realtor's association
    (C) hire only realtors
    (D) none of the above

14. What are the broker's responsibilities under the 1968 Fair Housing Act?
    (A) to show all houses to all prospects
    (B) to treat all prospects equally
    (C) both A and B
    (D) neither A nor B

15. In order to be recorded, a deed must be in writing and must
    (A) be signed by the grantee
    (B) state the actual purchase price
    (C) be acknowledged
    (D) be free of all liens

16. Which of the following is NOT a good reason why real property taxes are so popular?
    (A) Real estate ownership is easy to hide.
    (B) Real estate is valuable.
    (C) Real estate is easy to find.
    (D) Real estate can be foreclosed to provide payment of unpaid tax levies.

17. The purpose of Regulation Z is to
    (A) set the maximum interest rates that may be charged
    (B) let borrowers know the cost of credit
    (C) both A and B
    (D) neither A nor B

18. Which of the following contractual arrangements would be unenforceable?
    (A) A agrees to buy B's house.
    (B) A agrees with B that B shall steal money from C.
    (C) A agrees to find a buyer for B's car.
    (D) A agrees with B that B shall make restitution to C for money stolen by B.

19. The two parties to a lease contract are the
    (A) landlord and the serf   (C) lessor and the lessee
    (B) rentor and the rentee   (D) grantor and the grantee

20. When a person deliberately lies in order to mislead a fellow party to a contract, this act is
    (A) fraud
    (B) misrepresentation
    (C) legal if no third parties are involved
    (D) all right if the lie is not written into the contract

21. A contract that transfers possession but not ownership of property is
    (A) a special warranty deed   (C) an easement
    (B) an option   (D) a lease

22. Egbert owns a building in life estate. Upon Egbert's death, ownership of the building will go to Ethel. Ethel is a
    (A) remainderman   (C) common tenant
    (B) life tenant   (D) reversionary interest

23. A person owning an undivided interest in land with at least one other, and having the right of survivorship, is said to be a
    (A) tenant in common   (C) joint tenant
    (B) tenant at will   (D) tenant at sufferance

24. A person who has some rights to use land, but not all possessory rights, is said to have
    (A) an interest in land   (C) a life estate in land
    (B) an estate in land   (D) a tenancy in common

25. Which of the following is NOT corporeal property?
    (A) fee simple real estate   (C) easement
    (B) leasehold   (D) fixture

26. A listing contract that says the broker will receive a commission no matter who sells the property is called
    (A) an open listing
    (B) a net listing
    (C) an exclusive agency listing
    (D) an exclusive right to sell listing

27. Which of the following best describes an installment or land contract?
    (A) a contract to buy land only
    (B) a mortgage on land
    (C) a means of conveying title immediately while the purchaser pays for the property
    (D) a method of selling real estate whereby the purchaser pays for the property in regular installments while the seller retains title to the property

28. Ms. Maloney has a 3-month option on 20 acres at $2,000 per acre. She may
    (A) buy the property for $40,000   (C) not buy the land
    (B) sell the option to another   (D) all of the above

29. The mortgagor's right to reestablish ownership after delinquency is known as
    (A) reestablishment   (C) equity of redemption
    (B) satisfaction   (D) acceleration

30. A broker must place funds belonging to others in
    (A) his office safe, to which only he knows the combination
    (B) a safety deposit box
    (C) an account maintained by the Real Estate Commission
    (D) a trust, or escrow, account

31. A licensee's license can be revoked for
    (A) closing a deal
    (B) intentionally misleading someone into signing a contract that she ordinarily
        would not sign
    (C) submitting a ridiculous offer to a seller
    (D) all of the above

32. Capitalization is a process used to
    (A) convert income stream into a lump sum capital value
    (B) determine cost
    (C) establish depreciation
    (D) determine potential future value

33. The number of square feet in 1 acre is
    (A) 64,000   (C) 440
    (B) 460   (D) 43,560

34. When changed surroundings cause an existing house to lose value, there is
    (A) physical deterioration   (C) functional obsolescence
    (B) economic obsolescence   (D) all of the above

35. An appraisal is
    (A) a forecast of value   (C) a prediction of value
    (B) an estimate of value   (D) a precise estimation of value

36. A lien for unpaid property taxes
    (A) can be sold at auction
    (B) takes priority over all other liens
    (C) cannot exist unless taxes are at least 36 months overdue
    (D) is a form of adverse possession

37. The prohibitions of the 1968 Fair Housing Act apply to privately owned housing
    when
    (A) a broker or other person engaged in selling or renting dwellings is used
    (B) discriminatory advertising is used
    (C) both A and B
    (D) neither A nor B

38. According to Regulation Z, to cancel a credit transaction the borrower must inform the lender, within 3 days,
    (A) by phone
    (B) in writing
    (C) both A and B
    (D) neither A nor B

39. A agrees to trade his car to B in exchange for a vacant lot that B owns.
    (A) This is a valid contractual agreement.
    (B) This is not a contract because no money changes hands.
    (C) This is not a contract because "unlike" items can't be traded.
    (D) This is not a valid contract because the car is titled in A's name.

40. A percentage lease requires the tenant to pay
    (A) a percentage of taxes and insurance
    (B) a percentage of net income as rent
    (C) a percentage of sales as rent
    (D) none of the above

41. A seller of real estate is also known as the
    (A) vendee
    (B) grantor
    (C) vendor
    (D) grantee

42. An estate at will is
    (A) a limited partnership
    (B) a tenancy of uncertain duration
    (C) an inheritance by will
    (D) a life tenancy

43. A hands B a deed with the intent to pass title and orally requests B not to record the deed until A dies. When is the deed valid?
    (A) immediately
    (B) when B records the deed
    (C) when A dies
    (D) never

44. A quitclaim deed conveys only the interest of the
    (A) guaranteed
    (B) property
    (C) claimant
    (D) grantor

45. A gross lease requires the tenant to pay rent based on
    (A) gross sales
    (B) net sales
    (C) gross profit
    (D) none of the above

46. The recording of a deed
    (A) passes the title
    (B) insures the title
    (C) guarantees the title
    (D) gives constructive notice of ownership

47. The law that requires most real estate contracts to be written to be enforceable is the
    (A) Statute of Limitations
    (B) Statute of Frauds
    (C) Statute of Written Real Estate Agreements
    (D) Law of Property

Model Examination 2

48. In the absence of an agreement to the contrary, the mortgage normally having priority will be the one that
    (A) is for the greatest amount
    (B) is a permanent mortgage
    (C) was recorded first
    (D) is a construction loan mortgage

49. A net listing is one
    (A) that requires the broker to seek a net price for the property
    (B) that is legal in all states
    (C) that most ethical brokers prefer to use
    (D) in which the broker's commission is the amount by which the sale price exceeds the agreed-upon net price the seller desires

50. Under Regulation Z, a borrower may have the right to cancel, within 3 days,
    (A) a second mortgage on his dwelling
    (B) a first mortgage loan used to purchase his dwelling
    (C) a home-improvement loan more than 1 year old
    (D) none of the above

51. Which of the following does not terminate an agency relationship?
    (A) making an offer
    (B) death of either party
    (C) resignation of agent
    (D) destruction of subject matter

52. The 1968 Fair Housing Act protects against housing discrimination on the basis of
    (A) race and color
    (B) race, color, and religion
    (C) race, color, religion, and national origin
    (D) race, color, religion, national origin, sex, familial status, and handicap

53. A person who dies leaving no will is said to have died
    (A) intestate   (C) unbequeathed
    (B) without heirs   (D) unwillingly

54. From the point of view of the grantee, the safest kind of deed that can be received is a
    (A) general warranty deed   (C) quitclaim or release deed
    (B) special warranty deed   (D) trustee's deed

55. What is NOT an essential element of a valid contract?
    (A) offer and acceptance   (C) lack of ambiguity
    (B) capacity of participants   (D) legal objective

56. A freehold estate is
    (A) an estate acquired without paying anything
    (B) any leasehold
    (C) any estate wherein one may use the property as one wishes
    (D) an estate of uncertain duration

57. In order to do business, a licensee must
    (A) make proper application for a license
    (B) pass a licensing examination
    (C) have a license issued by the appropriate state agency
    (D) all of the above

58. When a loan is assumed on property that is sold,
    (A) the original borrower is relieved of further responsibility
    (B) the purchaser becomes liable for the debt
    (C) the purchaser must obtain a certificate of eligibility
    (D) all of the above

59. An estoppel certificate is often required when a
    (A) mortgage is sold to an investor
    (B) property is sold
    (C) property is being foreclosed
    (D) mortgage is assumed

60. Which of the following will not terminate a lease?
    (A) performance   (C) surrender
    (B) breach   (D) vacancy

61. The adjustment process in the direct sales comparison approach involves the principle of
    (A) contribution   (C) variable proportions
    (B) diminishing returns (D) anticipation

62. A contract in which A agrees to allow B to use A's real estate in return for periodic payments of money by B is a
    (A) deed   (C) lease
    (B) contract of sale   (D) mortgage

63. Dower rights assure that
    (A) a husband receives a certain portion of his deceased wife's estate
    (B) wives and, in some states, children receive a certain portion of a deceased husband's or father's estate
    (C) a homeowner cannot lose his entire investment in his home
    (D) husbands and wives share equally in property acquired during marriage

64. When an individual holds property past the expiration of a lease without the landlord's consent, the leasehold estate she has is a
    (A) tenancy at sufferance   (C) common of pasturage
    (B) freehold estate   (D) holdover tenancy

65. A broker's unlicensed secretary
    (A) may sell property providing he does it under the broker's direct supervision
    (B) may sell or negotiate deals so long as he does not leave the office
    (C) may refer interested clients to the broker or her employed licensees
    (D) all of the above

Model Examination 2

66. An ARM is an
    (A) alternative reliable mode
    (B) automobile repair mechanic
    (C) adjustable-rate mortgage
    (D) authentic riparian model

67. Which of the following is NOT required of an agent with respect to his principal?
    (A) to be loyal
    (B) to act in person
    (C) to account for the agent's own personal finances
    (D) to act in the principal's best interests

68. Tenancy in severalty refers to
    (A) ownership by one person only
    (B) ownership by two persons only
    (C) ownership by at least three persons
    (D) a special form of joint ownership available only to married couples

69. A person who has permission to use land, but has no other rights, has
    (A) tenancy at sufferance   (C) license
    (B) tenancy in common   (D) fee simple estate

70. When tastes and standards cause an existing house to lose value, there is
    (A) physical deterioration   (C) functional obsolescence
    (B) economic obsolescence   (D) all of the above

71. A rule-of-thumb method for determining the price a wage earner can afford to pay for a home is to multiply her annual income by
    (A) 1½   (C) 4
    (B) 2½   (D) 6

72. A real estate license, once received,
    (A) remains in effect indefinitely
    (B) is good for a limited period of time
    (C) must be filed in county records
    (D) may be inherited by the holder's spouse

73. Which of the following is most accurately described as personal property?
    (A) a fixture   (C) an improvement
    (B) a chattel   (D) realty

74. A real estate broker is a
    (A) general agent   (C) secret agent
    (B) special agent   (D) travel agent

75. A broker may use escrow moneys held on behalf of others
    (A) for collateral for business loans
    (B) for collateral for personal loans
    (C) for salary advances to licensees in his employ
    (D) none of the above

76. Which of the following forms of deeds has one or more guarantees of title?
    (A) quitclaim (C) warranty
    (B) executor's (D) special form

77. The highest price a buyer is willing, but not compelled, to pay and the lowest price a seller is willing, but not compelled, to accept is
    (A) estimated value (C) marginal value
    (B) economic value (D) market value

78. To be valid, a deed need NOT necessarily be
    (A) signed (C) sealed
    (B) written (D) delivered

79. A person who receives title to land by virtue of having used and occupied it for a certain period of time, without actually paying the previous owner for it, receives title by
    (A) will (C) alienation
    (B) descent (D) adverse possession

80. A conventional mortgage is
    (A) amortizing
    (B) guaranteed by the FHA
    (C) not guaranteed by a government agency
    (D) approved by the VA

81. The party to whom a deed conveys real estate is the
    (A) grantee (C) beneficiary
    (B) grantor (D) recipient

82. Which is NOT considered a permanent attachment to land?
    (A) anything growing on it
    (B) fixtures
    (C) chattels
    (D) anything built on the land

83. The main appeal of VA mortgages to borrowers lies in
    (A) low interest rates (C) unlimited mortgage ceiling
    (B) minimum down payments (D) easy availability

84. For which reason is a deed recorded?
    (A) to insure certain title (C) to meet a state requirement
    (B) to give notice to the world (D) to save title insurance cost

85. Ownership of real property is transferred
    (A) when the grantor signs the deed
    (B) when the grantor's signature has been notarized
    (C) when the deed is delivered
    (D) when the correct documentary stamps are put on the deed and canceled

86. A valid contract of purchase or sale of real property must be signed by the
    (A) broker (C) seller only
    (B) agent and seller (D) buyer and seller

87. A sublease is a
   (A) lease made by a lessor
   (B) lease made by a lessee and a third party
   (C) lease for basement space
   (D) condition of property

88. "Hand money" paid upon the signing of an agreement of sale is called
   (A) an option
   (B) a recognizance
   (C) earnest money
   (D) a freehold estate

89. Market value appraisals assume that
   (A) the purchaser pays all cash (no mortgage financing)
   (B) FHA or VA financing is employed
   (C) the appraiser can determine the types of financing involved
   (D) the financing, if any, is on terms generally available in that area

90. A licensed salesperson
   (A) must work under the supervision of a broker
   (B) can collect commission payments only from his broker
   (C) must have his license held by his employing broker
   (D) all of the above

91. If the property is assessed at $180,000 and the millage rate is 32.5, the tax is
   (A) $58.50
   (B) $585
   (C) $5,850
   (D) $58,500

92. Smith sold three lots for a total of $90,000. The first lot sold for 1½ times the price of the second lot. The second lot sold for twice the price of the third lot. How much did the first lot sell for?
   (A) $15,000
   (B) $30,000
   (C) $45,000
   (D) $90,000

93. Aaronson owns a 44-acre tract of land. In order to develop it, he must set aside 10% of the area for parks and must use 6.6 acres for streets, drainage, and other uses. If the minimum permissible lot size is 7,500 sq. ft., what is the maximum possible number of lots Aaronson can lay out?
   (A) 191
   (B) 180
   (C) 293
   (D) 81

94. Velez borrowed $7,500 for 4 years, paying interest every quarter. The total amount of interest she paid was $2,700. What was the annual interest rate?
   (A) 9%
   (B) 10%
   (C) 27%
   (D) 36%

95. Jim sold a parcel of land for $164,450. He made a profit of 43%. What was his purchase price?
   (A) $82,755.00
   (B) $93,736.50
   (C) $115,000.00
   (D) $164,450.00

96. Anne referred a customer to Connie, who sold the customer a house for $139,500. Connie paid Anne a referral fee of 12% of Connie's commission. If Anne received $1,171.80, what was the rate of the commission on Connie's sale?
    (A) 5%
    (B) 6%
    (C) 6½%
    (D) 7%

97. What monthly rent must Sam get on his land in order to earn an annual return of 11% on the $210,000 that he paid for the land? Assume that the tenant pays all property taxes.
    (A) $275
    (B) $1552
    (C) $1925
    (D) $23,100

98. Smith bought three lots for $10,000 each. If they increase in value by 25% each year *compounded*, in how many years will she be able to sell one of the lots for as much as she originally paid for all three?
    (A) 4
    (B) 5
    (C) 6
    (D) 7

99. How many acres are contained in a rectangular tract of land measuring 1,700 ft. by 2,100 ft.?
    (A) 81.96
    (B) 92.91
    (C) 112.01
    (D) 115.00

100. A backyard measures 100 ft. by 80 ft. The house is 40 ft. wide. A fence 4 ft. high is to be built around the yard, with the width of the house as part of the barrier. If fence fabric is $1.80 per square yard, how much will the necessary fence fabric cost?
    (A) $64
    (B) $256
    (C) $288
    (D) $2,304

Model Examination 2

Model Examination 3
SALESPERSON

See page 486 for the answer key. Math problems are worked out on page 492.

1. An appraisal is
   (A) a forecast of value
   (B) a prediction of value
   (C) an appraiser's opinion of value
   (D) a statement of exact value

2. The number of square feet in 1 acre is
   (A) 640
   (B) 45,630
   (C) 43,560
   (D) 53,460

3. How is the *gross rent multiplier* calculated?
   (A) market value/market rental
   (B) monthly payment/market rental
   (C) market rental/market price
   (D) sales price/market price

4. A perfectly rectangular tract of land contains exactly 10.6 acres. The measurement on one side is 181 ft. To the nearest foot, how deep is the tract?
   (A) 255 ft.
   (B) 385 ft.
   (C) 1,817 ft.
   (D) 2,551 ft.

5. What is the maximum number of 8,000-sq.-ft. lots that can be platted from a 17.1-acre tract if 19% of the land must be used for streets and parks?
   (A) 17
   (B) 62
   (C) 75
   (D) 93

6. Laws that set minimum construction standards are
   (A) building codes
   (B) zoning codes
   (C) environmental laws
   (D) condemnation laws

7. Which of the following is NOT an appraisal approach?
   (A) cost
   (B) trade
   (C) sales comparison
   (D) income

8. Value is determined by
   (A) supply and demand
   (B) asking prices
   (C) interest rates
   (D) active brokers

9. Permission for land use not normally permitted by the zoning classification of the property is
   (A) a differential
   (B) a zone change
   (C) a variance
   (D) an egregement

10. Smith sells a tract of land 400 ft. by 665 ft. for $17,100. To the nearest dollar, what is the price per acre?
    (A) $2,800
    (B) $2,950
    (C) $3,117
    (D) $3,228

11. In Green's city, the property tax rate is 71 mills, based upon 30% of the market value of the property. Green just paid $170,000 for a home. What will the tax be?
    - (A) $3,621
    - (B) $4,470
    - (C) $7,317
    - (D) $12,070

12. When changes in taste cause kitchen fixtures to become less desirable, there is
    - (A) physical deterioration
    - (B) functional obsolescence
    - (C) economic obsolescence
    - (D) all of the above

13. The income approach is generally most suitable for appraising
    - (A) commercial and investment property
    - (B) single-family homes
    - (C) heavily mortgaged property
    - (D) heavily insured property

Questions 14–16 concern the following situation:

Mr. Jones died, leaving Mrs. Jones the right to use, occupy, and enjoy his real estate until her death, at which time their son Willis would receive a fee simple estate in the real estate.

14. Mrs. Jones is a
    - (A) remainderman
    - (B) life tenant
    - (C) joint tenant
    - (D) tenant in common

15. Willis is a
    - (A) remainderman
    - (B) life tenant
    - (C) joint tenant
    - (D) tenant in common

16. Mrs. Jones has a
    - (A) fee simple estate in joint tenancy with Willis
    - (B) fee simple estate as tenant in common with Willis
    - (C) life estate
    - (D) reversionary interest

---

17. A building 40 ft. by 22 ft. has exterior walls 10 ft. high. There are 13 windows, 4 sq. ft. each, and a door measuring 48 sq. ft. One gallon of paint covers 400 sq. ft. If the door and the windows are not to be painted, how many gallons of paint are needed to give the walls *two* full coats?
    - (A) 2.85
    - (B) 5.7
    - (C) 3.1
    - (D) 6.2

18. Bernini borrows $12,000. He pays $210 each quarter in interest. What is the annual interest rate on this loan?
    - (A) 1.75%
    - (B) 5.75%
    - (C) 7%
    - (D) 8.5%

19. A freehold estate is
    - (A) an estate acquired without paying anything for it
    - (B) an estate always acquired by adverse possession
    - (C) an estate of uncertain duration
    - (D) any leasehold estate

20. A person who appears to own a piece of real estate, but actually does not, has
    - (A) good title
    - (B) recorded title
    - (C) constructive notice
    - (D) color of title

21. A real estate broker is
    - (A) a general agent
    - (B) an attorney-in-fact
    - (C) a special agent
    - (D) an agent provocateur

22. Contracts made by a minor are
    - (A) void
    - (B) voidable by the minor
    - (C) voidable by all parties
    - (D) voidable by adult parties

23. The parties to a deed are
    - (A) vendor and vendee
    - (B) testator and testatee
    - (C) grantor and grantee
    - (D) offeror and offeree

24. Ms. Levy has the choice of renting a house for $1,800 per month, including utilities, or for $1,400 per month if she pays the utility bills. Average utility bills are $3,840 per year, but Ms. Levy feels she can reduce this by 35%. How much *per month* does she expect to save by paying the utility bills herself?
    - (A) $0
    - (B) $120
    - (C) $144
    - (D) $192

25. Salesman O'Hara gets 50% of the first $50,000 of commissions he brings in and 60% of all above that amount in 1 year. Last year he sold $2,750,000 of real estate, all at 7% commission. How much did O'Hara get to keep?
    - (A) $192,500
    - (B) $115,500
    - (C) $110,500
    - (D) $85,500

26. A quitclaim deed conveys only the interest of the
    - (A) grantor
    - (B) claimant
    - (C) quittor
    - (D) property

27. Which of the following will NOT terminate a lease?
    - (A) breach
    - (B) performance
    - (C) vacancy
    - (D) surrender

28. One discount point is equal to
    - (A) 1% of the sale price
    - (B) 1% of the loan amount
    - (C) 1% of the interest rate
    - (D) none of the above

29. Which of the following is NOT covered by title insurance?
    - (A) forged deed
    - (B) deed by incompetent
    - (C) tornado damage
    - (D) undisclosed heirs

30. Ownership of realty by one person is
    - (A) tenancy in severalty
    - (B) conjoint tenancy
    - (C) tenancy by the entirety
    - (D) tenancy sole

31. Green made an offer to purchase real estate from Blue. The offer gave Blue 7 days to consider it. Two days later, without hearing anything from Blue, Green found another property that he liked better. Green then wanted to withdraw his offer to Blue.
    - (A) Green had to wait until the 7 days had passed.
    - (B) Green was required to notify Blue of his desire to withdraw the offer, and to give Blue "reasonable time" to accept or reject it.
    - (C) Green could withdraw the offer immediately.
    - (D) none of the above

32. The secondary mortgage market is the market
    (A) for second mortgages
    (B) in which existing mortgages are bought and sold
    (C) in which junior mortgages are originated
    (D) for older, low-interest loan assumptions

33. A landowner leases her land to a lessee, who in turn leases the land to a sublessee. Who holds the *sandwich lease*?
    (A) landowner
    (B) lessee
    (C) sublessee
    (D) none of the above

34. The covenant whereby a person warrants that he is the possessor and owner of property being conveyed is the covenant of
    (A) seizin
    (B) habendum
    (C) possession
    (D) further assurance

35. Title to land passes
    (A) on the date shown on the deed
    (B) upon recordation of the deed
    (C) when the deed is signed
    (D) upon delivery of the deed

36. Provisions for defeat of the mortgage are found in the____clause.
    (A) alienation
    (B) acceleration
    (C) foreclosure
    (D) defeasance

37. All mortgages are
    (A) due on sale
    (B) security for a debt
    (C) recorded
    (D) none of the above

38. A fixture is
    (A) anything that cannot be removed from the real estate without leaving a hole
    (B) anything the property owner says is a fixture
    (C) anything necessary to the proper and efficient use of the real estate
    (D) none of the above

39. Byrd lives in an apartment owned by Lyon. The lease has expired, but Byrd has stayed on and continues to pay rent to Lyon. This is an example of tenancy
    (A) by remainder
    (B) at will
    (C) at suffrance
    (D) in common

40. Which of the following is NOT real estate?
    (A) a flagpole affixed to a house
    (B) a tomato crop not ready to harvest
    (C) a greenhouse
    (D) all of the above *are* real estate

41. The law that requires that all transfers of ownership rights to real estate be in writing is the
    (A) Statute of Frauds
    (B) Statute of Limitations
    (C) Parol Evidence Rule
    (D) Statute of Liberties

42. After paying a 6½% commission, Jackson received net proceeds of $336,132.50 on the sale of his home. What was the sale price?
    (A) $21,848.60
    (B) $357,981.10
    (C) $359,500.00
    (D) $375,000.00

43. When a valid lease of real estate exists, and the rent is paid on time, which of the following is false?
    (A) The lessor cannot move in and use the property until the lease expires.
    (B) The lessee possesses the right of occupancy.
    (C) The lessee holds the fee to the real estate.
    (D) The lessor has a reversionary interest in the real estate.

44. The clause in a mortgage note that allows the lender to demand immediate payment in full of the remaining balance, if payment of the note is not made as contracted, is the____clause.
    (A) alienation
    (B) acceleration
    (C) foreclosure
    (D) amortization

45. All of the following should be recorded EXCEPT
    (A) an easement
    (B) a 20-year lease
    (C) a mortgage
    (D) a 6-month lease

46. In a typical mortgage loan transaction, the mortgagee is the
    (A) lender
    (B) borrower
    (C) appraiser
    (D) closing agent

47. Which of the following has access to documents that have been recorded in the public records?
    (A) prospective buyers
    (B) prospective lenders
    (C) appraisers
    (D) all of the above

48. Ms. Anderson sold a tract of land. After paying a 9% commission and paying 3% of the selling price in taxes, fees, and closing costs, she ended up with $176,000. What was the sale price of the land?
    (A) $181,280
    (B) $191,840
    (C) $197,120
    (D) $200,000

49. Farley's warehouse measures 52 ft. by 36 ft. The walls are 9 in. thick, and there are 13 support pillars inside the building, each 6 in. by 6 in. What is the area, in square feet, of the *net* interior floor space?
    (A) 1,739
    (B) $1,742^1/_4$
    (C) $1,803^5/_{16}$
    (D) $1,806^9/_{16}$

50. Title that establishes ownership of real estate in a reasonably clear manner upon examination of the public records is____title.
    (A) owner's
    (B) marketable
    (C) equitable
    (D) quiet

51. A certain property has no road frontage; however, there exists a recorded right of access across a neighboring parcel of land. This right is
    (A) a conditional title
    (B) an entroversion
    (C) an easement
    (D) a defeasance

52. An estate that may be terminated by any party at any time is an estate
    (A) for years
    (B) at will
    (C) in possession
    (D) in termination

53. If the commission in a listing contract is arranged so that the broker receives all of the purchase price in excess of a certain figure, the listing is a(n)____listing.
    (A) open
    (B) net
    (C) gross
    (D) multiple

54. Which of the following does NOT have the right of survivorship?
    (A) tenant in common
    (B) joint tenant
    (C) tenant by the entirety
    (D) all *have* the right of survivorship

55. In a VA loan transaction, to whom is the discount (if any) paid?
    (A) the VA
    (B) the lender
    (C) the broker
    (D) the buyer

56. What agency administers VA loan guarantees?
    (A) Veterans Authority
    (B) Virginia Association of Realtors
    (C) Department of Veterans Affairs
    (D) Veterinarians Association

57. A building that Montez leases is destroyed by an earthquake. Under common law,
    (A) the lease is no longer enforceable
    (B) Montez needn't pay rent until the building is rebuilt
    (C) Montez must rebuild the building, but may deduct the cost from the rent
    (D) Montez must continue to pay rent until the lease expires

58. Which of the following is neither real estate nor a fixture?
    (A) ceiling
    (B) chandelier on ceiling
    (C) light bulb in chandelier
    (D) light switch

59. Real estate brokers and salespeople should be familiar with
    (A) common law
    (B) agency law
    (C) license law
    (D) all of the above

60. Which of the following is NOT always a right possessed by an owner of a fee simple estate?
    (A) possession
    (B) easement
    (C) occupancy
    (D) disposition

61. Which of the following would NOT be considered commercial real estate?
    (A) office building
    (B) condominium home
    (C) shopping center
    (D) doctors' office complex

62. Smith wishes to develop a subdivision containing 55 lots averaging 10,500 sq. ft. each. An average of 1380 sq. ft. of street, sidewalk, and other space must be provided for each lot. What is the minimum number of acres that Smith will need?
    (A) 12
    (B) 14
    (C) 15
    (D) 17

63. Which of the following instructions from a seller may NOT be complied with by a real estate broker?
    (A) Don't put up a for sale sign in the yard.
    (B) Don't present offers for less than the listing price.
    (C) Don't show the property to persons who do not speak English.
    (D) Don't show the property on religious holidays observed by seller.

64. Real estate brokers' commissions usually are set by
    (A) the local board of realtors
    (B) the laws of the state
    (C) agreement with other brokerage firms
    (D) agreement between property owner and broker

65. When a licensed salesperson advertises property for sale,
    (A) the name of the broker must be mentioned
    (B) only the salesperson's name must be mentioned
    (C) the name of the property owner must be revealed
    (D) the price must not be mentioned

66. Which form of listing does NOT allow the seller to sell her listed property by herself without paying the listing broker a commission?
    (A) open listing
    (B) exclusive right-to-sell listing
    (C) multiple listing
    (D) exclusive agency listing

67. A broker has a listing the terms of which allow him to earn a commission only if he finds a buyer before the seller or another broker does. This is an example of
    (A) an open listing
    (B) an exclusive right to sell listing
    (C) a net listing
    (D) an exclusive agency listing

68. Part of an addition that Sam builds to his home turns out to be on land belonging to June. This is an example of
    (A) accretion
    (B) riparian rights
    (C) easement
    (D) encroachment

69. Tina has the legal right to use Fred's driveway for her lifetime. Tina has
    (A) a life estate
    (B) an easement in gross
    (C) a license to use
    (D) a riparian right

70. Simpson wishes to install wall-to-wall carpeting in his home, which measures 42 × 28 ft. The outside walls are 6 in. thick, and the interior walls are 4 in. thick. There are 135 linear ft. of wall inside the home. The two bathrooms (each with interior measurements of 9 ft. × 6 ft.) and the kitchen (12 ft. × 12 ft.) are not to be carpeted. If installed carpeting costs $13.95 per square yard, how much will the job cost?
    (A) $1,255.50
    (B) $1,222.95
    (C) $1,506.60
    (D) $1,715.85

71. Ms. Farrell contracts to buy a house for $330,000. She pays $9,000 in earnest money and applies for a 75% loan. How much more money will she need to make up the purchase price of the home?
    (A) $80,250
    (B) $73,500
    (C) $64,500
    (D) $29,250

72. Leo allows Lemmie to stay in Leo's house while Leo is on vacation, but Lemmie must leave when Leo returns. Lemmie has
    (A) a short-term lease
    (B) a proprietary right
    (C) a license
    (D) an easement

73. An estate that has an indefinite duration is
    (A) a freehold estate
    (B) a renewable leasehold
    (C) an estate at suffrance
    (D) a nonfreehold estate

74. How many 100 ft. × 100 ft. lots can be made out of a 3-acre plot of land?
    (A) 6
    (B) 11
    (C) 13
    (D) 43

75. A lot sold for $225 a front foot. If the lot was 96 ft. deep and had an area of 6,336 sq. ft., how much did the lot sell for?
    (A) $11,770
    (B) $14,256
    (C) $14,850
    (D) $21,600

76. A "legal description" of land must
    (A) be sufficient to identify the property
    (B) carry measurements to the nearest inch
    (C) show the area of the land being described
    (D) all of the above

77. Increase in the size of a plot of land because of soil deposited by the flow of a stream is called
    (A) accretion
    (B) riparian right
    (C) depletion
    (D) amortization

78. If an offer is *rescinded*, it is
    (A) revised
    (B) altered
    (C) terminated
    (D) accepted

79. Which of the following is NOT necessarily required in a deed?
    (A) acknowledgment
    (B) grantee's signature
    (C) date
    (D) description of real estate

80. Government's right to regulate land use derives from
    (A) escheat
    (B) just compensation
    (C) police power
    (D) eminent domain

Model Examination 4
BROKER

See page 486 for the answer key. Math problems are worked out on page 493.

1. The number of dollars remaining each year after cash expenses are deducted from cash rent receipts and other property income is
   (A) cash-on-cash
   (B) cash depletion
   (C) cash amortization
   (D) cash flow

2. The market value of a house is $350,000. If property is assessed at 20% of market value and the annual tax rate is 80 mills, how much is the tax?
   (A) $5,600
   (B) $10,700
   (C) $17,500
   (D) $28,000

3. Loss of value because a property is located in a rundown neighborhood is known as
   (A) physical deterioration
   (B) functional obsolescence
   (C) economic obsolescence
   (D) none of the above

4. Which of the following is NOT realty?
   (A) a 50-year lease
   (B) a fee simple estate
   (C) an easement in gross
   (D) a life estate

5. Which of the following is adequate recitation of consideration in a deed?
   (A) "For ten dollars and other valuable consideration"
   (B) "For natural love and affection"
   (C) the actual amount of consideration paid
   (D) all of the above

6. One type of depreciation generally is NOT curable. This type of depreciation is
   (A) physical deterioration
   (B) functional obsolescence
   (C) economic obsolescence
   (D) all of the above

7. Which of the following can enter into a listing agreement, in his own name, to sell real estate for a fee?
   (A) a licensed salesperson
   (B) a licensed broker
   (C) a trustee
   (D) none of the above

8. A licensed salesperson who wishes to sell her own property must
   (A) list the property with her broker
   (B) inform prospective purchasers that she is the owner
   (C) not list the property with anyone because of possible conflict of interest
   (D) not take the listing herself

Questions 9–13 refer to the following situation:

Robby buys a condo from Juan. The price is $150,000. Robby gets a VA loan for 80% of the purchase price. The loan discount paid by Juan is three points. The broker's commission on the sale is 6%. The contract interest rate on the VA loan is 4%.

9. Assuming that there are no closing costs other than those cited above, how much does Juan end up with?
   (A) $109,200
   (B) $136,500
   (C) $137,400
   (D) $139,200

10. What is the dollar amount of the discount?
    (A) $2,340
    (B) $2,700
    (C) $3,600
    (D) $4,500

11. What is the lender's approximate effective rate of return on the loan?
    (A) 7%
    (B) 4.375%
    (C) 4%
    (D) 3.625%

12. Who pays the discount on the VA loan?
    (A) Juan
    (B) Robby
    (C) the broker
    (D) the VA

13. To whom is the discount paid?
    (A) the broker
    (B) the lender
    (C) the VA
    (D) the FHA

---

14. A designated agency occurs when
    (A) a broker assigns a licensee within the firm to work with a buyer or seller in a transaction in which the original licensee represents both parties
    (B) a seller chooses one licensee to show the property and designates a different licensee to negotiate with potential buyers
    (C) a buyer asks a broker to assign one of the firm's agents to work with him as a buyer's agent
    (D) none of the above

15. Which of the following both originate mortgage loans and service them?
    (A) mortgage bankers
    (B) savings and loan associations
    (C) commercial banks
    (D) all of the above

16. Which of the following can be used as security for the payment of a debt?
    (A) mortgage
    (B) deed of trust
    (C) release of lien
    (D) A and B only

17. A lender may refuse to make a mortgage loan because of the
    (A) inability of the borrower to repay
    (B) location of the property
    (C) both A and B
    (D) neither A nor B

18. A mortgage held by the seller of the mortgaged property is
    (A) a purchase money mortgage
    (B) a satisfaction piece
    (C) a lien dependent
    (D) a joint tenancy

19. A recorded instrument that concerns ownership rights to realty
    (A) gives constructive notice
    (B) notifies the public of the claims made in it
    (C) must be notarized or acknowledged
    (D) all of the above

20. Jones acquires a fee simple estate to land belonging to Green because Jones used and occupied the land openly for a period of time, unmolested by Green. This is
    (A) an easement in gross   (C) an estoppel
    (B) an adverse possession   (D) a subrogation

21. A person who has another's power of attorney is called
    (A) an agent in place   (C) a lawyer
    (B) a real estate broker   (D) an attorney-in-fact

22. The right of the state to take title to real estate for which no legal owner can be found is called
    (A) police power   (C) eminent domain
    (B) tenancy   (D) escheat

23. Zach dies without a will. According to the laws of the state, Zelda receives title to Zach's real estate. Zelda has received
    (A) title by descent   (C) an easement
    (B) clouded title   (D) legacy title

24. A person may void a contract if it
    (A) was entered into under duress
    (B) was entered into with a minor
    (C) turned out to be a bad deal
    (D) all of the above

25. Which of the following real estate contracts can be unilateral?
    (A) a lease   (C) a mortgage
    (B) a contract of sale   (D) none of the above

26. Which of the following has no warranty?
    (A) executor's deed   (C) general warranty deed
    (B) quitclaim deed   (D) trustee's deed

27. A worker who is not paid for work that improved real estate may file a
    (A) suit for quiet title   (C) mechanic's lien
    (B) lis pendens   (D) satisfaction piece

28. What is the cash-on-cash ratio for a property that has a cash flow of $16,900 and an initial investor's cash equity of $130,000?
    (A) 7.69%   (C) 0.12
    (B) 0.219   (D) 0.13

29. What percent of a square mile is 200 acres?
    (A) 27.5%
    (C) 31.25%
    (B) 43.478%
    (D) 10%

30. When a property is foreclosed, which claim takes first priority?
    (A) tax lien
    (C) second mortgage
    (B) first mortgage
    (D) mechanic's lien

31. A parcel of land is 440 ft. by 817 ft. How many acres does it contain?
    (A) 17
    (C) 11.67
    (B) 8.25
    (D) More than 75

32. Which of the following is a specific lien?
    (A) a judgment
    (C) a lease
    (B) a mechanic's lien
    (D) none of the above

33. Real estate is
    (A) land and buildings
    (B) land and all permanent attachments to it
    (C) land only
    (D) land and everything growing on it

34. In an agency relationship, the employer is called the
    (A) seller
    (C) principal
    (B) buyer
    (D) broker

35. Real estate licenses, once received, are
    (A) valid indefinitely
    (C) inheritable
    (B) filed in the county record office
    (D) valid for a limited period only

36. In a lease contract, the tenant is the
    (A) lessee
    (C) leasee
    (B) lessor
    (D) leasor

37. Consideration that has value only to the person receiving it is
    (A) no consideration
    (C) valuable consideration
    (B) good consideration
    (D) good and valuable consideration

38. A general warranty deed protects the grantee against a loss by
    (A) casualty
    (C) defective materials
    (B) defective title
    (D) all of the above

39. A lease that requires the tenant to pay operating expenses of the property
    is a ____ lease.
    (A) gross
    (C) net
    (B) flat
    (D) step

40. A house is valued at $55,560 for property tax purposes. This is the
    (A) assessed value
    (C) market value
    (B) appraised value
    (D) replacement value

41. Taxes are due on October 15 of the year in which they are assessed. Tax rate is 38 mills. Assessed value is $48,500. If a sale of the property is closed on July 15, then at settlement (using the statutory year)
    (A) seller owes buyer $998.29
    (B) buyer owes seller $998.29
    (C) seller owes buyer $844.71
    (D) seller owes buyer $1,843.00

42. The mortgagor's right to reestablish ownership after foreclosure is called
    (A) acceleration
    (B) resatisfaction right
    (C) equity of redemption
    (D) redemption provenance

43. Regulation Z
    (A) sets maximum interest rates on mortgage loans
    (B) determines discounts on VA loans
    (C) allows borrowers to repay loans ahead of time without penalty
    (D) requires that borrowers be informed of the cost of credit

44. Which of the following statements is true?
    (A) a tenancy at will may be terminated at any time by either tenant or landlord.
    (B) GRM stands for gross reproduction method.
    (C) a tenancy in severalty involves a married couple.
    (D) all of the above

45. Which of the following represent(s) functional obsolescence?
    (A) no electrical outlets in some rooms
    (B) one bathroom in a 12-room house
    (C) both A and B
    (D) neither A nor B

46. An appraisal is
    (A) a forecast of value
    (B) an estimate of value
    (C) a prediction of value
    (D) a statement of exact value

47. At settlement, the buyer paid the seller $250.16 toward the annual tax bill of $763.20. If taxes are assessed for the calendar year and must be paid by July 15, what was the date of the settlement?
    (A) April 28
    (B) September 2
    (C) March 30
    (D) can't be determined

48. Which of the following statements is false?
    (A) A tax lien takes priority over all other liens.
    (B) In a closing statement, earnest money is an item likely to be credited to the buyer.
    (C) Joint tenants have the right of survivorship.
    (D) none of the above

49. If a borrower defaults on the payments to a mortgage loan, which clause allows the lender to demand immediate payment in full of the entire remaining loan balance?
    (A) defeasance
    (B) subrogation
    (C) acceleration
    (D) due-on-sale

50. Which of the following has the right of survivorship?
    (A) joint tenant
    (B) tenant in severalty
    (C) tenant in common
    (D) life tenant

51. In the covenant of seizin the
    (A) mortgagee states that he is foreclosing
    (B) lessor states that the lessee has not abided by the lease contract
    (C) grantor states that she owns the estate being transferred
    (D) lessee states that he is being evicted

52. Escheat is
    (A) the right to cross someone else's land to get to the road
    (B) a variety of fraud exclusive to real estate
    (C) the right to inherit if there is no will
    (D) none of the above

53. A lot is 75 ft. wide and contains 825 sq. yd. How deep is it?
    (A) 6 rods   (C) 32 yd.
    (B) 88 ft.   (D) ¹⁄₁₆ mi.

54. A broker's license is suspended for 6 months. The broker's two salespersons
    (A) also lose their licenses for 6 months
    (B) may continue to operate the broker's business
    (C) may, upon proper application, transfer their licenses to another broker
    (D) must place their licenses on inactive status for 6 months

55. One acre is equal to
    (A) 45,360 square feet   (C) 43,560 square feet
    (B) 54,630 square feet   (D) 17,810 square yards

56. The largest "bundle of rights" to real estate is a____estate.
    (A) leasehold   (C) life
    (B) fee simple   (D) homestead

57. In an exclusive right-to-sell listing,
    (A) only one broker is authorized to act as the seller's agent
    (B) if the seller finds the buyer, the seller still must pay the broker a commission
    (C) both A and B
    (D) neither A nor B

58. Salesperson Lois sold a house for $132,000. If her broker received 60% of the commission, and Lois's 45% share of that amount was $2,316.60, what was the commission rate charged on the sale?
    (A) 6%   (C) 7%
    (B) 6.5%   (D) 7.5%

59. A ¼-acre lot sold for $120,000. What was the price per square foot?
    (A) $11.02   (C) $22.00
    (B) $2.75   (D) $18.20

60. To prove that he is entitled to a commission, a broker must show that
    (A) he was licensed throughout the transaction
    (B) the price was a fair one
    (C) all liens on the property have been settled
    (D) all of the above

61. A broker receives two offers on the same property at the same time. She should
    (A) submit both offers
    (B) submit the better offer while trying to improve the other one
    (C) submit the better offer and reject the other one
    (D) reject both offers

62. Since the broker is the seller's agent, he may
    (A) accept an offer on behalf of the seller
    (B) solicit offers for the seller's listed property
    (C) try to negotiate better terms before submitting an offer
    (D) work to get the buyer the best possible price

63. Which of the following is NOT an "improvement" to land?
    (A) building   (C) orchard
    (B) driveway   (D) tomato crop

64. Which of the following is (are) usually exempt from property taxes?
    (A) a post office   (C) a public school
    (B) a hospital   (D) all of the above

65. Real estate brokers advertise the most
    (A) on radio and TV   (C) in magazines
    (B) in newspapers   (D) on billboards

66. Which of the following is (are) evidence of involuntary alienation?
    (A) deed in foreclosure   (C) both A and B
    (B) quitclaim deed   (D) neither A nor B

67. Which of the following is a nonfreehold estate?
    (A) fee simple estate   (C) life estate
    (B) leasehold estate   (D) none of the above

68. Sam's land has an easement to cross Karen's land to get to the lake. Sam subdivides his land into two parcels and sells one to George.
    (A) The easement no longer exists.
    (B) Sam's remaining land retains the easement, but George's does not.
    (C) Both Sam's remaining land and George's land have the easement rights.
    (D) Land benefiting from an easement cannot be subdivided.

69. A lease that specifies certain increases in rent over the life of the lease is a _____ lease.
    (A) reappraisal   (C) step
    (B) net   (D) percentage

70. A lease in which the tenant's rent is based at least in part upon his gross business revenues is a _____ lease.
    (A) reappraisal   (C) step
    (B) net   (D) percentage

71. Which level of government does NOT usually enact zoning laws?
    (A) federal   (C) county
    (B) state   (D) city

72. A court will appoint____to settle and manage the estate of a person who dies intestate.
    (A) a trustee
    (B) an executor
    (C) an administrator
    (D) an attorney-in-fact

73. An unlicensed person who shares a real estate commission may be in violation of
    (A) federal law
    (B) license law
    (C) zoning law
    (D) common law

74. Millie wants to buy a cottage costing $147,000. For the loan she wants, she needs a 10% down payment and must pay a 1% origination fee, 2 points discount, and a 0.5% PMI fee. How much money does she need to obtain this loan?
    (A) $14,700.00
    (B) $19,330.50
    (C) $19,845.00
    (D) $25,284.00

75. The interest rate on a loan is 6%. The interest for the month of April was $312.50. What was the loan balance at the beginning of April?
    (A) $52,083
    (B) $55,799
    (C) $60,000
    (D) $62,500

76. Usury is defined as
    (A) collecting more interest than is allowed by law
    (B) building a structure that extends over someone else's land
    (C) selling property for less than the asking price
    (D) selling real estate without a license

77. Mortgage loans guaranteed or insured by the federal government include
    (A) conventional loans
    (B) all ARM loans
    (C) VA loans
    (D) all of the above

78. In a settlement statement, accrued interest on an assumed loan is treated as
    (A) credit to buyer, debit to seller
    (B) credit to both buyer and seller
    (C) credit to seller and doesn't appear on buyer's statement
    (D) debit to buyer, credit to seller

79. Sam wants to build a patio 60 ft. by 20 ft. and 4 in. thick. How many cubic yards of concrete will he need?
    (A) 12.4
    (B) 14.8
    (C) 120
    (D) 400

80. A real estate license may be revoked for
    (A) failing to account for money belonging to others
    (B) submitting an offer for much less than the asking price
    (C) representing both buyer and seller without the consent of both
    (D) either A or C

Model Examination 5
BROKER

See page 486 for the answer key. Math problems are worked out on page 495.

1. Will openly occupied Ward's land for a period of time, without interference from Ward, and then received fee simple title to the land. This was an example of
   (A) an easement in gross
   (B) adverse possession
   (C) estoppel
   (D) subrogation

2. Max has Beth's power of attorney. Max is called
   (A) an agent in place
   (B) a real estate broker
   (C) a lawyer
   (D) an attorney-in-fact

3. The right by which the state takes title to real estate for which no legal owner can be found is
   (A) police power
   (B) tenancy
   (C) eminent domain
   (D) escheat

4. Which of the following types of deeds has no warranty?
   (A) executor's
   (B) quitclaim
   (C) general warranty
   (D) trustee's

5. Louise does work on Joe's house, but is not paid. She may file a
   (A) mechanic's lien
   (B) satisfaction piece
   (C) notice of foreclosure
   (D) sheriff's auction

6. What is the cash-on-cash ratio for a property having a cash flow of $8,360 and an initial investor's cash equity of $76,000?
   (A) 0.10%
   (B) 0.105
   (C) 0.11
   (D) 0.12

7. What percent of 1 square mile is 96 acres?
   (A) 21%
   (B) 19.6%
   (C) 15%
   (D) 12%

8. Which claim is paid first at a foreclosure?
   (A) tax lien
   (B) first mortgage
   (C) second mortgage
   (D) mechanic's lien

9. In an agency relationship, the principal is the
   (A) seller
   (B) buyer
   (C) broker
   (D) employer

10. In a lease contract, the landlord is the
    (A) leasee
    (B) leasor
    (C) lessee
    (D) lessor

11. If consideration has value only to the person receiving it, it is
    (A) personal consideration
    (B) good consideration
    (C) valuable consideration
    (D) good and valuable consideration

12. A lease that requires the landlord to pay operating expenses of the property is a ____ lease.
    (A) gross
    (B) flat
    (C) net
    (D) step

13. Taxes are due on June 1 of the year in which they are assessed. Tax rate is 41 mills. Assessed value is $53,250. If a sale of the property is closed on August 15, then at settlement (using the statutory year)
    (A) seller owes buyer $818.72
    (B) buyer owes seller $818.72
    (C) buyer owes seller $1,364.53
    (D) seller owes buyer $1,364.53

14. A properly done appraisal is
    (A) an authentication of value
    (B) an estimate of value
    (C) a prediction of value
    (D) a statement of exact value

15. If Murphy defaults on the payments to his mortgagee, under which clause may the lender demand immediate payment in full of the entire remaining loan balance?
    (A) defeasance
    (B) subrogation
    (C) acceleration
    (D) due-on-sale

16. Which of the following does NOT have the right of survivorship?
    (A) joint tenant
    (B) tenant in severalty
    (C) tenant by the entirety
    (D) all of the above

17. An easement can be
    (A) the right to cross someone else's land to get to the road
    (B) a variety of fraud exclusive to real estate
    (C) the right to inherit if there is no will
    (D) none of the above

18. A broker's license is revoked. The broker's salespeople
    (A) also have their licenses revoked
    (B) may continue to operate the broker's business
    (C) may, upon proper application, transfer their licenses to another broker
    (D) must place their licenses on inactive status for a year

19. In an exclusive right-to-sell listing,
    (A) only one broker is authorized to act as the seller's agent
    (B) if the seller finds the buyer, the seller still must pay the broker a commission
    (C) the broker must use her best efforts to solicit offers
    (D) all of the above

20. Among the broker's functions, he may
    (A) accept an offer on behalf of the seller
    (B) solicit offers for the seller's listed property
    (C) try to negotiate better terms before submitting an offer
    (D) work to get the buyer the best possible price

21. Which of the following is an "improvement" to land?
    (A) rezoning
    (B) driveway
    (C) orchard
    (D) all of the above

22. Which of the following is a nonfreehold estate?
    (A) fee simple estate
    (B) leasehold estate
    (C) life estate
    (D) dower estate

23. The rent for Sam's store is based at least in part upon Sam's gross business revenues. Sam's lease is a ____ lease.
    (A) reappraisal
    (B) net
    (C) step
    (D) percentage

24. What is usury?
    (A) collecting more interest than that allowed by law
    (B) building a structure that extends over someone else's land
    (C) selling property for less than the asking price
    (D) selling real estate without a license

25. Joe wants to build a patio 20 yd. by 20 ft. and 6 in. thick. How many cubic yards of concrete will he need?
    (A) 22.2
    (B) 40.0
    (C) 20.0
    (D) 400

26. The number of square feet in 1 acre is
    (A) 640
    (B) 43,560
    (C) 45,360
    (D) 53,460

27. How is the *gross rent multiplier* calculated?
    (A) market value/market rental
    (B) monthly payment/market rental
    (C) market rental/market price
    (D) sales price/market price

28. Minimum allowable construction standards are established by
    (A) building codes
    (B) zoning codes
    (C) environmental laws
    (D) condemnation laws

29. An allowed land use that is NOT normally permitted by the property's zoning classification is
    (A) a dispensation
    (B) a zone change
    (C) a variance
    (D) a restrictive covenant

30. Peeling paint and loose floorboards are examples of
    (A) physical deterioration
    (B) functional obsolescence
    (C) economic obsolescence
    (D) both A and B

31. The sales comparison approach is generally most suitable for appraising
    (A) commercial and investment property
    (B) single-family homes
    (C) heavily mortgaged property
    (D) heavily insured property

32. A feature of a freehold estate is that it
    (A) is acquired without paying anything for it
    (B) is always acquired by adverse possession
    (C) has uncertain duration
    (D) is any leasehold estate

33. A person who has the appearance of owning land, but does not own it, has
    (A) good title   (C) constructive notice
    (B) recorded title   (D) color of title

34. A contract entered into by a minor can be
    (A) void   (C) voidable by all parties
    (B) voidable by the minor (D) voidable by adult parties

35. Which of the following will NOT terminate a lease?
    (A) surrender   (C) vacancy
    (B) performance   (D) breech

36. In mortgage lending, one discount point is equal to
    (A) 1% of the sale price   (C) 1% of the interest rate
    (B) 1% of the loan amount   (D) 1% of the commission

37. Hooper's offer to purchase Looper's real estate stated that the offer would become void if not accepted within 5 days. The day after the offer was made, having heard nothing from Looper, Hooper wanted to withdraw his offer.
    (A) Hooper had to wait until the 5 days had passed.
    (B) Hooper was required to notify Looper of his desire to withdraw the offer, and to give Looper "reasonable time" to accept or reject it.
    (C) Hooper could withdraw the offer immediately.
    (D) none of the above

38. In a real estate transaction, title to land passes
    (A) on the date shown on the deed
    (B) upon recordation of the deed
    (C) upon notarization of the deed
    (D) upon delivery of the deed

39. A fixture is
    (A) anything that cannot be removed from the real estate without leaving a hole larger than 6 in.
    (B) anything the seller says is a fixture
    (C) anything needed for the proper use of the real estate
    (D) none of the above

40. The law that requires that all transfers of ownership rights to real estate be in writing is the
    (A) contract act   (C) Statute of Recordation
    (B) Statute of Limitations (D) Statute of Frauds

41. All of the following should be recorded EXCEPT
    (A) a deed of trust   (C) an executor's deed
    (B) a 20-year lease   (D) a contract of sale

42. In a typical mortgage loan transaction, the mortgagor is the
    - (A) lender
    - (B) borrower
    - (C) appraiser
    - (D) closing agent

43. A salesperson sold a property for $106,000. If the broker received 50% of the commission, and the salesperson's 60% share of that amount was $2,544, what was the commission rate charged on the sale?
    - (A) 7%
    - (B) 7.5%
    - (C) 7.75%
    - (D) 8%

44. An estate that any party can terminate at any time is an estate
    - (A) for years
    - (B) at will
    - (C) in possession
    - (D) leasehold entailed

45. A listing contract says that the seller receives $125,000, and the broker receives all of the purchase price over $125,000 as his commission. This is a(n) _____ listing.
    - (A) open
    - (B) net
    - (C) multiple
    - (D) exclusive

46. Jones leases a building that is damaged by a storm. Under common law,
    - (A) the lease is no longer enforceable
    - (B) Jones needn't pay rent until the building is repaired
    - (C) Jones must repair the building, but may deduct the cost from rent
    - (D) Jones must continue to pay rent until the lease expires

47. In each locality, real estate brokerage commissions are determined by
    - (A) the local board of REALTORS®
    - (B) the laws of the state
    - (C) the board of estimate
    - (D) agreement between property owner and broker

48. A lot sold for $980 a front foot. If the lot was 132 ft. deep and had an area of 6,468 sq. ft., how much did the lot sell for?
    - (A) $64,680
    - (B) $57,710
    - (C) $48,000
    - (D) $39,000

49. Which of the following is required for "mutual agreement" in a contract?
    - (A) offer and acceptance
    - (B) proper consideration
    - (C) description of the land
    - (D) legal form

50. In most states, a 6-month lease
    - (A) must be in writing
    - (B) need not be written
    - (C) may not be in writing
    - (D) ought not to be written

51. The expenses of settlement are
    - (A) paid by the broker
    - (B) paid by the seller
    - (C) negotiated between buyer and seller
    - (D) paid by the buyer

52. In most states a primary source of revenue for local government is
    - (A) income taxes
    - (B) sales taxes
    - (C) property taxes
    - (D) severance taxes

53. The purpose of real estate licensing laws is to protect
    (A) salespersons
    (B) lawyers and legislators
    (C) developers
    (D) the general public

54. A broker in a no-agency broker relationship,
    (A) may offer both buyer and seller confidential information about the other
    (B) does not have an agency relationship with either buyer or seller
    (C) deals only with transactions that do not involve leasing
    (D) all of the above

55. Salesperson Jones pockets an earnest money deposit and is found out. Jones's broker must
    (A) report the incident to the state attorney general
    (B) repay the money if Jones cannot do so
    (C) pay Jones's legal fees, if Jones is charged with a crime
    (D) both A and B

56. Listed real estate should be advertised in the name of the
    (A) owner
    (B) salesperson
    (C) broker
    (D) closing agent

57. A 2.6-acre lot sold for $188,000. What was the price per square foot?
    (A) $1.19
    (B) $1.55
    (C) $1.66
    (D) $1.82

58. Hamilton's broker license is revoked by the real estate commission. Hamilton may
    (A) apply for a salesperson's license
    (B) appeal the revocation to the courts
    (C) wait 6 months and apply for reinstatement
    (D) continue to operate his business until his existing listings are sold or have expired

59. Commissions from the sale of real estate
    (A) must be divided equally between broker and salesperson
    (B) must be divided equally among all participating brokers
    (C) are not taxable income
    (D) none of the above

60. Which is the superior lien?
    (A) tax lien
    (B) first mortgage
    (C) junior mortgage
    (D) mechanic's lien

61. A tenancy in severalty exists when
    (A) one person owns real estate
    (B) husband and wife own real estate together
    (C) any related persons own real estate together
    (D) none of the above

62. Which of the following is not a test of a fixture?
    (A) manner of attachment
    (B) intent of the person who put it there
    (C) cost of the item
    (D) custom in the community

63. During the life of the life tenant, the remainderman has
    (A) an easement in gross
    (B) a reversionary interest
    (C) a fee simple estate
    (D) a renewing leasehold estate

64. At settlement, the seller paid the buyer $351.00 toward the annual tax bill of $972.00. If taxes are assessed for the calendar year and must be paid by July 15, what was the date of the settlement?
    (A) May 10
    (B) August 20
    (C) July 15
    (D) can't be determined

65. When parties to a contract agree to amend the contract, the document they prepare and sign is called a
    (A) deed amendment
    (B) satisfaction piece
    (C) novation
    (D) relinquishment

66. What kind of estate is received if the deed states that the grantor grants to the grantee "and his heirs and assigns forever"?
    (A) fee simple
    (B) leasehold
    (C) life estate
    (D) nonfreehold

67. A deed that conveys only the interest of the grantor is a
    (A) general warranty deed
    (B) bargain and sale deed
    (C) quitclaim deed
    (D) special warranty deed

68. A real estate license should be
    (A) carried in the licensee's wallet
    (B) posted at the Real Estate Commission
    (C) posted in a public place in the broker's office
    (D) posted in the licensee's home

69. The usefulness of the cost approach in appraisal may be limited if the subject property is
    (A) a new structure
    (B) functionally obsolescent
    (C) in an inactive market
    (D) proposed construction

70. A tenant paid rent at the beginning of the month; the property sold in the middle of the month. To prorate rent at settlement, you would
    (A) credit the buyer
    (B) debit the seller
    (C) both A and B
    (D) neither A nor B

71. Which of the following is considered a "finance charge" for the purposes of Regulation Z?
    (A) title insurance fee
    (B) deed preparation fee
    (C) monthly payment
    (D) none of the above

72. A person who is employed by a broker to rent property, but not to sell it,
    (A) must be licensed
    (B) need not be licensed
    (C) must have a special rent-only license
    (D) must be a licensed broker

73. The process whereby a person may have her real estate sold to pay a debt or claim is called
    (A) lien
    (B) foreclosure
    (C) covenant
    (D) defeasance

74. A person who owns an undivided interest in real estate with at least one other person, and has the right of survivorship, is called a
   (A) tenant in severalty
   (B) life tenant
   (C) tenant in common
   (D) joint tenant

75. Which is NOT considered real estate?
   (A) fixtures
   (B) trees
   (C) chattels
   (D) sidewalk

76. A person who dies and leaves no will is said to have died
   (A) without heirs
   (B) intestate
   (C) unbequeathed
   (D) unherited

77. A broker must keep funds entrusted to her, but belonging to others, in
   (A) an office safe to which only she has the combination
   (B) a savings account in the name of the person whose money it is
   (C) a trust or escrow account
   (D) a special account managed by the state

78. When a party to a contract has deliberately lied in order to mislead the other party(ies) into agreeing to the contract, this action is an example of
   (A) fraud
   (B) misrepresentation
   (C) duress
   (D) defeasance

79. If a party to a contract acts so as to make performance under the contract impossible, this action is an example of
   (A) discharge of contract
   (B) performance of contract
   (C) abandonment of contract
   (D) breach of contract

80. A minor may be bound by the courts to contracts for
   (A) personal property
   (B) realty only
   (C) necessaries
   (D) rent

81. Edgar purchases a condo costing $232,500. The loan requires a 15% down payment, an origination fee of 0.75%, 2.25 points discount, and a 0.5% PMI fee. How much money does Edgar need for these expenses?
   (A) $23,250.00
   (B) $28,995.75
   (C) $41,791.88
   (D) $43,012.50

82. A makes an offer to buy B's real estate. B makes a counteroffer to A.
   (A) A is bound by his original offer.
   (B) A must accept the counteroffer.
   (C) A's original offer no longer exists.
   (D) A may not counteroffer back to B.

83. A contract of sale of real estate must be signed by
   (A) buyer and seller
   (B) broker, buyer, and seller
   (C) buyer only
   (D) broker only

84. In a contract of sale, the seller is the
   (A) grantor
   (B) vendee
   (C) grantee
   (D) vendor

85. Which of the following statements is true?
    (A) To be valid, a contract of sale must be signed by the broker, if a broker assists in the transaction.
    (B) A corporation may be a party to a contract of sale.
    (C) A contract of sale need not be written if it is closed within 1 year.
    (D) A person who is an attorney-in-fact must also be an attorney-at-law.

86. Which of the following must be included in a deed?
    (A) proper description of the real estate
    (B) street address, if the real estate is a house
    (C) area of the land ("more or less")
    (D) all of the above

87. A deed is recorded
    (A) to give public notice
    (B) to insure title
    (C) to satisfy the law
    (D) to avoid extra taxes

88. The part of a deed that defines or limits the quantity of estate granted is the
    (A) habendum
    (B) premises
    (C) equity
    (D) consideration

89. A final payment larger than the intermediate payments to a note is called
    (A) an escalator
    (B) an amortization
    (C) a balloon
    (D) a reappraisal

90. The interest rate on a loan is 5.125%. The interest for the month of July was $891.20. What was the loan balance at the beginning of July?
    (A) $200,000
    (B) $207,480
    (C) $208,671
    (D) $221,223

91. A conventional mortgage loan is
    (A) self-amortizing
    (B) not government insured/guaranteed
    (C) approved by the FHA
    (D) uninsurable

92. The mortgage with the highest priority is usually the one
    (A) with the highest unpaid balance
    (B) with the highest original loan amount
    (C) with the highest interest rate
    (D) that was recorded first

93. The seller of real estate takes a note secured by a mortgage on the real estate as partial payment. The mortgage is
    (A) sale financed
    (B) a purchase-money mortgage
    (C) a secondary mortgage
    (D) a first lien

94. An ad valorem tax is based on
    (A) the taxpayer's income
    (B) the sale price of the article taxed
    (C) the size and/or weight of the article
    (D) the value of the article taxed

95. A person who is too young to be held to a contract is called
    (A) minority-impaired
    (B) youthful
    (C) unavailable in law
    (D) incompetent

96. A contract in which rights to use and occupy real estate are transferred for a specified period of time is
    (A) a deed
    (B) an easement
    (C) a life estate
    (D) a lease

97. Whenever all parties agree to the terms of a contract, there has been
    (A) mutual agreement
    (B) legality of object
    (C) consideration
    (D) competency

98. Recording a deed
    (A) passes title
    (B) gives constructive notice
    (C) insures title
    (D) removes liens

99. Multiple listing
    (A) causes lost commissions
    (B) is a listing-sharing organization of brokers
    (C) is illegal in some states
    (D) is a violation of antitrust law

100. A contract that gives a person the right to buy during a specified time, but carries no obligation to do so, is
    (A) a sale contract
    (B) a land contract
    (C) an option
    (D) a bargain and sale

Model Examination 5

Model Examination 6
BROKER

See page 487 for the answer key. Math problems are worked out on page 496.

1. Jack wants to buy a house costing $111,500. The loan requires a down payment of $17,250, plus 1.5% origination fee, 2 points discount, and a 0.75% PMI fee. How much money does he need for these expenses?
   - (A) $17,250
   - (B) $19,665.25
   - (C) $21,988.75
   - (D) $21,255.63

2. The interest rate on a loan is 5.5%. The interest for the month of April was $884.50. What was the loan balance at the beginning of April?
   - (A) $173,555
   - (B) $192,983
   - (C) $210,000
   - (D) $225,000

3. Usury is defined as
   - (A) selling listed property for less than the seller's asking price
   - (B) selling real estate without a license
   - (C) collecting more interest than is allowed by law
   - (D) acquiring an easement by adverse possession

4. Ms. Simpson's broker license is revoked by the real estate commission. Ms. Simpson may
   - (A) apply for a salesperson's license
   - (B) appeal the revocation to the courts
   - (C) wait 6 months and apply for reinstatement
   - (D) continue to work her existing listings

5. Real estate commission payments
   - (A) must be divided equally among all participating brokers
   - (B) must be paid directly to the salesperson
   - (C) must be divided equally between broker and salesperson
   - (D) none of the above

6. Which is the superior lien in the event of foreclosure?
   - (A) tax lien
   - (B) first mortgage
   - (C) junior mortgage
   - (D) home equity loan

7. A tenancy in severalty exists when
   - (A) husband and wife own real estate together
   - (B) any related persons own real estate together
   - (C) one person owns real estate
   - (D) the tenant has the right to sublet

8. Which one of the following is not a test of a fixture?
   - (A) manner of attachment
   - (B) intent of the person who put it there
   - (C) time of attachment
   - (D) custom in the community

9. Angel wants to build a driveway 70 ft. by 12. ft. and 5 in. thick. How many cubic yards of concrete will he need?
   (A) 9.6
   (B) 11.8
   (C) 13
   (D) 84

10. So long as the life tenant is alive, the remainderman has
    (A) an easement in gross
    (B) a reversionary interest
    (C) a fee simple estate
    (D) a renewing leasehold estate

11. A deed conveying only the grantor's interest is
    (A) a general warranty deed
    (B) an absolute deed
    (C) a quitclaim deed
    (D) a special warranty deed

12. A real estate license should be
    (A) posted in the licensee's home
    (B) carried in the licensee's car
    (C) posted at the Real Estate Commission
    (D) posted in a public place in the broker's office

13. The usefulness of the cost approach in appraisal may be limited if the subject property is
    (A) a new building
    (B) functionally obsolescent
    (C) in an inactive market
    (D) under construction

14. A landlord receives rent at the beginning of the month. The property is sold 10 days later. To prorate rent at settlement, you should
    (A) credit the buyer
    (B) credit the seller
    (C) both A and B
    (D) neither A nor B

15. Which of the following is considered a "finance charge" for purposes of Regulation Z?
    (A) title insurance fee
    (B) deed preparation fee
    (C) monthly payment
    (D) prepaid interest

16. Which method of advertising do real estate brokers use the most?
    (A) radio and TV
    (B) magazines
    (C) newspapers
    (D) billboards

17. Which of the following is a nonfreehold estate?
    (A) fee simple estate
    (B) leasehold estate
    (C) life estate
    (D) qualified fee simple

18. A lease that spells out specific increases in rent during the term of the lease is a ____ lease.
    (A) reappraisal
    (B) net
    (C) step
    (D) percentage

19. A clause in a percentage lease that allows the lessor to cancel the lease if the lessee's revenues are not at least a minimum amount is a ____ clause.
    (A) nonperformance
    (B) net
    (C) defeasance
    (D) recapture

20. Zoning laws are usually NOT enacted by ____ government.
    (A) federal
    (B) state
    (C) county
    (D) city

21. A court appoints a(n) ____ to settle and manage the estate of a person who dies intestate.
    (A) trustee
    (B) executor
    (C) administrator
    (D) attorney-in-fact

22. A lot 59 ft. 6 in. wide contains 535.5 sq. yd. How deep is the lot?
    (A) 5.33 rods
    (B) 88 ft.
    (C) 27 yd.
    (D) 0.03 mi.

23. A broker's license is suspended for 6 months. Salespersons whose licenses are held by this broker
    (A) may apply to transfer their licenses to another broker
    (B) must place their licenses on inactive status for 6 months
    (C) also lose their licenses for 6 months
    (D) may continue to operate the broker's business

24. The largest "bundle of rights" to real estate is a ____ estate.
    (A) remainder
    (B) fee simple
    (C) life
    (D) homestead

25. One of broker Mack's salespeople sold a condo for $164,000. Mack received 48% of the commission and paid his salesperson 55% of that amount. How much did Mack keep, if the commission rate was 7%?
    (A) $2,479.68
    (B) $3,030.72
    (C) $5,166.00
    (D) $6,314.00

26. A 1.6-acre lot sold for $25,100. What was the price per square foot?
    (A) $3.61
    (B) $0.36
    (C) $1.88
    (D) $2.29

27. A broker who receives two offers on the same property at the same time should
    (A) reject both offers
    (B) submit both offers to the property owner
    (C) submit the better offer while trying to improve the other one
    (D) submit the better offer and reject the other one

28. As the seller's agent a broker may
    (A) reject an offer on behalf of the seller
    (B) work to get the buyer the best possible price
    (C) solicit offers for the seller's listed property
    (D) try to negotiate better terms before submitting an offer

29. Which of the following is not an "improvement" to land?
    (A) building
    (B) sidewalk
    (C) corn crop
    (D) flower bed

30. Unlicensed persons who receive shares of real estate commission payments may be in violation of
    (A) federal law
    (B) license law
    (C) zoning law
    (D) common law

31. A person who is employed by a broker to rent property, but not to sell it,
    (A) must be licensed
    (B) needs not be licensed
    (C) must have a special rent-only license
    (D) must be a licensed broker

32. Which of the following statements is true?
    (A) A person who is an attorney-in-fact must also be an attorney-at-law.
    (B) To be valid, a contract of sale must be signed by the broker.
    (C) A corporation may be a party to a contract of sale.
    (D) A contract of sale need not be written if it is closed within 1 year.

33. Which of the following must be included in a deed?
    (A) street address, if the real estate is a house
    (B) area of the land ("more or less")
    (C) proper description of land and improvements
    (D) proper description of land

34. A deed is recorded
    (A) to give public notice
    (B) to insure title
    (C) to satisfy the law
    (D) to avoid extra taxes

35. The clause that defines or limits the quantity of estate granted in a deed is the
    (A) habendum
    (B) premises
    (C) addendum
    (D) consideration

36. In a mortgage, the contract specifies payments of $2,000 a month, and a final payment of $220,000 at the end of 10 years. The final payment is called
    (A) an escalator
    (B) an amortization
    (C) a balloon
    (D) a parachute

37. The process by which real estate is sold to pay debts or claims is known as
    (A) lien
    (B) foreclosure
    (C) covenant
    (D) defeasance

38. A person who owns an undivided interest in real estate with at least one other person, without the right of survivorship, is called a
    (A) tenant in severalty
    (B) life tenant
    (C) tenant in common
    (D) joint tenant

39. Brokers often hold funds belonging to others. They must keep these funds in
    (A) an office safe to which only the broker has the combination
    (B) a savings account in the name of the person whose money it is
    (C) a trust or escrow account
    (D) a special account managed by the state

Model Examination 6

40. When a party to a contract unintentionally misleads the other party(ies) into agreeing to the contract, this action is an example of
(A) fraud
(B) misrepresentation
(C) duress
(D) defeasance

41. If a party to a contract is responsible for making performance under it impossible, this action is an example of
(A) specific performance
(B) breach of contract
(C) abandonment of contract
(D) nonperformance of contract

42. At settlement, the buyer took over the seller's 1-year property insurance policy, which had been purchased on February 1 for $324.00. If the seller was credited for $63.00 at settlement, what was the settlement date?
(A) May 10
(B) November 20
(C) July 19
(D) can't be determined

43. A minor may be bound by the courts to contracts for
(A) personalty only
(B) realty only
(C) rent only
(D) necessaries

44. Sally makes a counteroffer in response to Joe's offer to buy her lot.
(A) Joe may not counteroffer back to Sally.
(B) Joe is bound by his original offer.
(C) Joe must accept the counteroffer as is, reject it, or let it expire.
(D) If Joe makes a counteroffer, Sally may accept Joe's original offer.

45. A contract of sale of real estate must be signed by
(A) buyer only
(B) broker, buyer, and seller
(C) buyer and seller
(D) broker only

46. In a quitclaim, the seller is the
(A) grantor
(B) vendee
(C) grantee
(D) vendor

47. If a property has more than one mortgage on it, the one with the highest priority is usually the one that
(A) has the highest interest rate
(B) was recorded first
(C) has the highest unpaid balance
(D) has the highest original loan amount

48. The seller of real estate takes a note secured by a mortgage on the real estate as partial payment. The mortgage is
(A) sale financed
(B) a purchase-money mortgage
(C) a secondary mortgage
(D) a first lien

49. The market value of a house is $86,000. If property is assessed at 35% of market value and the annual tax rate is 42 mills, how much is the tax?
(A) $1,264.20
(B) $2,102.40
(C) $3,511.00
(D) $3,612.00

Questions 50–53 refer to the following situation:

May buys a condo from Ray. The price is $77,900. May gets a VA loan for 90% of the purchase price. The loan discount paid by Ray is 2.5 points. The broker's commission on the sale is 6%. The contract interest rate on the VA loan is 3.75%.

50. What is the dollar amount of the discount?
    (A) $759.53
    (B) $1,182.20
    (C) $1,752.75
    (D) $1,947.50

51. What is the lender's approximate effective rate of return on the loan?
    (A) 6.25%
    (B) 7.25%
    (C) 4.0625%
    (D) 3.5%

52. Who pays the discount on the VA loan?
    (A) May
    (B) Ray
    (C) the broker
    (D) the VA

53. To whom is the discount paid?
    (A) the broker
    (B) the lender
    (C) the VA
    (D) May

---

54. An ad valorem tax is based on
    (A) size and/or weight of article taxed
    (B) value of article taxed
    (C) taxpayer's income
    (D) sale price of article taxed

55. Whenever all parties agree to the terms of a contract, there has been
    (A) reality of consent
    (B) legality of object
    (C) consideration
    (D) competency

56. A contract that gives someone the right to buy during a specified time, but carries no obligation to do so, is
    (A) a sale contract
    (B) a land contract
    (C) an option
    (D) a bargain and sale

57. Jones made an offer to buy Smith's real estate. Smith signed the offer and left it on the desk while she went out to get some takeout chicken. While she was out, Jones called and left a message saying he was withdrawing the offer.
    (A) A contract of sale exists between Jones and Smith.
    (B) A contract between Jones and Smith exists, but it is not a contract of sale.
    (C) A contract doesn't exist, but Smith had a "reasonable time" to accept Jones's offer and create a contract.
    (D) There is no contract between Smith and Jones.

58. A property in a rundown neighborhood may lose value because of
    (A) physical deterioration
    (B) functional obsolescence
    (C) economic obsolescence
    (D) red lining

59. Which of the following is realty?
    (A) a 1-year lease
    (B) an equitable title
    (C) a land contract
    (D) a life estate

60. Which of the following can adequately describe the consideration in a deed?
    (A) "For ten dollars and other valuable consideration"
    (B) "For natural love and affection"
    (C) the actual amount of consideration paid
    (D) all of the above

61. Which type of depreciation generally is not curable?
    (A) physical deterioration   (C) economic obsolescence
    (B) functional obsolescence   (D) all of the above

62. What is the cash-on-cash ratio for a property that has a cash flow of $32,300 and an initial investor's cash equity of $222,750?
    (A) 7.05%   (C) 0.145
    (B) 0.0705   (D) 0.113

63. What percent of a square mile is a lot 1,085 ft. by 900 ft.?
    (A) 28.5%   (C) 3.5%
    (B) 18.494%   (D) 1.57%

64. In a real estate transaction, broker Lucille had an agency contract to represent the buyer. Broker Maurice had an agency contract to represent the seller.
    (A) Lucille is a buyer's agent.
    (B) Maurice has a listing contract with the seller.
    (C) Lucille is a designated agent.
    (D) both A and B are true.

65. Cortez got fee simple title to land that had belonged to Leone by using and occupying it openly for a certain time, unknown to and unmolested by Leone. This is an example of
    (A) estoppel   (C) an easement in gross
    (B) subrogation   (D) adverse possession

66. Baker gives Able his power of attorney. Able is called
    (A) an agent in place   (C) a lawyer
    (B) a real estate broker   (D) an attorney-in-fact

67. The right by which the state takes title to real estate for which no legal owner can be found is called
    (A) police power   (C) eminent domain
    (B) tenancy   (D) escheat

68. Moe receives title to Zoe's real estate after Zoe dies without a will. Moe has received
    (A) title by descent   (C) an easement
    (B) clouded title   (D) legacy title

69. A parcel of land is 1,077 ft. by 608 ft. How many acres does it contain?
    (A) 14.9   (C) 13.22
    (B) 9.88   (D) More than 15

70. Of the following instruments, the one with no warranty is the
    (A) executor's deed   (C) general warranty deed
    (B) quitclaim deed   (D) trustee's deed

71. A worker who is not paid for work that improved real estate may file a
    - (A) labor judgment
    - (B) novation
    - (C) mechanic's lien
    - (D) lis pendens

72. When a property is foreclosed, which of the following claims takes first priority?
    - (A) due, but unpaid, property taxes
    - (B) mortgage dated June 11, 2009
    - (C) general lien
    - (D) mortgage dated July 22, 2010

73. In an agency relationship, the employer is called the
    - (A) seller
    - (B) agent
    - (C) principal
    - (D) broker

74. If consideration in a deed has value only to the person receiving it, it is
    - (A) no consideration
    - (B) good consideration
    - (C) valuable consideration
    - (D) good and valuable consideration

75. A lease that does not require the tenant to pay any of the operating expenses of the property is a ____ lease.
    - (A) gross
    - (B) flat
    - (C) net
    - (D) step

76. Sam's contractor quotes "per square foot" costs of $102.20 for the first 1,600 sq. ft. of house, $84.50 for square footage over 1,600, $45.00 for basements, $58.40 for attached garages. Sam wants a 2,100 sq. ft., two-story house, with a basement, and a 420-sq. ft. attached garage. What price (to nearest $1,000) will the contractor quote for the entire job?
    - (A) $254,000
    - (B) $278,000
    - (C) $292,000
    - (D) $324,000

77. A house is valued at $371,650 for tax purposes. This is the
    - (A) assessed value
    - (B) appraised value
    - (C) market value
    - (D) replacement value

78. Simmy buys a house and gets a mortgage loan for $128,000 to pay for it. Simmy becomes a
    - (A) vendor
    - (B) mortgagor
    - (C) lessee
    - (D) mortgagee

79. A function of Regulation Z is to
    - (A) determine discounts on VA loans
    - (B) set maximum interest rates on mortgage loans
    - (C) allow borrowers to repay loans ahead of time without penalty
    - (D) require that borrowers be informed of the cost of credit

80. An investor purchased three lots. Lot A cost $22,000, lot B cost 2.5 times the cost of A, and lot C cost half the cost of B. She then sold lots A and B for 25% more than the cost of all three lots. If she then sold lot C for twice its cost, what was her total profit (to the nearest $100)?
    - (A) $38,200
    - (B) $53,600
    - (C) $67,600
    - (D) none of the above

Model Examination 7
APPRAISER

See page 487 for the answer key. Math problems are worked out on page 498.

NOTE: The last 25 questions are for general certification only.

1. The present and future demand for a property and its absorption rate is considered in a
   - (A) letter appraisal
   - (B) market feasibility study
   - (C) market segmentation
   - (D) highest and best use analysis
   - (E) transmittal letter

2. The appraiser's final value estimate should be based on
   - (A) an average of three value indications obtained by the three approaches to value
   - (B) a weighing of the reliability of the information analyzed in each of the three approaches to value
   - (C) the average of the three closest comparable sales
   - (D) the most sophisticated guess technique
   - (E) adjustments for most recent indicators in the local market

3. The appropriate time adjustment is concluded to be an increase of 7% per year compounded. The time adjustment for a comparable sales property that sold for $80,000 two years ago is
   - (A) −$11,592
   - (B) −$11,200
   - (C) −$5,600
   - (D) +$11,200
   - (E) +$11,592

4. The criteria for determining highest and best use include all of the following EXCEPT
   - (A) physical possibility
   - (B) financial feasibility
   - (C) legal permissibility
   - (D) probable use
   - (E) effect on community welfare

5. The broad forces affecting value do NOT include
   - (A) physical
   - (B) life-style
   - (C) political
   - (D) social
   - (E) economic

6. The certification of value section of an appraisal report states everything EXCEPT that
   - (A) the appraiser has no interest in the property
   - (B) the fee is not contingent upon any aspect of the report
   - (C) the facts are correct to the best of the appraiser's knowledge
   - (D) last year the property was appraised by another person
   - (E) the property was personally inspected by the appraiser

7. One implication of competition and excess profit is that
   (A) there is a certain optimum combination of land, labor, capital, and entrepreneurship
   (B) an estimate of value should be based on future expectations
   (C) abnormally high profits cannot be expected to continue indefinitely
   (D) maximum value accrues to real estate when social and economic homogeneity are present in a neighborhood
   (E) the direct sales comparison approach becomes compelling

8. Cost indexes offered by standardized services are used to
   (A) derive units of comparison
   (B) catalog building components
   (C) estimate operating expenses
   (D) update past costs into current costs
   (E) estimate the local consumer price index

9. A summary appraisal report
   (A) contains many items that are not considered in practice
   (B) is an appraisal report prepared for a client
   (C) summarizes the items that might be used in practice
   (D) may be based on hypothetical or assumed data
   (E) should be prepared on a nontypical property to show appraisal expertise

10. In real estate a *submarket* is
    (A) a group of salespersons who deal mostly in the same type of property
    (B) a group of sales that occur at the same time
    (C) a group of similar properties in the same area
    (D) a small portion of the market of similar properties
    (E) an area where sandwiches on French bread are eaten

11. The fact that rents for equally desirable space tend to be set by the market reflects the principle of
    (A) balance
    (B) substitution
    (C) externalities
    (D) consistent use
    (E) conformity

12. The fee for an appraisal assignment is
    (A) based on a percentage of the final value estimate
    (B) agreed upon during the preliminary study stage
    (C) determined after the appraisal is completed
    (D) set by the fee schedule of the local board of Realtors®
    (E) set by a fee scale from the Real Estate Commission

13. The last step in the appraisal process is to
    (A) write the report
    (B) reconcile all data
    (C) analyze the data
    (D) inspect the property
    (E) set the fee to be charged

14. The form in which a formal appraisal is presented is called
    (A) a presentation of value
    (B) an appraisal log
    (C) an appraisal report
    (D) a value certification
    (E) a narrative report

15. A formal appraisal report must include the
    (A) date of the value estimate
    (B) signature of the appraiser
    (C) identification of the property appraised
    (D) certification
    (E) all of the above

16. The highest and best use of land as if vacant forms part of the basis for
    (A) mortgage-equity analysis
    (B) a property rights adjustment
    (C) an operating expense estimate
    (D) the cost approach
    (E) the square footage approach

17. Identifying and studying submarkets of a larger market is called
    (A) market research
    (B) market survey
    (C) market agglomeration
    (D) market segmentation
    (E) market data

18. The identification and study of a pertinent market is called
    (A) market analysis
    (B) neighborhood review
    (C) property research
    (D) market reflection
    (E) market interaction

19. Which of the following is (are) important for good appraisal communication?
    (A) word choice
    (B) reading level
    (C) grammatical correctness
    (D) clarity
    (E) all of the above

20. All of the following are true EXCEPT
    (A) real property is a type of service
    (B) value is dependent on market conditions
    (C) a good or service has no value in exchange unless it possesses certain economic and legal characteristics
    (D) the price representing value is usually quoted in terms of money
    (E) real estate may be sold for all cash or financed

21. In estimating the market value of a comparable sale, an appraiser must consider all of the following EXCEPT
    (A) whether the transaction was made in cash, terms equivalent to cash, or other precisely revealed terms
    (B) whether the property had reasonable exposure in a competitive market
    (C) whether a fair sale was transacted, with neither the seller nor the buyer acting under duress
    (D) whether the replacement cost of the property corresponds to its market value
    (E) whether the seller was related to the buyer

22. In preparing an appraisal report, your analysis concludes that one of the approaches to value is not applicable to this particular case. You should
    (A) omit the approach altogether
    (B) base the approach on hypothetical data
    (C) state that the approach is not relevant
    (D) state that the approach is not applicable, explain the reasons for this contention, and provide supporting data
    (E) find another approach so as to include three approaches

23. In the cost approach the site is valued as if it were
    (A) vacant and available for development to its highest and best use
    (B) improved and suited for its intended use or development
    (C) developed and operating
    (D) attractively landscaped
    (E) without nearby utilities

24. *Investment value* is best described as
    (A) market price
    (B) market value
    (C) the cost of acquiring a competitive substitute property with the same utility
    (D) the present worth of anticipated future benefits to a certain entity
    (E) value in exchange

25. Location decisions involve analysis on which three levels?
    (A) general, specific, detailed
    (B) country, state, community
    (C) residential, commercial, industrial
    (D) country, state, county
    (E) region, neighborhood, site

26. The length of a tract of land along a street is called
    (A) depth   (D) abutment
    (B) width   (E) lineage
    (C) frontage

27. The most comprehensive type of appraisal report is
    (A) a restricted report   (D) a self-contained report
    (B) a summary report   (E) an unbiased report
    (C) a letter report

28. The principle of____states that a buyer will not pay more for a site than for another equally desirable one.
    (A) anticipation   (D) balance
    (B) imbalance   (E) conformity
    (C) substitution

29. The principle of anticipation is
    (A) future oriented
    (B) past oriented
    (C) the "as of" date for an appraisal
    (D) the anticipated loan-to-value ratio for the subject property
    (E) similar to the principle of substitution

30. The principle of_____states that value levels are sustained when the various elements in an economic or environmental mix are in equilibrium.
    (A) anticipation
    (B) equivalence
    (C) substitution
    (D) balance
    (E) highest and best use

31. Price and value are
    (A) not necessarily the same
    (B) synonymous
    (C) different, depending on financing terms
    (D) almost the same in an inactive market
    (E) interchangeable in a report

32. The purpose of a(n)_____is to analyze a property's potential for success.
    (A) feasibility study
    (B) marketability study
    (C) market segmentation study
    (D) appraisal report
    (E) need study

33. A use must be_____to be considered as a possible alternative for highest and best use.
    (A) physically and legally possible and financially feasible
    (B) physically and legally possible
    (C) already in existence and legal
    (D) physically possible and appropriate
    (E) legal and profitable

34. An appraiser
    (A) determines price
    (B) defends value
    (C) estimates price
    (D) estimates value
    (E) determines value

35. The objective of the appraisal should be stated in the report because
    (A) the market needs it
    (B) it defines the problem and identifies the value sought
    (C) it identifies the function of the report
    (D) it absolves the appraiser of liability
    (E) there are too many definitions of market price

36. The value estimate provided in an appraisal
    (A) changes with the use to which it is put
    (B) changes with the function of the appraisal
    (C) remains the same regardless of use
    (D) depends upon the use or function of the appraisal
    (E) always reflects market value

37. Population increases_____demand for housing.
    (A) depress the
    (B) are incapable of stimulating the
    (C) have no effect on the
    (D) are likely to create a
    (E) are determined by the

38. Environmental hazards that an appraiser must be conscious of include all of the following EXCEPT
    (A) asbestos
    (B) radon
    (C) Drano
    (D) urea formaldehyde
    (E) PCBs

39. In analyzing the economic environment and market area, it is best to
    (A) start at the general level and work down to the specific
    (B) start at the specific and work up to the general level
    (C) limit the analysis to the national level
    (D) limit the analysis to the local level
    (E) generally consider traffic flow

40. The first step in the appraisal process is to
    (A) define the problem
    (B) gather data
    (C) analyze data
    (D) determine the approaches to the value
    (E) make a final value estimate

41. Combining two or more sites in order to develop one site with a greater value than the individual sites have separately is called
    (A) synergy
    (B) plottage
    (C) surplus land
    (D) excess land
    (E) highest and best use of land

42. Assemblage is
    (A) always reflected in the market value
    (B) the act of bringing two or more smaller lots into common ownership for use
    (C) inappropriate for parcels containing 10 or more acres
    (D) uneconomical
    (E) illegal

43. Typically, land is appraised by the
    (A) square foot
    (B) front foot
    (C) acre
    (D) all of the above
    (E) none of the above

44. It is ____ for an appraiser to receive or pay finder's or referral fees.
    (A) reasonable
    (B) unethical
    (C) necessary
    (D) customary
    (E) convenient

45. A sale between relatives is considered
    (A) an arm's length transaction
    (B) a purely comparable sale
    (C) an open market sale
    (D) a distorted sale
    (E) a good deal

46. What of the following is true about zoning?
(A) It reflects the expectation that government will preserve property values.
(B) It is based on the right of government to regulate for health, morals, welfare, and safety.
(C) It is inappropriate for parcels with mixed uses.
(D) It represents an effort to establish the land's highest and best use.
(E) It represents the right to reuse property.

47. For an appraiser to use the assistance of another appraiser is
(A) inconsiderate
(B) unethical
(C) illegal
(D) ethical
(E) questionable

48. It is ____ to provide a value range to a client who requests it and understands its meaning and use.
(A) foolish
(B) appropriate
(C) unethical
(D) approximate
(E) difficult

49. Any recent sale of a subject property being appraised
(A) should be considered confidential
(B) cannot, under any circumstances, be considered in estimating the current market value of the property
(C) should be discussed in the appraisal report
(D) was not an arm's length sale
(E) should be used as a comparable sale, though adjusted for its time and terms

50. The dimensions of a warehouse are customarily measured from
(A) the roof line
(B) the midpoint of the exterior walls
(C) the inside of finished walls
(D) the outside of finished walls
(E) the foundation slab

51. The construction of a luxury home in a neighborhood almost completely developed with one- and two-bedroom apartments would
(A) produce external obsolescence
(B) be called an underimprovement
(C) result in plottage value
(D) result in neighborhood amenities
(E) be reasonable or appropriate

52. The most detailed, complex, costly, and time-consuming method of cost estimation is the
(A) quantity survey
(B) trade breakdown
(C) comparative unit
(D) unit in place
(E) comparable unit

53. An improvement's remaining economic life
    (A) is its chronological age
    (B) is its effective age
    (C) is the period over which the improvements are expected to generate benefits
    (D) is effective age minus chronological age
    (E) is effective age plus chronological age

54. The cost approach is most applicable when the property being appraised
    (A) has old improvements
    (B) has relatively new improvements that represent the highest and best use of the land
    (C) suffers substantial functional obsolescence
    (D) is more costly than the surroundings
    (E) has many older features that make interesting reading in a report

55. Price per front foot is
    (A) a physical unit of comparison
    (B) not as accurate as price per acre
    (C) rarely used in residential site analysis
    (D) an accurate guide to site marketability
    (E) useful when there are few physical differences between sites

56. Which is the last step in reconciliation?
    (A) identify which of the three approaches to use
    (B) apply the three approaches to the data collected
    (C) apply judgment to the data collected
    (D) review previous work and analysis
    (E) select a final estimate of value

57. The highest and best use of a site is its
    (A) existing use
    (B) most probable use
    (C) immediate next use
    (D) synonymous with ordinary and necessary use
    (E) different from most probable use

58. Markets in residential real estate are
    (A) equivalent to those for securities
    (B) related to physical boundaries
    (C) local
    (D) physically obscure
    (E) found by courthouse sales

59. Inflation tends to increase the value of
    (A) fixed-income securities
    (B) mortgages
    (C) deeds in lieu of foreclosure
    (D) real estate
    (E) debts

60. Real estate markets
    (A) are international in scope
    (B) meet none of the criteria of a perfect market
    (C) are centralized in nature
    (D) consist of used property only
    (E) are well developed in former Communist countries

61. The subject property has 85% occupancy. What conclusion would you most likely draw if the typical occupancy rate in the area was 95%?
    (A) Advertising is average.
    (B) The rents are high.
    (C) The rents are low.
    (D) Management is good.
    (E) New construction will occur soon.

62. The fact that the value of a property tends to equal the cost of an equally desirable substitute is an example of the principle of
    (A) balance   (D) diminishing returns
    (B) substitution   (E) supply and demand
    (C) contribution

63. Population flow to different regions of the United States will change primarily because of
    (A) changing economic opportunities
    (B) environmental control legislation
    (C) rezoning legislation
    (D) state tax policies
    (E) air conditioning in the Sunbelt

64. When each alternative use requires the same capital investment, the use that maximizes the investment's _____ on a long-term basis is the highest and best use.
    (A) diversified portfolio   (D) potential gross income
    (B) operating expenses   (E) occupancy rate
    (C) net operating income

65. What would be the indicated value of a property that rented for $750 per month, using a monthly gross rent multiplier of 100, if the expenses attributable to the property were $115 per month?
    (A) $75,670   (D) $61,125
    (B) $75,000   (E) $13,750
    (C) $68,750

66. Which of the following criteria most completely defines "highest and best use"?
    (A) physically possible, legally acceptable, and generating a higher present land value than any other use
    (B) legally authorized, politically viable, and socially acceptable
    (C) physically possible, comparable to other uses in the neighborhood, and legally authorized
    (D) comparable to other local uses, physically possible, and generating a higher present land value than any other use
    (E) the tallest and most beautiful structure that can be placed on the land

67. The total income anticipated from income property operations after vacancy and collection allowances and operating expenses are deducted is
    (A) net operating income
    (B) before-tax cash flow
    (C) effective gross income
    (D) potential gross income
    (E) property residual income

68. Which principle of value best affirms that value is the present worth of expected future benefits?
    (A) supply and demand
    (B) balance
    (C) substitution
    (D) anticipation
    (E) conformity

69. Which principle of value best affirms that the maximum value of property generally cannot exceed the cost of its replacement?
    (A) increasing and decreasing returns
    (B) supply and demand
    (C) substitution
    (D) balance
    (E) anticipation

70. Which of the following would be classified as a tangible rather than an intangible amenity?
    (A) pride of ownership
    (B) a sense of security
    (C) a free dishwasher
    (D) work satisfaction
    (E) clean air

71. Which type of property is subject to ad valorem taxation?
    (A) property owned by a religious organization and used for a religious purpose
    (B) new industrial plants that state and local governments have induced, with tax exemption as an incentive, to locate within their jurisdictions
    (C) commercial property with more than 50% nonprofit tenants
    (D) state colleges and universities
    (E) a state capitol

72. Compared with other assets, real estate is
    (A) immobile
    (B) expensive
    (C) long-lived
    (D) mortgagable
    (E) all of the above

73. All of the following are sources of comparable sales EXCEPT
    (A) public records
    (B) brokers
    (C) buyers and sellers
    (D) mortgage servicers
    (E) appraisers

74. An allowance for vacancy and collection loss is estimated as a percentage of
    (A) net operating income
    (B) before-tax cash flow
    (C) effective gross income
    (D) potential gross income
    (E) after-tax cash flow

75. The annual net operating income from an apartment house is $11,000. If a capitalization rate of 11% is used, the indicated market value is
    (A) $126,000
    (B) $176,000
    (C) $100,000
    (D) $242,000
    (E) $2,420

The remaining 25 questions are for general appraisal certification only.

76. Which of the following statements is true of a *gross lease*?
    (A) The tenant pays all operating expenses.
    (B) The landlord pays all operating expenses.
    (C) This lease is used only for commercial properties.
    (D) Rent rises with the cost of living.
    (E) This lease must be drafted by an attorney.

77. A forecast using discounted cash flow analysis would include
    (A) income, vacancy, and operating expenses
    (B) an economic analysis
    (C) reversion at the end of the holding period
    (D) discounting expected future cash flows to a present value
    (E) all of the above

78. In discounted cash flow analysis, the reversion to be received at the end of the holding period is
    (A) a separate cash flow
    (B) an annuity in arrears
    (C) an ordinary annuity
    (D) a percentage of annual income
    (E) an amount to be capitalized in perpetuity

79. A $1,000,000 property will have a 70% loan at an 8% annual mortgage constant. What must the net operating income be to produce a 12% cash-on-cash return?
    (A) $120,000   (D) $84,000
    (B) $56,000   (E) $700,000
    (C) $92,000

80. Income capitalization is the term used to describe the process of estimating the value of income property by studying expected future income. This process
    (A) converts the net income of a property into its equivalent capital value
    (B) reflects the time value of money by reducing or discounting future income to its present worth
    (C) focuses on the present worth of future benefits
    (D) uses market interest rates
    (E) all of the above

81. To earn 12% on your investment, what should you pay for a property that earns $6,000 per month and has operating expenses of $1,250 per month?
    (A) $475,000   (D) $333,333
    (B) $150,000   (E) $400,000
    (C) $229,166

82. The land development method is used to estimate the value of vacant acreage that is ready to be subdivided. This method requires
    (A) the study of current sales of subdivided lots
    (B) the projection of land development costs
    (C) RTC approval
    (D) both A and B
    (E) none of the above

83. A technique of income capitalization in which the analyst need not distinguish interest rates from capital recovery rates, but that is most useful for comparable income properties, is
   (A) direct capitalization
   (B) building residual
   (C) land residual
   (D) bank of investment
   (E) internal rate of return

84. Cash-on-cash return is
   (A) the annual cash flow divided by the equity investment
   (B) an internal rate of return that represents annual income and all gains or losses prorated to an effective annual amount
   (C) a percentage or decimal rate that, when divided into a periodic income amount, offers a lump-sum capital value for income
   (D) a value that does not change with time
   (E) none of the above

85. Which report is usually NOT prepared by a real estate appraiser?
   (A) marketability study
   (B) economic study
   (C) feasibility study
   (D) mineral valuation study
   (E) highest and best use

Questions 86–89 are based on the information below.

You are appraising a 40-acre tract of unimproved land. The size is zoned for single-family residential use. All utilities are available along the street on which the land fronts. The engineers who will plat the proposed subdivision told you that 20% of the land area will be used for streets and sidewalks. Zoning will permit four lots per acre of net developable land after deducting streets. Research indicates that lots similar to those that will be available on the subject land will sell for $18,000 each and that the entire tract can be developed and sold in 1 year. You find that 40% of the sale price of each lot must be allocated to selling cost, overhead, contingencies, carrying cost, and developer's profit, and that 2,000 feet of streets (including water, storm sewer, and sanitary sewer lines) must be installed at a cost of $80 per foot.

86. What is the number of lots to be developed?
   (A) 40
   (B) 128
   (C) 80
   (D) 88
   (E) 32

87. What is the gross amount that will be realized from the sale of all the lots?
   (A) $720,000
   (B) $2,304,000
   (C) $1,440,000
   (D) $1,584,000
   (E) $576,000

88. What is the cost of installing streets, water, and sewer lines?
   (A) $16,000
   (B) $32,000
   (C) $64,000
   (D) $160,000
   (E) none of the above

89. What is the amount of selling cost, overhead, contingencies, carrying cost, and developer's profit?
   (A) $921,600
   (B) $576,000
   (C) $288,000
   (D) $633,600
   (E) none of the above

Questions 90–93 are based on the information below:

A 100-unit apartment complex includes 40 one-bedroom units that rent for $950 and 60 two-bedroom units that rent for $1,150 monthly. The vacancy rate is 5%; miscellaneous income is $5,000 annually. Operating expenses amount to $400,000. The mortgage loan requires payments of $630,000 annually.

90. Potential gross income is
    (A) $1,289,000
    (B) $112,000
    (C) $107,000
    (D) $1,284,000
    (E) cannot be calculated from the information given

91. Effective gross income is
    (A) $1,224,800
    (B) $1,220,000
    (C) $824,800
    (D) $107,000
    (E) cannot be calculated from the information given

92. Net operating income is
    (A) $1,224,800
    (B) $824,800
    (C) $424,800
    (D) none of the above
    (E) cannot be calculated from the information given

93. Before-tax cash flow is
    (A) $1,030,000
    (B) $824,800
    (C) $194,800
    (D) none of the above
    (E) cannot be calculated from the information given

Questions 94–97 are based on the following information:

A building contains 50 one-bedroom units and 150 two-bedroom units. The one-bedroom units rent for $550 monthly; two-bedroom are $675. The vacancy rate is 7%; operating expenses are estimated at 40% of effective gross income. There is $2,000 annual income from vending machines.

94. Potential gross income is
    (A) $64,375   (D) $717,425
    (B) $1,547,000   (E) none of the above
    (C) $1,545,000

95. Effective gross income is
    (A) $64,375   (D) $1,438,850
    (B) $1,547,000   (E) none of the above
    (C) $1,545,000

96. Net operating income is
    (A) $64,375
    (B) $268,970
    (C) $863,310
    (D) $719,425
    (E) none of the above

97. Operating expenses are
    (A) $1,545,000
    (B) $54,075
    (C) $2,000
    (D) $719,425
    (E) $575,540

---

98. In one step of the land residual technique, the building capitalization rate is applied to the known building value to estimate the
    (A) highest and best use of the site
    (B) cost of the building
    (C) income needed to support the land
    (D) net operating income needed to support the building
    (E) land value

99. The basic formula for property valuation via income capitalization is
    (A) $V = IR$
    (B) $V = I/R$
    (C) $V = R/I$
    (D) $V = SP/GR$
    (E) $V = I/F$

100. All of the following lease provisions are advantageous to the lessee EXCEPT
    (A) an escape clause
    (B) a renewal option
    (C) a purchase option
    (D) an escalation clause
    (E) none of the above

Model Examination 8
APPRAISER

See page 487 for the answer key. Math problems are worked out on page 499.

1. In economics, the four factors of production are
   (A) land, labor, capital, and improvements
   (B) land, labor, capital, and entrepreneurship
   (C) land, labor, capital, and money
   (D) land, improvements, labor, and materials
   (E) land, labor, site, and improvements

2. The law of supply and demand is
   (A) a basic economic principle
   (B) legislated by Congress
   (C) seldom used in the appraisal process
   (D) not applicable in the short term
   (E) all of the above

3. Which of the following is NOT an agent of production?
   (A) land
   (B) transportation
   (C) labor
   (D) capital
   (E) entrepreneurship

4. Political forces affecting value may include
   (A) life-styles and living standards
   (B) topography
   (C) athletic levels and recreation facilities
   (D) government spending and taxation policy
   (E) primary registration and turnout

5. What are the two categories of tangible property?
   (A) real property and personal property
   (B) intangible property and real property
   (C) real estate and intangible property
   (D) legal and illegal investments
   (E) open and shut transactions

6. Zoning is an exercise of the
   (A) equity courts
   (B) police powers
   (C) Environmental Protection Agency
   (D) right of condemnation
   (E) right of escheat

7. Which of the following types of property is subject to ad valorem taxation?
   (A) property owned by a religious organization and used for a religious purpose
   (B) new industrial plants that state and local governments have induced, with tax exemption as an incentive, to locate within their jurisdictions
   (C) commercial buildings leased in part by nonprofit foundations
   (D) state colleges and universities
   (E) a state capitol

8. A person owning less than the entire bundle of rights has
   (A) escheat
   (B) a fee simple title
   (C) a partial interest
   (D) personal property
   (E) a fee tail

9. A metes and bounds description begins and ends with the
   (A) street and house number
   (B) block number
   (C) point of beginning
   (D) grid coordinates
   (E) iron pin

10. A(n) _____ identifies a property in such a way that it CANNOT be confused with any other property.
    (A) coded map book
    (B) legal description
    (C) narrative appraisal
    (D) full city survey
    (E) engineering report

11. All of the following statements are true EXCEPT
    (A) real property is a type of service
    (B) value is dependent on market conditions
    (C) a good or service has no value in exchange unless it possesses certain economic and legal characteristics
    (D) the price representing value is usually quoted in terms of money
    (E) real estate may be sold for all cash or financing arranged

12. All of the following will affect the market value of a property EXCEPT
    (A) political factors
    (B) legal use restriction
    (C) acquisition cost to present owner
    (D) economic factors
    (E) social concerns

13. Market value is _____ the same as selling price.
    (A) always
    (B) never
    (C) sometimes
    (D) usually
    (E) none of the above

14. Price is
    (A) market value
    (B) most probable sales price
    (C) investment value
    (D) a historical fact
    (E) all of the above

15. Functional utility depends on
    (A) zoning
    (B) wear and tear on the structure
    (C) tastes and standards
    (D) age of the equipment
    (E) insurance requirements

16. Value in use is
    (A) subjective
    (B) objective
    (C) readily measurable
    (D) a market phenomenon
    (E) synonymous with market price

17. The value added to total property value by a particular component is an example of the principle of
    (A) substitution
    (B) anticipation
    (C) change
    (D) contribution
    (E) conformity

18. The concept that the value of a particular component is measured by the amount that its absence would detract from the value of the whole is
    (A) opportunity cost
    (B) substitution
    (C) competition
    (D) contribution
    (E) conformity

19. The market loss caused by depreciation in an older structure may be offset by all of the following EXCEPT
    (A) architectural interest
    (B) historical registration
    (C) strong demand relative to supply
    (D) strong supply relative to demand
    (E) renovation of the structure

20. Studying appraisal helps a person
    (A) to improve value estimation skills
    (B) to pass the real estate brokers' license examination
    (C) to understand other real estate courses
    (D) to communicate with appraisers
    (E) all of the above

21. A dramatic change in short-term demand for real estate in the local market is likely to immediately precipitate
    (A) construction
    (B) price changes
    (C) conversions
    (D) activity
    (E) no change in supply

22. The area and community analysis section of an appraisal report
    (A) should "sell" the community
    (B) should describe the community objectively
    (C) is a study by the state's industrial development commission
    (D) considers the negative aspects only
    (E) considers the positive aspects only

23. In analyzing the economic environment and market area, it is best to
    (A) start at the general level and work down to the specific
    (B) start at the specific and work up to the general level
    (C) limit the analysis to the national level
    (D) limit the analysis to the local level
    (E) generally consider traffic flow

24. Which of the following reports is usually NOT prepared by a real estate appraiser?
    (A) marketability study
    (B) economic study
    (C) feasibility study
    (D) transportation network study
    (E) valuation study

25. An appraisal of a specific-purpose property for insurance purposes would depend most heavily on
    (A) book value
    (B) cost estimate
    (C) land value
    (D) highest and best use
    (E) specialty value

26. The first step in the appraisal process is to
    (A) define the problem to be solved
    (B) gather relevant data
    (C) analyze the data
    (D) inspect the property
    (E) set the fee to be charged

27. An appraisal is
    (A) an estimate of net realizable value
    (B) always concerned with the market value
    (C) an appraiser's opinion of market value
    (D) a precise statement of value
    (E) a broker's comparative sales analysis with further detail

28. The "as of" date in an appraisal report is
    (A) the date to which the value applies
    (B) immaterial to the value estimate
    (C) the date on which the report is delivered
    (D) the date on which the property will be conveyed
    (E) the anticipated closing date

29. Sales data descriptions of an appraisal report contain
    (A) details about each comparable sale
    (B) an analysis of the data, using the value approaches
    (C) the investigation of market forces
    (D) analysis of the street each comparable property is on
    (E) zoning details

30. All of the following are ways to delineate a neighborhood EXCEPT
    (A) natural barriers   (D) streets
    (B) utility service   (E) income characteristics
    (C) political boundaries

31. All of the following are sources of comparable sales EXCEPT
    (A) public records   (D) mortgage servicers
    (B) brokers   (E) appraisers
    (C) buyers and sellers

32. Which of the following criteria most completely define "highest and best use"?
    (A) legally authorized, politically viable, and socially acceptable
    (B) physically possible, comparable to other uses in the neighborhood, and legally
        authorized
    (C) physically possible, legally permissible, financially feasible, and generating a
        higher present land value than any other use
    (D) comparable to other uses in the neighborhood, physically possible, and generating
        a higher present land value than any other use
    (E) the tallest and most beautiful structure that can be placed on land

33. The three basic approaches used to estimate value are
    (A) use, exclusion, and disposition
    (B) cost, sales comparison, and use
    (C) cost, sales comparison, and market data
    (D) cost, sales comparison, and production
    (E) cost, sales comparison, and income capitalization

34. Units of comparison are used in
    (A) only the sales comparison approach
    (B) only the cost approach
    (C) only the income capitalization approach
    (D) A, B, and C
    (E) the appraisal of special-purpose properties only

35. Final value estimates should be rounded to reflect the
    (A) absence of good data
    (B) property's location
    (C) fact that a selling price will probably be a round number
    (D) lack of precision associated with an opinion
    (E) high value of real estate

36. When reconciling the adjusted sales prices of comparables, the greatest emphasis should be given to
    (A) the average
    (B) the median
    (C) the mode
    (D) the mean of A, B, and C
    (E) none of the above

37. Which of the following forms of appraisal report is NOT recommended?
    (A) completely filled-in institutional form
    (B) telephone conversation
    (C) letter report
    (D) long narrative report
    (E) demonstration

38. Which of the following approaches would probably be given the most weight in appraising a large office building?
    (A) reproduction cost
    (B) subdivision development
    (C) replacement cost
    (D) income capitalization
    (E) market absorption

39. The form in which a formal appraisal is presented is called
    (A) a presentation of value
    (B) an appraisal log
    (C) an appraisal report
    (D) a value certification
    (E) a narrative report

40. The form of an appraisal report
    (A) has no influence on the appraisal process
    (B) is the same, regardless of the problem
    (C) is set by the amount of the fee
    (D) is determined by the appraiser
    (E) determines the appraisal framework

41. The effective age and the useful life of a building represent judgments made by the
    (A) appraiser
    (B) property owner
    (C) tax assessor
    (D) buyer
    (E) insurer

42. The period over which existing improvements are expected to continue to contribute to property value is their
    (A) effective age
    (B) remaining economic life
    (C) remaining physical life
    (D) period of diminishing returns
    (E) chronological age

43. For a building, *effective age* is best defined as
    (A) the average age of the roof
    (B) the actual age divided by the age-life
    (C) the age of other property in equivalent condition and utility
    (D) the chronological age of the building
    (E) the period over which the building may be effectively used

44. The *utility* of real estate is its
    (A) attractiveness to the trained observer
    (B) longevity
    (C) capacity to satisfy human needs and desires
    (D) effective demand
    (E) remaining economic life

45. In appraising a residence, adjustments are NOT made to the comparable property for
    (A) age
    (B) lot value
    (C) assessed valuation
    (D) terms of sale
    (E) size

46. When a site has improvements on it, the highest and best use
    (A) is not definable
    (B) is its existing use
    (C) is its potential use
    (D) depends on whether or not the existing use is changeable
    (E) may be different from its existing use

47. To be considered as a comparable, a property
    (A) must have been sold within the past 5 years
    (B) must be competitive with the subject
    (C) must have been sold by an open-market transaction
    (D) must be a similar color
    (E) both B and C

48. The direct sales comparison approach is better than the income or cost approach because
    (A) fewer comparable properties are required, so it is easier to outline the results to clients
    (B) there are fewer mathematical calculations, so there is less chance of mathematical errors
    (C) the market for real estate is slow to change
    (D) it is always easier to obtain data for the direct sales comparison approach
    (E) none of the above is true

49. The appraisal of an established 20-year-old motel on a road with numerous competitive motels would most likely be based on the
    (A) square foot area of improvements
    (B) number of units
    (C) reproduction cost
    (D) gross rent multiplier
    (E) occupancy rate

50. In applying gross rent multiplier analysis to the subject property, the appraiser would use the
    (A) market rental
    (B) actual rent being paid
    (C) rent currently asked by the owner
    (D) rent offered by a potential tenant
    (E) rent listed in advertising the property

Questions 51–56 are based on the following information:

Factor	Subject	Comparable 1	Comparable 2	Comparable 3
Price		$90,000	$88,500	$87,000
Living area (sq. ft.)	1,500	1,600	1,450	1,400
Condition	Good	Fair	Excellent	Good
Garage	One-car	Two-car	One-car	Two-car
Time of sale	Now	Last year	Last year	This year

Adjusted Sales Price: Prices have been rising by 5% per year in the area for this type of property.

Other Adjustments: Each square foot of livable area is judged to be worth $30; condition grades are fair, good, and excellent, with each difference in condition grade worth 5%; a two-car garage is judged to be worth $1,500 more than a one-car garage.

51. What is the size adjustment for Comparable 1?
    (A) +$1,500
    (B) −$1,500
    (C) 0
    (D) +$3,000
    (E) −$3,000

52. What is the size adjustment for Comparable 2?
    (A) +$1,500
    (B) −$1,500
    (C) 0
    (D) +$3,000
    (E) −$3,000

53. What is the condition adjustment for Comparable 1?
    (A) 0
    (B) +$4,500
    (C) −$4,500
    (D) +$9,000
    (E) −$9,000

54. What is the condition adjustment for Comparable 2?
    (A) 0
    (B) +$4,425
    (C) −$4,425
    (D) +$8,850
    (E) −$8,850

55. What is the garage adjustment for Comparable 2?
    (A) 0
    (B) +$1,500
    (C) −$1,500
    (D) +$3,000
    (E) −$3,000

56. What is the garage adjustment for Comparable 3?
    (A) 0
    (B) +$1,500
    (C) −$1,500
    (D) +$3,000
    (E) −$3,000

Model Examination 8

57. In estimating the market value of a comparable sale, an appraiser must consider all of the following EXCEPT
   (A) whether the transaction was made in cash, terms equivalent to cash, or other precisely revealed terms
   (B) whether the property had reasonable exposure in a competitive market
   (C) whether a fair sale was transacted, with neither the seller nor the buyer acting under duress
   (D) whether the replacement cost of the property corresponds to its market value
   (E) whether the seller was related to the buyer

58. The terms of financing, whether good or bad,
   (A) have no effect on the market price
   (B) have no effect on the market value
   (C) have no effect on affordability
   (D) depend on fiscal and monetary policy
   (E) should be ignored when adjusting comparables

59. Adjustments for the property rights conveyed, financing, conditions of sale, date of sale, and location are often made to the _____ of the comparable property.
   (A) unit price
   (B) actual sales price
   (C) price per square foot
   (D) gross income multiplier
   (E) cash equivalent value

60. Cumulative percentage adjustments may be used
   (A) when the characteristics are interdependent
   (B) when the characteristics are independent
   (C) when dollar figures are available
   (D) when unimproved properties are being appraised
   (E) under no circumstances

61. The best unit of comparison for vacant land is
   (A) the square foot
   (B) the total lot
   (C) a combination of square foot and front foot units
   (D) the linear foot
   (E) the unit considered important by the market

62. You are asked to appraise a vacant building lot. The neighborhood is about 75% built-up. Most lots in the area are from 55 ft. to 65 ft. wide; the lot under appraisal is 60 ft. Comparable sales indicate that lots are selling at $120 to $150 per front foot. What is a good estimate of the price range for this lot?
   (A) $9,000–$11,000
   (B) $7,200–$9,000
   (C) $5,400–$6,750
   (D) $6,600–$7,600
   (E) $6,600–$11,250

63. In appraising a residential property by the cost approach, the appraiser considers the
    (A) sales prices of comparable properties
    (B) depreciation of the land
    (C) depreciation of improvements
    (D) potential for new competition
    (E) potential misuse of this approach

64. In the cost approach, ____ is deducted after estimating the cost to reproduce an existing structure.
    (A) land cost
    (B) cost to maturity
    (C) depreciation
    (D) cash equivalence
    (E) personal property value

65. External or economic obsolescence can be caused by all of the following EXCEPT
    (A) economic factors
    (B) political factors
    (C) social factors
    (D) factors within the property
    (E) legal factors

66. Economic obsolescence in a residence does NOT result from
    (A) an outdated kitchen
    (B) construction of a freeway near the property
    (C) the presence of an earthquake fault nearby
    (D) building restrictions in the community
    (E) factors external to the subject property itself

67. Reproduction or replacement cost includes all of the following EXCEPT
    (A) direct or hard costs
    (B) indirect or soft costs
    (C) entrepreneurial profit
    (D) fixed and variable expenses of operations
    (E) elevator shafts

68. In analyzing obsolescence, the test of curability of a component in a building is whether the cost to cure is no greater than the
    (A) expected increase in value
    (B) reproduction cost new
    (C) replacement cost
    (D) installation cost
    (E) economic life of the new component

69. Which of the following is NOT a type of depreciation?
    (A) entrepreneurial loss
    (B) external obsolescence
    (C) physical deterioration
    (D) functional obsolescence
    (E) economic obsolescence

70. Estimation of accrued depreciation and obsolescence does NOT involve
    (A) physical deterioration
    (B) economic obsolescence
    (C) financial structure
    (D) functional obsolescence
    (E) wear and tear

71. In appraisal, accrued depreciation is really an estimate of
    (A) physical deterioration
    (B) diminished utility
    (C) book depreciation
    (D) capital recovery
    (E) sinking fund factor

72. The cost approach is NOT useful for
    (A) checking value approaches
    (B) appraising institutional or special-use properties
    (C) estimating the value of new property
    (D) appraising older homes in an active market
    (E) insurance appraisals

Questions 73–75 are based on the following information:

An appraiser noted the following about a rental home:

needs exterior paint	$750 cost to cure
needs new water heater	$250 cost to cure
has one bath in market for two	$4,000 capitalized rent loss
has poor floor plan	$2,500 capitalized rent loss
is located next to a convenience store	$1,200 capitalized rent loss

73. How much is curable physical deterioration?
    (A) $250
    (B) $750
    (C) $4,000
    (D) $2,500
    (E) none of the above

74. How much is functional obsolescence?
    (A) $250
    (B) $1,000
    (C) $6,500
    (D) $7,700
    (E) none of the above

75. How much is environmental obsolescence?
    (A) $250
    (B) $750
    (C) $1,200
    (D) $2,500
    (E) $4,000

Questions 76 through 100 are for general appraisal certification only.

76. An appraisal of a freestanding store and the land it occupies is an unbiased estimate of the value of an interest in
    (A) personal property
    (B) mortgages
    (C) real estate
    (D) personal property and land
    (E) real estate plus business value

77. The term *vertical interests* does NOT refer to rights to
    (A) subsurface mineral extraction
    (B) the construction of railroad tunnels
    (C) the use and regulation of air space
    (D) subdivision and development
    (E) the construction of buildings over railroad yards

78. Inflation tends to increase the value of
    (A) fixed-income securities
    (B) mortgages
    (C) deeds in lieu of foreclosure
    (D) tangible long-lived investments
    (E) debts

79. With an amortized mortgage loan,
    (A) interest only is paid until maturity
    (B) some principal is repaid with each payment
    (C) the entire principal is repaid before maturity
    (D) equal amounts of principal are repaid each period
    (E) there is a balloon payment at maturity

80. When each alternative use requires the same capital investment, the use that maximizes the investment's____on a long-term basis is the highest and best use.
    (A) diversified portfolio
    (B) operating expenses
    (C) net operating income
    (D) potential gross income
    (E) occupancy rate

81. Land purchased for $50,000 cash appreciates at the rate of 15% compounded annually. About how much is the land worth after 5 years? Disregard taxes, insurance, and selling expenses.
    (A) $100,000
    (B) $87,500
    (C) $57,500
    (D) $37,500
    (E) $7,500

82. A land speculator expects that a certain 100-acre tract can be sold to a subdivider 4 years from now for $10,000 per acre. If holding and selling costs are disregarded, what cash price today (rounded to the nearest $1,000) would allow the speculator to realize a 15% compounded annual rate of return on the entire tract?
    (A) $572,000
    (B) $5,000
    (C) $600,000
    (D) $6,000
    (E) none of the above

83. Gross income multipliers are generally considered part of
    (A) the cost approach
    (B) the direct sales comparison approach
    (C) the income capitalization approach
    (D) the insurance approach
    (E) none of the above

84. Use of a gross rent multiplier is valid when the subject and comparable properties have similar
    (A) potential gross incomes
    (B) effective gross incomes
    (C) net operating incomes
    (D) operating expense ratios
    (E) cash flows

85. Time-distance relationships between a site and all relevant origins and destinations are called
    (A) access roads
    (B) transit facilities
    (C) ingress and egress
    (D) linkages
    (E) synergies

Model Examination 8

86. The land on which a 10-year-old house is located is valued at $28,000, and the reproduction cost of the dwelling is $92,000. Straight-line depreciation is 2% per year, applied to the building only. If there is no other obsolescence, what is the indicated value of the property?
   (A) $96,000
   (B) $101,600
   (C) $117,000
   (D) $117,700
   (E) $120,000

87. An allowance for vacancy and collection loss is estimated as a percentage of
   (A) net operating income
   (B) before-tax cash flow
   (C) effective gross income
   (D) potential gross income
   (E) after-tax cash flow

88. Effective gross income is income after an allowance for
   (A) depreciation
   (B) operating expenses
   (C) cash expenditures
   (D) both A and B
   (E) none of the above

89. In discounted cash flow analysis, the reversion to be received at the end of the holding period is
   (A) a separate cash flow
   (B) an annuity in arrears
   (C) an ordinary annuity
   (D) a percentage of annual income
   (E) an amount to be capitalized in perpetuity

90. To earn 12% annual cash return on a cash investment, what should you pay for a property that earns $4,000 per month and has operating expenses of $1,250 per month?
   (A) $150,000
   (B) $275,000
   (C) $229,166
   (D) $333,333
   (E) $400,000

91. In selecting an overall capitalization rate for an income-producing property, the appraiser will consider all of the following EXCEPT
   (A) return on invested capital
   (B) risk factors
   (C) return of invested capital
   (D) the interest rate on the existing loan, which was arranged last year
   (E) the interest rate prevailing in the market

Questions 92–95 are based on the following information:

A 200-unit apartment complex includes 80 one-bedroom units that rent for $475 and 120 two-bedroom units that rent for $575 monthly. The vacancy rate is 5%; miscellaneous income is $5,000 annually. Operating expenses amount to $400,000. The mortgage loan requires annual payments of $630,000.

92. Potential gross income is
   (A) $1,289,000
   (B) $1,284,000
   (C) $112,000
   (D) $107,000
   (E) none of the above

93. Effective gross income is
    (A) $1,224,800
    (B) $1,220,000
    (C) $824,800
    (D) $107,000
    (E) none of the above

94. Net operating income is
    (A) $1,224,800
    (B) $1,220,000
    (C) $824,800
    (D) $424,800
    (E) none of the above

95. Before-tax cash flow is
    (A) $1,030,000
    (B) $824,800
    (C) $424,800
    (D) $194,800
    (E) none of the above

---

96. To obtain the present value of a series of incomes, a(n)____rate is applied.
    (A) discount
    (B) income
    (C) overall capitalization
    (D) equity capitalization
    (E) stated

97. A fast-food chain could buy the building and land necessary for a new outlet for $200,000. Instead, an investor bought the property for this amount and leased it for $2,000 per month over a 20-year term. Rent is payable at the end of each month. What yield to maturity is implied by the lease, assuming that, at the end of 20 years, the property is still worth about $200,000?
    (A) 8%
    (B) 10%
    (C) 12%
    (D) 14%
    (E) 15%

98. When market rent is less than contract rent, the difference is known as
    (A) overage rent
    (B) excess rent
    (C) percentage rent
    (D) gross rent
    (E) slippage rent

99. If a particular buyer requires a recapture of the building portion of the purchase price in 25 years, what is the indicated recapture rate for the building, assuming straight-line recapture?
    (A) 0.25%
    (B) 2%
    (C) 4%
    (D) 20%
    (E) 25%

100. In a high-rise, 100-unit apartment building there is a basement laundry area that brings in $100 monthly from the concessionaire. The laundry income is
    (A) included, as miscellaneous income, in potential gross income
    (B) included, as other income, in effective gross income
    (C) deducted from effective gross income
    (D) added to before-tax cash flow
    (E) distributed to the maintenance workers

Model Examination 9
APPRAISER

See page 488 for the answer key. Math problems are worked out on page 501.

NOTE: The last 25 questions are for general appraisal certification only.

1. Natural or manmade features that affect a neighborhood and its geographic location are ____ influences.
   (A) social
   (B) economic
   (C) government
   (D) environmental
   (E) legal

2. The four broad forces influencing value are
   (A) utility, transferability, demand, and supply (scarcity)
   (B) governmental, economic, social, and political
   (C) supply, demand, location, and popular taste
   (D) governmental, economic, social, and physical
   (E) police power, eminent domain, taxation, and escheat

3. The federal government is active in which of the following areas?
   (A) housing and urban development
   (B) environmental protection
   (C) monetary and fiscal policy
   (D) secondary mortgage market encouragement
   (E) all of the above

4. Population increases____demand for housing.
   (A) depress the
   (B) are capable of diminishing the
   (C) have no effect on the
   (D) can create a
   (E) are determined by the

5. In eminent domain, "just compensation" means
   (A) the fair market value of the property
   (B) the current market value plus compensation for anticipated future benefits
   (C) the market value when the property was bought by the current owner
   (D) the insurable value
   (E) none of the above

6. The right of government or quasi-government units to take private property for public use upon the payment of just compensation is
   (A) escheat
   (B) condemnation
   (C) eminent domain
   (D) estoppel
   (E) an unconstitutional practice

7. ____ is the exercise of the right of government to take private property for public use.
   (A) Condemnation
   (B) Certified appraisal
   (C) Immediate justice
   (D) Land removal
   (E) both A and B

8. The fullest and most common type of estate in realty is
   (A) fee tail
   (B) mortgage
   (C) supra leasehold
   (D) community property
   (E) fee simple

9. An estate in severalty is ownership by
   (A) more than two parties
   (B) two parties
   (C) one or two parties
   (D) one party
   (E) two or more parties with right of survivorship

10. Which of the following is evidence of real estate ownership?
    (A) title
    (B) defaulted mortgage
    (C) estate
    (D) fee simple
    (E) tenancy

11. The concept of value in exchange assumes that
    (A) supply does not affect market value
    (B) a commodity is traded in a marketplace, and for that reason prices may be measured objectively
    (C) value can be determined without exposure in a marketplace
    (D) the real estate appraiser can be held liable if the property does not sell in a reasonable time for the appraised value
    (E) the property value will support a reasonable mortgage debt

12. The definition of market value in appraisal does NOT include
    (A) payment in cash or equivalent
    (B) exposure in the market
    (C) informed parties
    (D) topography of the property
    (E) probable price

13. "Value in exchange" is most closely related to
    (A) value in use
    (B) market value
    (C) investment value
    (D) sentimental value
    (E) none of the above

14. Which statement is FALSE?
    (A) Value in use may be lower than value in exchange.
    (B) Market price is the amount actually paid for a good or service, a historical fact from a particular transaction.
    (C) Cost represents the amount paid for the construction of a building or the amount paid for its acquisition.
    (D) Value in use may be far higher than value in exchange.
    (E) The appraiser must be professionally designated for the value to be accurate.

15. The three common types of legal description are
    (A) metes and bounds; recorded lot, block, and tract; and government rectangular survey
    (B) government rectangular survey, private survey, and house number
    (C) metes and bounds, acreage blocks, and government rectangular survey
    (D) land survey, building survey, and depreciation
    (E) short legal, average legal, and long legal

16. Valuation of property for real estate tax purposes results in
    (A) assessed value
    (B) appraisal
    (C) a special assessment
    (D) a millage rate
    (E) none of the above

17. ____ can render existing supply obsolete and less valuable.
    (A) Inflation
    (B) Interest rates
    (C) Employment
    (D) Income levels
    (E) Changes in tastes and standards

18. One implication of competition and excess profit is that
    (A) a certain optimum combination of land, labor, capital, and entrepreneurship exists
    (B) an estimate of value should be based on future expectations
    (C) abnormally high profits cannot be expected to continue indefinitely
    (D) maximum value accrues to real estate when social and economic homogeneity is present in a neighborhood
    (E) the direct sales comparison approach becomes irrelevant

19. Because real estate markets deal with different desires and needs, they are said to be
    (A) fractionated   (D) submarketed
    (B) structured   (E) spacious
    (C) segmented

20. Demand for real estate clearly exists when
    (A) population and employment are on the rise
    (B) there is desire or need for space, plus available mortgage financing
    (C) there is desire or need for space, plus ability to pay
    (D) purchasing power increases
    (E) farm prices rise

21. A mortgage is
    (A) a gift from the mortgagee
    (B) a transfer of real estate to a financial institution
    (C) any loan
    (D) a pledge of real estate as collateral for a loan
    (E) a cloud on the title to real estate

22. The portion of the loan payment for recapture of the investment capital in a mortgage is
    (A) principal, interest, taxes, and insurance
    (B) principal reduction or amortization
    (C) interest and principal payment
    (D) negative amortization
    (E) mortgage banking

23. An appraisal is
    (A) an establishment of value
    (B) a prediction of sales price
    (C) a mathematically precise forecast of value
    (D) an estimate of rental levels
    (E) an estimate of value

24. An appraiser
    (A) determines value
    (B) determines price
    (C) estimates value
    (D) measures price
    (E) forecasts price

25. An appraiser
    (A) determines rent rates
    (B) sets value
    (C) suggests financing
    (D) estimates value
    (E) inspects electrical, mechanical, and plumbing for working condition

26. The ____ establishes the market conditions prevailing when the appraisal is made.
    (A) statement of limitations
    (B) statement of conclusions
    (C) introductory note
    (D) transmittal letter
    (E) date of the value estimate

27. Analysis of a location involves which three levels?
    (A) general, specific, detailed
    (B) country, state, community
    (C) residential, commercial, industrial
    (D) country, state, county
    (E) region, neighborhood, site

28. Market data are used
    (A) in the direct sales comparison approach
    (B) in the income approach
    (C) in the cost approach
    (D) in statistical analysis
    (E) all of the above

29. The cost approach is most applicable when the subject property
    (A) has new improvements that represent the highest and best use
    (B) is in an active local market for similar properties
    (C) produces a positive cash flow
    (D) is in an area where many comparable properties have recently been sold
    (E) exhibits a great deal of functional obsolescence

30. In preparing an appraisal report, your analysis concludes that one of the approaches to value is not applicable to this particular case. You should therefore
    (A) omit the approach altogether
    (B) base the approach on hypothetical data
    (C) state that the approach is not relevant
    (D) state that the approach is not applicable, explain the reasons for this contention, and provide supporting data
    (E) find another approach so as to include three approaches

31. Reconciliation involves
    (A) averaging the unadjusted sales prices of comparables
    (B) recalculating all data
    (C) averaging all estimates derived, weighting each according to its importance
    (D) placing primary emphasis on the estimate deemed most reliable
    (E) averaging estimates from the three approaches, giving each equal weight

32. Cost and market value are more likely to be almost the same when properties are
    (A) new   (D) syndicated
    (B) old   (E) appraised
    (C) depreciated

33. In appraisal, reconciliation is
    (A) an estimate of value
    (B) one of the three approaches used in estimating value
    (C) a process of reevaluation that leads to the final value estimate
    (D) an assurance of checkbook accuracy
    (E) a process that is similar to correlation in statistics

34. The essential elements of an appraisal report
    (A) usually follow the scope of work
    (B) vary with the type of report
    (C) depend on the client's needs
    (D) depend on the fee charged
    (E) depend on the number of comparables located

35. A restricted appraisal report
    (A) contains many items that are not included in the usual report
    (B) is an appraisal report prepared for a fussy client
    (C) is generally the least detailed report
    (D) may be based on hypothetical or assumed data
    (E) should be prepared on a nontypical property to show appraisal expertise

36. A parcel of land that is improved to the point of being ready to be built upon is called
    (A) realty
    (B) land
    (C) a site
    (D) terrain
    (E) a location

37. Before performing a site inspection, an appraiser should
    (A) gather basic information about the site
    (B) know the reasons for the site inspection
    (C) have a map or drawing of the site
    (D) have writing materials for taking notes
    (E) all of the above

38. Environmental hazards that an appraiser must be conscious of include all of the following EXCEPT
    (A) asbestos
    (B) radon
    (C) Drano
    (D) urea formaldehyde
    (E) dry cleaning chemicals

39. The term that denotes the attractiveness and usefulness of a property is
    (A) price estimate
    (B) highest and best use
    (C) location
    (D) functional utility
    (E) value in use

40. Combining two or more sites in order to develop one site with a greater value than the individual sites have separately is called
    (A) assemblage
    (B) plottage
    (C) surplus land
    (D) excess land
    (E) highest and best use of land

41. In the cost approach, the valuation of land involves the principle of
    (A) conformity
    (B) contribution
    (C) highest and best use
    (D) marginal productivity
    (E) variable proportions

42. The highest and best use of land is the reasonable use
    (A) to which land is currently being put
    (B) to which land can be put without adverse effect over the short term
    (C) to which land can most profitably be put over the short term
    (D) to which land can most profitably be put over the long term
    (E) whereby land will become agriculturally productive

43. The direct sales comparison approach should be used
    (A) without exception
    (B) on residential properties only
    (C) on residential and income properties
    (D) in all cases where comparable sales are available
    (E) on vacant land

44. The direct sales comparison approach involves
    (A) analyzing sales
    (B) comparing properties that have recently been sold to a subject property
    (C) analyzing market rentals
    (D) both A and B
    (E) none of the above

45. If the monthly rental for the subject property is $575 and the gross rent multiplier is 127, what estimate of value is indicated?
    (A) $74,750
    (B) $75,000
    (C) $72,925
    (D) $73,125
    (E) $73,000

46. The direct sales comparison approach
    (A) uses the replacement cost of improvements, added to a comparable vacant land value
    (B) uses data on recent sales of comparable properties
    (C) uses the income-producing capability of the property
    (D) involves multiple listing service data
    (E) requires at least three comparable sales for application

47. What is the indicated value of a property that rents for $750 per month, using a monthly gross rent multiplier of 110, if the expenses attributable to the property are $125 per month?
    (A) $75,670
    (B) $82,500
    (C) $68,750
    (D) $61,125
    (E) $13,750

48. A 7-year-old residence is currently valued at $72,000. What was its original value if it has appreciated by 60% since it was built?
    (A) $27,000
    (B) $37,800
    (C) $45,000
    (D) $115,200
    (E) none of the above

49. For residential property, market value appraisals assume that
    (A) the purchaser pays all cash; no money is borrowed
    (B) an FHA or VA mortgage is used
    (C) a purchase money mortgage is considered
    (D) the value estimate is based on no special financing
    (E) the seller pays no more than five points

50. In considering comparable sales in direct sales comparison appraisal,
    (A) the seller's motivation is significant
    (B) the date of sale is significant
    (C) the proximity of the properties is most important
    (D) both A and B
    (E) none of the above

Questions 51–53 are based on the following information:

Seven comparables have been found for a single-family dwelling being appraised and gross rent multipliers calculated from the sales prices as follows:

Comparable	GRM
1	125
2	125
3	127
4	127
5	127
6	128
7	130

51. What is the mean GRM?
    (A) 125
    (B) 126
    (C) 127
    (D) 128
    (E) 130

52. What is the median GRM?
    (A) 125
    (B) 126
    (C) 127
    (D) 128
    (E) 130

53. What is the mode for the GRMs?
    (A) 125
    (B) 126
    (C) 127
    (D) 128
    (E) 130

_____

54. Land prices are analyzed and adjusted in the sales comparison process. These adjustments may involve
    (A) adding or subtracting lump-sum amounts
    (B) adding or subtracting percentages
    (C) accumulating percentages
    (D) using several units of comparison
    (E) any of the above

55. The adjustment process in the direct sales comparison technique involves
    (A) identifying the similarities between properties and adjusting the sales prices
    (B) analyzing the comparables and adjusting the prices for similarities
    (C) identifying the significant differences between the subject and comparable properties and adjusting the sales prices of the comparables for differences
    (D) locating competitive properties and ranking them in the order of desirability
    (E) adjusting the subject to be like the comparables

56. In the cost approach, the site is valued as if it were
    (A) vacant and available for development to its highest and best use
    (B) improved and suited for its intended use or development
    (C) developed and operating
    (D) attractively landscaped
    (E) lacking nearby utilities

57. The direct sales comparison approach is especially suitable for appraising land zoned for which of the following types of use?
    (A) single-family residential
    (B) commercial
    (C) industrial
    (D) multifamily residential
    (E) any of the above

58. All of the following are accepted classifications of accrued depreciation for appraisal purposes EXCEPT
    (A) functional obsolescence
    (B) economic obsolescence
    (C) accounting allocation
    (D) physical deterioration
    (E) external obsolescence

59. Accrued depreciation can be defined in appraisal terms as
    (A) an increase in value from inflationary gains
    (B) a total loss in value from all causes
    (C) diminished utility from trade imbalance
    (D) competitive pressures
    (E) functional form changes

60. The cost estimates used in appraisal typically reflect
    (A) wholesale costs
    (B) current cost levels
    (C) typical costs to build a building like this subject
    (D) the actual historic cost of the building being appraised
    (E) both B and C

61. Cost indexes are used to
    (A) derive units of comparison
    (B) catalog building components
    (C) estimate operating expenses
    (D) update past costs into current costs
    (E) estimate the local consumer price index

62. The most detailed, time-consuming, and costly method of estimating cost new is
    (A) unit of comparison   (D) unit-in-place
    (B) quantity survey   (E) segregated cost
    (C) trade breakdown

63. In calculating depreciation, a limitation of the age-life method is that it
    (A) tends to ignore physical deterioration
    (B) cannot be used with estimates of cost new
    (C) is based on replacement cost rather than reproduction cost
    (D) tends to ignore functional and economic obsolescence
    (E) is difficult to compute

64. Two baths are required to serve a three-bedroom house if
    (A) the appraiser believes they are necessary
    (B) the selling price is more than $75,000
    (C) two baths are demanded by a typical purchaser of a three-bedroom house in the given market
    (D) four or more persons will live in the house
    (E) one of the bedrooms is at the opposite end of the house from the other two

65. Which is the most precise yet least used cost estimation method?
    (A) index method
    (B) quantity survey method
    (C) comparative square foot method
    (D) unit-in-place method
    (E) segregated cost method

66. A defect is considered curable if
    (A) major structural alterations are not required
    (B) the cost of the cure represents more than 25% of the remaining utility
    (C) the cost to cure the condition is less than or equal to the anticipated addition to value
    (D) the cost to cure increases the remaining economic life of the improvement
    (E) the cure is in conformity with building codes

67. External or economic obsolescence is normally NOT
    (A) curable by the owner, the landlord, or the tenant
    (B) discovered during the neighborhood analysis portion of appraisal
    (C) evident in both land and buildings
    (D) caused by forces outside the property
    (E) also called environmental obsolescence

68. A house built in 1980 and appraised in 2015 would have
    (A) a useful life of 35 years
    (B) a chronological age of 35 years
    (C) an effective age of 35 years
    (D) an economic age of 35 years
    (E) a 35-year-old replacement cost

69. In one step of the land residual technique, the building capitalization rate is applied to the known building value to estimate the
    (A) highest and best use of the site
    (B) cost of the building
    (C) income needed to support the land
    (D) net operating income needed to support the building
    (E) land value

70. An example of partial interest is
    (A) a life estate
    (B) a leasehold estate
    (C) a lengthy attention span
    (D) a short attention span
    (E) both A and B

71. A condominium is
    (A) a type of mortgage on real estate
    (B) a building like a cooperative
    (C) a legal concept of ownership
    (D) a zero-lot-line house
    (E) a style of housing

72. Clarity and accuracy contribute to the
    (A) quality of an appraisal   (D) final value estimate
    (B) quantity of evidence   (E) appearance of the report
    (C) appraisal fee

73. If an appraiser is asked to undertake an assignment on a property type with which she has no previous experience and is otherwise unfamiliar, she should
    (A) refuse the assignment
    (B) accept the assignment, thereby expanding her abilities, but reduce the fee
    (C) ask the client to hire another appraiser to help her
    (D) associate herself with another appraiser experienced in this type of assignment and inform the client of this fact
    (E) get the necessary computer software to solve the problem

74. Real estate markets are composed of
    (A) buyers only   (D) buyers and sellers
    (B) sellers only   (E) appraisers and counselors
    (C) types of property

75. Real estate supply factors include
    (A) the current housing supply   (D) both A and B
    (B) new construction activity   (E) none of the above
    (C) tax depreciation allowances

The remaining 25 questions are for general appraisal certification only.

76. The mortgage constant is a function of all of the following EXCEPT
    (A) the term of the loan
    (B) the borrower's income level
    (C) the interest rate
    (D) the term of amortization
    (E) It is a function of all of the above.

77. The benefit(s) forgone from a project that cannot be built is (are) called
    (A) anticipation   (D) surplus productivity
    (B) substitution   (E) marginal cost
    (C) opportunity cost

78. The debt coverage ratio
    (A) is federally approved for residential valuation
    (B) can be applied uniformly to all properties
    (C) is the most equitable method of determining a cap rate
    (D) indicates the safety of the loan
    (E) is generally less than 1.00

79. The____is a key safety factor for the lender.
    (A) maturity term
    (B) sales price
    (C) loan-to-value ratio
    (D) age of the improvements
    (E) land value

80. A parcel of land is sold for $115,000. If it appreciated at 12% per year, and the seller held it for four years, how much did the seller pay for it (disregard taxes, selling costs, etc.)?
    (A) $60,000
    (B) $101,000
    (C) $73,000
    (D) $62,500
    (E) $81,700

81. A 30-year-old building with an effective age of 20 years has a total life expectancy of 50 years. How much depreciation has occurred?
    (A) 10%
    (B) 20%
    (C) 40%
    (D) 60%
    (E) none of the above

82. A plot of land, 100 ft. × 200 ft., along an interstate freeway, is situated 12 miles north of the central business district of a city with a population approaching 1 million. Which of the following would be the highest and best use of the land?
    (A) service station
    (B) convenience store
    (C) two-story office building
    (D) medical office building
    (E) there is not enough information to make a determination

83. A $2 million shopping center is purchased with a 75% loan-to-value ratio mortgage, payable monthly over 25 years at 12% interest. It generates $205,000 annual net operating income. The land is considered to be worth $500,000; the balance of cost is represented by land improvements. What is the improvement ratio?
    (A) 25%
    (B) 50%
    (C) 75%
    (D) 100%
    (E) none of the above

84. The adjustment for below-market-rate financing may provide an estimate of
    (A) market price
    (B) cash equivalence
    (C) property price
    (D) creative financing
    (E) replacement cost

85. Land or site appraisals assist in
    (A) the sale and purchase of land
    (B) land development
    (C) ad valorem and income tax situations
    (D) all of the above
    (E) none of the above

86. Overall rate of return is
    (A) the annual net operating income divided by the purchase price
    (B) annual income and all gains or losses prorated to an effective annual amount minus an internal rate of return
    (C) a percentage or decimal rate that, when divided into a periodic income amount, offers a lump-sum capital value for the income
    (D) an income that is unchanging with time
    (E) none of the above

87. All of the following are used in the valuation of income-producing property EXCEPT
    (A) rental rates
    (B) operating expenses
    (C) income taxes
    (D) net leasable area
    (E) vacancy and collection allowance

88. A $1 million property will have a 75% loan at an 8% annual mortgage constant. What must the net operating income be to produce a 12% cash-on-cash return?
    (A) $75,000
    (B) $127,500
    (C) $90,000
    (D) $150,000
    (E) $750,000

89. If a particular buyer requires a recapture of the building portion of the purchase price in 25 years, what is the indicated recapture rate for the building, assuming straight-line capture?
    (A) 0.25%
    (B) 2%
    (C) 4%
    (D) 20%
    (E) 25%

90. In a high-rise 100-unit apartment building there is a basement laundry area that brings in $100 monthly from the concessionaire. The laundry income is
    (A) included, as miscellaneous income, in potential gross income
    (B) included, as other income, in effective gross income
    (C) deducted from effective gross income
    (D) added to before-tax cash flow
    (E) distributed to the maintenance workers

91. In an appraisal of income property, which of the following items should be excluded from the expense statement?
    (A) mortgage loan interest payments
    (B) ordinary and necessary current expenses
    (C) projected replacement reserve
    (D) management fees
    (E) advertising expenses

Questions 92–95 are based on the following information:

A building contains 25 one-bedroom units and 75 two-bedroom units. The one-bedroom units rent for $550 monthly; two-bedrooms are $675. The vacancy rate is 7%; operating expenses are estimated at 40% of effective gross income. There is $1,000 annual income from vending machines.

92. Potential gross income is
   (A) $773,500
   (B) $772,500
   (C) $719,425
   (D) $64,375
   (E) none of the above

93. Effective gross income is
   (A) $773,500
   (B) $772,500
   (C) $719,425
   (D) $64,375
   (E) none of the above

94. Net operating income is
   (A) $64,375
   (B) $286,970
   (C) $431,655
   (D) $719,425
   (E) none of the above

95. Operating expenses are
   (A) $1,000
   (B) $54,075
   (C) $287,770
   (D) $719,425
   (E) none of the above

---

96. Which approach involves an investigation of the rent schedules of the subject property and the comparables?
   (A) cost approach
   (B) just compensation evaluation
   (C) income approach
   (D) comparable rent approach
   (E) all of the above

97. Property free and clear of indebtedness is offered for sale. The property is net-net leased (the tenant pays all operating expenses) for $90,000 per year under a 30-year lease. Rent is payable annually at the end of each year. The building cost $850,000, including a developer's profit and risk allowance; the land cost $100,000, and its value is well established by comparable sales. It is estimated that the building will be worth only about half its current cost at the end of the lease term, and that the land will remain constant in value over that period. A 10% discount rate is considered appropriate. Using the building residual technique estimate the value of the building.
   (A) between $250,000 and $300,000
   (B) between $300,000 and $750,000
   (C) between $750,000 and $1,000,000
   (D) between $1,000,000 and $1,500,000
   (E) not within any of the above ranges

98. Which of the following statements is true of a *gross lease*?
    (A) The tenant pays all operating expenses.
    (B) The landlord pays all operating expenses.
    (C) This lease is used only for commercial properties.
    (D) Rent rises with the cost of living.
    (E) This lease must be drafted by an attorney.

99. Land purchased for $100,000 cash appreciates at the rate of 15%, compounded annually. About how much is the land worth after 5 years? Disregard taxes, insurance, and selling expenses.
    (A) $200,000   (D) $75,000
    (B) $175,000   (E) $15,000
    (C) $115,000

100. An allowance for vacancy and collection loss is estimated as a percentage of
    (A) net operating income   (D) potential gross income
    (B) before-tax cash flow   (E) after-tax cash flow
    (C) effective gross income

Model Examination 10
SALESPERSON AND BROKER

See page 488 for the answer key. Math problems are worked out on page 502.

1. When estimating the market value of the subject house, which is 20 years old, which of the following would be of importance?
   (A) replacement cost new
   (B) reproduction cost new
   (C) market value of recently sold comparable properties
   (D) market value less depreciation

2. To appraise a house valued at over $1,000,000 in a federally related transaction, the person performing the appraisal would need to
   (A) be state certified
   (B) be federally licensed
   (C) be MAI designated
   (D) have 10 years' experience in appraisal

3. The subject house being appraised has a swimming pool and a garage. The appraiser estimates that a pool contributes $20,000 to the value and a garage contributes $15,000. A recent sale in the neighborhood for $300,000 is similar except that it has a garage but no pool. The adjusted value of the comparable house is
   (A) $300,000   (C) $320,000
   (B) $315,000   (D) $335,000

4. An appraiser opines that a commercial property, if fully leased, would produce $20,000 per month in rent. A vacancy allowance of 9% is applied, and by using a capitalization rate of 12%, the market value of the property is estimated at
   (A) $1,820,000   (C) $1,516,667
   (B) $1,666,666   (D) $2,400,000

5. A main goal of an appraiser is
   (A) measuring obsolescence
   (B) rendering a market value opinion
   (C) narrative reporting
   (D) meeting sales contract amount

6. A major factor in appraising a business opportunity is the
   (A) net income   (C) number of customers
   (B) number of employees   (D) owner's expertise

7. Prices of comparable sales are adjusted
   (A) to the subject property
   (B) upward if the comparable is inferior to the subject
   (C) downward if the comparable is superior to the subject
   (D) all of the above

8. All other things being equal, the cost per square foot of a two-story house compared to a one-story house having the same square footage
   (A) is less
   (B) is more
   (C) is the same
   (D) depends on height

9. Ellen bought a half-acre lot at $10 per square foot and built a house 50′ × 50′ for $75 per square foot. Her total cost
   (A) was $405,300
   (B) was $623,100
   (C) was $236,550
   (D) cannot be determined from information given

10. Wear and tear is a form of loss in value called
    (A) physical deterioration
    (B) functional obsolescence
    (C) deferred maintenance
    (D) economic obsolescence

11. In which appraisal approach does the appraiser estimate the land value separately from improvements?
    (A) cost
    (B) sales comparison
    (C) income
    (D) depreciation

12. Which is *not* an appraisal approach?
    (A) sales comparison approach
    (B) income capitalization approach
    (C) cost approach
    (D) depreciation approach

13. An appraiser should
    (A) raise or lower the appraised value to the contract amount
    (B) determine the price
    (C) be impartial
    (D) be a member of the broker's firm

14. The best way for a broker acting as a dual agent to minimize his or her risk is to
    (A) hire an attorney
    (B) obtain written permission from both parties to act for both sides
    (C) read the state's real estate law
    (D) provide full disclosure to all parties

15. When representing a buyer in a real estate transaction, a broker must disclose to the seller all of the following *except*
    (A) the buyer's motivation
    (B) the broker's relationship with the buyer
    (C) any agreement to compensate the broker out of the listing broker's commission
    (D) the broker's agreement with the buyer

16. Broker Herman must have an escrow account
    (A) before the state licensing agency will issue his broker's license
    (B) when he holds earnest money
    (C) before his agents can work
    (D) when his personal account is overdrawn

17. Which of the following best describes the role of a broker who seeks a buyer?
    (A) general contractor
    (B) independent contractor
    (C) special agent
    (D) attorney-in-fact

18. How is a buyer's broker typically paid?
    (A) by the buyer at closing
    (B) by a finder's fee paid outside of closing
    (C) by the buyer prior to closing
    (D) by the listing broker through a commission split

19. The rate of commission on a real estate sale is
    (A) typically 6% of the selling price
    (B) mandated at various rates by brokerage law
    (C) paid to the salesperson, who gives 50% to the broker
    (D) negotiable between the broker and (typically) seller

20. As a general rule, escrow money received by the broker
    (A) is given to the seller on signing the contract
    (B) may be spent by the broker for repairs to the property
    (C) is deposited in the broker's trust account soon after receipt
    (D) is shared equally by the broker and salesperson

21. An unlicensed employee of a broker who prepares an advertisement to sell a house
    (A) is free to do so
    (B) must have the broker's prior written approval
    (C) must become licensed
    (D) must accurately describe the house

22. An owner who sells property that he developed
    (A) may engage an unlicensed sales staff who receive commissions
    (B) may engage an unlicensed sales staff who receive salaries only
    (C) must acquire a broker's license
    (D) must acquire a salesperson's license

23. In a no brokerage agency relationship, the seller or buyer
    (A) is responsible for the broker's acts
    (B) is not responsible for the broker's acts
    (C) is not considered a customer of the broker
    (D) is an agent of the broker

24. In a no brokerage agency arrangement, parties give up their rights to a broker's
    (A) undivided loyalty
    (B) honest dealings
    (C) use of skill and care
    (D) accounting for funds

25. Some ways to terminate a brokerage relationship are
    (A) agreement between the parties
    (B) fulfillment of the contract
    (C) expiration of the term
    (D) all of the above

26. A broker with no agency relationship may assist
    (A) buyer
    (B) seller
    (C) both buyer and seller
    (D) all of the above

27. *Prima facie evidence* refers to evidence that is good and sufficient on its face to
    (A) sell real estate
    (B) buy real estate
    (C) establish a given fact
    (D) file a lawsuit

28. Brokerage representation may legally include
    (A) a broker working for the seller
    (B) a broker working as a single agent for buyer or seller (but not both in the same transaction)
    (C) broker representing neither buyer nor seller but facilitating the transaction
    (D) all of the above

29. A salesperson is _____ of the broker.
    (A) an agent
    (B) an employee
    (C) a paid contractor
    (D) a Realtor

30. Termination of a brokerage relationship may occur as a result of
    (A) bankruptcy of the principal or customer
    (B) death of either party
    (C) destruction of the property
    (D) all of the above

31. When a broker is an agent of the owner, the salesperson is
    (A) a Realtor
    (B) an independent contractor
    (C) a subagent
    (D) an employee

32. A single agent must
    (A) deal honestly and fairly
    (B) be loyal
    (C) provide full disclosure
    (D) all of the above

33. A person who wishes to sell his or her own house
    (A) must employ a broker
    (B) must employ a salesperson
    (C) must employ a Realtor
    (D) may employ any of the above, but is not required to do so

34. Which of the following, when performed for others, are included as real estate services for the purposes of determining licensure requirements?
    (A) buying and selling property
    (B) renting and leasing property
    (C) auction or exchange of property
    (D) all of the above

35. *Dual agency* is defined as an arrangement in which
    (A) the same broker represents both the buyer and the seller
    (B) the broker is the seller
    (C) the salesperson and the broker split the commission
    (D) the listing broker and selling broker cooperate with each other

36. When a broker serves in a single agent capacity, his obligations to the customer include
    (A) loyalty
    (B) confidentiality
    (C) obedience
    (D) all of the above

37. If a broker uses a title company to hold escrow deposits, the broker must turn over the funds
    (A) on the same day
    (B) in the same time frame as would be required if the broker maintained the account
    (C) when convenient
    (D) at the end of each month

38. If a buyer and seller reach oral agreement over the price and terms of a contract but seek a broker's help to complete written contract forms, the relationship with the broker is likely to be
    (A) single agent
    (B) transaction agent
    (C) no brokerage relationship
    (D) any of the above

39. A single agent relationship provides a _____ with a seller.
    (A) fiduciary relationship
    (B) transaction agency
    (C) no business relationship
    (D) subagency

40. When a real estate attorney wants to earn a commission for performing real estate services, he or she must
    (A) become a Realtor
    (B) obtain a real estate license
    (C) join a franchise
    (D) be a member of the bar association

41. It is a good practice for a broker to prequalify
    (A) a prospective buyer
    (B) a seller
    (C) a sales agent
    (D) all clients

42. Herb is 17 when he signs a contract to lease a small house. After the property manager accepts his offer, the lease contract is
    (A) void
    (B) voidable by Herb
    (C) voidable by either party
    (D) illegal

43. Carol is buying a house and has 30 days in which to obtain a financing commitment as specified in the sales contract. The contract states that Carol must notify the seller within that period if she cannot arrange financing, or risk default if she does not close. The contract states that "time is of the essence" applies to financing approval. Which is true?
    (A) Carol can arrange financing at her convenience.
    (B) The financing approval is automatically extended.
    (C) The lender must check Carol's credit references.
    (D) Carol must adhere to the stated time frame, which will end at 11:59 P.M. on the 30th day.

44. Harry gives Sam a $5,000 payment and a written agreement stating that, on July 1 of the following year, Harry will purchase the property from Sam for $150,000 cash, or Sam may keep the money. This transaction is
    (A) a lease with an option to purchase
    (B) a purchase contract with a delayed settlement
    (C) an option agreement
    (D) a limited partnership

45. Sally has shown Rebecca 11 homes, and Rebecca has selected one and made an offer. An hour later Rebecca changes her mind. Which of the following is true?
    (A) Rebecca has already committed to the first seller and cannot withdraw.
    (B) Rebecca may withdraw the offer but will forfeit the earnest money.
    (C) The broker earned a commission.
    (D) Rebecca may withdraw before the seller accepts the offer.

46. A bank acquired property through foreclosure. Upon sale of the property, the bank covenants and warrants the property's title only against defects occurring during the bank's ownership. This conveyance is a(n)
    (A) administrator's deed   (C) special warranty deed
    (B) general warranty deed   (D) covenant deed

47. A deed is the instrument used to convey ownership of
    (A) personal property   (C) real property
    (B) short-term use of real estate   (D) any of the above

48. Which of the following is a voluntary alienation of real property?
    (A) escheat   (C) foreclosure
    (B) condemnation   (D) a deed of trust

49. Developers subdivide land and assign lot and block numbers to identify lots in the subdivision. This is a legal description known as
    (A) a block party   (C) developer plat
    (B) recorded plat description   (D) lot survey method

50. A township is
    (A) 36 square miles   (C) a small city
    (B) one square mile   (D) 640 acres

51. What is the type of legal description that uses imaginary lines of meridians and baselines?
    (A) metes and bounds   (C) lot and block
    (B) recorded plat   (D) rectangular survey

52. Broker Barb is acting as a buyer's agent for Joe. Joe asks whether any people of a certain race live in a specific neighborhood. How should Barb respond?
    (A) She should advise Joe that, under fair housing laws, she cannot provide that information.
    (B) She should advise Joe of the race of all the neighbors she is aware of.
    (C) She should advise Joe that he should contact the demographic agency to obtain the information.
    (D) She should advise Joe to contact the school district to obtain the information.

53. A broker has contacted owners in a certain subdivision and advised them that several members of a particular race have bought homes in the area. The broker has offered to list properties at a reduced rate and encouraged the owners to sell quickly. This is
(A) steering
(B) profiling
(C) blockbusting
(D) scaring

54. Mortgage lenders may not discriminate on the basis of age, but they need not lend to
(A) parents of more than two children
(B) childless couples
(C) part-time workers
(D) minors

55. Ellen owns a two-family house and lives in one side. She wants to advertise the other side as nonsmoking. Can she legally do so?
(A) yes, because the right to smoke is not protected by law
(B) yes, because she owns the house
(C) no, because a property owner cannot advertise discriminatory practices
(D) no, because smoking is perfectly legal

56. A tenant applicant confined to a wheelchair is interested in renting a patio home. A request is made to the landlord to allow the tenant to build an access ramp. Which of the following is true?
(A) The tenant's application may be rejected.
(B) The landlord must allow the tenant to make the modification at the tenant's expense.
(C) The landlord is required to pay for modifications to the property to accommodate the access.
(D) The landlord may collect an additional deposit to assure compliance.

57. No federal fair housing laws are violated if a landlord refuses to rent to
(A) families with children
(B) tenants of Indian descent
(C) deaf persons
(D) college students

58. The federal ban on discrimination based on familial status is intended to provide equal access to rentals for
(A) unmarried couples under 25
(B) people with children
(C) single tenants
(D) the elderly

59. The Real Estate Settlement Procedures Act (RESPA) applies to
(A) all real estate financing
(B) contracts for deed
(C) second mortgages only
(D) financing of one- to four-family residences

60. The Civil Rights Act of 1866 prohibits
(A) zoning
(B) redlining
(C) open housing
(D) racial discrimination

61. If a landlord refuses to rent to a minority prospective tenant with a poor credit record,
    (A) federal fair housing laws are violated
    (B) the minority applicant should report this violation
    (C) there is no violation
    (D) the landlord may face a significant fine

62. Sullivan wants to rent an apartment but is confined to a wheelchair. At Sullivan's request, the landlord
    (A) must build a ramp at the landlord's expense
    (B) must build a ramp at Sullivan's expense
    (C) need do nothing
    (D) must reduce the rent to Sullivan's affordability level

63. A seller asks his broker about the race of a potential buyer. The broker
    (A) must answer the question if a single agent
    (B) violates fair housing laws if he answers the question
    (C) may answer the question because of the Constitutional right to free speech
    (D) may tell the seller but no one else

64. Broker Bob is showing houses to Joe Chen, who is of Chinese ancestry. Bob shows Joe houses in a neighborhood of predominantly Chinese-American residences because Bob thinks Joe would feel more at home there. This is
    (A) illegal steering under fair housing laws
    (B) superior and tactful service
    (C) done for Joe's benefit
    (D) effective sales technique

65. Where the dominant population base of an area consists of minorities,
    (A) brokers need not be concerned with fair housing laws
    (B) brokers must still observe fair housing laws
    (C) there are no reporting requirements
    (D) violation of fair housing laws is not possible

66. The Civil Rights Act of 1968 prohibits
    (A) integration
    (B) greenlining
    (C) discrimination in housing
    (D) school busing

67. *Familial status* refers to
    (A) families with two or more children
    (B) families with children under age 18
    (C) the earning capacity of the family
    (D) RESPA

68. Casualty insurance is
    (A) a financing expense
    (B) a capital expenditure
    (C) a fixed expense
    (D) a variable expense

69. A retail tenant in a mall pays monthly rent and additional amounts for property maintenance, taxes, utilities, and cleaning services. This is known as a
    (A) net lease
    (B) percentage lease
    (C) ground lease
    (D) gross lease

70. Broker Morris has a written agreement with Sarah Lee to find a one-story house with three bedrooms and two baths in Lancaster. What type of agreement does broker Morris have?
    (A) an open buyer's agent agreement
    (B) a dual agent agreement
    (C) an exclusive buyer's agent agreement
    (D) an agency agreement

71. Which of the following would terminate a listing agreement?
    (A) death of the broker
    (B) revocation of the salesperson's license
    (C) an offer to purchase
    (D) expiration of the salesperson's license

72. The Floyds' home was listed with a broker, but they located a buyer and sold the property themselves. However, they were still obligated to pay a brokerage fee. What kind of listing had they agreed to?
    (A) a net listing   (C) an exclusive right to sell
    (B) an open listing   (D) a multiple listing

73. If the agent has not located a buyer by the end of the listing period, what happens?
    (A) The listing is automatically extended for an additional 30 days.
    (B) The listing price is reduced by 10%.
    (C) The agency relationship terminates.
    (D) The broker can charge for advertising.

74. A contract in which an owner promises to pay compensation to a broker for providing a buyer but may give listings to other brokers is known as
    (A) an exclusive right to sell   (C) an open listing
    (B) a net listing   (D) multiple listing

75. Stephen, a salesperson associated with broker Bob, lists a house for sale for $320,000, with 6% commission due at closing. Three weeks later, the owner accepts an offer of $300,000, brought in by Stephen. Bob's practice is that 45% of commissions goes to the office and the remainder to the salesperson. How much will Stephen make on the sale?
    (A) $18,000   (C) $9,500
    (B) $10,560   (D) $9,900

76. Before Mary listed her house, she reserved the right to sell the property to anyone she found without paying a broker. What kind of listing is this?
    (A) exclusive right to sell   (C) multiple
    (B) exclusive agency   (D) open

77. Roger has contracted with three brokers to sell his ranch. He has agreed to pay a commission to the broker who brings a ready, willing, and able buyer and who meets his terms. This is a(n)
    (A) exclusive listing   (C) open listing
    (B) exclusive right to sell   (D) multiple listing

78. The listing broker will receive a commission fee of 6% on the first $250,000 of the sale price and 4% on any amount above $250,000. If the property sells for $450,000, how much is the total commission?
    (A) $15,000
    (B) $18,000
    (C) $27,000
    (D) $23,000

79. Which of the following is included in an agent's responsibilities to the party the agent is *not* representing?
    (A) The agent must disclose all material facts to the other party.
    (B) The agent owes no loyalty to the other party.
    (C) The agent must provide all information about the principal.
    (D) The agent must advise the other party.

80. Broker Barb listed Tony's house and subsequently showed it to her sister, who made an offer to purchase. What is Barb's responsibility of disclosure?
    (A) No disclosure is required.
    (B) Barb must disclose her family relationship to the purchaser.
    (C) No disclosure is required if the property is sold at the list price.
    (D) It is a violation of fiduciary duty for Barb to show the property to a relative.

81. The seller has agreed to pay two points to the lending institution to help the buyers obtain a mortgage loan. The house was listed for $320,000 and is being sold for $300,000. The buyers will pay 20% in cash and borrow the rest. How much will the seller owe to the lender for points?
    (A) $6,400
    (B) $4,800
    (C) $5,120
    (D) $6,000

82. The lender's underwriting criteria specify a maximum housing expense to income ratio of 28%. If the applicant proves annual earnings of $75,000 in the previous year, and that salary is continuing, the maximum monthly PITI would be
    (A) $2,100
    (B) $1,750
    (C) $2,800
    (D) $2,100

83. Which of the following is an advantage of a biweekly mortgage payment plan?
    (A) The borrower pays less per month in return for a longer term.
    (B) It is equivalent to 12 monthly payments each year.
    (C) There are lower interest rates.
    (D) The loan is paid off sooner than it would be with 12 monthly payments.

84. Common covenants found in a mortgage include all of the following except
    (A) keep the property in good repair
    (B) pay all current real estate taxes
    (C) provide unlimited access to the mortgagee
    (D) not damage any improvements securing the loan

85. The function of the Federal Housing Administration (FHA) is to
    (A) lend money
    (B) insure loans
    (C) guarantee loans
    (D) buy loans

86. The buyer who agrees to pay an existing loan but does not take personal responsibility
    (A) assumes the loan
    (B) takes the property subject to the loan
    (C) subordinates the loan
    (D) forecloses on the loan

87. In general, the lien with first claim on the real estate is the
    (A) largest one
    (B) one that is signed
    (C) one that was recorded first
    (D) one that is foreclosed

88. When a borrower is required to maintain an escrow account with the lending institution, money in that account may be used to pay the homeowner's
    (A) Realtor
    (B) utility bills
    (C) property taxes or insurance
    (D) life insurance

89. After Harvey bought his apartment, he started receiving his own property tax bills. This indicates that he has bought into a
    (A) condominium
    (B) cooperative
    (C) leasehold
    (D) syndicate

90. Mr. and Mrs. Buyer asked broker Bob about the best way to take title to the property they had agreed to buy. What should Bob do?
    (A) Advise the Buyers to ask their parents.
    (B) Advise the Buyers to contact an attorney.
    (C) Have his accountant advise the Buyers of the best way to take title.
    (D) Advise the Buyers to contact the county recorder.

91. Helen and David, who are not married, want to buy a house together. To ensure that if one dies, the other will automatically become the full owner, their deed must state that they are
    (A) tenants in common
    (B) tenants in severalty
    (C) tenants by the entirety
    (D) joint tenants

92. Real property is
    (A) the land
    (B) the land, the improvements, and the bundle of rights
    (C) the land and the right to possess it
    (D) the land, buildings, and easements

93. A house has a built-in bookcase and elaborate chandelier. The buyer is also getting a dinette set and a table lamp. Which is correct?
    (A) The built-in bookcase and chandelier are included in the real estate contract. The lamp and dinette set are chattels and are sold separately.
    (B) All the items must be included in the real estate contract.
    (C) The chandelier is real estate; the other items must be sold on a bill of sale.
    (D) All of the items are real estate because they are sold with the house.

94. Manmade additions to land are known as
    (A) chattels   (C) easements
    (B) trade fixtures   (D) improvements

95. Land can be owned apart from the buildings on it under the arrangement known
    as a
    (A) net lease   (C) remainder
    (B) life estate   (D) ground lease

96. No one seems to own the vacant land next to Mary's house, so she has used it for a
    pasture for many years. She may have a good chance of obtaining ownership by
    (A) poaching   (C) adverse possession
    (B) foreclosure   (D) eminent domain

97. An abstract of title contains
    (A) the summary of a title search
    (B) an attorney's opinion of title
    (C) a registrar's certificate of title
    (D) a quiet title lawsuit

98. In order to reach the beach, the Smiths have a permanent right-of-way across
    their neighbor's beachfront property. The Smiths own
    (A) an easement   (C) a deed restriction
    (B) a license   (D) a lien

99. Zoning ordinances typically regulate the
    (A) number of occupants allowed per dwelling unit
    (B) uses of each parcel of land
    (C) maximum rent that may be charged
    (D) building code

100. The business relationship between broker and salesperson for income tax purposes
    is usually
    (A) employer-employee   (C) single agent
    (B) independent contractor   (D) self-employment

Answer Keys and Explanations

Following are answer keys to all the model examinations in Chapter 24. A final section contains explanations of all the arithmetic questions in all the examinations.

MODEL EXAMINATION 1

1. D	13. A	25. D	37. B	49. C	61. C	73. C
2. B	14. C	26. C	38. C	50. C	62. C	74. B
3. C	15. B	27. C	39. B	51. B	63. C	75. C
4. D	16. B	28. C	40. B	52. C	64. C	76. C
5. D	17. A	29. A	41. B	53. B	65. B	77. A
6. A	18. D	30. B	42. A	54. A	66. B	78. D
7. B	19. C	31. B	43. D	55. A	67. A	79. B
8. C	20. A	32. A	44. D	56. B	68. A	80. A
9. B	21. C	33. A	45. C	57. B	69. A	
10. C	22. B	34. B	46. C	58. C	70. D	
11. A	23. B	35. A	47. C	59. C	71. B	
12. A	24. B	36. A	48. D	60. D	72. D	

MODEL EXAMINATION 2

1. B	16. A	31. B	46. D	61. A	76. C	91. C
2. D	17. B	32. A	47. B	62. C	77. D	92. C
3. D	18. B	33. D	48. C	63. B	78. C	93. A
4. B	19. C	34. B	49. D	64. A	79. D	94. A
5. D	20. A	35. B	50. A	65. C	80. C	95. C
6. B	21. D	36. B	51. A	66. C	81. A	96. D
7. B	22. A	37. C	52. D	67. C	82. C	97. C
8. B	23. C	38. B	53. A	68. A	83. B	98. B
9. C	24. A	39. A	54. A	69. C	84. B	99. A
10. D	25. C	40. C	55. C	70. C	85. C	100. B
11. C	26. D	41. C	56. D	71. B	86. D	
12. C	27. D	42. B	57. D	72. B	87. B	
13. D	28. D	43. A	58. B	73. B	88. C	
14. B	29. C	44. D	59. A	74. B	89. D	
15. C	30. D	45. D	60. D	75. D	90. D	

MODEL EXAMINATION 3

1. **C**	13. **A**	25. **C**	37. **B**	49. **A**	61. **B**	73. **A**
2. **C**	14. **B**	26. **A**	38. **D**	50. **B**	62. **C**	74. **C**
3. **A**	15. **A**	27. **C**	39. **B**	51. **C**	63. **C**	75. **C**
4. **D**	16. **C**	28. **B**	40. **B**	52. **B**	64. **D**	76. **A**
5. **C**	17. **B**	29. **C**	41. **A**	53. **B**	65. **A**	77. **A**
6. **A**	18. **C**	30. **A**	42. **C**	54. **A**	66. **B**	78. **C**
7. **B**	19. **C**	31. **C**	43. **C**	55. **B**	67. **A**	79. **B**
8. **A**	20. **D**	32. **B**	44. **B**	56. **C**	68. **D**	80. **C**
9. **C**	21. **C**	33. **B**	45. **D**	57. **D**	69. **B**	
10. **A**	22. **B**	34. **A**	46. **A**	58. **C**	70. **A**	
11. **A**	23. **C**	35. **D**	47. **D**	59. **D**	71. **B**	
12. **B**	24. **D**	36. **D**	48. **D**	60. **B**	72. **C**	

MODEL EXAMINATION 4

1. **D**	13. **B**	25. **D**	37. **B**	49. **C**	61. **A**	73. **B**
2. **A**	14. **A**	26. **B**	38. **B**	50. **A**	62. **B**	74. **B**
3. **C**	15. **D**	27. **C**	39. **C**	51. **C**	63. **D**	75. **D**
4. **C**	16. **D**	28. **D**	40. **A**	52. **D**	64. **D**	76. **A**
5. **D**	17. **A**	29. **C**	41. **A**	53. **A**	65. **B**	77. **C**
6. **C**	18. **A**	30. **A**	42. **C**	54. **C**	66. **A**	78. **A**
7. **B**	19. **D**	31. **B**	43. **D**	55. **C**	67. **B**	79. **B**
8. **B**	20. **B**	32. **B**	44. **A**	56. **B**	68. **C**	80. **D**
9. **C**	21. **D**	33. **B**	45. **C**	57. **C**	69. **C**	
10. **C**	22. **D**	34. **C**	46. **B**	58. **B**	70. **D**	
11. **B**	23. **A**	35. **D**	47. **B**	59. **A**	71. **A**	
12. **A**	24. **A**	36. **A**	48. **D**	60. **A**	72. **C**	

MODEL EXAMINATION 5

1. **B**	16. **B**	31. **B**	46. **D**	61. **A**	76. **B**	91. **B**
2. **D**	17. **A**	32. **C**	47. **D**	62. **C**	77. **C**	92. **D**
3. **D**	18. **C**	33. **D**	48. **C**	63. **B**	78. **A**	93. **B**
4. **B**	19. **D**	34. **B**	49. **A**	64. **A**	79. **D**	94. **D**
5. **A**	20. **B**	35. **C**	50. **B**	65. **C**	80. **C**	95. **D**
6. **C**	21. **B**	36. **B**	51. **C**	66. **A**	81. **C**	96. **D**
7. **C**	22. **B**	37. **C**	52. **C**	67. **C**	82. **C**	97. **A**
8. **A**	23. **D**	38. **D**	53. **D**	68. **C**	83. **A**	98. **B**
9. **D**	24. **A**	39. **D**	54. **B**	69. **B**	84. **D**	99. **B**
10. **D**	25. **A**	40. **D**	55. **B**	70. **C**	85. **B**	100. **C**
11. **B**	26. **B**	41. **D**	56. **C**	71. **D**	86. **A**	
12. **A**	27. **A**	42. **B**	57. **C**	72. **A**	87. **A**	
13. **B**	28. **A**	43. **D**	58. **B**	73. **B**	88. **A**	
14. **B**	29. **C**	44. **B**	59. **D**	74. **D**	89. **C**	
15. **C**	30. **A**	45. **B**	60. **A**	75. **C**	90. **C**	

MODEL EXAMINATION 6

1. **D**	13. **B**	25. **A**	37. **B**	49. **A**	61. **C**	73. **C**
2. **B**	14. **A**	26. **B**	38. **C**	50. **C**	62. **C**	74. **B**
3. **C**	15. **D**	27. **B**	39. **C**	51. **C**	63. **C**	75. **A**
4. **B**	16. **C**	28. **C**	40. **B**	52. **B**	64. **D**	76. **B**
5. **D**	17. **B**	29. **C**	41. **B**	53. **B**	65. **D**	77. **A**
6. **A**	18. **C**	30. **B**	42. **B**	54. **B**	66. **D**	78. **B**
7. **C**	19. **D**	31. **A**	43. **D**	55. **A**	67. **D**	79. **D**
8. **C**	20. **A**	32. **C**	44. **C**	56. **C**	68. **A**	80. **D**
9. **C**	21. **C**	33. **D**	45. **C**	57. **D**	69. **D**	
10. **B**	22. **C**	34. **A**	46. **A**	58. **C**	70. **B**	
11. **C**	23. **A**	35. **A**	47. **B**	59. **D**	71. **C**	
12. **D**	24. **B**	36. **C**	48. **B**	60. **D**	72. **A**	

MODEL EXAMINATION 7

1. **B**	16. **D**	31. **A**	46. **B**	61. **B**	76. **B**	91. **A**
2. **B**	17. **D**	32. **A**	47. **D**	62. **B**	77. **E**	92. **B**
3. **E**	18. **A**	33. **A**	48. **B**	63. **A**	78. **A**	93. **C**
4. **E**	19. **E**	34. **D**	49. **C**	64. **C**	79. **C**	94. **C**
5. **B**	20. **A**	35. **B**	50. **D**	65. **B**	80. **E**	95. **D**
6. **D**	21. **D**	36. **C**	51. **A**	66. **A**	81. **A**	96. **C**
7. **C**	22. **D**	37. **D**	52. **A**	67. **A**	82. **D**	97. **E**
8. **D**	23. **A**	38. **C**	53. **C**	68. **D**	83. **A**	98. **D**
9. **C**	24. **D**	39. **A**	54. **B**	69. **C**	84. **A**	99. **B**
10. **C**	25. **E**	40. **A**	55. **A**	70. **C**	85. **D**	100. **D**
11. **B**	26. **C**	41. **B**	56. **E**	71. **C**	86. **B**	
12. **B**	27. **D**	42. **B**	57. **B**	72. **E**	87. **B**	
13. **A**	28. **C**	43. **D**	58. **C**	73. **D**	88. **D**	
14. **C**	29. **A**	44. **B**	59. **D**	74. **D**	89. **A**	
15. **E**	30. **D**	45. **D**	60. **B**	75. **C**	90. **D**	

MODEL EXAMINATION 8

1. **B**	16. **A**	31. **D**	46. **E**	61. **E**	76. **C**	91. **D**
2. **A**	17. **D**	32. **C**	47. **E**	62. **B**	77. **D**	92. **B**
3. **B**	18. **D**	33. **E**	48. **E**	63. **C**	78. **D**	93. **A**
4. **D**	19. **D**	34. **D**	49. **B**	64. **C**	79. **B**	94. **C**
5. **A**	20. **E**	35. **D**	50. **A**	65. **D**	80. **C**	95. **D**
6. **B**	21. **B**	36. **E**	51. **E**	66. **A**	81. **A**	96. **A**
7. **C**	22. **B**	37. **B**	52. **A**	67. **D**	82. **A**	97. **C**
8. **C**	23. **A**	38. **D**	53. **B**	68. **A**	83. **B**	98. **B**
9. **C**	24. **D**	39. **C**	54. **C**	69. **A**	84. **D**	99. **C**
10. **B**	25. **B**	40. **A**	55. **A**	70. **C**	85. **D**	100. **B**
11. **A**	26. **A**	41. **A**	56. **C**	71. **B**	86. **B**	
12. **C**	27. **C**	42. **B**	57. **D**	72. **D**	87. **D**	
13. **C**	28. **A**	43. **C**	58. **B**	73. **E**	88. **E**	
14. **D**	29. **A**	44. **C**	59. **B**	74. **C**	89. **A**	
15. **C**	30. **B**	45. **C**	60. **A**	75. **C**	90. **B**	

MODEL EXAMINATION 9

1. D	16. A	31. D	46. B	61. D	76. B	91. A
2. D	17. E	32. A	47. B	62. B	77. C	92. B
3. E	18. C	33. C	48. C	63. D	78. D	93. C
4. D	19. C	34. A	49. D	64. C	79. C	94. C
5. A	20. C	35. C	50. D	65. B	80. C	95. C
6. C	21. D	36. C	51. C	66. C	81. C	96. C
7. A	22. B	37. E	52. C	67. A	82. E	97. C
8. E	23. E	38. C	53. C	68. B	83. C	98. B
9. D	24. C	39. D	54. E	69. D	84. B	99. A
10. A	25. D	40. B	55. C	70. E	85. D	100. D
11. B	26. E	41. C	56. A	71. C	86. A	
12. D	27. E	42. D	57. E	72. A	87. C	
13. B	28. E	43. D	58. C	73. D	88. C	
14. E	29. A	44. D	59. B	74. D	89. C	
15. A	30. D	45. E	60. E	75. D	90. B	

MODEL EXAMINATION 10

1. C	16. B	31. C	46. C	61. C	76. B	91. D
2. A	17. C	32. D	47. C	62. B	77. C	92. B
3. C	18. D	33. D	48. D	63. B	78. D	93. A
4. A	19. D	34. D	49. B	64. A	79. B	94. D
5. B	20. C	35. A	50. A	65. B	80. B	95. D
6. A	21. B	36. D	51. D	66. C	81. B	96. C
7. D	22. B	37. B	52. A	67. B	82. B	97. A
8. A	23. B	38. C	53. C	68. C	83. D	98. A
9. A	24. A	39. A	54. D	69. A	84. C	99. B
10. A	25. D	40. B	55. A	70. C	85. B	100. B
11. A	26. D	41. A	56. B	71. A	86. B	
12. D	27. C	42. B	57. D	72. C	87. C	
13. C	28. D	43. D	58. B	73. C	88. C	
14. B	29. A	44. C	59. D	74. C	89. A	
15. A	30. D	45. D	60. D	75. D	90. B	

ANSWER EXPLANATIONS—ARITHMETIC QUESTIONS

Model Examination 1

6. If the tax is based on 20% of the appraised value of $25,000, then the tax is based on
$$0.2 \times \$250,000 = \$50,000$$
City tax is 50 mills, or 5%, so
$$\$50,000 \times 0.05 = \$2,500 \text{ city tax}$$
County tax is 40 mills, or 4%, so
$$\$50,000 \times 0.04 = \$2,000 \text{ county tax}$$

7. This is a sidewalk question; remember not to count the corners twice. The total sidewalk area is 320 ft. × 5 ft. = 1,600 sq. ft. Since the sidewalk is 6 in., or half a foot deep, the cubic measure is 800 cu. ft. Also, 1 cu. yd. contains 27 cu. ft. (3 ft. × 3 ft. × 3 ft.), so the total number of cubic yards is
$$800 \text{ cu. ft.} \div 27 \text{ cu. ft.} = 29.63 \text{ cu. yd.}$$

21. After depreciating for 8 years at 3% per year, the building has lost 24% of original value (8 × 0.03 = 0.24). This means that it is now worth the remaining 76% of its original value. If that sum is $190,000, then the original value is
$$\$190,000 \div 0.76 = \$250,000$$

22. Six percent of $200,000 is 0.06 × $200,000 = $12,000. Interest for a single month would be $12,000 ÷ 12, or $1,000. Therefore, of the $1,200 *first* payment, $1,000 goes to interest, leaving $200 to reduce the principal. This means that Flaherty will pay interest on $199,800 the second month. Figuring the same way, we get a monthly interest charge of $999 for the second month on that amount; this will leave $201 by which the second monthly payment will reduce the principal.

38. Annual rent is $8,500 × 12 = $102,000. Taxes are based on 40% of appraisal of $470,000, or 0.4 × $470,000 = $188,000. The tax rate is 75 mills, or $7^1/_2\%$, so the tax is
$$0.075 \times \$188,000 = \$14,100$$
This represents 13.8% of the annual rent ($14,100 ÷ $102,000).

39. Total appreciation is $599,000 − $420,000 = $179,000. Total percent appreciation is $179,000 ÷ $420,000 = 42.619%. Average over 4 years is
$$42.619\% \div 4 = 10.65\%$$

45. The 11 lots originally cost a total of 11 × $21,000 = $231,000; Perkins sells 7 lots for a total of $28,000 more than that, or $231,000 + $28,000 = $259,000. The average sale price would be
$$\$259,000 \div 7 = \$37,000$$

50. The house is a combination of two rectangles: one is 50 ft. × 24 ft. (1,200 sq. ft.) and the other, smaller part jutting out to the bottom is 24 ft. × 16 ft. (384 sq. ft.). You get the 16 ft. measurement by subtracting the 24 ft. of the short side of the house from the 40 ft. of the long side.
$$1,200 \text{ sq. ft.} + 384 \text{ sq. ft.} = 1,584 \text{ sq. ft.}$$

51. The lot is 120 ft. × 75 ft. = 9,000 sq. ft. The area taken by the house is
$$1,584 \text{ sq. ft.} \div 9,000 \text{ sq. ft.} = 0.176 = 17.6\%$$

59. This figure is a trapezoid. The top (T) and bottom (B) are of unequal lengths, while the height (H) does not change. The formula for this figure is
$$\text{Area} = \tfrac{1}{2} \times (T + B) \times H$$
The area of the lot, then, is
$$\tfrac{1}{2} \times (110 \text{ ft.} + 160 \text{ ft.}) \times 200 \text{ ft.} = \tfrac{1}{2} \times 270 \text{ ft.} \times 200 \text{ ft.} = 27{,}000 \text{ sq. ft.}$$
If the lot is sold for $78,300.00, the price per square foot is
$$\$78{,}300.00 \div 27{,}000.00 = \$2.90$$

60. The salesperson's $15,120 was 60% of total commission, so
$$\$15{,}120 \div 0.6 = \$25{,}200 \text{ total commission}$$
Since the sale price was $315,000, the *rate* of commission was
$$\$25{,}200 \div \$315{,}000 = 0.08 = 8\%$$

65. First find the value of the house alone. Land is 15% of the total value, which means that the house is 85% of the total ($100\% - 15\% = 85\%$). Then the house is worth
$$0.85 \times \$188{,}000 = \$159{,}800$$
If the house has 1,733 sq. ft., the cost per square foot is
$$\$159{,}800 \div 1{,}733 \text{ sq. ft.} = \$92.21$$

66. First find the amount of the total commission:
$$0.065 \times \$140{,}700 = \$9{,}145.50$$
If Jones can keep 42% of this, then the broker must get to keep the remaining 58%. Therefore, the broker's share is
$$0.58 \times \$9{,}145.50 = \$5{,}304.39$$

67. $\text{Area} = 90 \text{ ft.} \times 60 \text{ ft.} = 5{,}400 \text{ sq. ft.}$, and $\$6{,}300 \times 12 \text{ mo.} = \$75{,}600$ per year. Annual rent per square foot is
$$\$75{,}600 \div 5{,}400 \text{ sq. ft.} = \$14.00$$

70. The lot value has increased by 800%. Don't forget that the lot was worth 100% of its value in 1993, so if it has gone up by 800%, then today it is worth 900%, or 9 times, its original value.
$$9 \times \$20{,}000 = \$180{,}000 \text{ lot value today}$$
Similarly, since the house is worth 40% more, today it is worth 140% of its original value:
$$1.4 \times \$130{,}000 = \$182{,}000 \text{ house value today}$$
House and lot together are worth $180,000 + $182,000 = $362,000 today.

74. There are two ways of answering this question.
(A) You can figure the commissions on $350,000 and $315,000 and subtract.
$$0.06 \times \$350{,}000 = \$21{,}000$$
$$0.06 \times \$315{,}000 = \$18{,}900$$
$$\$210{,}000 - \$189{,}000 = \$2{,}100, \text{ the correct answer}$$
(B) You can subtract $315,000 from $350,000 and get $35,000, which is the difference in price. The broker will lose the commission on that amount, so
$$0.06 \times \$35{,}000 = \$2{,}100, \text{ also the correct answer}$$

75. One acre contains 43,560 sq. ft., so
$$1\tfrac{1}{4} \times 43{,}560 \text{ sq. ft.} = 54{,}450 \text{ sq. ft.}$$

Model Examination 2

91. The millage rate of 32.5 is 3.25%, so tax on $180,000 is
$$0.0325 \times \$180,000 = \$5,850$$

92. Let the price of the *third* lot be P. The price of the second lot, then, will be $2 \times P$. The price of the first lot will be $1\frac{1}{2} \times 2 \times P$. All three cost $90,000, so
$$P + (2 \times P) + (1\frac{1}{2} \times 2 \times P) = \$90,000, \text{ or } 6 \times P = \$90,000$$
Therefore, $P = \$90,000 \div 6 = \$15,000$. The price of the second lot was twice that, or $30,000. The third lot was $1^1/_2$ times the second lot, or $45,000.

93. If Aaronson uses 10% of the 44 acres for parks, he will use 4.4 acres. Add that to the 6.6 other acres that must be used for streets, etc., and you get a total of 11 acres not devoted to lots. This leaves 33 acres, or $33 \times 43,560$ sq. ft. $= 1,437,480$ sq. ft. for lots. If each lot must be at least 7,500 sq. ft., then the maximum number of lots is
$$1,437,480 \text{ sq. ft.} \div 7,500 \text{ sq. ft.} = 191.664, \text{ or } 191 \text{ full lots}$$

94. Velez paid $2,700 interest over 4 years; this comes to $675 per year ($2,700 ÷ 4). The annual interest rate was
$$\$675 \div \$7,500 = 0.09 = 9\%$$

95. If Jim made a profit of 43%, then he sold the land for 143% of its purchase price. The purchase price was
$$\$164,450 \div 1.43 = \$115,000$$

96. Anne's $1,171.80 was 12% of Connie's commission, which must have been $1,171.80 ÷ 0.12 = $9,765. If the sale price was $139,500, the rate of commission was
$$\$9,765 \div \$139,500 = 0.07 = 7\%$$

97. Eleven percent of $210,000 is $23,100.
$$\$23,100 \div 12 = \$1,925 \text{ monthly}$$

98. How many years will be required for $10,000 to compound to $30,000 at 25% per year?
One year: $1.25 \times \$10,000 = \$12,500$
Two years: $1.25 \times \$12,500 = \$15,625$
Three years: $1.25 \times \$15,625 = \$19,531$
Four years: $1.25 \times \$19,531 = \$24,414$
Five years: $1.25 \times \$24,414 = \$30,518$
It will take about 5 years.

99. Area $= 1,700$ ft. $\times 2,100$ ft. $= 3,570,000$ sq. ft.
$$3,570,000 \text{ sq. ft.} \div 43,560 \text{ sq. ft.} = 81.96 \text{ acres}$$

100. The backyard is 100 ft. + 80 ft. + 100 ft. + 80 ft. = 360 ft. around. From this we subtract the 40 ft. taken up by the house, to get 320 lineal ft. of fence needed. If the fence is 4 ft. high, it will have 320 ft. $\times$ 4 ft. = 1,280 sq. ft. of fence fabric; 1,280 sq. ft. is 142.222 sq. yd.
$$142.222 \text{ sq. yd.} \times \$1.80 = \$256.00 \text{ total cost}$$

Model Examination 3

4. The number of square feet in 10.6 acres is
$$10.6 \times 43,560 \text{ sq. ft.} = 461,736 \text{ sq. ft.}$$
If one side of the tract is 181 ft., the other must be
$$461,736 \text{ sq. ft.} \div 181 \text{ ft.} = 2,551.0276 = 2,551 \text{ ft., rounded off}$$

5. The number of square feet in 17.1 acres is
$$17.1 \text{ acres} \times 43,560 \text{ sq. ft.} = 744,876 \text{ sq. ft.}$$
If 19% must be set aside, 81% is left for lots, or
$$0.81 \times 744,876 \text{ sq. ft.} = 603,349.56 \text{ sq. ft.}$$
If each lot must have at least 8,000 sq. ft., the maximum number of lots is
603,399.56 sq. ft. ÷ 8,000 sq. ft. = 75.4, or a maximum of 75 full lots

10. Area = 400 ft. × 665 ft. = 266,000 sq. ft.
266,000 sq. ft. ÷ 43,560 sq. ft. = 6.1065 acres
$17,100.00 ÷ 6.1065 acres = $2,800.29, or $2,800 per acre

11. Taxable value = $170,000 × 0.30 = $51,000
Since 71 mills is the same as a tax rate of 7.1%, the tax is
$$0.071 \times \$51,000 = \$3,621$$

17. A building that is 40 ft. × 22 ft. is 124 ft. around (40 + 22 + 40 + 22). The total wall area is 124 ft. × 10 ft., or 1,240 sq. ft. From this we subtract the 52 sq. ft. of windows (4 sq. ft. × 13) and the 48 sq. ft. of door to get 1,140 sq. ft. of wall area needing paint. One gallon of paint covers 400 sq. ft. For one coat of paint we need 1,140 sq. ft. ÷ 400 sq. ft. = 2.85 gal., so two coats will require twice as much, or 5.7 gal.

18. Annual interest = $210 per quarter × 4 = $840. The interest rate is
$$\$840 \div \$12,000 = 0.07 = 7\%$$

24. Ms. Levy will pay $400 less rent per month if she pays the utility bills herself. Average bills are $3,840 per year, which is $320 per month ($3,840 ÷ 12). Levy thinks she can reduce this by 35%, which means that she expects to pay only 65% of the $320 monthly average, or 0.65 × $320 = $208. She saves $400 on rent and expects to pay $208 of that for utilities, so she expects to save $192 per month.

25. Total commissions brought in by O'Hara = 7% × $2,250,000 = $192,500. He gets 50% of the first $50,000 (or $25,000) *plus* 60% of the rest. In his case, the rest is $142,500.
$$0.6 \times \$142,500 = \$85,500$$
To this we add his $25,000 share of the first $50,000 to get a total income for him of $110.500.

42. If Jackson paid a 6½% commission, then the $336,132.50 he has left represents the remaining 93½% of the sale price. The sale price then must be
$$\$336,132.50 \div 0.935 = \$359,500$$

48. Ms. Anderson paid out a total of 12% of the selling price in fees, so her $176,000 is the 88% of the sale price that she has left. Therefore, the sale price was
$$\$176,000 \div 0.88 = \$200,000$$

49. The 9-in.-thick walls are ¾ ft. thick. Therefore, the interior dimensions of the floor are 50½ ft. × 34½ ft. (remember, the walls are at *both* ends):

$$50.5 × 34.5 = 1,742.25 \text{ sq. ft. gross,}$$

from which we subtract the area taken up by the pillars. They are each ½ ft. × ½ ft., or ¼ sq. ft. Their total area is

$$13 × ¼ \text{ sq. ft.} = 3¼ \text{ sq. ft.}$$

Subtracting this amount from 1,742.25 leaves a net of 1,739 sq. ft.

62. The lots contain 10,500 sq. ft. each and must each have 1,380 sq. ft. additional amenity. Therefore, Smith will need a minimum of 11,880 sq. ft. for each lot (10,500 sq. ft. + 1,380 sq. ft.). Since he wants 55 lots, he will need at least 55 × 11,880 sq. ft. = 653,400 sq. ft.; 653,400 sq. ft. ÷ 43,560 sq. ft. = 15 acres exactly.

70. Interior gross dimensions are 41 ft. × 27 ft. = 1,107 sq. ft. (Remember to subtract 6 in. of outside wall from each end.) Interior wall area is ⅓ ft. × 135 ft. = 45 sq. ft. Each bathroom is 54 sq. ft. The kitchen is 144 sq. ft. This is a total area of 297 sq. ft. *not* to be carpeted, leaving 810 sq. ft. because 1 sq. yd. contains 9 sq. ft. (3 ft. × 3 ft.), the total number of square yards to be carpeted is 810 sq. ft. ÷ 9 sq. ft. = 90 sq. yd. At $13.95 per square yard, the total cost is $1,255.50 (90 sq. yd. × $13.95).

71. To determine how much Ms. Farrell still needs, we subtract from the $330,000 purchase price the $9,000 earnest money payment and the 75% loan. The loan is 75% of $330,000, or $330,000 × 0.75 = $247,500. $330,000 less $9,000 is $321,000. Subtracting the $247,500 loan leaves $73,500 needed.

74. A lot 100 ft. × 100 ft. contains 100 × 100 = 10,000 sq. ft. The 3-acre plot contains 43,560 × 3 = 130,680 sq. ft.; 130,680 ÷ 10,000 = 13.068, or 13 full lots.

75. The width of the lot is 6,336 ÷ 96 = 66 ft. At $225 a front ft. the lot would sell for 66 × $225 = $14,850.

Model Examination 4

2. Assessed value is 20% of $350,000 × 0.2 = $70,000. 80 mills is 8%.

$$$70,000 × 0.08 = $5,600$$

9. We must subtract the broker's commission and the loan discount from the $50,000 sale price, since seller (Juan) must pay both.

$$6\% \text{ of } $150,000 \text{ is } $150,000 × 0.06 = $9,000 \text{ commission.}$$

Loan is 80% of $150,000. $150,000 × 0.80 = $120,000 loan. Discount is 3 points, or 3% of $120,000. $120,000 × 0.03 = $3,600.

Total payments by Juan are $9,000 commission + $3,600 loan discount, or $12,600.

$$$150,000 − $12,600 = $137,400$$

10. In question 9, we found the loan discount to be $3,600.

11. We figure the *effective* rate to the lender of a mortgage loan by adding *⅛ of 1%* to the *contract* interest rate for each *one* point of discount paid on the loan. The contract interest rate is 4%; there are 3 points discount. Thus, the effective rate is 4% + ⅜%, or 4⅜% (4.375%).

28. Cash-on-cash ratio is the annual cash return received, divided by the cash spent (original equity) to acquire the investment.
$$\$16,900 \div \$130,000 = 0.13$$

29. One square mile contains 640 acres.
$$200 \div 640 = 0.3125, \text{ or } 31.25\%$$

31. One acre contains 43,560 sq. ft. The tract in this problem is 440 ft. × 817 ft. = 359,480 sq. ft. Then
$$359,480 \div 43,560 = 8.253 \text{ acres, or } 8.25 \text{ rounded}$$

41. The sale is closed July 15, but the taxes aren't due until October 15. Therefore, the taxes haven't been paid; the buyer will have to pay the full year's tax bill on October 15. So *seller pays buyer* at closing.
Assessed value is $48,500; tax rate is 38 mills (which is 3.8%, or 0.038). So the year's tax is 48,500 × 0.038 = $1,843.00.
Seller owned property for exactly 6½ mo. (January through June, and half of July). So seller owes buyer 6.5 mo. of taxes. One month of taxes is $1,843 ÷ 12 = $153.583; 6.5 × $153.583 = $998.29.

47. In this problem we have to determine how long the buyer owned the property. We know he owned it at the end of the year. We calculate time from his tax payment, and then figure backwards from December 31 to determine the date of settlement. Remember: the settlement date is considered a day that the *seller* owned the property. The total tax bill is $763.20; $763.20 ÷ 12 = $63.60 per month; $63.60 ÷ 30 = $2.12 per day.
First we determine how many *whole months* the buyer owned the property by dividing the buyer's share of taxes ($250.16) by the monthly tax share of $63.60; $250.16 ÷ $63.60 = 3.93333. Thus, the buyer owned the property for 3 whole months (October, November, and December) and then some. Now we know that the settlement occurred sometime in September.
We subtract the 3 whole months worth of taxes from the buyer's share; 3 × $63.60 = $190.80; $250.16 − $190.80 = $59.36. The buyer also owned the property for $59.35 "worth" of September.
$59.36 ÷ $2.12 = 28 of September's 30 days. Thus, the closing had to be on 30 − 28 = 2 of September.

53. Since 1 sq. yd. is 3 ft. × 3 ft. = 9 sq. ft., 825 sq. yd. is 825 × 9 = 7,425 sq. ft.; 7,425 ÷ 75 = 99 ft. None of the answers is 99 ft., but three choices are expressed in measures other than feet: 1¹⁄₁₆ mi. is 5,280 ÷ 16 = 330 ft., which is *not* 99 ft.; 32 yd. is 32 × 3 = 96 ft., *not* 99; 6 rods is 16.5 × 6 = 99 ft., the correct answer.

58. First we find the amount of the total commission. Lois's share of $2,316.60 was 45% of the total her firm received. Then $2,316.60 ÷ 0.45 = $5,148, Lois's firm's share, which was 60% of the total; $5,148 ÷ 0.6 = $8,580 total commission.
The house sold for $132,000; $8,580 ÷ $132,000 = 0.065, or 6.5%

59. Because ¼ acre contains 43,560 ÷ 4 = 10,890 sq. ft.,
$$\$120,000 \div 10,890 = \$11.02, \text{ or } \$11.00 \text{ rounded}$$

74. We have to calculate the down payment, the origination fee, the discount, and the PMI fee and then add all of these to get the answer.
Down payment is 10%. $147,000 × 0.10 = $14,700 down payment
Origination fee, discount, and PMI fee all are calculated as part of the *loan amount* (not the sales price). The loan will equal the sales price less the down payment, or $147,000 − $14,700 = $132,300 loan amount.
Origination fee (1%) is $132,300 × 0.01 = $1,323.00
Discount (2%) is $132,300 × 0.02 = $2,646.00
PMI fee (0.5%, or ½%) is $132,300 × 0.005 = $661.50
$14,700 + $1,323.00 + $2,646.00 + $661.50 = $19,330.50

75. We have to calculate the *monthly* interest rate, because we are given a monthly interest payment; 6% ÷ 12 = 0.5% = 0.005. The interest payment of $312.50 is 0.5% of the loan amount.
$$312.50 ÷ 0.005 = \$62{,}500$$

79. We have to determine the number of cubic yards in the patio. First we determine the number of cubic feet. The patio is 60 ft. × 20 ft. = 1,200 sq. ft. It is 4 in. thick = 4/12 ft. or ⅓ ft. So 1,200 ÷ 3 = 400 cu. ft. is the *volume* of the patio. Since 1 cu. yd. is 3 × 3 × 3 = 27 cu. ft.,
$$400 ÷ 27 = 14.82 \text{ cu. yd., or } 14.8 \text{ rounded}$$

Model Examination 5

6. Cash-on-cash ratio is annual cash return received, divided by the cash spent (original equity) to acquire the investment.
$$\$8{,}360 ÷ \$76{,}000 = 0.11$$

7. Because 1 sq. mi. contains 640 acres,
$$96 ÷ 640 = 0.15, \text{ or } 15\%$$

13. The sale closed August 15, but the taxes were due on June 1. Therefore, the taxes have already been paid by the seller. So *buyer pays seller* at closing, to reimburse the taxes already paid.
Assessed value is $53,250; tax rate is 41 mills (which is 4.1%, or 0.041). So the year's tax is 53,250 × 0.041 = $2,183.25.
Seller owned property for exactly 7.5 mo. (January through July, and half of August). So buyer owes seller the taxes for the remaining 4.5 mo. of the year that the buyer will own the property. One month's taxes amount to $2,183.25 ÷ 12 = $181.9375; 4.5 × $181.9375 = $818.719, or (rounded) $818.72 that buyer owes seller.

25. Because 20 yd. is 20 × 3 = 60 ft., the area of the patio is 60 × 20 = 1,200 sq. ft. The patio is 6 in., or ½ ft., thick. Then 1,200 × 0.5 = 600 cu. ft., the *volume* of the patio. One cubic yard is 3 × 3 × 3 = 27 cu. ft. Therefore, Joe will need
$$600 ÷ 27 = 22.22, \text{ or (rounded) } 22.2 \text{ cu. yd. of concrete}$$

43. First we find the amount of the total commission. Salesperson's share of $2,544 was 60% of the total the firm received. $2,544 ÷ 0.6 = $4,240 for the firm's share, which was 50% of the total. $4,240 ÷ 0.5 = $8,480 total commission.
Because the house sold for $106,000,
$$\$8{,}480 ÷ \$106{,}000 = 0.08, \text{ or } 8\%$$

48. We have to determine the number of front feet in the lot, and multiply that number by $980 to determine the price the lot sold for.

$$6,468 \div 132 = 49 \text{ front ft. } 49 \times \$980 = \$48,020, \text{ or } \$48,000 \text{ rounded}$$

57. $188,000 ÷ 2.6 acres = $72,307.69 per acre

$$\$72,307.69 \div 43,560 = \$1.65997, \text{ or } \$1.66 \text{ rounded}$$

64. We have to determine how long the seller owned the property. We know he owned it at the beginning of the year. We calculate time from his tax payment, and then figure from January 1 to determine the date of settlement. Remember; the settlement date is considered a day that the *seller* owned the property. The total tax bill is $972. $972 ÷ 12 = $81 per month

$$\$81 \div 30 = \$2.70 \text{ per day}$$

First we determine how many *whole months* the seller owned the property by dividing his share of taxes ($351) by the monthly tax share of $81; $351 ÷ $81 = 4.33333. Thus, the seller owned the property for 4 whole months (January through April) and part of May, the month in which settlement must have occurred.

Now we subtract the 4 whole months worth of taxes from the seller's share; 4 × $81 = $324, and $351 − $324 = $27. So the seller also owned the property for $27 "worth" of May. $27 ÷ $2.70 = 10 of May's 31 days (statutory year). Thus, the closing had to be on May 10.

81. We have to calculate the down payment, the origination fee, the discount, and the PMI fee and then add all of these to determine the answer.

Down payment is 15%; $232,500 × 0.15 = $34,875 down payment

Origination fee, discount, and PMI fee all are calculated as part of the *loan amount* (not the sales price). The loan will be the sales price less the down payment, or $232,500 − $34,875 = $197,625 loan amount

Origination fee (0.75%) is $197,625 × 0.0075 = $1,482.19 rounded

Discount (2.25%) is $197,625 × 0.0225 = $4,446.56 (rounded)

PMI fee (0.5%, or ½%) is $197,625 × 0.005 = $988.13 (rounded)

$$\$34,875 + \$1,482.19 + \$4,446.56 + \$988.13 = \$41,791.88$$

90. We have to calculate the monthly interest rate, because we are given a monthly interest payment; 5.125% ÷ 12 = 0.42708% = 0.0042708. The interest payment of $891.20 is 0.42708% of the loan amount.

$$\$891.20 \div 0.0042708 = \$208,671 \text{ rounded}$$

Model Examination 6

1. We know the down payment and must calculate the origination fee, the discount, and the PMI fee and then add all of these to determine the answer.

Origination fee, discount, and PMI fee all are calculated as part of the *loan amount* (not the sales price). The loan will be the sales price less the down payment, or $111,500 − $17,250 = $94,250 loan amount.

Origination fee (1.5%) is $94,250 × 0.015 = $1,413.75

Discount (2%) is $94,250 × 0.02 = $1,885.00

PMI fee (0.75%) is $94,250 × 0.0075 = $706.88 (rounded)

$$\$17,250 + \$1,413.75 + \$1,885.00 + \$706.88 = \$21,255.63$$

2. We have to calculate the monthly interest rate, because we are given a monthly interest payment; 5.5% ÷ 12 = 0.45833% = 0.0045833. The interest payment of $884.50 is 0.45833% of the loan amount.

$$\$884.50 \div 0.0045833 = \$192,983 \text{ rounded}$$

9. The area of the driveway is 70 ft. × 12 ft. = 840 sq. ft. The driveway is 5 in., or $^5/_{12}$ ft., thick; 5 ÷ 12 = 0.41667 ft. thick. Then 840 × 0.41667 = 350 cu. ft. (rounded), the *volume* of the driveway. Because 1 cu. yd. is 3 × 3 × 3 = 27 cu. ft., Joe will need
$$350 ÷ 27 = 12.96, \text{ or (rounded) 13 cu. yd. of concrete}$$

22. Because 59 ft. 6 in. = 59.5 ft. and 535.5 sq. yd. = 535.5 × 9 = 4,819.5 sq. ft., we have 4,819.5 ÷ 59.5 = 81 ft. of depth. This answer is not one of the choices. However, three of the answers are expressed in measures other than feet: 0.03 mi. is 0.03 × 5,280 = 158.4 ft.; 5.33 rods is 5.33 × 16.5 = 87.95 ft. Both of these choices are incorrect. However, 27 yd. is 27 × 3 = 81 ft., which is correct.

25. The commission was 7%; $164,000 × 0.07 = $11,480 total commission. Mack's 48% share is $11,480 × 0.48 = $5,510.40; 55% of that was paid to the salesperson, leaving 1 − 0.55 = 0.45 or 45% for Mack.
$$\$5,510.40 × 0.45 = \$2,479.68$$

26. Because 1.6 acres is 1.6 × 43,560 = 69,696 sq. ft.,
$$\$25,100 ÷ 69,696 = 0.3601, \text{ or } \$0.36 \text{ rounded}$$

42. We have to determine how long the seller owned the property, and then figure from February 1 (the day the insurance policy was purchased) to determine the date of settlement. Remember, the settlement date is considered a day that the *seller* owned the property.
The total bill was $324; $324 ÷ 12 = $27 per month, and $27 ÷ 30 = $0.90 per day
First we determine how many *whole months* of the policy year the buyer owned the property. We divide her share of the policy cost ($63) by the monthly share of $27; $63 ÷ $27 = 2.33333. Thus, the buyer owned the property for 2 whole months and part (0.3333) of a third; 0.3333 × 30 = 10 more days. The policy expires January 31, so the buyer's 2 full months are December and January. Since she had already owned the policy for 10 days at the beginning of December, the settlement must have occurred in November. 30 − 10 = 20 of November.

49. Assessed value is 35% of $86,000; 0.35 × $86,000 = $30,100. Since 42 mills is 4.2%,
$$0.042 × \$30,100 = \$1,264.20$$

50. The discount is based on the *loan amount*. The loan is 90% of $77,900; 0.9 × $77,900 = $70,110. The discount is 2.5 points, or 2.5%.
$$0.025 × \$70,110 = \$1,752.75$$

51. For every 1 point discount paid, we increase the *effective* rate of return to the lender by $^1/_8$%, or 0.125%. The contract interest rate is 3.75%, and there are 2.5 points; 2.5 × 0.125 = 0.3125%, which we add to the contract rate.
$$3.75\% + 0.3125\% = 4.0625\%$$

62. Cash-on-cash ratio is the annual cash return received, divided by the cash spent (original equity) to acquire the investment.
$$\$32,300 ÷ \$222,750 = 0.145 \text{ rounded}$$

63. There are 1,085 × 900 = 976,500 sq. ft. in the lot. Because 1 sq. mi. contains 5,280 × 5,280 = 27,878,400 sq. ft.,
$$976,500 ÷ 27,878,400 = 0.035, \text{ or } 3.5\% \text{ rounded}$$

69. The area is $1,077 \times 608 = 654,816$ sq. ft., and $654,816 \div 43,560 = 15.0325$ acres. The only acceptable answer, therefore, is "more than 15."

76. This problem isn't difficult, but it requires several calculations. It is wise to leave time-consuming problems such as this one until after you have answered the simpler questions.

    We have to calculate the cost of the house, basement, and garage and then add them together.

    House: First 1,600 sq. ft. cost $\$102.20 \times 1,600 = \$163,520$. There are $2,100 - 1,600 = 500$ additional sq. ft. to pay for. $500 \times \$84.50 = \$42,250$ additional. $\$163,520 + \$42,250 = \$205,770$ for the house.

    Basement: Note that this as a two-story house. Therefore, the basement will be only *half* the area of the house, or $2,100 \div 2 = 1,050$ sq. ft.; $1,050 \times \$45.00 = \$47,250$ for the basement.

    Garage: $420 \times \$58.40 = \$24,528$

    $\$205,770 + \$47,250 + \$24,528 = \$277,548$, or \$278,000 to the nearest \$1,000

80. First we calculate the cost of the lots. We know A costs \$22,000. B costs 2.5 times that amount; $2.5 \times \$22,000 = \$55,000$. C costs half the price of B; $\$55,000 \div 2 = \$27,500$. So $\$22,000 + \$55,000 + \$27,500 = \$104,500$, the cost of all three lots.

    A and B were sold for 25% more than this amount, or 125% of this amount, or $1.25 \times \$104,500 = \$130,625$. C was sold for twice its cost; $\$27,500 \times 2 = \$55,000$.

    Thus, $\$130,625 + \$55,000 = \$185,625$, the amount all three lots sold for. $\$185,625 - \$104,500 = \$81,125$. However, this is not one of the answer choices. Therefore, "none of the above" is correct.

Model Examination 7

3. $1.07 \times 1.07 = 1.1449$, which is 14.49% increase. Then
$$0.1449 \times \$80,000 = \$11,592$$

65. The expenses don't matter, since GRM applies to gross rental, without regard for expenses.

    Therefore, value = rent $\times$ GRM, or
$$\$750 \times 100 = \$75,000$$

75. Value = NOI / rate:
$$\$11,000 \div 0.11 = \$100,000$$

79. Property is worth \$1,000,000. A 70% loan is \$700,000, which leaves \$300,000 equity. An 8% constant applied to the loan is $\$700,000 \times 0.08 = \$56,000$. A 12% cash-on-cash return to the \$300,000 equity is $\$300,000 \times 0.12 = \$36,000$. The mortgage constant payment + cash on cash return = NOI, so
$$\text{NOI} = \$56,000 + \$36,000 = \$92,000$$

81. Monthly NOI is $\$6,000 - \$1,250 = \$4,750$. Annual NOI is $\$4,750 \times 12 = \$57,000$.
$$\$57,000 \div 0.12 = \$475,000 \text{ value}$$

86. Developable land = 80% of 40 acres, or 32 acres.
    Four lots per developable acre:
$$4 \times 32 = 128 \text{ lots}$$

87. There are 128 lots at $18,000 each:
$$128 \times \$18,000 = \$2,304,000$$

88. Cost of installing 2,000 feet of streets, etc., at $80 per foot:
$$2,000 \times \$80 = \$160,000$$

89. These expenses amount to 40% of total sales:
$$\$2,304,000 \times 0.4 = \$921,600$$

90. Monthly rents: $40 \times \$950 = \$38,000$; $60 \times \$1,150 = \$69,000$; $\$69,000 + \$38,000 = \$107,000$.
Potential annual gross income = $\$107,000 \times 12 = \$1,284,000$

91. Effective gross income is potential gross income plus miscellaneous income, less vacancy.
Vacancy is 5% of potential gross rent: $\$1,284,000 \times 0.05 = \$64,200$ vacancy
$$\$1,284,000 + \$5,000 - \$64,200 = \$1,224,800$$

92. NOI is effective gross less operating expenses:
$$\text{NOI} = \$1,224,800 - \$400,000 = \$824,800$$

93. Before-tax cash flow is NOI less mortgage servicing:
$$\$824,800 - \$630,000 = \$194,800$$

94. Monthly rents: $50 \times \$550 = \$27,500$; $150 \times \$675 = \$101,250$; $\$27,500 + \$101,250 = \$128,750$
Potential annual gross income = $\$128,750 \times 12 = \$1,545,000$

95. Effective gross income is potential gross income plus miscellaneous income, less vacancy.
Vacancy is 7% of potential gross rent: $\$1,545,000 \times 0.07 = \$108,150$ vacancy
$$\$1,545,000 + \$2,000 - \$108,150 = \$1,438,850$$

96. NOI is effective gross less operating expenses, which are 40% of effective gross, so NOI is 60% of effective gross:
$$\text{NOI} = \$1,438,850 \times 0.6 = \$863,310$$

97. Operating expenses are 40% of NOI:
$$\$1,438,850 \times 0.4 = \$575,540$$

Model Examination 8

51. Comp 1 is 100 sq. ft. larger than subject, so adjustment will be negative. -100 sq. ft. at $30:
$$100 \times \$30 = -\$3,000$$

52. Comp 2 is 50 sq. ft. smaller than subject, so adjustment will be positive: $+50$ sq. ft. at $30:
$$+50 \times \$30 = +\$1,500$$

53. Comp 1 is one condition grade worse than subject, so adjustment ($+5\%$) will be positive:
$$\$90,000 \times +0.05 = +\$4,500$$

54. Comp 2 is one condition grade better than subject, so adjustment (-5%) will be negative:
$$\$88,500 \times -0.05 = -\$4,425$$

55. Comp 2 and subject have same garage situation, so no adjustment is made.

56. Comp 3 has 2-car garage, subject has 1-car, so adjustment is negative: $-\$1,500$.

62. Subject is 60 feet wide, front footage comps are $120 to $150 per front foot. 120×60 = $7,200.
$$\$150 \times 60 = \$9,000, \text{ so } \$7,200 \text{ to } \$9,000 \text{ is indicated range}$$

73. Exterior paint ($750) and water heater ($250) are the items of curable physical deterioration; they add up to $1,000. No answer of $1,000 is given, so the correct answer is "none of the above."

74. Functional obsolescence items are one bath ($4,000) and poor floor plan ($2,500); these add up to $6,500.

75. Location next to convenience store ($1,200) is the only environmental item given.

81. $(1.15)^5 \times \$50,000 = 1.15 \times 1.15 \times 1.15 \times 1.15 \times 1.15 \times \$50,000 = 2.011 \times \$50,000$, or $100,000 rounded.

82. Expected sale price in 4 years: 100 acres $\times$ $10,000/acre = $1,000,000. Today's value would be $1,000,000/(1.15)_4$; $(1.15)_4 = 1.15 \times 1.15 \times 1.15 \times 1.15 = 1.749$.
$$\$1,000,000 \div 1.749 = \$571,753, \text{ or } \$572,000 \text{ rounded}$$

86. Building has depreciated 2% a year for 10 years, or 20% total; thus it's worth 80% of reproduction cost: $92,000 \times 0.8 = $73,600. Add $28,000 land value to get answer of $101,600.

90. Cash return per month: $4,000 $-$ $1,250 = $2,750; $2,750 \times 12 = $33,000 per year.
$$\$33,000 \div 0.12 = \$275,000$$

92. Monthly rents: $80 \times \$475 = \$38,000$; $120 \times \$575 = \$69,000$; $\$38,000 + \$69,000 = \$107,000$.
$$\text{Potential annual gross income} = \$107,000 \times 12 = \$1,284,000$$

93. Effective gross income is potential gross income plus miscellaneous income, less vacancy.
Vacancy is 5% of potential gross rent: $1,284,000 \times 0.05 = $64,200 vacancy
$$\$1,284,000 + \$5,000 - \$64,200 = \$1,224,800$$

94. NOI is effective gross less operating expenses:
$$\text{NOI} = \$1,224,800 - \$400,000 = \$824,800$$

95. Before-tax cash flow is NOI less mortgage servicing:
$$\$824,800 - \$630,000 = \$194,800$$

97. Since it is assumed that the property will keep its value of $200,000 for the entire 20 years, use simple capitalization. Annual rent is $24,000; value is $200,000:
$$\$24,000 \div \$200,000 = 0.12, \text{ or } 12\%$$

99. Recapture rate is 100%/25 years = 4% per year.

Model Examination 9

45. Value = rent × GRM:
$$\$575 \times 127 = \$73,025, \text{ or } \$73,000 \text{ rounded}$$

47. When using GRM, you ignore expenses, so don't pay any attention to the $125 monthly expenses. Just use the monthly rent of $750. Value = rent × GRM:
$$\$750 \times 110 = \$82,500$$

48. The residence is now worth 160% of what is was worth when it was built:
$$\$72,000 \div 1.6 = \$45,000$$

51. To find the mean, add the seven GRMs, divide by 7:
$$(125 + 125 + 127 + 127 + 127 + 128 + 130) \div 7 = 889 \div 7 = 127$$

52. The GRMs are already arranged in order; the median is the one in the middle (the fourth): 127.

53. The mode is the value that appears most often. Since 127 appears three times, more than any other GRM value, the mode is 127.

80. Purchase price will be $115,000/(1.12)^4$. $(1.12)^4 = 1.12 \times 1.12 \times 1.12 \times 1.12 = 1.574$.
$$\$115,000 \div 1.574 = \$73,084 = \$73,000 \text{ rounded}$$

81. Effective depreciation is figured for 20 out of a total of 50 years, or 20/50 = 0.4 = 40%.

83. You are given more information than you need. Improvement ratio is value of improvements/total property value. Since total value is $2,000,000 and land is worth $500,000, improvements are worth $1,500,000.
$$\$1,500,000 \div \$2,000,000 = 0.75 = 75\%$$

88. Loan is 75% of value: $1,000,000 × 0.75 = $750,000. 12% constant: $750,000 × 0.12 = $90,000. There is $250,000 of equity, for which 15% cash-on-cash is desired: $250,000 × 0.15 = $37,500.
   NOI will have to be mortgage payment + desired cash return:
$$\$37,500 + \$90,000 = \$127,500$$

89. Recapture rate is 100%/25 years = 4% per year.

92. Monthly rents: 25 × $550 = $13,750; 75 × $675 = $50,625; $13,750 + $50,625 = $64,375.
$$\text{Potential annual gross income} = \$64,375 \times 12 = \$772,500$$

93. Effective gross income is potential gross income plus miscellaneous income, less vacancy.
   Vacancy is 7% of potential gross rent: $772,500 × 0.07 = $54,075 vacancy
$$\$772,500 + \$1,000 - \$54,075 = \$719,425$$

94. NOI is effective gross less operating expenses, which are 40% of effective gross.
   NOI is 60% of effective gross:
$$\$719,425 \times 0.6 = \$431,655$$

95. Operating expenses are 40% of NOI:
$$\$719,425 \times 0.4 = \$287,770$$

97. Land value is $100,000; 10% of that ($10,000) is return to land, so $90,000 − $10,000 = $80,000 is the return to the building. This implies a value of a little less than $800,000 for the income over 30 years ($80,000/0.1), *plus* the present value of a reversion of about $400,000, which wouldn't be very much. The range $750,000 to $1,000,000 clearly is correct.

99. Value will be $(1.15)^5 \times \$100,000 = 2.011 \times \$100,000 = \$201,100 = \$200,000$ rounded.

Model Examination 10

3. Comparable sold for $300 without a garage. Add $20,000 for garage = $320,000.

4.
$20,000 monthly rent × 12	$ 240,000 annual
Vacancy rate at 9%	−21,600
Net rental income	$ 218,000
Divide by 0.12 capitalization rate	$1,820,000

9.
Lot = 43,560 × $10 × ½	$217,800
House = 50 × 50 = 2,500 × $75	187,500
Total	$405,300

78.
6% of $250,000 =	$15,000
4% of $200,000 =	8,000
Total	$23,000

81.
$300,000 × (1.00 − .20 = .80)	$240,000 mortgage
2 points = 2% of mortgage	× .02
Points	$4,800

82.
$75,000 × .28	= $21,000
Divide by 12 months	= $1,750

Index

Notes